The Scarecrow Author Bibliographies

1. John Steinbeck (Tetsumaro Hayashi).   1973.
2. Joseph Conrad (Theodore G. Ehrsam).   1969.
3. Arthur Miller (Tetsumaro Hayashi). 2d ed.   due 1976.
4. Katherine Anne Porter (Waldrip & Bauer).   1969.
5. Philip Freneau (Philip M. Marsh).   1970.
6. Robert Greene (Tetsumaro Hayashi).   1971.
7. Benjamin Disraeli (R. W. Stewart).   1972.
8. John Berryman (Richard W. Kelly).   1972.
9. William Dean Howells (Vito J. Brenni).   1973.
10. Jean Anouilh (Kathleen W. Kelly).   1973.
11. E. M. Forster (Alfred Borrello).   1973.
12. The Marquis de Sade (E. Pierre Chanover).   1973.
13. Alain Robbe-Grillet (Dale W. Fraizer).   1973.
14. Northrop Frye (Robert D. Denham).   1974.
15. Federico García Lorca (Laurenti & Siracusa).   1974.
16. Ben Jonson (Brock & Welsh).   1974.
17. Four French Dramatists: Eugène Brieux, Francois de Curel, Emile Fabre, Paul Hervieu (Edmund F. SantaVicca).   1974.
18. Ralph Waldo Ellison (Jacqueline Covo).   1974.
19. Philip Roth (Bernard F. Rodgers, Jr.).   1974.
20. Norman Mailer (Laura Adams).   1974.
21. Sir John Betjeman (Margaret Stapleton).   1974.
22. Elie Wiesel (Molly Abramowitz).   1974.
23. Paul Laurence Dunbar (Eugene W. Metcalf, Jr.).   1975.
24. Henry James (Beatrice Ricks).   1975.
25. Robert Frost (Lentricchia & Lentricchia).   1976.
26. Sherwood Anderson (Douglas G. Rogers).   1976.
27. Iris Murdoch and Muriel Spark (Tominaga and Schneidermeyer).   1976.
28. John Ruskin (Kirk H. Beetz).   1976.
29. Georges Simenon (Trudee Young).   1976.
30. George Gordon, Lord Byron (Oscar Jose Santucho).   1977.
31. John Barth (Richard Vine).   1977.

GEORGE GORDON, LORD BYRON:

*A comprehensive bibliography of
secondary materials in English,
1807-1974*

by

OSCAR JOSÉ SANTUCHO

with

A Critical Review of Research
by
CLEMENT TYSON GOODE, Jr.

The Scarecrow Author Bibliographies, No. 30

The Scarecrow Press, Inc.
Metuchen, N.J.   1977

PR
4381
.S27

Library of Congress Cataloging in Publication Data

Santucho, Oscar José.
George Gordon, Lord Byron : a comprehensive bibliography of secondary materials in English, 1807-1974.

(The Scarecrow author bibliographies ; no. 30)
Includes index.
1. Byron, George Gordon Noël Byron, Baron, 1788-
1824--Bibliography. I. Goode, Clement Tyson, 1929-
joint author.
Z8139.S27 [PR4381] 016.821'7 76-41006
ISBN 0-8108-0982-6

CONTENTS

FOREWORD

Only a generation ago readers and writers seemed to be more concerned with Byron the man than with Byron the author. Within the last twenty years biographical study has surely achieved a culmination, at least for a few decades; and many of the poems have also recently been given the scrutiny, the exegesis, and the evaluation they deserve.

But there have long been some uncomfortable gaps in Byron literature. While making a survey of the publications about the poet, Professor W. W. Pratt in the mid-fifties deplored the lack of a "technical bibliography [or] anything approaching it." Every Byron student, engaged in whatever investigation, has always, as Professor Santucho says in his preface, had to assemble individually his own catalogue of secondary articles and books by consulting the familiar but incomplete pioneers in the area and then by sweeping repeatedly through stacks of the annual lists issued by several journals and associations.

Some years ago Professor Santucho determined to simplify this process. He searched many libraries and collections here and in England and inspected a vast array of volumes in order to assemble and organize over 5000 items of Byroniana. His diligence and patience have supplied an indispensable tool for Romantic writers and scholars.

Professor Clement T. Goode, Jr., of Baylor University, has augmented the usefulness of this massive compilation by providing us with a comprehensive introduction, a guide that directs us along orderly paths through the vast forest of bibliographical entries. Professor Goode therefore has simplified our use of this book by his chronological exposition and assessment of the contribution made by each major period during the past century and a half of scholarship and criticism on Byron and his work.

Whatever future direction scholars may take in their

study of Byron, their journey should therefore now be made easier. Surely anyone who undertakes a re-interpretation of Byron's relevance to present or future eras will enlist the aid of the present bibliography. This book should also make the interlocking tasks of an editor, historian, annotator, and critic move along more rapidly than did the variorum editions of Don Juan and Cain with their notes and essays on sundry pertinent subjects. Moreover, in the spring 1971 issue of The Wordsworth Circle Professors Thorslev and Stillinger have justly called for further attempts to relate more thoroughly the five major English romantic poets to each other, to the host of once popular, but now forgotten, writers of that era, and to their entire cultural milieu; and to reinforce in greater detail their powerful immediacy, the value of their vision and their affirmation for our own time. He who seriously accepts some of these challenges will in the course of his endeavor exploit all available guides to the records of the past, and be grateful for the labor-saving rewards provided by Professor Santucho's compilation and Professor Goode's introduction.

In this storehouse one may meet and absorb the notions and tastes, the fashions and prejudices of workaday journalists, of thoughtful commentators, of angry or sentimental men, of the obscure and the anonymous, of the clever, the voluble and the magisterial. Every bibliography can be full of discoveries, can contain the beginnings of many potential directions for exploration which may lead one almost endlessly into paths where few have penetrated.

T. G. Steffan
Austin, Texas, 1976

PREFACE

For a long time all Byron students have painstakingly had to consult several annual bibliographies which include Byron references in order to proceed with their research, knowing that this laborious consultation was the sine qua non of all research and the only sure way not to duplicate what other scholars in the field had accomplished.

Up to 1924 there was no bibliography of Byron criticism per se, if we may disregard that first attempt at bibliography contributed to Notes and Queries in 1886 by John Taylor of the Library of Bristol and augmented copiously the same year by Richard Edgcumbe in the same periodical. The J. P. Anderson bibliography appended to Roden Noel's Life of Byron in 1890 dealt with Byron criticism, but it consisted of material compiled from the British Museum alone. Not until 1924, with Samuel Chew's Byron in England, was there an attempt to compile something like a complete bibliography of Byron studies; it came as a fitting anniversary tribute for the poet. Since that time only Escarpit and Marchand in the fifties have attempted a bibliography more extensive than the usual perfunctory "minimum" list of sources found at the end of books about Byron. Even the lists compiled by these two men do not purport to be complete but only a compilation of the sources read for or employed in their work. Such scholarly publications as ELH, PQ, ELN, and K-SJ--especially the last--have been compiling reasonably comprehensive bibliographies of the Romantic poets and in particular since 1937. Still there has been no systematic check of the earlier bibliographies for verification or for completeness, nor have they been brought together into one volume for the convenience of the scholar.

The latter is still handicapped by having to make a cross-check and fresh compilation for each new topic that he initiates, plus having to fill in gaps. And there is always the gnawing suspicion that the earlier bibliographies might not be complete or that his topic may have already been dealt with.

The present project is an attempt to overcome these difficulties and to make the collection as nearly complete as possible by covering all available ground. However, this bibliography is confined to printed material, whether published or not, about Byron and his work, written in the English language alone, and covering a period from 1807, the date of the earliest critical reference found, to the end of 1974.

There are, naturally, some limitations in the scope of this work which should be pointed out at the beginning. The reader will not find here most of the brief notices of Byron utilized by standard biographical encyclopedias or those found in countless anthologies or in histories of literature that present only a superficial account of the life and works of the poet. Also omitted are American and British M. A. theses or papers read at meetings of scholarly societies but not yet published. All listings of records of Byron's poetry or of songs composed from his work have been left out, too, as have been items relating to his iconography and illustrations to his works. Finally, no newspaper accounts about Byron will be found here.

Except for these omissions, the objective has been to provide all the secondary source material of Byron scholarship to date. Some primary material has been included, especially when it was a landmark in Byron scholarship or heavily reviewed. Collections of the poems or of the letters, where introductions or descriptions of the collections are found, have been included; but the casual reprint of a letter or poem in some periodical or collection when not accompanied by an editorial comment has been omitted. As Byron is a central figure of the English Romantic period, he reflects many aspects of the culture of the period and has connections with other literary figures. Therefore a good many publications have been included--like the histories of Regency England and the diaries and letters of his contemporaries where he is mentioned--which, while not primarily concerned with Byron, serve to show in some significant way this centrality and these connections. However, it would have been futile to record every book with a passing reference to him, even when the aim is inclusiveness; consequently a rule has been observed of incorporating only books with at least five or more passing references, unless for some reason the reference was considered important enough on its own merits to deserve inclusion.

The general procedure followed in compiling this bibliography was to exhaust all the available indexes and the more specialized bibliographies listed at the beginning of the bibliography under "Sources Used." Each item therein contained, located either under the section listed as Byron or in a cross-reference, was carefully written down on cards and the information noted was checked against the original article or book for relevance to the present bibliography, for accuracy, and for annotations where necessary.

Two volumes were especially rewarding in opening new avenues of research: Newman I. White's The Unextinguished Hearth and Ward's Index and Finding List of Serials Published in the British Isles, 1798-1832. These two books supplied the names of numerous periodicals not listed by Poole's Index. Research of these periodicals yielded a number of items previously unknown, and they have been incorporated in this bibliography. It should be noted in passing that this bibliography had been nearly completed long before Reiman's The Romantics Reviewed was published in 1972. Besides contributing a few entries to the present bibliography, Reiman's monumental work was used to double-check the entries common to his work and mine. All partial bibliographies and footnotes found in the books and articles listed in this bibliography were also checked for items that might properly belong here, and these were introduced if they conformed to the limitations set down, so the user of this bibliography need not bother to look there.

Further research uncovered the names of libraries rich in Byron material, here and abroad. Immediate correspondence was established with those abroad, and a visit to each of the American libraries became indispensable. The British Museum microfilmed two scrapbooks of contemporary criticism of Byron; the Bristol Public Library cooperated fully by sending three similar scrapbooks in view of the impossibility of microfilming them; the Birmingham Public Library sent a Xerox copy of all of its Byron holdings; and both the Roe Collection at Newstead Abbey and the Nottingham Public Library supplied copies of their card catalogues and microfilms of all their material that had a place in this bibliography. The major libraries in the United States were researched personally, and the results of the research have been incorporated in this bibliography. The few libraries that could not be visited personally furnished Xerox copies of whatever material they held of Byron not already included in this bibliography.

Although the arrangement and the style adopted for this bibliography will be easily recognizable, it is important to underscore some points. The chronological arrangement was adopted in order to avoid the inevitable repetition that would ensue if a system of categories had been employed. Furthermore, for the sake of clarity, the 165 years covered were divided into ten major chapter divisions which, in spite of their artificiality, do reveal a definite pattern in the development of Byron scholarship. The titles of the chapters and the dates should be self-explanatory in revealing these trends. Each chapter division is then broken down year by year, and the alphabetical arrangement prevails within each year.

References have been annotated when the title does not give an inkling of the nature of the material involved or when information in the title needs to be supplemented in some way. These brief annotations are enclosed in square brackets following the entry and are descriptive rather than critical. They range in length from one word to a whole sentence or two, sometimes quoted from the article itself, giving the substance of the study. Articles whose contents are evident from the title or are of a very general nature about Byron's life or works have not been annotated at all. Dr. Goode's review of research complements these annotations.

When the material has not been handled personally because of unavailability in American libraries, and therefore the accuracy of information in the entry cannot be vouched for, an asterisk has been placed in front of the item. Most of the items contained herein, however, have been located and checked.

Brackets have been used to include the name of the author of an article or book originally published anonymously but whose identity has already been ascertained. For articles from Blackwood's, for instance, the authorship or real names attributed by Alan L. Strout have been adopted. For writers using pseudonyms, the real names have been set up in the body of the bibliography after using such sources as Laing's Dictionary of Anonyms and Pseudonyms or Cushing's Initials and Pseudonyms and his Anonyms. In the index, the reader will find a "See under" after the pseudonym that will refer him to the real name.

Books with different titles on both sides of the Atlantic have been recorded with both titles in the same entry. The same holds true for data relating to city and publisher.

Contrary to the practice adopted by the Library of Congress, dates of publication of books have not been bracketed if they can be found anywhere in the book. When the date has been ascertained from external evidence, then brackets have been used, followed by a question mark if the date is only approximate or is an educated guess, or is listed as such on the title page itself. If the date has been only approximately determined by omission of the last digit, the book will be found listed alphabetically under the year beginning the decade. Thus, a book dated 192? will be found under 1920.

If a periodical has gone through several series in its lifetime, the series are numbered, starting with the second series, 2nd, 3rd, etc., whereas if it has only gone through two series, then the second series is called "new series" and is abbreviated "n. s." If two periodicals are known by the same name, such as Horizon or the Literary Journal, some identification is used about one of them only, preferably the place of publication which is included in parentheses immediately following; e.g., Horizon (N. Y.).

In almost every case the complete pagination of a periodical article or book chapter has been given. Wherever page references are not given, it is to be understood that various passages in the book refer to Byron and that the reader should consult the index of the volume in question.

No attempt has been made to list reprints of articles or books not dealing with Byron in their totality. But for those directly relevant to Byron, the following method has been generally adopted:

a) If an article or review is reprinted in other periodicals or in a book containing collected articles by the same writer, the reprint is noted under the original date of publication, but it will not be found again, in general, under the year when it was reprinted. However, if the article is reprinted in a book containing essays by different writers, collected by one or two editors, it will be found under the year when it was reprinted, not under the original date, though notice is given of year of original publication.

b) In the case of books that have seen several editions with no changes, only the year of the first edition is listed. After 1950, however, important books on Byron have been reprinted, and they are then noted twice, first under the year of original publication and then under the year of reprint.

It will be noticed that reviews in English of books dealing exclusively with Byron are listed and that these have been put in block form, a review per line, chronologically arranged, although the alphabetical arrangement had to be used when the dates of the reviews exactly coincided. Order of preference in the chronological arrangement when periodicals coincide for the same year proceeds from big units of time to smaller ones; i.e., from annual periodicals, to quarterlies, to monthlies, to weeklies.

It is hoped that the user of this bibliography will find in it more, rather than less, than he expected to find.

ACKNOWLEDGMENTS

It is a pleasure to acknowledge my many debts to the Byron scholars and the many institutions who have given me help with the compilation of this bibliography. My appreciation also goes to all previous and present compilers of bibliographies who naturally made my task easier.

I cannot overlook the kindness of several Byron scholars whose unlimited generosity in regard to advice, material, and encouraging words I cannot too greatly emphasize. I am indebted to Dr. Truman G. Steffan for letting me use the microfilms of two scrapbooks from the British Museum and some from the Roe-Byron Collection at Newstead Abbey, not to mention his enthusiasm over my project and the kind words of his preface to this work. I would wish to recognize the loan made by the late Dr. William H. Marshall of a microfilm of The London Liberal, unobtainable in this country. The advice of Drs. Willis Pratt and Leslie Marchand is gratefully acknowledged.

The several libraries that have contributed all the Byron material they contained are listed on a separate page (following "Sources") and thanks are due to them all. The librarians of these institutions have given their time generously and faithfully. I feel that especial mention is due to Mr. Charles Dwyer and Miss Catherine Blow, who, during two summers of research conducted at the University of Texas, were thoughtful of my interest, generous with information and prompt to answer questions. I am greatly indebted to Mr. M. A. Young's ability as a bibliographer, which he displayed in some work he undertook for me with material from the Birmingham Public Library in England. I am also indebted to Mr. David E. Gerrard, the Curator of Newstead

Abbey, for helping in several ways to make this bibliography as complete as possible. I wish to express special thanks to Mr. W. S. Haugh, from the Bristol Public Library, for showing praiseworthy desire to cooperate in this project by sending me three scrapbooks which he would probably not have allowed out of his reference shelf under any other circumstances. A special word of thanks goes to Mrs. Inger Tavernise of the William R. Perkins Library at Duke University for her boundless generosity. I also wish to thank Mr. Pawel Depta of Harvard University for varied and indispensable aid. Likewise I wish to express my gratitude to Miss Carolyn E. Jakeman of the Houghton Library at Harvard for calling my attention to materials and making them accessible to me. I am also specially indebted to Miss Connie Sacco and Mr. Frank Orser, both of Yale University, for their personal assistance. I am also particularly indebted to Messrs. Robert G. Kirkpatrick, Edwin G. Wilson and Lewis Schwartz, and Rae Ann Nager, all involved in the editing of the Keats-Shelley Journal, for letting me use the proof copies of the 1972 Journal before it saw print.

To Baylor University and Quinnipiac College I am particularly grateful for the grants they provided that made finishing this project possible.

Dr. Clement T. Goode, Jr., from Baylor University, not only directed this project from its inception, but also contributed the review of research. To him and his wife Jane, who put endless hours into proofreading, go my sincere thanks.

O. J. Santucho
Quinnipiac College

PART I

A CRITICAL REVIEW OF RESEARCH

by
Clement Tyson Goode, Jr.
Baylor University

1. Byron's Lifetime, 1807-1824

"It was the best of times, it was the worst of times" is Dickens' way of describing the period into which Byron was born. The poet's biography--with the euphoria of sudden fame turning into the agony of vilification and forming a presage of the waves of successes and disappointments that followed--makes him appear a true citizen of his age. Perhaps Dickens' phrase may be extended as well to the long publication history that has attended Byron. Not only do the years undulate with acclaim and notoriety, but each era contains its detractors and champions of the poet and his work.

The bibliographical portion of this volume is the cumulative record of what has been said about Byron in English, and the present survey is intended as a guide through this research. The latter is an attempt to see the palimpsest beneath the listing, an effort to chart the way through the various periods of Byron scholarship, marking significant lines of development, noting works of intrinsic merit or historical importance, and tracing sundry trends. The whole may be seen as a brief history of the critical fortunes of the poet.

The first chapter in this history traces the reaction during Byron's own lifetime. His star rises quickly, and the man and his work become in a very short time household words for thousands of his countrymen and a topic for curious fascination abroad. Letters crisscross, diaries note, poems attest, recorded conversations tell--all reveal his hold upon the public of his day. But the bulk of commentary and the most accurate barometer of his reputation during the years 1807-1824 are the reviews that trail after every work that he published. Donald H. Reiman has provided the researcher a resource tool of inestimable value by collecting the majority of these contemporary reviews in his nine-volume The Romantics Reviewed (1972), five volumes of which are devoted to "Byron and Regency Society Poets." As the story of Byron's contemporary reception is well known, only the highlights need be pointed out here.

Hours of Idleness and English Bards and Scotch Reviewers mark the beginning; they represent action and reaction on Byron's part. The former work is presented to the
world in 1807 via a "Preface" that exhibits both the mingled
emotions of a teen-ager and the high ambitions/dread fears
of a first author. Every possible hedge against failure is
contained therein--the author is only nineteen, the poems are
merely an idle pastime, etc. --and Byron obviously hopes for
leniency from the critics. In most cases they oblige him;
for the overwhelming majority of reviews are favorable, even
if their complimentary nature is often couched in the empty
critical rhetoric of the times and seems frequently a conces-
sion to the author's youth or his rank. The general tenor
is that the writer possesses ability and shows promise for
his years. A few reviewers demur at his amatory subject
matter and urge him to use his talents for more worthwhile
purposes. Byron was pleased with his acceptance, but of
course the negative reviews were the ones that remained in his
mind. Only three were predominantly unfavorable, though
two or three others were mixed, and jests and gibes appear
in the other notices. The Monthly Mirror, quipping mainly
on the vulnerable points of Byron's "Preface" and the incor-
rectness of his Latin, had fun in general at the young writer's
expense:

> We know little of the peerage, and nothing of Lord
> Byron's family, but we shrewdly guess that he is
> descended from Lord Lovett, who, as our nurse
> once told us, walked and talked half an hour after
> his head was cut off, which piece of ingenuity of
> his ancestor he has improved upon, by actually
> writing in the very same predicament.

And this sort of badinage the poet took in stride. The mocking, sarcastic wit of the Satirist's Hewson Clarke was understandable (ill will between the two began at Cambridge where
they were contemporaries) though hardly fair. But when the
Edinburgh Review, with its powerful influence and Whig affili-
ations, "cut to atoms ... my little fabric of fame" (L & J,
I, 183), Byron was driven to an anger (its intensity later
verified by Hobhouse and Medwin) that could find relief only
by repayment in kind. With English Bards and Scotch Reviewers the poet is no longer a teen-ager physically or men-
tally; he is a worthy adversary, and he turns the laughter,
quips, and caustic wit back upon the reviewers. The literary response to his new volume manifests a significant change
in tone. Gone are the condescending attitude and the easy
humor; a new respect has replaced these. Virtually all the

reviews are positive, and English Bards is compared favor-
ably with Pope's Dunciad and Gifford's Baviad and Maeviad.
With the attention of the critics thus arrested, the future publications of Lord Byron are assured of serious consideration.

Byron enters upon the years of fame with the publication of Childe Harold I and II in 1812. The keynote is the
poet's own "I awoke one morning and found myself famous."
The claim is no exaggeration, for a letter quoted by Leslie
Marchand (Byron: a Biography, I, 335) fully verifies the
fact: "The subject of conversation, of curiosity, of enthusiasm almost, one might say, of the moment is not Spain or
Portugal, Warriors or Patriots, but Lord Byron! ... [Childe
Harold] is on every table...." The quarto edition of 500
copies was sold out in three days. Not just a fashionable
social occurrence, the poem was also a literary event of
some importance. The reviews are numerous and highly
complimentary. The term genius repeatedly occurs, as it
often does in the polite commentary of the day, but this time
it is coupled with wishes for the author to publish something
worthy of his talents and powers, something epical. Appreciation is already being shown for such Byronic elements as
descriptions of the sublime in nature, striking imagery, im-
petuous feeling, bold and original thought. Aside from admonishments of a political or religious nature, and aside
from differences of opinion about Byron's use of the Spenseri-
an stanza and archaic ornamentation, the critics are mostly
concerned about the absence of plot and the strangeness of
the hero who exhibits anti-heroic traits, who provides no unity,
and who seems to serve no purpose but to convey Byron's
sentiments. The confusion developing from the latter--i.e.,
is Byron the hero or not?--raises for the first time the issue
of personal biography in Byron's works, perhaps the central
issue in the long history of Byron criticism. As a measure
of Byron's new-found stature, both the Edinburgh Review and
Quarterly Review, the two most influential review periodicals
of the day, give Byron's work significant notice, as they will
continue to do regularly hereafter.

The six romances written to capitalize on the success
of Childe Harold appear with such astonishing rapidity between
1813 and 1816 that several reviewers apologize for not being
able to keep abreast of them, and some express alarm lest
the poet should satiate his public. Edition after edition of
The Giaour is sold. The Bride of Abydos appears, and the
British Critic reports shortly that it "is now in the hands of
nearly the whole English nation." The popularity of The Corsair on the morning of its nativity is unprecedented, 13,000

copies being sold according to the European Magazine. Byron's poetic supply is sustained by Lara, The Siege of Corinth,
and Parisina; but the public demand starts to lessen, and the
satiation prophecy mentioned earlier begins to come true.

Byron's critical reputation during these years is tied
closely to the popular reaction. The reviewers at first seem
to be carried along by the universal fervor. Even though
faults are liberally singled out in The Giaour (lack of structure, disreputable hero, lack of moral point, labored simi-
les), Byron's talent is eulogized and the piece is generally
esteemed. The Bride of Abydos, with a more normal structure, fewer obscurities, and a "softer" emphasis, is regarded
even more highly; but at the same time the moral criticism
becomes insistent, carping begins about the similarity of the
heroes to Childe Harold, and a lone voice wishes that the
poet would follow his declaration not to obtrude any more of
his effusions upon the public. The tenor of these last remarks is amplified upon the appearance of The Corsair but so
is the critical appreciation of this romance, the favorite thus
far of the reviewers; and a critical dialogue is established,
with several journals praising the moral value of the poem
and urging Byron not to withdraw from publication. Still,
the unfavorable trend continues with Lara and The Siege of
Corinth, and it finally overwhelms the favorable with Parisina.

The subject matter of Parisina accounts for the peculiar vehemence directed against it, particularly that from the
moral and religious critics who never tire of calling Byron
to account for wasting his God-given talent and for not pro-
ducing something of great spiritual and ethical value. But
some of the charges have become cumulative and help explain the decline in critical favor of both the poetry and the
poet. The formulaic nature of the hero and the poems, and
Byron's trifling with the muse and the public in reneging on
his repeated promise of poetic abstinence are the central foci
of discontent. Other puissant charges concern the disagree-
able hero and subject matter, the careless grammar, the uneven verse, and the imitative nature of the romances, though
these are as frequently countered by affirmations of the
"strongly-conceived hero" and passions and descriptions, the
"extraordinary energy and vigor" of the language, the great
facility of the verse, and the originality in conception of the
poems. These pro and con lines of debate will recur in future Byron criticism. The poet's departure from England in
1816 seems to be the final touch to the perfect bell curve of
his reputation during the years 1812-1816.

The period bracketed by the third and fourth cantos
of Childe Harold (1816-1818) is a time of restoration on firm-
er ground of Byron's poetic repute. Out of the ashes of his
personal life and literary reputation, the poet responds with
the greatness for which the critics had been clamoring and
produces three of his finest romantic achievements. The
critical reaction marks a significant turn. The strictures
against Childe Harold III are singularly uncreative; they are,
in fact, identical to those leveled against the romances, with
the added fault of domestic linen aired. But the favorable
reviews give evidence of a deeper and more thoughtful appreciation of the poem--of its finely-wrought passion wedded to
natural scenery, its vigor of thought, its mellowing down to
a human and ethical level--and quickly overwhelm the negative strains. The poem is considered superior to anything
yet written by Byron, and the poet is again elevated with
superlatives.

Manfred merits more careful consideration. It seems
to represent a literary reversal, as the general feeling runs
heavily against the work. Examination shows, however, that
certain sensitive areas--the egocentric hero, the unfortunate
subject matter, the question of morals--and the strange nature of the piece are the major causes of the dissatisfaction.
Becoming increasingly evident is the fact that a number of
reviewers who are committed to a fixed theory about Byron's
genius or a particular political view are unable to deal with
the poet's rapid changes in form and style. But it is clear
that the work has made a deep impression and that Byron
has lost none of his stature; beneath the surface, perceptive
and appreciative comments are in evidence, and a few reviews of outstanding quality show that they have met the
challenge of the poem.

When the last canto of Childe Harold is published, old
prejudices are laid aside and the piece is acknowledged as
"the finest of them all" (Edinburgh Review). Accolades are
heaped upon the completed project in remarkable unanimity
of opinion: "the finest, beyond all comparison, of Byron's
poems" (Blackwood's); "the most original [poem] in the
language, both in conception and execution" (Edinburgh Review); "[Childe Harold] will hereafter rank with the first and
best compositions which our own or any other country has
ever produced" (Northern Star); "a work, which ... is plainly destined to live for ever" (Scots Magazine). The few unfavorable reviews, such as in the perennially negative
British Critic and British Review, now seem hopelessly out

of step and are fully revealed in their bias.   Led by Jeffrey,
Scott, and John Wilson, the appraisals of Byron's work have
developed to a point of remarkable literary acuteness and
sensitivity; the reviews are now more fully attuned to Byron's
purposes, his hero, and his work.   At this particular high
moment, the acme of Byron's poetic career, he is acknowledged as England's foremost poet.   Opinion will change radically with succeeding publications that cross public moral,
political, or religious predispositions.   But with the completion of Childe Harold the poet has risen above his contemporary judges--"the lash of those critics who dip their pens in
acid or gall, can never affect a poet of Lord Byron's description" (Belle Assemblée)--and is safely ensconced in the fir-
mament, as more than one journal prophetically implies that
he will last beyond the age.

        Though Byron had experimented with a variety of ap-
proaches in his eleven-year public career, nothing represented so radical a departure from the Byronic "norm" as
Beppo, published anonymously just two months before Childe
Harold IV.   Born of an anecdote told on a summer evening
at La Mira, the poem seemed innocuous enough.   Personally,
it was a light tribute to Byron's felicitous liaison with Italian
social life and customs and perhaps a psychological sign of
his emergence into the sun again.   Publicly, it was a farewell to Childe Harold* and a literary trial balloon.   As the
latter test, it could hardly have been more successful.   Its
good-natured satire, relaxed mood, absence of political or
religious threat, and easy verse won instant approval from
the critics.   Even Byron's staunch old enemy, the British
Critic, if it did not laugh outright, managed at least a respectable smile.   But as a prelude to Don Juan, no one, not
even Byron, realized how momentous this "jeu d'esprit" was.
Byron intended Don Juan to be 'a little quietly facetious upon
every thing"; however, the first two cantos of his "epic,"
published July 15, 1819, turn out to be a literary bombshell.
As long as Byron's ottava rimas were "harmless and happy,"
the critics enjoyed them; but when Don Juan stepped on moral
and religious toes, the old anger welled up again.   Fearing
defection from orthodoxy with a paranoia born of the French
Revolution, the Tory and religious journals set upon poem
and poet with a series of blistering attacks, using the knock-
about political rhetoric of the time.   Byron is described as

---

*Though published slightly earlier, Beppo was written after
the first draft of Childe Harold IV had been completed.

"a cool, unconcerned fiend" (Blackwood's), who deliberately
attempts "to seduce to the love of evil which he has chosen
as his good" (Eclectic Review). The poem is defined as a
"narrative of degrading debauchery in doggrel rhyme" (British
Critic) and described as a satire against all cherished insti-
tutions--"religion, morality, the social order, [and] domestic
feeling" (New Monthly Magazine). Some of the reviews, notably the one in the New Monthly Magazine, are more offensive
than the material they castigate.

Two years later Cantos III-V appear; and these sections receive more of the same abuse, though there are one
or two signs of reaction to the intensity of the conservative
vituperation and a like number of liberal journals have become less favorable than before. Both the Edinburgh Review
and the Quarterly Review break long silence and exercise
their powerful influence on the issue of Don Juan, generally
agreeing with the opponents of the poem but with fair judgment and without rancor. In the midst of all the high feeling aroused and the vehemence written, nearly every review
has generous praise for Byron's genius and talent. The Eclectic Review perhaps best expresses the mixed feelings of
the critics: "[Don Juan] is impossible not to read without
admiration, yet ... it is equally impossible to admire without
losing some degree of self-respect." Teresa's injunction on
Byron in 1821 not to write any more stanzas of Don Juan
placed a temporary stay on both verses and critical outrage.

Actually, Byron had already partially turned from his
masterpiece, after its disheartening reception, to begin ex-
perimenting with drama in 1820-1821. Manfred had not been
a conventional drama but a poetic drama, recognized as such
by the author and relegated to that species by the critics;
but at the time that it had appeared, the hope was expressed
that Byron would try his hand at something suitable for the
stage. It seemed only natural that he should, since the public saw his talent in part as dramatic and since the poet
himself had been interested in the theater from his youth.
In a brief but intense creative period of slightly over a year,
Byron produced three historical dramas--in an attempt to
reform the English stage along classical lines, rather than
to present actual stage pieces--and the powerful Biblical
drama of Cain.

As far as the critical notice is concerned, the author
might have spared himself the trouble. Marino Faliero,
Byron's first orthodox play, was anticipated eagerly and read

avidly. Even though the journals are about equally divided
in opinion, the reception was less than enthusiastic; the
praise of the favorable reviews seems pre-conceived and the
tribute in the unfavorable articles is perfunctory. The negative arguments are far more convincing of current opinion
and are an accurate indicator of the fate of The Two Foscari
and Sardanapalus. As Byron was committed to a particular
view and dramatic course, the handwriting is already on the
wall. The dramas, then, were thought of collectively as
failures and far below the author's customary standard. If
Byron was on a new tack, the critics either refused to see
it or to allow it. Apparently judging the plays by contemporary stage fare, they found them lacking in what they were
accustomed to in drama: "attractive passions," probability,
variety of interest. Virtually every aspect of the plays as
drama receives a journalistic buffeting: their tragic label is
questioned, the plots are "ill-constructed," the characters
"improbable," the speeches "tedious," even the choice of historical subject matter "unmanageable." The recurrent word
is "heaviness," or variants thereof: "laborious," "prolix,"
"tedious," "verbose," "dull," "flat," "monotonous." The
dramas were too somber and metaphysical, too long and
carefully detailed, too artfully woven for contemporary taste.
And so Byron's grand experiment at reform ends with the
echo of "Lord Byron is not now, and perhaps is not destined
to be, a master of his new vocation" (Edinburgh Monthly Review). If the results of the three historical dramas are
poor, the aftermath of Cain, in an entirely different mold,
is worse. The power and poetry of the work are granted,
but blasphemy is now added to Byron's former sins of immorality and political and domestic impiety; the story of the
reaction to Cain, which seems to reach national proportions,
is really a chapter in itself. But the immediate response is
endless variations on the theme of blasphemy and Byron's
debasement of his splendid powers.

Ironically, at the moment that Byron's literary immortality is assured with the consummation of Childe Harold,
his contemporary reputation begins to decline. The fact is
not so noticeable with the initial cantos of Don Juan, for
there is still strong acknowledgment of his eminence as a
poet. With the historical dramas, however, there is an almost total disappointment of expectations. Cain, containing
"blasphemy," turns public opinion farther away, though Byron's power as a poet and his great gifts are still recognized.
The publication of The Vision of Judgment serves as a reverse Rubicon for his reputation. The reviews, in a body,

oppose the satire and greet it with such epithets as "shock-
ing" and "profane"; the steady journalistic warnings to the
poet of "one day going too far" seem finally to have come
true. The effrontery of political heresy joined to the sins of
immorality and blasphemy is too much to bear, and The Liberal as a foil only worsens matters. The intensity of feeling can be measured by the Investigator's declaration of
"warfare against Lord Byron, and the infidel writers of the
day. " The heat is transferred to the literary criticism of
the poem, which labels Vision of Judgment as generally inferior in quality. Something now has definitely been lost; the
major journals discreetly ignore the poem, and Byron's greatness is being spoken of in the past tense. The lesser dramas
of Werner, Heaven and Earth, and The Deformed Transformed,
published separately over the next several months bring regard for the poet very close to the point of derision: "Lord
Byron has ceased to be dangerous; he is beginning to be ridiculous" (British Critic). Because two of the plays are
based largely upon other literary works, they are accused of
being merely prose translated into more prose and beyond
literary criticism. Of more serious import are comments
suggesting that Byron is showing "symptoms of an exhausted
mind" and "of genius sinking into a premature decay. "

    The remaining cantos of Don Juan, which appear in
groups of two's and three's until the end of the poet's life,
suffer the same maltreatment as before; the rhetoric, no
doubt through long practice, has grown even more colorful
in describing Byron as "the Poet--Laureate of Lust" or "a
wretched debauchee ... wallow[ing] in the sty of his own lux-
ury, in words and in description, like a drivelling dotard"
(Literary Gazette). Arrested points of praise or compliment
may still be found, but largely moral and religious "cant"
and political bias have replaced critical standards of judgment. Only an isolated review by Francis Jeffrey and a
letter by William Maginn in Blackwood's approach genuine
literary criticism. Personal references to the decline of
Byron's ability and reputation continue, and other names
than his are spoken of in the first rank. Cantos XV and
XVI of Don Juan are published March 26, 1824, Byron's
death cuts off further notice of his work, and suddenly his
fame rests in the hands of posterity.

2. Death and Aftermath, 1824-1839

When Lord Byron breathed his last in that lonely room at Missolonghi with the ever-faithful Fletcher at his side and the news had gone forth from that household to reach the Western world, the reaction was both simple and complicated; but in either case it was overwhelming. Initially there was sincere and immediate grief. This reached everyone: from the close friends, the servants, the physicians, the Greek troops and citizens associated with Byron at Missolonghi, to the friends and relatives and the vast crowd that attended the body all along its processional from its arrival on the Thames to its final burial in the family vault at Hucknall Torkard.

Even before the body was laid to rest, however, reaction had begun to stray from the path of pure and simple grief. Perhaps it began with the doctors' decision to perform an autopsy instead of simply the necessary embalmment, this action apparently taken to settle the differences among them concerning the cause of Byron's death; later two of these physicians--Millingen and Bruno--sent bills of £100 each for this service. But the same reaction can be seen in ever-widening circles: in Trelawny's shift from sincere sentiment to self-laudation at Byron's expense in his letters to Mary Shelley and in his self-aggrandizing aims in Greece; in the Greek citizens' desire for Byron's lungs for their church of San Spiridione; in the unpleasant quarrel involving Hobhouse, Murray, and Moore over the burning of Byron's unpublished Memoirs; in Lady Byron's attitude toward the Memoirs; in the refusal by the Dean of Westminster Abbey to allow Byron's burial there; in the specious explanations among the titled for not attending the funeral; in the change of the grief-stricken Fletcher to leading actor in Byron's final death scene; and certainly in Teresa's almost side-show antics in later years. In short, reaction hardens into motive, grief shifts to exploitation. The reasons given might be stated as positive or negative; but in each instance the

motives, if not venal, are at least selfish. The pattern of
the reactions to Byron's death is really the epitome for the
publications that appear about him in the year of his demise
and the decade and a half that follows--the first phase in the
critical fortunes of Byron after his death.

First comes the grief, the years 1824 and 1825 largely marking this phase. The shock of Byron's death is regis-
tered by the great glut of print that appears immediately
after the news arrives in England. Exclusive of reviews,
more books, pamphlets, and articles appear about him in
1824 than in any year for the next 100 years, the bulk of
this matter coming expectedly in the latter half of the year.
The almost-universal public concern is demonstrated by the
wide range of journals that carry information on Byron,
some 34 in all for this year alone; all England seemed to
mourn. As befits a time of sorrow, memory and mention
turn to the man himself; and virtually all material of 1824
is biographical in nature, more than 80% of the total in fact.
The death itself receives the lion's share of attention; and
all aspects--the final illness, the opening of the body, the
hours immediately following death, the arrival of the body
in England, preparations for the burial, the funeral, the
will--all are lugubriously dwelt upon as each journal vies
for the notice of the public. But the biographical demand
and supply are great and range wide: from anecdotes--of
which there are a half-dozen interesting tidbits on such
matters as Byron's Grecian orphan or a letter to Colonel
Stanhope on Byron's escape from the Turks--to a large number of generalized biographical accounts, effusive appreciations, and wide-ranging considerations of his character and
morals. In between the scope of these are items dealing
with such specialized interests as Byron's family, his relations with other people (Southey, Scott, Moore, Murray,
etc.), his first love and marriage, his separation, his relation to a certain place (as Greece), the burning of his Memoirs.

The year 1825 is still a period of grief, but of grief
beginning to wane. There is a drop in print by about a
fourth, though the year still represents the next largest production of writings on the poet until 1869. The death has
been fairly well mined by now, so the references are fewer.
It is still a topic of interest, but it is considered more at
leisure and at some distance: a poem composed on the occasion, a general assimilation of materials about his death,
reflections on the reasons for such general grief. The next

year the subject will not be discussed at all, nor thereafter
except in the general biographical consideration of the poet.
But the biographical interest of 1824 is still maintained; if
anything, the percentage is even higher, for the slack in specific interest in the death is taken up with the more general
consideration of the subject's life. The pattern followed is
basically that of 1824: anecdotes, general biographical accounts, appreciations, assessments of Byron's character and
genius, and the ever-present concern over his morals and
salvation. The specialized interests, too, are quite similar:
Byron's relation with other people, especially Southey; Byron
and Greece, with an increase of interest here; Byron's infidelity; the Memoirs, etc. The amount of criticism of Byron's
work these first two years is understandably negligible, consisting mainly of six or seven generalized considerations that
deal with an evaluation of the poetry, Byron's works "viewed
in connection with Christianity and the obligations of social
life," the immorality of his writing, and the probable fate of
his work. More particular considerations of Byron's work
compare it with that of another poet (e.g., Burns, Moore,
Scott) or speak specifically to a poem as Don Juan or The
Vision of Judgment. Most of the latter-type criticism, however, appears in one volume, Byroniana. Bozzies and Piozzies, which has a series of 14 "critiques" and/or "notes" on
11 of the poems.

    Once the period of grief ends, the remainder of this
decade and the next are largely given over to a different
kind of reaction to Byron's death, the attempt to capitalize
on the event, to exploit the materials of an association with
a famous personality. This type of reaction begins even before the decent period of grief has ended, with the appearance
of two books in a matter of weeks after the news of Byron's
death has become widely known. These notorious volumes
are R. C. Dallas' Recollections of the Life of Lord Byron,
from the Year 1808 to the End of 1814 and Thomas Medwin's
Journal of the Conversations of Lord Byron ... at Pisa, in
the Years 1821 and 1822. Untypical of the years of grief,
they nevertheless caused the most stir (eliciting ten and 18
reviews respectively), primarily because of their sensational
nature; and they are the longest-lived material of these
years, remaining still some of the most important documents
for a contemporary, firsthand knowledge of the poet.

    Dallas was a sort of unofficial literary adviser and
agent for Byron in the years 1808-1814, but the relationship
was to his profitable satisfaction as Byron gave him some of

the copyrights to the volumes that he helped see through the press. Normally a thoroughly upright man, he acted completely out of character in the publication of his book. Spurred apparently by literary aspirations and greed for money, he handled his publication with such haste and obtuseness that it caused much friction, involved him in a law suit with Hobhouse, and even lowered the quality of his book. The volume is not without value; for its inaccuracies, though substantive, are few and its transcribed conversations could not be completely fabricated. But it is distorted on two counts. First, the letters of Byron to his mother and the author have been transposed into third person narrative (Dallas was attempting to evade legally the injunction brought by Hobhouse forbidding publication of these letters) and thereby have lost the character of the whole, though the information is preserved.* Second, Dallas had several personal grievances against Byron (from which the poet has since been exonerated) that caused at times an unnecessarily hostile tone in the book.

Medwin, on the other hand, did not know Byron in England, but only for a period of four months or so in 1821 and 1822 during Byron's Pisan residence when he "Boswellized" his subject. His motives for hastening his volume into print after three weeks' composition at Geneva were the same as Dallas', with the additional desire for notoriety; the latter he hoped to capitalize on--and did--in subsequent volumes. His writings more than matched those by Dallas for animus provoked, since he managed to offend all the principals involved. The Journal is probably the most controversial of the firsthand accounts because the inaccuracy of known facts-- beginning with the title page--is so egregious as to cast doubt on the whole piece (Hobhouse alone notes fifty errors in his condemnatory article in the Westminster Review). Ironically, Medwin gained a rather formidable reputation because the hue and cry against him was so great that he actually stirred public sympathy, and because the Continent depended upon him for its first views of Byron, and because Galt and later biographers drew upon him. Whether Medwin willfully misrepresented some aspects of the record or was merely a good-natured blunderer as far as facts were concerned may be debated; at least his reporting seems to be accurate in its general tone, and he is still valuable for

---

*The original version of the book with the letters intact was nevertheless translated and published in French, then in English, in France the next year.

furnishing some realistic glimpses of Byron and catching
much of the elusive spirit of his conversation.

Dallas and Medwin were merely the first of the com-
mercializers. But the precedent is entirely clear now. Acquaintances from every period of Byron's life will step forth
to present their view of the famous man. The methods might
not be as crude nor the motives as obvious, but there will
be the same desire to trade on the dead poet's name and the
results will often be as full of mischief. A small minority
will try to defend Byron and vindicate his memory.

The Greek experience understandably produced a large
number of these traffickers in notoriety, for this was Byron's
last and most attractive venture and he was associated closely with a rather large group of individuals under circumstances that very nearly forced camaraderie. Edward Blaquiere and George Finlay were harmless enough. The former was sent out by the newly-formed London Greek Committee
to gather information in 1823, met Byron in Genoa, and
urged him to go to Greece. After the poet's death he made
a second trip to Greece, collected materials, and published
his Narrative of a Second Visit to Greece (1825), based
largely on secondhand sources. Since a large part of his
account was obtained from Byron's valet, Fletcher, it is affirmative toward Byron. Finlay, the important future Greek
historian, was fresh from Göttingen and the university and
on his way to Greece to satisfy his deep interest in the
Greek struggle for independence when he stopped both at
Cephalonia and Missolonghi to enjoy Byron's conversation.
Apparently he caught something of Byron's true nature in his
"Reminiscences of Lord Byron" (1825), for Hobhouse found
in it the verisimilitude of his friend as he remembered him.
But it is for the description by Pietro Gamba, Teresa's
younger brother and Byron's companion in revolution in Italy
and Greece, that Hobhouse reserves his highest praise; he
calls Gamba's A Narrative of Lord Byron's Last Journey to
Greece (1825) the most interesting and authentic of the primary accounts. Gamba was the poet's most ardent admirer
and probably the closest to him, enjoying something like a
brotherly relationship. The chevalier of the entire group,
he was a model of deportment throughout the days of grief.
Unlike some of the others, he seems to have been actuated
in his enterprise by the sincerest motives of friendship and
regard for Byron. The accuracy of his account is usually
accepted; and his portrait is the most sympathetic to Byron
and helpful in seeing the general situation in Greece from
Byron's point of view.

Colonel Stanhope and William Parry represent the military components at Missolonghi and counterpoint each other in their persons and views. Stanhope was apparently given authority equal to Byron's by the Greek Committee and was under the same roof with Byron for a brief time. Though they shared confidences, they were at odds almost from the beginning. Stanhope was the earnest and idealistic reformer who impractically believed in fighting by importing education and printing presses and hoped for a government of absolute democracy for the Greeks. The realistic and practical Byron realized the impossibility of this approach, but he nevertheless managed to get along with the "typographical colonel" as he called him. Stanhope's Greece in 1823 and 1824 (1825) is full of pretension and self-inflation and is slanted wholly against Byron's views in an effort to promote his own; but it is not altogether unfavorable to Byron personally.

William Parry, Byron's rough-and-ready practical military associate at Missolonghi, sought to counteract Stanhope and the attacks of others by setting the record straight and thereby vindicating Byron's memory in The Last Days of Lord Byron (1825). He was in an advantageous position to do this because Byron had taken an immediate liking to him, they had shared the same military and policy views, and, according to Parry, in the last two and a half months of Byron's life "there was no person in whom he placed more confidence than in me." Parry's rendition is a healthy counterblast to the disparaging accounts, the most moving of all descriptions of Byron's deathbed, and on the whole the most vigorous and convincing eyewitness statement of Byron's final struggles in Greece. Because his version was rough and straightforward, and because he was so frank, some of the people he offended--Stanhope, Trelawny, Millingen--denigrated his character and account by presenting him as ignorant, constantly drinking, and common. Later in his life the legitimacy of his authorship was questioned and he actually died in a madhouse. But today his account stands high: Byron's letters, Gamba, and other trustworthy sources corroborate his claims; and most of his estimates of persons (with the notable exception of Finlay), situations, and events have been substantiated.

Julius Millingen, who was sent by the Greek Committee and set up a hospital at Missolonghi, was one of several physicians who treated Byron in his last illness. He later sided with the Turks and used his Memoirs of the Affairs of

Greece (1831) not only for personal vindictiveness--against
Trelawny notably--but also to gain preferment with the enemy
by attacking the Greeks and Byron's own motives. Apparently his scheme worked, for he was made official court physician to the Sultan the next year. Unfortunately for Byron,
Millingen used him as the mouthpiece for his attacks on both
Trelawny--helping to create an implacable enemy for the
poet in this quarter--and the Greeks. The attacks on the
latter are much too intense, but in substance support can be
found for them in Byron material.

        The firsthand accounts that appear during this time
deal with periods other than the Greek in the poet's life.
For the one immediately preceding Missolonghi there appeared in 1830 an interesting volume by a young Scottish
army doctor named James Kennedy; its title was Conversations on Religion with Lord Byron and Others. In a series
of seven or eight private interviews with Byron, and several
more with others present, Kennedy tried to convert Byron
and his audience to orthodox Christianity over a period of
several months beginning on August 10, 1823, and ending
when Byron moved on to Missolonghi. When he projected
his book, his intentions were apparently not for exploitation
but for purposes of converting his readers, for the conversations with Byron were to occupy only a quarter of a larger design outlining the principles of Christianity. Death cut
off his plan, and his widow edited the conversations in the
present form. Despite the skeptical feeling of some about
Byron's position in these discussions, the poet, though
amused, trusted this Scotsman, treated him kindly, and
seemed to respect his earnest and sincere belief. There is
no reason to doubt the reliability of these conversations, as
Kennedy was as honest and scrupulous a recorder as any of
Byron's firsthand witnesses; and the picture conveyed of Byron's deep religious interest coupled with his skepticism of
certain orthodox tenets is vouched for by Lady Byron, Teresa, and others.

        For the period in Italy at Genoa the "most gorgeous"
Lady Blessington is the contemporary witness. With a past
that precluded her entry into the first ranks of society, this
single-minded, socially ambitious woman had created her own
rival society in England. From the moment that she arrived
in Genoa in 1823, she was determined to draw Lord Byron
into her social and conversational web; and she was eminently successful. The number of their meetings during the
April and May days that the Blessingtons were in Genoa is

uncertain, but it was probably about 21, some of which were
by accident. The immediate motive for her serialized account of these conversations published in the New Monthly
Magazine in 1832 and 1833 seems to have been desire for
money, as was the case with the reprint in book form in
1834 and a later version called The Idler in Italy (1839); but
personal social attack and praise through the mouth of Byron
are certainly part of her game as well. Other motives--judg-
ing from the portrait she presents of Byron--may simply be
in the realm of her psychological makeup; for she treats him
with such condescension at times as to divest him of all
charisma, and we are left with the patronizing "poor Byron"
as she calls him, a depiction that is to have considerable influence throughout the century, unfortunately. Teresa, in
her unpublished life of Byron, sums up what she considers
the flaws of the Conversations: "We will say only that it
contains few pages on which the untrue, the premeditated,
the artificial, and even the impossible do not substantially
dominate" and "what is reprehensible is to have placed in
Lord Byron's mouth (when he was no longer able to defend
himself) what she thought concerning a great many things
and people and in this way to avoid their malice. " With all
of its flaws, the Conversations still remains, along with
Medwin's Journal, one of the two most interesting contemporary accounts of Byron. It is long on insight; though short
on conversational validity, it is unique in being the only
book-length record by a woman.

Growing out of the Pisan period in Byron's life, besides Medwin's Conversations already mentioned, is Leigh
Hunt's Lord Byron and Some of His Contemporaries (1828),
the most openly vindictive of all the eyewitness accounts.
Hunt had arrived at Pisa on July 1, 1822, to implement the
plans Byron and Shelley had projected for a journal to be
called The Liberal. Shelley, Hunt's main patron, drowned
one week later. From this point the relationship between
Byron and Hunt went steadily downhill and the fortunes of
The Liberal with it. Hunt's book need never have been published; it seems to have come about by accident because of
his misadventures with monetary advances made by his publisher for a project on which Hunt reneged. In order to
make reparation, Hunt decided to deliver an account of his
relations with Lord Byron; so partly his motives are pecuni-
ary. A deeper motive is revealed, however, once he becomes engaged on the project--that is, injured pride. He
gives vent to hatred of long standing, built up largely on
two counts: aristocratic slights--real or imagined--on the

part of Byron, and Byron's parsimoniousness toward him.
The former charge is exaggerated since Byron's letters reveal no hatred of Hunt even though the two did have their
differences. The latter charge is disproved by Byron's known
generosity toward Hunt. If much of Hunt's injury is imaginary, his bitterness is not. The portrait of his subject is
so distorted and false as to be libelous today; for he makes
Byron out to be, among other things, avaricious, hypocritical, cowardly, jealous, superstitious, arrogant, insincere,
inept in conversation, bumbling in social situations. Not
only does he attack Byron, but Hobhouse, Moore, or anyone
who has a favorable word for Byron; and all is done under
the guise of modesty, honest frankness, and other such com-
pliments that Hunt pays himself. It is a mean effort and un-
worthy of its author. Twenty-two years later Hunt tries to
make amends in his Autobiography by offering apology; but
one suspects that it is more a plea for sympathy in old age
than genuine repentance, for he mainly tries to excuse himself and actually retracts nothing. At any rate it comes
twenty-two years too late; his virulence has already prejudiced readers against Byron, and some of his accusations
have become apocrypha almost impossible to controvert.
Lord Byron and Some of His Contemporaries represents the
low watermark for the period of the firsthand estimates of
Byron.

One good result comes from Hunt's maliciousness.
Two years later appears Thomas Moore's Letters and Journals of Lord Byron. It is inevitable that the eyewitness activity after Byron's death should culminate in a full-scale
biography by one who knew and was on intimate terms with
him for a large part of his life. Hunt's publication, which
presumed in this direction, might have been forestalled altogether, or at least limited to brief treatment, if Moore
had not been plagued by obstructions, enmity against him,
quarrels and reconciliations, changes of publishers, so that
by 1828 an impasse seems to have been reached. Hunt's
appearance in print accomplished a small miracle by consoli-
dating the different factions--particularly Moore, Murray,
and Hobhouse--so that the former was finally able to bring
this whole enterprise to completion. Too often Moore's contribution to Byron studies is either overlooked, since his
work has been almost entirely superseded, or passed off as
rather vapid but harmless, Moore himself being seen merely
as a "joiner of materials." Actually, his piece is a landmark at the time for a number of reasons. For one thing,
it enjoyed semi-official status since it was sanctioned by

Murray and Hobhouse; the immediate family, under the circumstances, probably never could have agreed on an "official" biographer. Also, Moore managed to collect an astonishing amount of material notwithstanding the proximity to
Byron's death, the enormous current interest, and the great
monetary value of any documents by or connected with the
poet. Through a combination of diligence, personal charm,
utilization of his own renown, and reliance on pressure in
high places, he garnered 561 letters, the journals and "Detached Thoughts," and various verses. Perhaps most important today are the dozens of interviews that Moore engi-
neered with people who knew his subject, for these yielded
anecdotes about and conversations with Byron that do not appear elsewhere and add to the contemporary flavor of the
work that still makes it valuable. For the first time, too,
a full-length portrait of Byron was presented, and it was by
someone who was neither so close as to be violently prejudiced in his behalf nor so familiarly distant (like Hunt) as to
be hostile. So it was reasonably balanced; and if it tips the
scale in favor of Byron, then it serves as a valuable counter-
weight to the anti-Byron material that had prevailed before.
This is not to say that there are no faults, for Moore does
tamper and suppress. But if he is favorable to Byron, he
is also discreet where Lady Byron is concerned; if he is
apologetic, he still shows Byron's faults; and if he moralizes,
he also disclaims by innuendo. Altogether, the portrait is
one that has not been invalidated. The simple fact is that
Moore's life of Byron dominates this posthumous period of
Byron criticism, and it does so primarily by worth rather
than notoriety. As mentioned, it is the culmination of the
contemporary accounts, the fullest, the most balanced, the
best. But it also marks the beginning of serious, full-scale
biographies of Byron. Moore did his job well enough to forestall any comparable biography for fifty years, and it really
was not completely surpassed until twentieth-century biographers made use of the Coleridge/Prothero edition and later
discoveries.

        John Galt in The Life of Lord Byron (1830) ostensibly
continues the full-scale biographical line already begun so
well by Moore; for he states that his book is intended to
supplement the latter's, in particular by dwelling on the intellectual side rather than the factual and by correcting its
"too radiant and conciliatory" likeness of Byron. The term
"ostensibly" is used because Galt does not really launch a
full and original biography of his own; he merely lifts the
larger part of his material from Moore and the contemporary

but chronologically-limited accounts already published. His
major claim to genuine authenticity rests on the portion of
his book that deals with knowledge of Byron on his first tour
of the East in 1809 and 1810 when the two met on at least
three occasions and were in proximity for a total of six or
seven weeks. Because of his familiarity with this period and
his own experiences in the East at the same time, he fleshes
out this segment of his work to the abnormal proportion of a
third. His "biography," then, is more honestly another eye-
witness account of a particular period of Byron's life, even
written for the monetary motive usually prompting these
recollections; and the lasting value of the piece lies in the
recounting of this period. Galt vitiates much of the value
of his account in his aim to "correct" Moore's "sunny side"
portrayal; for his effort consists fairly consistently of a
bringing down of Lord Byron, although he does appreciate
the poetry. His negative bias seems to have come mainly
from the difference in rank of the two men and from some
personally deprecatory remarks of Byron that he had read in
Moore's biography. As legitimate biography, then, Galt's
book must rank low; Moore calls it a "wretched thing" and
Hobhouse says "[Byron] was not the mean tricky creature you
have represented him to have been." As influence, unfortunately, it must rank quite high--not as high as Moore's biography officially, but for the public at large it quickly became standard because of the style (Galt was a novelist),
price, and length--and it was reprinted into the twentieth
century. For these reasons it is important for promoting
such erroneous views of Byron as the underestimation of his
motives in going to Greece and his plagiarisms.

The mesmeric hold upon the public of Byron's personality rather than his work is especially evident in this
period. All important items are biographical in nature,
either personal accounts on a limited scale or full biographies; and the biographical percentage of the residue remains
about the same as that during the initial years of grief. The
items that might be loosely designated as critical are so few
that no general patterns emerge, nor may any be singled
out as particularly worthy of note. So discussion has centered on the figures considered in the preceding paragraphs
who knew Byron in varying degrees of intimacy, who present
the most important documents concerning him for the period,
and whose accounts are the bases for future conceptions and
misconceptions. Many of these presentations of the poet are
slanted for personal reasons, so that one cannot as yet see
Byron plain; in some cases it will take almost to the present

day to determine who was telling the truth and who came closest to the real Byron. Motives for a particular bias may be monetary need, justification of personal views, desire for notoriety, self-inflation, a personal grudge, or pride; but whatever the motive, the end was the same--exploitation. It is enough to give the period its character. In light of this summary, the prediction that Finlay makes is peculiarly apropos: "I believe that, for some time, he [Byron] will not be dealt with more fairly than during his life.... Time will put an end to all undue admiration and malicious cant.... It will then be possible to form a just estimation of the greatness of his genius and his mind, and the real extent of his faults."

The firsthand accounts will go on for a while--Trelawny, Hobhouse, Teresa must still be heard from--but the majority are now out, and the main biographical lines have been laid down. If the preceding period seems to end with a tapering off of interest in Byron and with the forces representing denigration firmly in command, whether they be the shrill tones of Hunt or the patronizing disparagement of Blessington and Galt, then there is still Mazzini's ringing prophecy in 1839 that Byron will be remembered.

3. Decline in Interest and Reputation, 1840-1868

For the moment Mazzini's words are blown in the wind. The struggle between the admirers and detractors of Lord Byron for supremacy following his death seems to have been won, for the time being at least, by the latter. Hunt's blasts and Lady Blessington's innuendoes are the final stage in his demotion; the public thereafter no longer seems to have found him even worthy of interest. What follows is a long, three-decade period of decline. The light comes dangerously close to flickering out; there is almost a second and more final death for Byron. This state of affairs, however, cannot be laid entirely at the door of the Dallases, Medwins, Stanhopes, Hunts, and Blessingtons; there are other reasons for the decline. In part, at least, it must be due to the natural course of events, the gravitational law applied to literature that what goes up must come down. It was inevitable that there would be something like an equal reaction to the extraordinary reputation that Byron enjoyed in his own day, that a literary god was bound to be replaced by another, that the Romantic spirit and vogue that he epitomized would metamorphose into a wholly different world, that the young Turks who followed him in their youth would be turning from him as they grew older.

Evidence for the decline already existed before 1840. One might suspect its beginning as early as 1827 when only five items relating to Byron appeared, a striking contrast to the mountain of information from 1824-1826; but then Hunt's attack came the next year and the accounts of Galt, Kennedy, and Moore in 1830 to allay the suspicion. Still, in 1831 and the next three years the output is not what one would expect, even with Hunt, Millingen, and Blessington to keep the publicity alive. But from 1835 to 1839 it is obvious that a decline really has set in. With the years 1840-1868 the decline is firmly established; there are one-third fewer entries for approximately twice the number of years as in the preceding era of Byron studies. No single year produces over

24

twelve items that deal with Byron if one excepts the answers
to queries; some years have only two entries (1847-1848),
some only three (1841-1843). The years 1841-1848 have the
dubious distinction of representing the absolute nadir of Byron interest; never before nor after would interest fall this
low. It seems fantastic now that the man who was a byword
in England and on the Continent for so many years, who
quite possibly was the most famous man of his day, should
so quickly suffer this eclipse. The 40's, 50's, and 60's
make it plain that Byron is going to have to be rediscovered.

Commensurate with the loss of interest in Byron during these decades is the decline in his reputation. It can be
seen from several different angles. To be expected is the
continuance but gradual decline in numbers of the contemporary firsthand accounts; most of them follow the disparaging
line already established. Trelawny's Recollections of the
Last Days of Shelley and Byron, published in 1858, is no
exception. Trelawny is one of the few major contemporary
associates of Byron who did not produce his account until
some decades later, possibly to forestall any denial of his
claims since many of the participants in the drama of Byron's and Shelley's lives had now died. His is the major
item in the years under discussion. Joseph Severn refers
to Trelawny as a "camelion" and as "Lord Byron's jackal."
This estimate seems to be accurate on both counts; for at
Byron's death Trelawny writes, "The world has lost its
greatest man, I my best friend," and within four months he
is saying that Byron is better off dead. The Recollections
are the culmination of a sustained campaign to belittle Byron
in every respect, beginning as far back as 1831 when Trelawny appealed to Claire Clairmont for help in deflating the
poet's fame ("to dissipate the cant and humbug about Byron,"
he calls it). While extremely vivid and picturesque, his
book is a potpourri of inaccuracies and concocted stories
that produces an overall unpleasant effect of Byron--indolent,
proud, parsimonious, worldly, cynical, insincere--and the
little sympathy that he does show is removed from the later
version of 1878 entitled Records of Shelley, Byron and the
Author. In part Trelawny's continuing prejudice may be explained by the revelation to him in the books by Kennedy
and Millingen (whom he passionately detested) of Byron's
references to him as untruthful; in part it may also be explained by his own ego and proclivity to shift with the tides
of public taste.

Medwin and Hunt are contemporaries who are heard
from again. The former, in his Life of Percy Bysshe

Shelley (1847), turns on Byron somewhat from his more ami-
able tone in his Conversations.   Hunt in his Autobiography
(1850) removes some of the more offending pages of his earlier attack and apologizes; he still maintains, however, that
he wrote no fictions but only what he felt or thought to be
true.   Two more contemporaries need to be noticed: Thomas
Campbell and Samuel Rogers.   The former is important because of his defense of Lady Byron after Moore's Life appeared; his posture then and in 1849 in the publication of his
Life and Letters is attack by innuendo.   Rogers was an in-
veterate London gossip, responsible for some of the apocryphal stories in circulation about Byron, but his references to
Byron in his Table Talk of 1856 at least are not unkind.

        The decline in Byron's reputation can also be seen
from the angle of the new young writers who will make up
the Victorian generation.   They begin with stunning expressions of grief and a sense of loss at Byron's death that border on adulation.   Bulwer-Lytton, Carlyle, Jane Welsh,
Tennyson--the words of all attest to the grip Byron held
upon their young minds; Jane Welsh compares his passing to
the sun or the moon having gone out of the heavens.   Once
the trauma of the event has passed and some of the bloom
is off their youthful ardor, they begin to follow the general
downward curve of his reputation set by his squabbling contemporaries.   Carlyle is perhaps symptomatic of the shift in
sensibility among the rising Victorians.   His references to
Byron show him sympathetic up to 1828, though he feels the
poet did not live long enough to realize fully his potential.
In 1828, however, his opinion begins to change, and he sees
him as an "English Sentimentalist and Power-man"; by 1830
he is convinced that Byron's fame will not endure because he
is false, theatrical, insincere, and never really gave any
productive thought to mankind; by the time he writes Sartor,
he is prepared to admonish his audience to "Close thy Byron;
open thy Goethe. "

        About the same time that Carlyle is finding a Victori-
an identity by rejecting his past represented by Byron, other
emerging young writers are doing the same.   There is a rising tide of condemnation.   Newman (1829) speaks out to con-
demn the Childe Harold type of poetry as mere eloquence and
Byron himself for lacking versatility, religious principle, and
poetic feeling.   While Macaulay (1831) is the first to make
the astute observation of the split in Byron between the Classic and Romantic and though he does grant Byron credit for
excellence in his descriptive and meditative passages, he

really represents the rising middle-class point of view which
is largely unsympathetic to Byron. So effectively does he
harp on what he considers Byron's flaws in his review of
Moore's <u>Life</u> that those he singles out have become critical
dogma almost to the present day: e.g., the egocentric quality of Byron's work, his lack of dramatic effectiveness, the
careless structure of his tales, his weakness in characterization, his "system of ethics, compounded of misanthropy
and voluptuousness." The same year, Bulwer-Lytton, in the
preface to his <u>The Siamese Twins</u>, is making a plea for a
new school of poetry, a new expression to fit the times.
The trend continues with Henry Taylor's anti-Byronic estimate (1834) in which he condemns especially the lack of intellectual content in Byron's work; the latter in fact becomes
another stock complaint for the rest of the century.

        As the swing into the Victorian period continues, with
its common denominator of middle-class morality, its complacency, its passion for moral reform, its optimistic trust
in material progress, it turns even farther from Byron.
Thackeray's agitated attack in his <u>Notes of a Journey</u> in
1846, with his famous comment that Byron never wrote from
the heart, represents the dead center of the decline in Byron's reputation among the Victorians. By this time most
of the Victorians have repudiated the poet or will do so
shortly: Ruskin in the 50's (Byron is among the "powerful
and popular writers in the cause of error," and "the mass of
sentimental literature ... [is] headed by the poetry of Byron"); Tennyson in the 60's ("Byron's merits are on the surface," and later "Byron is not an artist or a thinker, or a
creator in the higher sense, but a strong personality");
Browning in the 70's (as a result of Alfred Austin's praise
of Byron and attack on Browning); Swinburne later.

        Thackeray's essay is central also in that shortly
thereafter, though the condemnation of Byron continues, it
is abated somewhat and tempered with positive remarks.
With Augustus and Charles Hare at mid-century, criticism
is still largely condemnatory, for they follow mainly Macaulay's line of comment concerning Byron's egotism ("the
prince of egotists") and lack of dramatic ability. Bagehot,
too, is condemnatory in this decade when he dismisses Byron with two sentences ("Lord Byron tried this kind of composition in <u>Manfred</u>, and the result is an evident failure,"
and "it was the instinct of Byron to give in glaring words
the gross phenomena of evident objects"), and in the next
decade when he expands his comment into a more careful

consideration in order to criticize Byron's exaggeration and
his romances. But Ruskin, after a brief anti-Byronic period,
begins to notice some good traits: Byron's sympathy with
justice, his kindness, courage, and humanizing pity; and in
Ruskin's later writing he offers some of the most perceptive
comment on Byron's work up to that time. And George Borrow, while he notes that Byron with his assumed melancholy
and his fame (dependent in part on his being an aristocrat)
helped dethrone himself with his "mouthings and coxcombry,"
still believes that he had fire and emotion and would be re-
instated again. As the generation of the 50's grows more
disillusioned with events and conditions, many begin to remember Byron's uncompromising liberalism, and the attitude
toward him changes even more radically, especially Arnold's.
The latter acknowledges Byron's "pageant of his bleeding
heart" and feels that he lacked in intellect, culture, and
ideas; but still, Arnold proclaims, he had genius and was
"the greatest natural force, the greatest elementary power
... since Shakespeare. " Perhaps even more important, Arnold feels Byron was relevant in that he belonged "to that
which is the main current of the literature of modern
epochs ... [he tried to] apply modern ideas to life. " Kingsley recognizes the loss of Byron's influence but defends him
by noting his "artistic good taste, his classical polish, his
sound shrewd sense, his hatred of cant, his insight into humbug ... [his] habit of being always intelligible ... [his] most
intense and awful sense of moral law--of law external to himself. "

By the decade of the 60's there is still criticism; but
with Meredith's cry for more Byron and less Tennyson, and
with Swinburne's eloquent "Preface" wherein he praises Byron's sincerity, his firm grasp on nature, his focus on human interest, and the total achievement of his works (while
downgrading only his dramatic power), one feels that the
corner has been turned and that a revival of interest and an
upswing in the poet's reputation are just ahead. In spite of
all the turning away from the poet by the Victorians, they
are never really far from him; they turned away a moralistic
and complacent cheek when it was fashionable to do so, but
the other glowed with the evident influence and effect he had
upon them, even Carlyle. The Hares in 1851 state that Byron "magnifies himself by speaking with bitter scorn of all
things"; perhaps this statement explains in part the Victorian
attitude toward Byron--a very ambivalent one at best--and in
part his decline in their view.

A quick statistical count reveals this period as again overwhelmingly biographical in interest, with roughly 100 items on and 11 general appreciations of Byron. But the nature of these biographical items is revealing and gives us another angle on the decline of Byron interest in this period. Many of these items are not really concerned with Byron directly at all; instead, they are reminiscences or recollections, memoirs, autobiographies, letters, journals--lives of other people who mention Byron only in passing reference. The biographical items concerned directly with Byron are in the main anecdotes, Byron's relation to a place, and biographical sketches, especially in encyclopedias and histories of poetry. This evidence is further testimony to Byron's decline. But other explanations may be in order. The reason for the lack of more substantial biographical work, one must suppose, is at least partly due to the gradual trailing off of the firsthand accounts--though Hobhouse and Teresa are still to be heard from. Then, too, there is Moore's biography with its intimidating array of primary source material; nothing much new is being uncovered from which to compile a better work.

One trend in the period, though a slight one and probably a result of the lack of new materials on Byron, is the tendency to look more at his poetry. Aside from the critical comment already noted--which includes a few items of solid merit--there are a half-dozen general estimates of Byron's work, a few items on miscellaneous aspects of his poetry, and 65 or so on particular pieces. The figures are deceiving, however, in that most of the latter are of the N & Q variety. After the biographical exploration succeeding Byron's death, then, there is an indication of a turning to the work now, though the man and personality still hold the center of the stage. The criticism is in the main peripheral and not of lasting value and will be a long time coming of age, but at least it reveals a slight current in this direction.

4. Revival of Interest, 1869-1897

The period from 1840 to 1868 ended with three items for the final year, just one item short of the lowest output ever for a single year of scholarship on Byron. The present period opens with 68 items--the highest total since the year of the poet's death and a spectacular indicator that a Byronic revival is underway. The reason for such a cataclysmic shift in attention is not hard to find; at the epicenter is a revelatory publication of the Byron scandal, and whirling around it is the heat of controversy inevitably engendered.

The publication is by Harriet Beecher Stowe, and it first appeared in September 1869 as a twenty-page lead article entitled "The True Story of Lady Byron's Life" in Macmillan's Magazine in England and in The Atlantic Monthly in America; a year later it was expanded into book form with new evidence for her charges and replies to her numerous critics. The work was bred, first, by what Mrs. Stowe considered the alarming dissemination of Byron's poetry (which she looked upon unfavorably) through a number of unauthorized editions as well as the issuance of John Murray's popular Pearl Edition; and, second, by what she claimed was a too-attractive picture of Lord Byron and an unfair view of Lady Byron in Teresa Guiccioli's Lord Byron jugé par les témoins de sa vie (apparently an after-thought as her article had been completed and in the printer's hands before she read this account). The motives for her book, then, are those of the crusader; as Leslie Stephen says, "she thought that by blasting [Byron's] memory she might weaken the evil influence of his writings, and shorten his expiation in another world." It is, in fact, the crusading tone and manner of the whole narrative that make it seem dated, even humorous, today; but the matter was serious enough at the time and caused a sensation.

Actually, Mrs. Stowe may not have been the first to bring forward publicly the charge of incest. John Fox pre-

ceded her by several months with two responsible articles
that examine the marriage problem. He concludes that the
offense on Byron's part was of sufficient severity to make
the separation irrevocable; he may be implying incest in an
example that he gives of just cause why a wife might leave
her husband, but he discreetly avoids naming the cause and
later takes Mrs. Stowe to task for doing so. Altogether Fox
wrote four articles surveying the issue--centering on Byron,
his wife, the marriage, and the problem of the incest--and
these would have been important except for Mrs. Stowe's
more sensational publication. Mrs. Stowe had the advan-
tages of a popular magazine with wide circulation and her
famous name; so to her must go the credit for stirring up
the discord and for giving the major impetus to the revival
of interest in Byron.

        Ironically, the two most important items for the year
1869 focus on Lady Byron and Teresa Guiccioli: the one,
Mrs. Stowe's account of Lady Byron; the other, Teresa's
view of Byron in English translation, My Recollections of
Lord Byron. The one portrays the poet in the darkest colors
possible, in what must be considered an extreme attack; the
other paints him primarily in rosy hues, in an opposite extreme of hero worship. But the year clearly belongs to Mrs.
Stowe. Teresa's account seems to elicit no interest other
than the reviews, though two articles do appear about her
for the year--one of a general nature and one claiming that
Byron went to Greece to get away from her. Mrs. Stowe's
account, on the contrary, releases a fury of interest. Of
the 68 items listed for the year, more than 40 deal with the
controversy, a startling 60 per cent of the year's total output on
Byron. Most are articles dealing with the principals involved in the scandal, with correspondence relating to it,
with Mrs. Stowe herself, or with the progress of the controversy.

        But a surprising number of books come into print
almost overnight, seven in all. One is on Medora Leigh;
the remainder purport to be summaries of the entire controversy from one point of view or another. The approach may
be under the guise of a fair and objective appraisal, with
such words in the title as "compiled from the best authorities"; or it may be out and out sensational, appealing on the
basis of the scandalous side of the whole business. In either
case nearly all the material is favorable to Byron, for the
overwhelming public reaction was disapproval of Mrs. Stowe's
revelations. The range of the latter is from disapproval of

her motives, to vindication of Lord Byron, to satire and
parody of the revelations themselves. Fox is the most notable writer aligned on the same side as Mrs. Stowe, though
one or two others show disapproval of Byron or defend the
revelations as perfectly justified in the interests of literary
history. Both sides take an extreme approach; only the
Athenaeum for September 11, 1869, makes a plea for sanity
by urging reservation of judgment until all charges are proved.

     The controversy continues through the next year; the
added fuel this time is the enlarged version of "The True
Story," printed in book form as Lady Byron Vindicated.
Again interest generated may be gauged by the total number
of articles and books on Byron that appear, over 40 this
time. The number is down from the preceding year but
otherwise represents the highest figure since 1825. The
number devoted to the Stowe issue is down considerably but
is not far from half the total if one excludes 11 N & Q items
related to one query. So the issue is still a burning one,
though it is beginning to subside. Articles remain in the
majority; but books continue to come out on the scandal and
even increase in percentage, the most important being the
account of the separation written forty years earlier by Hobhouse but now privately printed for the first time. Sides
are still assumed though the positions taken are less extreme,
another indication of heat beginning to die down. The next
year only one item appears, John Fox's Vindication of Lady
Byron, which is mainly a reprint of his Temple Bar articles
of 1869 and remains the lone book that supports Mrs. Stowe.
Not until ten years later is the subject brought up again; and
the entry is not on the scandal but an N & Q exchange over
varying contemporary accounts of the separation, in particular those of Mrs. Morrell and Medwin. Thereafter items
appear sporadically--two in 1885, two in 1887, one in 1897--
and most of these relate to the scandal rather than focus on
it. The only publication directly related is that of J. C.
Jeaffreson in the Athenaeum, September 19, 1885, which contains 24 letters from Augusta to Hodgson that bear evidence
against Mrs. Stowe. So after a bright blaze across the sky,
the Stowe scandal quickly burns itself out.

     If the Stowe issue is for practical purposes dead after
1870 until the end of the century, it has at least served the
useful purpose of reviving interest in Byron. With interest
revived, albeit along controversial lines, the remainder of
the century may be seen, not as the aftermath of the Stowe
scandal, but as a new thrust or movement that establishes

interest on a more stable and permanent basis. The most obvious testament to this fact is the large increase in publications about the poet after matters settle down again to a more normal indication of interest. The average number of items that appear from 1871 to the end of the century is about 20 per year. While this figure is understandably less than the number appearing in 1869 and 1870, it is well in advance of the average of seven for the twenty-nine-year period preceding these years; and the latter average would be even less if the multiple N & Q entries for these years were omitted.

A further clue indicating the establishment of a more permanent interest in Byron is the direction taken by biographical study, which remains the area of greatest interest through the rest of the period. Of course there is the expected potpourri of items dealing with widely scattered biographical topics: Byronic relationships (Mary Chaworth, Caroline Lamb, Moore, Trelawny, Shelley--with a number of items on the latter association because of the rise in Shelley's reputation and Shelleyan studies), Byron and Greece, Byron and the stage, the Byron memorial (an area of noticeable concentration with nine items, including a book by Richard Edgcumbe in 1883), and the usual anecdotes and minor Byroniana. But two aspects are new to this era. First, there is an overwhelming welter of biographical material in the nature of recollections, reminiscences, memoirs, diaries, letters, table talk from people who had known or remembered Byron. The most important resemble the personal accounts that flooded the market immediately succeeding his death; these are the Personal Reminiscences (1875) of William Harness, Byron's Harrow acquaintance whose friendship he kept up while he was in England, and the Memoir (1878) of Francis Hodgson, the Cambridge tutor and friend to whom Byron was even closer. Both are positive in outlook without being slanted and reveal the best side of Byron in his early friendships; the Memoir is the more important because of the new letters and verse that it contains.

The great majority of these reminiscent accounts, however, are not this directly related and do not purport to be as intimate nor as detailed as the earlier, firsthand treatments, that is, reproductions of Byron's very conversation or character and opinions in some way. A number of this group did have contact with the poet personally in varying degrees of importance, but their reminiscences usually

offer comment on him in the larger context of their lives
and careers instead of focusing on him directly--e.g., those
of Sir George Sinclair (1870), Sir Henry Holland (1872),
George Ticknor (1876), Crabb Robinson (1877), John Wilson
Croker (1884), James Hogg (1885), John Murray (1891),
Claire Clairmont (1893), and John Gibson Lockhart (1897).
The remainder of these reminiscences--and by far the greatest in number--are by people who had no direct contact with
Byron at all; but because he was part of the times in which
they lived and because his name had attained a great deal of
notoriety again, they felt compelled to write about him.
Since they are not well known in relation to Byron, there is
no need to mention their names. But the sum total of all
these memoirs is important, not only for what they contribute
to the store of Byron knowledge and that of his times, but
because they dominate publications on Byron until the end of
this era and give it in large part its character, forming about
one-third of the total. Besides adding more fragments to the
mosaic of Byron's life and thought, they clearly demonstrate
the growing interest in and acceptance of Byron once again.

      The second new aspect of studies biographical, a re-
vitalized interest in comprehensive biography, demonstrates
the same conclusion. Thomas Moore's work had intimidated
biographers for forty years and no full-scale biography had
been attempted; but beginning in 1870, four appear by the
end of the century. Two are large tomes and attempt to be
inclusive: Karl Elze's Lord Byron, A Biography (1870) is
the earlier and a plodding work; it presents some new material and documents, though it has been completely superseded today. J. C. Jeaffreson's The Real Lord Byron (1883)
offers some new material also, but his effort is marred by
his peculiar theories and by his concentration on the worst
side of Byron's character while ostensibly trying to correct
the wrongs done to the poet. The two briefer biographies
that appear, each written for a series, are better. John
Nichol's Byron (1880), for the "English Men of Letters"
series, adds little that is new, places too much trust on
Stanhope and Blessington, offers scant criticism, and needs
modification in some of its conclusions; but as a brief and
convenient summary of Byron's life and accomplishment, it
still stands. Roden Noel's Life of Lord Byron (1890), in
the "Great Writers" series, is less as biography, since the
author follows Jeaffreson's work too closely, but more as
criticism since he adheres to the same lines of his earlier
astute essay "Lord Byron and His Times" (1873) in St. Paul's
Magazine and also because he was a practicing poet himself.

These biographies are of slight importance today, but they
do manifest the continuance of interest in Byron after the
Stowe revelations. They attempt to make use of the new materials and items that had come to light and to make a general assessment of the life and achievement of the poet; the
fact that they failed in the larger context of time is probably
due to their closeness to the unresolved Stowe scandal and
their lack of definitive materials with which to work.

If the biographical studies furnish evidence of the establishment of interest in Byron, they do not guarantee the
poet's fame. A shift in that direction, however, may be
seen in the estimates that appear after 1870 when the Stowe
issue has died down. The number itself is impressive and
further testimony to the stabilizing and sustaining of interest
in Byron, for the total amounts to about 26 per cent of the published materials as opposed to five to ten per cent in preceding
periods. It would seem then that the cause célèbre of 1869-
1870, arousing the considerable interest that it did, also
evoked a massive reappraisal of the poet. There is some
distance now from the decline which set in during Byron's
own period and after, and he can be viewed more dispassion-
ately. The young of his own day, having grown old, tended
to ignore his faults and remember him fondly; while the
Victorians, having firmly established themselves, would not
need to be as combative as formerly. The change in opinion,
accordingly, is startlingly favorable; in fact, the swing in
that direction is almost as far as it had been in the reverse
direction earlier.

The first estimate to appear is The Poetry of the
Period (1870) by Alfred Austin. His appreciation of Byron
is admirable, particularly in his emphasis on such lofty
matters as Byron's sublimity of thought, his grasp of the
eternal aspects of nature, and his treatment of man's struggle with nature; but he holds Byron up with such verve as
an example to the major Victorians that one shudders lest
reaction should set in, which is exactly what happens shortly in the cases of Swinburne and Browning. John Morley
enlarges Austin's praise in a masterful essay first published
in the Fortnightly Review (1870) without committing his blun-
der of damning the Victorians. His appraisal is so rational
and astute that many of his ideas have become commonplace:
e.g., Byron is the most enormous force of his time; he is
the embodiment of the revolutionary principle and his poetry
is a revolutionary force in itself; he is the enemy of a society "which only remembered that man had property, and

forgot that he had a spirit"; he is the revealer of a "dis-
tinctively modern scorn and aversion for the military spirit";
he is "one of the most rational of men" but in his interest
as mover places passion over intellect; Byron does not sooth
but agitates us; there is the "genuine modernism of his poetic
spirit"; he has "a quality of poetical worldliness in its enlarged and generous sense of energetic interest in real transactions"; his influence is continental rather than insular.
Morley's essay is amplified by its memorable prose and remains a minor classic in Byron criticism.   Plainly, Byron
can now be looked upon with favor again; and instead of being deprecated by or compared unfavorably with the Victorians, the trend is reversed in the 70's and Byron is now
lauded at their expense.   This tendency has already been
noted in Austin's work; and it may be further seen in that of
Joseph Devey, William Minto, and one signing himself the
"London Hermit."

     The 80's are ushered in auspiciously with evaluations
by John Ruskin, Richard C. Jebb, and John Addington Symonds.   Ruskin remains one of the most articulate spokes-
men for Byron among the Victorians as he clears him in
"Fiction, Fair and Foul" of much of the opprobrium concerning his morality and ethics that had clogged criticism from
the beginning of his career.   In a competent study of Byron's
Grecian venture, Jebb further clears the poet of the cynical
charges lodged against his motives and sincerity in that
cause.   Symonds' "Lord Byron" contains reservations but
still attests to Byron's greatness.   The climax of the new
acclaim Byron was enjoying comes in the famous "Preface"
by Matthew Arnold to Poetry of Byron that appears in 1881--
not so much in the extravagance of the appreciation as in the
fact that Arnold, one of the most important poets and critics
in the Victorian period, was willing to grant Byron his fame.
Arnold's appraisal is balanced, for he does not overlook what
he considered such faults of Byron's as his personal posing,
his lack of constructive criticism of society, the weakness in
the formal aspect of his poetry.   But at the same time Arnold sympathized with and found comfort in Byron's revolt
from the complacency, narrowness, and conformity--Philis-
tinism he calls it--of his own day; he is moved to appreciation of Byron's "sense for what is beautiful in nature, and
... in human action and suffering"; and he rises to positive
eulogy in referring to his "splendid and imperishable excellence of sincerity and strength" which is manifested through
a poetry that is direct and forceful in energy.   But Arnold
overreached himself in his famous prophecy that Byron and

Wordsworth would be the first names when England came to
"recount her poetic glories," and drew down fire upon his
head from a number of sources.   His immediate reviewers--
William Ernest Henley, Alfred Austin, and William Hale
White--went right on praising Byron and in fact scored Arnold, not for his praise, but in essence for not going far
enough.   But other critics like Swinburne, George Saintsbury,
and to a certain extent Andrew Lang presented a different
stance and reacted with rancor.   Swinburne especially is
noteworthy; for he replaces his earlier view of Byron as
stated in his "Preface" of 1866 with an outburst in 1884 that
borders on hysteria, the apparent reason being that Arnold
dared raise Byron higher than Coleridge and Shelley.   The
reaction of these latter critics, though heated, does not really alter the current as far as reappraisal of Byron is concerned.   For the moment, at least, interest in the poet has
been restored, he has been accepted (he still does not have
his niche in Westminster, but he is included in the Encyclopaedia Britannica in 1876 and Dictionary of National Biography
in 1886), and he has even been accorded a noteworthy place
among the stellar lights of the nation's heritage.

     Meanwhile consideration of particular works by the
poet goes on quietly, making fewer headlines but gathering
in volume and reflecting the rise in interest.   Almost a
gross of items appears, treating about 30 different pieces.
These figures represent nearly double the number of specific
works treated and more than twice the number of total entries concerning them that appeared in the preceding period
of study.   The Childe Harold cantos, representing the popular romantic side of the poet, receive the largest share of
attention, as they have since Byron's death; but Don Juan is
beginning to attract a significant amount of notice.   English
Bards and The Prisoner of Chillon also enjoy considerable
discussion, though this is less a trend than is the shift
toward Don Juan.   Several of these studies are book length,
but only the little volume by William Gerard, Byron Re-
studied in His Dramas (1886), need be mentioned.   Since
most of the criticism of particular works is of the N & Q
variety, it is less significant in quality than it is in volume.
The tendency toward development in criticism continues,
then; but, like Thursday's child, it still has far to go.

     More immediately indicative of things to come is a
new interest that begins to take form gradually over the entire period and is almost premonitory of the great era in
Byron research to follow.   Undoubtedly it, too, is a part of

the outgrowth initiated by the Stowe scandal and the forces
at work in Byron's favor over these years; but there is a
fresh impetus here as well, a building up toward something.
This new thrust manifests itself in the turning back to primary source materials, especially the poetry, and the collecting of new materials concerning Byron, most notably the
letters.

A return to reading Byron's poetry has already been
hinted at with the publication of Murray's "Pearl Edition" of
Byron's works in 1857, an edition issued to circumvent publishers who would take advantage of the lapse in the copyrights on Byron's poetry. But even this event does not suggest the wholesale return to the poetry that takes place in
the period under discussion. The renewed interest is reflected in the numerous editions appearing with a kind of
gathering momentum: the publication of the works by J.
Dicks in 1869, the editions edited by William Minto and
William Michael Rossetti in 1870, the reissue of Murray's
edition in 1867 and again in 1873, the appearance of William
Scott's edition in 1874 and later in 1883 and 1890, Matthew
Arnold's controversial edition of selections from Byron's
poetry in 1881, Henry F. Tozer's edition of Childe Harold's
Pilgrimage in 1885, which is also reprinted in 1891 and
1907, the two-volume edition of the works for "The Canterbury Poets" series edited by Mathilde Blind (1886), as well
as several American editions published. Byron's poetry
never really ceased to be read; but the personal scandal
seemed to make his poetry more attractive than ever, and
with growing acceptance came a heightened awareness of his
works.

Perhaps more suggestive of the new sense of direction and of more lasting value is the collection of fresh Byroniana, particularly letters, and the general movement
toward accumulating accurate data and materials. The impulse can be seen even in the Stowe years. In 1869 alone
there are four notices concerning several of Byron's unpublished letters; the correspondence is late--mainly 1823--and
to Douglas Kinnaird and J. J. Coulmann, though the letter
Byron drew up at La Mira, August, 1817, on the separation
is also printed. Sharpe's London Magazine prints "Letters,
Etc. , of Lord Byron" in several installments this same year.
So a respectable amount of this type of material is produced
in the first year of this period when the major focus is on
the life and scandal. After the scandal dies down, interest
is sustained until the end of the century, when it builds to

a climax. During this span 11 separate notices appear of
14 unpublished letters (two later proved to have been published) which range in date from an 1808 letter to Hodgson
to an 1824 letter to Barff; other important addressees are
Lady Byron, John Murray, James Wedderburn, and John
Hunt.

Even more significant are the collections of unpublished letters that appear in book form over the same time
span. In 1884 Letters Written by Lord Byron During His
Residence at Missolonghi is printed privately; it is a collection of letters written from January to April, 1824, to
Samuel Barff of Zante, who, along with Charles Hancock,
an English merchant residing at Cephalonia, cashed Byron's
bills and handled his business during his last year. The
collection edited by H. S. Schultess-Young in 1872, The Unpublished Letters of Lord Byron, is much more valuable
though fraught with problems (some of the material is taken
from the Major Byron forgeries in the British Museum).
Prothero largely dismisses the volume, but some of the
letters are genuine as they had already been published by
Moore; and Samuel Chew believes that the long series of
letters to the mysterious "L" (whom Byron ostensibly se-
duced) are genuine, along with some other possibilities in
the collection addressed to Shelley.

Potentially the most valuable collection of all was
that begun in 1896 by William Ernest Henley, who planned
to edit Byron's complete works. The problem was that a
cooperative arrangement could not be worked out with Murray for use of his vast collection of letters and materials,
a fact which doomed the project from the start. After the
appearance of Henley's first volume in 1897, Murray was
forced into publication of his own edition of Byron's works,
Henley's publisher withdrew support, and the editor had to
terminate his project. As it was, he expanded the number
of Byron letters and brought a lively and vigorous style to
the editorial apparatus; but the impossibility of his position
can be appreciated by comparing the number of letters in
his volume down to August 22, 1811 (88 letters), to the
number in Murray's edition (168 letters) for a similar time
period. The important phenomenon here is not the failure
of these publications, but the fact that they were undertaken.
Obviously interest in Byron is growing; and this burgeoning
attention to his letters is directly reflected in the publication
of the first one-volume collection of his letters for a general
audience, the collection edited by Mathilde Blind in 1887.

The gradual build-up toward something of major importance becomes even more apparent when one fits into the
evidence the busy activity in collecting information about Byron's works and gathering the materials themselves. Clues
may be picked up as early as 1869 with the appearance of
"Editions of Byron and Byroniana" in the American Bibliopolist. There is a lag until 1877 when several articles by
Liecester J. Warren appear, one in the Athenaeum dealing
with the "MSS of Childe Harold, Canto III," and several
others in an exchange in N & Q involving a listing of early
editions of English Bards and Scotch Reviewers. Again there
is a lag, though shorter this time, when in 1883 Richard
Edgcumbe publishes "Byron's Version of 'Tu Mi Chamas'"
and prints the verses found in Lady Lansdowne's album at
Bowood. Then in 1885 interest begins to accelerate and
lasts until the end of the century.

Editions absorb the most attention. In 1885 a lengthy
exchange occurs in the Athenaeum over "The Byron Quarto
of 1806 and its Variants," and in the same year Richard Edgcumbe and others describe in N & Q their copies of the first
edition of Hours of Idleness. In succeeding years George
Blackledge and others carry on an exchange in N & Q concerning the edition of Byron's works with the Finden illustrations (1886); W. H. Downing writes about an 1820 edition of
Byron's works published in Philadelphia by M. Thomas (1888);
J. Cuthbert Welch and others deal in N & Q with Byron's
works that were issued in paper covers (1889); the same author and Edward Peacock exchange views on the third edition
of English Bards and Scotch Reviewers (1890); a heated exchange dealing with the identity of the editor of the edition of
Byron's Life and Works published by Murray in 1834 occurs
in N & Q in 1891; and in 1894 in the Athenaeum may be
found an equally long series of articles that are concerned
with the bibliography of the different editions of English
Bards and Scotch Reviewers.

Over this same period considerable interest is also
manifested in establishing a more nearly accurate canon of
Byron's works. In 1886 W. Roberts initiates this activity
by publishing "Poems Attributed to Byron" in N & Q; his
article is quickly followed by eight additional articles in the
same journal which append further items to his list. The
accuracy of particular poems is the concern of Henry T.
Wake (1887) and John E. Norcross (1888). The former eli-
cits a long series of replies to his query about a missing
stanza in Childe Harold that Byron himself seems to have

indicated in his Zwickau edition of the poem.   Norcross
prompts several replies to his query concerning missing
stanzas in "Ode to Napoleon Buonaparte. " A Byronic fragment beginning "What matter the pangs of a husband and
father" is held up for scrutiny in 1893; and in 1894 Henry T.
Wake, along with four others, wonders about the authenticity
of the "Mountain Violet. "

        Finally, throughout the same period, solid evidence
of interest in Byron bibliography is apparent.   John Taylor
in 1886 publishes an initial list in N & Q; and in eight subsequent articles Richard Edgcumbe both expands this list
with his own compilation of items for a Byron bibliography
and establishes the classification he would use.   This specialized interest quickly comes of age when J. P. Anderson
publishes his "Bibliography" in Roden Noel's Life of Lord
Byron in 1890; this list is the most important one until the
appearance of Samuel C. Chew's Byron in England nearly 35
years later.   Toward the end of this era, J. H. Slater includes a section on "Lord Byron" in his Bibliographical Survey of the Works of Some Popular Modern Authors (1894).

        In summary, interest in Byron has been revived by
the Stowe scandal, and that interest has been established in
the succeeding years.   Moreover Byron's reputation has
taken a turn for the better; and even if it has not been fully
restored, at least he is now accepted as a poet.   Along with
acceptance has come interest in the gathering and reassessing
of materials concerning the poet and his work.   The time is
now ripe for a collected edition of all the poet's works that
have been accumulated and accounted for over the years.
The result--to come in the next era--is more than was bar-
gained for: the important Coleridge/Prothero edition has
been prepared for and is waiting in the wings.

5. Incentive to Scholarship, 1898-1923

The Coleridge/Prothero edition more than merits the
advance buildup of the preceding period, for this work inaugurates the modern era in Byron studies. This landmark in
Byron scholarship begins in 1898 with the first volume of the
poetry and two volumes of the letters and journals. The publication of the poetry continues at the rate of one new volume
per year until its completion in 1904; the one-volume version,
minus Coleridge's notes, follows in 1905, and thereafter the
authoritative edition of Byron's poetry is available to the
general public. The letters and journals set is completed
earlier; the third volume appears in 1899, the fourth in
1900, and the last two volumes in 1901. With the letters
and poetry reasonably complete, something approaching an
authentic, full-length picture of Byron may now be seen.

Coleridge based his text on the six-volume The Works
of Lord Byron published by John Murray in 1831, as it followed "the text of the successive issues of plays and poems
which appeared in the author's lifetime, and were subject to
his own revision, or that of Gifford and other accredited
readers." Since a number of variae lectiones had been detected over the years, Coleridge made a fresh collation of
all the manuscripts which had passed through Moore's hands
plus the manuscripts of all other important plays and poems
except for Heaven and Earth, The Blues, and Morgante Maggiore; the printed results, including canceled lines, are of first
importance. Of more dubious worth is the punctuation because Coleridge, asserting that this matter was more Gifford's responsibility in the published texts than Byron's,
made a fresh appraisal based primarily on meaning and interpretation. The edition advances the known canon of Byron's work by at least 30 hitherto unpublished poems, including a considerable fragment of the third part of The
Deformed Transformed and 14 stanzas of the unfinished
seventeenth canto of Don Juan. The latter is the most noteworthy of these additions, but the real significance of the

total lies more in rendering the edition inclusive than in presenting works of any particular literary merit.   The value of
this authoritative text is rounded off by the inclusion of Byron's notes, many published for the first time, and the editor's own valuable apparatus garnered from research in the
Dictionary of National Biography and minute examination of
the literature, magazines, and the newspapers of the period.

  Prothero's assignment as editor of the letters and
journals was not necessarily easier; but it was infinitely
more attractive and had more immediate effect because of
the vast amount of new material that was available to him,
primarily from Murray's rich archives.   Only two substantial collections of Byron's letters had appeared before, if
one discounts the promising Henley edition of 1897 which was
aborted after one volume; the first was Moore's Life, which
printed 561 letters, and the other was FitzGreene Halleck's
American edition of Byron's Works (1847), which increased
the number to 635.   Prothero was able nearly to double this
figure with his total of 1,198 letters, an increase of 563; in
addition, he was also able to present the correct or complete texts of a number of letters that Moore had either
garbled or published only in part.   This edition does have
limitations: first, Prothero was not permitted much of the
Lovelace material and what he was allowed to publish was
from copy supplied by the Earl and therefore subject to suspicion; second, he was able to collate most of the new material from the original, but not all of the older material
found in Moore, Dallas, Hunt, Galt, and Hodgson.   Prothero
provides valuable support for the letters with his notes marshalled from the Dictionary of National Biography and from
a mass of material that was accumulated by the father and
grandfather of the present publisher.   In addition, he includes a vast array of important documents by way of supplementary appendices.   Despite editorial flaws in both publications, Coleridge and Prothero performed their tasks well
enough for their editions to remain standard to the 1970's.

  The effect of the Coleridge/Prothero edition (hereafter referred to also as the Murray edition) must be seen
from two different perspectives for one to understand it fully.
The immediate effect is not what one would expect. · During
the seven-year time span covering the publication of this
milestone in the study of Byron, there is little direct stimulation other than reviews; the rash of new publications that
one would anticipate does not materialize.   The reviews
themselves, however, are another matter.   Those that appear

when the first three volumes are published in 1898 dwarf the
like of anything published since Byron's death and are on a
par with the reviews of Moore's Life in 1830, which had the
double advantage at the time of Byron's recent death and his
international reputation. Fourteen major journals cover the
event, some with three reviews of the three volumes published; the total number of reviews is more than the remaining publications on Byron for the year. The violently abusive review, such as Lionel Johnson's of the first volume of
the poems, is the exception rather than the rule and is apparently based on personal spleen; "H. L." effectively answers it in "The Spectre of Byron at Venice" the next year.
The general range over the seven-year duration of publication is from disfavor with Byron in some of the early reviews, to grudging acceptance in the mid-years of publication (exemplified by Sir Alfred C. Lyall in 1900), to genuine
regard and praise in the final years (perhaps best seen in
the laudatory comments of Churton Collins in 1905). The
notices in The Athenaeum almost exactly follow this curve.
By the time the final volume of the Murray edition has been
published, it has become crystal clear that, while arguments
might continue about the man and his work, there will no
longer be any doubt about Byron's significance or the fact
that he will continue to be read.

    Other than the reviews and a very fine essay of appre-
ciation by Stephen Phillips (1898), which was apparently
written to counteract some of the hostile reviews, the only
immediate reaction to the Murray edition seems to have been
three notices of a Byron revival, all appearing in the initial
year of publication. These are somewhat belated, as the revival had actually been going on for some time, but they are
tied to the appearance of the Coleridge/Prothero volumes
and are testimony to their importance. Brander Matthews
notes that there are signs of a revolution in Byron's favor.
W. P. Trent, in a more significant evaluation, sees no
permanent favorable or popular revival but points out that
as a result of the Coleridge text, students can now see Byron as a better technical artist than before; while acknowledging the inferiority of Byron's earlier work, he recognizes
the genius, versatility, and vigor of the latter, particularly
Don Juan, and sees in Byron a tremendous force, the poet
of an age. The most important of these three notices is
"The Wholesome Revival of Byron" by Paul Elmer More.
He finds Byron "wholesome" personally in that he never deceived himself as Shelley perhaps did in the confidence of
his own morality (hence the immorality of Byron's work is

much exaggerated); and Byron is "wholesome" artistically in
that the classical element of intellect in his work rescues
him from the vague and over-subtilized design, style, and
use of metaphor found in the poetry of his contemporaries
(notably Shelley), and the "breadth and mental scope" of his
treatment of nature, plus the human sympathy found therein,
save him from the overrefined nature-cult trivialities of the
age (seen especially in the verse of Wordsworth and Tennyson).

Aside from these notices and the reviews, one waits
in vain during these seven years for further sign of reaction; none is forthcoming. Any creative new interest based
on the Murray edition will apparently commence only after
the entire publication has been completed. From the vantage point of the first seven years of this period and the immediate reaction, then, the Murray edition is more a culmination than a beginning. All the directions initiated in the
preceding era by the Stowe controversy are brought to maturity in these volumes: they fully culminate the interest
begun by Stowe; they manifest the recognition of Byron as
an important figure of England's literary past and lay for-
ever the ghost that he would be forgotten; they climax the
serious collecting of Byron material by being inclusive;
they are vivid testimony, as an authoritative text worthy of
any major poet, of Byron's acceptance. The double focus
on Byron the man, prompted by Stowe, and Byron the poet,
prompted by the stirring of interest in Byron's work later
in the period, finds natural fulfillment in the double-barreled
Coleridge/Prothero edition that is in turn premonitory of the
main trunklines of Byron consideration from this time on.

The other angle from which to view the effect of the
Murray edition in order to understand it more fully is the
long-term view; the real significance of the edition lies in
this direction. This effect is delayed until the entire collection has been completed in 1904; it then begins to operate almost immediately. The first important signs can be seen in
1905 as both Coleridge and Prothero begin to capitalize on
the edition, the former with a one-volume issue of the poetry, the latter with an article on "The Goddess of Wisdom
and Lady Caroline Lamb." The same year, W. A. Bettany
edits a volume, The Confessions of Lord Byron, which is a
collection of Byron's "private opinions of men and matters"
taken exclusively from the Letters and Journals. By far the
most significant sign is a publication by Lord Lovelace, the
grandson of Byron; this is the important volume of Astarte.

After 1905 the Murray edition belongs to the public; but already the principal means of utilization of the new volumes
have become apparent: occasional publications by the editors
which will bear the stamp of their authority, exploitation of
the materials of the edition itself, and stimulation to the production of new material. As the Coleridge/Prothero work
is years ahead of its time, far outdistancing in worth what
had preceded it, it provides a solid foundation on which to
build. For this reason it represents not only the culmination of much of what had gone on in Byron studies before,
but also a time of new beginnings. It is to Byron scholarship what the year 1816 is to Byron's poetry--a watershed,
a time of coming of age and maturity.

Most fundamental is the beginning of a new period of
fresh interest and excitement in Byron. If the interest en-
gineered by the Stowe controversy was sputtering or at least
was not fully stabilized, the publishing event of 1898-1904
served to fuel it again and sustain it for the next 20 years.
There is a slight drop in average number of items published
--from 20 to 18--but the figures are so close one could say
a stable level of output had been achieved.

The single item causing the most stir of the entire
period is Astarte, which was brought out in two editions that
span the era, the first in 1905 by Lord Lovelace, and the
second revised by his wife in 1921. No doubt prompted by
the Murray edition, Astarte helps fill in some key omissions
therein by including important letters and documents from
Lord Lovelace's own rich collection of primary materials.
The 1905 version was a small and virtually private edition,
only a few copies being sold to secure copyright. The motive for publication, if his wife's later account in Ralph,
Earl of Lovelace, a Memoir (1920) is to be believed, was
more or less to exculpate his grandmother from the abuse
and injustice (largely magnified in his own mind as a result
of his upbringing and closeness to her point of view) that he
believed had been heaped upon her as a result of the separation and subsequent misunderstandings. But in performing
this "service," the book, with no sympathy for Byron and
utter disregard for his point of view, brings again the Stowe
charge before the public after it had for practical purposes
been laid aside as an unresolved issue. In actuality the book
does not prove the charge as it purports to do with certain
evidences that it produces. But it so clouds the issue with
its pedanticism, its semi-fictionalized account of Byron, its
incorporation of laborious matter that is not directly related,

its aura of official sanction, that it carried an oddly convincing ring to it and confirmed the deed in the eyes of a
number of people.

The argument of Astarte was seriously weakened the
next year with the appearance of several essays in Lord Byron and His Detractors. Therein E. H. Pember showed the
weakness of the evidence produced; John Murray, IV, completely refuted Astarte's attack on the Murray family, and
Lord Ernle [Prothero] also replied. Richard Edgcumbe, in
his Byron: The Last Phase (1909), showed at least an alternate possibility by interpreting the addressee of the crux
letter of May 17, 1819 as Mary Chaworth-Musters, who is
alleged to be the secret love of Byron, the mother of Medora
Leigh, and the cause of the separation. The theory carried
enough weight to convince, at least partially, Francis Gribble
in his superficial work The Love Affairs of Lord Byron
(1910) and Samuel C. Chew in his The Dramas of Lord Byron
(1915).

If the first edition of Astarte missed the mark, the
revised edition of 1921 by the Countess Lovelace came closer; for she omitted some of the earlier incumbrances, such
as the attack on the Murrays and matter not directly related,
arranged the original material better, and added 31 letters
from Byron to Augusta and three to his wife. The full
range of personality of the poet is revealed in the letters,
but the proof still falls short of being substantiative. The
most important fact, though, is that many more people were
convinced, including the important authority Lord Ernle ("The
End of the Byron Mystery," 1921), who found the innocence
of Byron less easy to maintain in the light of the second edition of Astarte and the unpublished letters to Lady Melbourne.
Whatever the motives of the Lovelaces in publishing Astarte,
the excitement caused by the book and the new interest that
it in turn generated cannot be denied.

One of the most immediate and important effects of
the Astarte volumes was the publication in 1922 of the complete series of Melbourne letters themselves by John Murray,
IV, in Lord Byron's Correspondence; with the appearance of
these volumes the proof of Byron's guilt finally becomes
more circumstantial. In spite of editorial tampering with
the material (silent omissions, bowdlerization), the edition
is doubly important not only for the proof furnished but also
because of the large addition to the canon of Byron correspondence, an area recognized as being of major literary im-

portance in Byron's work since the publication of the Prothero edition.   All of the important letters from the 500-
letter bequest (1914) of Lady Dorchester, the daughter of
Hobhouse, are here published for the first time, including
letters to Lady Melbourne, Hobhouse, and Douglas Kinnaird.
They cover the period from his first tour in 1809, but they
are mainly concerned with the years of fame in London society and his residence abroad after the separation.   Murray
claimed in his introduction that he and his house were devoted to Byron's literary, not personal, side; nevertheless,
the Correspondence seems intended in part at least as a rejoinder to Astarte.   The reverse was actually accomplished,
for these two volumes stirred up a hornet's nest of debate--
eliciting more reviews than any single item of the entire
period--and even seemed to support the incest charge.   The
famous April 25th letter of 1814, with its reference to "not
an 'Ape' " ten days after the birth of Medora Leigh, seemed
conclusive proof to many authorities; and this one sentence
remains the most incriminating evidence against Byron.
Even this sentence, however, is subject to an alternate interpretation, as Miss Doris Langley Moore has recently
shown.   And also to be considered is Hobhouse's Recollections of a Long Life (1909), edited by Lady Dorchester, with
its important documents including the author's account of the
separation, which seems to run counter to the Astarte
charges.   Inconsistencies, mysteries, confusion remain, and
the issue is not finally resolved; but the Correspondence
probably makes it as decisive as it will ever be.

     If the Murray edition of Byron's works marks a new
period of attention to and excitement about Byron, it is a time
of other beginnings as well.   A new beginning in biographical study was also initiated.   The letters and journals now
open the way for Byron to speak for himself, whereas before
the multitudinous conversations, recollections, memoirs,
reminiscences, diaries, etc. had all spoken for him.   Any
true portraiture had become impossible with the extreme accounts of, charges against, and distortions of Byron made by
earlier writers.   Also, Thomas Moore's biography, which
had the benefit of the first mass of Byron letters and materials, left the rest of the nineteenth century biographers
very little new to build upon.   One is shocked really by the
dearth of Byron biography throughout the century, in the
light of the mark made by the man upon his entire age; and
the four full-scale biographies that do appear are so seriously limited in either scope or quality that they are merely of
historical interest today.   With the publication of the letters

and journals one can now see him, if not plain, then at least with a greater degree of clarity. Astarte, regardless of how one interprets the facts, also brings matters into sharper focus with the new materials that it adds. A turning point, then, has been arrived at in Byron biography.

One may quickly brush aside William Graham's Last. Links with Byron, Shelley, and Keats (1898), which is not really an attempt at biography at all, but a reprint of two articles from the preceding period. These grew out of some conversations that the author had with Jane Clairmont in 1878 in Florence. Her reminiscences are expectedly hostile, and much of her account has been disproved by her own letters. Likewise, The Pilgrim Poet: Lord Byron of Newstead (1911) by Albert Brecknock is of no more than topographical and local interest. But Richard Edgcumbe's Byron: The Last Phase (1909) is significant enough to mark the first real sign of things to come in the way of biography, although it is encumbered by an essay dealing with a fantastic theory concerning the separation and the Stowe charges. The part dealing with "the last phase, " Byron's life in Greece, is biography in the good sense of the term, in that it is a professional marshalling and judicious handling of the evidence of the Greek years. The quality of the book is such that, although it has been superseded by later facts and evidence, it still retains value as a sympathetic counterpoise to Harold Nicolson's rather cold and dispassionate treatment of the same subject. The book also heralds a new phase in Byron biography to come--the host of thoroughly professional but highly specialized book-length accounts of a restricted portion of the poet's life.

The fully-ripened biographical fruit of the Murray edition and the activity that followed, including Astarte, is Ethel Colburn Mayne's two-volume Byron (1912). There are faults to be sure--she accepts too readily the incest charges on evidence that she claims is irrefutable but which is still too flimsy to be acceptable; she manhandles documentary facts to support her point of view, which is usually Lady Byron's and may account for the entrée she gained into the Lovelace circle; and her effusive style is distracting at times--but the positive values of her text far outweigh these drawbacks. Most of the facts are there, primary material from the Murray edition and Astarte is heavily drawn upon, and her critical comments are usually incisive and perceptive. The book quickly becomes authoritative; it is as if one had stepped suddenly from the horse-and-buggy period of biography into

the modern era of the automobile. The 1924 revision and
abridgment into one volume draws upon the valuable new material found in the Correspondence edited by Murray, the revised edition of Astarte, and In Whig Society (1921) by Mabell, Countess of Airlie, the latter containing fresh material
from the Holland House circle. Accordingly, earlier flaws
are remedied--such as the revised judgment of Trelawny,
the correction of the rather ugly Hoppner business, and
better documentation for the Byron "problem"--and the book
becomes even more satisfying as a biography. For years it
remained the fullest and best account of the poet, and it
still retains value as an excellent and very full one-volume
survey.

The Murray edition would seem to be the great culminating effort of the trend in collecting materials that developed during the last quarter of the century; and it was this.
But looking back on the results that came after, one can see
that it was in itself a time of new beginning in this area also. An edition of this magnitude not only consolidated the
advances that had been made but dramatically ushered in a
period nonpareil for the gathering and publication of Byron
materials. Like a magnet the Murray edition attracted into
publication such remaining major collections of Byron materials as those found in the two editions of Astarte, Lord Byron's Correspondence, Recollections of a Long Life, and In
Whig Society; collectively these represent major advances,
particularly in the area of letters. Still another volume,
From the Unpublished Letters of Lord Byron, was published
in Venice in 1915 and purports to present unpublished letters.
William Polidori's diary, one of the last unpublished contemporary accounts of Byron and an informative document on
the Continental trek to Switzerland and the days spent there,
also makes its appearance in an edition based on a bowdler-
ized transcript edited by William Michael Rossetti (1911).

Less spectacular individually, but important nevertheless in toto, are the myriad of everyday items that are also
drawn forth throughout the entire period and that help to
render it a bonanza period in the collection of Byroniana.
Most significant are the letters--only 11 entries appear, but
30 items are noted. They range in date from 1801 to 1824;
since Byron's earliest letter was written toward the end of
1798, they very nearly span his letter-writing career. The
addressees number 17, plus some who are unidentified; many
of these are important personages in the poet's life--Hob-
house, Hodgson, Kinnaird, Dallas, Webster, Croker, Murray,

Hoppner. The Murray edition seems to have given more
purpose and direction to this area of activity; for the range,
number and importance of the letters have significantly advanced. Testimony to the ranking importance of the letters
now in Byron's overall work is the separate article devoted
to them that appears in the Encyclopedia Americana for 1918
by W. J. Dawson. No major poetic discovery outside of the
Coleridge/Prothero edition occurs in this period; but a few
minor unpublished poems are added to the canon, notably
"King of the Humbugs, " "Address to the Sun, " and the poem
beginning "Again deceived! Again betrayed!" Two other
poems--"To My Dear Mary Anne" and "Ah Memory, Torture
Me No More"--are authenticated by Henry Buxton Forman
in an article in the Athenaeum for June 11, 1904. The minor importance of these pieces is indicative of the superlative nature of the Coleridge edition which includes everything
of major importance in Byron's poetry. The continuing interest in collecting information about editions goes on in several publications by Gilbert Redgrave (1899), N. Herz (1909),
J. T. Andrews (1919), G. H. Healey (1919), and H. C. Roe
(1919), as they offer data, corrections, descriptions, etc.,
of editions of English Bards and Scotch Reviewers, Bride of
Abydos, Don Juan, and Fugitive Pieces. Finally, as a manifestation of this interest in collecting Byron materials and
information concerning them, one may note John Murray's
published list of manuscripts and autographs in 1898, Ottokar Intze's list of catalogs of various Byron collections and
catalog of his separate works in 1914, and Samuel Chew's
list of apocrypha in 1919.

The sense of a beginning may also be felt in the area
of Byron's poetry, not only in editions but in consideration
of his work as well. With a decent text and an authentic
canon now, the door is open for the wider dissemination of
Byron's poetry through subsequent editions that are based
upon Coleridge's work. Particularly noteworthy are the
one-volume editions with general introductions that appear.
The number is impressive for one thing--an average of more
than one every two years--and is testimony to Byron's popularity on the rise. But perhaps more significant is the element of quality added to these numbers; for the editors include some names that command scholarly respect, either
established or emerging: E. H. Coleridge, R. H. Stoddard,
A. Symons, Leslie Stephen, William P. Trent, Will D. Howe,
Hardin Craig, William Dick, H. J. C. Grierson. Even
though these one-volume editions are no longer of significant
value, the importance of these editors bodes well for Byron
in the future.

With the poetry of Byron coming into wider dissemination and wider respect, the door is also open for a more serious and scholarly assessment of his work and worth as a poet. One can detect some new movement both in the consideration of specific poems and in the more general assessments. Significance in the former does not lie in numbers; in fact, there appears to be a considerable falling off, from 133 to 59 items. Nor does importance lie in the subject nature, which is still much the same as formerly (authorship, sources, autobiography, theme, interpretation, morality, query, etc.); nor in the range, which is approximately the same--21 works represented, with Childe Harold (14), Don Juan (10), Manfred (five) and Cain (five) being the poems most frequently dealt with, the latter two replacing English Bards and The Prisoner of Chillon of the preceding period in interest. What really matters is that most of the N & Q material, which largely made up the 133 figure, is now gone in this period; the 59 items remaining actually represent a larger percentage of more substantial articles. The general works of a critical nature on the poetry cover the usual broad spectrum of topics--themes, humor, the Byronic hero, grammar/rhyme/prosody/rhythm, Italian and Hellenic elements, war poetry, literary indebtedness, influence on other literary figures, Byron as critic, etc.--with some concentration of items (ten) comparing Byron to other literary figures. But the really notable contribution in this area lies in the important items that deal with a phase of Byron's work such as the oriental tales, the dramas, the lyrics, the satires. Martha P. Conant's The Oriental Tale in England (1908) and Edward Bliss Reed's English Lyrical Poetry (1912) mention such of Byron's work as is appropriate for their purposes. But three other special studies help redress the biographical emphasis in Byron scholarship and make a significant start toward the solid critical work that will soon emerge in Byron study. Claude M. Fuess's judgments in his Lord Byron as a Satirist in Verse (1912) come too early to be of value today and have been superseded by more sophisticated assessments; but his volume still has value in its historical account of the two satiric traditions, English and Italian, that Byron followed. Samuel C. Chew (1915) essays the first study of the whole group of Byron's dramas, if one discounts William Gerard's earlier brief survey; and Chew's traditional study very nearly remained the only full account until recently. The study of Byron as Critic (1923), by Clement T. Goode, is thorough and workmanlike; serving as a foundation for later illumination of the topic, it still remains the only full treatment in English.

The final material to be surveyed in this era points
up one overwhelming fact that has been evident and referred
to repeatedly. The span from 1898 to 1923 is the period of
Byron's arrival. Every sign--the Murray edition, the
heightening of interest, the advancement in biography, the
extraordinary gains in the collecting of material, the popularity of the poetry, the enclave in criticism--adds up to
this fact. At the beginning of the period Byron is acknowledged and tolerated, like a bastard child. By the end
he has moved into his full legitimacy of respect and recognition. The standard encyclopedias readily incorporate him,
such as Chambers's Cyclopaedia of English Literature (1903)
and the important eleventh edition of the Encyclopaedia Britannica (1910), wherein E. H. Coleridge is responsible for the
entry. The multifarious literary histories that appear are
too numerous to single out; but all accord the poet ample
space, including the elaborate English Literature, an Illustrated Record (1903) by Richard Garnett and Edmund Gosse
and the prestigious Cambridge History of English Literature
(1914) where F. W. Moorman makes the assessment.

Part of Byron's recognition is due to the series of
excellent studies that appear concerning the Romantic Movement itself. After W. L. Phelps's pioneering effort in 1893,
the following emerge in rapid order: The Romantic Triumph
(1900), T. S. Omond; A History of English Romanticism in
the Nineteenth Century (1901), H. A. Beers; Main Currents
in Nineteenth Century Literature (1901), Georg Brandes (who
makes Byron the master pattern for the central tendencies
of the Romantic Period); The Romantic Revolt (1907), C. E.
Vaughan; The Romantic Movement in English Poetry (1909),
Arthur Symons; A Survey of English Literature: 1780-1830
(1912), Oliver Elton (who produces a comprehensive and perceptive essay remarkable for its time); The Drift of Romanticism (1913), P. E. More; Currents and Eddies in the English
Romantic Generation (1918), F. E. Pierce; Rousseau and Romanticism (1919), Irving Babbitt. These are important studies
and men; they reveal that the Romantic Period is undergoing
careful research and assessment and that, consequently, Byron's position is being understood better and appreciated
more.

Perhaps the final mark of status for one to achieve
is to become a source of influence oneself. The older
studies of influence on Byron and the accusations of plagiarism diminish markedly during these years; suddenly there
is a rash of studies devoted to Byron's influence: on a

certain locale--Eastern Europe, America (W. E.
Leonard's important and exhaustive study, Byron and Byronism in
America, 1905), Germany, Spain, Italy--on a particular individual (Grabbe, Espronceda, Goethe), or on a movement
(Nahum Sokolow, History of Zionism, 1919).   In literary
scholarship Byron has not only arrived, he has begun to
move as a force in his own right.

6. Centennial, 1924-1925

The centenary of Byron's birth went unnoticed except
for an article in The Nation by George E. Woodberry in
which he took note of the lack of interest and traced and
tried to explain the decline in Byron's reputation in England;
he concluded with the following benediction: "[Byronism] has
gone by ... he is a poet no one can love, and he left a
memory that no one can admire, and there is none of his
works that receives the meed of perfect praise. "

It was not so with the centenary of Byron's death.
Such a deluge of material is produced that it represents the
most extensive production of Byron scholarship for a single
year down to this time--109 items, as opposed to 78 for the
year of his death and 68 for the first year of the Stowe controversy. The outpouring is to be expected, not only because of the occasion but because of the renewed interest
since the last quarter of the preceding century. Only about
20 items state or imply celebration of the centenary directly
in the title; but of course most of the remainder are called
forth by the event. The commemorative articles may be
passed over as in the main occasional and duly respectful;
the one exception is by Howard Mumford Jones in the Yale
Review, which adds significance by tracing Byron's artistic
lineage from the eighteenth century and his Scottish heritage
and concludes by seeing him as the "first modern man in
British poetry. "

The five commemorative books that appear are mainly collections of one kind or another. Two are collections
of addresses by their respective authors, Demetrius Caclamos and Cumberland Clark. Two more are collections of a
diverse nature: The Celebration of the Centenary of Lord
Byron's Death by the University of Athens, 1824-1924,
which contains centenary speeches, odes, and miscellanea,
some in English and some in Greek; and the collection edited
by Walter A. Briscoe, Byron, The Poet, which contains reprints of material by several important writers, addresses

delivered in tribute to Byron, and other essays written especially for the book.   The latter volume is marred by the
fact that some of its "addresses and essays" are merely
summaries of lectures or "notes" reprinted from larger
works, many of the longer essays are amateurish and are
on limited subjects, and the shorter essays by illustrious
names treat their complex subjects only superficially.   Only
two items in this large collection are of any real value--one
by Grierson on "Byron and English Society," which traces
not only Byron's conflict with "aristocratic society, its politics and morals," but also offers delicate insight on the effect of the evangelical religion of Byron's youth on his
thought and poetry; and the Foundation lecture by Arthur
Quiller-Couch which seeks to separate the grain from the
chaff in Byron's work by using a dividing date of April 25,
1816, when Byron left England.   The fifth book, actually a
centenary pamphlet, is H. W. Garrod's Byron: 1824-1924;
it is not on a par with his volume on Wordsworth, and most
of his major points--including his contention that Byron's
fault lay in his superstition, which "shadows all his thinking"--now seem at best debatable.

        Of the large number of appreciative essays drawn
forth by the centenary but not exclusively celebrating it per
se, several are worthy of note, though not especially noteworthy: C. H. Herford gives Byron a fairer hearing in
"Lord Byron" than in his earlier Age of Wordsworth; Rev.
H. H. Henson is more concerned with Byron's ethics than
his work; F. J. Hopman has a two-part article in which he
considers Byron's personal characteristics in the first part,
and in the second measures Byron's poetry by four a priori
categories that he sets up for a great poet (seer, powerful
and lofty imagination, constructive genius, and gift of poetic
transformation) and finds him ranking not very high; Hilaire
Belloc in "On Byron" speaks of the "marriage of intelligence
with the magic of words" in Byron's poetry and blames the
reader for the shifts in his popularity; Osbert Burdett offers
as the "Verdict on Byron" that his real genius is to be
found in the letters and journals; Lord Ernle, out of his
rich experience with Byron, writes on "The Cosmopolitan
Poet" and "The Poetry of Byron"; Howard Mumford Jones,
again, offers a popular survey of "The Influence of Byron";
H. J. C. Grierson reprints his "Lord Byron: Arnold and
Swinburne" wherein he rebalances Arnold's "overestimation"
by recognizing Byron's limitations as an artist, but eloquently rescues him from the "underestimation" of Swinburne and
concludes that "English poetry would be greatly the poorer

without the passionate, humorous, essentially human voice
that declaims in Childe Harold and flows like a torrent in
Don Juan"; H. C. Minchin finds Byron's writing "instinct
with power, as well as with the flaming gift of satire"; S. F.
Gingerich feels that "the great law of fatality" drove Byron
from Wordsworth to the world of satire and irony in which
his poetry terminates; Alan D. McKillop, too, feels that Byron's real reputation lies in his satires; Samuel C. Chew
talks about "Byron in America": the effects of his death
upon and his attitudes toward America, his contacts with
Americans, and his influence on America via several items
of Byronism that W. E. Leonard had overlooked. Generally,
then, comments are favorable with reservation; and there
are few outright demurrers. Surprisingly, in a number of
the articles the emphasis is on Byron's classical side, indicating that this strong trend begun in the last quarter of the
nineteenth century is continuing. Besides these items that
are directly or loosely connected with the commemorative
occasion, a number of other items remain.

The crucial years in Byron study, the years that turn
on staggering events, generally focus on biographical matter;
and the centenary year is no exception. Aside from the
material already considered and a few general articles of a
critical nature--which compare Byron with Shakespeare or
Goethe, deal with Byron on the stage, consider the theme of
sorrow in his work, analyze Byron as satirist, find Byron's
genius not in the satiric nor the romantic but in "the true
comic spirit," which Mr. G. R. Elliott finds in the "Stoical
acceptance of life, with concentration of poetic mood and
form"--and aside from only three items that deal with particular works (Vision of Judgment, The Waltz, Don Juan), the
remainder of the material for the year consists of biographical items, almost 50 per cent of the whole.

The biographical articles contain nothing of unusual
value; the subject matter may be conveniently divided into
four general categories: those dealing with Byron and people
related to him (Ada, Teresa, Moore, the Murrays, Goethe,
Southey, Stowe, his bodyguard, his loves), those dealing with
places visited or mentioned in his work (Southwell, London,
Venice, Italy, Missolonghi, Greece, Hucknall Torkard, the
United States), those dealing with periods of his life (the
happy years, the last years), and those dealing with somewhat morbid interests (his lameness, the last illness). More
unusual is the prodigious number of book-length biographical
studies of Byron that are published in this one year. Some

are quick and obviously intended to capitalize on the centenary itself; these are ephemeral and are of little value today. R. L. Bellamy's Byron the Man is concerned only
with presenting the poet in his biography and ignores any
critical account of his works. John Murray, IV, treats of
the relationship between his famous grandfather and Byron in
his Byron and John Murray. Harold Spender's Byron and
Greece is mainly an autobiographical record of Byron's two
visits to Greece with a brief introduction; extracts from the
letters, journals, and poetry are used in chronological arrangement to show that Byron's love for Greece was an important influence in his life and gave it its one heroic touch.
A Scot, J. D. Symon, is perhaps a bit chauvinistic in his
Byron in Perspective, which places undue emphasis on the
Scottish background of the poet, Aberdeen in particular, and
its subsequent influence on his life and poetry; the "background" is the most valuable part of the book and makes use
of some new material, but the heavy accent that it receives
renders it disproportionate to the rest of the narrative.
The book by Clement Wood, Byron and the Women He Loved,
need only be mentioned to illustrate the popular and sensational bias that was still of interest to the public.

        Three specialized biographical or topical accounts,
however, do make a significant addition to the Byron canon
of studies. The first of these is Harold Nicolson's Byron:
The Last Journey which covers again the ground of Richard
Edgcumbe's book, Byron: The Last Phase, but draws upon
new material (the Dorchester papers and Dr. Bruno's diary
describing Byron's last illness) and a firsthand study of important locales; therefore it supersedes Edgcumbe's work on
the factual side. The latter, however, is still of value for
the warmth and sympathy of its treatment; for Nicolson, in
attempting to explode the popular romantic aura attached to
the Grecian venture and to replace it with a more realistic
picture, is rather cool and detached. He shows that Byron
was not motivated purely by love of Greece and that the
heroic episode at Missolonghi was really simply "a succes-
sion of humiliating failures"; but his realistic relief heightens
even more Byron's courage and perseverance. Dora Neill
Raymond's The Political Career of Lord Byron remains the
fullest treatment of this topic almost by default. It is important for the compendious gathering of material on the
subject, under the foci of Byron's speeches in the House of
Lords, his relations with Italian revolutionaries, and his
Greek experience of 1823-1824; but it is uncritical in its
handling of the material and uninspired in its style. The

third book, The Byron Mystery, is by Sir John C. Fox, the
son of the man who preceded Mrs. Stowe in her charges of
incest and then supported her in his Vindication of Lady Byron (1871). Fox is a lawyer, and he approaches the problem by a thorough review of the entire history of the matter
from the period of rumor, following Lady Byron's flight, to
the revelations of 1869, to the indecisive period that followed,
to Astarte with its new evidence and counter charges, to the
Correspondence of 1922. His analysis of the evidence is
weighed in favor of Lady Byron as follows: Byron and Augusta did commit incest before his marriage (this fact was
admitted, repented of by Augusta, and forgiven by Lady Byron); Byron attempted it again after the marriage, Lady Byron fled, the separation followed, and the subsequent relationship of Augusta and Lady Byron is thus accounted for.
The presentation marshals most of the facts that could be
used in a court against Byron; it was, accordingly, accepted
by most authorities. But the decision is still not satisfactory
to those who find Byron too complex a human being to be
judged on legal evidence alone.

The year 1925 may also be considered part of the
centenary, for the momentum of the event is enough to carry
it on for another year; but there is a sharp drop-off in every
category. Several items dealing specifically with the occasion
may still be found. The general estimates that take advantage of the event are still being produced, three of which deserve attention: R. W. Chambers' Ruskin (and others) on
Byron notices Ruskin's lifelong admiration of Byron, suggests
that the poet was his master in the Don Juan/Fors Clavigera
type of freewheeling periodic address to the nation, but defends vigorously the post-war society that Byron and Shelley
attacked in their poetry. Oliver Elton, in one of the best of
the interpretive essays, accepts the permanent interest in
Byron the man and therefore proceeds to evaluate his poetry; by carefully sifting out the best in Byron, he answers
certain questions that he had posited as follows: Byron not
only can tell a story but he ranks as one of the four or five
best in verse in England; he is a fine lyric poet, though he
has suffered by comparison with the generically different
lyric talent of Shelley; he has "command of beauty in language"; his poetry has grandeur; and The Vision of Judgment,
Don Juan, and much of his prose demonstrate that he does
possess humor. J. G. Robertson's study of Byron is appreciative in an oblique way, for it is a detailed and able critical survey of the relationship of Goethe and Byron which
shows not only Byron's sincere respect for Goethe but the

latter's almost idolatrous homage to the younger man that
climaxes in the Euphorion episode of the Second Part of
Faust.

Book-length biographical studies are still part of the
momentum of the centenary, and still of decidedly uneven
quality. The restricted subject of Leslie P. Pickering's
Lord Byron, Leigh Hunt and the "Liberal" is self-evident,
and E. Barrington's Glorious Apollo is a fictionalized biography along sensational lines. Of real merit, however, is
the appearance of John Drinkwater's The Pilgrim of Eternity,
which is well researched and based on original material.
Drinkwater attempts to present the portrait of "a living personality" extended over the "full term of Byron's life,"
freeing it from the melodrama and sentimental perversions
of it, yet capturing it in all of its complexity with the fundamental conflict of antagonistic forces. The book attempts to
be fair about the Byron "problem" and represents perhaps
the best of the efforts to rescue the poet from this calumny.
Although not primarily critical in purpose, the book's inte-
gral comments on Byron's work are incisive, sane, and
astute; Drinkwater is the first to rehabilitate Cantos III and
IV of Childe Harold from the oblivion to which critics were
beginning to consign them, and his recognition of the merit
of Byron's historical dramas is almost prophetic. Despite
some flaws, this book still holds up and remains one of the
better one-volume biographies. The remaining biographical
and critical items of this year are of limited scope and need
not be paused upon.

Deserving separate treatment for these centenary
years are a few items that bring to maturity a specialized
interest in Byron study that had been growing for some time,
that is, bibliography. The compilation of A Descriptive Catalogue of an Exhibition of Manuscripts and First Editions of
Lord Byron (1924) by R. H. Griffith and H. M. Jones and
the Bibliographical Catalogue of First Editions, Proof Copies
and Manuscripts of Books by Lord Byron (1925) manifest
this interest. Richard Ashley Rice (1924) presents a good
brief survey of "Lord Byron's British Reputation," concluding that Byron's position at the time was not substantially
different from that after his death, since "psychological so-
phistications" had merely been exchanged for "frank hypoc-
risies" without any resultant change in opinion, as the dilemma of the genius and the man was still apparent. Rice
is also concerned with Byron's psychology and thought; his
commentary was rewarding at the time, but is largely out-

dated now.   The most important bibliographical item is
Samuel C. Chew's Byron in England (1924).   Despite inevitable minor errors of fact in a work of this nature, it is an
indispensable work for the study of Byron's reputation in
England, offering a survey with supportive references and
"the largest list of English Byroniana" down to its time.
It is a work of indefatigable effort; and anyone who is interested in Byron bibliography, including the present surveyor,
must turn to him.   It stands as a fitting monument for Byron in the year of his centenary.

7. Literary Pause, 1926-1934

    The centenary was a prolific but in backward glance
not a banner occasion for Byron studies. On the whole, one
is disappointed, for only Chew's volume--and perhaps Drinkwater's, although it has been surpassed in biographical facts
--has stood well the test of time. The first quarter of the
century was a great era, the greatest to this point in Byron
study; but the centenary in no way caps it as a fitting climax. In fact there is more a tapering off in everything except quantity. Nor does the centenary inaugurate a new dispensation; if anything there follows a literary pause, a pause
which lasts for almost a decade.

    The pause is primarily in the area of quality; nothing
is produced of the magnitude of the Murray edition, nor anything of a sensational nature like Stowe's accusation or the
publication of Astarte. The most noteworthy work appearing
during the decade is Thomas J. Wise's A Bibliography of the
Writings in Verse and Prose of George Gordon Noel, Baron
Byron (1933). This volume is an important and useful tool,
not to be demeaned in any way; but at the same time its position as the pre-eminent work of the period is indicative of
a general slackening in creativity. This slackening is further evidenced by the rehashing of material that was current
much earlier. John C. Fox, II (1930) and Michael Monahan
(1926), for example, are concerned with reviewing Astarte
some years after the fact, "Byron's Lameness" is still being
discussed in the Mentor for 1927, and Arnold's essay is being criticized as late as 1931 by Cyril Barnard. The reprinting of considerable material from earlier years points
to the same conclusion; for one finds a number of contemporary reviews, a chapter from Moore's biography, two articles by James Louis Garvin from the Observer of 1924, as
well as other items. But if there is a pause on the side of
quality and a slackening in creativity, there is no letup in
publication activity itself. In sheer volume the entries-per-
year average is up considerably from that before the

centenary, about 28 items per year versus 18 before.   So
the centenary has at least aroused a great deal of interest.

The area of biographical interest is typical of the
period as a whole.   There are no great biographies, but
there is a lot of biographical activity, a higher percentage
than during the 1898-1921 period.   This fact is probably to
be accounted for immediately by the centenary occasion and
in the longer view by the large accumulation of primary
source material since the last quarter of the nineteenth century.   A number of book-length biographies, or books with
a biographical slant, appear but none to match the quality of
the earlier Mayne and Drinkwater biographies.   Albert
Brecknock follows up his The Pilgrim Poet: Lord Byron of
Newstead (1911) with Byron: A Study of the Poet in the
Light of New Discoveries (1926); and since the author is a
resident of Nottingham and librarian of Hucknall Torkard,
he writes with feeling for Byron and with familiarity of the
topography, but otherwise the book is superficial and even
unclear as to what the "new discoveries" are.   Lord Byron:
Roman einer Leidenschaft (1929), by Kasimir Edschmid, was
translated and published in America the next year as The
Passionate Rebel: The Life of Lord Byron; the book is comprehensive but more in the manner of a novel, as the German title suggests.   The biography by André Maurois, Byron
(1930), is more significant than the preceding and contains a
small amount of new material; but it is now primarily interesting for its French point of view.   In spite of the author's
imposing list of sources and documents consulted, the book
is largely a popularization.   Sympathetic, readable, easy-
going in style, it nevertheless takes liberties with chronology,
romanticizes occasionally, cavalierly omits important aspects
of Byron's life and work, and accepts with insouciance Byron's worst sins.   The latter acceptance may be simply Gal-
lic unconcern, but it does mark a turning away from the
narrow focus of fascination with or outrage about these matters to a more tolerant attitude and a willingness to place
Byron's aberrant behavior within the broader social outlook
of the day and the total view of the man and his work.   A
more limited treatment is Peter Quennell's Byron (1934) in
the "Great Lives Series"; it remains a fairly good brief
critical biography, though it absorbs too readily Medwin,
Trelawny, and the contemporary Venetian accounts.   It accepts Astarte as conclusive, deflates somewhat the Byron
legend by showing Byron as its author and victim, and points
to Childe Harold, Don Juan, and English Bards as Byron's
best poetry.   It is a prelude to the author's later and more

impressive work. A somewhat different biography--if indeed
it can be called that at all--is Charles Du Bos's Byron and
the Need of Fatality, published in Ethel Mayne's translation
in 1932. Where other biographies range widely, this book
restricts itself but probes deep; it is an intensive psychological study of the four years from the publication of Childe
Harold in 1812 to the poet's departure from England in 1816.
Du Bos is interested in the state of mind that led to incest
and its effects on Byron's life and work. He is not concerned with the poetry per se except as it relates to his
character; the Journals he considers to be the poet's masterpiece. The volume is largely speculative by its very nature,
and it rides its thesis too hard and emphasizes the Calvinistic background of predestination too much; but it is a provocative book and at times enlightening.

        Perhaps because biographers such as Mayne and
Drinkwater had utilized so effectively the primary material
that had recently become available, and because not enough
new and important material had appeared to justify reappraisal or full-scale study, several writers restricted themselves
to a more limited aspect of the poet's life. The scope of
their work may be judged by mention of the titles: Lord
Byron's Helmet (1927) by Maud Elliott; Bowles, Byron and
the Pope-Controversy (1927) by J. J. Van Rennes; Shelley
and Byron: A Tragic Friendship (1934) by Isabel Clarke.

        Minor items of a particular biographical nature, main-
ly articles, appear in quantity and tend to fall into certain
categories as in preceding eras: Byron and other people
(Landor, Shelley, Isaac Nathan, Theodore Hook, Moore,
Murray, Hunt, Charlotte Dacri, Lady Byron, Caroline Lamb,
Millingen, Coleridge, Canning, Scott, Teresa), Byron and
places (Athens, Ravenna, Geneva, Pisa, Greece), the morbid (Byron's lameness, his inferiority complex, his nervous
instability, his last illness, his death), Byron's opinions on
subjects (drama, politics, English society), anecdotes, and
various miscellanea (memoirs, his monument to Boatswain,
pronunciation of his name, his reading, Byron in Glenarvon).
The general biographical assessments of Byron are found in
addresses, general essays, general defenses, but mainly in
the introductions to one-volume editions during this period.

        The biographical work of most significance is not di-
rectly on Byron at all but on those people associated with
him in some way, some of major importance and some of
minor. No fewer than seven books appear dealing with these

figures in Byron's life, and the quality ingredient missing in
Byronic biography may be found in part here. Armistead
Gordon's Allegra: the Story of Byron and Miss Clairmont
(1926) is really not as limited as the title implies, for it
uses the Claire Clairmont relationship as the center for a
loose biographical account of the poet's life as a whole; the
book is readable but makes no real contribution to scholarship. The central episode is treated with sympathy but is
more favorable to Claire than usual; elsewhere the book
places undue stress on Byron's Scottish background and relationship to Shelley. Of a more lasting value is The Life
and Letters of Anne Isabella, Lady Noel Byron by Ethel
Mayne, published in 1929. It remains the authorized family
view, Miss Mayne being allowed access to the important
Lovelace papers for the first time and the Countess of Lovelace contributing an "Introduction" and "Epilogue" in which
she traces the ancestry and descendants of Lady Byron.
Letters during the engagement are included in one appendix,
and material clarifying the marriage settlement is incorporated in another. The biography is important for seeing
things from the Lovelace perspective, but allowance must be
made for this fact and the lack of probing behind the face
value of the evidence. Edmund Blunden's Leigh Hunt: A
Biography (1930) is still the best biography of Hunt in English, though it falls short of being definitive by failing to
draw fully upon several American collections including the
rich Luther Brewer collection. The book does make use of
much new material, however, and presents a balanced account not only of Hunt but of the many acquaintances whom
he pulled into his circle in his nearly sixty-year career.
Other volumes appearing which deal with Byron's associates
are as follows: Roy Clark, William Gifford (1930); Elizabeth
Jenkins, Lady Caroline Lamb (1932); Michael Sadleir, Blessington-D'Orsay (1933); and Joan Haslip, Lady Hester Stanhope (1934). These seven books treating Byron's acquaintances amount to a major area of literary activity during the
period.

        The pause that this period seems to represent is also
evident in the treatment of primary materials, for no great
edition is published nor are any great collections exposed to
public view for the first time. Nevertheless, a great deal
of collecting and assimilating of Byron materials is going on.
The collecting of letters continues, though at a slower rate.
In fact, only seven new letters, widely scattered over Byron's
life and each to a different person (Ridge, Moore, Wedderburn Webster, Alessandro Guiccioli, Hoppner, an unknown

addressee, and E. Church), are revealed, besides some new
material excerpted from unpublished letters in a series of
articles by George Paston in "New Light on Byron's
Loves..." (1934). The assimilation of the letters already
collected since the publication of the Murray edition, however, moves right along; and the literary pause is effectively utilized for this purpose. Numerous articles appear in
this enterprise, and the culmination of this interest is
marked by the appearance of three volumes of letters.
Seventeen Letters of George Noel Gordon Lord Byron to an
Unknown Lady, 1811-1817 (1930), edited by Walter Peck,
while revealing the increased interest in Byron's letters, is
suspect; for it draws upon the earlier collection of The Unpublished Letters of Lord Byron (1872) by H. S. Schultess-
Young, which is known to be at least partly spurious. The
one-volume selections of the letters by V. H. Collins (1927)
and R. G. Howarth (1933) are more representative and make
Byron's letters available to a wide spectrum of readers for
whom the Prothero edition had been out of reach. They are
concrete testimony both to the growing recognition of the
letters as meritorious in themselves and to the gathering
public interest in them.

        The activity in collecting and assimilating Byron ma-
terials goes beyond interest in the letters; some real gains
are made in other areas. The most significant item is A
Bibliography of the Writings of ... Byron (1932-33) compiled
by Thomas J. Wise, which remains the most complete bibliography of Byron's first editions; other Byroniana such as
TLS letters, facsimile title pages, etc. are included but are by
no means complete. Unfortunately the author's notoriety for
faking material renders some of his listings suspect. Elkin
Mathews issues Byron and Byroniana: A Catalogue of Books
in 1930. Important primary source material also appears
for the first time with E. S. De Beer and Walter Seton's
"Byroniana: The Archives of the London Greek Committee"
(1926) and Lord Ernle's editing of The Ravenna Journal
(1928). Besides these substantial additions, a number of
articles also aid the research, adding bits and pieces to the
complex puzzle. Some of these deal with manuscripts
(Temple Scott, 1927; Marcel Kessel, 1931). Others deal
with first editions (J. C. Butterwick, 1931; Jacob Schwartz,
1931) or other editions (E. H. Hespelt, 1927; Charles J.
Sawyer and F. J. Darton, 1927). H. W. M. (1927) presents
a bibliographical study on the printing of Childe Harold IV.
M. J. Ryan (1928) deals with Byron's prefaces. The abundance of this material points to a later need for drawing all

of these and subsequent findings together. But at this stage
it is a continuation of the interest begun in the last quarter
of the preceding century and part of the additional impetus
provided by the Murray edition.

Substantial critical endeavor on Byron and his works
is still not forthcoming. The general estimates continue in
such accounts as histories of English literature (Louis Cazamian, 1927; Lafcadio Hearn, 1927), histories of the literature of the century (John M. Stuart-Young, 1929; B. I.
Evans, 1934), histories of the Romantic Movement or aspects thereof (G. H. Crump, 1927; Hoxie N. Fairchild, 1928
and 1931; Ernest Bernbaum, 1930), histories of Neoclassi-
cism or aspects thereof (Sherard Vines, 1930; George Kitchin, 1931) and innumerable general essays. These general
estimates and revaluations of Byron's work continue to increase as they had done in the 1898-1922 era and the Stowe
period before that; in fact there are about the same number
in this eight-year period as in the preceding twenty-five-
year period.

Criticism of specific pieces or a particular phase of
Byron's work increases during the period by a third, although
not a single book-length study is published. Diversity is
mainly the key, with 17 poems dealt with in some 31 items;
Childe Harold, Don Juan, and Manfred still maintain their
popularity and are the major items of interest. Studies
treating a special phase of Byron's work are diverse and
largely insignificant; but one interest blossoms fully and
represents a major contribution--the fascination with the
Byronic hero. The latter aspect is encompassed in a series
of fine studies of special phases of the pre-Romantic and
Romantic movements, particularly the Gothic: Eino Railo,
The Haunted Castle (1927); Hoxie N. Fairchild, The Noble
Savage (1928); Eleanor Sickels, The Gloomy Egoist (1932);
Mario Praz, The Romantic Agony (1933). Criticism of the
work rather than the man is on the upswing, then, though
nothing of any real direct substance is produced yet. The
feeling is strong, however, that this activity is leading toward something of significance in the near future, a feeling
analogous to that which preceded the emergence of the
Coleridge/Prothero edition after a quarter century of activity
and collecting materials.

Three more trends of the period deserve mention;
two are continuations of trends noticed earlier, and one represents a fresh interest. The sudden rush continues of one-

volume selections of Byron's work that appeared after the
Coleridge edition, but in a modified form. Instead of consisting almost exclusively of poetry, these now include a
miscellany of primary source material, such as those edited
by Walter Littlefield (1926), Hamish Miles (1930), D. M.
Walmsley (1931), and R. A. Rice (1933); or they contain exclusively selections from the letters and journals, such as
those edited by V. H. Collins (1927) and R. G. Howarth
(1933); or they deal solely with one work, such as Frank
Ristine's edition of Don Juan (1927) and Frederick Carter's
edition of Manfred (1929). Thus the student or general reader is assured of a more balanced selection of Byron's production, and the letters have become accepted not only as
useful primary tools but as works of literary worth in themselves.

        Continuing in a big way is the trend, already noted,
of moving away from influences on Byron (one notable exception being F. W. Stokoe's German Influence in the English
Romantic Period: 1788-1818 [1926] which reveals for Byron
a superficial German influence, mainly through Goethe,
Schiller, Wieland, and Gessner) to Byron's influence on
others; by now it has branched out into many interesting
variations. There are studies of his influence or fame in
various countries, including France, Germany, Scandinavia,
Yugoslavia, Iceland, and the United States. Essays and
books deal with his influence on such literary or public fig-
ures as Emily Brontë, Disraeli, Shelley, Von Zedlitz, and
Victor Hugo. Direct imitations of specific works are studied,
such as the continuations of Don Juan and an imitation of
Lara. Interest even extends to the actual representations of
Lord Byron in fiction, as in Caroline Lamb's Glenarvon
(Mary B. Whiting, 1930) and Howard Gordon Page's The
Shattered Harp (D. R. F. , 1929), and on the stage, as in
Alicia Ramsey's Byron (D. R. F. , 1929).

        One final trend that seems to begin with this period
and that marks a new phase in Byron study, albeit a minor
one, is the renewed interest in contemporary reviews and
views of Byron. Albert Mordell (1926), Miriam Thrall
(1934), and G. L. Nesbitt (1934) study contemporary journals
that deal with Byron and his works; the latter two are concerned with Fraser's and the Westminster Review respectively. Contemporary reviewers who were connected with Byron
are also studied; R. B. Clark treats of William Gifford
(1930) and M. C. Hildyard edits Lockhart's Literary Criticism (1931). Edmund Watson (1931) reprints comments that

reveal Byron and his literary contemporaries as they appeared
to each other.   And J. C. Metcalf reprints a chapter from
Moore's life of Byron in showing The Stream of English Biography (1930).   This trend represents an area that has not as
yet been covered in the re-study of Byron and his age; as
such it adds still another piece to the picture of the poet and
his time.

8. Modern Critical Beginnings, 1935-1945

The years 1935-45 mark the first significant period of criticism in Byron publication. To be sure, there has been criticism all along, some of it of a high order; but much of it has been tied to the poet's personality and hence is defensively pro or con. Some of the better criticism came in Victorian commentary or genteel essays; but most of these remained general and rarely got down to objective cases. Too much of the commentary that has directed itself to the business of Byron's poetry has been of a peripheral nature or has dealt with issues that were less than central--Byron's plagiarisms, the morality (more often the immorality) of his writing, criticism of his grammar, pronunciations, speculation (what did Lara see?), identifications, parodies. In short, surprisingly little work to this point has been done in interpreting Byron's poetry; most of the book-length studies, lacking the perspective that later work and editing have made possible, have faded, and the numerous articles, being confined to the minutiae of a word, phrase, or line, are of little real value. The need has now arrived for centrally-important exploratory studies of the poet's works themselves.

T. S. Eliot seems to have been the first to recognize the need with his pioneering essay, "Byron," of 1937; as the initial piece in this new direction, it merits close attention. Eliot notes that Byron's life has now been brought into proper perspective, but not his poetry: "Byron ... would seem the most nearly remote from the sympathies of every living critic: it would be interesting, therefore, if we could have half a dozen essays about him, to see what agreement could be reached. The present article is an attempt to start that ball rolling." Eliot sees Byron through Scottish lenses, finding the most important element in his makeup a perversion of Calvinism into a kind of diabolistic mixture of Shelley's Prometheus and Milton's Satan that allows the poet to have things both ways--"as an individual isolated and superior to

other men because of his own crimes, and as a naturally
good and generous nature distorted by the crimes committed
against it by others. " This split is the frame for Eliot's
article. Within this context he finds certain vices and virtues in Byron's work. The vices noted are traditional: one
is Byron's attempt to be poetical, which results in falseness
and superficiality ("insincerity" to an earlier age) and is
best exemplified by Childe Harold; the other major fault is
Byron's deficiency in language, which Eliot considers a failure amounting to a defect in sensibility.

  The Byronic virtues that Eliot describes are a different matter. Here he breaks new ground and intimates a
sense of the excitement of discovery. There is audacity in
considering the romances at all; Eliot not only finds positive
value in them but rates Byron a superb narrative artist,
ranking only behind Chaucer and Coleridge. The success of
these tales, he says, stems from "a torrential fluency of
verse and a skill in varying it from time to time to avoid
monotony" plus a "genius for divagation. " The first point is
a rather commonplace judgment, but the latter is highly original and turns a heretofore-considered defect into a correct-
ly-recognized asset. Eliot boldly proclaims Don Juan as Byron's greatest poem primarily because it unites all of Byron's
strengths. The picaresque first half is "of the best kind"
and rarely fails; the last four cantos are "at the head of Byron's works" because the satire there is particular and precise and the subject matter gives him an opportunity to develop a genuine emotion--i.e., hatred of hypocrisy. Eliot
believes these latter cantos are unique in the English language,
along with the dedicatory stanzas to Southey which he labels
"one of the most exhilarating pieces of abuse in the language."
Eliot's essay is genuinely critical. Because there are no
prior claims on him, he is able to overturn some outdated
concepts and to open up other avenues for exploration. His
comments are full of remarkably astute observations; even
when he seems most wrong, he provokes new insight ("if
Byron had distilled his verse, there would have been nothing
whatever left"). This essay stands as one of the seminal
pieces in modern Byron criticism.

  Eliot's essay did not garner the direct response for
which he had hoped, but undoubtedly the magic of his name
helped make Byron's work critically respectable again and
must account in part for the flowering of criticism that followed. If nothing else, his piece was the trumpet of a
prophecy and showed that the proper time for this important

area of Byron study had finally arrived. Back when Arnold
made his famous prediction, there was some reasonable
doubt as to whether Byron would have a future at all. The
point was still worth debating when the turn of the century
came. But the Murray edition had given Byron his place in
the sun: his work had been collected and presented in a full-
scale edition. Biographers had built upon that in a very
nearly definitive way. A centennial celebration had brought
him honor and homage. Now with the poet safely ensconced
it was only logical for the thoughtful distillation process of
criticism to begin.

    Though Eliot sounded the trumpet, he was actually
not the first to initiate this period of modern critical beginnings. This distinction belongs to W. J. Calvert, whose
book, Byron: Romantic Paradox (1935), was frowned on at
the time because biography was too strong an emphasis to
allow for separate interpretation of the work. Eliot was to
bolster Calvert's position the next year with his essay and
comment that he was not concerned with Byron's private life.
This new critical view--which was not really an attempt to
overthrow biographical interpretation so much as simply to
look at the work squarely--was to gain in legitimacy until
finally accepted in the 1960's. Calvert's general thesis, the
Neo-classic/Romantic paradox in Byron's nature and work,
had been recognized before, by Byron himself in fact; but no
one had investigated it as thoroughly nor applied it as formi-
dably to his entire corpus. Calvert first establishes the
paradoxical nature of Byron the man, a nature in which two
personalities meet: "the one immediate, spontaneous, emotional, partly self-conscious and partly naïve--in a word,
contemporary--and the other rational, sophisticated, conservative, partly naïve and partly self-conscious--a man of traditions to which he must sometimes, even by force of will,
return." He shows further that Byron was the child of two
centuries, a poet who wrote Romantically but critically held
himself to be the heir and champion of the Age of Reason
and the School of Pope; therefore, he feels, Byron was a
man at constant warfare with himself, not certain in which
of two opposite and irreconcilable camps his temperament
lay, though it really lay in both. It is this warfare carried
out in Byron's poetry that is Calvert's particular concern.
He traces it from the poet's early English Bards and Hints
from Horace, which reveal his eighteenth-century heritage;
to the popular romances of 1812-1816, which express his
Romantic side but violate his Neoclassical sense of poetry's
true function and worth; to the high seriousness of Childe

Harold, which nevertheless continues his Romantic self-expression; to the carefully constructed historical dramas that exhibit his faith in Pope, though they are still tinged with his Romantic style. Byron marches to maturity bearing the burden of this self-conflict between his passion for individuality and his rational desire for social wholeness. With Don Juan a resolution is finally effected; and in this masterpiece the two sides of the man are completely and successfully merged. Calvert's book is important, a milestone in a way: it dared to separate the work from the events of the poet's life; its commentary, while not outstanding in itself on particular works, helped lead the way in the critical approach to Byron; and it utilized the paradox approach to the man and work so thoroughly and convincingly that it is largely responsible for establishing this highly influential view. Interestingly enough, Calvert and Eliot are independently in step on the first two of these points.

Whether Eliot and Calvert actually started something with their work or merely articulated earliest what was inevitable anyway perhaps cannot be firmly established, but they set the pattern for the period. Eliot's article in particular seems a blueprint for the concentrations of interest. One major center of interest is on Byron's romances, for the first time; and since they had been held in such low esteem formerly, the correlation seems more than coincidental. Wallace Cable Brown produces four articles that help in understanding the background of Byron's romances, three of these indirectly by demonstrating the popularity of English travel books about the Near East from 1775-1825 and by showing the relationship of these to the minor poetry and prose fiction of the period. The fourth, "Byron and English Interest in the Near East" (1937), is directly related and describes not only how Byron's romances grew out of this travel-book milieu with its emphasis on accuracy and liveliness of style but how they in turn influenced later specimens of the genre as a model. A complementary article by Harold Wiener, "Byron and the East: Literary Sources of the 'Turkish Tales' " (1940), adds further to our understanding of the romances by studying Byron's sources and the use that he made of them, though the author admits that these were only secondary to the poet's personal experience. W. Edward Farrison deals with "The Popularity of Byron's Metrical Tales" (1938).

The most critically innovative article on the romances, however, along with Eliot's comments, is G. Wilson Knight's

compact "The Two Eternities" (1939), an article much in
advance of its time and anticipatory of his later Byron
studies.   Like Eliot and Calvert, he eschews the biographical for the critical; like the former he finds worth in the
romances, and like the latter he concentrates on the two
sides of Byron's personality and work.   One of the eternities that Knight finds is in Byron's life: "He lives that
eternity which is art.   He is more than a writer: his virtues and vices alike are precisely those entwined at the
roots of poetry.   He is poetry incarnate.   The others are
dreamers: he is the thing itself. "   The other eternity may
be found in Byron's work.   It occurs when he finally accom-
plishes a matching of the inner psychological and spiritual
life--which he achieved in the romances--with the meaningful
external action--which he achieved in Childe Harold via nature.   Knight gives the reader rich insights along the way
into such varied aspects of Byron's art as theme, action,
psychology, imagery, and style.

        Another notable concentration of critical interest in
this period, foreshadowed by Eliot's article, is Byron's satire, especially the particular satire Don Juan.   F. R.
Leavis (1936) claims that the tradition of Augustan satire
ended with Byron in English Bards.   He believes that Byron
was unable to command the essentials of the Augustan mode
(decorum, order, elegance, consistency) and that he therefore developed his own peculiar Romantic mode, exemplified
in Vision of Judgment.   David Worcester in The Art of Satire
(1940) simply follows the lead set forth by Leavis in assessing Byron's place in the satirical tradition; he too believes
that Byron followed the path of formal eighteenth century satire in his English Bards, then developed thereafter his own
manner from the Italian art of improvvisatore.   Worcester
abbreviates Byron's effect on the satiric tradition as follows:
"with Byron, formal satire died, " "in Byron's melodramatic
despair are the first hints of cosmic irony, " and "historically, Don Juan is one of the few English representatives of
the secondary, Tieckian variety of romantic irony. "   This
assessment remains the conventional view until G. M. Ridenour
later shows clearly that Don Juan is in part modeled along
Augustan lines; and the view of Byron's epic as primarily
ironical is challenged repeatedly in the 1950's and 60's.
Northrop Frye also includes Byron in his discussion of "The
Nature of Satire" (1944).   Ronald Bottrall in 'Byron and the
Colloquial Tradition in English Poetry" (1939) is not so much
concerned with Byron's satire as satire as he is with the
style of Byron's satires, in particular the rhythm and word

order. For this approach he studies Byron in the context of
a colloquial tradition in English poetry which manifests rhythms of colloquial speech when there is a live poetic drama
in the period, but in non-dramatic periods takes its form in
a poetry-substitute for drama that uses a large canvas, tells
a story, and utilizes vivid dialogue. Byron fits into the tradition after he has matured to objectivity following his exile:
by this time he already has the narrative ability, he now
finds his technique in the aristocratic colloquial speech of
his letters and journals, and he uses for his canvas the
European scene and civilization. The author's unique viewpoint enables him to offer a number of original and constructive comments about Byron's style, though his zeal for his
theory leads him astray in his criticism of Childe Harold.
Bottrall echoes Eliot's essay in many respects, including the
comparison of Byron to Chaucer as a storyteller and the
consideration of Don Juan as Byron's masterpiece.

When Bottrall states that Don Juan is "the greatest
long poem in English since The Dunciad," he is merely epit-
omizing the gathering enthusiasm of the period for the work.
Recognition of its central importance actually began during
the Victorian period, but not until this critical era does it
win the accolade over Childe Harold and Byron's romantic
poems. Four articles deal with it: Alan L. Strout ("Lockhart on Don Juan," 1940) publishes for the first time correspondence between Lockhart and John Wilson Croker that
identifies Lockhart as the author of the Letters to the Right
Honorable Lord Byron, instead of Bentham as the Blackwood's group wanted the public to believe. Margaret McGing
finds "A Possible Source for the Female Disguise in Byron's
Don Juan" (1940) in Miss Tully's Narrative of Ten Years'
Residence at Tripoli in Africa, which she believes is more
authentic than the account of Captain Gronow who claimed
that it was derived from the actual adventures of a prankster,
Dan Mackinnon, whom Byron may have known. John Waller's
"A Defence of Don Juan" (1938) is against the charges of the
poem's indelicacy and inferior workmanship. The most interesting of the articles is E. D. H. Johnson's "Don Juan in
England" (1944), which shows that Byron, by extending his
strictures against the Regency moral and social code (especially its hypocrisy and cant) to the English in general,
seriously miscalculated the moral temper and views of his
vast middle-class audience; the fact that he castigated the
majority for the delinquencies of the aristocratic minority
accounts for the outrage that greeted the poem. In addition
to these articles there is generous mention and discussion of

Don Juan in the more general studies; and there is a book-
length account of the legend and the hero in John Austen's
The Story of Don Juan (1939).

The capstone for this entire arch of activity, however,
consists of two books which are devoted exclusively to Don
Juan. Elizabeth Boyd's monograph (1945) is the more general guide and is solid and thorough; it attempts to study the
poem as a separate entity and to work backwards to a general assessment of the mind of Byron, the latter object being
ably accomplished in the succinct concluding chapter. Her
treatment of the poem includes a survey of the externalities
of Byron's poetic career as these led to the making of Don
Juan (essentially a trek to total artistic independence on Byron's part--from society, politics, the critics, Murray, even
the trammels of self); a literal synopsis, canto by canto,
without any attempt to elaborate ironic or aesthetic values;
a history of Byron's plans for the poem and the gradual evolution of its form and purpose; a description of "Don Juanism,"
or the complexity of style to be found; a discussion of the
themes of the piece, including the "grand theme" of Nature
vs. Civilization or Reality vs. Appearance; and a rewarding
discussion of Byron's reading and the use to which he put
that reading in Don Juan, a usage which included not only
suggestions for enriching the situations, sentiments, and
characterizations but also for the cultivation of many of his
ideas.

Paul Trueblood's book (1945) is less comprehensive;
in fact, it is three studies selected from several which the
author states may later be used for an introduction to a
critical edition of Don Juan. The first of these traces the
origin and evolution of the poem from the "sportive satire"
of the early cantos to the serious social criticism of the
later ones as Byron's satiric genius flowered with his at-
tainment of spiritual and creative maturity. The specific
factors hastening the maturation process from December
1820 to June 1822 are seen to be Teresa, the example of
Henry Fielding, and the influence of Shelley. The second
section represents a thorough investigation of the contemporary reception of Don Juan. Trueblood presents the English
periodical reviews (17 more than Coleridge listed) from August 1819 to April 1824 in order to measure the criticism in
the "light of the dominant critical prejudices of the period, "
and to study the effect of the reviews on Byron as they
caused him to modify his plans and effect the final changes
in the poem. In the last section of his book Trueblood tries

to determine if Byron's avowed purpose in Don Juan--as "a
Satire on abuses of the present states of Society"--and performance are one.   In a twofold approach he first distinguishes the objects of Byron's satire, which he catalogues
helpfully under the headings of individuals, England and
things English, and social institutions and modern society in
general; he then evaluates the significance of Byron's work,
first defending it against the charges of negativism, cynicism,
misanthropy, and immorality, and concludes by finding Don
Juan a positive "epic-satire of all insincerity and all that ob-
structs human freedom." These monographs by Boyd and
Trueblood, complementing each other as they do, firmly establish the importance of Don Juan and make a significant
start in the direction of full-scale study of this much neglected masterpiece.

      There is no interest concentration in the remaining
studies of particular works during this period; criticism is
almost perfectly distributed through 11 articles that deal
with ten poems.   Most of these may be passed over quickly.
William S. Ward in "Byron's Hours of Idleness and Other
than Scotch Reviewers" (1944) summarizes 17 contemporary
reviews (16 original and one derivative), finds 11 favorable,
three unfavorable, two about evenly divided, and indicates
that Byron must have been unaware of the Satirist and
Monthly Mirror reviews since they were almost as deroga-
tory as the Edinburgh Review.   Two minor poems receive
attention: "Byron's Epitaph to Boatswain" (1943) is shown
by B. R. McElderry, Jr., to belong possibly to a minor literary fad of the time, thus countering interpretations that
make it part of the Childe Harold mood or claim that it
demonstrates Byron's artificiality, as Boatswain died three
weeks after the epitaph; and Roy P. Basler corrects "The
Publication Date, and Source of Byron's 'Translation of a
Romaic Love Song' " (1937) from Coleridge's "Childe Harold,
1814 (Seventh Edition)" to Hobhouse's Journey through Albania
(1813), noting at the same time some minor variations of
texts.   Concerning Byron's lyrics, Edith Sitwell in A Poet's
Notebook (1943) considers "So We'll Go No More A-Roving"
great poetry, and C. G. Brouzas writes of "Teresa Macri,
the 'Maid of Athens' " (1945).   Childe Harold arrives at its
dark tower in this period, with only three items appearing:
J. E. discusses the circumstances of its composition in
"Childe Harold's Pilgrimage" (1940), George Hamilton writes
of "Hamlet or Childe Harold?" (1944), and Harold Nicolson
(1943), in a privately printed English Association Presiden-
tial Address, uses the poem to sift through Byron's fashionable

but insincere romanticism to his genuinely realistic, modern,
and universal vein of disillusionment--it is Byron's reaction
to this latter, in anger or in love, that gives to his poetry
its " 'excellence of sincerity and strength.' " Of Byron's
dramas, T. H. V. Motter (1935) re-estimates the stage
value of Byron's Werner; Paul Siegel discusses and compares
the idea of " 'A Paradise Within Thee,' in Milton, Byron,
and Shelley" (1941) and argues that the treatment of the inner
world of each illumines the character of the author in each
case; and E. D. H. Johnson, in the most substantial of all
these articles, offers "A Political Interpretation of Byron's
Marino Faliero" (1942) in which the sympathy displayed for
both conspirators and patrician judges and the inability of
the Doge to offer a constructive solution for the evils of
government are seen as the projections of Byron's own uncertainties, for he was sympathetic with the radical Carbonari in Italy but hostile to the English radical reform movement, and he recognized the evils of the monarchy in England
but at the same time the danger attendant on the democratic
form of government that the Carbonari would bring. Finally,
a brief discussion of The Vision of Judgment by L. E. Nelson
in Our Roving Bible (1945) forms the springboard for remarks on Byron and the Bible and religion.

One other area of criticism remains to be discussed--
the broader, more general critical studies. Except for one
important segment of these, most may simply be fitted into
the general pattern noted in earlier periods. There are the
usual capsule assessments which do not necessitate mention.
There are the surveys that fit Byron into the European Romantic context, as Albert Guerard's Preface to World Literature (1940) and Emery Neff's A Revolution in European Poetry, 1660-1900 (1940). There are the surveys of English
literature like B. Ifor Evans' English Literature: Values
and Traditions (1942), which is too brief to be of much value,
or like George Sampson's The Concise Cambridge History of
English Literature (1941) and H. J. C. Grierson and J. C.
Smith's A Critical History of English Poetry (1944) which
offer somewhat fuller treatment. There are the more specialized treatments of the Romantic period like B. Ifor Evans'
Tradition and Romanticism (1940), which fits Byron into
Evans' concept of the continuity and compromise that per-
sists from age to age in English literature, from the Neoclassical to the Romantic; or like J. W. Beach's A Romantic
View of Poetry (1944) and Mary M. Colum's From These
Roots (1937), which deal with the Romantics' ideas about
poetry; or like F. L. Lucas's The Decline and Fall of the

Romantic Ideal (1936), which sees Byron and his work as healthy but tinged with the decadence that is part of the later decline of Romanticism.

But one new development in this area of general criticism stands out in its importance--treatises that deal with particular topics or ideas of the Romantics. Joseph Warren Beach furnishes a classic study of The Concept of Nature in Nineteenth-Century English Poetry (1936) wherein he finds Byron the least transcendental of the major Romantics. Since he considers Byron's approach to nature as being through feeling and not intellect, he finds that the poet prefers nature wild (to flee from society and man), sublime (to find a match for his own elemental passions, to lose himself in the wild and free forces of nature), or Arcadian (to restore himself to innocence and "natural" passion). Oddly enough, despite Byron's stress on the emotions, he is the greatest popularizer of the sentiment associated with the philosophy of nature, largely because of the Shelleyan or Wordsworthian influence he expresses in Childe Harold III. A book of equal stature, Douglas Bush's Mythology and the Romantic Tradition in English Poetry (1937), takes favorable note of Byron's Neoclassic side and finds his use of myth confined largely to that of Prometheus; moreover Byron's usage of myth is mainly remote from the idealistic and symbolical use of his contemporaries. Byron's use of the Promethean myth also plays a large part in Albert Guérard's "Prometheus and the Aeolian Lyre" (1944), which analyzes the Romantics' stress on Promethean individualism along with their paradoxical desire for submersion of the rational self in Nature. In studies dealing exclusively with Byron, M. T. Jamil discusses the "Philosophy in Lord Byron" (1938) in a three-part study. And E. W. Marjarum presents an important study of Byron's religious opinions in Byron as Skeptic and Believer (1938), pointing up a Calvert-type paradox between Byron's Calvinistic heritage and receptivity to religious and metaphysical currents of his own day, and his relations to eighteenth-century rationalism. Because of the paradox, any conclusions reached must be tenuous; but Marjarum believes that Byron was more consistently in line with the eighteenth-century Deists (qualified by Byron's doubts about the immortality of the soul and his emphasis on the emotions), though he might be temporarily swayed by Wordsworth and Shelley as he was in 1816. Finally, mention should be made of several articles, without naming them, that concern Byron's idea and treatment of freedom; most of these were called forth by the event that dominates the last years of this era.

Even though the critical side of Byron study contains the most significant advances made during this period, other areas of scholarship manifest interesting developments. Two important trends are discernible in the area of biography. The one of most consequence has to do with the lesser figures associated with Byron rather than with the poet himself. Actually it is a continuation of the activity begun so significantly in the preceding period with the publication of seven books on these lesser figures. This activity continues with such gusto--the number of books more than doubling--that the results make this one of the major developments of this period. The cause, one may surmise, is that the new material on Byron has now been exposed and competently mined; accordingly, biographers have apparently switched to these lesser figures where untapped material is abundant. Some of these figures are important enough to justify biographical treatment in their own right; but these biographies--Jack Simmons' Southey (1945), H. J. C. Grierson's Sir Walter Scott, Bart. (1938), R. G. Grylls' Mary Shelley (1938), and those on Thomas Moore by Seamus MacCall (1935), H. M. Jones (1937), and L. A. G. Strong (1937)--enrich our knowledge of Byron by offering the point of view of the other side.

The remaining biographical accounts are certainly inspired, in part at least, by interest in Byron and range through his life of acquaintances: Mary Chaworth, Byron's first love and Alastor (Frances Scheidacker, 1935); Lord Brougham, Byron's shadowy nemesis from the beginning of his career (G. T. Garratt, 1935); Isaac Nathan, the young composer of the music for Hebrew Melodies (O. S. Phillips, 1940, in a pretentious and trivial account); Lady Bessborough, the concerned mother in the Caroline Lamb affair (Ethel Mayne, 1939; and also the Earl of Bessborough, 1940); Caroline Lamb herself (David Cecil, 1939, relying on unpublished family papers in a vivid but unfair account); Claire Clairmont, mistress in England and Switzerland and architect of the rise and fall of Byron's friendship with Shelley (R. G. Grylls, 1939, utilizing some new material in a semi-fictionalized biography that is reliable in historical details); Allegra, the unfortunate issue of the Clairmont affair (Iris Origo, 1935); Teresa Guiccioli (Austin K. Gray, 1945, whose account suffers by comparison with Origo's superior rendition); Trelawny, superficial friend in Italy and foe after Byron's death (Margaret Armstrong, 1940, in a generally unfavorable account); John Wilson Croker, Secretary to the Admiralty and diviner of the authorship of Don Juan (M. F. Brightfield, 1940); and, beyond Byron's death, Harriet

Beecher Stowe (Catherine Gilbertson, 1937, and also Forrest
Wilson, 1941).

The journals reflect this same trend of interest as
articles appear on Fletcher (Harold Nicolson, 1937), the
Holland House Circle (Agnes Repplier, 1936, and also the
Earl of Ilchester, 1937), John Murray (TLS, 1943), and
Alessandro Guiccioli, husband of Teresa (Iris Origo, 1935).
The logical extremity of this interest is reached with publication on figures so minor that they border on the obscure
in the life of Byron. Two of the innumerable women who
carried on infatuated, one-sided correspondences with him
are treated: Harriette Wilson, who met the poet at the
Water's Masquerade in 1814 and was one of the most famous
courtesans of the day, is the object of a biography (A. M.
Thirkell, 1936) and an article that studies and publishes her
letters for the first time (Peter Quennell, 1935); and Henrietta d'Ussieres, whom Byron arranged an assignation with in
1814, is also treated through her correspondence (Peter
Quennell, 1938). Finally, there is a well-documented biography that rounds out the shadowy figure of the Rev. Colonel
Finch, a minor associate of Byron and Shelley in Italy
(Elizabeth Nitchie, 1940), and an article on an American who
visited Byron when he was sick at Missolonghi (Una Pope-
Hennessy, 1938). The fever of activity on these related
figures peaks in this era, though there will continue to be
notable contributions made from time to time in later periods.

The other important development in biographical study
centers on Byron himself. One searches in vain for the
competent, full-length biography drawing on newly-discovered
material that one has come to expect since the turn of the
century; by now most of the material has been utilized, and
biographers are content to let Mayne and Drinkwater stand
for awhile. First-rate biographies are still being produced,
but with a difference; this era marks the real beginning of
highly specialized treatments of specific periods of Byron's
life in studies that are well researched, skillfully written,
and infinitely more complete than the counterpart sections in
a full biography. The method has been used to good effect
before--Harold Nicolson's treatment of the Grecian episode,
for example--but there seems to be more of a legitimate
trend, more purpose and direction beginning with this period.
The two well-known volumes by Peter Quennell that treat
Byron: The Years of Fame (1935) and Byron in Italy (1941)
are the showcase examples, and they set the pattern for the
type in the next period. They are the most thorough accounts

of their respective periods--July 1811 to April 1816, and
April 1816 to 1823 when Byron leaves Italy for Greece--until
Marchand. Some new material is drawn upon, notably Hobhouse's annotated copy of Moore's Life and selected letters
(from the Murray archives) written by Byron's "enthusiastic
... public," although nothing is furnished that was not already known except some support for the suspicion of Byron's
homosexuality. Quennell's strength is mainly in his retelling
of the old material: the sketch of scenes and people sur-
rounding Byron are vivid, picturesque, and even fascinating
at times; and Byron's temperament and character are portrayed from a balanced perspective and with occasional pene-
tration. But when Quennell goes beyond this realm to explain Byron's effect on the Victorian age in The Years of
Fame or to assess the Romantic Movement in Byron in Italy,
he overreaches himself, and his arguments detract greatly
from his book. Curiously enough, in the earlier volume
Quennell only mentions Byron's poetry in passing, the very
factor that accounts for "the years of fame"; and when he
does render a critical judgment, it is peremptory (on the
romances) or flippant (on Childe Harold) and usually erroneous, as later opinion shows. Quennell is more disposed
toward Byron's satirical side; consequently there is better
balance between character and career in his second volume,
and his critical judgments are more thoughtful. These two
volumes will be remembered, but primarily because of the
excellence of their style, the lively and lucid retelling of the
events of Byron's life and personality.

Other than the two trends noted, there is a general
drop in biographical activity for the period in both numbers
and quality. The only other book to be mentioned is Frances
Winwar's The Romantic Rebels (1935), which is one of her
popularized group biographies that worked fairly well with
the Pre-Raphaelites because they formed a homogeneous group
but becomes diffuse with the more diverse Romantics. Keats
and Shelley are praised at the expense of Byron and Wordsworth.

The articles dealing with some biographical aspect of
Byron are fairly numerous but are exactly what one has
come to expect--phases of the life, comparisons or relations
with other people, associated places, etc.--and are generally
undistinguished. Four, however, are worth singling out,
three of them by one man, David V. Erdman. In his initial
article, "Byron's Stage Fright: ..." (1939), Erdman poses
the question "Why did Byron write plays 'to reform the stage'

--and then violently protest against their being staged?" The answer to this question, he believes, is also the clue to the entire Byronic paradox in both his life and work. He finds the answer in Byron's inferiority complex and his attempt to resolve it by formulating "a paradoxical life-plan to cope with a paradoxical situation"; i.e., to attract attention and thus prove his superiority through verse, prose, voice, and at the same time to build an elaborate defense against the possibility of failure. Erdman illustrates his point briefly by reference to Byron's life and poetry, proceeds at some length to show it operative in his career as an actor and protesting playwright, and climaxes his discussion with Marino Faliero as his main case in point. Significantly, Byron's second and third classical tragedies were written under the illusion that Marino was enjoying a successful run.

Erdman's next two articles deal with Byron and politics and seemingly have no relation to his first article, but in the background of both is Erdman's thesis about Byron's psychological mechanism of paradox. "Lord Byron and the Genteel Reformers" (1941) deals specifically with the political scene in England during the short time in which Byron took a serious interest in politics, with Lady Oxford's political tutelage of a coterie of genteel reformers and Byron in particular (reversing the traditional opinion of her role with Byron), and with Byron's relation to the radical aristocrats of the time and to the cause of Princess Caroline. "Lord Byron as Rinaldo" (1942) traces Byron's political interest and career from his earliest schoolboy ambition to distinguish himself as orator and statesman, to the disappointment at his seating in Lords, to his determination to enter upon a parliamentary career in 1812 and even in 1813, and to his final political apathy as the result of a sense of failure because of a series of disillusioning experiences that gradually eroded his role-concept of himself as Spokesman through Parliament to the world beyond. The psychoanalytical angle of these articles may seem a bit too forced and pat at times, but Byron's political interests and activities have been researched in great detail and are presented lucidly and fully in a firm line of argument. Bertrand Russell's oft-printed essay, "Byron and the Modern World" (1938), covers something of the same ground, defining Byron as an aristocratic rebel and depicting the circumstances causing his make-up. Russell sees Byron, however, as enormously important when measured as a nineteenth-century force of change; for he is the prime figure in the movement "aimed at liberating human personality from the fetters of social convention and social morality. "

A quick survey of the advances made in the area of
primary materials reveals nothing of major significance.
For Byron letters, Lady Charnwood's Call Back Yesterday
(1938) contains items from her collection which were written
by numerous Romantics including Byron but which had not
been previously accessible; Olybrius presents "A Letter of
Byron" (1938) to Lord Erskine, September 10, 1823; and
"Tenbury Discoveries, No. III" (1941) contains a letter from
Byron to Hoppner, dated December 7, 1819. As new Byron
originals become scarce, activity shifts to the figures associated with Byron, similar to the shift of interest in the
area of biography; and the material is more important here.
The letters of the Byron-Caroline Lamb relationship are
printed in Lady Bessborough and Her Family Circle (1940);
15 letters (plus two summaries) from Mary Shelley to Byron,
as well as numerous valuable references to the poet, are included in The Letters of Mary W. Shelley (1944), edited by
Frederick L. Jones; two collections of letters already mentioned from young ladies during the years of fame, Harriette
Wilson and Henrietta d'Ussieres, are published separately in
Cornhill (1935, 1938) by Peter Quennell. The latter co-edits
with "George Paston" (Emily Morse Symonds) "To Lord Byron": Feminine Profiles (1939) which includes "unpublished
letters, 1807-1824" from 13 women correspondents, though
much of the material is reprinted from Paston's series of
articles in Cornhill (1934)--none of the letters touch on Byron's work and very little biographical novelty is evident.
There are additional odds-and-ends letters from major and
minor figures in Byron's life, some of which are revealing,
such as the letter from Moore to Hobhouse written from
Newstead in 1828, which shows Moore's animus toward Hunt
and his unenthusiastic attitude toward Hobhouse. Consideration of the sum of Byron's letters may be found in Edgar
Johnson's One Mighty Torrent (1938) and Horace Gregory's
Shield of Achilles (1944).

Several new poems or lines are attributed to Byron,
wondered at, or debated publicly: "To Her Who Best Can
Understand Them," found in Washington Irving's commonplace-
book, initiated by F. P. Smith (1936) and answered by George
S. Hellman (1944), who in turn raises considerable opposition; "Literal Version of a Later Literal Effusion," found
among Disraeli's papers, initiated by C. L. Cline (1942) and
also stimulating controversy; three poems found in the seven
scrapbooks at Duke (George Harwell, 1937); two lines attributed by Keats to Byron (K. J. B., 1943); and a couplet that
Moore picked up at Harness's house while compiling his Byron

biography (Olybrius, 1943). Single-volume collections of Byron's work have diminished considerably; only one general
collection, edited by Sir Arthur Quiller-Couch (1940), appears. The earlier editions were competently edited and
will stand for awhile longer. One new angle, however, is
noticeable--i.e., the publication of Byron's poetry in single
volumes according to its romantic or satiric side. This approach seems to be part of the general movement in this direction that was begun by Calvert's influential book; at any
rate the results are good as the volumes by Bredvold (1935),
Chew (1936), and Joan Bennett (1937) illustrate.

The remaining publications that deal with primary
source material are the usual potpourri of notations on manuscripts, editions, reviews, and forgeries, with the exception
of three important catalogs: The Roe-Byron Collection,
Newstead Abbey (1937), which lists the items bequeathed by
Herbert C. Roe to Nottingham; Byron: 1788-1938 (1938),
which records the Huntington Library exhibition in observation of the sesquicentennial of Byron's birth; and the British
Museum General Catalogue of Printed Books (1939, updated
1959-66), which lists the British Museum holdings of editions,
translations, biographies, critical works, and miscellaneous
Byroniana. The Cambridge Bibliography of English Literature (1941) with its Supplement (1957) and new edition (1969)
is helpful in its listing by H. G. Pollard of editions, as
well as secondary materials on Byron, though it is by no
means complete.

Discussion of the last period in Byron study ended
with two minor trends that had begun to assume a degree of
importance; this section may conclude with notice of these
same two trends, for interest in both is retained. The first,
contemporary views and reviews, is centered more in reviews this time as shown by the following: W. S. Ward (1944)
summarizes the seventeen reviews of Hours of Idleness,
H. H. Clark (1940) treats the reviews in the North American
Review, A. L. Strout deals with John Bull's Letter (1942),
and A. J. App (1937) and Henri Peyre (1944) discuss Byron's
clash with the reviewers. Evident, too, is the fact that
there is less reprinting this time and more emphasis on
scholarly research and comment.

The second trend, which burgeoned so fully in the
preceding period and completely reversed the earlier emphasis from influence on Byron to Byron's influence itself, continues at the same rapid pace. Since the Victorians were

too close to Byron to admit this fact, effort is seemingly re-
doubled now to make up for the oversight. Of the five items
that continue the older interest, only A. P. Hudson's "Byron
and the Ballad" (1945) and W. J. Phillips' France on Byron
(1941) need be singled out. Byron's influence, on the other
hand, quickly overwhelms the preceding in numbers. His
effect on continents (Europe) and countries (France, Holland,
Germany, Russia) is studied at about the same ratio as before. Interest in his influence on individuals doubles, with
pieces on Brontë (Helen Brown, 1939), Browning (B. B.,
1944), Bryant (A. I. Ladu, 1939), Churchill (R. G. W.,
1943), Flecker (Geoffrey Tillotson, 1942), Fanny Kemble
(Margaret Armstrong, 1938), Mácha (René Wellek, 1937),
Patmore (B. B., 1944), Poe (R. P. Basler, 1937), and
Whitman (J. J. Rubin, 1939). There are the inevitable imitations and sequels, mainly of Childe Harold and Don Juan.
The offshoot for still another direction in Byron's influence
can be seen in G. H. Hamilton's "Eugène Delacroix and
Lord Byron" (1943) and R. E. French's "Lord Byron in Romantic Music" (1941). Studies by Stephen A. Larrabee (1943)
and Edmund Blunden (1942) also relate Byron to the arts,
though do not deal specifically with his influence thereon.
This interest in Byron's influence and relation to the fine
arts will be developed in later periods.

Whereas the period from 1926-1934 represented a
pause in literary quality though not in quantity, this period
reverses the process and represents a pause of sorts in
quantity. The actual average per year of Byron material is
down in this decade from 28 items per year to about 23, the
low activity of the war years accounting for the decline;
otherwise the average would have remained about the same.
So there is no appreciable loss of interest in Byron, merely
a lull until the war is over. But the loss in quantity is
more than made up for in quality. The large amount of
significant secondary material that is produced suggests that
merit and quality are beginning to catch up with the revolution in primary source material that had been uncovered
earlier in the century.

9. Byronic Reorientation: Renaissance
    in Primary Source Materials,
    1946-1956

        After World War II is over, the flow of Byron publi-
cations begins to rise, as one would expect; it quickly surpasses the pre-war level. If the interest quotient were
plotted on a graph, the bar would show a steady and rather
striking swing upward: through the 20's for the first three
years, a surge into the 30's for the next five, and a second
surge into the 40's for the next two. The period ends with
a high of 53 items, a fact which augurs well for the succeeding decade.

        The most important work accomplished in this period
concentrates on primary materials, both in the publication
and interpretation of them. Scholarship seems to have come
full circle since the turn of the century in moving through a
zodiac of achievement in primary materials, biography, acclaim, criticism, and back to primary materials again. To
be sure, the present era is not as momentous as the one
that brought the Murray Edition, Astarte, and the Correspondence; but a renaissance of sorts is effected with the discovery of new material of consequence.

        The showcase pieces are The Last Attachment (1949)
by Iris Origo, which opens up the very important Gamba papers to an English-speaking audience for the first time, and
Byron: A Self-Portrait (1950), edited by Peter Quennell;
both are valuable for the letters they include and render this
area of research especially prominent. Iris Origo, by virtue of her Italian nationality, rank, and ability, was eminently suited to handle the Gamba papers; her narrative is the
first full account of Byron and Teresa Guiccioli and acts as
a perfect foil for the material which she presents. The
Gamba material itself is extensive and includes 156 letters
and notes written by the poet to Teresa (all but 17 of which
are in Italian and printed in full in a separate appendix) as
well as numerous other letters within the Gamba circle,
Teresa's 1700-page "La Vie de Lord Byron en Italie"

(apparently the third and most extensive version, succeeding
the earlier ones given by her to Moore and Lamartine),
letters to Teresa after Byron's death (the most relevant to
Byron being those from Lady Blessington, John Murray,
Thomas Campbell, Thomas Moore, Alfred D'Orsay, and John
Pigot), and various official papers that shed much light on
Teresa's separation from her husband in 1820. Besides the
Gamba material, Origo also relies upon material dug out of
the Italian official archives and the secret archives of the
Vatican (which reveal for the first time the full extent of the
involvement of Byron and the Gambas in the Italian political
intrigues of the time), upon documents found in the Keats-
Shelley Memorial Library in Rome, upon letters in the Pierpont Morgan Library and the great John Murray collection,
and upon papers of Count Rangone, who collected current
anecdotes about Byron. With such thorough and painstaking
research and with the views of both principals fully exposed
for the first time, Origo was able to deliver an account of
the 'last attachment" that is both reliable and balanced. In
reality the book encompasses much more than the liaison; it
ripples out to include Byron's gradual absorption into all the
intricacies of Italian social and political life. Questions re-
main--Count Guiccioli's motives with regard to Byron, some
of the attitudes and actions of the political authorities--but
so many problems are settled (the sincerity of Byron's love,
the stabilizing effect of the match upon him, the salutary influence of Teresa upon his work) that the portrayal of this
phase of the poet's life is likely to remain the definitive
treatment for some time.

Peter Quennell's Byron: A Self-Portrait is a collection of 375 Byron letters, all of the diaries, and Detached
Thoughts. The poet's entire letter-writing career is spanned
in these two volumes, from his "first letter I ever wrote"
to those sent from Greece; consequently, a more immediate
sense of his growth to maturity is attained than in Prothero's
six volumes. Byron is allowed to speak for himself, with
only a cogent biographical summary by the editor to introduce each chronological phase of his life. One might desire
a different emphasis here and there--more of the Venice and
Ravenna years, less of the poet's adolescence and frivolity
in London--but the collection is representative. Of enduring
worth in these volumes--since any selection of Byron's
letters is apt to catch the wit, the seriousness, the spon-
taneity that are uniquely his--is the ample supply of unpublished matter incorporated. The editor claims 56 new letters
and the restoration of suppressed portions from 36 others.

However, the first figure needs scaling down as several of
these letters had already appeared in Origo's volume and
Prothero's edition, and at least one letter is a forgery, perhaps another; as for the restored letters, many are still
censored with asterisks at the request of the manuscript own-
ers. Quennell's work as editor is not as felicitous as his
accomplishments as Byron biographer: his introduction of
the new material is only incidental, the restored portions of
the letters are not indicated in the text, errors in transcrip-
tion are frequent, numerous texts are taken from inferior
printed sources instead of available manuscripts, and the annotations are quixotic rather than systematic and contain errors. The reader is not disappointed with the additions
themselves; although no new interpretations are afforded,
they do flesh out in robust fashion the several facets of the
man already known.

    One more substantial collection of letters appears;
these letters are included in Leslie Marchand's article, "Lord
Byron and Count Alborghetti" (1949), an interesting example
of literary detective work on a hitherto unlisted figure in Byron biography. The Count was Secretary General of the Pa-
pal Legation at Ravenna, a lay official who was second in
command after the Cardinal Legate and hence a person of
power and influence. Marchand places the eight unpublished
letters of Byron to the Count and the 19 of the Count to Byron against the general background of Byron's life at Ravenna (a key period in his biography) and convincingly shows
that the Count played a vital role in the poet's affairs during
his two years in the city. Besides performing many ser-
vices for Byron, this figure seemed ready at hand for any
emergency: exercising his influence with the Pope to win
for Teresa favorable terms in the separation proceedings,
extricating Byron's servant from a difficult situation with the
authorities, helping Teresa to escape from Ravenna when the
political authorities threatened her. His supplying Byron
with information from the Cardinal's own mailbag explains
how Byron kept well informed about political developments on
the Continent and in England, and how he knew so much about
official surveillance of his activities. Many cloudy references
in Byron's letters to his friends at this time may now be
properly understood, and his apparent immunity to arrest in
the sticky Carbonari business now becomes comprehensible.

    Only a few other isolated letters by Byron come to
light: five to Robert Wilmot (his first cousin and advisor to
Lady Byron during the separation proceedings), one to Lady

Frances Wedderburn Webster in which he acts as domestic
"pacificator," one addressed to the editor of the Courier attacking Southey but wisely suppressed, one to Dr. James
Alexander (his physician at Genoa) which rather mysteriously
inquires about a house, and others to Dallas, Somerville,
Hoppner, the Greek patriot Nicholas Karvellas, and an
unknown correspondent.   Unpublished letters by Byron's associates are in moderate evidence, but only those contained
in three articles need be singled out: Willis Pratt supplements Origo's book with his "Twenty Letters of the Countess
Guiccioli Chiefly Relative to Lord Byron" (1951), one letter
being written in English to Lady Blessington in 1832, and
the rest in French to Emma Fognani (wife of the portrait
painter) between 1863 and 1872 and here presented in manuscript translation by the Fognanis' son and his wife; these
letters are of interest in showing Teresa's continuing attachment to Byron's memory.   Leslie Marchand (1955) draws
upon two unpublished letters from Trelawny and one from
Captain Daniel Roberts (all dated in August, 1822) that deal
with the burning of Shelley's body, to show clearly that
Trelawny altered his story in his later manuscript and published accounts so that he would appear solely responsible
for the burial preparations.   Payson Gates (1953) prints the
text of a Leigh Hunt letter (with additions and corrections by
Byron) to his nephew H. L. Hunt in which he appraises the
first number of The Liberal, outlines plans for the second
number, and comments on matters of interest to his London
co-workers.   Some other letters published are merely reprints, such as those in the commemorative volume In Memory of Lord Byron's Sojourn at St. Lazarus which collects
all of Byron's letters mentioning the Armenian Convent, or
Byron's letter to the editor of Galignani in which he wittily
refutes that paper's announcement of a work to appear by
Lord Byron on vampires.   Jacques Barzun's edition of The
Selected Letters of Lord Byron (1953) is an adequate reprinting for classroom use but offers nothing new except the editor's own graceful and cosmopolitan essay, "Byron and the
Byronic in History," in which he sees Byron as a wondrous
"archetype of Man."

        Occupation with Byron's letters beyond the realm of
gathering and publishing new material takes several forms.
Some important cataloging of materials in the Rare Book
Collection at the University of Texas is done by Guy Steffan
in two articles.   In "Byron Autograph Letters" (1946) he
catalogues and comments on 71 letters, a promissory note,
a "demise," and Byron's will stipulating his wish to be buried

with his dog at Newstead.   His analysis of the letters reveals them as representative not only of Byron's entire public career but of his correspondents, his interests, and his
activities as well.   Over 50 of the letters are deemed worthy
of publication, 45 of which have not appeared in print before
and eight more of which correct Prothero's text.   In his second article Steffan performs the same task for the 121
"Autograph Letters and Documents of the Byron Circle"
(1945-1946).   Of these, 58 are letters written by members
of the "family," 39 or 41 are from or to lawyers, and the
remainder are from members outside of the family (Caroline
Lamb, Teresa Guiccioli, Mary Shelley, Trelawny, etc.).
The bulk of the correspondence has to do with the daily frus-
trations--usually financial--that beset the family.

Several other articles offer commentary on Byron's
letters: C. Keith (1946) traces the making of Byron as a
letter writer, finds Byron the reader and literary critic most
prominent in the letters, and states that Byron moves "up
and down the ladder of humanity, more familiarly than any of
the other great letterwriters."   Edmund Wilson (1952, in a
reprint) considers the Correspondence and defends Byron
from the adverse charges resulting from its publication.
Mario Praz (1950) deals with Byron's letters to Teresa.
Joshua Whatmough (1956) submits two of Byron's letters to
statistical analysis to show how legends can be dispelled.

Finally, one small group of items deals with forgeries
of Byron letters.   Two of these are by Theodore Ehrsam
(1951, 1954) on the most famous of Byron forgers, Major Byron.
Two more are by Charles Hamilton, who comments generally
on Byron forgeries (1954) and also warns of the facsimile
(1955), using Byron's letter to Galignani on The Vampyre as
his case in point.   Add to this group the article by T. J.
Brown (1953), utilizing a facsimile illustration of Byron's
handwriting to detect faked literary manuscripts, and the
well-documented history by Herbert Greenberg (1946) of the
Harvard Library's forged copy of Byron's "Ossian's Address
to the Sun," and the matter of forgery becomes a minor
corollary interest to the period's concern over primary materials.

To turn from the heady business of the new letters
uncovered in this renaissance to the poetry is to turn down
a blind alley.   There are editions in abundance, with seemingly every major English and American publisher of a standard series of literary texts adding a selection from Byron

to its list.   In England there are the "Crown Classics" (ed.
Patric Dickinson, 1949), "Everyman" (ed. Guy Pocock,
1948), "Penguin Poets" (ed. A. S. B. Glover, 1954), and
"Nonesuch" (ed. Peter Quennell, 1949) editions; and in America there are the "Rinehart Editions" (ed. E. E. Bostetter,
1951) text, and two volumes in the "Modern Library College
Editions" series (ed. Louis Kronenberger, 1949 and Leslie
Marchand, 1951).   One can always quarrel with the selections; but most of these texts are competently edited and introduced, some with marked originality, for example Dickinson's introduction.   But one looks in vain for new material.
There is only a pittance to be found--Ward Pafford's (1952)
printing of the Yale Manuscript "To Those Ladies," a 12-
quatrain poem of 1806 which fits not only into Byron's complex pattern of response to the criticism of Fugitive Pieces
but foreshadows his later shifting and paradoxical attitude to
the reception of his work; and T. G. Steffan's very thorough
presentation (1948) of the Pierpont Morgan Library Manuscript version of Byron's "The Edinburgh Ladies Petition and
Reply," complete with manuscript description, printed text,
scholarly analysis, and recondite survey of the scientific
knowledge of the period which the poem was satirizing.   Two
other poems are not new, but W. T. Bandy shows that Byron's "Stanzas on the Death of the Duke of Dorset" (1949)
and his lines to Lady Blessington (1948) appeared earlier
than believed--the former in the Edinburgh Annual Register
for 1824 (Bandy prints the text with variants and argues for
its superiority over the standard version) and the latter in
Les Annales romantiques for 1827-28 and again in the Monthly Magazine for 1829 (Bandy prints Lady Blessington's reply
but not Byron's lines since they are in substantial agreement
with the accepted text).   There is very little to savor here
in the way of fresh discovery.

     When one turns to the work done on the primary ma-
terials in poetry, however, he discovers the rest of the
renaissance here.   To T. G. Steffan must go the accolade
in this movement; for he not only catalogs "The Byron Poetry Manuscripts in the Library of the University of Texas"
(1947) but also produces a series of close studies of Byron's
revisions of Canto I of Don Juan that will lead straight to
the impressive Variorum Edition (which he edits with Willis
Pratt) in the next period.   His survey of poetry manuscripts
in the University of Texas Library reveals 59 manuscripts
(60 are catalogued but one turns out to be a copy of "To
Night" by Joseph Blanco White) which may be divided into
three categories: 37 manuscripts of Byron's poetry, 16

manuscripts of Lady Byron's and six manuscripts of occasional poems by other writers who utilize Byron as their
subject.   The highlights of the collection are the 13 manuscripts of poems and two drafts of the preface to Hours of
Idleness from the Southwell period, Ode to Napoleon and The
Siege of Corinth from the later English period, and Sardanapalus, Cain, Don Juan VIII, and The Island from the Italian
years.   This study by Steffan, which is part of a world cen-
sus of Byron poetry manuscripts, completes his cataloging
of the University of Texas Byron materials (vide supra his
two earlier surveys); and he uses this piece as a plea for a
cooperative effort in locating all extant Byron manuscripts.

     Steffan's five articles that deal wholly or in part with
Byron's revisions of Canto I of Don Juan are the seminal
pieces for his contribution later to the Variorum Edition.
The Pierpont Morgan Library Manuscript of the first draft
and a British Museum manuscript of a few scattered stanzas
are the bases for these studies.   In the first article, "Byron
at Work on Canto I of Don Juan" (1947), Steffan approaches
the composition of the Canto through the external avenues of
the letters and manuscript which mutually corroborate and
clarify each other; in the process he is able to correct the
dating by Moore and Coleridge (from September 6-November
1, 1818 to July 3-September 6) who had erroneously followed
Byron's note on his fair copy rather than his first draft dating.   He also explores a third avenue of approach to the
Canto, the internal avenue of psychological forces that control the composition; by exploring the personal, environment-
al, ideological factors affecting Byron, he shows how these
confuse and produce a complex state of mind and feeling that
account for much in the poem.   The next three articles are
closely complementary studies of different facets of Byron's
revisions.   One centers on the "Ms. Rhyme Revision of
Canto I of Don Juan" (1948) and shows that despite Byron's
fluency with rhyme his best effects came from second effort.
The poet tries to retain the rhyme within the stanza when re-
vising, but there is a high rate of change in the couplet
where he did most of his revision anyway and where there
was no danger of cumulative damage.   The next article concentrates on "The Extent of Ms. Revision of Canto I of
Don Juan" (1949) as seen especially in the lines of the poem.
The manuscript reveals that Byron composed rapidly and
corrected rapidly for the most part, even penning alternate
possibilities at times for the London Synod to decide upon;
but revisions are more extensive than formerly believed.
About 46 per cent of the final published lines have been

corrected; the couplets (particularly the seventh line) plague
him the most, over two-thirds of them needing revision, and
the middle lines in the rest of the stanza cause him the next
greatest trouble. The final and climactic article of this
group, "Byron Furbishing Canto I of Don Juan" (1949), tries
to determine the principles and standards that governed Byron's revisions. It finds that in passages where thinness occurs the poet revises to incorporate more substance; in one-
word or phrasal changes his aim is nearly always to be
more incisive, through the specific, the concrete, the exaggerated, even the sensational in order to serve the purposes
of his art; in tone, since his poem is conversational, he revises toward the colloquial manner occasionally. The last
of these five articles, "Byron's Focus of Revision in His
Composition of Don Juan" (1952), overlaps with the preceding
article in finding that Byron manages most easily in his narrative and dialogue passages as well as in his conversational
passages; and that his hardest work was in passages of psychological analysis, physical description, personal engagement, images and allusions, and trifling frivolity. But in
the later article Steffan extends Byron's "focus of revision"
from Canto I to the first seven cantos and draws the same
conclusion. Steffan, through minute study and analysis of
the manuscript, is able to explode such legends about Byron
as the sprezzatura artist, to correct many facts, and to
offer pragmatic insight into both the nature of the man and
the mind and methods of the artist.

    A brief miscellany of other work relevant to the pri-
mary materials of Byron's poetry may be cited. Steffan
adds further to his already solid accomplishment with Byron
manuscripts, this time with a study of Byron's revisions in
Beppo (1953). Again the Pierpont Morgan Library Manuscript is used, and his procedure and conclusions closely
approximate those of the earlier articles. This is one of
the best of his studies and is especially interesting in that it
shows Byron consciously at work "on a novelty that was soon
to become his natural and most compelling habit of expression." Andrew Rutherford finds Coleridge's description of
Murray's copy of "An Early Ms of English Bards and Scotch
Reviewers" (1956) inadequate and inaccurate; accordingly, he
presents a full description, proves that the manuscript is
not the first draft as Coleridge maintained but the third
draft, and corrects Coleridge's dating of the manuscript
from before Byron read the Edinburgh Review attack to at
least a month after. In the matter of editions, T. C. Duncan Eaves (1946) notes that Murray's two-volume edition of

Select Works of the Right Honourable Lord Byron, 1823, is
not recorded in Coleridge. And Alex. Bridge (1951) identifies the editor of the Memoirs of the Life and Writings of
Lord Byron, "George Clinton, Esq.," as in reality James
Bacon.

     To be expected, perhaps, is the paucity of new Byron
prose materials. Only "An Italian Pocket Notebook of Lord
Byron" (1949) and "Byron's 'Fantastic' Will of 1811" (1951)
come to light; both are commented on by Willis Pratt and
are contained in the University of Texas collection. The
former turns out to be Byron's account book, with inter-
leaved memorabilia, of monies received and expended plus
other memoranda from December 1819, when Byron was at
Venice, to July 1820, when he had moved to Ravenna, after
which time it came into Teresa's possession and records
certain emotional moments in her liaison with the poet from
1822 until after his departure for Greece in the following
year. The "fantastic will" is one in which Byron stipulates
that he be buried with his dog at Newstead; it is drawn up
by a legal clerk and signed by Byron on every page. Byron's
"Observations on an Article in Blackwood's Magazine" had
already been printed in the Murray edition; but Philip Daghlian (1947), with the aid of the manuscript in the Yale University Library and the page proofs revised by Byron, attempts
to piece together the entire history of the manuscript,
proofs, and publication of this reply by Byron to a review
of Don Juan in Blackwood's--a reply that was never published
during his lifetime.

     The deficiency in new Byron prose material is com-
pensated for by that found among his circle and contemporaries. The circle materials are particularly rich. The
Italian Journal of Samuel Rogers (ed. J. R. Hale, 1956);
Frederick L. Jones' edition of Mary Shelley's Journal (1947)
with her valuable insights into Byron's activities and character; the same editor's edition (1951) of the journals and
letters of Maria Gisborne and Edward E. Williams, with the
latter standing revealed as much closer in friendship to Byron than formerly assumed; Lorraine Robertson's publication
of unpublished passages from "The Journal and Notebooks of
Claire Clairmont" (1952)--all are issued in this period.
Claire and her journals receive a slight concentration of interest with articles by Herbert Huscher (1955) and Marcel
Kessel (1951).

Contemporary prose accounts about Byron and his activities are more plentiful though less centrally important;
they offer interesting glimpses of and sidelights on the poet.
In England there is Mrs. Arbuthnot, who records in her
Journal of Mrs. Arbuthnot, 1820-1832 (1950) gossip about
Byron's vices and Caroline Lamb's reaction to Medwin's
Conversations; there is Leigh Hunt, who notes his reactions
to Thomas Moore's Life of Byron (Sylva Norman, 1953); and
the most interesting is Benjamin Robert Haydon's largely
sympathetic marginalia on his copy of Medwin's Journal (Duncan Gray and Violet Walker, 1956), notes that are especially
helpful since he knew Shelley, Keats, Moore, Murray, Hunt,
and Scott (the publisher of the Champion who caused Byron
much damage at the time of the separation) and is able to
provide different points of view on Byron's activities and
much current gossip in London circles about the poet. Widely scattered Continental reactions also attest to Byron's contemporary charisma. In Venice during March 1819 an unknown observer, in obvious fascination, pens a surprisingly
accurate and intimate record of Byron's habits, domestic
situation, and literary activity in his copy of Childe Harold
(C. L. Berry, 1956). From Germany, Goethe's comments
on Byron are always interesting and are dealt with by D. F.
S. Scott (1950) and John Hennig (1949) in "Early English
Translations of Goethe's Essays on Byron. " A Russian
source on Byron's activities in the Greek revolt is noted by
Claude Jones (1956). Both prose and poetic Greek reactions
to Byron and his death are printed by James Notopoulos
(1955). Even the American lawyer, George Ticknor (1947),
writes his impressions of Byron in his Journal.

Although the area of primary materials overshadows
that of biography, there is still considerable activity in the
latter area. The full-length biographies that have been so
noticeably lacking in the last period are suddenly prevalent
here; no fewer than five appear. Some of these are true
children of the age in the lucrative supply of new materials
they furnish and could easily have been discussed earlier,
as The Last Attachment in fact was. The two most important wear their "biography" with a difference, so much so
that they almost seem examples of the emperor's new
clothes. They are biographies, however, in the sense that
they deal with the sum total of the poet's life; it is in the
fresh arranging of their materials that their uniqueness lies.

The first of these, G. Wilson Knight's Lord Byron:
Christian Virtues (1952), is the more radical in its departure;

Knight confesses that he does not "make any pretensions to
biographical skill of the more conventional kind. " Instead
his biography is a study of genius ("[Byron is] the supreme
genius of our era"), not the life of a genius but the thing
itself manifested in action through Byron as a personality of
challenging poetic importance. Knight's method merits attention both because of its unusual nature and because it will
be used again by the author in two later books on Byron.
Knight puts great stock in his evidence--in fact, he criti-
cizes former biographers for "too much biographical skill
with too little reliance on evidence"--and he includes the
range of Byron's poetry and prose and the important firsthand accounts in his sources. The unreliability of many of
the latter is now widely recognized, and one might criticize
the author for non sequitur reasoning except that in his unique
approach he seems to be concerned less with the truth of the
fact per se (the aim of the conventional biography) than with
the fact's truth--i. e. , the effect of Byron's genius on these
people--in which case his use of this evidence is acceptable.
Knight's method is to reduce narrative and comment to a
minimum and mass his evidence about certain essential foci
that he considers central to his study. In this way the
massed facts and quotations, released from their normal
temporal associations, may be "seen afresh as themselves";
no attempt is made to prove anything beyond them, and the
evidence alone is the argument--i. e. , "the art and argument [lie] rather in selection and structure than in any explicit deductions. " The result, then, is not the biographical story of a life but a "mosaic of evidence regarding qualities. " By now it should be obvious that Knight is applying
his well-known "spatial" method, which he has used effectively in his books on Shakespeare, in order to see beyond
Byron the man to the more eternal qualities of genius. The
new "interest centres" that Knight finds in the consideration
of his subject are as follows: love of animals ("Byron is
our greatest poet of animal life"), wide range of reading,
especially in history ("the greatest historical poet in Western
literature"), courage, etc. The author has carefully appended an index of these qualities. To enumerate them in
isolation is to reduce all to absurdity; for, ultimately, it is
his method that heightens, supports, and pleads for credence.
And it is his method that seems to have made this the most
controversial book on Byron of the decade (as Knight says,
however, no review has found an error in his work) and one
of the most controversial of all books on Byron.

The major charges against the volume are that it
uses a card-index approach and arrives at frozen attitudes
rather than a living personality, that it sees only one side
of the man (the virtues--the vices are to come in a later
book) whereas all sides are needed to form a moral judgment,
that it resolves Byron's contrarieties by calling them merely
parts of a dual nature, and that its praise is overextravagant
and amounts to idolatrous hero-worship. These are sound
and reasonable charges, if one were judging the book as
"conventional biography." But Knight stresses that it is not,
and he could easily refute these charges by saying simply
that he is not after the temporal man and personality but the
eternal genius. The book may not be a perfect one, but it
is certainly seminal, as Knight's "Preface" clearly indicates
that he intended it to be; and time has vindicated him in a
manner since some of his views have now gained widespread
recognition (e.g., his interpretation of "Julian and Maddalo").
The book is also intended as a corrective of current tendencies that Knight sees exemplified in Quennell, Nicolson, and
Origo.

     In an odd sort of way Ernest J. Lovell's His Very
Self and Voice (1954) shares kinship with Lord Byron:
Christian Virtues. Both purport to be new kinds of biography,
both depend on a massing of primary and/or contemporary
materials, both predominantly let the evidence speak for itself, both claim to get at the real Byron through his impression on others, both approaches will be extended in future volumes; but in the end, of course, they are different in aim,
tone, and result. Lovell pursues the elusive character of
Byron through his talk, since he was the conversationalist
par excellence in an age that placed a premium on this art.
Man and age met at this point, and the impact of one upon
the other resulted in a record of over 150 contemporary accounts of Byron as talker in over 180 sources. Lovell attempts to marshal these (with the exception of the Medwin
and Blessington conversations, which he reserves for later
treatment) into a unified and coherent narrative of Byron's
conversational life, preserving his words (direct and indirect)
as well as the manner or style of speaking so as to provide
a faithful transcript of the poet's actual voice and personality.
The larger aim of the book is, by presenting these many
conflicting accounts, to gain a more comprehensive understanding of, and thereby to come closer to, the honest truth
of the man in the daily drama of his life. The result offers
a Pirandello-like approach to this truth rather than an idealistic one. Like Knight's book, Lovell's is controversial; and

again the controversy centers on the method of approach.
Objectors feel that the book is divided in aim between being
an inclusive scholarly work and a piece condensed for popular appeal; furthermore, Byron as brilliant conversationalist
fails to materialize, and the real man is buried under a
mass of conflicting and prejudiced testimony. If the book
fails to give us Byron's "very self and voice," the fault
would seem to lie more with the chroniclers than with the
editor. What we do have is a comprehensive collection of
widely scattered contemporary accounts, many of them unpublished or difficult of access, which reveal the effect of
Byron in all of his variety of personality and range of conversation on the people of his own day. The collection is
set off with excellent notes and an exceptionally fine introduction which presents a resumé of each of Byron's major
acquaintances.

The three "conventional" full-length biographies are
mainly a re-treading of familiar ground. Eileen Bigland's
Passion for Excitement (1956) is a popularization, but it is
not as sensational as the title implies. She has gone to
Byron's letters and journals, the major eyewitness accounts,
and the standard biographies; so she stays reasonably close
to the facts. Instead of attempting anything new, she seeks
to recreate, by selecting and choosing from the sources, "a
vivid and masterful portrait of the man and his extraordinary life," for which purposes she has employed a novelistic
style. Since Byron, with a View of the Kingdom of Cant and
a Dissection of the Byronic Ego (1948) is by C. E. Vulliamy,
a professional biographer, it too is meant for a popular
audience. He undergirds his rather loose biography with
approximately the same sources as Bigland, but the results
are different. Bigland intrudes in a personal way only in
her style, but Vulliamy intrudes his personality into every
aspect of the book. He is a man of very broad and varied
interests, and much of what he has to say is of value--e.g.,
the British view of such elusive terms as cant and Byronism
--but ultimately he vitiates his biography by his own personality. What one ultimately gets is not Byron, but Vulliamy. Finally, one should mention Duncan Gray's modest
little volume, The Life and Work of Lord Byron (1946), one
of the "Newstead Abbey Publications" (No. 4).

The restricted biographies of the last period--a fledg-
ling trend noted--become even more restricted in the present
decade as Byron research becomes increasingly specialized:
from Byron: The Years of Fame to Byron at Southwell

(1948), from Byron in Italy to Byron, Shelley, and their Pisan Circle (1952). The Southwell phase in Byron's life is one that is largely neglected in favor of the later years of his maturity and achievement; but it does represent the all-important formative stage of Byron as a poet. The University of Texas is especially blessed with manuscripts and letters belonging to this period; Willis Pratt presents these in the first scholarly monograph, Byron at Southwell, to be based upon the Texas collection. The book's scholarly apparatus has been criticized as disconcerting to the narrative, but the "Foreword" explains the purpose of the narrative as only a lucid frame for properly arranging and understanding the documents now made available for the first time. These new materials include not only several poetry manuscripts and letters from Byron, his mother, and lawyers, but all variants and cancelled readings from printed texts as well; one manuscript has particular charm, Elizabeth Pigot's original parody of Old Mother Hubbard, "The Wonderful History of Lord Byron and his Dog," with its watercolor illustrations. Pratt's book alters no currents but it makes a number of modest contributions: the letters reveal new details concerning the printing of Fugitive Pieces and Poems on Various Occasions, Elizabeth Pigot emerges as the most important influence on Byron in these embryonic years, the emotional ties between Byron and William Harness are closer than realized, something of the comic spirit of Don Juan may be detected in the unprinted "Prim Mary Ann" (though it is harder to see in "To Miss H."), and the comparisons of manuscripts and printed texts help to show something of Byron's methods of composition.

Clarence Cline recognized the need for a full-scale biography that an age flourishing in newly-discovered materials inevitably brings; his Byron, Shelley, and Their Pisan Circle is "an attempt to write a segment of that biography," in this case the brief but important Pisan period (1821-1822) in the lives of Byron and Shelley. Cline shows the gathering of this brilliant group, largely because of Shelley; shows Byron, the eldest, assuming the social leadership with his rides, pistol practice, and weekly dinners, and later the moral leadership as reflected in the Taafe affair; and shows finally the disintegration of the colony. But it is the Taafe affair that is the focal point of the book; for Cline has exhausted virtually all of the evidence, including the unpublished correspondence (in the University of Texas collection) of Byron and Taafe to Edward Dawkins (the British Chargé d'Affaires) which presents their respective sides of the case;

the unpublished autobiography, letters, and documents of
Taafe in the possession of his great-granddaughter; extensive
correspondence from Murray's archives involving the principals; the unpublished (at the time) journal of Edward Williams
in the British Museum; the mass of court records from the
State Archives at Pisa, Florence, and Lucca; plus supplementary matter from the Keats-Shelley Memorial Library,
the Carl Pforzheimer Collection, the Morgan Library, and
the Berg Collection.   No revolutionary discoveries are made,
but certain speculative matters are cleared up or corrected:
the complex interrelationships of the Pisan group are now
better understood; with regard to the pivotal dragoon affair
the precise sequence of events is made clear, the man responsible for the dragoon's wound is most certainly Byron's
servant Papi, and the obscure figure of Taafe is at last de-
lineated in full; finally Origo's confirmation of Byron's sus-
picions about Italian authorities aiming at him through the
Gambas is further supported.   The thoroughness of Cline's
research has enabled him to accomplish his goal, for this
book is likely to remain the authoritative account of the Pisan period.

      Two other limited studies are restricted in a differ-
ent way, rather than by locale where Byron spent a certain
portion of his life.   One, William Borst's Lord Byron's
First Pilgrimage (1948), is much broader in scope and more
fluid as it involves the details of Byron's Continental tour of
1809-11.   Borst wisely holds his recapitulation of the familiar material leading up to the tour--the facts, Byron's character and accomplishment, the Childe Harold attitudes already present in the poet--to the briefest of introductions.
Then he moves into largely unexplored territory for the main
portion of his study, which is a kind of factual guide (emphasizing the actuality of Byron's art) to Childe Harold I and II.
The accumulation of historical, geographical, political, military, and other data is impressive and illuminating; and Borst
goes to such neglected sources as contemporary travel records, memoirs, materials in Portuguese, Greek, French,
German, and obscure histories and records of the pertinent
countries involved to gather his information.   The book is
also a "consideration of the effect of his experiences upon
the mind and character of the poet"; and Borst concludes
that Byron gained the following from his Eastern odyssey:
future material, an emotional refuge, intolerance of English
insularity, a broader outlook especially in politics and social
matters, a more cosmopolitan view, and a locale congenial
to his temperament for the future.   The book remains the
fullest record to date of this particular tour.

The final limited study does not involve a place or a journey at all but a relationship. E. M. Butler's Byron and Goethe (1956), after an interesting essay noting the remarkable parallels in the lives and careers of the two men, traces the entire history of this curious literary relationship, which is a little like an uneasy courtship at a distance since the two men never meet. Byron furnished the stimulation by force of his work and hypnotic life (Goethe believed the versions in Glenarvon and The Giaour were actual), and Goethe supplied the passion. Reminiscent of the scenario from a romantic movie, the whole affair is tracked through a maze of besetting difficulties--accidents, chance, delays, letters gone astray, Byron's almost futile attempt to dedicate a work to Goethe, the German's alternating chills and fever --until something like a happy ending is reached with re- demption for Byron in Greece and a final burst of vigor for Goethe in his old age.

The interest in full-scale studies of Byron's associ- ates and acquaintances that began in earnest after the Cen- tenary and developed rapidly during the next two decades be- gins to decline somewhat, though not drastically as 12 still appear. Some of these deal with figures treated in earlier book-length accounts: David Cecil turns again to Melbourne (1954); curiously, Lady Bessborough, who had two books devoted to her in the preceding period, is the object of still another by D. M. Stuart, Dearest Bess (1955); Mary Shelley again receives treatment, this time by Elizabeth Nitchie (1953); and Trelawny is the object of two studies, by S. J. Looker (1950) and Glynn Grylls (1950). Several fig- ures receive extended treatment for the first time: William Harness (C. M. Duncan-Jones, 1955), Francis Jeffrey (J. A. Greig, 1948), John Gibson Lockhart (M. Lockhead, 1954), and Count D'Orsay (W. Connely, 1952). John Cam Hobhouse and Ugo Foscolo are not only newly considered but are dis- tinguished by a pair of books, wholly or in part, on each. The delay in Hobhouse interest is rather surprising since he was Byron's best and most loyal friend; Michael Joyce fi- nally gives him his due in My Friend H. (1948). Joyce un- abashedly allots Byron considerable space because of the friendship, but he is content with only "the man as Hob- house knew him" and does not attempt a full portrait. The work is thorough and makes use of the existing Hobhouse collections, including material still in family hands; of the unpublished matter the most interesting item is the diary en- try of 1812 describing how Hobhouse prevented Lord Byron from eloping with Caroline Lamb. Foscolo crosses the path of Hobhouse in an unpleasant episode rendered by E. R. Vincent in Byron, Hobhouse, and Foscolo (1949). This book is concerned with a double collaboration on Childe Harold IV: that of Hobhouse with Byron to provide exposition for the Italian subject matter in the poem since Byron had no time for it, and that of the Italian poet Foscolo with Hobhouse to provide an essay on contemporary Italian literature since Hobhouse had no knowledge of the subject. The result was a disaster for Hobhouse; Foscolo's essay received the approbation, Hobhouse received the criticism from Italy when Foscolo's authorship was suspected (by mutual agreement Foscolo had been a silent partner), and a potential friendship was destroyed amid the ensuing pressures and misunderstandings over payment. Vincent prints many unpublished letters of the chief actors as well as extracts from Hobhouse's personal diary. The method he uses is similar to that employed by Willis Pratt in Byron at Southwell, where a graceful narrative acts as a frame for the new materials. Vincent supplements his rendition of this episode with a fuller volume on Foscolo, Ugo Foscolo: An Italian in Regency England (1953).

Of the immense quantity of articles of a loose biographical nature appearing throughout the period, an unusually large percentage is devoted to Byron's relationship with other people or to his acquaintances. The variety of persons represented is amazing and hardly anyone is mentioned twice. There is a supply of the familiar names that one has come to expect: Caroline Lamb, Lady Byron, Moore, Shelley (with four articles), Teresa, Lady Blessington, Goethe, even Captain Chamier. But it is the array of new faces that makes this area particularly noteworthy; they fill in many gaps, and the total is even greater than in the last period when this interest was pursued with such avidity. Willis Pratt follows up his monograph on the Southwell period by concentrating entirely upon "Byron and Elizabeth Pigot" (1949); rewriting, condensing, and refocusing his material, he explores more fully his earlier suggestion of Elizabeth's important formative influence on Byron as he traces the poet's development from its tenuous Southwell beginnings to its set course with the publication of English Bards and Scotch Reviewers. Iris Origo's "The Innocent Miss Francis and the Truly Noble Lord Byron" (1952) tells the story of Eliza Sarah Francis, one of Byron's infatuated admirers, and her half-dozen romanticized tête-à-têtes with him in London just before his marriage; the documents were found by Origo among the Gamba papers as a result of

"Eliza's" correspondence with Teresa in 1863-64. D. J.
Rulfs (1950) records Byron's admiring comments on Edmund
Kean and the relation of the two to Drury Lane; and R.
Findlater (1955) includes Byron in his study of another theatrical figure, Grimaldi the clown, whom Byron came to know
at private dinner parties and Covent Garden. George Whalley
(1951) discusses the Byron-Coleridge relationship in general
and Byron's request that Moore review Coleridge's "two
volumes of Poesy and Biography" in particular. Oblique relations with public officials are included in studies by Paul
M. Zall (1953), who shows how Byron and others felt the
oppressive force of Lord Eldon's censorship, and D. M.
Stuart (1953), who designates Byron as the most effective of
contemporary poets railing against the Prince Regent. Oddly
enough, obscure interests sometimes run parallel at the same
time: two articles appear during this decade on J. W. Dalby, the bookseller, and his relation to the Romantic poets
(Willis Pratt, 1947; and Edmund Blunden, 1952); and three
more have to do with Byron and the Armenian monks of San
Lazzaro (M. T. Greene, 1955; N. Maxoudian, 1955; L. K.
Kristof, 1956). Acquaintances in Italy are dealt with: Ernest Lovell attempts a complete survey of the important
"Byron and Mary Shelley" (1953) relationship (largely neglected by her biographers) by including in his scrutiny her
diaries and novels in addition to the biographical facts; he
finds a unifying thread through it all, that Byron became to
her a "symbol of one of her most deeply felt needs, that of
a Father-lover, the desired pillar of masculine power and
authority. " Lovell's article is a follow-through of his "Byron and the Byronic Hero in the Novels of Mary Shelley"
(1951), wherein he detected biographical overtones. Iris
Origo (1950) proceeds from her The Last Attachment to con-
centrate on one aspect of that affair, the delightful story of
the governess Fanny Silvestrini who acts as go-between for
the lovers. And Thomas Pyles touches upon Byron's Venetian mistresses in "Margarita, Marianna and the Countess
of Blessington" (1949). In Greece Byron stayed in the
Macri home on his first tour; C. G. Brouzas completes with
three publications the study that he began in the last period
of Teresa (the supposed original of Byron's "Maid of Athens")
and her family.

The remaining essays of a biographical nature represent a heterogeneous assortment. Some describe Byron's
abilities: as swimmer (Harold Nicolson, 1951), as pugilist
(L. J. Henkin, 1947), as student of Armenian (D. B. Gregor,
1951). Many more describe his faults: his epilepsy (J. E.

Bryant, 1953; F. McEachran, 1954), his neurosis (P. Bottome, 1949), his borderline insanity (W. N. Brown, 1952), his "ailments" (P. M. Dale, 1952). His lameness, a perennial topic of interest, is of particular concern in this era: P. Tompkins approaches the topic through "Byron's Shoes" (1954) and W. R. Bett (1951) through its connection with his genius; H. C. Cameron (1949) sees its cause in a mild form of Little's Disease which leaves no deformity but causes a stiffness and awkwardness in movement; Leslie Marchand (1956) seems to have cleared up the matter once and for all with his survey of the evidence and conclusion that it was a club foot and that Byron's right foot was the one affected. The possibility of a more serious defect is raised by G. Wilson Knight in three articles (1954, 1956) dealing with the authorship of the "Don Leon" poems which were printed in 1866 and which make an apology for homosexuality and reveal an intimate knowledge of Byron's private life; the contingency of Byron's homosexuality, Knight believes, could explain the separation, the burning of the Memoirs, and passages in "Julian and Maddalo."

Another group of studies concentrates on specific biographical episodes in the poet's life: Guy Boas (1954) is interested in Byron at Harrow; Dora Jean Ashe (1953) disproves the traditional idea (based mainly on Gillman's statement) that Byron supported Coleridge's application for the production of Remorse at Drury Lane in 1812--Byron was not even on the committee at the time; Gilbert Highet (1954), in a slight but urbane piece, suggests that the reason for the "extraordinary variations in [Byron's] outlook and his personality" was his starvation diet; C. E. M. Roberts (1946) treats of the visit of "Byron ... [to] the U.S. S(hip) 'Constitution' " in 1822, which was of consequence in his relations with Goethe; Leslie Marchand produces two articles (1952, 1955) that deal with the burning of Shelley's body, stressing especially Trelawny's accounts; W. S. Dowden, also in two articles (1955), shows that Byron's allusions to Austrian surveillance of his activities and fear of his political significance were not ungrounded; Byron's last words are recorded by E. S. LeComte (1955), and Amice Lee (1955) makes several references to Byron's burial; finally, W. M. Parker (1947) provides the interesting gossip following Byron's death that the autobiography was merely blank paper.

The relationship of Byron with other places, usually a prevalent topic in these brief biographical surveys, is not as conspicuous as formerly; and of these, Greece receives

most of the attention with studies by S. B. Liljegren (1953),
Henry Raynor (1954), Terence Spencer (1954), and Douglas
Dakin (1955).   Two other locale studies merit brief comment: John Cameron traces "Byron's Association with Scotland" (1946), from his Aberdeen boyhood, to his later repudiation in English Bards and Scotch Reviewers and poems
against Lord Elgin, to his final more positive attitude. Heinrich Straumann's two-fold aim in Byron and Switzerland
(1949) is to give an account of Byron's residence and tours
there in 1816 and to ascertain the relationship of the experience to the poetry by comparing the impressions in the
letters and journals with the creative result.

Certain opinions and attitudes of Byron's are the object of several studies that round out this section on Byron:
his adulation of Pope (G. Wilson Knight, 1954), his reaction
to the laureateship (K. Hopkins, 1954), his devotion to freedom (R. W. , 1952), his revolutionary expressions regarding
English politics in the years following the defeat of Napoleon
and his influence on events there (D. V. Erdman, 1947), and
his consistent hatred of oppression and espousal of liberty for
man throughout his life and work (W. S. Dowden, 1950).

The years 1946-1956 do not represent a significant
period in Byron criticism, the emphasis lying elsewhere.
Not a single book appears that may be considered genuinely
critical, the closest being Ernest J. Lovell's Byron: The
Record of a Quest (1949).   This work does deal with Byron's
poetry, but it is more directly aimed at his concept and
treatment of nature.   Lovell sees Byron's "quest" as religious in that he was seeking peace of mind, psychological in
that he hoped to find this peace in the dissolution of his own
wretched identity, and intellectual in that a solution had to be
found in a system that would satisfactorily relate God, man,
and nature for him.   At times Byron seemed to find his
answer in the complete acceptance of nature, as when he
came under Shelley's influence in Switzerland; and certain
almost instinctive ideas and qualities within his mind im-
pelled him in this direction--his rebelliousness, desire for
a retreat from the world, deism, "mobility. " But this
quest was to end finally in failure because other traits--his
Calvinism, comic view, worldliness, sense of guilt, genuine
unhappiness, and above all his "sense of fact"--operated to
urge him in the opposite direction.   Lovell traces the various conflicts and failures that Byron went through in arriv-
ing at this final position: the conflict between country and
town (Byron preferred finally the latter), the failure of the

picturesque tradition for him (after it became vulgarized and
artificial), vacillation between the hope of finding a spiritual
cure in nature and the sense of nature's denial of this to all
but the spiritually pure and virtuous (the Zeluco theme), and
the philosophical opposition between the benevolent creation
of the Deists and the hostile view of nature of the Calvinists
(both of which Byron could equally espouse). But if Byron
failed to find happiness and a satisfactory philosophical solution, he did manage to wring achievement out of his failures
by increasing his "awareness of the comic vision, which
enabled [him] to view the world honestly, without oversimplification, in all its immense complexity and so do justice to
his own consciousness of it. "

        Though no trailblazing books of a critical nature ap-
pear on Byron in these years, it is not a retrogressive period; there is a generous supply of briefer studies that wedge
open areas for criticism, offer new approaches or new insights, and project new opportunities for the future.   In
these studies, the most notable area of contribution is that
which carves out a certain block of Byron's work and holds
it up to scrutiny or isolates a certain aspect or quality of
his work for comment.   Byron's prose is viewed with freshness and sensitivity by G. Wilson Knight (1953), who considers it from the vantage point of drama.   He believes that
Byron developed the solid Augustan bases of his prose style
in the historical commentary of Childe Harold I and II with
its maturity of judgment and dignity of phrase; it was in his
Parliamentary speeches that he learned something of the art
of drama.   His letters and journals reveal the full maturity
of his dramatic prose style; and Knight analyzes these for
their dramatic elements, compares them in style with that
of Shakespeare, and illustrates from them with close study
of vivid examples.   Knight sees Byron's prose as a blend of
the Dionysian and Apollonian to be found in Nietzsche's definition of drama, with emphasis upon the former.

        Byron's lyrics have been largely neglected; therefore
L. C. Martin attempts to redress this oversight in his "Byron Foundation Lecture" for 1948.   Acknowledging the traditional charges against Byron's lyrics of egotism and facility,
Martin sees positive good in them when the latter conveys a
headlong sense of immediacy and the former communicates a
sincerity and strength that lie with the elemental and universal.   But Byron is at his best when he transcends both personality and fluency to write on such universal themes as
"liberty or endurance, or the power of man to rise above

his mortal nature" in the sublime or grand style as Arnold
understood it. Then he ranks "among the masters of the
English impersonal lyric. "

    Byron's dramas to this point have rarely been given
serious consideration, either as stage pieces in his own day
or as important works of art since; but in this period they
draw some attention. G. Wilson Knight (1950), in a prelude
to his later more important work on Byron's dramas, calls
them "the most important poetic dramas in English between
the seventeenth century and our own time" and suggests an
annual Byron Festival. George Rowell mentions them in his
survey of The Victorian Theater (1956). Arthur Norman and
Patricia Ball get down more to specific cases. The former
illustrates the dramatic quality of the "Dialogue in Byron's
Dramas" (1954) and regards it "of such fine mettle as to
place him among the foremost of verse dramatists. " Ball
brings astute insight to and has the same enthusiasm for her
subject as Knight; indeed, she proclaims her article as a
"follow up and support [for] Mr. Knight's pioneer efforts. "
She calls Byron's plays "Byronic Drama" (1955), emphasizing
their uniqueness, and lists the characteristics of the type.
The stage history of Byron's dramas is also noted, with the
suggestion that it was the avant-garde nature of these pieces
that caused his edict against their production and not some
elaborate psychological reason (see David Erdman, "Byron's
Stage Fright"). The dramas are seen as peculiarly relevant
today not only because they are historically authentic but because they grapple with the same political and social problems.

    Byron's skill as parodist has long been recognized but
little reckoned with; C. V. Wicker (1954) gives a push in
this direction with his listing of Byron's parodies preceded
by illustrative comment. Full appreciation of Byron as a
satirist was a long time in coming, but its dramatic triumph
was witnessed in the preceding period. Additional valuation
is now found in studies by E. D. Mackerness (1947), who
traces Byron's evolution as a satirist and his development of
a proper vehicle for his art, surveys the targets of his
barbs, and establishes the positive standards that regulated
his comment and pulled it into a coherent philosophy; and also by Marius Bewley, who finds "The Colloquial Mode of Byron" (1949) more in the English tradition than the Italian (as
Ronald Bottrall and others have believed)--not the English
tradition represented by Pope and the Augustans, but that of
the Caroline poets in the seventeenth century.

Those studies that isolate one element of Byron's
work for comment are not as significant as the preceding
and, with one exception, need only a side glance in passing.
Carl Lefevre sustains the conspicuous interest in Byron's
heroes begun in the 1926-1934 period, considering "Lord Byron's Fiery Convert of Revenge" (1952) as a type of the Byronic hero. Using The Siege of Corinth as his archetypal
pattern, he describes the renegade aristocrat, the representative plot, and the protagonist's aspiration (self-expression)/
achievement (self-destruction) conflict that is resolved in the
final holocaust; then he shows the development of this the-
matic type through The Corsair, Lara, and Marino Faliero.
More briefly, it is seen to be fully present in three other
pieces (The Giaour, The Bride of Abydos, and Parisina) and
at least partially in 11 others. This study is provocative
because of its viewpoint, but its categorical nature causes it
to be one-sided and to miss much of the complexity of these
poems. Mario Praz's The Hero in Eclipse in Victorian
Fiction (1956) traces the fortunes of the Byronic hero in the
English and Continental fiction of the later nineteenth century,
showing that the figure is considerably diminished to meet
the bourgeois demands of the Victorians. P. J. Scharper
(1952) finds marked similarities in the Byronic hero and
Hemingway's adolescent hero, though he feels Byron's type
is more subtle and intellectual. The great difference, he
believes, is that Byron matured at 30, looked back at his
hero with a detached view, and laughed at him in Don Juan;
Hemingway never arrived at this point. Such isolated phenomena in Byron's work as his interest in rivers is traced
by P. R. Butler (1954); and his use of the sea as a symbol
of eternity is observed by John Bourke (1954). Gilbert
Highet places Byron in The Classical Tradition (1949), and
Lesley Blanch (1956) discusses his amalgamation of the ex-
otic trend as "a medium, a way to exalt and dramatize the
tragedies of his characters." The technical aspects of Byron's art come in for consideration, with Donald Davie treating his diction (1952) and syntax (1955), and Bernard Groom
(1955) also discussing the latter.

The brief critical pieces that deal with a specific
work are legion and, in the absence of more extensive
studies, they do make an important contribution albeit in a
quieter way. Perhaps in keeping with the special interest
in primary materials during the era, the overwhelming majority of these are concerned with tracking down a Byronic
passage, allusion, or incident to its original source. These
are too numerous to pursue; but parallels, reminiscences,

etc. , are found for poems ranging from Oscar of Alva to
The Island (ten poems in all), and six sources are found for
parts of Don Juan alone.

    The remainder of these articles and essays offer a
variety of approaches to the poems under consideration,
which extend in a fairly representative way throughout Byron's literary career. Ward Pafford (1951) is interested in
the dating of Hours of Idleness and nails down Coleridge's
nebulous publication date to the last week in June 1807,
through Byron's letters to Elizabeth Pigot; later he establishes the date even more precisely by means of a presentation copy to Byron's mother inscribed June 25, 1807. Rose
Macaulay (1946), in her book on Portugal, includes a chapter on Byron's visit and the account of it in Childe Harold I
and II; and W. B. Stanford (1954) finds one of the five poetic
voices in Tennyson's "Ulysses" is that of Childe Harold in
its "mood of peevish discontent with normal life, ... romanticized description of himself ... and ... determination
'to drink life to the lees. ' " Aside from the anthology pieces,
Byron's Hebrew Melodies has largely been ignored; Joseph
Slater (1952) remedies this situation very nicely with thorough
coverage of the background and nature of the volume. Slater
traces the origin of the collection to a fashion made popular
by George Thomson (of Burns fame), the publication of national melodies accompanied by verses of popular contemporary poets; he then proceeds to give an account of the origin,
composition, and fortunes of the volume itself; and he concludes with the surprising revelation that the poems are not
religious in character but nationalistic, foreshadowing Byron's
later interest in political causes in Italy and Greece. Byron's fragmentary ghost story published with Mazeppa is
placed by Richard Switzer (1955) in the larger context of the
origin of Polidori's Lord Ruthwen and The Vampyre and its
progeny.

    Manfred is discussed by Robert Estrich and Hans
Sperber (1952), and by Arthur Wormhoudt (1956) in his char-
acteristic Freudian approach; but Bertrand Evans (1947) offers the most influential study of the drama. He corrects
earlier scholarship that placed Manfred in the tradition of
the Gothic novel on the basis of superficial resemblances but
failed to explain the transition from villain in the novels to
hero in the poetry. The proper line of descent, he clearly
shows, is from Gothic drama which shaped the ultimate Manfred from Walpole's simple object of terror in a mise en
scène of terror, to the villain whose black deeds served less

to frighten the heroine than to harrow his own soul, to the
sympathetic villain because of his remorse (demanded by the
leading actors and censors), to the Byronic hero by intensi-
fication (remorse to heroic action for purposes of expiation).
The major dilemma of hero/sin was solved by Byron in
leaving the sin "half unexplained." The story upon which
"Byron's 'Beppo' " (1948) is based was first discovered by
Leslie Marchand in Hobhouse's diary; the source, ironically,
is the husband of Marianna Segati and not, as E. H. Coleridge conjectured, an episode in the history of Colonel Fitzgerald and the Marchesa Castiglione that was mentioned in a
letter to Moore.

Cain, which Stanislavski thought enough of in the
nineteenth century to produce (David Magarshack, 1950),
maintains its reputation in the twentieth as evidenced by its
inclusion in Joseph T. Shipley's Guide to Great Plays (1956).
Constantine Stavrou (1955) compares Milton's and Byron's
devils; since Byron was never convinced of the justness of
God's ways to man he "did not embody in his devil all that
was not God. Cain is a conflict between doubt and denial
rather than between God and Satan." Of Byron's stage
tragedies, Sardanapalus is treated by Elsie Butler (1955),
who deals with the dedication to Goethe, and by R. Tsanoff
(1949), who speaks of Byron's use of imagination in this
play; The Two Foscari is considered a failure as drama and
theater, by W. G. Bebbington (1953), but a success as poetry because of the powerful speeches and the Byronic identification with the hero Jacopo. Both T. O. Mabbott (1946)
and Arthur Dickson (1946) explicate the third stanza of "On
This Day I Complete My Thirty-Sixth Year": Mabbott analyzes Byron's "symbolic and suggestive" lines from outside
the poem and finds the images "consonant with nature and
classical tradition; with application to Byron's personal situation, and that of Greece." Dickson explains the stanza within
the context of the poem as a variation of what Byron has already stated three times--i.e., "though I am still subject to
passionate love, I am no longer capable of inspiring it in
others."

Don Juan, consistent with the shift in interest of
critics in the last period, continues to dominate the emphasis of these shorter critical pieces. The important manuscript studies of Guy Steffan have already been discussed.
Don Juan is considered as a European figure by Salvador de
Madariaga (1946); he ranks him with Faust, Don Quixote,
and Hamlet as one of the European immortals, stressing the

special relationships between Hamlet/Don Quixote and Faust/
Don Juan, and traces his European tradition along with Byron's contribution to it. The latter he has reservations
about, for only "an idle Englishman would think of turning
Don Juan into a tourist"; and although the rhythm is "exhilarating" and the style "impertinent," the hero does not "gain
anything in symbolic value or vigor." C. M. Bowra (1949)
stresses that Byron is unique among the Romantics in his
abandonment of the imagination in favor of a more realistic
art modified by the spinal quality and power of his wit.
When Byron outgrew his romantic side and found his proper
vehicle in Don Juan, he wrote his masterpiece; for it contains the truth about himself (his personality entire in all of
its complexity of emotion and intellect), the truth about contemporary life (the whole panorama which he hoped to correct), and the truth about his era, i. e. , the themes and
topics of the Romantics subjected to his own critical mind.
The poem is viewed as comedy by Mark Van Doren (1946),
who thinks that it is a brilliant miss, yet "we never quite
decide that he is wasting our time." Arthur Wormhoudt
(1949) takes a psychoanalytical approach, following the singular theories of Edmund Bergler who believes that many human actions can be explained by problems encountered in
breast feeding, and sees the key to Byron's complex psychological makeup and the answer to the deepest problem in
Don Juan as lying on "the oral level of regression." Of the
studies that are concerned with particular parts of Don Juan,
Steffan (1947) continues his exhaustive research on the first
canto, this time exploring the "complicated area of Byron's
personal history and Venetian environment" as they contributed to "the reality of experience that went into the first
canto"; and in another article (1952) he shows how the murder of the military commandant of Ravenna outside Byron's
door on December 19, 1820, is translated into the circumstantial accounts found in the letters to Moore and Murray
and finally is transmuted into the poetry of stanzas 33-39 of
Canto V. P. E. Wheelwright discusses "The Isles of
Greece" (1954). Finally, in studies in a minor key, Autrey
N. Wiley (1949) points out how the makers of the "Incomparable Oil Macassar" (a popular French hair oil at the
time) complacently accepted Byron's reference in Canto I as
an advertisement for their product, and Frank Stiling (1949)
explains the pharmacology of the two prescriptions imbedded
in Canto X, xli, along with the proper pronunciation and
scansion of the Latin terms.

General critical assessments of Byron and his work--
of the type that may be found in histories of English literature and histories of the Romantic Movement--are more prevalent than usual, in fact about double the number found in
the last period. S. C. Chew (1948) and J. W. Beach (1950)
both allot appropriate space for the poet in their histories of
nineteenth- and twentieth-century literature, as do A. T.
Rubinstein and A. C. Ward in The Great Tradition in English
Literature (1953) and Illustrated History of English Literature
(1955) respectively. Limitations of space and necessity for
resumé virtually prohibit any chance for original contribution
in these surveys. Treatment is even briefer in the more
specialized histories such as English Poetry (1952) and Science and English Poetry (1950) by Douglas Bush, and A Short
History of English Drama (1948) by B. I. Evans. Historians
of the Romantic Movement or aspects thereof, working within
a narrower topical frame, are able to probe somewhat deeper. Graham Hough in The Romantic Poets (1953) presents a
balanced and compact survey of Byron's life and achievement;
but some valuable commentary on the poet's early work and
the satires is marred by an almost total lack of regard for
the dramas and Childe Harold III. With a plea for a return
to Byron's poems, letters, and journals for fresh insight,
Herbert Read (1951) first gives a diagnosis of Byron's state
of mind out of which grew his work, and then discusses the
literary output itself, interspersing commentary with liberal
quotations. In the more restricted histories, Allardyce Nicoll discusses Byron's plays in the context of A History of
Early Nineteenth Century Drama (1930) and Bertrand Evans
places the poet's appropriate dramatic pieces in the tradition
of the Gothic Drama From Walpole to Shelley (1947). In the
area of criticism, M. W. Abrams (1953) mentions briefly
Byron's comments regarding theory but finds that he had
little effect on the critical tradition; René Wellek (1955) discusses Byron's practical criticism, centering mainly on the
Bowles controversy. The promising development of the last
decade--treatises on particular topics or ideas of the Ro-
mantics--fails to keep pace in the present. An article appears on "The Persian Poetry Fad in England, 1770-1825"
(J. D. Yohannan, 1952) and another on "Timelessness and
Romanticism" (Georges Poulet, 1954); but only H. N. Fairchild's Religious Trends in English Poetry (1949), which
traces the conflict in Byron between skepticism and belief,
has any real weight, and it is handicapped by a too-assertive
religious bias.

The budding trends with which discussion of the last
two periods ended may be noticed once again, for they now
seem to have assumed importance as major interest areas
for scholarly research. The first of these, centering on attention to Byron in his own day, has tripled in numbers and
in significance. Only the volume edited by John Wain (1953)
contains reprint material: reviews by Jeffrey, Scott, John
Wilson, and Lockhart of Childe Harold III and IV, Manfred,
Don Juan, and Byron's plays. The rest are new studies of
the contemporary journals and journalists for their comments
on Byron: the Monthly Magazine (W. S. Dowden, 1951), the
London Literary Gazette (R. W. Duncan, 1956), the London
Magazine (E. L. Brooks, 1956; Josephine Bauer, 1953), the
Windsor and Eton Express and General Advertiser (Noel
Scott, 1950 and 1955; W. G. Bebbington, 1956), Lockhart
(Marion Lockhead, 1954), and Jeffrey (James A. Greig,
1948). The reactions to the first two cantos of Don Juan
are mentioned in Obscenity and the Law (1956) by Norman
St. John-Stevas; but the first defender of the poem from the
charge of immorality is detected by Elmer Brooks (1956) in
the person of John Scott instead of Harry Franklin as formerly believed. W. S. Ward (1949) presents the serious reactions of William Roberts, editor of the British Review, to
Byron's good-humored jest in Canto I of Don Juan about having bribed him for a favorable review, with the result that
Roberts makes himself appear even more ridiculous. Byron's little known and puzzling " 'George Russell of A. ' " is
shown by R. M. Wardle (1950) to have possibly been the result of the less-than-favorable reviews that were appearing
in Blackwood's regularly throughout 1821; Byron may have
wanted to settle some scores with the magazine by setting up
this straw Blackwoodian and hacking him to shreds. The
crowning achievement of this trend is the publication by A.
L. Strout (1947) of what S. C. Chew has called "the most
interesting of all contemporary bits of Byroniana," John
Bull's Letter to Lord Byron, a remarkably perceptive pamphlet recognizing the greatness of Don Juan. Strout accom-
panies this edition with the literary background of the three
great periodicals and their reviewers, publishes for the first
time the Croker/Lockhart correspondence which definitely
establishes the latter as the author of the "Letter," and includes a bibliography and appendices, the most important of
which contains all contemporary allusions to Byron appearing in Blackwood's between 1817-1825 and thereby furnishes
a "seismic chart" of contemporary reaction to Byron.

The second trend, evidences of Byron's influence,
has now almost completely replaced the earlier reverse interest of influences on Byron which was so prominent in the
nineteenth century, though parallels to the work of Fray Luis
de Léon, Vincenzo Monti, Dryden, Sterne, Chatterton, Rousseau, Monk Lewis, and Maturin are noted. Studies of the
effect of Byron's work on countries, such as Norway, Germany, Poland, Russia, Croatia, Spain, and America, have
almost doubled; several of these areas have not been touched
before. The number of items showing Byron's impact on
certain individuals is equally impressive, the total again
nearly twice that of the last period. Especially interesting
is the rapid expansion of the circumference of this group,
for of the sixteen individuals dealt with, only Emily Brontë
(M. Evans, 1948; D. J. Cooper, 1952) and Walt Whitman
(S. J. Kahn, 1956) are repeated from the two preceding dec-
ades. The variety and number of individuals treated is
again noteworthy: Keats (R. Gittings, 1956), Shelley (B. W.
Griffith, 1956), Lamartine (C. M. Lombard, 1955), Büchner
(R. Majut, 1955), Annette Von Droste-Hülshoff (Sister M.
Rosa, 1948), Leopardi (Iris Origo, 1953), a Slavonic author
(G. Apel, 1956), Pushkin (C. M. Bowra, 1951; M. Montagu-
Nathan, 1953), Lermontov (W. J. Entwistle, 1949; J. T.
Shaw, 1956), Emerson (K. B. Taft, 1954), Melville (E.
Fiess, 1952), Chivers (C. H. Watts, 1956), and Faulkner
(C. Grenier, 1956). The spin-off interest that developed in
this area in the preceding period, Byron's influence in the
fine arts, is sustained and up slightly: in music, Eric Blom
(1954) registers Byron's mark left on music and musical set-
tings, and Glyn Court (1956) shows that Byron's effect on the
life and work of Berlioz was negligible; in art, G. H. Hamilton's three studies (1949, 1952, 1954) examine the inspiration of Byron on Delacroix, and Robert Sencourt shows "Certain Affinities of Turner" (1951) with Byron.

Imitations of Byron's work are not so much noticed
by critics, with the exception of Edmund Blunden's discussion
of an imitator of Beppo and Don Juan (1955), as is the influence
of Byron's personality on some of the novels of his day: the
anonymous novel Harold the Exile is based on his early life (W.
S. Dowden, 1951), Caroline Lamb's Glenarvon is her view of
the affair with Byron (Clarke Olney, 1956), and the novels
of Mary Shelley have already been noted (see Lovell
above).

Three articles that offer a selective bibliographical
survey of publications on Byron appear in the 50's, indicating

both an attempt to supplement Chew (who ended his survey
with Lord Byron's Correspondence of 1922) and a need to
cope with and order the growing stockpile of Byron research.
Ernest Bernbaum's piece (1952) allots under four pages to
Byron and so is of limited use, but the author does offer an
interesting comparative chart that shows Byron ranking behind
Keats and Shelley in total publications. The articles by Leslie Marchand (1952, updated in 1960) and Willis Pratt (1958)
are genuine surveys and are hence more serviceable; both
are published, in part at least, in the next period, but the
materials they survey belong to the present era. Pratt
shows that by 1956 the gap between Byron publications and
those dealing with Keats and Shelley has considerably narrowed. The great revolution in Byron scholarship and criticism in the period to follow will alter the Romantic map of
research even further.

         The dramatic rise in Byron publications noted at the
beginning of this chapter has no watershed event like the
Stowe revelations or the Murray edition to explain it. But
a pattern has become evident in the preceding discussion
that might perhaps offer some elucidation. A highly productive and highly influential "Texas school" emerges out of the
publications of this period. The University of Texas collection of Byron materials is especially rich--293 manuscripts
of this collection are detailed by Willis Pratt in Lord Byron
and His Circle (1947) and over 30 more are listed in "Lord
Byron and His Circle: Recent Manuscript Acquisitions"
(1956)--and it has yielded some fine Byron returns. Along
with its manuscript treasures, the University has also been
fortunate in having on its campus a remarkable group of
scholars who began their concentrated work on Byron during
this decade. The names of Ernest Lovell, Willis Pratt, and
Truman Guy Steffan constantly recur in the important scholarly work of these years; with the additional work of Clarence
Cline, who published a book and an article during this span,
the list becomes even more impressive. The final tally
amounts to four books, one descriptive catalog, 26 articles,
plus reviews; and the crowning achievement of this activity,
the four-volume Variorum Edition of Don Juan, is not included, though it should be, since it is not published until
the next year.

         Two figures completely outside of the Texas circle
begin to raise their voices at this time also: Leslie Marchand and G. Wilson Knight. Marchand's publications
through articles, reviews, and an edition of Byron's poems

are frequent and give promise of much to come.   The work
of Knight (one book and six articles) is highly controversial,
brilliant at times, and influential; already he is exposing
some of the ideas that he will develop into major studies in
the next period.

Both of these factors--the activity of the Texas school,
and of Marchand and Knight beyond this school--seem to account directly and/or indirectly for the significant increase
in Byron work.   The next period largely bears the stamp of
Marchand's authority, with Knight continuing to act as a
stimulus to Byron scholarship with his revolutionary ideas
and methods, and the Texas scholars continuing to make substantial contributions; but the present decade clearly belongs
to the Texas scholars.   They form the vanguard of Byron
research in this era; and through their productiveness and
vitality they help shape, influence, and give the present period its distinctive character.

10. Balance Restored: Renaissance in Biography
     and Criticism, 1957-1972

     The publications on Byron during this period are so
voluminous that any detailed plotting of "currents and eddies"
would be impractical; the whole would be lost in an estuary
of confusion. An adequate sense of direction might be maintained by restricting consideration to books alone. These
most nearly approximate the mainstream since they are the
significant repositories of the particular author's ideas,
many developed from earlier articles; and they also represent the present building on accumulated information and
ideas from the past. Articles, essays, and pamphlets number in the hundreds; omission of these is regrettable, for
many attain a sophisticated level of professional competence
and/or originality. But the book-length studies are so
numerous and are of such significant quality that exclusive
devotion to them seems justified. They will be discussed in
some detail, both because they represent the position of contemporary scholarship on Byron and because the particular
issues they present are as important as the larger trends of
which they are a part. Proportion of treatment for individual volumes is not necessarily a measure of importance but
often an indicator of complexity. These books reveal a number of trends that will be noted, but most of these may be
drawn into two major areas of achievement in which this era
ranks pre-eminent: biography and criticism.

     The name that stands first when biography is con-
sidered is Leslie A. Marchand. His activity of the preceding decade matures into a magnum opus by anyone's estimate:
the indispensable, three-volume Byron: a Biography (1957).
The stature of his accomplishment can be measured by the
ten years of steady research and work that went toward its
completion. The two gravest problems he faced were the
great mass of material left by Byron and his contemporaries
and the ambiguities about the poet's life. The researcher's
own indefatigable efforts overcame the first problem, for he

retraced every step of Byron's wanderings, discovered new
sources, and examined each existing piece of evidence available.   His list of acknowledgments is a roll call of all the
great Byron collections in America and England, the only
notable exception being the Lovelace Papers, whose contents
he had to derive secondhand from Fox, Mayne, Maurois,
and of course the first Earl of Lovelace.   The second problem, the actual writing of the life, was even more formidable.
Marchand copes with it by insisting on the absolute authenticity of his material for one thing, verifying it from the original sources wherever possible and thereby correcting many
former errors and omissions, particularly in Byron's published letters.   In addition, he presents his account as im-
partially as he is able.   The result is about as accurate and
balanced an account as possible until more evidence is uncovered.

Interpretation of the main outlines of Byron's life is
not appreciably altered; instead there is a general filling in
of detail, a solid sense of authority.   Marchand does manage
to communicate more than the factual account of a life lived,
he projects an intuitive sense of a personality developing
and burning itself out with life.   The problem of proportion
might be debated; but Marchand's large allotment to beginnings and the youthful period is the fullest treatment to date,
and the account of the Greek expedition and after, an absorbing narrative in its own right, seems justified as the climax
of the book and the life.   As for the marriage problem,
Marchand presents his version as fairly as he can, pointing
out the lack of legal evidence from most witnesses, but opt-
ing finally in favor of the incest on the circumstantial evidence of Byron's own letters.   Each individual could wish
for more on this phase or that (the historical and political
background of Italy and Greece at the time, Byron's relation
to the theater, the reactions to Don Juan and Cain); but these
neglected areas are offset by new light shed on Byron's fi-
nances or the clarification of many personal relationships.
A more serious oversight is the lack of attention to Byron's
keen intellectual history.   In the final analysis, however,
Marchand has fulfilled his stated justification for writing the
book--that is, to include the new and to re-evaluate the old--
and he has updated Byron's life and personality for the present age.   He has presented the details of the life unflinch-
ingly, but he has not lost sight of the personality.   And in
the end it is this personality that really matters.

If the matter of an up-to-date, perhaps definitive biography (if such is ever possible with Byron's life) is settled
by Marchand's achievement, the ghost of the marriage problem is far from being laid. Something of the fervor of the
Stowe/Astarte years returns with the spate of biographies
that appear which deal directly with this crux. G. Wilson
Knight's Lord Byron's Marriage: The Evidence of Asterisks
appears the same year as the Marchand biography; but there
all resemblance ends. His is the promised extension of his
spatial approach to biography, utilized in Lord Byron:
Christian Virtues and now applied to Byron's vices. To appreciate Knight's approach, one must wrench apart one's
conventional ideas of biography, must, in fact, radically re-
order his thinking as to what biography actually is. Knight
sees Byron's life as the incarnation of poetry, as so extraordinary that it involves something of the mystery and complexity of a work of art; therefore the biographer must em-
ploy imaginative rather than conventional means to first understand, then present that life and personality. A complete
chronological picture is discarded in favor of the moment of
frozen apogee (the method of art)--in this case Lord Byron's
marriage--that explains all that has gone before and predicates
all that is to come. Uncovering new material is not as important as re-examining the old, in a sort of Rashomon approach that is multi-angled; and the sequential arrangement
of facts is not as important as the evidence that these facts
reveal, so there is a constant departure from and return to
the marriage as the focal center.

If Knight's approach is a radical departure from the
traditional, his resultant theory is even more so. He concentrates on "the one factor that has never been satisfactorily
explained"--Lady Byron's sudden change of attitude toward
her husband--and on the piece of evidence most often ne-
glected--the Don Leon poems--in order to see if the two interlock and if the rest of the evidence can fall into place
around this center. As he explains it, Lady Byron's change
of attitude leads directly into all the mysteries concentered
about the marriage problem, the separation, and the aftermath. The Don Leon poems, probably written by George
Colman, a possible drinking crony of Byron's at the time of
the marriage, reveal intimate knowledge of Byron's marital
activities, particularly on his wedding night. The two considerations interlock at the point of homosexuality, not incest; the latter, Knight believes, was simply an elaborate
ruse to cover up the former, which was a capital offense in
England at the time. The specific clue provided by the Don

Leon poems is the intimation of sodomy practiced with men
and carried over into the marriage with Annabella. Knight
applies this factor to a "number of issues left unresolved
by the explanation of incest" and offers a logical explanation
for each. To substantiate his claims, he examines in close
detail the lives, characters, motives, correspondence, and
work of his principals, indexing and cross-indexing his evidence in the familiar mosaic pattern of his spatial method.
At the minimum his thesis is plausible, arrived at by logical,
perhaps ingenious, reasoning and close examination of the
facts; at its maximum it could be brilliant if ever proved
irrevocably true. But for the moment, with its many suppo-
sitions, it must be labeled highly speculative. Still, he has
raised serious questions about the incest line of reasoning
and about Annabella as a witness, has strengthened the suspicion of Byron's homosexuality, has made some astute
guesses about the principals and perhaps even offered some
illumination of their character, has forced attention on the
Don Leon poems and certain facts usually glossed over; and
through it all he has managed to be reasonably fair to Annabella and Augusta and has never lost sight of the real genius
and worth of Byron.

The remarkably different conclusions of Marchand and
Knight regarding the marriage problem, based essentially
upon the same evidence, crystallize the fact that the issue
will not likely be settled without the aid of further documents.
Needless to say, the importance of the Lovelace Papers, the
last major aggregate of unpublished materials, becomes
greatly magnified; and the period looks to them with antici-
pation as the potential touchstone for clearing up all mysteries bearing upon the marriage. The absence of the Lovelace Papers is not as serious a handicap to Knight as to
Marchand. Knight's approach, together with his shrewd comment that any statement by Annabella after her departure
could not be considered reliable evidence, really preempts
any argument against his theory when and if the collection
should appear.

Actually, disclosure of its contents was not long in
forthcoming; two scholars were granted unrestricted access
and published their results within five years. Doris Langley
Moore's The Late Lord Byron (1961) was the first-fruits.
Beginning with an authoritative account of the destruction of
the defense, the burning of Byron's Memoirs, she proceeds
to show how Lady Byron devoted a lifetime to her own self-
justification in the marriage/separation business. In the

beginning, according to Moore, Annabella collected any and all evidence of the most heinous kind to justify her separation, as the "minutes" of her interview with Caroline Lamb (who hypocritically accuses Byron of incest, of fathering Medora, and of "the practice of unnatural crime") and her attempts to extract a confession of incest from Augusta show; and then, in the rest of her life, she tried to thwart any potential spokesman for Byron's case by preventing or controlling biographies and by preoccupying herself "with her own rectitude." The resultant picture of Annabella is unpleasant, revealing self-righteousness, coldness, calculation, selfishness, hypocrisy; but it is a corrective for the patently false view of her as a paragon of virtue. Moore has no patience with Knight's view of the marriage problem: "Lady Byron ... was not in that condition of imbecile ignorance which would be essential, in any epoch, to enable a wife to mistake unnatural relations for natural relations." Her own assessment is that regardless of the specific reason(s), both individuals were unhappy, a fact that made the separation inevitable; further, after it had become a reality, Annabella negated all possibility of return by having talked too much to too many "in confidence." Concerning the possibility of the incest in particular, Moore is low key, admitting the possibility but pointing to only one slender thread of evidence-- the letter to Lady Melbourne, which itself is capable of an innocuous interpretation.

Though access to the Lovelace Papers leads to inevitable comment on Annabella, the marriage, the separation --and Moore's volume does make an important contribution to the marriage controversy--The Late Lord Byron is really a study of the incredible reaction that followed Byron's death for the subsequent twenty years or so, when the "posthumous dramas" of the subtitle take place among those who had known the poet--wife, sister, friends, acquaintances, enemies. Since the author draws on a considerable amount of unpublished material from the Lovelace Papers and Hobhouse collection (new material is also published from the Murray archives), Lady Byron and Hobhouse figure as the chief characters in the dramatis personae, with Lady Byron more in the role of antagonist and Hobhouse as protagonist and dogged defender of his friend's reputation, even though his own motives at first are not as pure as they could be. The view of Augusta is one of human ineptitude, doing what she can to protect her brother's memory and preserving some measure of self-respect. Byron himself, lacking substance, remains a shadow; but as prime mover of all events he plays well the

role of Caesar's ghost.   The emergent "shadowgraph" of his
character is better than one has come to expect, not that
his sins are forgiven, but that so much myth and apocryphal
slander about him are exploded for the first time.   As the
chief culprits in the defamation and calumny, the innumerable biographers and memoirists of the time play out their
often mean and petty roles (but not unimportant roles, since
their accounts affect Byron's reputation for the next 130
years) of self-aggrandizement, self-vindication, revenge,
venality, acquisitiveness, and human weakness ad infinitum.
Moore exposes each in turn: Hunt and Trelawny unsparingly
as the worst offenders; Stendhal, Blessington, Galt, and Stanhope less scathingly; Medwin and Dallas more lightly still,
as they are less malicious in their distortion and errors.
On the other hand, Teresa Guiccioli, Pietro Gamba, and
William Parry are treated well, as Moore feels that their
words stand closer to the truth about Byron's character.
The most serious charge against Moore's work is that she
attacks with too much relish and praises with too obvious a
bias.   The author readily admits to the bias, but it is an
educated bias backed by an impressive range and depth of
scholarship and documentation that render her conclusions
convincing.

        Considerable controversy in the columns of TLS at-
tended the publication of Moore's book, but the fray was
mainly a battle of personalities and not a serious indictment
of the work itself.   The book has, in fact, won the endorse-
ment of the scholarly community.   One fact is certain: future biographers will have to deal with this study, particularly with regard to the eye-witness accounts of Byron's life,
since their credibility has now been considerably lessened.
In the final analysis The Late Lord Byron assures a more
sympathetic treatment and fairer appraisal of Byron's story
in the future by broadening the base of the evidence.

        The second scholar to have unrestricted access to
the Lovelace Papers was Malcolm Elwin.   He replaced Doris
Langley Moore as official literary advisor when Lady Wentworth died and the collection passed into the hands of Lord
Lytton.* Arrangements were made for Elwin to catalog the

---

*Because Doris Moore's entrée to the collection passed with
the death of Lady Wentworth, Elwin can describe his version
as "the first fully documented account of Byron's marriage
and separation based on unrestricted use of the Lovelace
Papers."

entire collection--a mass of material covering 150 years and
amounting to 170 volumes in typescript--and to write or edit
a projected seven books based upon the extensive holdings.
Because the marriage/separation is the axis about which the
collection rotates, it is only fitting that the first volume
should deal with this involvement; and because the assemblage
of most of the pertinent documents resulted from Annabella's
careful and painstaking collecting of verifiable evidence to
justify her actions, the focus quite naturally is upon her.
The book recounts her history up to the point when she becomes Lord Byron's Wife (1962) and through the crises ensuing from that relationship until Byron leaves England. In
the process Elwin depicts the parents who molded her, particularly the forceful mother, and relates their story in full
for the first time. Out of Annabella's youthful years emerges
the portrait of a bright and cultivated but supremely self-
centered and spoiled only child. By the time she has pursued Byron into a proposal, having first put him in his place
by a refusal, the traits have become fixed--vanity, humor-
less sobriety, strait-laced piety, a facility for self-justifica-
tion, a penchant for highly critical analyses of others--that
would likely doom any marriage, especially with one of Byron's temperament. Elwin follows the emphasis of his material, treating in detail the years from 1810, when the
couple met, through 1815. The greatest amount of concentration, however, is reserved for the first four months of
1816, the months dealing with the separation, when the documents and correspondence (as many as twelve letters in a
single day) virtually form a daily record.

   Elwin allows the letters and documents to speak for
themselves while he modestly assumes the secondary role of
narrator and editor, filling in the background by way of
notes and offering his own commentary unobtrusively. The
side of his book that portrays Annabella and her family,
based as it is upon the large quantity of previously unpublished material, is new and informative; together with his
later volume on the Milbankes it will likely remain definitive. The part that deals specifically with the marriage/
separation makes no startling or new revelations; in fact,
the conclusions arrived at by Elwin are much the same as
Moore's: it was a marriage that never should have been;
once consummated it could never last, for both were supremely unhappy. The separation seems to have arisen not
from incest or homosexuality, though there is the distinct
possibility that these may have existed, but from a multi-
plicity of causes, mainly resulting from two opposite

personalities in an impossible situation. Sympathy does
shift to Byron after the separation when it is shown that
Annabella plots and plans with a phalanx of family, confi-
dantes, and legal attorneys (Lushington is more prominent
than formerly realized) and stands clearly revealed as selfish, calculating, hypocritical, supremely self-righteous,
and bent only upon justifying herself; in this light Byron's
query as to the cause rings with peculiar force. He was
certainly capable of forgiveness; but his "Dearest Bell"
letters for reconciliation fail to beat back the dark of her
steady, turgid flow of self-vindication. The new Augusta
letters to Annabella in the month after the latter leaves alter her "Dowdy Goody" or "Goose" image and disclose her
as "perhaps too easily moved to tenderness, but she could
maintain grace in adversity, and always there was a perva-
sive charm that rendered her eminently lovable. " Elwin's
competent handling of a staggering array of material is especially meritorious; for he has marshalled it intelligently,
kneaded it into a lucid narrative, and maintained an objective perspective in the process.

     With the long-awaited Lovelace Papers now authorita-
tively presented and drawn upon in two studies, those ex-
pecting a sensational revelation or desiring an absolute verification of some past theory have been doomed to disappointment. Annabella and the Milbankes stand clearly revealed
for the first time, some former uncertainties and questions
are cleared up, a better perspective of the entire situation--
both marriage and separation--is gained, and a further re-
dressing of the balance in favor of Byron has occurred, with
Annabella now among the detractors lined up by Doris Moore
as unreliable witnesses. But many of the old enigmas are
still around--permanently it would now seem--and Byron remains as great a mystery as before. As the subsequent
controversy in the TLS manifests, those so choosing may
still offer their unique solutions or speculate as they see fit.
G. Wilson Knight and Michael Joyce are heard from again;
but in light of the general agreement on fundamental issues
by Moore and Elwin, they are listened to less attentively
than before.

     The preceding are the most consequential of the bio-
graphical studies produced during this period, either because
of their definitiveness or because of their signal importance
at this particular point in Byron scholarship. They furnish
enough new evidence and fresh reassessments to make this
era one of the most imposing in biographical accomplishment

in the long history of Byron publication. Add to the list a
host of other biographical studies, running the gamut of literary quality, and one is impressed with the quantity of biographical activity as well. Three areas of concentration are
noticeable: the general biographies, those limited to a special aspect or period of the poet's life, and those centering
around associates of Byron.

Some of the general biographies are of no scholarly
significance and need be mentioned only to show the continuing fascination that Byron's life holds for a wide-ranging
popular audience. N. K. Wells' George Gordon, Lord Byron (1960) offers nothing of any particular distinction for an
adult audience. Geoffrey Trease's Byron: A Poet Dangerous
to Know (1969) is rather novel in that it purports to be the
first attempt to introduce Byron's life to youthful readers.
In spite of its aura of daring, it is responsibly done, with
its dialogue consisting of Byron's own words or inscribed
thoughts and feelings. Aside from its helpful map of Byron's European tours and journeys, however, its value is
restricted to the high school audience for which it was intended. Derek Parker's Byron and His World (1968), part
of the "Famous Lives" series, is another matter entirely;
it is of interest to the Byron scholar and general public
alike. The arrangement is in the manner of a brief but informative biography with illustrations, but its main emphasis
and true value lie in its fine aggregate of pictures. One
could accurately call it a visual biography, recreating Byron's life, times, and poetry through strong, often striking
visual impressions. The pictures themselves, frequently accompanied by appropriate quotations from Byron's work, are
made up of paintings, etchings, engravings, cartoons (all the
famous Cruikshanks are here), photographs, and pencil
sketches. These vividly delineate the whole teeming gallery
of people, places, buildings, scenes, dogs, and notices associated with Byron's life. Some glaring errors concerning
Shelley and his circle mar the written account, but the pictures speak eloquently and are the real treasure which the
rest of the volume merely houses.

Still one other general biography needs to be mentioned. At the very end of this period, when the definitive
nature of Marchand's monumental biography is being jeopar-
dized by the unexpected appearance of the Lovelace material
and studies based upon it, this eminent scholar reasserts
his authority by publishing Byron: A Portrait (1970), following the example set by N. I. White twenty-five years earlier

in condensing his two-volume Shelley into a single volume.
Basically Marchand's purpose is to distill the old and to incorporate the new that is significant in order "to give the
essence of Byron's dramatic career and engaging personality
... drawn from the most recent research and authentic
sources." The major principles followed in the distillation
process are to allow Byron to lay down the main biographical lines himself through his own verse and prose, especially the letters, and then to fill in with colors from the ample
supply of contemporary revelations about the poet so that a
true "portrait" emerges. Incorporation of new matter largely takes form in the insights and details gained from the recently published studies by Moore and Elwin. The only
hitherto unpublished particulars to be included concern the
authentication of Byron's residence in the Piazza di Spagua
in Rome in 1817 and the rediscovery of Byron's name on a
column at Delphi. Quite naturally Marchand has drawn free-
ly upon his original study, retaining what remains pertinent
but modifying where necessary for accuracy, clarity, or an
altered judgment. He has remained as objective as before,
explaining or interpreting where necessary but not obtruding
upon the reader. The general revision and inclusion of new
material, particularly the Lovelace matter, bring Marchand's
work thoroughly up-to-date once again. It is now likely to
remain for some time to come simply the best one-volume
biography of Byron yet published.

Of the restricted accounts of Byron's life, those dealing with the marriage have already been given prominent
mention. James Barbary's The Young Lord Byron (1965),
its contents designated by its title, is really a novel for the
young. Of those remaining, William H. Marshall's Byron,
Shelley, Hunt and "The Liberal" (1960) represents the only
notable study of a specific episode in the poet's life. It is
a workmanlike piece that supersedes the earlier treatment
by Leslie P. Pickering (1925) and also the accounts included
in the larger general biographies of the participants by Edmund Blunden, Newman I. White, and Leslie Marchand.
Marshall stresses that his role is that of the historian rather
than the critic; consequently his dual emphasis is on the
ephemeral history of The Liberal in full, and the concurrent
history of the individuals both in the venture and in their relationships. If in his massing of facts and details something
of the spirit of the journal itself is lost, as well as the political excitement of the times that elicited and surrounded it,
the study makes up for the lack by its completeness. The
author attempts to bring together all the materials--manuscripts

in the United States and England, contemporary periodical
reactions, published primary source material mainly from
twentieth-century editions of letters and journals--that relate
the story of The Liberal. Equally important is the balanced
treatment of the participants, for Marshall avoids the pit-
falls of earlier renditions that tended to apologize either for
Byron or Hunt. With the majority of facts settled and the
personalities in perspective, The Liberal may now be properly understood for the first time. Marshall shows us clearly
its reasons for being, the history of its publication, its content and makeup, its reception (including appendices of press
notices and contemporary parodies), the economic aspect,
and the complicated reasons for its failure. Not without
value is the insight gained into the actual production of a
journal during the tumultuous period.

    Concerned not so much with a limited episode as with
a limited aspect of Byron's life is the study by Bernard Grebanier, The Uninhibited Byron: An Account of His Sexual
Confusion (1970). The "sexual confusion" has reference to
the heterosexual/homosexual tendencies in Byron's nature.
This subject matter has unfortunately tended to dominate
much of the popular and scholarly consideration of Byronic
biography; so it was probably unavoidable that a book of this
nature would ultimately appear. Formerly, however, projected theories usually concentrated upon one aberration at a
time, with proper scholarly caution in the light of evidence
that was often less than circumstantial. Grebanier embraces
them all without question. The evidence which he makes
large claims for as being original or overlooked--the trau-
matic experience with May Gray; contemporary fiction about
Byron and Caroline Lamb, including her two novels; the
autobiography of Medora Leigh and her very moving final
letter to her mother; Byron's schoolboy poems; unpublished
portions of the poet's letters; the Don Leon poems--has all
been reckoned with before, though Grebanier does conveniently reprint the Don Leon poems in toto. The author has
tentatively planned two books: the present one encompasses
the subject to the breakup of Byron's marriage, with its
theme being Byron's "sexual confusion, which began in his
childhood and worked havoc on himself and almost everyone
connected with him, and which made the success of his marriage wholly improbable"; the second will ostensibly continue
the story through Venice and end with his departure for Ravenna to commence his liaison with Teresa. The sexual side
of Byron's biography is important, but it is a limited aspect.
Grebanier, not only by according it his major concern but by

simplistically accepting all charges at face value, has made
it seem gargantuan. The human side that Leslie Marchand,
Doris Langley Moore, and Elwin Moore find is missing here.

Some excellent items may be found among the publications on Byron's associates, even though the gradual decline from the peak of interest in the 1935-1945 decade continues in this period. Twelve volumes still represent a
sizable concentration of interest. Two or three of the biographies are responsibly done and long overdue; but the most
significant items are the editions of primary materials that
appear, adding to an already fine harvest garnered in this
period. These studies might be conveniently organized into
two groups: an inner circle of associates intimately connected with Byron and an outer circle of friends and acquaintances.

The poet's in-laws would probably object to being
placed in the inner circle; but protocol dictates that they
should be. Malcolm Elwin, in the continuing project of editing the important Lovelace Papers, has produced an absorbing narrative of The Noels and the Milbankes (1968) through
their letters for twenty-five years, 1767-1792. The letters
are previously unpublished and involve six primary correspondents: Annabella's mother and father, her mother's two
sisters and brother (Elizabeth, Sophia, and Thomas Noel),
and her mother's Aunt Mary Noel, who reared the three
girls after her mother's death in 1761. The letters lack the
controversy and consequent importance of the marriage material, and they do not pretend to literary significance since
they were not self-consciously composed for posterity. But
they are revelatory in several small ways: of the times
(specifically the latter part of the eighteenth century into
which Byron was born) with its society, customs, and gossip
of the privileged class; of the general caliber of the Noel
family itself; and, most important, of the parents and the
atmosphere they created for an upbringing that produced Annabella Milbanke.

Augusta, the one true feminine thread through Byron's
life, is represented for the first time by a book-length study,
My Dearest Augusta (1968) by Peter Gunn. The story is familiar but gains a certain freshness with its concentration on
Augusta and with the material rearranged accordingly. Byron, of course, still looms large in the account; but the portrait of Augusta is now full-length and detailed, beginning
with the genealogy and carrying through to her final sorrows

involving Medora and Annabella.   A very different Augusta
emerges from behind the cardboard stereotype of the past;
she now seems attractive and lively, warm-hearted and hu-
mane.   Letters provide much of the validity and immediacy
of the book.   But the general scholarly procedure is open to
question: certain letters are taken out of context and ridden
rather hard to prove a thesis, the incest is accepted without
question, and although impressive sources are acknowledged
they are nowhere specifically cited.

Augusta's daughter, Medora Leigh, also receives full
biographical treatment for the first time, four years later,
by Catherine Turney in Byron's Daughter (1972).   An almost
identical assessment could be made of this book.   The parts
of her story that impinge upon the lives of the principals
(Augusta, Byron, Annabella) are already well-known, though
distorted through widely-divergent perspectives.   It seems
only fair that "Libby" should have her say.   Turney is helpful in bringing together most of the printed materials that
bear on her life as well as some unpublished information;
the shift in view produces some interesting results, particularly when some of Byron's letters are read from this vantage point.   The book must be used with caution, however,
for the author's bias about the central issue is evident from
her title, Augusta is rendered one-dimensional again, evidence is handled at times irresponsibly, and numerous errors may be detected in her documentation.

Both Claire Clairmont and Caroline Lamb, members
of Byron's inner circle by virtue of brief periods of intimacy
with the poet, receive attention.   Claire is represented by
the more significant item, The Journals of Claire Clairmont
(1968), edited by Marion Kingston Stocking.   The picture of
Claire presented is only two-dimensional, cluttered as it is
with daily trivia and mere surface events rendered staccato.
The journals actually are more directly pertinent to the
Shelleys, since four of them record events from the year
1814, when Claire eloped with Mary and Shelley, to the
latter's death in 1822, with intervals; one of the intervals is
the year 1816.   The importance to Byron, then, lies not in
the surface cataloging of events but in seeing Claire more
clearly.   Unfortunately there is too much light, for none of
the mystery of the woman who could sway Byron into a relationship and maneuver two of the greatest poets of the day
into a deep and abiding friendship is revealed, although the
intellectual side is suggested by the cumulative list of books
she records in her day-to-day reading.   The journals--six

in number, including two Russian journals when Claire was
a governess for the partial years 1825-1827--and the two
leaflets from 1828 and 1830 are masterfully edited with an
exact text and an introduction (history and description), biographical framework (to aid the general reader), full annotations, and useful appendix, charts, lists, etc. Both the
Noel-Milbanke letters and these journals are of second-line
importance; as the territory will not likely be covered again,
it is fortunate that both have been definitively edited.

Henry Blyth's biography of Caroline Lamb, Caro, The
Fatal Passion (1972), does not merit serious scholarly attention; it falls somewhere between Elizabeth Jenkins' biography
of 1932 and Doris Leslie's novel, This for Caroline, of 1964.
The important facts are accounted for, but the accent is primarily on the sensational presented in a popular style. He
dislikes Byron ("he is treated [by biographers] as a mature
adult, which he never was") and he apologizes for all of
Caroline's behavior on the pseudo-psychological grounds of
immaturity, instability, and ill-health. The general shallow-
ness may be seen in the evaluation of his subjects as children and in his assessment of his book as "an essay on the
problems of growing up." The whole is devoid of footnotes;
and despite acknowledgment of the Salmond Collection, nothing new is visible except some sketches by Caroline which
are not without charm.

Studies that deal with Byron's outside circle of associates number about the same and may be dealt with in two
groups: close friends of the poet and short-term acquaintances. The period sees two books directed to the Byron-
Shelley relationship: John Buxton's Byron and Shelley (1968)
and A. B. C. Whipple's The Fatal Gift of Beauty (1964).
Buxton's justification for repeating this oft-told tale is that
"their biographers have inclined to favour one at the expense
of the other, and so to distort our understanding of both."
Since he considers the friendship the most important relationship in the life and work of each, he attempts to deliver
an undistorted account of both the history of the friendship
and the general literary bonds of interest existing between
the two poets. The story is narrowed primarily to the six
years of the intermittent relationship--from the 1816 meeting in Switzerland to Shelley's death in 1822--in order to
allow for more intensive coverage. Unfortunately the intensity is dissipated by the author's methodology of utilizing a
factual framework that becomes excessive to link up the
significant moments of felicity between his two principals.

With such a lateral direction taken, some character complexity and potential depth of understanding are lost; but Buxton
does trace fully and faithfully the history of the friendship,
incorporating pertinent quotations from the letters, journals,
and contemporary accounts. His treatment of the literary
relationships is tenuous, only a beginning; but the final compact pages of the book suggest lines that can profitably be
developed in the future. A. B. C. Whipple's version of the
friendship is strictly biographical, and his emphasis is
slightly different. Byron's reference to Italy's "fatal gift of
beauty" becomes the title and touchstone of his book as he
seeks, in recounting the narrative of the four brief Italian
years shared by the two men, to show how the country inspired Byron and Shelley to their greatest work and at the
same time doomed each of them. Both books are intended
for the general public; but Buxton's is the more scholarly,
even though it does contain errors, lacks documentation, and
fails to capitalize on the latest developments.

Thomas Moore, an equally close friend of Byron and
neglected for almost thirty years, is suddenly represented
by three publications, two adding to the trove of primary materials of the era. The Letters of Thomas Moore in two
volumes (1964), edited by Wilfred S. Dowden and covering
the correspondence of Moore from 1793-1847 in 1,323 letters,
is an important plus; for many of the letters are to or about
Byron or his circle, and the difficulties Moore faced in as-
sembling his historically enduring biography of the poet are
clearly revealed. The Journal of Thomas Moore, 1818-1841
(1964), edited by Peter Quennell, need only be mentioned as
it contains mainly reprint material. Miriam Allen de Ford's
handbook, Thomas Moore (1967), in "Twayne's English Authors Series," is the first volume on Moore since the separate biographies by Jones and Strong in 1937, both of which
emphasized his life. De Ford's book does not replace either
but supplements them nicely by attempting a compact critical
appraisal of Moore's work and an isolation of that which is
of permanent value.

Captain Medwin and Lady Blessington, brief acquaintances of Byron in Italy, are treated in three publications. Ernest J. Lovell has edited Medwin's Conversations
of Lord Byron (1966) and Lady Blessington's Conversations
of Lord Byron (1969), the most important conversational records of the poet, as part of a projected enterprise he announced fifteen years earlier in the "Introduction" to His
Very Self and Voice. These three volumes comprise a

complete record of Byron's conversational life. The importance of the Medwin and Blessington records extends beyond
the conversational fact; they are generally considered the
most interesting of the eye-witness accounts, they played havoc with other contemporary impressions of Byron, and they
have exercised a heavy influence on all subsequent biographers. The major problem with both of these conversations
is their reliability. When first published, they were among
the most controversial of all contemporary accounts; after
Byron's generation had passed, they began to assume re-
spectability until by the opening of the present period their
authority stood quite high. Recently Doris Langley Moore
has raised such questions about the integrity of the authors
as to threaten the credibility of their accounts all over again.
Lovell has done a real service in rescuing these conversations from disrepute and restoring them to a proper balance
and perspective. He has given us an accurate text in both
cases: for Medwin's Conversations he uses the author's own
annotated copy of his "New Edition" of 1824 (the third London edition) which was intended for a new and final edition;
for Lady Blessington's Conversations he follows the London
edition of 1834, using Teresa Guiccioli's copy and incorporating her valuable markings and annotations, and he collates
this text with the installments in The New Monthly Magazine
and Literary Journal, July 1832-December 1833. Furthermore, he has solved the problem of accuracy by laying out
virtually all the cross-referencing evidence available, published and unpublished, in notes so that the reader may use
his own judgment. Some of the data is so massive --in the
Medwin volume for instance--that this material has to be
arranged in antiphonal fashion with the text itself; almost
every paragraph thus receives its reverberating commentary.
Lovell's own evaluation of Medwin as careless rather than
malicious, and of his work as accurate in its general makeup and tone, and Lovell's understanding recognition of the
true grain of Lady Blessington's sympathetic identification
with Byron and her impressive insights into his character
beneath the chaff of her own social motives seems sensible
and just. His judgments are enhanced by the weight behind
them of in-depth studies of his two subjects: Medwin in a
general biography, Captain Medwin: Friend of Byron and
Shelley (1962), and Lady Blessington in a long (114 pages)
and sensitive "Introduction" which explores in full her relations with Byron and the origins and motives behind her
book. In short these two rich sources of material on Byron, beclouded for years, are now restored to usefulness
and may be employed with a fair degree of confidence.

Lovell's volumes represent scholarship at its best and together with His Very Self and Voice bid fair to establish him
as the leading authority on the contemporary accounts of Byron.

The high significance of this period in biographical
scholarship is obvious. A number of particularly knotty
problems, if not solved, have been brought for the moment
at least to a point of satisfactory resolution: the matter of
a definitive biography, the marriage issue, the reliability of
such Byronic witnesses as Captain Medwin and Lady Blessington, the clarification of the personal relations involved in
The Liberal venture. Much new material has come to light
in the process of coping with these issues, some of it quietly substantiative and some of it revolutionary in its importance, such as the Lovelace Papers, so that all of the
pivotal resource material on Byron is gradually being accumulated into publication. Significant as this period is in
biographical accomplishment, however, achievement in another area is of such impressive proportions that it rivals
if not surpasses the biographical in importance and thereby
also stamps its character upon the age. The area is that
of criticism; and if it had its true beginnings in the thirties
and early forties, it has waited until now to reach its maturity. With Byron's life in large part settled, scholarly attention has definitely swung to his work and art.

Two general books on Byron's poetry signal this new
trend, and they make their appearance with the ringing in of
the sixties: Paul West's Byron and the Spoiler's Art (1960)
and Andrew Rutherford's Byron: A Critical Study (1961). In
part at least these publications demonstrate that the criticism of the early years of the era is still of a piece with
that initiated in the 1935-1945 decade. A page even seems
to have been taken from T. S. Eliot in that both books
claim to re-focus on the poetry instead of the biography,
both consider the romances seriously again, and both advo-
cate the satires at the expense of Byron's romantic work.
The tradition is there, and it will continue strongly in succeeding years. However, these texts also contain modifications and new areas of interest that will be explored as the
period advances. These two books are vastly different in
organization and style. West's compact little volume, with
its machine gun-like spraying of ideas and its verbal pyro-
technics, inaugurates the decade with a flourish. It is a
book both original and eristic--at the same time brilliant
and erratic, intellectual and dogmatic, stimulating and

controversial. West's main concern is with Byron's farce
with language which he sees as finally and fully manifested
in Don Juan. He summarizes Byron in three words--elimi-
nation, farce, paradox--but only the first two are pertinent
to his study. By elimination he refers to Byron's personality
as a sensitive man "who for social and psychic reasons had
to eliminate ties and sensibility" in order not to feel obliged
to anything--subject matter, people, things, his role, his
reputation. Farce is Byron's "elimination" applied to his
writing; the personality dictates the style and genre. Only
in farce can he be totally free and thus most himself: farce
exists in his personages, who become things and are thus
not "obliged" in any way, and in his language where he can
exercise to perfection the spoiler's art of the title. Don
Juan, the pinnacle of Byron's farce, is not considered in an
extended analysis per se; instead, commentary is woven into
the discussion of his central thesis as he pursues it through
the following areas: Byron's life as it relates to his poetry,
his attitude toward his art and his working out of an aesthetic, his development through the use of different verse forms
(especially in Childe Harold), and general commentary on the
romances and plays. Each of these areas is related to Don
Juan as West proceeds so that the book does not focus on the
epic directly so much as it shows how Byron eventually got
there.

     Andrew Rutherford's Byron is less spectacular but
more methodical, thorough, and balanced. It ranks with
West's study as a pioneering book, for it offers commentary
for the first time work by work over Byron's major canon.
Scope did not allow for sustained criticism in each case
(except for Don Juan) but the book is an important step
toward more detailed critical treatment of specific works
later on. Rutherford's central thesis is that Byron was
searching all of his life for a poetic manner suited to his
personality, genius, station, and experience. Since the emphasis is on the poetry, only the biographical material
necessary for understanding Byron's attitude toward poetry
and that accounting for the fluctuations in the character and
content of his work is admitted. Rutherford treats briefly
the strengths and weaknesses of the poems to mid-1817,
seeing them as flawed experiments in Byron's search, with
the exception of The Prisoner of Chillon which he labels the
best of Byron's non-satiric works. He contends that Byron
found his true mode in the ottava rima form of Beppo, where
he could write not merely as a "romantic poet, but a sophisticated man of the world." Thereafter Rutherford

concentrates on the three major works in this style, elimi-
nating the dramas and all other pieces as "inferior in quality" or "misguided experiment," and finds in Don Juan Byron's
most substantial achievement but in The Vision of Judgment
his masterpiece.

In spite of their differences, these two pioneering
studies touch at many points, demonstrating a cohesiveness
in this early criticism: both disclaim Byron's life in favor
of his work, yet both rely on biographical material and psy-
chologize considerably in explaining the poetry; both take Byron's statements concerning his art literally and establish
their central theses accordingly; both have quite a bit to say
about the personae, which will become an increasingly important topic in the discussion of Byron's work; both view
the non-satiric pieces largely as flawed experiments on the
way toward perfecting a method or a style; both consider the
satires not only as the culmination of Byron's work but also
as his most natural mode and hence his highest achievement.
In part these books preserve and extend the older critical
tradition as noted; but in part they open up new avenues:
the New Critical approach seems just around the corner with
the disclaimer of the biographical and the close analysis of
specific passages; some of the significant romantic pieces
like the later Childe Harold and Manfred, in acting as worthy
opponents to the satires, seem bordering on rediscovery; appreciation of certain isolated non-satiric pieces like The
Prisoner of Chillon suggests other possibilities; relatively
untapped areas like the dramas are held up for renewed
scrutiny. Of course there are numerous gauntlets to be
taken up against West's charges--that Byron was no thinker,
had no philosophy nor commitment, reflected an essentially
negative attitude toward life, abdicated from the deeper human pity, lacked any kind of organization in his writing, exhibited a sameness in his variety but no development in his
work, and showed greatness only in his satires; and against
Rutherford's charges of shoddy workmanship in the romances,
of the inferiority of the dramas, of the essential failure of
Childe Harold and Manfred, of the superiority of The Prisoner of Chillon and The Vision of Judgment, of the reduction
of all the non-satiric work to mere "experiment." Both
books are indeed controversial, but they are stimulative;
they manage to do what Eliot had hoped for back in 1937.
As a measure of their value as stimulus, one can point to
the reviews; for they share honors in eliciting more reviews
than any single volume on Byron down to their time.

Handbooks are usually a fair indicator of a healthy critical climate, and they barometer accurately the state of affairs in this decade. No fewer than four are produced; and if Rutherford's general study, though not directly a handbook, were included, they would chronologically blanket the critical era. All four are in the traditional handbook mold that incorporates biography in varying degrees and discusses the poems along introductory lines for the general reader, though each has its own variations and there are differences in quality. Leslie Marchand's Byron's Poetry: A Critical Introduction (1965), in the "Riverside Studies in Literature" series, is the most comprehensive and thorough. The key word for this book is balance, both in subject matter and treatment. Marchand deals with the biographical/milieu part with a sure hand, treating it with easy competence and resonance; in fact, his relating of the biography to the poetry (he relates it, not narrates it) is one of the major strengths of his book. His discussion of the poetry (approached individually and by generic groups in approximately chronological order) offers no revolutionary theories by his own acknowledgment; but it is usually solid, dependable, and above all judicious, perhaps representing best the academic view of Byron's poetry at the time it was published. Paul Trueblood's Lord Byron (1969) in "Twayne's English Authors Series" is intended for a broader audience, "to encourage understanding and appreciation of the personality and work of one of the most attractive and 'modern' of the Romantic poets. " He compresses well the essential details of Byron's life and work and conveys the whole in a popular style. His emphasis is divided about equally between biography and criticism, with the latter forming appropriate resting points within the chronological framework of the former. He is much indebted to Marchand for the biographical portions of his text. For the literary parts, he includes consideration of "the genesis of each work, its subject matter, structure, style, and relationship to the poet's total poetic production"; he incorporates recent critical views of Byron, relying mainly on Calvert, Rutherford, Marshall, Joseph, and Boyd. Francis M. Doherty's Byron (1969) is part of the "Arco Literary Critiques" series. Upholding the inseparability of Byron's life and work, Doherty sees three Byrons--the one of the letters, the one of the romantic poems, and the one of the great satires--and "[all] three Byrons can appear in the same place side by side. " After giving the factual background of Byron's life in a dozen pages, he discusses the work by genres and poems in an approximate chronological order, as Marchand had done, working in the letters as

he proceeds. His central movement is from Byron as derivative poet, woodenly projecting only parts of his personality
and mind into his work, to Byron as plastic genius presenting
the whole truth about man. Mainly student-oriented, the
text is made up basically of a plot-summary approach; but
it is not condescending, as the publisher's preface to the
series most decidedly is. John D. Jump's Byron (1972),
one of the initial titles in the new "Routledge Author Guides,"
excels in two of the format areas of the series (times and
life) but is uneven in the third (works). Jump's reconstruc-
tion of Byron's historical/cultural milieu, which he presents
as an "Age of Revolutions" (historical, political, economic,
social), and Byron's life, which he handles with remarkable
objectivity (yet opts for the incest) and thoroughness, are
both jewels of compression and genuinely effective as guides.
The chapter on Byron's prose is less as guide but more as
perceptive essay (which it in fact originally was). Only with
Jump's discussion of Byron's poetry does one have reservations. Commentary on the ottava rima poems is praiseworthy and certainly adequate for introductory purposes, with
Don Juan being properly accented. But the author's bias
against Byron's romantic poems, obvious from his downgrading comments and space allotment (18 pages for the 1812-
1818 poems versus 75 pages for the three late satires), ne-
gates the purpose of the volume and seems strangely archaic
coming as it does after the critical revolution of the 60's.

These handbooks do not particularly advance the critical movement so much as they perform an incremental func-
tion--gathering up and focusing current ideas and opinions
(sometimes literally, as in Trueblood's book), re-enforcing
certain other positions as Byron's weakness as a thinker and
his carelessness in composition (Marchand), or nurturing
such seedling ideas as the value of Byron's romantic pieces
or the modernity of the poet (Marchand).

If West and Rutherford signal an important return to
criticism in Byron studies, then William H. Marshall in his
The Structure of Byron's Major Poems (1962) helps to con-
firm the trend. His book may be considered along with Paul
Elledge's Byron and the Dynamics of Metaphor (1968), since
the one influenced the other and both share much in common.
Both follow implicitly the critical tradition of the thirties and
forties, already evident in West's and Rutherford's work and
now rapidly being established as the twentieth-century view.
Both take a step beyond their immediate predecessors, however, in eschewing biography almost exclusively, in concentrating their focus on the poetry to a highly restricted but

basic area (structure for Marshall, metaphor for Elledge),
and by intensifying their analysis to virtually a New Critical
approach. All of these aspects become highly controversial
issues in the period.

Marshall offers his study in the belief that Byron's
poetry has not received a fully objective reading; he feels
that his predecessors have been sidetracked by a search for
biographical facts, for theological or ethical value, for influences, for socio-cultural relationships. Marshall grounds
his study in the view that Byron avoided any system of belief
throughout his life. This factor, he feels, reflected "a
fundamental split between skepticism and the impulse to believe and belong" in the poet and accounted in his work for
the avoidance of Classicism (since it implies acceptance of
an order) and for the abandonment of his quest for meaning
in nature and the Universe in favor of acceptance of the im-
perfection of Self and Man's consciousness as an end in itself. Byron therefore gradually emerges as an ironist--i.e.,
"one aware of the limits of human capacity and the absurdity
of many forms of human activity"--and irony becomes the
key to a study of his poetry. The specific form that Byron
relies upon most seriously is dramatic irony, which is the
perfect mode of expression for the paradoxical Byronic universe, made up neither of credible absolutism nor acceptable
relativism, and the "Byronic Hero," who can neither worship nor accept guilt. In a close structural analysis of most
of Byron's major poems--with heavy stress upon the persona
because of the dramatic aspect--Marshall tracks Byron's development (contrary to West's denial) from English Bards and
Childe Harold I and II, which reveal no sustained intellectual
or dramatic structure; through three of the early romances,
which show Byron's transitions from mere narrative structure utilizing characters largely as allegorical figures to a
situation of dramatic irony and dramatic intensity in the
characters of Parisina; then through Byron's middle period
when the poet perfects his dramatic and ironic techniques in
a half dozen of his major poems written between 1816-1819;
and lastly through the poet's final phase where Byron uses
his structural technique of dramatic irony with greatest artistic integrity in Don Juan.

Although Elledge's Byron appears six years later, at
the very height of the new critical wave, the author still
finds it necessary to justify a primarily aesthetic study, so
strongly ingrained is the biographical/critical approach to
Byron's production. His point of departure is the recognition

of a fundamental and conscious dichotomy as the most dis-
tinguishing feature of the poet's thought and work, "a vacillation between the poles of orthodox dualism and romantic
monism." This position seems to come in a rather straight
line from Calvert's "romantic paradox," through West's "absolute or farce," through Marshall's "split between skepticism
and the impulse to believe and belong." Elledge's view is
different, however, in that he sees the matter not in the
negative light of "inconsistency" or "insincerity," but as the
oscillation of a temperament too flexible and encompassing
to be straitjacketed by a simple metaphysical system. He
sees Byron moved instead by mobilite, to yield to "present
impressions," to render with absolute fidelity the factual and
emotional truth of the moment. Control for the poet comes
through an intellectual construct in the work of art.

The particular construct Elledge has chosen for his
study is Byron's use of metaphor, an important area since
it accords perfectly with the poet's dual nature and unifies
his intellectual and imaginative faculties, it complements and
reinforces his themes through connotative richness, and it
underlies structure in its establishment of complex relationships. Elledge defines metaphor broadly in order to be as
inclusive as possible of the general principle of comparison
in Byron's works. He chooses representative poems from
each of three periods--The Corsair, Lara, and Parisina for
1813-15 years, The Prisoner of Chillon, Childe Harold III,
and Manfred from 1816-17, and Marino Faliero, Sardanapalus,
and Cain from 1820-21--for close analysis of metaphoric
patterns. He finds that Byron relies primarily upon a quar-
tet of juxtaposed polarities--fire/clay, light/dark, organic
growth/mechanical stasis, and the counterpart or Doppelgänger (again emphasizing the concern with Byron's persona in
this period)--polarities he uses to figure forth the basic dichotomy of human nature and at the same time the tragedy
of man in finally being unable to reconcile the antithetical
impulses of his nature. With Marshall, Elledge clearly
sees development in Byron's work, more in the systematic
growth of artistic craftsmanship, however, than in the linear
progression toward discovering and perfecting a certain mode.

Even though Marshall and Elledge present two entirely different studies, their close proximity in premises, point
of view, ideas, approach, conclusions, even the poems
treated, should be obvious. Their importance to the critical
trend can be seen in several ways. They realize many of
the tendencies suggested in the earlier efforts by West and

Rutherford: they make the break from biographical criticism
even more decisive and win respect for the aesthetic study
on its own merits; they exploit the methods of New Criticism
to distinct advantage; the romances and dramas are given extended analytical coverage; further untapped areas are explored, such as the dramatic monologues (Marshall) and the
historic dramas (Elledge); non-satiric works, besides The
Prisoner of Chillon, are found meritorious; the resurrection
of Childe Harold III and Manfred now seems assured.   In
addition, by affirming some central ideas of their predecessors, Marshall and Elledge lend strong support to these
views.   There is agreement with West and Rutherford on the
dualism or split in Byron's nature that prevented him from
accepting a single metaphysical view of the universe.   There
is agreement as well that he met failure in trying to reconcile the dichotomy, having to settle finally for the truth of
existence, the reality of mortal man made up of irreconcilable opposites; both writers are, however, more positive in
how they view this final position.   All four authors hold Don
Juan to be the ultimate expression of this final position and
Byron's most significant achievement, though there is much
variation of opinion as to exactly what type of expression it
is.   The departures of Marshall and Elledge from their predecessors are as important as their agreements: they con-
centrate on the non-satiric pieces even while acknowledging
the greatness of the ottava rima poems, they open up more
completely the complexities of Byron's persona, they shift
attention away from style to other important areas like structure and metaphor, and in so doing they prove that Byron
was a conscious artist and did show development in his work.
These two studies contribute, finally, to the maturing process,
the helping of Byronic criticism to come of age.   Earlier
cut-and-dried positions like Calvert's sharp break between
Byron's Romantic and Neo-classic poems, followed to an extent by West and Rutherford, no longer seem defensible.
Categorical references in the early 60's to Byron's lack of
thought, insincerity, inconsistency, "shoddy workmanship,"
accidental artistry, non-satiric "pulp" will have to be modified.   One may quarrel with individual interpretations by
these two authors--as later critics will--or find their approaches too neatly schematized; but their studies do lead
the reader to the poetry and enable him to understand it
better.

     What has been a trend now rapidly accelerates into a
full-fledged movement as the decade progresses.   Critical
books appear with astonishing rapidity: at first one per

year, then, after a mid-decade lull, one appears in 1967,
two the next year, and four in 1969--sixteen appear in all
for the entire period.   The vanguard books have performed
their function admirably--stimulating, provoking, influencing.
By the mid-sixties the heart of the movement has been
reached, and the criticism has attained a high degree of maturity and sophistication.   The four texts to be considered
next all confront the totality of Byron's poetry, and all are
cardinally important.

M. K. Joseph's excellent volume, Byron the Poet
(1964), fills a special kind of role in the critical movement.
With the new dawning, criticism has had the privilege of
relatively uninhibited freedom to say or do what it pleases,
although certain consistent threads have been observable; the
result has been widely differing opinions, controversy, and
a fragmented and diffused picture of Byron's work.   Inevitably
the need arises to pause, sort through to the centrally important, and advance from a more solid base.   Joseph's book
effectively meets this need.   In the first place it is comprehensive, omitting little of any real importance in Byron's
work except the lyrics.   It thus has the distinct advantage,
lacking in some other studies, of a complete overview of
Byron's poetry from a consistent viewpoint.   Some depth,
of course, is sacrificed; but the author largely overcomes
this handicap by compression and concentration on essentials.
The loss is felt mainly in the tales, dramas, and satires,
where he has to take the pieces in aggregate; but no loss is
felt in Don Juan, which is accorded more space than George
M. Ridenour's entire monograph on the poem.   The effectiveness of Joseph's book as synthesis is one of its most useful
assets.   The author has been trained in the Oxford tradition;
and he carefully grounds his analysis of Byron's work in
scholarship, not so much original as synthetic.   Each poem
is seen from every angle of significance--biography, composition and publication, sources, traditions, genres, manuscript revisions, stanza form, style, etc.--in order to provide a maximum matrix for interpreting the piece properly.
The result is an amazingly thorough, compact, and graceful
synthesis of the kernel of twentieth-century critical commentary in every important area.   At the same time Joseph has
made the material his own by disagreeing and judiciously
correcting, or agreeing and extending.   He has not so much
held the mirror up to the age as he has provided an instru-
ment for it to take cognizance of itself.   The preceding is
not to underestimate the originality of Joseph's work, which
is primarily manifested in both innumerable perceptive insights

and illuminating comments ("the Vision bears something of
the same relation to Don Juan that Shaw's 'Don Juan in Hell'
bears to the rest of Man and Superman") and in the larger-
scale commentary on such scantily noticed pieces as Childe
Harold IV or the discussion of Cain and its relation to Byron's other work. The full range of Joseph's rich amalgam of
fresh observations and scholarship may be seen in the Don Juan
section, where he is at his best; no single treatment of the poem
could be exhaustive, but he makes it seem very nearly so.
The sections on the narrator and Byron's handling of his
imagery should be singled out for their excellence.

The most original contribution of all, as far as
the movement itself is concerned, is Joseph's sympathetic
and positive approach to Byron's poetry. The swing has
been in this direction: from a grudging recognition of
some little excellence in Byron's work, mainly in the
satires, to a wider recognition of worth that seems obliged
to balance every good with something negative, now finally
to Joseph's view. The author may find more unity in
Byron's thought and work than is palatable to some, may
insist too much on Byron as a moralist at the expense
of his ironical/cynical side, but Joseph has with some
temerity advanced a strong, affirmative view. It will
now stand as a viable position with which to contend. Because of its comprehensive nature, its valuable synthetic
quality, and its sympathy and fairness to the poetry, Byron the Poet may remain for some time the standard introduction to Byron's poetry.

Robert Gleckner's Byron and the Ruins of Paradise
(1967) appears next chronologically. Along with Joseph's
volume, it is the most intensive general study of Byron's
poetry published to this point. Both authors see Byron as
a developing, conscious artist--Joseph, more generally in
matters of themes, structure, poetical form, as well as in
Byron's experiments with different genres, conventions, and
meters; Gleckner, more intensively in personae and Byron's
struggle for form. In their overall view of the work, however, the two differ markedly; for Gleckner, while just as
sympathetic as Joseph, sees Byron's position as essentially
negative throughout his career. The basis for the latter's
belief is the recurrent metaphor of the fall in Byron's poetry, which Gleckner sees not as the usual theological fall
associated with original sin and inherited damnation but as a
gradually evolving myth of "man's eternal fall and damnation
in the hell of human existence." Man has been exiled alone

into the world for no apparent reason--the paradoxical act of
a God "who punishes as evidence of his love"--where man is
made wretched not only by the evil in his nature but also by
his own goodness gone awry. Gleckner traces the idea as
it slowly evolves from a strong sense of loss in Hours of
Idleness, gradually darkens into melancholy in Childe Harold
I and II, deepens into pessimism in the tales with the reali-
zation that Eden is irrevocably lost and that even the good
in man leads to destruction, worsens in the lyrics of 1814-
1816 with the recognition that no escape is possible and that
man's only hopes of immortality--the mind and Mankind--
are doomed to sorrow, tragedy, and death; it finally reaches
despair in the later work where one can only counter inevitable defeat through creating, either by wringing order out
of chaos and thus asserting one's own godhead (later Childe
Harold and Manfred) or by laughing that one may not weep
(the ottava rima poems). Equally important in Gleckner's
discussion is his thorough and ingenious plotting of Byron's
struggle to find a suitable vehicle for expressing his vision.
He traces it mainly through the way the different voices,
roles, and points of view relate to the structure of the various poems, from the early fictional point of view and pre-
occupation with personae in Hours of Idleness to the final
reality of the poet standing forth as his own subject, as
"both creator and creature, world and man, observer and
participant, seer and seen," exhibiting dramatically the essential war of man within himself.

     Gleckner is on to something and he pursues his aims
intelligently. At the same time, however, he opens the lid
to a number of critical barbs: that his view is too exclusive, too forced at times to maintain his thesis, and too
blind to other critical considerations in the poetry; further,
that his reading of Byron's poetry as absolute vision of deso-
lation and despair is to ignore the redemptive aspects of
Childe Harold III and IV and to seriously misread the satires by seeing Don Juan as a grim and "depressing fable
for our time" and Beppo's laughter as "merely the mask of
despair." Nevertheless, these reservations are largely over-
shadowed by the achievement of Gleckner's book. He com-
bines much of the best of the decade, a fine balance of
scholarship and acute original insight brought out through the
New Critical approach; and he brings Byron criticism to a
high level of sophistication. To this point no prior scholar
has done more to reduce to order the problem of Byron's
personae, nor has anyone dealt more effectively with the
lyrics, the Oriental Tales, and Childe Harold in showing

their important contribution as stages in Byron's development toward effective form and voice for his vision. He tilts against some old windmills, such as the idea that Byron's letters are more sincere than his poetry, that he is attitudinizing in his early poetry, that his satires represent a sharp break from his earlier work, that the non-satiric pieces must be treated with condescension; and he overturns a few. But decidedly the most remarkable achievement of Gleckner's book--making this a landmark work--is the recognition of coherence in the full canon of Byron's poetry. Where previously critics had seen a fundamental shift in Byron's direction from the romantic pieces to the satires, Gleckner sees the poetry all of a piece with a consistent metaphysical overview and an essentially unified progressive development toward the expression of it.

Even though Fiery Dust: Byron's Poetic Development (1968), by Jerome McGann, and Byron and the Ruins of Paradise present opposite views about Byron's poetry, the two books share much in common and the former represents the next logical step in the critical advance of the period. Fiery Dust, in fact, represents the ultimate position toward which the criticism of this decade has been evolving. These statements will become comprehendible if one first understands what McGann is doing. Basically his volume is a study of the development of Byron's poetry with emphasis concentered in the different kinds and stages of Byronic self-expression and the central importance of the latter as it relates to Byron's themes and style. The author has organized his book as a collection of cohesive essays in order to allow freer range for a wide spectrum of approaches: manuscript, autobiographical, analytical, mythical, theological. Each essay presents an interpretation of a particular work or two but at the same time contributes to the centrally important topic of Byron's self-dramatization. The five sections deal in order with the following: Hours of Idleness and the genesis of the myth of Byron's dramatized self; the four cantos of Childe Harold (about one-third of the book), which McGann considers Byron's most crucial poem since it contains the most information about himself and his ideas and since it spans the important years of his poetic development; four tales (The Giaour, The Prisoner of Chillon, Mazeppa, The Island) and five dramas (Marino Faliero, The Two Foscari, Sardanapalus, Cain, and Heaven and Earth) which cover the same years as Childe Harold and which show the development of his art and ideas as they undergo generic change; and Beppo which represents Byron's final stage and the Don Juan manner.

Because there are too many oratories in McGann's
edifice for easy survey, one must keep to the main lines of
style and theme (his transcept and nave) in order to perceive
the whole. The five divisions of the book define roughly the
modal stages of Byron's "egoistic imperatives." With Hours
of Idleness he makes his first fumbling attempt at injecting
his mythologized self into the poetry, an artifice derived in
part from his models (Moore and Stangford) and partly in
keeping with his lifelong belief that true poetry must convey
feeling to the reader--that is, the poem must possess the
sense of a living present and presence. This first effort is
inept and all on the surface, but it prefigures his later poetic
direction. With Childe Harold Byron places his second-self
at the very center of the work so that he is both subject--
the poem is the immediate record of his life--and form--the
poet as protagonist narrating the story is a living personality
in a continuum of events that are contemporaneous with the
act of narration. Since the future and ultimate outcome are
unknown to him, his story becomes the personal odyssey of
his own moral development gained through important self-
discoveries and renewals perceived piecemeal along the way,
until by the end of Canto IV he is able "to offer the reader
... a revelation that is at once his interpretation of the
meaning of his own history and his vision of man's fate as
well." In the tales, most notably The Giaour, McGann
shows how Byron was able to objectify his self-dramatization through a character like the oral balladeer. The device
of the oral poem enables the balladeer to assume all the
roles--making tone rather than pure description carry the
burden of Byron's all-important "feeling"--and thus deliver
a virtuoso performance which in turn catches the reader up
in a "gaze of wonder." The plays need not be dwelt upon
because Byron sublimates his autobiographical tendencies into
the action of the play itself, Sardanapalus furnishing the most
relevant example. The Don Juan manner, analyzed through
Beppo, is Byron's most complex and self-conscious style;
the poet, confident in his power as improvisatore, shifts his
emphasis from the personality behind the poem to the actual
dramatization of self. Story, reality of events, personae,
even the words are subordinate to the presence and performance of Lord Byron himself so that the reader leaves
the poem convicted of his contact with a particular man and
a fascinating personality.

The major theme of Byron's poetry, running from
first to last, as McGann shows, is the poet's attempt to
cope with the dual nature of the universe and man. Unlike

the normal Platonist who aspires to the higher world at the
expense of the lower, Byron attempts to unite the two
worlds. All of his protagonists strive for a unified redemp-
tion, but most are unable to attain it. Some, like the Giaour
and the heroes of the tales, are "unregenerate Promethean
men" who are consumed by their own vital energy in heredi-
tary rage; others, like the Prisoner of Chillon, give up the
struggle of life, abnegate moral responsibility, and reside in
"spiritual inertia"; still others, as the figures in the dramas
who are trapped in an evil system or inhibited by a traditional orthodoxy from accepting life or love, cannot attain a
union but can at least reject the system or question the orthodoxy and thus gain a kind of freedom through self-
knowledge. In certain crucial works, however, the heroes
are able to bring about a resolution, indicating that Byron
was able to meet and solve the problem of duality. For
Childe Harold the answer lies in his discovery that the goal
he seeks is not a place, or an achievement, or death, but
the act of pilgrimage itself; only in the continuum of life,
with its amenities and sorrows but at the same time its felicitous moments of illumination, can the individual find the
possibility for infinite self-re-creation and renewal through
the powers of the mind--and thus triumph over despair, decay, and death. Mazeppa achieves fulfillment by mastering
both himself and life; for him death is the mother of life
and he gains life by ceasing to struggle against it; but at the
same time, by understanding the temporal process ("all
things reach their appointed end") and not attempting to im-
pose his will upon events, he is able to master the shifting
stratagems of Fate. The Island shows that an earthly paradise is possible through love; but to attain it the individual
must choose love over life, must not allow himself to be divided into conflict by "entropic" forces, and must pursue his
ideal with such relentless commitment that he is able to
burst through the limits of space/time and achieve identification with nature in a life of ecstasy within but beyond the
reach of the mutable world. Although Sardanapalus has
achieved perfect self-possession for himself by resolving the
conflict between power and pleasure and following the example of nature, he is unable to bring about a "Saturnian
Age" for his people because the conflict is still inherent in
the political state. Nevertheless, he is victorious through
the manner of his death, which images to future generations
his Messiah-like trope for a new dispensation. In Beppo
Byron himself as the poet-raconteur is the norm of the fulfilled man. His perfect man-of-the-world manner is really
the verbal expression of the perfect man of the world that

he is, for he has learned to reconcile the spiritual with the
material in life itself. Paradise is here, in the wedding of
fire and dust; the ideal is in the real and in its capacity for
endless reduplication in physical form. So the fulfilled man
is not the one who seeks beyond materiality but the one who
finds his ideal in the infinite capability of the natural world.

In the natural evolutionary process of this decade,
with studies becoming ever more comprehensive, detailed,
and sophisticated, it seems inevitable that the intensity of
the critical interest would produce a book like Fiery Dust.
Each new addition to the critical canon has advanced the efforts of its predecessors toward fuller understanding of Byron's work. Even though McGann has not read Gleckner, it
is evident from what has been said that they are working
along similar lines in many respects, even concentrating on
much the same material. But whereas Gleckner has astute-
ly taken Byron's full canon and discovered coherence in it,
both metaphysical and aesthetic, his conclusion is a negative
view for Byron. McGann, on the other hand, by resolving
the problem of the poet's duality, is able to go one step
further and see the poet's overall position as eminently positive. Moreover, the totally affirmative attitude of McGann
toward Byron's work--that is, viewing it as a coherent whole,
as positive in outlook, and as poetically worthy in its individual components--represents the ultimate resting point
toward which the decade has been moving. In this light
Fiery Dust may be seen as a brilliant culminating achievement. It is not a final position in the continuing study of
Byron's poetry; but the boundaries of Byron criticism have
now been stretched to accommodate the full range of critical
perspectives.

McGann's study is of such importance as a culminating work for much of the critical activity of the period that
further description of its achievement in this direction is
necessary. A particularly divisive area has always been
the presence and extent of Byron himself in his work, a
factor which has resulted in not one but several gordian
knots. McGann's study makes common sense suggestions
for severing these: it provides a resolution for the sensitive biography-vs.-criticism issue in the interpretation of
Byron's poetry by taking the very logical mean position that
the poet dramatized himself through his poetry, as a mythologized narrator, raconteur, or improviser; coaxially, it
offers a solution to the question of Byron's poetic sincerity,
which has divided critics from the beginning, by removing

the poet from the realm of personal judgment and asking that
the poetry be simply "accepted, and read, as a self-drama-
tizing vehicle"; as a further corollary, it culminates the decade's interest in Byron's personae by carefully distinguish-
ing Byron's dramatized self as "myth" rather than "persona."
The book also acts in a culminative way for the critical reassessment going on in specific areas of Byronic material
outside the ottava rima poems: the period's recovery work
on Childe Harold is beautifully climaxed with McGann's meticulous and thorough treatment that establishes at once the
coherence and integrity of the whole work and recognizes
the poem for the masterpiece that it is; much of the early
promise found in Byron's romances and dramas is fulfilled
also in McGann's highly intelligent readings, especially of
The Giaour, Mazeppa (though the ending is not reconciled),
The Island, Sardanapalus, and The Two Foscari; and he continues the steady flow of "rediscovered" Byron poems of the
60's with his analysis of The Two Foscari, though his real
service in this area is extensive re-enforcement of the gains
of other critics. The era's fruitful endeavor on Byron's
aesthetic comes together in McGann's revelation that Byron
did have one (instead of "flawed experiments" on the way to
the Don Juan style), that it was consistent, and that it was
developmental in that he was perfecting forms of the mythologized self for the Don Juan manner. Also, in keeping with
the gradual movement of the period from the view that Byron had no formal or consistent philosophy to recognition of
a metaphysical overview--the main problem being the apparently insoluble dichotomy in the poet's thinking--McGann
shows that Byron kept the duality but resolved it into a unified humanistic scheme, presenting a superlative exegesis of
Byron's theological views along the way.

Michael Cooke's study the next year reinforces the
final position reached by McGann--the totally affirmative
view of Byron's work--while at the same time it advances
the critical movement one more important step. Cooke's
metaphoric title, The Blind Man Traces the Circle (1969),
refers to Byron's groping progress in his poetry from youthful transcendence and loss, through a circumstantial and in-
comprehensible world, back to something like his true home,
with an affirmative resolution that was seeded in the beginning. It is the classic Romantic circle and, generally, what
this study is about. But the subtitle reference to "patterns
and philosophy" is more direct; for it denotes that he, too,
like his predecessors in these important comprehensive
studies, is concerned with the development of theme and

form in Byron's full canon. The "philosophy" is the larger
design of the piece, offering a key to mind and poetry, and
can be traced in the curve of the book's six chapters: Byron's initial position is idealistic, for his philosophical/sub-
jective lyrics from Hours of Idleness and Hebrew Melodies
celebrate the Romantic vision of harmony between mind and
Nature; but the vision is forfeited to circumstance and his
own will. His long pilgrimage for recovery or discovery
begins with Nature (Childe Harold III), emblematic locus for
his seeking mind of various emotional and moral sanctuaries;
he is frustrated here, partly because conflict exists in Nature, partly because the questing (questioning) mind eventually loses its power to reconcile. From the external world
he is forced inward upon his existential self and trust in the
firmness of his will; but expected triumph does not come
through self-assertion and defiance, for a series of heroic
encounters (Manfred, Cain, Ode to Napoleon) between autono-
mous mind-as-will and "strong reality" leave him with the
same antinomy--now seemingly in the nature of things--as
before. "Strong reality" subsumes all else as he carries
his unquenchable hope and a relentless process of analysis
into the world of disordered fact (Mazeppa and Don Juan)
and, having glimpsed the totality of disunity (rather than an
apocalyptic unity), emerges out of the abyss with a sense of
poise that does not demand solutions but holds it proper to
"ponder boldly" (Childe Harold IV). This position is spun into
a philosophy of skepticism in Don Juan, where uncertainty is
not only accepted but nourished as the purest truth from the
world of fact, neither vice (Beppo) nor virtue (Don Juan) being excepted; but a qualifying "personality" emerges in the
process to demonstrate the "limits of skepticism." Byron's
final position (The Two Foscari, Siege of Ismail cantos, and
The Island) merges the intellectual candor of the skeptical
attitude and the personal commitment of the humanistic personality (together Childe Harold IV's "ponder boldly") into an
affirmative resolution--existential, not philosophical--by
means of a third option to the skeptical poles of religion and
rationalism which Cooke calls counter-heroic (i. e. , counter
to the desperate activity or passivity of the heroic and idio-
satiric respectively) and defines as "to be principled and hu-
mane in action, to acknowledge without collapse the normal
perplexities and corruptions of existence, to profit and be
honored by the opportunity of confronting the self and the universe through suffering." A good part of Cooke's energy is
directed to Byron's methodology, the "patterns" aspect of his
title. The word has a double edge, for he employs it not
only to denote particular stylistic relationships in specific

works, but to show how Byron used these strategems--mainly structure and imagery--to establish or reflect the various stages of his philosophical progress.

Although Cooke attempts to distinguish his study by reference to its synthesizing approach, the latter is really very similar to that of Joseph, Gleckner, and McGann in several respects--it ranges through the Byronic repertory, it offers a total view of the work along with detailed analyses of specific pieces, it demonstrates a developing philosophy and a coherent methodology, and it resolves the problem of radical dualism in Byron's thought and work (in remarkably similar fashion to McGann's fusion of the duality into humanistic stoicism)--so it deserves to be placed among them.   Nevertheless, there is a difference, and this difference accounts for Cooke's most impressive contribution to the critical movement.   By shifting the emphasis from close interpretive reading of individual poems, with ideas emerging, to close, step-by-step appraisal of the philosophy itself, the poetry illustrating and supporting it, Cooke has managed for the first time to endow Byron's poetry with a philosophy and a name.   Not only has he determined and defined Byron's final philosophical position, but he has traced the poet's "stations" toward that eventual goal.   His approach may be less satisfying from the standpoint of a reading of individual poems, but it is more satisfactory from the perspective of Byron's overall mind and work.   Critics have expressed certain reservations about omissions (largely the tales and dramas), usage of material out of context, failure to link convincingly the lyrics with the final phase, and the very limited range of treatment for Don Juan; but these are reservations only and in no way negate the value of the book. A number of subsidiary gains add to its general worth; the most important are the recognition of kinship between certain Byronic works in philosophy or style or related concerns, new perspectives on some old problems (Byron's treatment of will, indecorum in Don Juan), the skillful use of imagery and structure to convey epistemological insights, and the proper alignment of the poet with the Romantic tradition (a curious scholarly oversight as late as M. H. Abrams' Natural Supernaturalism in 1971).

Each of the comprehensive critics has mapped his own unique route.   Along the main lines, however, they have moved with remarkable accord and have supplemented each other in a progressive way for the movement as a whole. Cooke is no exception: he opens up new avenues, provides

strong support for advances made--a case against coherence
and development in Byron's work would now be difficult to
maintain--and he provides a fitting capstone to these studies
by pinpointing Byron's philosophical development. The general studies have done their work well, for no more appear
during this era*--an implicit tribute to their effectiveness.
With this plateau reached, one has the feeling that criticism
can never go back to what it was before. To see how far it
has progressed, one need only place the achievements beside
West's important pioneering study.

A necessary corollary to the general reassessment of
Byron's poetry is concentrated study on individual poems.
Activity in this area is important throughout the period, the
work on the poems generating interest in the reassessment
and the reverse occurring as the general interest flows back
into continued activity on certain pieces and stirs initiative
on rediscovered poems. In keeping with the twentieth-century
evaluation of Don Juan as Byron's masterpiece, this work receives the lion's share of attention with six volumes concentrating on it. Because two of these precede or appear sim-
ultaneously with West's study, some claim could be made for
their actually initiating the critical trend of the period. At
any rate, one--the Don Juan Variorum Edition by T. G.
Steffan and Willis Pratt--appears in the same year as
Marchand's biography, a fortuitous paradigm of the double-
edged direction that scholarly activity will take in this era.

Byron's "Don Juan": A Variorum Edition (1957) is as
monumental in its domain as Marchand's Byron is in the
province of biography. Consistent with most of the landmark
pieces in Byron scholarship, it faces both backward and forward. Published a year earlier, it might have more of a
backward look: the brilliant culmination of the work of the
Texas school throughout the decade and the apogee of the
Don Juan interest in the century. Coming as it does the
next year, the emphasis seems more immediately future: a
definitive text is now at hand and a range of publications
will follow. The text itself is based on approximately 30
manuscripts and fair copies--a first draft for each canto,
fair copies of Cantos I-VIII (the first five in Byron's hand,
the rest in Mary Shelley's), plus various fragments; only
the fair copies of Cantos IX-XVI and perhaps some fragments
are missing, and they are not crucial since Byron did not
revise much from the first draft to the printed copy, even

---

*J. D. Jump's Byron appears in 1972 but is a handbook.

less so for the later cantos. Thorough manuscript data as
to ownership, location, size, dating, signatures, contents,
watermarks, housing, etc., are recorded in an appendix.
The authors adopt a conservative editorial policy, using the
first edition of each canto as the basic text and retaining
generally the inconsistencies in mechanics (due largely to
Byron's own indifference and the variant policies of Murray
and Hunt). Emendations fall into seven categories: corrections of printer's errors, occasional punctuation and spelling
changes for clarity, restoration of expurgated lines, modifications to accord with Byron's revisions for the 1833 edition
or his instructions for Cantos III-V for the fifth edition of
1822, and a switch from Roman to Arabic numerals (on manuscript authority) for stanza numbering. The reading format
sacrifices a bit of fluency for the sake of recording all manuscript readings and data, collated edition discrepancies,
and editorial comment immediately after each stanza; but the
result is an eminently usable scholarly tool.

     Besides making available more Don Juan manuscript
material than ever before, the Steffan/Pratt edition also provides more accumulated information concerning the poem by
way of commentary, notes, and other aids than previously
gathered. The reader thus benefits from both an authoritative text and an excellent foundation for study of Byron's
chef d'oeuvre. The first of the four volumes (volumes II
and III make up the Variorum Edition proper) is a tripartite
discussion--chronicle, composition, evaluation--by Steffan on
the "Making of a Masterpiece." The chronicle part is valuable both as a biographical matrix of everything Byron said
or did relating to the writing and publication of Don Juan and
as a summary of the aesthetic theories and literary opinions
wrung out of him during the months of controversy. The
facts alone are conveniently tabulated in an appendix. The
discussion of the composition of Don Juan, supported by the
author's meticulous scrutiny of the manuscripts, is the
longest and most original section of the book; it climaxes
Steffan's labors in this vineyard over the past decade, including and correcting some of his earlier material. By
assiduous perusal of the additions and revisions, he is able
to suggest a great deal about Byron's psychological and artistic motives, to show his mind and feeling at work on the
poem, and to throw significant light on the poet's artistic
methodology. It is a model study of the poetic process, of
how Don Juan became the great poem that it is, as well as
an overwhelming corrective (several appendices lend imposing tabular authority) of the view that Byron was an undisci-
plined artist. Steffan's last section shifts from how to why

Don Juan is a masterpiece, as he attempts to explain to a
wider audience, canto by canto, what Byron was trying to do.
Willis Pratt keeps pace with the rest of the edition by furnishing an impressive final volume of notes to the poem.
Included are Byron's first edition notes (along with manuscript
omissions, deletions, and interesting variants), some notes
from Moore's 1833 edition (which drew upon commentary of
Scott, Rogers, Lockhart, Campbell, and others) and from E.
H. Coleridge's edition, plus abundant information from the
editors' own store concerning people, places, events, references, allusions, etc., as well as translations. Pratt's
volume also contains a survey of English, Continental, and
American commentary on Don Juan. In an edition of this
magnitude errors are bound to creep in and omissions do
occur; but none brings discredit, and many are taken care
of in the second edition that appears in 1971. How much
the Variorum Edition was responsible for the plethora of
Don Juan criticism that follows cannot be measured; but
everything written thereafter comes under its aegis, and
Steffan's conclusions are used extensively to justify the new
awareness of Byron's conscious artistry.

        George M. Ridenour's The Style of "Don Juan" (1960)
is a worthy first offspring. Coming at the end of the discussion of the critical studies rather than at the beginning
where it belongs, its effects are somewhat muted. But in
1960 nothing like it had appeared before. Boyd's important
monograph on Don Juan had been primarily a scholarly treatment, and Trueblood's effort was in large part a survey of
selected Don Juan topics. Ridenour's work is criticism of
a high order. With no particular antecedents, it seems to
have skipped the slow evolving process of the general studies
and to have sprung full-blown. His approach is a fine blend
of scholarship and New Criticism (the most familiar pattern
of the era) as he discusses what he calls the style of Don
Juan. The term is not nearly as restricted as it sounds;
for he uses it to include tradition and a world view as well
as rhetorical means. His position, somewhat oversimplified,
is that Byron utilized the paradoxical possibilities in two
traditions (the Classical theory of styles and the Christian
doctrine of the Fall) and radically converted a third (the
heroic epic) for the same purposes in order to organize and
convey his conception of a universe that is paradoxical in all
of its elements, as clearly revealed in art (especially poetry)
and nature (particularly love). This stasis is rendered dy-
namic through three lines of movement in the poem which
roughly parallel the three organizing metaphors, which

illustrate further the paradoxical nature of things, and which
offer a resolving, but not redeeming, vision: 1) the narrative movement proper is the progress of Don Juan from innocence to experience; 2) the more central action is the gradually narrowing gap between the thoroughly knowledgeable persona and the protagonist, a rising movement that cancels out
categories like innocence/experience by the end; 3) the ultimate world view of the poet that emerges is the recognition
that the only value to be achieved out of an irrevocably dual
world is the unique response of the individual. Byron's response is "secular and social, and its artistic expression is
the plain manner of satire and conversation. "

    Besides being an astonishingly good critical treatment
of Don Juan at the time (it still stands up well), Ridenour's
book is also remarkably seminal in its suggestions of methodology, issues, and main lines of study that will be followed during the sixties. The methodology of intensive
analysis of structure, tone, metaphoric patterns, imagery,
characters as archetypes or allegorical figures may seem
commonplace now in Byron criticism; but it was new at the
time. Later important critical issues--Byron's personality
in his work; system or chaos in the poetry; Don Juan as satire, comedy, or irony; the exact epic nature of Don Juan--
all are struggled with by Ridenour. And a considerable list
could be drawn up of the period's major and minor interests
that are prefigured in The Style of 'Don Juan''; the most obvious, reduced to a topical list, are as follows: persona
(general, but cf. especially Gleckner and McGann), controlling metaphor of the Fall (cf. especially Gleckner), world of
fact (cf. especially Cooke), ambiguity and paradox (general,
cf. especially Cooke), dual universe (general), pessimistic
resolution in individual assertion (cf. especially Gleckner),
mobilité (cf. especially Elledge), improvisation (cf. especially Joseph and McGann), influence of Wordsworth's Ode (cf.
Cooke); even the stress on exploring neglected works can be
seen in Ridenour's careful analysis of "Ode to a Lady whose
Lover was killed by a ball..." and "To Romance. " Ridenour corrects a number of earlier critical opinions--e.g. ,
the contention by Worchester and Leavis that Augustan satire
ended with Byron--and such entrenched views as those which
claim that Don Juan lacks coherence or is intended primarily
to expose or demonstrate appearance vs. reality. In turn
he will stand corrected later by Cooke for his charges of
indecorum in certain parts of Don Juan and his statement
that Byron loses the world of reason. Fathered by Steffan
and Pratt, Ridenour's book becomes a worthy progenitor in
its own right.

The Steffan/Pratt edition and Ridenour's monograph
are the most important and influential of the Don Juan studies.
Four more publications testify to the continuing interest, but
these are more limited in scope and more eclectic in nature:
one is a history, one a study of influence, another a collection of critical essays, and the final one a concordance.
The first of these, Leo Weinstein's The Metamorphoses of
Don Juan (1959), is not really about Byron's poem but the
tradition from which it sprang, and for that reason it deserves notice. What makes it valuable is that it is the first
full scholarly treatment of the Don Juan legend* itself, super-
seding the pioneering efforts of George de Bévotte and the
work of a host of other scholars who have dealt with limited
portions of the legend.

András Horn's Byron's "Don Juan" and the Eighteenth-
Century English Novel (1962) picks up the numerous suggestions of influence mentioned by such critics as Grierson,
Boyd, Trueblood, Koeppel, Fuess, Escarpit, and others and
concentrates everything into a systematic analysis of Byron's
debt to Fielding, Sterne, and Smollett. He finds the major
link with Fielding to be an attitude, a strictly social morality
that implies tolerance on the one hand--to the extent of license on the part of the hero--and aptly defended by satiric
thrusts at conventional mores--and active humanitarianism on
the other. Sterne's influence is found mainly in the poem's
subjectivism, specifically in the all-pervading presence of
the author and in his assertions of will. In Smollett, or the
tradition that he represents, are to be found the picaresque
elements of the poem that conglomerate to give a sense of
epic totality: the piling up of incoherent pieces of reality;
the frame of travel, assuring variety; and the questing hero
immersed in life and unable to see beyond the present moment (McGann does a great deal with this concept in Childe
Harold). Horn's second aim is to locate behind these influences, in the manner of George Lukács, the determining
factors of background (found mainly in middle-class environment, political liberalism, and the contemporary revolutionary atmosphere) and personality that caused Byron to create
from them.

*At this point should be noted the exhaustive bibliographical
compilation by Armand E. Singer, The Don Juan Theme,
Versions and Criticism: A Bibliography (1965), which lists
specifically for Byron's poem 129 "critical" references plus
other scattered items that are pertinent.

The collection of essays on Don Juan (1969), edited
by E. E. Bostetter, is in the familiar "Twentieth Century
Interpretations" series. In spite of the drawbacks imposed
by the format of the series itself, which forces an editor to
seriously truncate important arguments and to wrench articles
out of a larger context, Bostetter has managed a respectable
product. The most influential twentieth-century commentators
to 1968 are represented (with the modest exception of himself
and Trueblood), and he is able to convey within his restricted
limits something of the spirited variety of opinion about Don
Juan's genre, style, and theme. Because McGann's and
Cooke's contributions were not available at the time, he
overstresses in his introduction the negative views of the
poem's conclusion; but he compensates with his own positive
affirmation. This collection is doubly helpful in Don Juan
studies in that it demonstrates the present importance of the
poem and it furnishes a sampling resumé of the best of contemporary thought about it. The fact that all but five and
one-half pages in the volume appeared during the years pres-
ently under discussion demonstrates how rapidly criticism
has come of age.

If the period has furnished a definitive text of Don
Juan, an authoritative history of the legend, and a body of
superior criticism,* the whole is rounded off with A Concordance to Byron's "Don Juan" (1967) edited by Charles Hagelman and Robert Barnes. It replaces Ione Young's concordance in this area and will likely remain definitive since
it is keyed to the Variorum Edition and is programed to
merge ultimately with a complete concordance to the definitive edition of Byron's poetry when it materializes.

Don Juan is not the only individual poem to receive
its just due during the modern critical span; Cain and the
Hebrew Melodies also receive expert treatment. Commensurate with the example set by the Variorum Don Juan, both
are presented in definitive texts and are, in fact, modeled
along the same variorum/critical lines, though each differs
considerably in its particular makeup. Steffan himself is
responsible for Lord Byron's "Cain" (1968), which is divided
into three sections. The variorum edition of the play forms
the middle part. For the text Steffan has collated all

---

*The bulk of this material is to be found in the general
studies considered earlier, and in certain important essays
and articles beyond the scope of this chapter but which are
represented in the Bostetter collection.

important editions (1821, 1833, 1837, 1904, 1905 Coleridge,
1905 More) with the original manuscript at the University of
Texas.   Only two significant content variances are uncovered:
the addition of three amplifying lines (441-3) to the 1821 edition sent in a letter to Murray, and the omission of 3-1/2
lines (163-66) that were probably considered blasphemous by
Murray and his advisers.   The majority of variations between the manuscript and the editions are minor and occur
in the area of punctuation and mechanics, where Byron tended
to be erratic and to defer to his publisher; Steffan eliminates
most of the manuscript capitalization, converts Byron's
superfluous dashes to periods, reduces his italics and apos-
trophes to those which are functional, and simplifies the
punctuation.   Precedent for most of these changes is found
in the 1821 and 1905 Coleridge editions; but Steffan goes beyond these editors in aiming for simplicity, consistency, and
logic.   The result is a more modern and readable text, but
in not following the strict manuscript and in not indicating
all of his modifications in the textual notes, Steffan has left
himself vulnerable to criticism.   The textual notes do contain the essential information (manuscript cancellations, 17
manuscript insertions of 42 lines, and undeleted variants)
and more (variants from the sundry editions and important
editorial comment).   Additional key aids for the Byron student are the 37 pages of annotations and the very nearly exhaustive bibliography.   The other two major parts of the
book are made up of 12 essays that touch most of the possible
areas of Cain study.   The first eight deal with the history of
the composition, publication, and argument of the play; the
theological doctrines attacked; characterization; transformation of Biblical material; imagery; language; metric; and a
description of the manuscript and Byron's insertions.   The
remaining section, comprising four essays, surveys critical
opinions from 1821 to the mid-1960's, from Byron's social
and literary circle and the reaction of the periodicals to the
Victorian and twentieth-century views.   The whole project
represents a Herculean achievement on Steffan's part and in
all probability stamps him as the current leading textual authority in Byron study.   Some reviewers have questioned
whether the task was worth doing, indicating that Byron's
most controversial work is still not fully accepted.   But this
variorum edition, the general revival of interest in Cain
since 1950, and recent intensive study of the play seem to
indicate that the corner has finally been turned and that a
respected future is in store for the work.

Byron's Hebrew Melodies have long been neglected, even during the present era when hardly a work of the poet's has been left critically unturned. Of the older studies, only Karl Buetler's dissertation of 1912 and Joseph Slater's article of 1952 stand out. Since 1960 Gleckner alone has given these lyrics serious comprehensive treatment, though Cooke has analyzed three of them and Marchand and Bernard Blackstone (pamphlet 219 for the British Council) have allotted them a few pages of survey. Thomas L. Ashton in Byron's Hebrew Melodies (1972) not only goes a long way toward correcting this deficiency but toward getting at the root of the problem itself. From the beginning, confusion has surrounded these lyrics, when Murray followed Isaac Nathan's first number of A Selection of Hebrew Melodies (1815) with Hebrew Melodies a month later, omitting the music and adding 12 new lyrics. To compound the confusion, each edition since that time has varied the contents. By straightening out the publishing history, establishing an edition of 30 authentic Hebrew Melodies, and furnishing a definitive text for the first time, Ashton has laid a solid foundation for future criticism and research. The critical portion of Steffan's Cain may have presented more of a challenge to the editor, but Ashton has the more difficult task in dealing with the manuscripts. In all he locates 47 extant manuscripts of 21 Hebrew Melodies, more than and including every manuscript consulted by previous editors. Since the bulk of these manuscripts belong to the lyrics composed at Halnaby and Seaham, the majority of the holographs remained there and passed into the Lovelace Collection, while Lady Byron's fair copies were sent to London and wound up in the Murray archives. The remaining few manuscripts were found at the British Museum, Harvard University, and the University of Texas. Ashton has collated these individual manuscripts with the editions published in Byron's lifetime and with the later authoritative editions (a total of 20); all decipherable variants and deletions are recorded for the first time. The latter clearly demonstrate Byron's attention to revision and re-enforce the conclusions of the Variorum Don Juan regarding the consciousness of the poet's artistry. For his copy-text the editor uses Hebrew Melodies for 24 of the lyrics, the first editions for five lyrics not contained therein, and Poems (1816) for "Bright be the place of thy soul" which embodied Byron's final revisions; the poems have been re-arranged in chronological order as nearly as discernible. Ashton's edition, together with his excellent calendars of manuscripts and editions, useful appendices of collated information, and helpful annotations (chiefly sources, allusions, related primary material, and prior editor's notes) and bibliography, is an impeccable example of editorial scholarship.

The critical portion of Ashton's book is divided into two parts: a biographical-historical section concerned with the evolution of the Hebrew Melodies, including background interest in national melodies at the time, Byron's involvement in Nathan's project, composition, establishment of chronology, publication, reaction, and aftermath; and a section of criticism on the lyrics proper, wherein Ashton makes some enlightening points in individual readings but ventures out on a critical limb in assessing the general tone of the lyrics as melancholy and defiant. If the post-publication pattern of the Steffan/Pratt Don Juan holds true, one can expect an increase in publishing activity on Cain and the Hebrew Melodies; the value of the first is far from being settled and Byron's lyric expression is just coming under serious scrutiny. By now it seems evident that the definitive Don Juan has also inaugurated a trend of critical/variorum editions of Byron's works; if so, the three published thus far furnish exemplary models.

As a brief addendum to the preceding studies of Byron's individual works, Lord Byron: Werner, A Tragedy (1970) should at least be mentioned. Actually it is more of a contribution to Victorian theater as it is "A Facsimile of the Acting Version of William Charles Macready," the prompt copy of one John Willmott and now in the Theater Collection of the Harvard College Library. Some pertinence to the present study may be found in the fact that the text is a first edition first issue of Werner (1923). The introduction by Marvin Spevack is oriented toward Macready; what material there is on Byron is either derived secondhand or represents the author's misgrounded opinions (e.g., Byron might have been great if he had not died early, and Macready vastly improved Byron's drama by rewriting it).

In these revolutionary years in Byron criticism, because the main thrust has been toward re-evaluating the whole of the poet's canon, energy and emphasis have gone into the general studies, with fall-out attention going to a few important individual works. For this reason only two specialized-interest or topical studies appear of any importance: Peter Thorslev's The Byronic Hero (1962) and G. Wilson Knight's Byron and Shakespeare (1966).

Thorslev's volume continues the practice so noticeable
in the last period of blocking out a particular area of Byron's
work for more intensive study. In this instance he gathers
up the researches on the Byronic hero of the past, particularly the burgeoning interest of the 1946-56 years, and absorbs them into his own very full and thorough treatment.
Basically his approach is through tradition, a study of the
eighteenth century-type heroes (the Child of Nature; the Hero
of Sensibility, manifested in the Man of Feeling or the
Gloomy Egoist; and the Gothic Villain) and the nineteenth
century types (the Noble Outlaw, Faust, Cain, Ahasueris,
Satan, and Prometheus) which form the more-or-less direct
line of descent for the Byronic hero. After tracing the origin, characteristics, and development of each of these types,
the author applies his information to the actual heroes in
Byron's work (Childe Harold, Giaour, Selim, Conrad, Lara,
Manfred, Lucifer, and Cain), shows the exact indebtedness
of each to the past, and draws his appropriate conclusions.
Curiously, in scholarship dealing with the Byronic hero, the
cart has preceded the horse in that a large body of material
considering the literary influence of the figure (in Victorian
literature, in the French Symbolists, in the work of important Russian novelists, in German poetry, in American
literature, etc.), as well as the cultural influence, was already in existence before Thorslev's book, which represents
the first full examination in English of both the antecedents
for and the actual hero in Byron's work. Thorslev has effectively shown the Byronic hero in his historical lineage (thus
separating out opinion which has linked him with a number of
history's villains from de Sade to Hitler), has exhibited him
in his proper Romantic matrix (the "last great age of heroes"),
and corrects some popular notions that had mushroomed out
of season (e.g., the views of Mario Praz). Thorslev struggles against the limitations imposed by a historical study of
this nature--narrowness, oversimplification, overcategoriza-
tion--by expanding his subject matter to include the wider
areas of the Romantic Movement and the heroic tradition itself; by so doing he provides not only a useful classification
of literary materials but a focus for wider application, including the relevancy to our own age and literature. At the
same time, he does not try to claim too much for his results, insisting only upon a general rather than a direct influence of the historical antecedents upon Byron. Published
in 1962 at the initial stage of critical ferment, The Byronic
Hero has been superseded in some of its judgments--the
value of Byron's romances, the confusion of theme in Manfred, the confusion of character in Childe Harold, etc.--but

at the same time it demonstrates foresight and astuteness
in its treatment of such later important ideas as Byron's
mobilité, the existential implications of his poetry, and Don
Juan as an optimistic poem.

Whereas Thorslev's study is traditional, Knight's
book, as one has come to expect, is anything but orthodox.
The title is innocuous enough, Byron and Shakespeare suggesting possibly a treatment of influence or a comparison of
the two as dramatists; but such is not the case. Knight is
attempting nothing less than to show that Byron lived in his
life and work what Shakespeare had accomplished through his
artistry. The proposition is a daring one and its execution
therefore the more remarkable. It is all part of Knight's
highly original spatial approach and his unique qualifications
as specialist on both Shakespeare and Byron. The volume
in fact culminates his study of each literary figure: for
Shakespeare, he maps the dramatist's entire artistic universe; for Byron, in revealing him as the incarnation of that
universe, he makes much clearer and more substantial his
earlier claims for the supremacy of his genius. Because
Knight's subject is elusive and his approach by necessity
imaginative and creative, his study is difficult to summarize
adequately in brief space. His overall concern is with genius, its essence as it were. He finds this matchless quality
in a few important literary figures of Western culture--Dante,
Milton, Swift, Goethe, Nietzsche, Ibsen, etc.--but its supreme manifestation he finds in Shakespeare because of the
comprehensive nature of his work. In part, then, Knight's
particular purpose is to demonstrate concretely this latter
fact. But the genius of Byron (not the man, the genius quality) approaches even closer to the ideal of all-encompassing
universality because it includes life as well. Knight believes
that Byron made explicit and purposive what Shakespeare arrived at through poetic (i.e., in the sense of being meta-
phorically veiled). The other part of his aim, then, is to
apply Shakespeare's universe to Byron's life and work.

The connection is easier to establish than one might
suppose, for Byron saturated himself in Shakespeare's plays
so thoroughly that Knight is able to marshall an imposing
array of biographical and literary similarities in his familiar
cluster method of evidence. He masses his facts, quotes,
and similarities around certain focal centers of relationship,
Shakespeare's plays furnishing the design, and Byron's life
and work the embodiment. At the beginning are the sonnets
(where the ideal may be found) and at the end Henry VIII

(which reflects the necessity of coming to terms with the
real world). In between are various counter-forces to society, individual integrity, and the ideal--tyranny (Hamlet),
comedic feelings (Falstaff, et al.), satanic impulses (Richard
III and Macbeth), alienation (Timon and Shylock), sexual in-
stincts (Anthony and Cleopatra, Othello), and mental tempest
or power (Prospero and Lear). Knight shows that, through
the lens of genius which transcends ordinary cultural codes,
each of these can be seen as a proper operative agent in
life and, by complementing or generating its opposite quality,
a necessary reconciling force in human nature. Knight's
spatial method of structured evidence deliberately avoids any
formal argumentative scheme (this would be "criticism,"
which he disavows in favor of "interpretation"); nevertheless,
his own implicit views are evident by the end: Genius in its
stretch toward absolute universality moves toward compre-
hensiveness in its metaphysic (both life itself and beyond the
human) and synthesis in its ethic (the reconciliation of the
opposite forces in every area of life into a golden middle
way); it is compounded of imaginative vision (Shakespeare)
reconciled to the terms of everyday existence (Byron). The
ultimate function of genius, then, leads to action, to set
man on the "golden path" toward greater human fulfillment.
Knight sees Byron's life and work directed to this end; and
for this reason he is superior to Shakespeare, not greater
as an artist but more fully realized as genius.

It is easy to see how Knight's views and claims can
be misunderstood. To view his study as one of Shakes-
pearean influence on Byron for example--and it has been
seen in this way and criticized for belaboring minuscule evidence and stretching credibility by references to Byron's
clairvoyance and astral walking--is to miss the point of his
spatial approach, which is more concerned with the effect of
facts as truth than the literal truth per se. His is not so
much a comparative study, though the work of Shakespeare
and Byron reciprocally illuminate each other in many striking ways, as a progressive study of genius. In this light
his references to Byron in larger-than-life terms--"Promethean figure," "the new Messiah," "man of some new order,
as yet unrecognized," "modern Europe's attempt at an evolutionary advance"--are understandable. The weaknesses to
be found are still largely the result of Knight's method, but
the high risks involved in such a method reap returns in
opening new avenues and offering a more comprehensive way
of looking at Byron. Despite reservations, it is an interesting study, widening understanding of both Byron and Shakespeare and, by bringing them together, transcending them

both.   Much of Knight's work on Byron has been prophetic.
Byron and Shakespeare was published in 1966; its complete
acceptance and enthusiastic appreciation of the poet seem to
foreshadow the general biographical and critical reversal of
fortunes in Byron scholarship in the 60's.

      Also ancillary to the general critical movement are
the collections.   Two appear--one early, one late--and they
supplement each other chronologically.   The selections in
Andrew Rutherford's Byron (1970), part of "The Critical
Heritage Series, " deal with the contemporary and near-con-
temporary critical reaction to the poet and are therefore
largely confined to the nineteenth century.   Paul West's collection, Byron (1963), part of the "Twentieth Century Views"
series, is made up entirely of twentieth-century commentary.
Rutherford, through careful editing and judicious selecting,
has managed to include in his volume nearly everything that
is important in the century; it is an exemplary collection
and a real boon to scholars.   Virtually all the generic types
of commentary are included--short notices, reviews, critical
essays, pamphlets, book-length studies, letters, journals,
table talk, projections in fiction, and verse notices--and the
criticism is representatively distributed throughout the chronological limits of his volume.   His range is from the very
beginning, with Brougham's 1808 review of Hours of Idleness,
to something like the end when Arthur Symons' interesting
critique of 1909 brings us to "the very threshold of 'modern'
criticism. "   The reviews come mainly from the prestige
journals, Edinburgh Review and the Quarterly, and to a lesser
extent from Blackwood's; the informal commentary is concentrated primarily in the major writers of the day and in John
Murray's Albermarle "Synod. "   Compact and helpful notes ac-
company many of the selections, and the introduction ties
everything together by tracing the history of contemporary reaction to Byron and its effect on the poet, and by considering Victorian criticism briefly under its major recurrent
themes.   It is satisfying to have all of these important materials under one roof; some of them are not easy to come
by, and together they reveal something about the contemporary
attitude toward Byron and his work, something about the
state of criticism at the time, and something about the perennial value of good criticism, as some of these pieces
stand up surprisingly well.   The collection by Paul West suffers by comparison, primarily because he is handicapped by
two factors.   Working within a frame one-third the size of
Rutherford's volume, he can hardly be inclusive of the important advances in twentieth-century scholarship.   Though

West attempts to sample material from each decade since
the 20's, rightly accenting the last two decades, the collection is heavy on British material, overbalanced toward style,
and more eclectic than representative. The most serious
factor limiting this miscellany, however, is that it appeared
at the beginning of the period and missed all the momentous
changes that were to affect Byron scholarship and criticism;
too, some of the essays, as those by Praz and Leavis, have
been corrected by later scholars as Thorslev and Ridenour.
The volume, as it now stands, has value in a few quality
essays but a second edition is in order.

Ione Young's A Concordance to the Poetry of Byron
(1965), as the last publication to be considered, seems particularly apposite. Even though this work was published in
1965, well into the computer age of technology, it was compiled by hand; explanation is given in the preface that the
project was begun in 1940 at the University of Minnesota with
a grant from the WPA. The result seems to be as reliable
as one could expect under the circumstances. The concordance is keyed to the Cambridge edition of The Complete
Poetical Works of Byron, edited by Paul Elmer More. The
pity is that Young's labors will be ultimately negated by
more recent computerized concordances based upon definitive
texts; the Hagelman/Barnes is already evidence of this trend.
In the meantime Young's product will be serviceable for a
number of years.

The year 1972 is by no means an arbitrary choice for
concluding this period and this survey.* In retrospect one
can see that biography, with the work of Marchand and the
opening up of the Lovelace material by Moore and Elwin,
has come to a point of equilibrium. Moreover, the splendid
revolution in criticism that distinguishes the era with its
vitality seems to have achieved most of its goals. The age
has indeed been a renaissance; and the view of Byron's
world--both his life and his work--will not be quite the same
again.

With the year 1973 a new phase in Byron studies has
definitely begun with the appearance of the first two volumes
of the projected new collected works. It seems appropriate
that Leslie Marchand should be the editor of Byron's Letters
and Journals and that he should help inaugurate the new era

_____

*The bibliography section has been extended through 1974 in
an effort to make the listing as current as possible.

with these two volumes. Jerome McGann, whose manuscript
work on Childe Harold is well known, will be the editor of
Byron's poetry. This enterprise, which will be in progress
for some time, will undoubtedly command attention during
the next few years, will characterize the era of which it is
a part, and will affect scholarship for decades to come.

The unveiling of the memorial stone in Westminster
Abbey in 1969, the formation of the Byron Society in 1971,
and the appearance of the Byron Journal in 1973 are demon-
strable signs that the poet's reputation has at last entered
upon its majority. The pilgrimage of Byron scholarship has
come far toward biographical and literary truth, has advanced through perilous moments and struggled painfully at
times. The trek will of course continue, for Jerome McGann
has taught us that the value of pilgrimage lies in the act itself, in epiphanies discovered along the way, rather than in
any final goal to be achieved. Work and time, the poet's
own twin admonishments to his pilgrim figure, have led to
the present pinnacle. The current phase of Byron studies,
with the golden 1957-1972 years joined to the laurel promise
of the projected new edition of the poet's works, represents
a high moment and a bright promise for the future.

PART II
A COMPREHENSIVE BIBLIOGRAPHY
OF SECONDARY MATERIALS
IN ENGLISH

by
Oscar José Santucho

Sources Used

General Indexes, Annual and
Specialized Bibliographies

A. L. A. Index to General Literature. Freeport, N.Y.: Books for
    Libraries Press, 1971.

Anderson, J. P. "Bibliography of Byron," in Roden Noel's Life
    of Byron. London: Walter Scott, 1890.

Annual Bibliography of English Language and Literature. Cam-
    bridge: Bowes & Bowes, 1921-present.

Annual Magazine Subject Index. Boston: Faxon, 1908-1949.

Atheneum Subject Index to Periodicals. London: The Atheneum,
    1915-1916.

Bernbaum, Ernest. "Lord Byron," Guide Through the Romantic
    Movement. New York: Ronald Press, 1930.

Birmingham Public Library. Catalogue of the Byron Collection
    Presented by R. Tangye, to Birmingham Public Library. [Eng.]

Blackwell, B. H. A Selection of Books from the Library of N. E.
    Leigh, with a Large Collection of the Works of Byron and
    Byroniana, on Sale by B. H. Blackwell, Ltd. Oxford: Black-
    well, 1930.

Boas, F. S. "Short Bibliographies of Wordsworth, Coleridge, By-
    ron, Shelley and Keats: Pamphlet No. 12 of the English As-
    sociation, 1912.

Boyle, Edward Melville. Catalogue of the Library of the Late E.
    M. Boyle of Philadelphia, Including the Famous Byron Collec-
    tion. New York: Anderson Galleries, 1919.

Briscoe, J. P. List of Books No. 14. Nottingham: Nottingham
    Public Library, 1890.

British Humanities Index. London: Library Association, 1963 to
    present.

British Museum. Department of Printed Books. Catalogue of
    Printed Books. London: Clowes & Sons, 1906.

Carpenter, Hazen C. A Selective Annotated Bibliography of the
    Major English Writers, 1789-1832. ("Special Bibliography
    Series," No. 6.) Colorado Springs: U.S. Air Force Acad-
    emy Library, 1959.

Catalogue of Books and Manuscripts at the Keats-Shelley Memorial
    House in Rome. Boston: G. K. Hall, 1969.

Chew, Samuel C. "Byron," The English Romantic Poets: A Re-
    view of Research. New York: Modern Language Association;
    London: Oxford University Press, 1950.

_____. "Byron," The English Romantic Poets: A Review of
    Research. Revised Edition. New York: Modern Language
    Association, 1956. Rptd. in 1966.

_____, and Ernest J. Lovell, Jr. "Byron," The English Roman-
    tic Poets: A Review of Research and Criticism. 3rd Re-
    vised Edition. Edited by Frank Jordan. New York: Modern
    Language Association of America, 1972.

_____. "Byron," A Literary History of England, ed. Albert C.
    Baugh. New York: Appleton-Century-Crofts, 1948. Rptd.
    with bibliography updated, in 1967.

_____. Byron in England: His Fame and Afterfame. London:
    John Murray, 1924.

Craig, Hardin (ed.). Byron's "Childe Harold, Cantos III and IV,
    "The Prisoner of Chillon," and Other Poems. New York:
    H. Holt & Co., 1913.

ELH. "The Romantic Movement: A Selective and Critical Bibliog-
    raphy." Baltimore: The Johns Hopkins Press, 1937-1949.

English Language Notes. "The Romantic Movement: A Selective
    and Critical Bibliography." Boulder, Colorado: University
    of Colorado, 1965-present.

Erlangen Universitat. Englischen Seminar. Byroniana und anderes
    aus dem Englischen Seminar zur begrussung der VII hauptver-
    sammlung des Bayerischen neuphilologen-verbades, Erlangen
    11, bis 13 April, 1912. Erlangen: M. Mencke, 1912.

Escarpit, Robert. Lord Byron: Un temperament litteraire.
    Paris: Le Cercle du livre, 1957.

Essay and General Literature Index. New York: H. W. Wilson
    Co., 1900-present.

Fogle, Richard Harter. "The Romantic Movement," Contemporary
    Literary Scholarship: A Critical Review, ed. Leary Lewis.
    New York: Appleton-Century-Crofts; London: Bell, 1958.

_____. Romantic Poets and Prose Writers. New York: Apple-
     ton-Century-Crofts, 1967.

Gay, Harry Nelson. A Collection of Titles, Compiled on Slips by
     H. N. Gay, Relating Especially to Byron, Keats, Shelley and
     Hunt. In the Houghton Library at Harvard University.

Gilbert, Judson Bennett. Disease and Destiny: A Bibliography of
     Medical References to the Famous. With Additions and an
     Introduction by Gordon E. Mestler. London: Dawsons of
     Pall Mall, 1962.

Green, David Bonnell, and Edwin Graves Wilson (eds.). Keats,
     Shelley, Byron, Hunt and Their Circles. A Bibliography,
     July 1st, 1950-June 30, 1962. Lincoln: University of Ne-
     braska Press, 1964.

Griffith, R. H., and H. M. Jones. A Descriptive Catalogue of an
     Exhibition of Manuscripts and First Editions of Lord Byron.
     Austin, Texas: The University of Texas Press, 1924.

Houtchens, Carolyn Washburn, and Lawrence Huston Houtchens.
     English Romantic Poets and Essayists. A Review of Research
     and Criticism. New York: Modern Language Association,
     1957. Rptd. in 1966.

Hutt, Charles. Catalogue of the Valuable Stock of Books of the
     Late Mr. Charles Hutt, Comprising an Extensive Collection
     of Works in All Classes of Literature. London: Dryden
     Press, 1889.

Index to Articles on Byron in Various Periodicals, English and
     American. K. 155 of the Roe Collection at Newstead Abbey.

Index to Book Reviews in the Humanities. Detroit: P. Thomson,
     1960.

International Index: A Guide to Periodical Literature in the Social
     Sciences and Humanities. New York: H. W. Wilson, 1907-
     1964.

Intze, Ottokar. Byroniana. Consisting of I. A List of Catalogues
     of Various Byron Collections, II. Catalogue of His Separate
     Works, III. An unpublished Letter by Byron Presented to the
     Members of the Allgemeiner Deutscher Neuphilologenverband,
     at Bremen, June, 1914. Birmingham, (Eng.): New Meeting
     Press, 1914.

Jack, Ian. English Literature, 1815-1832. Oxford: Oxford Uni-
     versity Press, 1964.

Jump, John. "Byron," English Poetry: Select Bibliographical
     Guides, ed. A. E. Dyson. London: Oxford University Press,

1971.

Keats-Shelley Journal. "Annual Bibliography." New York: Keats
 Shelley Association of America, 1952-present.

Kiell, Norman (ed.). Psychoanalysis, Psychology and Literature:
 A Bibliography. Madison: Wisconsin University, 1963.

Krug, Werner Gerhard. Lord Byron als Dichterische Gestalt in
 England, Frankreich, Deutschland und Amerika. Potsdam:
 R. Schneider, 1932.

Manchester. John Rylands Library. Catalogue of the Printed
 Books and Manuscripts.

Mathews, Elkin. Byron and Byroniana: A Catalogue of Books.
 London: E. Mathews, 1930.

_____. Catalogue of 18th Century Books and Modern First Edi-
 tions, Including a Collection of Byron and Byroniana, Offered
 for Sale by Elkin Mathews. London: E. Mathews, 1927.

Metzdorf, Robert Frederick (ed.). The Tinker Library. New
 Haven: Yale University Library, 1959.

M. L. A. "Bibliography." New York: Modern Language Association, 1947-1962.

_____. MLA International Bibliography. New York: Modern
 Language Association, 1963-present.

Paris. Bibliotheque Nationale. Departement des Imprimés. Catalogue Général des Livres Imprimés. Paris: E. Leroux,
 1897.

Peabody Institute. Baltimore. Catalogue of the Library, 1905.

Philological Quarterly. "The Romantic Movement: A Selective
 and Critical Bibliography, 1950-1964." Iowa City: University
 of Iowa.

Pollard, G. H. "Bibliography of Byron," Cambridge Bibliography
 of English Literature, ed. F. W. Bateson. Cambridge,
 (Eng.): At the University Press, 1941.

Poole's Index to Periodical Literature. Boston & New York:
 Houghton Mifflin Co., 1891-1908. (Including five supplements.)

Pratt, Willis W. Lord Byron and His Circle. A Calendar of
 Manuscripts in the University of Texas Library. Austin,
 Texas: The University of Texas Press, 1947.

Pratt Institute, Brooklyn. School of Library Service Lectures.

Quintana, Ricardo. Byron, 1788-1938. An Exhibition at the Huntington Library. San Marino, California, 1938.

Readers' Guide to Periodical Literature. New York: H. W. Wilson, 1900-present.

Roe-Byron Collection Catalogue. Nottingham, 1937.

Smith, Herbert F. A Guide to the Manuscript Collection of the Rutgers University Library.

Stephen, Leslie. "Lord Byron," Dictionary of National Biography. London: Smith, Elder & Co., 1886.

Subject Index to Periodicals. London: Library Association, 1915-1961.

Symons, A. J. A. Bibliographical Catalogue of First Editions, Proof Copies and Manuscripts of Books by Lord Byron, Exhibited at the Fourth Exhibition Held by the First Edition Club, January 1925. London: Printed for the Club, 1925.

U. S. Library of Congress. Library of Congress Catalog. A Cumulative List of Works Represented by Library of Congress Printed Cards.

Ward, William S. (comp.) Literary Reviews in British Periodicals, 1798-1820: A Bibliography with a Supplementary List of General (Non-Review) Articles on Literary Subjects. 2 vols. New York & London: Garland Publishing Co., 1972. (Companion volumes to Reiman's The Romantics Reviewed.)

Watson, George (ed.). "Byron," The New Cambridge Bibliography of English Literature. Vol. III. 1800-1900. Cambridge: at the University Press, 1969.

Wise, Thomas J. A Bibliography of the Writings in Verse and Prose of George Gordon Noel, Baron Byron, with Letters Illustrating His Life and Work, and Particularly His Attitude Towards Keats. 2 vols. London: Printed for Private Circulation Only, 1932-33.

_____. A Byron Library, a Catalogue of Printed Books, Manuscripts and Autograph Letters by George Gordon Noel, Baron Byron, Collected by Thomas James Wise. London: Printed for Private Circulation Only, 1928.

Woods, George B. English Poetry and Prose of the Romantic Movement. New York: Scott, Foresman & Co., 1916.

The Year's Work in English Studies.   London: Oxford University
        Press, 1919-present.

Scrapbooks of Contemporary Criticism

Album Containing Contemporary Notices and Criticisms of Byron's
        Writings, with Biographical References. K. 25 in the Roe-
        Byron Collection at Newstead.

British Museum Scrapbooks of Miscellaneous Clippings from News-
        papers and Periodicals.   2 vols.

"Byron and His Critics,"   Bristol Public Library Scrapbooks.

Duke University Rare Book Collection.   Seven Scrapbooks.

Fane, Henry A.   Scrapbook in the Roe Collection.   K. 38.

Libraries Researched

Baylor University   Iowa University
Birmingham Public Library   Johns Hopkins University
    (England)   Kent State University
Boston Atheneum   Library of Congress
Boston Public Library   Michigan University
Boston University   New York Public Library
British Museum   Newberry Library
Brooklyn Public Library   Nottingham Public Library
Chicago Public Library   Pennsylvania University
Chicago University   Princeton University
Cleveland Public Library   Rice University
Columbia University   Roe-Byron Collection at New-
Cornell University   stead Abbey
Duke University   Texas University
Harvard University   Yale University

ABBREVIATIONS

AL	American Literature
Aumla	Journal of the Australasian Universities Language and Literature Association
BMC	British Museum Catalogue
CBEL	Cambridge Bibliography of English Literature
CLA Journal	College Language Association Journal
CR	Contemporary Review
ELH	A Journal of English Literary History
ELN	English Language Notes
ER	Edinburgh Review
ES	English Studies
ILN	Illustrated London News
JEGP	Journal of English and German Philology
KR	Kenyon Review
K-SJ	Keats-Shelley Journal
KSMB	Keats Shelley Memorial Bulletin
MLJ	Modern Language Journal
MLN	Modern Language Notes
MLQ	Modern Language Quarterly
MLR	Modern Language Review
MP	Modern Philology
N&A	Nation and Atheneum
N&Q	Notes and Queries
NAR	North American Review
NR	New Republic
NS	New Statesman
NSN	New Statesman and Nation
NYHTBR	New York Herald Tribune Book Review
NYM	New York Magazine
NYRB	New York Review of Books
NYTBR	New York Times Book Review
PBSA	Publications of the Bibliographical Society of America
PMLA	Publications of the Modern Language Association
PQ	Philological Quarterly
QR	Quarterly Review
RES	Review of English Studies
SAQ	South Atlantic Quarterly
SEL	Studies in English Literature (Rice University)
SP	Studies in Philology
SR	Sewanee Review
SRL	Saturday Review of Literature

T&T	Time and Tide
TLS	Times (London) Literary Supplement
UTQ	University of Toronto Quarterly
UTSE	University of Texas Studies in English
VQR	Virginia Quarterly Review
YES	Yearbook of English Studies

1. BYRON'S LIFETIME, 1807-1824

1807

Byron, George Gordon, Lord. Hours of Idleness, a Series of
Poems, Original and Translated. Newark: Printed and Sold
by S. and J. Ridge, 1807.
Reviews:
Monthly Literary Recreations, III (July, 1807), 67-71.
Beau Monde, II (Sept., 1807), 88-90.
[John Higgs Hunt], Critical Review, 3rd ser., XII (Sept.,
1807), 47-53.
Universal Magazine, 2nd ser., VIII (Sept., 1807), 235-37.
British Critic, XXX (Oct., 1807), 436-37.
Satirist, I (Oct., 1807), 77-81.
Eclectic Review, III, Part II (Nov., 1807), 989-93.
Literary Panorama, III (Nov., 1807), cols. 273-75.
[G. E. Griffins], Monthly Review, 2nd ser., LIV (Nov.,
1807), 256-63.
Antijacobin Review, XXVIII (Dec., 1807), 407-408.
Gentleman's Magazine, LXXVII, Part II (Suppl. for 1807),
1217-19; ibid., LXXVIII, Part I (March, 1808), 231-33.
[L. Aikin], Annual Review, VI (1808), 529-31.
New Annual Register, XXVIII (1807), 379.
[Lord Brougham], ER, XI (Jan., 1808), 285-89. Rptd. in
Analectic Magazine, III (June, 1814), 469-73; separately
as an off-print as Extract of the Review of Lord Byron's
"Hours of Idleness" from the "Edinburgh Review," xxii,
which occasioned "English Bards and Scotch Reviewers,"
London: Printed for Wilton & Son, 1820; Literary and
Scientific Repository, I (Oct., 1820), 389-424; Polar Star,
III (1830), 22-25; Chautauquan, LXII (March, 1911), 114-
19.
Monthly Mirror, n.s., III (Jan., 1808), 28-30.
Satirist, II (May, 1808), 333-35. [Excerpts from other re-
views.]
Satirist, III (Aug., 1808), 78-86.
Portfolio (Dennie), 3rd ser., I (March, 1809), 258-61.
Poetical Register, Vol. for 1806-1807 (1811), pp. 538-39.

1809

Byron, George Gordon, Lord. English Bards and Scotch Reviewers.

A Satire. London: Printed for James Cawthorn, British Library, No. 24, Cockspur St. , 1809.
Reviews:
 Antijacobin Review, XXXII (March, 1809), 301-306; ibid. ,
  XXXVII (Sept. , 1810), 84-87. [2nd edition.]
 Gentleman's Magazine, LXXIX (March, 1809), 246-49; ibid. ,
  LXXX, Part I (Feb. , 1810), 156. [2nd edition.]
 British Critic, XXXIII (April, 1809), 410-11.
 Critical Review, 3rd ser. , XVII (May, 1809), 78-85.
 Eclectic Review, V, Part I (May, 1809), 481-84.
 Beau Monde, I (June, 1809), 245-46.
 Cabinet, 2nd ser. , I (June, 1809), 527-29.
 Literary Panorama, VI (June, 1809), 491-96.
 Satirist, V (July, 1809), 91-92. [Excerpts from other re-
  views.]
 New Annual Register for 1809, XXX (1810), 372.
 The Town, I (1810), 35-36.
 Portfolio (Dennie), 3rd ser. , V (May, 1811), 436-50.
 Poetical Register, Vol. for 1808-1809 (1812), 607-608.
 Town Talk, III (Aug. , 1812), 217-22; ibid. , III (Sept. , 1812),
  302-305; ibid. , III (Oct. , 1812), 372-77.
 Literary Journal, April 19, 1818, pp. 49-50; ibid. , May 3,
  1818, pp. 86-87; ibid. , May 10, 1818, pp. 98-99.
 Literary Chronicle, I (May 4, 1818), 86-87; ibid. , I (May 11,
  1818), 98-99.
 Ulster Register, IV (June 5, 1818), 491-495.

1811

Censor. "Lord Byron, " Satirist, VIII (May, 1811), 385-89.

"Lord Byron, " Scourge, I (March, 1811), 191-211.

1812

Byron, George Gordon, Lord. Childe Harold's Pilgrimage. A
 Romaunt. London: John Murray, 1812.
Reviews:
 [Francis Jeffrey], ER, XIX (Feb. , 1812), 466-77. Rptd. in
  Literary and Scientific Repository, I (Oct. , 1820), 398-424.
 [C. Dallas], Literary Panorama, XI (March, 1812), cols. 417-
  30.
 [George Ellis], QR, VII (March, 1812), 180-200. Rptd. in
  Literary and Scientific Repository, I (Oct. , 1820), 389-424.
 Scourge, III (April, 1812), 305-13.
 British Critic, XXXIX (May, 1812), 478-82.
 [T. Denman], Monthly Review, 2nd ser. , LXVIII (May, 1812),
  74-83.
 Gentleman's Magazine, LXXXII, Part I (May, 1812), 448-54.
 [W. Roberts], British Review, III (June, 1812), 275-302.

Christian Observer, XI (June, 1812), 376-87. Rptd. in
    Quarterly Theological Magazine and Religious Repository,
    I (1813), 154-68.
Critical Review, 4th ser. , I (June, 1812), 562-75.
Eclectic Review, VIII, Part I (June, 1812), 630-41.
Antijacobin Review, XLII (Aug. , 1812), 343-65.
Satirist, n. s. , I (Oct. , 1812), 344-58; ibid. , I (Dec. , 1812),
    542-50.
Town Talk, III (Oct. , 1812), 217-22; ibid. , III (Nov. , 1812),
    302-05; ibid. , III (Dec. , 1812), 372-77.
General Chronicle, VI (Nov. , 1812), 323-35.
Belle Assemblee, 2nd ser. , VI (Suppl. to Vol. VI, 1812),
    349-54.
New Annual Register for 1812, XXXIII (1813), 377.
Monthly Magazine, XXXIV (Jan. 30, 1813), 650-52.
Portfolio (Dennie), 4th ser. , I (Feb. , 1813), 192-98.

_____. The Genuine Rejected Addresses, Presented to the Com-
    mittee of Management for Drury Lane; Preceded by that
    Written by Lord Byron, and Adopted by the Committee.
    London: B. Macmillan, 1812.
Reviews of Byron's Address:
    A Critique on the Address Written by Lord Byron, Which Was
        Spoken at the Opening of the New Theatre Royal Drury Lane,
        October 10, 1812. London: T. Bailey, 1812.
    QR, VIII (Sept. , 1812), 172-81.
    Universal Magazine, 2nd ser. , XVIII (Oct. , 1812), 324-25.
    Examiner, Oct. 18, 1812, pp. 663-65.
    Antijacobin Review, XLIII (Dec. , 1812), 359-73.
    General Chronicle, VI (Dec. , 1812), 481-95.
    British Critic, XLI (Jan. , 1813), 72-73.
    Monthly Review, LXX (Feb. , 1813), 84-87.

                                1813

Byron, George Gordon, Lord. Waltz: An Apostrophic Hymn. By
    Horace Hornem, Esq. London: Sherwood Neely & Jones,
    1813.
Reviews:
    British Critic, LXI (March, 1813), 301-302.
    Critical Review, 4th ser. , III (March, 1813), 330-31.
    Gentleman's Magazine, LXXXIII, Part I (April, 1813), 348-49.
    Lady's Monthly Museum, 2nd ser. , XIV (April, 1813), 232-
        34.
    [C. L. Moody], Monthly Review, LXX (April, 1813), 432-33.
    Satirist, n. s. , II (April, 1813), 385-87.
    New Review, I (June, 1813), 636-38.
    New Annual Register for 1813, XXXIV (1814), 408-409.
    Literary Chronicle, June 14, 1821, pp. 441-42.

_____. The Giaour, a Fragment of a Turkish Tale. London:
    John Murray, 1813.

Reviews:
[T. Denman], Monthly Review, 2nd ser., LXXI (June, 1813),
   202-207.
Drakard's Paper, June 27, 1813, pp. 199-200.
Critical Review, 4th ser., IV (July, 1813), 56-68.
[Francis Jeffrey], ER, XXI (July, 1813), 299-309.   Rptd. in
   Analectic Magazine, II (Nov., 1813), 380-91.
Satirist, n.s., III (July, 1813), 70-88.
Antijacobin Review, LXV (Aug., 1813), 127-38.
Theatrical Inquisitor, III (Aug., 1813), 48-50.
Town Talk, V (Aug., 1813), 55-59.
Gentleman's Magazine, LXXXIII, Part II (Sept., 1813), 246-
   47.
Belle Assemblée, 2nd ser., VIII (Oct., 1813), 120-22.
[W. Roberts], British Review, V (Oct., 1813), 132-45.
Reasoner, I (Oct., 1813), 250-55. Cf. W. Gifford, ibid., I
   (Nov., 1813), 313-14. [A letter prompted by the October
   review.] Ibid., I (March, 1814), 494-96. [An answer to
   Gifford.] Ibid., I (April, 1814), 539-43. [Gifford's reply.]
   Ibid., I (June, 1814), 687-93. [A second reply to Gif-
   ford.]
Scots Magazine, LXXV (Oct., 1813), 769-73.
Christian Observer, XII (Nov., 1813), 731-37.
Eclectic Review, X (Nov., 1813), 523-31.
British Critic, XLII (Dec., 1813), 611-13.
New Review, II (Dec. 1813), 674-75.
New Annual Register for 1813, XXXIV (1814), 408-409.
[George Ellis], QR, X (Jan., 1814), 331-42.

_____. The Bride of Abydos. A Turkish Tale. London: John
   Murray, 1813.
Reviews:
Belle Assemblée, 2nd ser., VIII (Dec., 1813), 257-60.
Critical Review, 4th ser., IV (Dec., 1813), 653-58.
New Annual Register for 1813, XXXIV (1814), 408-409.
British Critic, 2nd ser., I (Jan., 1814), 34-50.
[George Ellis], QR, X (Jan., 1814), 343-54.
Gentleman's Magazine, LXXXIV, Part I (Jan., 1814), 51-53.
[J. Hodgson], Monthly Review, 2nd ser., LXXIII (Jan., 1814),
   55-63.
Reasoner, I (Jan., 1814), 357-64.
Scots Magazine, LXXVI (Jan., 1814), 48-51.
Theatrical Inquisitor, III (Jan., 1814), 355-60.
Tradesman, XII (Jan., 1814), 43-46.
[W. Roberts], British Review, V (Feb., 1814), 391-400.
Eclectic Review, 2nd ser., I (Feb., 1814), 187-93.
New Review, III (Feb., 1814), 111-17.
Monthly Museum, I (Feb., 1814), 287-90.
Satirist, n.s., IV (Feb., 1814), 145-59.
Antijacobin Review, XLVI (March, 1814), 209-37.
C., Analectic Magazine, III (April, 1814), 334-44.
[Francis Jeffrey], ER, XXIII (April, 1814), 198-229.
Literary Panorama, XV (April, 1814), cols. 370-78.

Portfolio (Dennie), 4th ser., III (April, 1814), 319-36.
[R. Bakewell], Monthly Magazine, XXXVII (May, 1814), 298-
  300.
Variety, Sept. 10, 1814, p. 5.

Hobhouse, John Cam. A Journey through Albania and Other
  Provinces of Turkey. London: J. Cawthorn, 1813.

T., C. "Sentiments on the First Perusal of The Giaour Infidel, "
  Gentleman's Magazine, LXXXIII, Part II (July, 1813), 4.

1814

Byron, George Gordon, Lord. The Corsair. London: John Mur-
  ray, 1814.
Reviews:
  Belle Assemblée, 2nd ser., IX (Feb., 1814), 81-83.
  [W. Roberts], British Review, V (Feb., 1814), 506-11.
  Critical Review, 4th ser., V (Feb., 1815), 144-55.
  European Magazine, LXV (Feb., 1814), 134-35.
  Gentleman's Magazine, LXXXIV, Part I (Feb., 1814), 154.
  [J. Hodgson], Monthly Review, 2nd ser., LXXIII (Feb., 1814),
    189-200.
  Scots Magazine, LXXVI (Feb., 1814), 124-27.
  Theatrical Inquisitor, IV (Feb., 1814), 105-108.
  Universal Magazine, 2nd ser., XXI (Feb., 1814), 129-36.
  Antijacobin Review, XLVI (March, 1814), 209-37.
  British Critic, 2nd ser., I (March, 1814), 277-96.
  Monthly Museum, I (March, 1814), 349-54.
  New Monthly Magazine, I (March, 1814), 149-51.
  Satirist, n.s., IV (March, 1814), 246-50.
  Christian Observer, XIII (April, 1814), 245-57.
  [J. Conder], Eclectic Review, 2nd ser., I (April, 1814), 416-
    26.
  [Francis Jeffrey], ER, XXIII (April, 1814), 198-229.
  New Review, III (April, 1814), 339-43.
  Reasoner, I (April, 1814), 549-57.
  [George Ellis], QR, XI (July, 1814), 428-43.
  Portfolio (Dennie), 4th ser., IV (July, 1814), 33-44; ibid.,
    IV (Sept., 1814), 271-86.
  Mentor, Aug. 16, 1817, pp. 149-53; ibid., Aug. 23, 1817,
    pp. 161-64.

_____. Lara, A Tale. Jacqueline, A Tale. London: John
  Murray, 1814.
Reviews:
  Critical Review, 4th ser., VI (Aug., 1814), 203.
  Entertaining Magazine, II (Aug., 1814), 432-36; ibid., II
    (Sept., 1814), 486-90.
  New Universal Magazine, I (Aug., 1814), 123-26.
  Scots Magazine, LXXVI (Aug., 1814), 608-11.
  Belle Assemblée, 2nd ser., X (Sept., 1814), 131-32.

Monthly Museum, II (Sept. , 1814), 220-24.

[J. Hodgson], Monthly Review, LXXV (Sept. , 1814), 83-92.

New Monthly Magazine, II (Sept. , 1814), 156-57.

British Critic, 2nd ser. , II (Oct. , 1814), 401-13.

[J. Conder], Eclectic Review, 2nd ser. , II (Oct. , 1814), 393-
      400.

[George Ellis], QR, XI (July, 1814), 428-57. [Published after
      Oct. 10, 1814.]

Lady's Monthly Museum, 2nd ser. , XVII (Nov. , 1814), 290-
      94.

Portfolio (Dennie), 4th ser. , VI (July, 1815), 33-56.

_____. Ode to Napoleon Buonaparte. London: John Murray,
      1814.

Reviews:
      Monthly Review, LXXIII (April, 1814), 433-35.

      Examiner, April 24, 1814, pp. 258-59.

      Antijacobin Review, XLVI (May, 1814), 441-47.

      British Critic, 2nd ser. , I (May, 1814), 433-35, 545-47.

      Critical Review, 4th ser. , V (May, 1814), 524-29.

      Eclectic Review, 2nd ser. , I (May, 1814), 516-20.

      Gentleman's Magazine, LXXXIV, Part I (May, 1814), 477.

      Literary Panorama, XV (May, 1814), 531-32.

      Monthly Museum, I (May, 1814), 501-502.

      New Review, III (May, 1814), 502-504.

      Scourge, VII (May, 1814), 410-17.

      Theatrical Inquisitor, IV (May, 1814), 286-89.

      Universal Magazine, 2nd ser. , XXI (May, 1814), 399-401.

      Reasoner, I (July, 1814), 735-38.

Candidus. "Byron's Plagiarisms," Monthly Magazine, XXXVII
      (June, 1814), 410-11.

Irving, Washington. "Lord Byron," Analectic Magazine, IV (July,
      1814), 68-73. [First American review that Chew knew existed
      but could not find. In it Irving hopes that Byron's poetic
      genius will "kindle up into a fervent and lasting flame. "]
      Rptd. in Poetical Works of Lord Byron, Boston: Cummings
      & Hilliard, 1814, pp. v-xi; Literary and Scientific Repository,
      I (Oct. , 1820), 289-424.

"Memoir of the Right Honourable George Gordon Byron," European
      Magazine, LXIV (Jan. , 1814), 3-4.

Strada. "Portraits of Authors. No. VI: Lord Byron," Champion,
      May 8, 1814, pp. 150-51.

                                1815

Byron, George Gordon, Lord. Hebrew Melodies. London: John
      Murray, 1815.

Reviews:
> British Lady's Magazine, I (May, 1815), 358-60.
> Lady's Magazine, XLVI (May, 1815), 226-27.
> Theatrical Inquisitor, VI (May, 1815), 377-78; ibid., VIII
> (June, 1816), 442-44.
> British Critic, 2nd ser., III (June, 1815), 602-11.
> Gentleman's Magazine, LXXXV, Part I (June, 1815), 539;
> ibid., LXXXV, Part II (Aug., 1815), 141.
> Augustan Review, I (July, 1815), 209-15.
> [J. Conder], Eclectic Review, 2nd ser., IV (July, 1815), 94-
> 96. Rptd. in Analectic Magazine, VI (Oct., 1815), 292-94.
> European Magazine, LXVIII (July, 1815), 37.
> New Universal Magazine, III (July, 1815), 37-38.
> [W. Roberts], British Review, VI (Aug., 1815), 200-208.
> Christian Observer, XIV (Aug., 1815), 542-49.
> Critical Review, 5th ser., II (Aug., 1815), 166-71; ibid.,
> 5th ser., III (April, 1816), 357-66.
> Lady's Monthly Museum, 3rd ser., II (Sept., 1815), 169-72.
> [F. Hodgson], Monthly Review, 2nd ser., LXXVIII (Sept.,
> 1815), 41-47.

"Biographical Memoir of the Right Honourable George Gordon Byron, Lord Byron," Lady's Magazine, XLVI (April, 1815), 151-
52.

"Some Account of the Right Honourable George Gordon, Lord Byron," New Monthly Magazine, III (July, 1815), 527-30.

Talfourd, Sir Thomas Noon. "An Attempt to Estimate the Poetical
Talent of the Present Age, including a Sketch of the History
of Poetry," Pamphleteer, V (1815), 413-71.

1816

Byron, George Gordon, Lord. The Siege of Corinth. A Poem.
Parisina. A Poem. London: John Murray, 1816.
Reviews:
> Critical Review, 5th ser., III (Feb., 1816), 146-54.
> Monthly Review, LXXIX (Feb., 1816), 196-208.
> Champion, Feb. 11, 1816, pp. 45-46.
> Belle Assemblee, XIII (March, 1816), 127-30.
> British Lady's Magazine, III (March, 1816), 181-83.
> [J. Conder], Eclectic Review, 2nd ser., V (March, 1816),
> 269-75.
> Gentleman's Magazine, LXXXVI, Part I (March, 1816), 241-43.
> Liverpool Magazine, I (March, 1816), 110-14.
> New Monthly Magazine, V (March, 1816), 148-49.
> Stage, n.s., I (March 2, 1816), 155-58; ibid., n.s., I (March
> 9, 1816), 167-69.
> Augustan Review, II (April, 1816), 380-88.
> British Critic, 2nd ser., V (April, 1816), 430-36.
> Theatrical Inquisitor, VIII (April, 1816), 276-83.

[W. Roberts], British Review, VII (May, 1816), 452-69.
Dublin Examiner, I (May, 1816), 9-20.
European Magazine, LXIX (May, 1816), 437-38.
Literary Panorama, 2nd ser., IV (June, 1816), 417-20.

_____. Poems on His Domestic Circumstances. London: R.
Edwards, 1816. [It contains a "Memoir of the Right Honour-
able Lord Byron," pp. 3-13.] London: John Murray, 1816.
Reviews:
Belle Assemblée, 2nd ser., XIII (April, 1816), 177-78.
John Scott, Champion, April 14, 1816, pp. 117-18; ibid.,
    April 21, 1816, pp. 124-25.
Augustan Review, II (May, 1816), 551-52.
[W. Roberts], British Review, VII (May, 1816), 510-13.
New Monthly Magazine, V (May, 1816), 344-45.
Scourge, XI (May, 1816), 376-80.
[J. Conder], Eclectic Review, 2nd ser., V (June, 1816), 595-
    99.
Farrago, No. 2, June 18, 1816, pp. 3-9.
Gentleman's Magazine, LXXXVI, Part I, (Suppl. to Part I,
    1816), 613.
Monthly Review, LXXXI (Sept., 1816), 95-96.
Antijacobin Review, LI (Dec., 1816), 374.

_____. Monody on the Death of the Right Honourable R. B.
Sheridan, Written at the Request of a Friend, to be Spoken
at Drury Lane Theatre. London: John Murray, 1816.
Reviews:
Examiner, Sept. 22, 1816, pp. 602-603.
Augustan Review, III (Nov., 1816), 474-82.
Eclectic Review, 2nd ser., VI (Nov., 1816), 502-506.
Monthly Review, LXXXI (Nov., 1816), 319-21.
New Monthly Magazine, VI (Dec., 1816), 441.
Theatrical Inquisitor, XI (Nov., 1817), 362-67.

_____. Childe Harold's Pilgrimage. Canto the Third. London:
John Murray, 1816.
Reviews:
Independent, I (Sept., 1816), 310-18.
[Sir Walter Scott], QR, XVI (Oct., 1816), 172-208.
Critical Review, 5th ser., IV (Nov., 1816), 495-506.
Dublin Examiner, II (Nov., 1816), 41-50.
Monthly Review, 2nd ser., LXXXI (Nov., 1816), 312-19.
Scots Magazine, LXXVIII (Nov., 1816), 849-54.
Portfolio, Political and Literary, Nov. 23, 1816, pp. 73-77;
    ibid., I (Dec., 1818), 266-68.
Champion, Nov. 24, 1816, p. 374.
British Critic, 2nd ser., VI (Dec., 1816), 608-15.
[Francis Jeffrey], ER, XXVII (Dec., 1816), 277-305.
Gentleman's Magazine, LXXXVI, Part II (Dec. 1816), 521-24.
Literary Panorama, n. s., V (Dec., 1816), cols. 409-13.
Monthly Magazine, XLII (Dec., 1816), 447-49.
Belle Assemblée, 2nd ser., XIV (Suppl. for 1816), 338-41.

British Lady's Magazine, V (Jan., 1817), 17-26.
Lady's Magazine, XLVIII (Jan., 1817), 12-18.
[W. Roberts], British Review, IX (Feb., 1817), 1-23.
Literary and Statistical Magazine for Scotland, I (Feb., 1817),
    75-81.
[J. Conder], Eclectic Review, 2nd ser., VII (March, 1817),
    292-304.
Portico, III (March, 1817), 173-84.
Christian Observer, XVI (April, 1817), 246-59.
American Monthly Magazine, I (May, 1817), 3-12.
[W. Phillips], NAR, V (May, 1817), 98-110.
Christian Miscellany, II (June, 1817), 270-77; ibid., II (July,
    1817), 317-24.
Portfolio (Dennie), 5th ser., III (June, 1817), 490-99.

_____. The Prisoner of Chillon, and Other Poems. London:
    John Murray, 1816.
Reviews:
    [Sir Walter Scott], QR, XVI (Oct., 1816), 172-208.
British Critic, 2nd ser., VI (Dec., 1816), 615-17.
Critical Review, 5th ser., IV (Dec., 1816), 567-81.
Dublin Examiner, II (Dec., 1816), 116-28.
[Francis Jeffrey], ER, XXVII (Dec., 1816), 305-10.
Monthly Review, 2nd ser., LXXXI (Dec., 1816), 435-38.
Champion, Dec. 1, 1816, 382-83.
Portfolio, Political and Literary, Dec. 7, 1816, 123-28.
British Lady's Magazine, V (Jan., 1817), 17-28.
Gentleman's Magazine, LXXXVII, Part I (Jan., 1817), 41.
Monthly Magazine, XLII (Jan., 1817), 546.
Theatrical Inquisitor, X (Jan., 1817), 43-48.
Lady's Magazine, XLVIII (Feb., 1817), 51-52.
New Monthly Magazine, VII (Feb., 1817), 57.
[J. Conder], Eclectic Review, 2nd ser., VII (March, 1817),
    292-304.
American Monthly Magazine, I (May, 1817), 3-12.
[W. Phillips], NAR, V (May, 1817), 98-110.

"General Review of Lord Byron's Poems," Analectic Magazine,
    VIII (Sept., 1816), 252-57.

Hunt, Leigh. "Distressing Circumstances in High Life," Examiner,
    April 21, 1816, pp. 247-50. [On the separation of Lord and
    Lady Byron.] Rptd. in Leigh Hunt's Literary Criticism, eds.
    Lawrence Houston Houtchens and Carolyn W. Houtchens. New
    York: Columbia University Press, 1956. Pp. 95-102.

"Lady Anne Isabella Byron," Ladies' Monthly Museum, 3rd ser.,
    III (June, 1816), 301-305.

"Lord Byron," Portico, II (Oct., 1816), 304-15; ibid., II (Nov.,
    1816), 386-98; ibid., II (Dec., 1816), 476-85; ibid., III (Jan.,
    1817), 53-62.

"Memoir," Poems on His Domestic Circumstances. By Lord Byron. London: William Hone, 1816. Pp. 3-6.

N., W. "Lord Byron's Poetical Character Examined," Monthly
Magazine, XLII (Sept., 1816), 113-15. [On The Giaour and
The Siege of Corinth.]

A Narrative of the Circumstances Which Attended the Separation of
Lord and Lady Byron; Remarks on His Domestic Conduct and
a Complete Refutation of the Calumnies Circulated by Public
Writers. London: R. Edwards, 1816.

*Nightingale, Joseph. "Life of the Noble Author," Poems on His
Domestic Circumstances. London: J. Bumpus, 1816.

"An Original Biography of Lord Byron," The Works of Lord Byron.
Including Several Poems Now First Collected. Together with
an Original Biography. 3 vols. Philadelphia: Moses Thomas, 1816. Pp. xi-xlii.

Scott, John. "The Examiner's Charges against The Champion,"
Champion, April 28, 1816, pp. 133-34.

_____. "The Pilgrimage of Living Poets to the Stream of Cas-
taly," Champion, April 7, 1816, p. 110.

"The Wrongs of Lady Byron, and Mrs. Mardyn's Letter and Lord
Byron's Farewell to England," Scourge and Satirist, XII
(July, 1816), 9-18.

                              1817

Byron, George Gordon, Lord. Manfred, a Dramatic Poem. London: John Murray, 1817.
    Reviews:
    [John Wilson], Blackwood's, I (June, 1817), 285-95.
    Critical Review, 5th ser., V (June, 1817), 622-29.
    Monitor, I (June, 1817), 170-76, 177-82.
    Scots Magazine, LXXIX (June, 1817), 449-53.
    Literary Gazette, June 21, 1817, pp. 337-38.
    Sale-Room, June 21, 1817, p. 200.
    Champion, June 22, 1817, p. 197.
    British Critic, 2nd ser., VIII (July, 1817), 38-47.
    [J. Conder], Eclectic Review, 2nd ser., VIII (July, 1817),
        62-66.
    Gentleman's Magazine, LXXXVII, Part II (July, 1817), 45-47.
    Monthly Magazine, XLIII (July, 1817), 547.
    Monthly Review, 2nd ser., LXXXIII (July, 1817), 300-307.
    Knight Errant, July 19, 1817, p. 46.
    [W. Roberts], British Review, X (Aug., 1817), 82-90.
    [Francis Jeffrey], ER, XXVIII (Aug., 1817), 418-31.
    European Magazine, LXXII (Aug., 1817), 150-52.

Lady's Monthly Museum, 3rd ser., VI (Aug., 1817), 90-95.
Theatrical Inquisitor, XI (Aug., 1817), 120-27.
American Monthly Magazine, I (Sept., 1817), 348-56.
Gloucestershire Repository, Oct. 17, 1817, pp. 409-10.
Portico, IV (Oct., 1817), 260-74.
Belle Assemblée, 2nd ser., XVI (Suppl. to 1817), 342-43.

_____. The Lament of Tasso. London: John Murray, 1817.
Reviews:
   Literary Gazette, July 26, 1817, pp. 49-50.
   Edinburgh Magazine, n.s., I (Aug., 1817), 48-49.
   Gentleman's Magazine, LXXXVII, Part II (Aug., 1817), 150-
      51.
   Monthly Review, 2nd ser., LXXXIII (Aug., 1817), 424-27.
   British Lady's Magazine, 2nd ser., I (Sept., 1817), 176-77.
   [J. Conder], Eclectic Review, 2nd ser., VIII (Sept., 1817),
      291-92.
   Monthly Magazine, XLIV (Sept., 1817), 153.
   Portico, IV (Sept., 1817), 206-208.
   Edinburgh Observer, Sept. 13, 1817, p. 12.
   American Monthly Magazine, I (Oct., 1817), 422-26.
   [J. Wilson], Blackwood's, II (Nov., 1817), 142-44.
   British Critic, 2nd ser., VIII (Nov., 1817), 488-93.
   Lady's Magazine, XLIV (Jan., 1818), 7-10.

"Byron's Imitations," British Stage and Literary Cabinet, I (Oct.,
   1817), 232-35.

"Byron versus Elgin," British Stage and Literary Cabinet, I
   (March, 1817), 63-64.

Clarke, Hewson. Lord Byron. The Legal Critics Refuted; or an
   Essay to Prove from the Argument of Lord Byron's Counsel,
   that "Childe Harold," and "The Prisoner of Chillon" are
   Mercenary Forgeries, and that the "Pilgrimage to the Holy
   Land" is a Genuine Production. London: Published by the
   Author, 1817.

Coleridge, Samuel Taylor. Biographia Literaria; or, Biographical
   Sketches of My Literary Life and Opinions. 2 vols. London:
   Rest Fenner, 1817.

"On the Nature of Lord Byron's Poetry," Literary Gazette, April
   5, 1817, pp. 162-63.

"On the Poetical Style of Lord Byron," Literary Gazette, March
   29, 1817, p. 145.

"On the Poetry of Scott and Byron," Scots Magazine, LXXIX (Jan.,
   1817), 26-27. [From the French.]

"State and Character of the Poetry of the Present Age: Burns,
   Cowper, Wordsworth, Byron, etc.," New Annual Register,
   1817, pp. 43-50.

1818

Byron, George Gordon, Lord.   Beppo, a Venetian Story.   London:
    John Murray, 1818.
Reviews:
    [Francis Jeffrey], ER, XXIX (Feb., 1818), 302-10.
    British Critic, 2nd ser., IX (March, 1818), 301-305.
    Monthly Review, 2nd ser., LXXXV (March, 1818), 285-90.
    Literary Gazette, March 14, 1818, pp. 162-64.
    Yellow Dwarf, March 28, 1818, pp. 101-102.
    Champion, March 19, 1818, p. 203.
    Edinburgh Magazine, n. s., II (April, 1818), 349-51.
    Literary Journal, April 5, 1818, pp. 17-18.
    Literary Panorama, 2nd ser., VIII (May, 1818), 239-42.
    [W. Roberts], British Review, XI (May, 1818), 327-33.
    Presbyter Anglicanus, Blackwood's, III (June, 1818), 323-29.
        Rptd. in Southern Literary Messenger, IV (April, 1838),
        269-72.
    Eclectic Review, 2nd ser., IX (June, 1818), 555-57.
    New England Galaxy, I (June 26, 1818), n. p.
    Monthly Magazine, XLV (July, 1818), 535.
    Edinburgh Reflector, July 1, 1818, p. 6.
    Gentleman's Magazine, LXXXVIII, Part II (Aug., 1818), 144-
        45.

_____. Childe Harold's Pilgrimage.   Canto the Fourth.   Lon-
    don: John Murray, 1818.
Reviews:
    [Sir Walter Scott], QR, XIX (April, 1818), 215-32.
    British Critic, 2nd ser., IX (May, 1818), 540-54.
    Catholic Gentleman's Magazine, I (May, 1818), 255-60; ibid.,
        I (June, 1818), 347-48.
    [J. Wilson], Edinburgh Magazine, n. s., II (May, 1818), 449-
        53.
    Lady's Magazine, XLIX (May, 1818), 203-206; ibid., (June,
        1818), 251-54.
    [John Wilson], Blackwood's, III (May, 1818), 216-18*. [Pagi-
        nation irregular. Asterisk actually used in Blackwood's.]
    Anti-Unionist, May 2, 1818, No. 14.
    Literary Gazette, May 2, 1818, pp. 273-77.
    [William Hazlitt], Yellow Dwarf, May 2, 1818, pp. 142-44.
    Literary Journal, I (May 3, 1818), 81-83; ibid., I (May 10),
        99-100.
    [J. Wilson], ER, XXX (June, 1818), 87-120.
    Monthly Magazine, XLV (June, 1818), 434-36.
    Northern Star (Sheffield), II (June, 1818), 469-77.
    Portico, V (June, 1818), 420-38.
    American Monthly Magazine, III (July, 1818), 206-10.
    [J. Conder], Eclectic Review, 2nd ser., X (July, 1818), 46-
        54.
    Gentleman's Magazine, LXXXVIII, Part II (July, 1818), 45-47.

[W. Roberts], British Review, XII (Aug., 1818), 1-34.
Literary Panorama, 2nd ser., VII (Aug., 1818), 718-22.
New Monthly Magazine, X (Sept., 1818), 156-60.
Theatrical Inquisitor, XIII (Sept., 1818), 217-21; ibid., XIII
    (Oct., 1818), 289-94.
British Lady's Magazine, 3rd ser., I (Nov., 1818), 221-24;
    ibid., I (Dec., 1818), 266-68.
Monthly Review, LXXXVII (Nov., 1818), 289-302.
Belle Assemblée, 2nd ser., XVIII (Suppl. to 1818), 340-42.
Fireside Magazine, I (Jan., 1819), 34. [Quotes from Monthly
    Review.]

A. "Observations on a Letter to Lord Byron," New Monthly Maga-
    zine, X (Aug., 1818), 31-33. [Answer to the letters by
    Presbyter Anglicanus published in Blackwood's for June, 1818.]

Dyce, Alexander. "Plagiarisms of Lord Byron," Gentleman's
    Magazine. LXXXVIII, Part I (Feb., 1818), 121-22. [In Lara,
    from Parnell, Pope, and The Mysteries of Udolpho.]

Hazlitt, William. "Lecture VIII: On the Living Poets," Lectures
    on the English Poets. London: Taylor & Hessey, 1818.
    Pp. 283-331. Rptd. in Literary Panorama, VIII (July, 1818),
    cols. 674-76. [The Byron section only is reprinted.]

Hobhouse, John Cam. Historical Illustrations to the Fourth Canto
    of Childe Harold: Containing Dissertations on the Ruins of
    Rome; and an Essay on Italian Literature. London: John
    Murray, 1818.
  Reviews:
    New Monthly Magazine, X (Sept., 1818), 160-62.
    Eclectic Review, 2nd ser., X (Oct., 1818), 323-36.
    Monthly Review, 2nd ser., LXXXVII (Nov., 1818), 298-302.
    Edinburgh Monthly Review, I (Jan., 1819), 110-18.
    British Critic, 2nd ser., XII (July, 1819), 23-40.

"On Byron's Plagiarisms from Mrs. Radcliffe," Monthly Magazine,
    XLVI (Aug., 1818), 20-21.

Stendhal, Count de [pseud. for Marie Henri Beyle]. Rome, Naples,
    and Florence in 1817. English Translation. Sketches of the
    Present State of Society, Manners, Arts, Literature, etc.,
    in These Celebrated Cities. London: Henry Colburn, 1818.

Vertumnus. "Lord Byron Vindicated from Alleged Plagiarism,"
    Gentleman's Magazine, LXXXVIII, Part I (May, 1818), 389-
    90.

Wilson, John. "Essays on the Lake School of Poetry," Blackwood's,
    III (July, 1818), 368-81. Rptd. in Southern Literary Messen-
    ger, IV (April, 1838), 268-69.

<u>1819</u>

Byron, George Gordon, Lord.   <u>Mazeppa, a Poem</u>.   London: John
     Murray, 1819.
<u>Reviews</u>:
     Bell's Weekly Messenger, June 13, 1819, p. 189.
     [J. Wilson?], Blackwood's, V (July, 1819), 429-32.
     [William Maginn], "John Gilpin and Mazeppa," Blackwood's,
          V (July, 1819), 434-39.
     Gentleman's Magazine, LXXXIV, Part II (July, 1819), 43-45.
     Lady's Magazine, L (July, 1819), 291-95.
     Monthly Review, 2nd ser., LXXXIX (July, 1819), 309-14.
     Theatrical Inquisitor, XV (July, 1819), 43-47; ibid., XV (Aug.,
          1819), 86-91.
     Green Man, July 3, 1819, pp. 53-56; ibid., July 10, 1819,
          pp. 62-63.
     Literary Chronicle, I (July 3, 1819), 97-99; ibid., I (July 10,
          1819), 117-19.
     Literary Gazette, July 3, 1819, pp. 417-19.
     Theatre, July 10, 1819, pp. 1-4.
     Kaleidoscope, I (June 29, 1819), 194. [Quotes from Literary
          Gazette]; ibid., II (July 3, 1920), 4 [Excerpts from The
          Scotsman]; ibid., II (Feb. 22, 1820), 130.
     Man of Kent, July 17, 1819, pp. 693-95.
     Champion, July 25, 1819, pp. 471-72.
     British Lady's Magazine, 3rd ser., III (Aug., 1819), 82-85.
     Eclectic Review, 2nd ser., XII (Aug., 1819), 147-56.
     Edinburgh Magazine, n.s., V (Aug., 1819), 145-52.
     Edinburgh Monthly Review, II (Aug., 1819), 214-18.
     Fireside Magazine, I (Aug., 1819), 305-307; ibid., I (Sept.,
          1819), 344-45; ibid., I (Sept., 1819), 349, 352, 355, 358.
          [Quotes other reviews.]
     Monthly Magazine, XLVIII (Aug., 1819), 57.
     New Monthly Magazine, XII (Aug., 1819), 64-67.
     Analectic Magazine, XIV (Nov., 1819), 405-10.
     Belle Assemblée, 2nd ser., XX (Supp. to 1819), 341-42.

_____.   Don Juan.   London: Thomas Davidson, 1819.
<u>Reviews</u>:
     Q., European Magazine, LXXVI (July, 1819), 53-56.
     Monthly Review, 2nd ser., LXXXIX (July, 1819), 314-21.
     Green Man, July 17, 1819, p. 69.
     Literary Chronicle, I (July 17, 1819), 129-30; ibid., I (July
          24, 1819), 147-149. Cf. Dramaticus, ibid., July 17, 1819,
          pp. 135-36.
     Literary Gazette, July 17, 1819, pp. 449-51; ibid., July 24,
          1819, pp. 470-73.
     Champion, July 25, 1819, pp. 472-73; ibid., Aug. 1, 1819,
          pp. 488-90.
     Kaleidoscope, II (July 27, 1819), 12. [Quotes from Literary
          Gazette.]
     British Critic, 2nd ser., XII (Aug., 1819), 195-205.
     [W. Roberts], British Review, XIV (Aug., 1819), 266-68.

Gentleman's Magazine, LXXXIX, Part II (Aug. , 1819), 152.
[J. G. Lockhart], Blackwood's, V (Aug. , 1819), 512-18.
Monthly Magazine, XLVIII (Aug. , 1819), 56.
W. C. , New Monthly Magazine, XII (Aug. , 1819), 75-78.
New Bon Ton Magazine, XXX (Aug. , 1819), 234-39.
Fireside Magazine, I (Sept. , 1819), 344-45, 353-54, 356.
   [Quotes from other reviews.]
Edinburgh Monthly Review, II (Oct. , 1819), 468-86.
Miniature Magazine, III (Oct. , 1819), 236-39.
[Leigh Hunt], Examiner, Oct. 31, 1819, pp. 700-702.
Analectic Magazine, XIV (Nov. , 1819), 405-10.
Portfolio (Dennie), 5th ser. , VIII (Nov. , 1819), 428.
T. , Western Review, II (Feb. , 1820), 1-16.
Investigator, III (Oct. , 1821), 353-60.
Investigator, V (Oct. , 1822), 334-38. Cf. "Canting Slander, "
   Examiner, Nov. 24, 1822, pp. 739-41; ibid. , Dec. 22,
   1822, pp. 804-806. [A defense of Don Juan against the
   attack of Investigator.]
Edinburgh Magazine, n. s. , IX (Aug. , 1821), 105*-108*.

Bowles, William Lisle. The Invariable Principles of Poetry, in a
   Letter Addressed to Thomas Campbell, Esq. , Occasioned by
   Some Critical Observations in His "Specimens of British
   Poets, " Particularly Relating to the Poetical Character of
   Pope. London: Longman, Hurst, Rees, Ormes and Brown,
   1819.

Campbell, Thomas. Specimens of the British Poets, with Biographical and Critical Notices, and an Essay on English Poetry.
   7 vols. London: John Murray, 1819.

Colton, Charles Caleb. Remarks, Critical and Moral, on the Tal-
   ents of Lord Byron and the Tendencies of "Don Juan. " With
   Notes and Anecdotes, Political and Historical. London:
   Printed for the Author, 1819.
   Review:
   Gentleman's Magazine, XC, Part I (April, 1820), 344-45.

"Critique on Modern Poets, " New Monthly Magazine, XII (Nov. ,
   1819), 377-81.

"Enquiry Respecting His Hints of Horace, " Monthly Magazine,
   XLVIII (Sept. , 1819), 110.

"Extract of a letter from Geneva, with Anecdotes of Lord Byron, "
   New Monthly Magazine, XI (April, 1819), 193-95. [Gossip
   about Lord Byron at Villa Diodati and on the composition of
   The Vampyre, attributed to him.]

[Hone, William?] "Don John, " or, Don Juan Unmasked; Being a
   Key to the Mystery Attending That Remarkable Publication;
   with a Descriptive Review of the Poem, and Extracts. London: William Hone, 1819.

Review:
Literary Chronicle, I (July 24, 1819), 149-50.

Irving, Washington. The Sketch Book of Geoffrey Crayon, Gent.
New York: Printed by C. S. Van Winkle, 1819-1820.

"Lord Byron's Poetry," Christian Observer, XVIII (Nov., 1819),
717-20.

"Memoir of the Right Honourable Lord Byron," The Works of the
Right Honourable Lord Byron. Comprehending All His Suppressed Poems, Embellished with a Portrait and a Sketch of
his Lordship's Life. 6 vols. Paris: Galignani, 1819. Pp.
i-viii.

Merivale, J. H. "Remarks on the Reviews of Don Juan," Blackwood's VI (Dec., 1819), 288-90.

Mitford, John. "Lord Byron's Travels in Greece," New Monthly
Magazine, XI (June, 1819), 388-92.

Mulock, Thomas. The Answer Given by the Gospel to the Atheism
of All Ages; Being Strictures Suggested Chiefly by the Works
Styled Theological, of the Late Thomas Paine. London: A.
A. Paris, 1819.

P., E. "Remarks Philosophical and Literary on the Poetry of Byron and Scott," Gentleman's Magazine, LXXXIX, Part II
(Oct., 1819), 315-17; ibid., LXXXIX, Part II (Nov., 1819),
397-400.

Wiffen, J. H. "On the Character and Poetry of Lord Byron,"
New Monthly Magazine, XI (May, 1819), 330-32.

X. "Observations on Lord Byron's Juvenile Poems, with Specimens," New Monthly Magazine, XI (Feb., 1819), 1-9.

1820

"Biographical Memoir of the Right Honourable George Gordon Byron, Lord Byron," London Magazine, I (Jan., 1820), 1-11;
ibid., I (Feb., 1820), 118-22.

Bowles, William Lisle. "Observations on the Poetical Character
of Pope; further Elucidating The Invariable Principles of Poetry, with a Sequel in Reply to Octavius Gilchrist," Pamphleteer, XVII (1820), 369-84; ibid., XVIII (1821), 213-58.

_____. "A Reply to the Charges Brought by the Reviewer of
Spence's Anecdotes, in the Quarterly Review, for Oct., 1820,
against the Last Editor of Pope's Works, and Author of 'A

Letter to Mr. Campbell, on The Invariable Principles of Poetry,' " Pamphleteer, XVII (1820), 73-96.

"Contemporary Authors, No. IX: Lord Byron," Monthly Magazine, I (Sept., 1820), 102-103.

"Essay on Song Writing," Blackwood's, VII (April, 1820), 32-35. [On Byron's Hebrew Melodies.]

Goethe, Johann Wolfgang von. "Manfred," London Magazine, I (May, 1820), 524-25. [Goethe's opinion of it.]

Lockhart, J. G. "Extracts from Mr. Wastle's Diary," Blackwood's, VII (June, 1820), 317-23. [On Don Juan.]

"Lord Byron, an Anecdote," Literary Chronicle, II (Jan. 22, 1820), 59-60.

"Lord Byron: His French Critics: The Newspapers and the Magazines," London Magazine, I (May, 1820), 492-97.

"Lord Byron," Literary Gazette, May 6, 1820, pp. 296-97. [A very favorable Parisian review of a French translation of Byron's works.]

Oxonian. The Radical Triumvirate; or, Infidel Paine, Lord Byron, and Surgeon Lawrence Colleaguing with the Patriotîc Radicals to Emancipate Mankind from All Laws, Human and Divine. London: Francis Westley, 1820.

"Poetry and Prose, by a Member of Parliament and Free Mason," London Magazine, I (Feb., 1820), 121-26. ["Lord Byron's poetry is neither that of imagination nor of intellect, in the first degree, but chiefly of sensibility."]

"Remarks on the Writings of Lord Byron, Particularly on the Poem of Don Juan," London Magazine, I (March, 1820), 269-70.

Stacy, John? A Critique on the Genius and Writings of Lord Byron, with Remarks on "Don Juan." Norwich: John Stacy, 1820.
Review:
European Magazine, LXXXVI (July, 1824), 9-14.

1821

Byron, George Gordon, Lord. Letter to **** ***** on the Rev. W. L. Bowles' Strictures on the Life and Writings of Pope. London: John Murray, 1821.
Reviews:
Literary Chronicle, III (March 31, 1821), 193-96.
Literary Gazette, April 7, 1821, pp. 213-15.

[Albany Fontblanque?], Examiner, April 29, 1821, pp. 267-
    69.
Y. [Pseud. for Henry Matthews], Blackwood's, IX (May,
    1821), 227-33.
British Critic, 2nd ser., XV (May, 1821), 463-74.
Edinburgh Monthly Review, V (May, 1821), 616-26.
Monthly Magazine, LI (May, 1821), 365.
Literary Gazette (Philadelphia), I (May 19, 1821), 315-18;
    ibid., I (May 26, 1821), 328-31; ibid., I (June 2, 1821),
    346-49.
Gentleman's Magazine, XCI, Part I (June, 1821), 533-34.
[William Hazlitt], London Magazine, III (June, 1821), 593-607.
Edinburgh Magazine, n.s., IX (Aug., 1821), *105-*108.
Antijacobin Review, LX (Aug., 1821), 577-83.
[W. H. Prescott], NAR, XIII (Oct., 1821), 450-73.

_____. Marino Faliero, Doge of Venice. An Historical Trage-
    dy, in Five Acts. With Notes. The Prophecy of Dante, a
    Poem. London: John Murray, 1821.
Reviews:
    Literary Gazette, Nov. 25, 1820, pp. 763-64. [Historical
        background of the play about to be published by Lord By-
        ron.]
    Edinburgh Magazine, n.s., VIII (Jan., 1821), 54-55.
    London Magazine, III (Jan., 1821), 68; ibid., III (May, 1821),
        489-98.
    [John Wilson], Blackwood's, IX (April, 1821), 93-103.
    Bell's Weekly Messenger, April 22, 1821, p. 121.
    Literary Chronicle, III (April 28, 1821), 257-62.
    Literary Gazette, April 28, 1821, pp. 259-63.
    Bon Ton Magazine, n.s., I (May, 1821), 43-51.
    British Critic, 2nd ser., XV (May, 1821), 463-74.
    European Magazine, LXXXIX (May, 1821), 437-43; ibid.,
        LXXIX (May, 1821), 452-53.
    [William Hazlitt], London Magazine, III (May, 1821), 550-54.
    *London Review and Literary Journal, May 1821, pp. 437-43.
    Monthly Review, 2nd ser., XCV (May, 1921), 41-50.
    New Monthly Magazine, 2nd ser., I (May, 1821), 725-28. [A
        review of The Prophecy of Dante alone.]
    [Leigh Hunt], Indicator, II (May 2, 1821), 233-40.
    Beacon, May 5, 1821, p. 143. [On The Prophecy of Dante
        alone.]
    Literary Gazette, IV (May 5, 1821), 277-79. [On the Prophecy
        of Dante alone.]
    [Albany Fontblanque?], Examiner, May 6, 1821, p. 285-86.
    Beacon, May 19, 1821, p. 159.
    Literary Gazette (Philadelphia), I (May 19, 1821), 319-20.
    [W. Roberts], British Review, XVII (June, 1821), 439-52.
    Drama, or Theatrical Pocket Magazine, I (June, 1821), 89-92;
        ibid., I (July, 1821), 114-20.
    Eclectic Review, 2nd ser., XV (June, 1821), 518-27.
    Ladies' Literary Cabinet, IV (June 2, 1821), 25-29.
    Literary Gazette (Philadelphia), I (June 9, 1821), 353-55.

[On The Prophecy of Dante alone.]
[J. Everett], NAR, XIII (July, 1821), 227-46.
[Francis Jeffrey], ER, XXXV (July, 1821), 271-85.
Monthly Magazine, LI (July, 1821), 524-28.
New Edinburgh Review, I (July, 1821), 237-56.
Western Review, IV (July, 1821), 321-28. [A review of The
  Prophecy of Dante. Philadelphia: M. Carey & Sons,
  1821.]
[Reginald Heber], QR, XXVII (July, 1822), 476-524. [Also a
  review of the other dramas.]
Monthly Magazine, LVIII (Dec., 1824), 430-31.

_____. Sardanapalus, a Tragedy. The Two Foscari, a Tragedy.
  Cain, a Mystery. London: John Murray, 1821.
Reviews of the three plays together:
  Belle Assemblée, 2nd ser., XXIV (Dec., 1821), 282.
[Albany Fontblanque?], Examiner, Dec. 23, 1821, pp. 808-
  10; ibid., Dec. 30, 1821, pp. 827-28.
Literary Gazette, Dec. 22, 1821, pp. 808-812; ibid., Dec.
  29, 1821, pp. 821-22; ibid., Jan. 5, 1822, pp. 4-5.
Edinburgh Magazine, n.s., X (Jan., 1822), 102-14.
European Magazine, LXXXI (Jan., 1822), 58-70.
[J. G. Lockhart], Blackwood's, XI (Jan., 1822), 90-92.
Monthly Review, 2nd ser., XCVII (Jan., 1822), 83-98.
Rambler's Magazine, I (Jan., 1822), 25.
[Thomas Noon Talfourd], London Magazine, V (Jan., 1822),
  66-71.
Literary Gazette, Jan. 5, 1822, pp. 4-5. Rptd. in Saturday
  Magazine, n.s., I (Dec. 22, 1821), 577-80.
[Francis Jeffrey], ER, XXXVI (Feb., 1822), 413-52.
Siluriensis [Pseud. for Colonel John Matthews], Blackwood's
  XI (Feb., 1822), 213-17.
Monthly Magazine, LIII (Feb., 1822), 10-15.
[W. Roberts], British Review, XIX (March, 1822), 72-102.
Leeds Correspondent, IV (March, 1822), 5-21; ibid., IV
  (April, 1922), 110-16.
British Critic, 2nd ser., XVII (May, 1822), 520-40.
[Reginald Heber], QR, XXVII (July, 1822), 476-524.
Investigator, V (Oct., 1822), 343-60.

Sardanapalus
  Gentleman's Magazine, XCI, Part II (Dec., 1821), 537-41.
  Literary Chronicle, III (Dec., 22, 1821), 799-802.
  Leeds Correspondent, IV (Jan., 1822), 5-21.
  Brighton Magazine, I (Feb., 1822), 198-206.
  Lady's Magazine, 2nd ser., III (Feb., 1822), 79-82.
  X. L. D., Kaleidoscope, n.s., II (Feb. 5, 1822), 241-43;
    ibid., II (Feb. 12, 1822), 254-55.
  Nemo, Manchester Iris, I (Feb. 9, 1822), 9-10.
  Portfolio (Dennie), 5th ser., XIV (Dec., 1822), 487-92.

The Two Foscari
  Kaleidoscope, n.s., I (Nov. 20, 1821), 158-59; ibid., n.s.,

I (Jan. 29, 1822), 238-39.
Literary Gazette (Philadelphia), I (Dec. 22, 1821), 813-15.
Literary Chronicle, III (Dec. 29, 1821), 815-17.
Gentleman's Magazine, XCII, Part I (Jan., 1822), 59-61.
Nemo, Manchester Iris, I (Feb. 16, 1822), 17-18.
Brighton Magazine, I (March, 1822), 304-309.
Lady's Magazine, 2nd ser., III (March, 1822), 150-53.
Leeds Correspondent, IV (April, 1822), 110-13.

Cain

Literary Gazette, Dec. 22, 1821, pp. 808-12; ibid., Dec. 29,
    1821, pp. 821-22.
*True Briton, Dec. 22, 1821, pp. 2-3.
Gentleman's Magazine, XCI, Part II (Supp. to 1821), 613-15.
*The Babbler; or, Weekly Literary & Scientific Intelligencer,
    I (Jan., 1822), 148-54.
Brighton Magazine, I (Jan., 1822), 72-79.
Lady's Monthly Museum, 3rd ser., XV (Jan., 1822), 38-41.
Literary Chronicle, IV (Jan. 5, 1822), 6-8.
Literary Speculum, I (Feb., 1822), 257-60.
[R. Carlile], Republican, Feb. 8, 1822, p. 192.
Kaleidoscope, n. s., II (Feb. 19, 1822), 258.
Nemo, Manchester Iris, I (Feb. 23, 1822), 25-26.
Examiner, Feb. 24, 1822, pp. 120-21; ibid., June 2, 1822,
    pp. 338-40.
[W. Roberts], British Review, XIX (March, 1822), 94-102.
Lady's Magazine, 2nd ser., III (March, 1822), 151-53.
Rambler's Magazine, I (March 1, 1822), 119.
Literary Gazette, March 16, 1822, pp. 166-67.
*Gridiron; or, Cook's Weekly Register, I (March 23, 1822),
    22-25.
Congregational Magazine, V (April, 1822), 202-206.
Imperial Magazine, IV (April, 1822), col. 379.
London Christian Instructor, V (April, 1822), 202-206.
Leeds Correspondent, IV (April, 1822), 113-16.
Eclectic Review, 2nd ser., XVII (May, 1822), 418-27.
Evangelical Magazine, XXX (May, 1822), 192-93.
P. P. P. [pseud. for George Croly?], Blackwood's, XI (June,
    1822), 740.
United States Literary Gazette, I (June 1, 1824), 54-57.
    [Also a review of The Deformed Transformed.]

_____. Don Juan.   Cantos III, IV, and V.   London: Thomas
    Davidson, 1821.
Reviews:
    European Magazine, LXXX (Aug., 1821), 181-85.
    Harry Franklin, Blackwood's, X (Aug., 1821), 107-15.
    Monthly Review, 2nd ser., XCV (Aug., 1821), 418-24.
    Literary Chronicle, III (Aug. 11, 1821), 495-97; ibid., III
        (Aug. 18, 1821), 514-16.
    Literary Gazette, Aug. 11, 1821, pp. 497-500; ibid., Aug.
        18, 1821, pp. 516-17.
    [Henry L. Hunt?], Examiner, Aug. 26, 1821, p. 538.

British Critic, 2nd ser., XVI (Sept., 1821), 251-56.
Monthly Magazine, LII (Sept., 1821), 124-29.
Literary Gazette (Philadelphia), I (Sept. 29, 1821), 609-12;
    ibid., I (Oct. 13, 1821), 641-44.
Imperial Magazine, III (Oct., 1821), cols. 945-48.
Investigator, V (Oct., 1822), 315-71.
Literary Speculum, I (Nov., 1821), 1-5.
[W. Roberts], British Review, XVIII (Dec., 1821), 245-65.
Gentleman's Magazine, XCII, Part I (Jan., 1822), 48-50.
[W. Maginn and J. G. Lockhart], Blackwood's, XIV (July,
    1823), 88-92.
Edinburgh Magazine, n. s., IX (Aug., 1821), *105-*108.

Aristarchus. "Vindication of Lord Byron's Poetry," Imperial Mag-
    azine, III (Sept., 1821), cols. 810-12.

"Authentic Particulars of Lord Byron's Habits at Venice," Bon Ton
    Magazine, I (May 1, 1821), 52-54.

"Biographical Sketches of Illustrious and Distinguished Characters:
    The Right Honourable George Gordon Byron, Lord Byron,"
    Belle Assemblée, 2nd ser., XXIV (Dec., 1821), 243-48.

Bowles, William Lisle. Two Letters to the Right Honourable Lord
    Byron, in Answer to His Lordship's "Letter to **** ***** on
    the Rev. William Lisle Bowles' Strictures on the Life and
    Writings of Pope": More Particularly on the Question, Whe-
    ther Poetry Be More Immediately Indebted to What is Sublime
    or Beautiful in the Works of Nature, or the Works of Art.
    London: John Murray, 1821. Rptd. with alterations in
    Pamphleteer, XVIII (1821), 331-400.

        . A Vindication of the Late Editor of Pope's Works, from
    Some Charges Brought against Him, by a Writer in the "Quar-
    terly Review," for October, 1820; with further Observations
    on "The Invariable Principles of Poetry"; and a Full Exposure
    of the Mode of Criticising Adopted by Octavius Gilchrist, Esq.,
    F.A.S. London: Printed by A. J. Valpy, 1821.

"Chaucer and Don Juan," Blackwood's, X (Oct., 1821), 295-98.

Fabius [pseud. for William Lisle Bowles]. "A Letter to the Right
    Honourable Byron, Protesting against the Immolation of Gray,
    Cowper and Campbell, at the Shrine of Pope," Pamphleteer,
    XVIII (1821), 571-84.

Gillespie, Reverend. "Burns, Scott, Byron and Campbell," Ka-
    leidoscope, n. s., I (Feb. 27, 1821), 273-74.

Hunt, Leigh. "Sketches of Living Poets," Examiner, July 29,
    1821, pp. 472-74. Rptd. in Literary Gazette (Philadelphia),
    I (Sept. 19, 1821), 615-17; Leigh Hunt's Literary Criticism,
    eds. Lawrence Houston Houtchens and Carolyn W. Houtchens.

New York: Columbia University Press, 1956, pp. 153-58.

John Bull [pseud. for John Gibson Lockhart]. Letter to the Right
Honourable Lord Byron. London: William Wright, 1821.
Review:
John Wilson, Blackwood's, IX (July, 1821), 421-26.

A Letter to R. W. Elliston, Esq. (Lessee of the Threatre Royal
Drury Lane), on the Injustices and Illegality of His Conduct
in Representing Lord Byron's Tragedy of "Marino Faliero."
London: Printed for J. Lowndes, 1821?

"Lord Byron, Don Juan and Thomas Davidson," Edinburgh Magazine, n.s., IX (Aug., 1821), *105-*109. [Asterisks are part
of the Edinburgh Magazine pagination.] Rptd. in St. Tamma-
ny's Magazine, Nov. 27, 1821, pp. 41-43. [On the circumstances attending the publication of Don Juan and an adverse
criticism of it.]

M., G. "Defence of Wordsworth," Imperial Magazine, III (Oct.,
1821), cols. 885-87. Cf. ibid., III (Oct., 1821), cols. 923-
25; ibid., III (Nov., 1821), cols. 978-83; ibid., III (Nov.,
1821), cols. 1016-32; ibid., III (Dec., 1821), cols. 113-24.
[A series of letters vindicating Byron at the expense of
Wordsworth and vice versa.]

_____. "On the Genius and Writings of Byron," Imperial Maga-
zine, III (March, 1821), cols. 254-57.

"Memoir of the Right Honourable Lord Byron," Lord Byron's
Works. 5 vols. Paris: Printed for Baudry, 1821. Pp. v-
xii. Rptd. in The Works of Lord Byron. 12 vols. Paris:
Printed for Baudry, 1823. Pp. 1-8.

Morgan, Lady Sydney Owenson. Italy. 3 vols. London: Henry
Colburn & Co., 1821.

"On the Controversy Respecting Pope and His Writings," Gentleman's Magazine, XCI, Part I (April 1821), 291-94.

"Plagiarisms of Lord Byron Detected," Monthly Magazine, LII
(Aug., 1821), 19-22; ibid., LII (Sept. 1821), 105-109. Rptd.
in Portfolio (Dennie), 5th ser., XIII (March, 1822), 250-54.

"Remarks on Childe Harold," Literary Speculum, I (Nov., 1821),
6-9.

S. "Lord Byron's Plagiarisms," Gentleman's Magazine, XCI,
Part I (April, 1821), 349-55. Cf. E. B., "Lord Byron Defended from the Charge of Plagiarism," ibid., XCI (Supp. to
Part I, 1821), 601-602. Atticus, ibid., XCI, Part I (Sept.,
1821), 228-29.

Scott, John. "Living Authors. No. IV: Lord Byron," London
    Magazine, III (Jan., 1821), 50-61.

"Some Observations on the Plagiarisms of Lord Byron," Literary
    Chronicle, III (April 7, 1821), 217-18; ibid., III (April 21,
    1821), 250-51.

T., T. "Controversy between Lord Byron and Mr. Bowles," The
    Gossip, Kentish Town, Aug. 11, 1821, pp. 185-88.

[Watson?]. Gordon, a Tale. A Poetical Review of "Don Juan."
    London: T. & J. Allman, 1821.
    Review:
    Imperial Magazine, IV (Jan., 1822), cols. 85-89.

Watts, Alaric A. "Examples of Lord Byron's Plagiarisms,"
    Literary Gazette, Feb. 24, 1821, pp. 121-24; ibid., March 3,
    1821, pp. 137-39; ibid., March 10, 1821, pp. 150-52; ibid.,
    March 17, 1821, pp. 168-70. Cf. John Bull, II (June 16,
    1822), 629. [An addition to Watts' list.]

Wilson, John. "Familiar Epistles to Christopher North: On
    Anastasius. By Lord Byron," Blackwood's, X (Sept., 1821),
    200-206.

                              1822

Byron, George Gordon, Lord. "The Vision of Judgment. Sug-
    gested by the Composition so Entitled by the Author of Wat
    Tyler," Liberal, I, 1822.
    Reviews:
    A Critique on "The Liberal." London: William Day, 1822.
    Literary Speculum, II (Oct., 1822?), 422-32.
    Gentleman's Magazine, XCII, Part II (Oct., 1822), 348-51.
    [T. N. Talfourd], Lady's Magazine, III (Oct., 1822), 565-69.
    New European Magazine, I (Oct., 1822), 354-63.
    [Albany Fontblanque?], Examiner, Oct. 13, 1822, pp. 648-52.
    Literary Chronicle, IV (Oct. 19, 1822), 655-58; ibid., IV (Oct.
        26, 1822), 675-77.
    Literary Gazette, Oct. 19, 1822, pp. 655-56; ibid., Oct. 26,
        1822, pp. 678-81; ibid., Nov. 2, 1822, pp. 693-95.
    Literary Museum, Oct. 19, 1822, pp. 405-406.
    Literary Register, Oct. 19, 1822, pp. 241-43; ibid., Oct. 26,
        1822, pp. 260-61.
    British Luminary and Weekly Intelligencer, Oct. 20, 1822,
        p. 754.
    John Bull, II (Oct. 27, 1822), 780-81.
    Edinburgh Magazine, n.s., XI (Nov., 1822), 561-73.
    Imperial Magazine, IV (Dec., 1822), cols. 1139-42.
    Monthly Magazine, LIV (Dec., 1822), 452; ibid., LIV (Jan.,
        1823), 538.
    London Liberal, I (1823), 43-56.

Investigator, VI (Jan., 1823), 76-89.
Monthly Censor, II (April, 1823), 452-58.

Bowles, William Lisle.   Letters to Lord Byron on a Question of
    Poetic Criticism.   Third Edition with Corrections to Which
    are Now First Added the Letter to Mr. Campbell, as far as
    Regards Poetical Criticism; and the Answer to the Writer in
    the "Quarterly Review," as far as They Relate to the Same
    Subject.   London: Hurst, Robinson & Co., 1822.

Britannicus.   Revolutionary Causes: With a Brief Notice of Some
    Late Publications; and a Postscript, Containing Strictures on
    "Cain."   London: Printed for J. Cawthorn, 1822.
    Review:
    Monthly Review, 2nd ser., XCVII (June, 1822), 203-10.

"Byron Anachronisms," Literary Gazette, March 2, 1822, p. 142.
    [In Sardanapalus.]

Carey, William.   "Coincidence not Plagiarism," Variae.   Histori-
    cal Observations on anti-British and anti-contemporarain Pre-
    judices.   Important Critical Coincidences of Lord Byron in
    1820; of Thomas Campbell, Esq. in 1818, with William Carey
    in 1809; and of Sir Walter Scott in 1821, with the Same in
    1805.   London: Published for the Author by James Macauley
    Carey, 1822.   Pp. 17-56.   [On the coincidences between
    Carey's A Letter to J. A., Esq., a Connoisseur in London
    and Byron's Letter to **** ***** on the Rev. W. L. Bowles'
    Strictures on the Life and Writings of Pope.]

"Cases of Walcot v. Walker; Southey v. Sherwood; Murray v.
    Benbow, and Lawrence v. Smith," QR, XXVII (April, 1822),
    123-30.   [On Cain.]

"Concerning Byron's Letter to Murray," Examiner, Oct. 27, 1822,
    p. 679.   [About a pretended letter sent by Byron to Murray
    disparaging Hunt.   Asks Murray to publish the forgery to
    exonerate himself.]

Harness, William.   The Wrath of Cain.   A Boyle Lecture Delivered
    at the Church of St. Martin-in-the Field.   London: Rivington,
    1822.   [Warns against the danger of Byron's publication in a
    skeptical age like theirs.]

Harroviensis.   A Letter to Sir Walter Scott, Bart., in Answer to
    the Remonstrance of Oxoniensis on the Publication of "Cain,
    a Mystery," by Lord Byron.   London: Printed for Rodwell
    and Martin, 1822.
    Review:
    Monthly Review, 2nd ser., XCVII (June, 1822), 203-10.

Lake, J. W.   "The Life of Lord Byron," The Works of Lord By-
    ron, Comprehending the Suppressed Poems.   16 vols.   Paris:

Published by A. & W. Galignani, 1822-1824. Vol. I, pp. 5-
106. [Reprinted in numerous American, French and German
editions.]

"A Letter of Expostulation to Lord Byron, on His Present Pursuits;
with Animadversions on His Writings and Absence from His
Country in the Hour of Danger," Pamphleteer, XIX (1822),
347-62.

"The Liberal," Literary Gazette, Nov. 2, 1822, pp. 694-95. [A
letter about the unoriginality in The Vision of Judgment.]

"Lord Byron," Belle Assemblée, 2nd ser., XXVI (Dec., 1822),
526*-527*. [Asterisks in Belle Assemblée.]

"Lord Byron," Brighton Magazine, II (July, 1822), 45-52.

"Lord Byron and The Liberal," Literary Museum, I (Dec. 14,
1822), 543-44.

"Lord Byron and Sir Walter Scott," Portfolio (Dennie), 5th ser.,
XIV (July, 1822), 86-87.

"Lord Byron: Letters on Cant," Brighton Magazine, II (July, 1822),
52-57; ibid., II (Aug., 1822), 182-84.

"Lord Byron's Cambolio," Blackwood's, XI (Feb., 1822), 162-65.
[A poetical criticism of Byron's poetry.]

McDermot, Martin. "A Letter to the Rev. W. L. Bowles, in Reply to His Letter to Thomas Campbell, Esq., and to His Two
Letters to the Right Honourable Lord Byron; Containing a Vindication of Their Defence of the Poetical Character of Pope,"
Pamphleteer, XX (1822), 119-44, 385-410.

"Odious Cant--George III and Lord Castlereagh," Examiner, Nov.
3, 1822, pp. 689-91; ibid., Nov. 10, 1822, pp. 705-707.

"On Liberality, True and False--The Liberal; Verse and Prose
from the South. Postscript to Lord Byron," Council of Ten,
II (Nov., 1822), 149-78. [Comments on Byron's Vision of
Judgment.]

"On the Respective Merits of Byron and Wordsworth," Imperial
Magazine, IV (May, 1822), cols. 416-39.

Oxoniensis [pseud. for H. J. Todd]. A Remonstrance Addressed
to Mr. John Murray Respecting a Recent Publication. London: Printed for F. C. & J. Rivington, 1822.
    Reviews:
        Christian Remembrancer, IV (Feb., 1822), 113-16.
        Monthly Review, 2nd ser., XCVII (June, 1822), 203-10.

P., E. "The Rhetoric of the Infidel School; or, Points of Re-
        semblance between Lord Bolingbroke and Lord Byron, "
        Gentleman's Magazine, XCII, Part II (Nov. , 1822), 398-403;
        ibid. , XCII, Part II (Dec. , 1822), 511-14.

Palaemon [pseud. for Col. John Matthews]. "Critique on Lord By-
        ron, a Poem, " Blackwood's, XI (April, 1822), 456-60. Rptd.
        in Maginn's Miscellanies: Prose and Verse, ed. R. W.
        Montagu, 2 vols. , London: Sampson Low, Marston, Searle
        & Rivington, 1885, II, 327-34; The Odoherty Papers, Anno-
        tated by Dr. Shelton Mackenzie, 2 vols. , New York: Red-
        field, 1855-1857, II, 219-25.

Philo-Milton. Vindication of the Paradise Lost, from the Charge
        of Exculpating "Cain, a Mystery." London: Printed for F.
        C. & J. Rivington, 1822.
        Review:
        Monthly Review, 2nd ser. , XCVII (June, 1822), 203-10.

"Portraitures of Modern Poets. No. II: Lord Byron, " Ladies'
        Monthly Museum, 3rd ser. , XV (Feb. , 1822), 86-91.

"Remarks on Byron and Wordsworth, " Imperial Magazine, IV
        (July, 1822), cols. 628-50.

"Remarks on the Life, Character and Writings of Lord Byron, "
        Gazette of Fashion, I (March 16, 1822), 103-105; ibid. , I
        (March 30, 1822), 135-37; ibid. , II (May 18, 1822), 36-38;
        ibid. , II (June 1, 1822), 67-69.

"Second Letter to Lord Byron on The Liberal, " Council of Ten, II
        (Dec. , 1822), 334-43.

T., J. "Lord Byron--Infidel Opinions--Influence of Education, "
        Gazette of Fashion, I (April 27, 1822), 211-12.

T., T. [pseud. for William Maginn]. "Tickler on Werner, "
        Blackwood's, XII (Dec. , 1822), 782-85. [Critique of Werner.]

Uriel, a Poetical Address to the Right Honourable Lord Byron.
        Written on the Continent: With Notes, Containing Strictures
        on the Spirit of Infidelity Maintained in His Works. An Ex-
        amination into His Assertion that "If 'Cain' is Blasphemous,
        'Paradise Lost' is Blasphemous." And Several Other Poems.
        London: Hatchard, Burton & Smith, 1822.
        Review:
        Investigator, V (Oct. , 1822), 352-60.

W. "Memoir of Living Poets: Lord Byron, " Imperial Magazine,
        IV (Aug. , 1822), cols. 751-59; ibid. , IV (Sept. , 1822), cols.
        816-25.

[Watkins, John]. Memoirs of the Life and Writings of the Right
    Honourable Lord Byron, with Anecdotes of Some of His Con-
    temporaries. London: Printed for Henry Colburn & Co. ,
    1822.
Reviews:
    Literary Chronicle, IV (June 1, 1822), 343-44; ibid. , IV
        (June 8, 1822), 360-62.
    Museum; or, Record of Literature, Fine Arts, Science, An-
        tiquities, the Drama, etc. , I (June 15, 1822), 113-15.
    Rambler's Magazine, I (July, 1822), 318-23.
    European Magazine, LXXXII (Sept. , 1822), 255-59.
    Belle Assemblée, 2nd ser. , XXVI (Supp. to 1822), 530-32.
    Gentleman's Magazine, XCIII, Part I (Feb. , 1823), 149.

                                1823

Byron, George Gordon, Lord.   "Heaven and Earth, " Liberal, II,
    1823.
Reviews:
    [Albany Fontblanque?], Examiner, Dec. 29, 1822, pp. 818-22.
    [John Wilson], Blackwood's, XIII (Jan. , 1823), 72-77.
    Edinburgh Magazine, n. s. , XII (Jan. , 1823), 9-16.
    Gentleman's Magazine, XCIII, Part I (Jan. , 1823), 43-44.
    [Thomas Noon Talfourd], Lady's Magazine, 2nd ser. , IV
        (Jan. , 1823), 19-21.
    Literary Chronicle, V (Jan. 4, 1823), 8-11.
    Literary Gazette, Jan. 4, 1823, pp. 2-5.
    Literary Museum, II (Jan. 4, 1823), 1-3.

_____. The Age of Bronze; or, Carmen Seculare et Annus Haud
    Mirabilis. London: Printed for John Hunt, 1823.
Reviews:
    Examiner, March 30, 1823, pp. 217-18.
    Edinburgh Magazine, n. s. , XII (April, 1823), 483-88.
    Monthly Review, C (April, 1823), 430-33.
    [John Wilson], Blackwood's, XIII (April, 1823), 457-60.
    Edinburgh Literary Gazette, I (April 5, 1823), 141-42.
    Literary Chronicle, V (April 5, 1823), 209-10.
    Literary Gazette, April 5, 1823, pp. 211-13.
    Literary Museum, II (April 5, 1823), 209.
    Literary Register, April 5, 1823, pp. 209-10.
    British Magazine, I (May, 1823), 114-19.
    Monthly Magazine, LV (May, 1823), 322-25.

_____. "The Blues, " Liberal, III, 1823.
Reviews:
    Literary Chronicle, V (April 26, 1823), 257-59.
    Literary Museum, II (April 26, 1823), 257-59.
    Literary Gazette, May 3, 1823, p. 275.
    Literary Register, May 3, 1823, pp. 273-75.
    John Bull, May 4, 1823, pp. 141-42.

_____. The Island; or, Christian and His Comrades. London:
Printed for John Hunt, 1823.
Reviews:
New Monthly Magazine, 2nd ser., VIII (1823), 136-41.
Lady's Magazine, 2nd ser., IV (June, 1823), 347-48.
[Albany Fontblanque?], Examiner, June 16, 1823, pp. 394-96.
Literary Chronicle, V (June 21, 1823), 385-87.
Literary Gazette, June 21, 1823, pp. 389-91.
Literary Museum, II (June 21, 1823), 385-86.
Literary Register, June 28, 1823, pp. 405-406.
British Critic, 2nd ser., XX (July, 1823), 16-22.
British Magazine, I (July, 1823), 195-200.
Monthly Review, 2nd ser., CI (July, 1823), 316-19.
New European Magazine, III (July, 1823), 47-51.

_____. Don Juan, Cantos VI, VII and VIII. London: Printed
for John Hunt, 1823.
Reviews:
Portfolio (London), I (1823), 330-33, 343-48.
[J. G. Lockhart], Blackwood's, XIV (July, 1823), 88-92.
Monthly Review, 2nd ser., CI (July, 1823), 319-21.
Literary Examiner, I (July 5, 1823), 6-12; ibid., I (July 12,
1823), 23-27.
Literary Chronicle, V (July 19, 1823), 451-53.
Literary Gazette, July 19, 1823, pp. 451-53.
Literary Museum, II (July 19, 1823), 452-53.
Literary Register, July 19, 1823, pp. 451-53.
British Critic, 2nd ser., XX (Aug., 1823), 178-88.
British Magazine, I (Aug., 1823), 273-76.
Edinburgh Magazine, n.s., XIII (Aug., 1823), 190-99.
B., Lady's Magazine, 2nd ser., IV (Aug., 1823), 462-64.
New European Magazine, III (Aug., 1823), 126-28.
John Bull, III (Aug. 31, 1823), 280.
Gentleman's Magazine, XCIII, Part II (Sept., 1823), 250-52.
Monthly Magazine, LVI (Sept., 1823), 112-15.
J. G. B., Minerva, II (Sept. 20, 1823), 190-91.

_____. "Morgante Maggiore." The Liberal, IV, 1823.
Reviews:
Literary Examiner, July 26, 1823, pp. 49-58.
Literary Chronicle, V (Aug. 2, 1823), 481-83.
Literary Museum, II (Aug. 2, 1823), 486-88.

_____. Don Juan, Cantos IX, X, and XI. London: Printed for
John Hunt, 1823.
Reviews:
Literary Examiner, I (Aug. 2, 1823), 65-70; ibid., I (Aug. 9,
1823), 81-85; ibid., I (Aug. 16, 1823), 105-10; ibid., I
(Aug. 23, 1823), 120-23.
Literary Chronicle, V (Aug. 30, 1823), 553-55.
Literary Sketch Book, Aug. 30, 1823, pp. 44-45; ibid., Sept.
6, 1823, pp. 56-58.
[J. G. Lockhart], Blackwood's, XIV (Sept., 1823), 282-93.

British Critic, 2nd ser., XX (Sept., 1823), 524-30.
British Magazine, I (Sept., 1823), 296-99.
Edinburgh Magazine, n.s., XIII (Sept., 1823), *357-*360.
   [Asterisks are in Edinburgh Magazine.]
Gentleman's Magazine, XCIII, Part II (Sept., 1823), 25-52.
Literary Gazette, Sept. 6, 1823, pp. 562-63.
Literary Museum, II (Sept. 6, 1823), 564-65.
Monthly Review, CII (Oct., 1823), 217-20.
J. G. B., Minerva, II (Nov., 1823), 247.
Monthly Magazine, LVI (Dec., 1823), 414-17.

_____. Don Juan, Cantos XII, XIII, and XIV. London: Printed
   for John Hunt, 1823.
Reviews:
   Knight's Quarterly Magazine, I (Oct., 1823), 337-48.
   Monthly Review, 2nd ser., CII (Oct., 1823), 217-21.
   Literary Examiner, I (Nov. 8, 1823), 289-94; ibid., I (Nov.
      15, 1823), 305-309; ibid., I (Nov. 22, 1823), 321-25; ibid.,
      I (Nov. 15, 1823), 337-41.
   British Critic, 2nd ser., XX (Dec., 1823), 662-68.
   New European Magazine, III (Dec., 1823), 530-34.
   Literary Chronicle, V (Dec. 6, 1823), 769-71.
   Literary Gazette, Dec. 6, 1823, pp. 771-73.
   Literary Museum, II (Dec. 6, 1823), 769-70.
   Literary Sketch-Book, Dec. 6, 1823, pp. 257-58; ibid., Dec.
      20, 1823, pp. 296-97.
   Monthly Review, 2nd ser., CIII (Feb., 1824), 212-15.
   Literary Register, Jan. 4, 1823, pp. 5-6; ibid., Jan. 11,
      1823, pp. 22-23.
   John Bull, III (Jan. 12, 1823), 14.
   Council of Ten, III (Feb., 1823), 89.
   [William Hazlitt], ER, XXXVIII (Feb., 1823), 27-48.
   Monthly Magazine, LV (Feb., 1823), 35-39.
   New Monthly Magazine, 2nd ser., VII (Feb., 1823), 353-58.
   Eclectic Review, 2nd ser., XIX (March, 1823), 216.
   Monthly Censor, II (April, 1823), 452-58.

_____. Werner, a Tragedy. London: John Murray, 1823.
Reviews:
   Literary Gazette, Nov. 23, 1822, pp. 740-42.
   Literary Chronicle, IV (Nov. 30, 1822), 753-57.
   Literary Museum, Nov. 30, 1822, pp. 487-500.
   Literary Register, Nov. 30, 1822, pp. 340-42.
   Museum; or, Record of Literature, Fine Arts, etc., I (Nov.
      30, 1822), 497-500.
   [Odoherty], Blackwood's, XII (Dec., 1822), 710-19.
   Drama, III (Dec., 1822), 324-32.
   Edinburgh Magazine, n.s., XI (Dec., 1822), 688-94.
   [Thomas Noon Talfourd], Lady's Magazine, 2nd ser., III
      (Dec. 31, 1822), 662-68.
   Monthly Review, 2nd ser., XCIX (Dec., 1822), 394-405.
   New European Magazine, I (Dec., 1822), 517-27.
   Examiner, Dec. 1, 1822, pp. 754-57; ibid., Dec. 8, 1822,
      pp. 771-74.

European Magazine, LXXXIII (Jan., 1823), 73-76.

Monthly Magazine, LIV (Jan., 1823), 504-507.

New Edinburgh Review, IV (Jan., 1823), 159-74.

Eclectic Review, 2nd ser., XIX (Feb., 1823), 148-55.

British Critic, 2nd ser., XIX (March, 1823), 242-50.

New Monthly Magazine, 2nd ser., VI (1822), 553-55.

Monthly Censor, II (April, 1823), 452-58.

"Account of Lord Byron, by a Citizen of the United States," Lady's
    Magazine, 2nd ser., IV (Sept., 1823), 535-36.

"Anecdotes of Lord Byron," Nic-Nac, I (March 29, 1823), 142;
    ibid., I (April 26, 1823), 172; ibid., I (June 14, 1823), 229;
    ibid., I (Oct. 25, 1823), 370-71.

"Autographs with Biographical Notices, III: Lord Byron," Mirror,
    I (March 22, 1823), 330-31.

Idoloclastes [pseud. for J. G. Lockhart?]. "Lord Byron and Mr.
    Landor," Blackwood's, XIV (July, 1823), 99.

Lacy, John [pseud. for George Darley]. "A Letter to the Drama-
    tists of the Day," London Magazine, VIII (July, 1823), 81-86;
    ibid., VIII (Aug., 1823), 133-41; ibid., VIII (Nov., 1823),
    530-38; ibid., VIII (Dec., 1823), 645-52. [Hostile remarks.]

"The Literary Police Office, Bow Street," London Magazine, VII
    (Feb., 1823), 157-61. [In an imaginary court, Byron is
    charged with a violent assault upon several literary gentle-
    men.]

"Lord Byron," Bell's Weekly Messenger, Sept. 8, 1823, p. 275.

"Lord Byron," John Bull, III (Aug. 10, 1823), 252-53. [Discusses
    the court injunction finally issued to protect Byron against the
    piracy of Don Juan.]

"Lord Byron: Don Juan," Portfolio (Dennie), 5th ser., XVI (Aug.,
    1823), 157-62.

"Memoir," Poems of His Domestic Circumstances, by the Right
    Honourable Lord Byron: To Which are Added Several Choice
    Pieces from his Lordship's Works. London: J. Limbird,
    1823. Pp. iii-vi.

Parry, Thomas. The Beauties of Lord Byron; with a Sketch of
    His Life and a Dissertation on His Genius and Writings. Lon-
    don: J. Sudbury, 1823.
    It contains:
        "A Sketch of his Life," pp. iii-xi.
        "Dissertation on the Works of Lord Byron," pp. 3-15.

"Recent Poetical Plagiarisms and Imitations," London Magazine,
    VIII (Dec., 1823), 597-604; ibid., IX (March, 1824), 277-85.
    [Finds a passage in Childe Harold, III, derived from Christa-
    bel.]

S., R. [pseud. for John Wilson? or J. Gillon?]. "The Candid,
    No. 1," Blackwood's, XIII (Jan., 1823), 108-24. [On The
    Vision of Judgment and The Liberal, I.]

_____. "The Candid, No. 2," Blackwood's, XIII (March, 1823),
    263-75. [On Heaven and Earth.]

Scott, Robert. "Memoir of Lord Byron," Manchester Iris, II
    (April 5, 1823), 111-12.

"Shipwreck," Edinburgh Literary Gazette, I (April 12, 1823), 165.

Simpson, Stephen. The Author's Jewel. Consisting of Essays,
    Miscellaneous, Literary and Moral. Philadelphia: Moses and
    Samuel Thomas, 1823.
    It contains:
        "Byron's Marino Faliero," pp. 27-34; "Byron's Tragedies,"
        pp. 11-25.]

"The Stars of Pisa," London Liberal, I (1823), 9-23. [Considers
    Byron the last man to work any serious effect on public opin-
    ion in England.]

Talfourd, Thomas Noon. "The Living Poets. No. 1: Lord By-
    ron," Lady's Magazine, 2nd ser., IV (Jan., 1823), 3-10;
    ibid., IV (April, 1823), 198-203.

                              1824

Byron, George Gordon, Lord. The Deformed Transformed; a
    Drama. London: Printed for J. and H. L. Hunt, 1824.
    Reviews:
        Weekly Literary Magnet, I (1824), 55-58.
        [Albany Fontblanque?], Examiner, Feb. 15, 1824, pp. 104-106.
        Literary Chronicle, VI (Feb. 18, 1824), 129-31.
        Literary Gazette, Feb. 28, 1824, pp. 131-33.
        Edinburgh Magazine, n. s., XIV (March, 1824), 353-56.
        London Magazine, IX (March, 1824), 315-21.
        Monthly Review, 2nd ser., CIII (March, 1824), 321-24.
        New European Magazine, IV (March, 1824), 255-60.
        Belle Assemblée, 2nd ser., XXIX (April, 1824), 170.
        British Critic, 2nd ser., XXI (April, 1824), 403-14.
        Atlantic Magazine, I (May, 1824), 62-68.
        Universal Review, I (May, 1824), 239-46
        United States Literary Gazette, I (June 1, 1824), 54-57. [Al-
            so a review of Cain.]

_____. Don Juan, Cantos XV and XVI. London: Printed for John and H. L. Hunt, 1824.

Reviews:
Somerset House Gazette and Literary Museum, I (1824), 407-408.

[Albany Fontblanque?], Examiner, March 14, 1824, pp. 163-64; ibid., March 21, 1824, pp. 179-80.

Monthly Review, 2nd ser., CIII (April, 1824), 434-36.

Literary Chronicle, VI (April 3, 1824), 215-17.

Literary Gazette, April 3, 1824, pp. 212-13.

2. DEATH AND AFTERMATH, 1824-1839

1824

"Anecdotes of Lord Byron," Mirror, IV (Supp. No. XCIX, 1824), 136-38.

"Anecdotes of Lord Byron," Portfolio (London), III (1824), 92-93.

"Appearances on Opening the Body of Lord Byron," Mirror, IV (Supp. No. XCIX, 1824), 136.

"Arrival of Byron's Body to England," New Monthly Magazine, 2nd ser., XII (Aug., 1824), 373.

B., J. G. "Lord Byron," Minerva, n. s., I (July 3, 1824), 205-206.

B., L. "Pierce Egan and Lord Byron," European Magazine, LXXXVI (July, 1824), 48-51. [Thinks Byron is not the author of Don Juan or Cain.]

"Biographical Account of Lord Byron," Literary Gazette, May 22, 1824, pp. 329-31.

"Biographical Particulars of Celebrated Persons Lately Deceased: Lord Byron," New Monthly Magazine, XII (June, 1824), 278-80.

Brydges, Sir Egerton. Letters on the Character and Poetical Genius of Lord Byron. London: Longman, Hurst, Rees, Orme, Brown & Green, 1824.
Reviews:
Literary Gazette, July 31, 1824, pp. 481-83.
Belle Assemblée, 2nd ser., XXX (Sept., 1824), 121-22.
Minerva, n. s., II (Jan. 29, 1825), 267-70.
J. G. Lockhart, Blackwood's, XVII (Feb., 1825), 137-44.
Monthly Magazine, LIX (April, 1825), 210-16.

"Byron and Burns; or a Voice from Tartarus," Edinburgh Magazine, 2nd ser., XV (Dec., 1824), 699-702. [A dialogue between Byron and Burns.]

"Byron and Greece," Mirror, IV (Supp. No. XCIX, 1824), 143.

"Byron and Southey, " Blackwood's, XVI (Dec., 1824), 711-15.

"Byron in Greece, " Mirror, IV (Supp. No. XCIX, 1824), 130-34.

Cato [pseud. for George Burgess]. Cato to Lord Byron on the Im-
    morality of His Writings. London: Printed for W. Wetton,
    1824.
Reviews:
    Gentleman's Magazine, XCIV, Part I (Jan., 1824), 49.
    British Review, XXII (Nov., 1824), 345-56.

"Character of Lord Byron, " Lady's Magazine, 2nd ser., V (June,
    1824), 331-32.

"The Characteristics of the Present Age of Poetry, " London Maga-
    zine, IX (April, 1824), 424-27.

Dallas, R. C. Recollections of the Life of Lord Byron, from the
    Year 1808 to the End of 1814; His Early Character and Opin-
    ions, Detailing the Progress of His Literary Career, and in-
    cluding Various Unpublished Passages of His Works. Taken
    from Authentic Documents, in the Possession of the Author.
    To Which is Prefixed an Account of the Circumstances Lead-
    ing to the Suppression of Lord Byron's Correspondence with
    the Author, and His Letters to His Mother Lately Announced
    for Publication. London: Printed for Charles Knight, 1824.
Reviews:
    Universal Review, II (Nov., 1824), 241-59.
    Literary Gazette, Nov. 20, 1824, pp. 738-41; ibid., Nov. 27,
        1824, pp. 758-60.
    Literary Chronicle, VI (Nov. 27, 1824), 753-54; ibid., VI
        (Dec. 4, 1824), 770-72.
    Examiner, Nov. 28, 1824, pp. 754-56.
    Lady's Magazine, 2nd ser., V (Dec., 1824), 651-54.
    Monthly Magazine, LVIII (Dec., 1824), 453-56.
    New Monthly Magazine, 2nd ser., XII (Dec., 1824), 552-53.
    John Cam Hobhouse, Westminster Review, III (Jan., 1825),
        1-35.
    United States Literary Gazette, I (March 15, 1825), 353-54.
    NAR, XXI (Oct., 1825), 300-59.

"Death of Lord Byron, " Bell's Weekly Messenger, May 17, 1824,
    p. 156.

"Death of Lord Byron, " Imperial Magazine, VI (June, 1824), cols.
    584-86.

"Death of Lord Byron, " Lady's Magazine, 2nd ser., V (May, 1824),
    275-76.

"Death of Lord Byron, and a Sketch of His Character, " Rambler's
    Magazine, I (June, 1824), 99-102.

Dibdin, Thomas F. The Library Companion; or, the Young Man's
    Guide, and the Old Man's Comfort, in the Choice of a Li-
    brary. 2 vols. London: Harding, Triphook and Lepard,
    1824. [Byron was the "assassinator of his own fame." At-
    tacks Don Juan but praises other productions.]

A Discourse on the Comparative Merits of Scott and Byron, as
    Writers of Poetry. Delivered before a Literary Institution
    in 1820. Glasgow: R. Malcolm 1824. ["With all his de-
    fects Byron stands as pre-eminent above that class of writ-
    ers of which Scott is the head."]

Dupin, Charles M. "On the Death of Lord Byron," Kaleidoscope,
    n.s., IV (June 15, 1824), 451-52.

"Family of Byron," Mirror, IV (Supp. No. XCIX, 1824), 140-41.

Fletcher, William. Lord Byron's Illness and Death as Described
    in a Letter from William Fletcher to Hon. Augusta Leigh.
    Original in the Roe Collection at Newstead Abbey. Rptd. in
    Portfolio (London), III (1824), 298-300; Westminster Review,
    II (July, 1824), 253-57; Lady's Magazine, 2nd ser., V (Aug.,
    1824), 441-43; Mirror, IV (Supp. No. XCIX, 1824), 134-36;
    Bell's Weekly Messenger, Aug. 16, 1824, p. 258; Polar Star,
    VI (1830), 156-57.

Full Particulars of the Much Lamented Death of Lord Byron, with
    a Sketch of His Life, Character and Manners. London: B.
    Dickinson, 1824.

Gordon, Sir Cosmo. The Life and Genius of Byron. London:
    Knight & Lacey, 1824. Rptd. in Pamphleteer, XXIV (1824),
    176-220.

*Grizzeldina. "Lord Byron, Ladies and Asmodeus," Literary
    Chronicle, VI (Nov. 27, 1824), 744-45. Cf. Jonathan Old-
    worth, ibid., VI (Nov. 27, 1824), 763.

Growler, Geoffrey. "To John Bull on His Sins," John Bull Maga-
    zine, I (Nov., 1824), 162-67. [On Lord Byron's Memoirs,
    his marriage, his departure from Lady Byron.]

Hobhouse, John Cam. Exposure of the Mis-statements contained
    in Captain Medwin's Pretended "Conversations of Lord Byron."
    London: John Murray, 1824.

"Imitation and Plagiarism," Weekly Literary Magnet, I (1824), 72-
    73. Cf. ibid., I (1824), 129-31. [Answer to above article,
    defending Byron against plagiarism.]

Juan. "Poetry No Fiction. No. VI: Don Juan," Belle Assemblée,
    2nd ser., XXX (Oct., 1824), 154-57. [On Haidée.]

"The Late Lord Byron," Kaleidoscope, n. s., IV (May 25, 1824), 397-98. [A memoir from the Irish Times.]

Layman [pseud. for Thomas Bailey, according to the BMC]. A Sermon on the Death of Byron. London: Longman, Hurst, Rees, Orme, Brown & Green, 1824.

Libra. "Lord Byron and Washington Irving," Portfolio (Dennie), 5th ser., XVIII (Aug., 1824), 95-96. [A plagiarism.]

"Life of Lord Byron," Mirror, III (Supp. No. LXXXV, 1824), 337-50. [At the end of article can be found: "Tributes from The Times, The Morning Chronicle, The Morning Herald, The British Press, The Star, The Globe and Traveller, and The Examiner," which were reprinted in Literary Speculum, I (Nov., 1821), 1-9.]

"Lord Byron," American Monthly Magazine, II (July, 1824), 68-71.

"Lord Byron," Bell's Weekly Messenger, July 5, 1824, p. 213. [Arrival of Byron's remains; his will.]

"Lord Byron," Bell's Weekly Messenger, July 12, 1824, p. 219. [Preparations before burial.]

"Lord Byron," Bell's Weekly Messenger, Oct. 25, 1824, p. 338. [Letter to Colonel Stanhope on Byron's escape from the Turks.]

"Lord Byron," Blackwood's, XV (June, 1824), 696-701. [Account of an interview with him in Genoa.]

"Lord Byron," Examiner, May 23, 1824, pp. 321-22. [On The Vision of Judgment.]

"Lord Byron," Examiner, June 6, 1824, pp. 353-54. [On the causes of the separation and a reprint of Sir Walter Scott's estimate of Byron.]

"Lord Byron," Minerva, n. s., I (July 24, 1824), 250-52.

"Lord Byron," Nic-Nac, II (May 22, 1824), 200-205; ibid., II (June 12, 1824), 219-21; ibid., II (July 10, 1824), 253-56.

"Lord Byron," Universal Magazine, XXI (March, 1814), 207. [A political account.]

"Lord Byron and His Disciples," American Monthly Magazine, II (Sept., 1824), 177-85.

"Lord Byron and His Writings," Minerva, n. s., I (Sept. 25, 1824), 395-98.

"Lord Byron: An Obituary Notice," Gentleman's Magazine, XCIV,
Part I (June, 1824), 561-68.

"Lord Byron," Portfolio (London), III (1824), 209-10. [An account
of the hours following Byron's death, from the notebook of a
young Englishman just returned from Greece.]

"Lord Byron in Greece," Westminster Review, II (July, 1824),
225-62. [On the last scenes of Lord Byron's life though it
purports to be a review of The Deformed Transformed.]

"Lord Byron's First Love and Subsequent Marriage," Lady's Magazine, 2nd ser., V (Oct., 1824), 543-44.

"Lord Byron's Grecian Orphan," Bell's Weekly Messenger, July 19,
1824, p. 232. [An anecdote.]

"Lord Byron's Letters," John Bull Magazine, I (Aug., 1824), 41-
42.

"Lord Byron's Poetical Soul," American Monthly Magazine, I
(April, 1824), 289-95. [An estimate of his poetry.]

M., J. "Lord Byron and Mr. Murray," Literary Chronicle, VI
(Nov. 13, 1824), 730-32.

McDermot, Martin. "Preliminary View," The Beauties of Modern
Literature in Verse and Prose; to Which Is Prefixed a Preliminary View of the Literature of the Age. London: Printed
for Sherwood, Jones, & Co., 1824. Pp. 1-104. [Deals with
Moore and Byron.]

Medwin, Thomas. Journal of the Conversations of Lord Byron,
Noted during a Residence with His Lordship at Pisa, in the
Years 1821 and 1822. London: Printed for Henry Colburn,
1824.
Reviews:
  Literary Magnet, II (1824), 365-68.
  Minerva, n. s., I (Aug. 14, 1824), 298-300; ibid., II (Dec.
    25, 1824), 186-88.
  Literary Chronicle, VI (Oct. 23, 1824), 673-75; ibid., VI
    (Oct. 30, 1824), 689-94; ibid., VI (Nov. 6, 1824), 709-12.
    Cf. ibid., VI (Nov. 20, 1824), 743-44. [Makes a correc-
    tion about the duel between Captain Stackpoole and Lieut.
    Cecil.]
  Literary Gazette, Oct. 23, 1824, pp. 673-75; ibid., Oct. 30,
    1824, pp. 694-96; ibid., Nov. 6, 1824, pp. 709-10; ibid.,
    Nov. 13, 1824, pp. 725-26.
  Examiner, Oct. 31, 1824, pp. 689-93.
  Edinburgh Magazine, n. s., XV (May, 1824), 607-*616. [As-
    terisk is in Edinburgh Magazine.]
  Gentleman's Magazine, XCIV, Part II (Nov., 1824), 434-42. Cf.
    Robert Southey, ibid., XCIV, Part II (Dec., 1824), 546-47.

Blackwood's, XVI (Nov. , 1824), 530-36. Cf. Harroviensis,
    ibid. , XVI (Nov. , 1824), 536-40.
Lady's Magazine, 2nd ser. , V (Nov. , 1824), 578-85.
London Magazine, X (Nov. , 1824), 449-62.
New Monthly Magazine, 2nd ser. , XI (Nov. , 1824), 407-
    15.
Universal Review, II (Nov. , 1824), 241-59.
Belle Assemblée, 2nd ser. , XXX (Dec. , 1824), 258.
Ladies' Monthly Museum, 3rd ser. , XX (Dec. , 1824), 304-
    306.
Atlantic Magazine, II (Jan. , 1825), 203-15.
John Cam Hobhouse, Westminster Review, III (Jan. , 1825),
    1-35.
United States Literary Gazette, I (Jan. 15, 1825), 289-92.
NAR, XXI (Oct. , 1825), 300-359.

*Milner, George. Speech on the Probable Fate of Lord Byron's
    Poetical Works, delivered at a Public Literary Society.
    Derby: Printed by J. Drewry, Iron-Gate, 1824.

"Missolonghi, May 2, " New Monthly Magazine, 2nd ser. , XII (Aug. ,
    1824), 355-56. [On the dissection of Byron.]

Murray, John, II. Notes on Captain Medwin's "Conversations with
    Lord Byron. " London: John Murray, 1824.

N. , R. "Personal Character of Lord Byron, " London Magazine,
    X (Oct. , 1824), 337-47. Rptd. in Portfolio (Dennie), 5th
    ser. , XIX (Feb. , 1825), 155-57; ibid. , XIX (March, 1825),
    198-214.

Oldworth, Jonathan. "Lord Byron-Mr. Moore: Byron's Autobi-
    ography, " Literary Chronicle, VI (June 12, 1824), 377-78.

"On the Genius and Writings of Lord Byron, " European Magazine,
    LXXXVI (July, 1824), 9-14.

"Original Anecdote of Lord Byron, " Belle Assemblee, 2nd ser. ,
    XXX (Nov. , 1824), 198.

"Particulars of the Destruction of Lord Byron's MSS of His Life, "
    Bell's Weekly Messenger, May 24, 1824, p. 164.

"The Public and Domestic Life of the Late Right Honourable George
    Gordon, Lord Byron, with an Authentic Account of His Resi-
    dence in the Greek Islands, " Portfolio (London), IV (Nov. 13,
    1824), 145-60.

"Recollections of Lord Byron, " Mirror, III (June 26, 1824), 417-
    23.

"Reflections on Viewing the Funeral of Lord Byron, " Portfolio
    (London), III (1824), 236-37.

"Remarks on the Death of Lord Byron," Edinburgh Magazine, n. s.,
   XIV (May, 1824), 611-12.

"Robert Burns and Lord Byron," London Magazine, X (Aug., 1824),
   117-22. Rptd. in Portfolio (Dennie), 5th ser., XVIII (Nov.,
   1824), 386-93.

S. "[Mistake Respecting Lord Byron]," Christian Observer, XXIV
    (Oct., 1824), 619-20. [Shelley, not Byron, wrote atheistic
    inscription in album at Hotel d'Anglaterre at Chamouni.]

Scott, Sir Walter. "The Death of Lord Byron," Edinburgh Weekly
    Journal, May 19, 1824. Rptd. in Pamphleteer, XXIV (1824),
    169-73; Literary Chronicle, VI (May 29, 1824), 345-46;
    Mirror, III (June 5, 1824), 377-79; Portfolio (London), III
    (1824), 118-20, Miscellaneous Prose Works of Sir Walter
    Scott, Bart., 6 vols., Edinburgh: Cadell & Co., London:
    Longman, 1827, IV, 393-461.

Sheppard, John. Thoughts, Chiefly Designed as Preparative or
    Persuasive to Private Devotion. London: G. & W. B. Whit-
    taker, 1824. [Note E of the first edition was reprinted as
    Note F, with the addition of a long postscript relating to the
    salvation of Lord Byron's soul, including a letter addressed
    by Sheppard to Byron, Nov. 21, 1821, and Byron's reply of
    Dec. 8.]

Simmons, J. W. An Inquiry into the Moral Character of Lord By-
    ron. New York: Bliss & White, 1824. Rptd. London: John
    Cochran, 1826.
    Reviews:
    American Monthly Magazine, II (Nov., 1824), 512-16.
    Atlantic Magazine, II (Dec., 1824), 98-104.
    Literary Chronicle, VIII (April 29, 1826), 268-69.

Styles, John. Lord Byron's Works Viewed in Connexion with
    Christianity, and the Obligations of Social Life: a Sermon
    Delivered at Holland Chapel, Kennington, July 4th, 1824.
    London: Printed for Knight & Lacey, 1824.
    Review:
    Kaleidoscope, n. s., V (Aug. 17, 1824), 49-50.

Tricoupi, Spiridion. "Funeral Oration on Lord Byron, Composed
    and Delivered by Mr. Spiridion Tricoupi," Literary Gazette,
    July 3, 1824, pp. 426-28. Rptd. in New Monthly Magazine,
    2nd ser., XII (Aug., 1824), 353-55; Mirror, IV (Supp. No.
    XCIX, 1824), 138-40.

*Vindex. Captain Medwin Vindicated from the Calumnies of the
    Reviewers. London: William Marsh, 1825.

1825

Ardelius. "Juaniana," London Magazine, XI (Jan., 1825), 82-95.

The Astrologer of the Nineteenth Century; or, Compendium of As-
trology, Geomancy and Occult Philosophy. London: W. C.
Wright, 1825. [Mentions the death of Byron, reflections in-
duced by his death, changes in his person, omens of his
death, an elegy to Byron, and an emblematic representation
of him.]

Benbow, William. A Scourge for the Laureate, in Reply to His In-
famous Letter of the 13th December, 1824, Meanly Abusive
of the Deceased Lord Byron. London: Benbow, 1825.

Blaquiere, Edward. Narrative of a Second Visit to Greece, Including Facts Connected with the Last Days of Lord Byron, Extracts from Correspondence, Official Documents, etc. London: Printed for Geo. B. Whittaker, 1825.
Review:
Literary Chronicle, VII (April 9, 1825), 225-26.

Bowles, William Lisle. A Final Appeal to the Literary Public,
Relative to Pope in Reply to Certain Observations of Mr. Roscoe, in His Edition of that Poet's Works, to Which Are Added,
Some Remarks on Lord Byron's Conversations, as Far as
They Relate to the Same Subject and the Author. In Letters
to a Literary Friend. London: Hurst, Robinson & Co.,
1825.

Brydges, Sir Egerton. An Impartial Portrait of Lord Byron, as a
Poet and a Man, Compared with All the Evidences and Writings Regarding Him, up to 1825. Paris: A. & W. Galignani,
1825.

_____. A Note on the Suppression of Memoirs Announced by the
Author in June, 1825; containing Numerous Strictures on Contemporary Public Characters. Paris: Printed by J. Smith,
1825.

_____. Recollections of Foreign Travel, on Life, Literature,
and Selfknowledge. 2 vols. London: Longman, Hurst, Rees,
1825.

"Byron and Southey," Literary Chronicle, VII (Jan. 8, 1825), 28-
29.

Byron in Greece. Printed Privately, 1825. ["Not published" on
the cover.]

Byroniana. Bozzies and Piozzies. London: Sherwood, Jones &
Co., 1825.

It contains:
"Critique on Corsair," pp. 42-43.
"Critique on Don Juan," pp. 100-104.
"Critique on English Bards and Scotch Reviewers," pp. 31-32.
"Critique on Hours of Idleness," pp. 20-23.
"Critique on Lara," pp. 44-47.
"Notes on Siege of Corinth," pp. 48-52.
"Notes to Cain," pp. 66-73.
"Notes to Corsair," pp. 33-41.
"Note to Age of Bronze," pp. 74-79.
"Note to Beppo," pp. 53-54.
"Note to Don Juan," pp. 83-99.
"Note to English Bards and Scotch Reviewers," pp. 24-30.
"Note to Mazeppa," pp. 55-57.
"Note to Ode to Napoleon Buonaparte," pp. 58-65.

Clinton, George [pseud. for James Bacon]. Memoirs of the Life
   and Writings of Lord Byron. London: James Robins Co.,
   1825.
Review:
   Dublin and London Magazine, I (Sept., 1825), 297-300.

Dallas, R. C. Correspondence of Lord Byron with a Friend, including His Letters to His Mother, Written from Portugal,
   Spain, Greece, and the Shores of the Mediterranean in 1809,
   1810, and 1811. Also Recollections of the Poet by the Late
   R. C. Dallas, Esq., the Whole Forming an Original Memoir
   of Lord Byron's Life, from 1808 to 1814. And a Continua-
   tion and Preliminary Statement of the Proceedings by Which
   the Letters Were Suppressed in England at the Suit of Lord
   Byron's Executors. 3 vols. Paris: A. & W. Galignani,
   1825.
Reviews:
   New Monthly Magazine, 2nd ser., XIII, Part I (Jan., 1825),
      106-11.
   Literary Chronicle, VII (Jan. 8, 1825), 28.
   Blackwood's, XVII (Feb., 1825), 146.
   United States Literary Gazette, II (June 1, 1825), 192-93.
   NAR, XXI (Oct., 1825), 300-359.

"Don Juan and Southey," Minerva, n.s., III (April 9, 1825), 7.
   [About dedication of Don Juan to Southey.]

Evans, John. "Dr. Evans on Byron's Infidelity," Monthly Repository, XX (Jan., 1825), 1-7.

_____. "Postscript on Lord Byron's Rejection of Christianity,"
   Tracts, Sermons and Funeral Orations; including an Attempt
   to Account for the Infidelity of Edward Gibbon, Esq., With a
   Postscript on Lord Byron's Prejudices against Revealed Religion. London: Baldwin, Cradock & Joy, 1825. Pp. 65-84.

F.   "Observations on the Character, Opinions and Writings of Lord
     Byron," Christian Observer, XXV (Feb., 1825), 79-87; ibid.,
     XXV (March, 1825), 151-58; ibid., XXV (April, 1825), 214-
     22; ibid., XXV (May, 1825), 281-88.

Gamba, Peter.   A Narrative of Lord Byron's Last Journey to
     Greece.   London: John Murray, 1825.
     Reviews:
        Literary Gazette, Jan. 22, 1825, pp. 49-51.
        J. G. Lockhart, Blackwood's, XVII (Feb., 1825), 144-49.
        Belle Assemblée, 3rd ser., I (March, 1825), 124.
        New Monthly Magazine, 2nd ser., XV (March, 1825), 125.

Hazlitt, William.   "Lord Byron," The Spirit of the Age.   London:
     H. Colburn, 1825.   Pp. 157-81.

Hooper, John.   "Defence of Byron," Newgate Monthly Magazine, II
     (Sept., 1825), 30-34.

[Iley, Matthew?].   The Life, Writings, Opinions and Times of the
     Right Hon. George Gordon Noel, Lord Byron: Including in
     Its Most Extensive Biography, Anecdotes, and Memoirs of the
     Lives of the Most Eminent and Eccentric, Public and Noble
     Characters and Courtiers of the Present Polished and En-
     lightened Age and Court of His Majesty King George the Fourth.
     In the Course of the Biography is Also Separately Given, Cop-
     ious Recollections of the Lately Destroyed Manuscript original-
     ly Intended for Posthumous Publication, and Entitled "Memoirs
     of My Own Life and Times," by the Right Hon. Lord Byron.
     By an English Gentleman, in the Greek Military Service and
     Comrade of His Lordship.   Compiled from Authentic Docu-
     ments and from Long Personal Acquaintance.   3 vols.   Lon-
     don: Matthew Iley, 1825.
     Review:
        Belle Assemblée, 3rd ser., I (Supp. to 1825), 294-97.

[Kilgour, Alexander, according to BMC].   Anecdotes of Lord By-
     ron, from Authentic Sources; with Remarks Illustrative of His
     Connection with the Principal Literary Characters of the Pre-
     sent Day.   London: Knight & Lacey, 1825.
     Review:
        Literary Chronicle, VII (May 21, 1825), 326.

The Literary Sketch-book; consisting of Reviews of Popular Works;
     Original Sketches of Characters, Manners and Society, Hu-
     morous, Satirical, and Sentimental; Historical Anecdotes;
     Poetry, Choice and Original; Specimens of Wit, Humour, etc.
     London: William Crawford, 1825.
     It contains:
        "Review of Don Juan, Cantos IX-XI," pp. 44-45, 56-57.
        "Review of Don Juan, Cantos XII-XIV," pp. 257-58, 296-97.
        "Sketch of Byron," pp. 273-74, 319-20.

Lockhart, J. G. "Remarks on the Character of Lord Byron,"
    Blackwood's, XVII (Feb., 1825), 131-51.

"Lord Byron," Christian Monthly Spectator (New Haven), VII (Sept.,
    1825), 450-52. [On the correspondence between Lord Byron
    and Mr. Sheppard.]

"Lord Byron," United States Literary Gazette, I (Jan. 15, 1825),
    300-301.

"Lord Byron at Florence," Lady's Magazine, 2nd ser., VI (Aug.,
    1825), 451-52.

"Lord Byron in a Storm," Minerva, n.s., II (Jan. 1, 1825), 203-
    204.

"Lord Byron's Character and Writings,"[1] NAR, XXI (Oct., 1825),
    300-359. Rptd. separately, London: Sherwood, Gilbert &
    Piper, 1826. [A review of Dallas' Recollections of the Life
    of Lord Byron, Dallas' Correspondence, and Medwin's Con-
    versations.]

"Lord Byron's Poems," NAR, XX (Jan., 1825), 1-47. [A review
    of the 1815 edition of Lord Byron's works published in New
    York.]

M., J. "Lord Byron. George Gordon Byron, Lord Byron of
    Rochdale, in the County of Lancaster," Annual Biography and
    Obituary, IX (1825), 254-327. [A biography of Byron.]

[Mudie, Robert]. "Death and Character of Lord Byron," Attic
    Fragments. London: Knight & Lacey, 1825. Pp. 46-55.

"North American Review, No. xlvi," Portfolio (Dennie), XIX (Feb.,
    1825), 121-25. [Analyzes the causes of the general regret
    felt at his death.]

The Olla Podrida. London: Lupton Relfe, 1825.
    It contains:
        "An Apology for Lord Byron," pp. 146-48.
        "On the Death of Lord Byron," pp. 342-44. [A poem.]
        "On Lord Byron's Don Juan," pp. 74-76.

"Original Anecdote of Lord Byron," Literary Chronicle, VII (June
    11, 1825), 377.

"Original Anecdotes of Lord Byron," Belle Assemblée, 3rd ser.,
    I (Jan., 1825), 15-16.

Parry, William. The Last Days of Lord Byron. London: Knight

---

[1]Yale University ascribes this article to W. Phillips, but Harvard
Library ascribes it to Andrews Norton.

& Lacey, 1825.
Reviews:
    Circulator, 1825, pp. 390-93.
    Literary Chronicle, VII (May 7, 1825), 289-91; ibid., VII
        (May 14, 1825), 309-11.
    Literary Gazette, May 7, 1825, pp. 290-92; ibid., May 14,
        1825, pp. 311-12.
    Belle Assemblée, 3rd ser., I (June, 1825), 263.
    Gentleman's Magazine, XCV, Part I (June, 1825), 517-21.
    Literary Magnet, IV (June, 1825), 131-32.
    Blackwood's, XVIII (Aug., 1825), 137-55.
    Leicester Stanhope, Examiner, April 2, 1826, p. 212.

"Sophia Hyatt, the White Lady," Mirror, VI (Oct. 8, 1825), 250-
    51. [A woman who avowed that her only pleasure consisted
    in roaming through Newstead and in tracing the spots that
    Byron had been familiar with.]

Stanhope, Leicester Fitzgerald Charles. Greece in 1823 and 1824;
    Being a Series of Letters and Other Documents on the Greek
    Revolution Written during a Visit to that Country.... Lon-
    don: Sherwood, Gilbert & Piper, 1825.
It contains:
    George Finlay, "Reminiscences of Lord Byron," pp. 501-29.
    Leicester Stanhope, "Sketch of Lord Byron," pp. 530-51.

Waddington, George. A Visit to Greece in 1823 and 1824. Lon-
    don: John Murray, 1825.

                                    1826

"Anecdote of Byron," Mirror, VII (March 18, 1826), 174. [An ac-
    count by West, the painter.]

Bowles, William Lisle. Lessons in Criticism to William Roscoe,
    Esq., F.R.S., Member of the Della Crusca Society of Flor-
    ence, F.R.S.L., in Answer to His Letter to the Rev. W. L.
    Bowles, on the Character and Poetry of Pope ... With fur-
    ther Lessons in Criticism to a Quarterly Reviewer. London:
    Hurst, Robinson & Co., 1826.

"Byron Papers," Blackwood's, XIX (March, 1826), 335-43. Rptd.
    partly in Literary Chronicle, VIII (Feb. 4, 1826), 75-76;
    ibid., VIII (Feb. 11, 1826), 92-93. [On Rousseau and Byron;
    Byron and Drury Lane, etc.]

Cartwright, John. The Life and Correspondence of Major Cart-
    wright, ed. Frances D. Cartwright. 2 vols. London: Henry
    Colburn, 1826.

A Cosmopolite. "Lord Byron in the Greek Islands," Dublin and
    London Magazine, II (Feb., 1826), 68-70.

Emerson, James, Count Pecchio, and W. H. Humphreys. A Pic-
    ture of Greece in 1825; as Exhibited in the Personal Narra-
    tive of James Emerson, Count Pecchio and W. H. Humphreys.
    2 vols. London: Henry Colburn, 1826.

"Essay on Lord Byron," Tales of Chivalry and Romance. Edin-
    burgh: James Robertson; London: B. Cradock & Joy, 1826.
    Pp. 291-99.

Hazlitt, William. Notes of a Journey through France and Italy,
    1824-1815. London: Hunt & Clarke, 1826.

Kelly, Michael. Reminiscences of Michael Kelly, of the King's
    Theatre and Theatre Royal Drury Lane. London: H. Col-
    burn, 1826.

*"Lecture on Byron," Metropolitan Quarterly Magazine, I (1826),
    457-78.

"Letters and Conversations of Lord Byron," Literary Chronicle,
    VIII (April 1, 1826), 200-202. [Extract from J. J. Coulman's
    Fragment of a Journey to Italy in 1823, published in a French
    periodical.]

"Lord Byron and His Writings," Spirit and Manners of the Age, I
    (June 24, 1826), 385-90.

"Lord Byron and Percy B. Shelley," Spirit and Manners of the Age,
    I (March 4, 1826), 144. [They were two important triflers
    and eminent madmen.]

"Lord Byron's Visit to the Sandwich Islands," Mirror, VII (March
    25, 1826), 185-86.

"Memoir of Lord Byron," Dublin and London Magazine, II (May,
    1826), 230-31.

N. , H. "Cant of Lord Byron," Spirit and Manners of the Age, I
    (June 17, 1826), 369-72.

"North American Review on Lord Byron's Works and Pinkney's
    Poetry," London Magazine, XIV (Feb. , 1826), 224-29.

"Observations on the Literary and General Character of Lord By-
    ron," Lady's Magazine, 2nd ser. , VI (March, 1826), 167.

"Original Anecdotes of Lord Byron," Edinburgh Magazine, n. s. ,
    XVIII (June, 1826), 704-706.

Palma, Count Alerino. Greece Vindicated; in Two Letters, to
    Which Are Added, by the Same Author, Critical Remarks on
    the Works Recently Published on the Same Subject by Messrs.
    Bulwer, Emerson, Pecchio, Humphrey, Stanhope, Parry and

Blaquiere. London: James Ridgeway, 1826.

Remarks on Cain. Not published, [1826?]. [In the Harvard Li-
    brary.]

"Sketches of Biography and Character: The Right Hon. Lord Noel
    Byron," Spirit and Manners of the Age, I (Feb. 25, 1826),
    113-18.

West, Edward. "Lord Byron's Last Portrait--with Records of His
    Conversation, etc., during his Sitting," New Monthly Maga-
    zine, 2nd ser., XVI (1826), 243-48.

"The Works of the Right Hon. Lord Byron," New York Review, II
    (April, 1826), 325-39. [A review of the 8 volume edition
    published by H. W. Pomeroy in Philadelphia in 1825.]

                                1827

B., J. "Lord Byron's Poetry," Monthly Repository, 2nd ser., I
    (Dec., 1827), 868-70.

"Byron and Other Poets Compared," Mirror, X (July 7, 1827), 2-3.

Country Curate [pseud. for Erskine Neale]. "The Sorrows of a
    Rich Old Man," The Living and the Dead. London: C.
    Knight, 1827. Pp. 161-96.

"Passages Marked in Montaigne's Essays, by Lord Byron," New
    Monthly Magazine, 2nd ser., XIX (Jan., 1827), 26-32; ibid.,
    2nd ser., XIX (March, 1827), 240-45.

[Smith, James]. "A Portrait: Lord Byron," New Monthly Maga-
    zine, 2nd ser., XIX (April, 1827), 382-84.

                                1828

Angelo, Henry. The Reminiscences of Henry Angelo. 2 vols.
    London: H. Colburn, 1828-1830. [Recollections of his fenc-
    ing master.]

Aston, James and Edward. "Dissertation on Lord Byron," Pompeii,
    and Other Poems. London: Longman & Co., 1828. Pp.
    169-83.

"Byron and Shelley," Censor, I (Oct. 4, 1828), 38-41; ibid., I
    (Oct. 18, 1828), 49-51.

"Byroniana," Literary Gazette, May 24, 1828, pp. 332-33; ibid.,
    June 7, 1828, pp. 364-65; ibid., June 14, 1828, pp. 380-81;
    ibid., June 21, 1828, pp. 395-96; ibid., Sept. 20, 1828,

pp. 604-605.

D'Israeli, Isaac. "Preface," The Literary Character, Illustrated
by the History of Men of Genius, Drawn from Their Own
Feelings and Confessions. 4th ed. London: Henry Colburn,
1828.

French, B. F. "Biographical Memoir," The Beauties of Lord Byron, Selected from His Works to Which Is Prefixed a Biographical Memoir of His Life and Writings. Philadelphia:
W. F. Geddes, 1828. Pp. iii-vii.

Howe, Samuel G. M. D. An Historical Sketch of the Greek Revolution. New York: White, Gallaher & White, 1828.

Hunt, Leigh. Lord Byron and Some of His Contemporaries; with
Recollections of the Author's Life and of His Visit to Italy.
London: Henry Colburn, 1828.
Reviews:
Lady's Magazine, 2nd ser., IX (Jan., 1828), 38-42.
Monthly Review, 3rd ser., VII (Jan., 1828), 300-12.
New Monthly Magazine, 2nd ser., XXII (Jan., 1828), 84-96.
Literary Gazette, Jan. 5, 1828, pp. 6-8; ibid., Jan. 19,
    1828, pp. 54-56.
Examiner, Jan. 27, 1828, pp. 51-53.
Dublin and London Magazine, IV (Feb., 1828), 23-29.
London Magazine, XXI (Feb., 1828), 211-33.
Monthly Literary Journal, Feb., 1828, pp. 46-53.
Blackwood's, XXIII (March, 1828), 362-408.
J. W. Croker, QR, XXXVII (March, 1828), 402-26.
Literary Magnet, IV (March, 1828), 18-41.
W. B. O. Peabody, NAR, XXVIII (Jan., 1829), 1-18. Rptd.
    partly in Extractor, II (April 11, 1829), 168-71; Polar
    Star, II (1829), 168-71.

"A Letter from Lord Byron Lately Brought to Light," Lady's Magazine, 2nd ser., IX (July, 1828), 384-85. [Dated at Monte-
nero, Villa Dupuy, June 10, 1822, to D'Israeli.]

"Lord Byron and the Bible," Imperial Magazine, X (Aug., 1828),
cols. 699-701.

"Lord Byron at Missolonghi," Mirror, XII (Oct. 18, 1828), 245-47.

"Lord Byron's First Love," Mirror, XII (Nov. 1, 1828), 286.

"Lord Byron's Interview with a Monk," Mirror, XII (Oct. 11, 1828),
239-40. Rptd. in Polar Star, n.s., III (1830), 120-21. [A
rather romanticized and highly improbable dialogue in which
Father Paul in Greece tries to persuade Byron to return to
England and to believe in God.]

"Lord Byron's Monument," Atheneum, Sept. 24, 1828, pp. 751-52; ibid., Oct. 1, 1828, pp. 767-68.

[Maurice, F. D.]. "Sketches of Contemporary Authors. No. XII: Lord Byron," Atheneum, April 8, 1828, pp. 351-52.

Sheldrake, T. "Lord Byron," Lancet, XIV (Sept. 20, 1828), 779-84. Rptd. as "Lord Byron-Theatricals," New Monthly Magazine, 2nd ser., XXIX (Sept., 1830), 294-303.

"Singular Anecdote of Lord Byron," Censor, I (Sept. 6, 1828), 14. [Byron shot at a schoolfellow for looking at his club-foot.]

"Sydney's Letter to the King"; and Other Correspondence, Connected with the Reported Exclusion of Lord Byron's Monument from Westminster Abbey. London: James Cawthorn, 1828.

                                    1829

Albrizzi, Isabella Teotochi. "Character of Lord Byron," Extractor, I (Feb. 7, 1829), 516-18. [A translation of a passage from her Ritratti Scritti.]

Gordon, Pryse Lockhart. "Sketches from the Portfolio of a Sexagenarian," New Monthly Magazine, 2nd ser., XXVI (Aug., 1829), 191-200. [On Lord Byron and Sir Walter Scott.] Rptd. in his Personal Memoirs: or, Reminiscences of Men and Manners at Home and Abroad, during the Last Half Century; with Occasional Sketches of the Author's Life; Being Fragments from the Portfolio of P. L. Gordon. 2 vols. London: Henry Colburn & R. Bentley, 1830.

"Lord Byron and M. Casimir Delavignie," Foreign Quarterly Review, IV (Aug., 1829), 470-83. [On Marino Faliero.]

Nathan, I. Fugitive Pieces and Reminiscences of Lord Byron: Containing an Entire New Edition of the "Hebrew Melodies," with the Addition of Several Never before Published; the Whole Illustrated with Critical, Historical, Theatrical, Political, and Theological Remarks, Notes, Anecdotes, Interesting Conversations, and Observations, Made by that Illustrious Poet: Together with His Lordship's Autograph; Also Some Original Poetry, Letters, and Recollections of Lady Caroline Lamb. London: Printed for Whittaker, Treacher & Co., 1829.

Newman, John Henry. "Poetry with Reference to Aristotle's Poetics," London Review, I (1829), 153-71. Rptd. in his Essays, Critical and Historical. 2 vols. London: B. M. Pickering, 1871. Pp. 1-29.

"Original of the Shipwreck in Don Juan," United Service Journal,

I (Feb., 1829), 221-27. [Reply to the A. A. Watts'
article of 1821 which appeared in the Literary Gazette.]
Rptd. in Extractor, I (Feb. 14, 1829), 556-59; Spectator,
CXXXIX (Nov. 26, 1927), 924-25.

"The Poetry of Thought. Lord Byron's Cain," London University
Magazine, I (1829), 144-57.

"Remarkable Deliverance of Lord Byron, from an uninhabited Island in the Adriatic Sea," Court Journal, I (Sept. 12, 1829),
308. Rptd. as "Singular Event in Lord Byron's Life," in
Polar Star, 2nd ser., I (1829), 370.

"Traits of Lord Byron," Polar Star, I (1829), 126-27.

1830

Byron, Isabella, Lady. Remarks Occasioned by Mr. Moore's "Notices of Lord Byron's Life." London: Richard Taylor,
printer, Red Lion Court, Fleet St., 1830. Rptd. in New
Monthly Magazine, XXVIII (April, 1830), 374-76.

"Byron and Shelley on the Character of Hamlet," New Monthly Magazine, 2nd ser., XXIX (Oct., 1830), 327-36. Rptd. in Polar
Star, V (1830), 416-21.

Campbell, Thomas. "Notices of the Life of Lord Byron by Mr.
Moore, and Remarks on those Notices by Lady Byron," New
Monthly Magazine, 2nd ser., XXVIII (April, 1830), 377-82.
Cf. "Byron and His Critics," Atheneum, April 10, 1830, pp.
209-10; Fraser's Magazine, I (April, 1830), 356-59; ibid., I
(May, 1830), 484-88; Monthly Magazine, 2nd ser., IX (April,
1830), 384-87; ibid., IX (May, 1830), 512-16. [Items related
to the Campbell article.]

Fairfield, Summer L. "The Young Poets of Britain," Abaddon,
the Spirit of Destruction; and Other Poems. New York:
Sleight & Robinson, 1830. Pp. 135-57.

Galt, John. The Life of Lord Byron. London: Colburn & Bentley,
1830.
Reviews:
Gentlemen's Magazine, C, Part II (Sept., 1830), 249-51.
Atheneum, Sept. 4, 1830, pp. 552-55.
H. Brougham, ER, LII (Oct., 1830), 228-30.
Fraser's Magazine, II (Oct., 1830), 347-70.
Monthly Magazine, 2nd ser., X (Oct., 1830), 399-402.
American Monthly Magazine, II (Dec., 1830), 594-602.
Monthly Review, 3rd ser., XV (Dec., 1830), 240-52.
Charles Webb Le Bas, British Critic, 4th ser., IX (April,
1830), 257-324.

See also:
       John Galt, "Galt's Life of Lord Byron," New Monthly Maga-
       zine, 2nd ser., XXIX (Oct., 1830), 386-87. [A letter
       from Galt to the editor.] Cf. John Cam Hobhouse, ibid.,
       XXIX (Nov., 1830), 502-503. [Letter: Hobhouse to editor.]

_____. "Pot versus Kettle. Remarks on Mr. Hobhouse and
       Mr. Galt's Correspondence Respecting Atrocities in the Life
       of Lord Byron," Fraser's Magazine, II (Dec., 1830), 533-42.
       [About Byron's having left Teresa destitute, which Hobhouse
       denied.]

Grant, Harding. Lord Byron's "Cain, a Mystery": With Notes,
       wherein the Religion of the Bible Is Considered in Reference
       to Acknowledged Philosophy and Reason. London: William
       Crofts, 1830.
       Reviews:
       Monthly Magazine, 2nd ser., X (Oct., 1830), 465-66.
       Fraser's Magazine, III (April, 1831), 285-304.

Hazlitt, William. Conversations of James Northcote, Esq., R.A.
       London: H. Colburn & R. Bentley, 1830.

Heber, Reginald. The Life of Reginald Heber, by His Widow. 2
       vols. New York: Protestant Episcopal Press, 1830. [Touches
       on Heber's reviews of Byron's works.]

Keightly, Thomas. History of the War of Independence in Greece.
       2 vols. Edinburgh: Constable & Co., London: Hurst,
       Chance & Co., 1830. Vol. II, pp. 181-84.

Kennedy, James. Conversations on Religion with Lord Byron and
       Others. Held in Cephalonia, a Short Time Previous to His
       Lordship's Death. London: John Murray, 1830.
       Reviews:
       Fraser's Magazine, II (Aug., 1830), 1-9.
       Monthly Review, 3rd ser., XIV (Aug., 1830), 475-89.
       Amateur (Boston), I (Aug. 21, 1830), 77-78.
       Monthly Repository, 2nd ser., IV (Sept. 1830), 605-13.
       Christian Remembrancer, XIV (May, 1832), 257-64.
       W. B. O. Peabody, NAR, XXXVI (Jan., 1833), 152-88.

"Lord Byron in Italy," Court Journal (London), April 10, 1830,
       pp. 226-28. [Specially translated from the Memoirs of a
       Celebrated French Woman.] Rptd. in Amateur, July, 1830,
       pp. 26-27.

Lord Byron Vindicated and Mr. Campbell Answered. London:
       Marsh and Miller, 1830. [In answer to Thomas Campbell's
       defense of Lady Byron in the New Monthly Magazine above.]

Moore, Thomas. Letters and Journals of Lord Byron, with Notices
       of His Life. 2 vols. London: John Murray, 1830.

Reviews of Vol. I:
Literary Gazette, Jan. 16, 1830, pp. 33-38; ibid., Jan. 23,
    1830, pp. 53-55; ibid., Feb. 13, 1830, pp. 100-101.
Mirror, XV (Supp. No. CDXI, 1830), 49-64.
Atheneum, Jan. 23, 1830, pp. 34-36; ibid., Jan. 30, 1830,
    pp. 49-50.
Asiatic Journal, 2nd ser., I (Feb., 1830), 145-55.
Blackwood's, XXVII (Feb., 1830), 389-420; ibid., XXVII
    (March, 1830), 421-54.
Gentleman's Magazine, C, Part I (Feb., 1830), 146-50.
Ladies' Museum, I (Feb., 1830), 107-10.
Monthly Magazine, IX (Feb., 1830), 183-97.
Monthly Repository, 2nd ser., IV (Feb., 1830), 125-28.
Monthly Review, 3rd ser., XIII (Feb., 1830), 217-37.
Fraser's Magazine, I (March, 1830), 129-43.
Thomas Love Peacock, Westminster Review, XII (April, 1830),
    269-304.
Hugh Swinton Legaré, Southern Review, V (May, 1830), 463-
    522. Rptd. as "Lord Byron's Character and Writings," in
    Writings of Hugh S. Legaré. 2 vols. Charleston, S. C.:
    Burgess & James, 1846. Vol. II, pp. 356-410.
Belle Assemblée, 3rd ser., XI (June, 1830), 289-91.
Western Monthly Review, III (June, 1830), 647-63.
W. O. B. Peabody, NAR, XXXI (July, 1830), 167-99. Rptd. The
    Literary Remains of the late W. B. O. Peabody. Boston:
B. H. Green; New York: C. B. Norton, 1850. Pp. 30-61.

Reviews of Vol. II:
Atheneum, Dec. 25, 1830, pp. 800-804; ibid., Jan. 8, 1831,
    pp. 22-24.
Belle Assemblée, 3rd ser., XIII (Jan., 1831), 72-79.
Gentleman's Magazine, CI, Part I (Jan., 1831), 64-67.
J. G. Lockhart, QR, XLIV (Jan., 1831), 168-226.
Edinburgh Literary Journal, II (Jan. 8, 1831), 19-23; ibid.,
    II (Jan. 15, 1831), 38-40; ibid., II (Feb. 5, 1831), 89-91.
Tatler, II (Jan. 12, 1831), 445-46; ibid., II (Jan. 13, 1831),
    449-51; ibid., II (Jan. 14, 1831), 453-55; ibid., II (Jan.
    15, 1831), 457-58.
Monthly Magazine, 2nd ser., XI (Feb., 1831), 145-59.
Monthly Review, 4th ser., I (Feb., 1831), 217-37.
New Monthly Magazine, 2nd ser., XXXI (Feb., 1831), 159-64.
Oliver Yorke, Fraser's Magazine, III (March, 1831), 238-52.
Charles Webb Le Bas, British Critic, 4th ser., IX (April,
    1831), 257-324. Rptd. separately as Review of the Life
    and Character of Lord Byron: London: J. G. Rivington,
    1833. [Both volumes are reviewed.]
Hugh Swinton Legaré, Southern Review, VII (May, 1831), 1-
    42. Rptd. as "Lord Byron's Letters and Journals," in
    Writings of Hugh S. Legaré, 2 vols. Charleston, S. C.:
    Burgess & James, 1864. Vol. II, pp. 411-48.
Thomas Babington Macaulay, ER, LIII (June, 1831), 544-72.
    Rptd. in Selections from the "Edinburgh Review," ed.
    Maurice Cross. 4 vols., London: Longman, Rees, 1833,

I, 548-68; Macaulay's Critical and Miscellaneous Essays,
5 vols., Philadelphia: Carey & Hart, 1841-1844, I, 328-
61.

G. W. Blagden, American Quarterly Observer, II (April,
1834), 291-308.

"Remarks on Byron's Sardanapalus," Blackwood's, XXVII (Feb.,
1830), 141-42.

Roche, Eugenius. London in A Thousand Years; With Other Poems.
London: Colburn & Bentley, 1830. [Contains a short letter
from Byron, dated July 21, 1807, not included in Prothero's
Letters and Journals.]

                                  1831

Bagnall, Edward. "Introductory Observations," Lord Byron, with
Remarks on His Genius and Character. Oxford: D. A. Tal-
boys, 1831.

Beste, John Richard Digby. "The Infidelity and Catholicism of
Lord Byron," Satires and Beggar's Coin. London: Hurst,
Chance & Co., 1831. Pp. 159-71.

Bulwer-Lytton, Edward George. The Siamese Twins. A Satirical
Tale of the Times, with Other Poems. London: Henry Colburn & Richard Bentley, 1831. [Differences between Byron
and his imitators.]

Hunt, Leigh. "Lord Byron, Mr. Moore, and Mr. Leigh Hunt,
with Original Letters not in Mr. Moore's Work," Tatler, II
(Jan. 11, 1831), 441-43. Rptd. in Leigh Hunt's Literary
Criticism, eds. Lawrence H. Houtchens and Carolyn W.
Houtchens. New York: Columbia University Press, 1956.
Pp. 302-43.

Inglis, Henry D. Switzerland, the South of France, and the Pyre-
nées in 1830. 2 vols. Edinburgh: Constable & Co., 1831.
[Contains an account of Byron's visit to the Castle of Chillon.]

Knowles, John. The Life and Writings of Henry Fuseli. 3 vols.
London: Henry Colburn & R. Bentley, 1831. [Byron asked
Fuseli where to find the subject of his picture of Ezzelin.]

"Lord Byron's English Bards and Scotch Reviewers," Atheneum,
Sept. 10, 1831, pp. 585-86. [Various readings of several
editions.]

"Lord Byron's Venetian Mistress," Olio, VII (Feb. 12, 1831), 86-
88. [A translation of Marquis di Salvo's Lord Byron en
Italie et en Grèce.]

Millingen, Julius. Memoirs of the Affairs of Greece; containing
    an Account of the Military and Political Events which Oc-
    curred in 1823 and Following Years. With Various Anec-
    dotes Relating to Lord Byron, and an Account of His Last
    Illness and Death. London: Printed for John Rodwell, 1831.
    Reviews:
        Monthly Review, 4th ser., I (Jan., 1831), 92-112.
        QR, XLIV (Jan., 1831), 168-226.
        A. V. Millingen, New Englander, XXXVIII (Sept. 1879), 637-
        54.

Percy. "Religious Opinions of Byron," New England Magazine, I
    (July, 1831), 63-68, 112-18.

"Performance of Byron's Tragedy Werner," New Monthly Magazine,
    2nd ser., XXXIII (Jan., 1831), 22.

"Remarks on the Unjust Conduct of the Public Toward Lord Byron,"
    Olio, VII (July 2, 1831), 404-406.

Williams, D. E. The Life and Correspondence of Sir Thomas
    Lawrence. 2 vols. London: Henry Colburn & Richard Bent-
    ley, 1831. [Lord Byron's Cain the subject of conversation.]

                                1832

Blessington, Marguerite Power Farmer Gardiner, Countess of.
    "Conversations of Lord Byron with Lady Blessington," New
    Monthly Magazine, XXXV (July, 1832), 5-23; ibid., XXXV
    (Aug., 1832), 129-46; ibid., XXXV (Sept., 1832), 228-41;
    ibid., XXXV (Oct., 1832), 305-19; ibid., XXXV (Dec., 1832),
    521-44; ibid., XXXVII (Feb., 1833), 214-22; ibid., XXXVII
    (March, 1833), 308-18; ibid., XXXVIII (June, 1833), 143-53;
    ibid., XXXVIII (July, 1833), 305-15; ibid., XXXIX (Sept.,
    1833), 33-46; ibid., XXXIX (Dec., 1833), 414-22.

[Chamier, Frederick]. The Life of a Sailor. 3 vols. London:
    R. Bentley, 1832.

"English Translation of Byron's Letter to the Pasha of Patras,
    Jan. 23, 1824," Mirror, XX (Nov. 3, 1832), 290.

Hamilton, Lady Anne. Secret History of the Court of England,
    from the Accession of George the Third to the Death of
    George the Fourth. 2 vols. London: W. H. Stevenson,
    1832.

"Lord Byron's Juvenile Poems," Fraser's Magazine, VI (Sept.,
    1832), 183-204. [A review of the first seven volumes of the
    14 volume edition of The Works of Lord Byron published by
    Murray in 1832.]

P. , A. "A Mystery--for the Byron Critics, " Monthly Magazine,
    2nd ser. , XIII (March, 1832), 291-97. [On the similarities
    between Pickersgills's The Three Brothers and Lord Byron's
    The Deformed Transformed.]

"A Roland for an Oliver, " Arnolds' Magazine of Fine Arts, III
    (May, 1832), 401-408. [On Lord Byron's opinion of paint-
    ing.]

Southey, Robert. "Two Letters concerning Lord Byron, " Essays,
    Moral and Political. 2 vols. London: John Murray, 1832.
    Vol. II, pp. 183-205. [To the editor of the Courier, 1822,
    1824.]

Taylor, John. Records of My Life. 2 vols. London: Edward
    Bull, 1832. [Personal reminiscences and letters.]

[Trelawny, Edward John]. Adventures of a Younger Son. 2 vols.
    New York: J. & J. Harper, 1832.

                            1833

Bulwer-Lytton, Edward George. England and the English. 2 vols.
    London: R. Bentley, 1833.

"A Cast of Casti, by Lord Byron, " New Anti-Jacobin, I (April,
    1833), 30-54. [A translation of Casti's Diavolessa (pp. 35-
    54) is presented as evidence that this poem is the source of
    Byron's Don Juan.]

"The Celebrated but Hitherto Unpublished Poem of Lord Byron on
    Mr. Rogers, " Fraser's Magazine, VII (Jan. , 1833), 81-84.
    ['Question and Answer" is introduced and quoted.]

Coleridge, Samuel Taylor. Specimens of the Table-Talk of the
    Late Samuel Taylor Coleridge, ed. H. N. Coleridge. New
    York: Harper, 1833.

Cross, Maurice (ed.). Selections from the "Edinburgh Review. "
    4 vols. London: Longman, Rees, 1833.
    It contains:
    Francis Jeffrey, review of Childe Harold's Pilgrimage, III, I
        pp. 191-99. Rptd. from ER, XXVII (Dec. , 1816), 277-
        310.
    Francis Jeffrey, review of Manfred, I, 477-88. Rptd. from
        ER, XXVIII (Aug. , 1817), 418-31.
    John Wilson, review of Childe Harold's Pilgrimage, IV, I
        447-59. Rptd. from ER, XXX (June, 1818), 87-120.
    Francis Jeffrey, a review of Sardanapalus, The Two Foscari,
        Cain, I, 199-207, 459-64. Rptd. from ER, XXXVI (Feb. ,
        1822).
    William Hazlitt, a review of Heaven and Earth, I, 207-10.

Rptd. from ER, XXXVIII (Feb., 1823), 27-48.

Cunningham, Allan. "Byron," Atheneum, Nov. 16, 1833, p. 771.
    Rptd. in his Biographical and Critical History of the British
    Literature of the Last Fifty Years, Paris: Baudry's Foreign
    Library, 1834, pp. 94-100; Literary Journal (Providence), I
    (May 31, 1834), 409.

Galt, John. The Autobiography of John Galt. 2 vols. London:
    Cochrane & M'Crone, 1833.

Halleck, FitzGreene. "Life of Lord Byron," The Works of Lord
    Byron, in Verse and Prose, including His Letters, Journals,
    etc., with a Sketch of His Life. New York: George Dear-
    born, 1833. Pp. xv-xxviii. [This life reprinted in 1835 &
    1837. It can also be found in The Works of Lord Byron.
    Hartford: S. Andrus & Son, 1847, 1848, 1850 and other edi-
    tions.]

Madden, Richard Robert. "Byron," The Infirmities of Genius, Il-
    lustrated by referring to the Anomalies in the Literary Char-
    acter, to the Habits and Constitutional Peculiarities of Men
    of Genius. London: Saunders & Otley, 1833. 2 vols. Vol.
    II, pp. 105-202.

Medwin, Thomas. The Shelley Papers: Memoir of Percy Bysshe
    Shelley. London: Whittaker, Treacher & Co., 1833.

T., L. "The Effect of Criticism on Authors," Mirror, XXII
    (Sept. 14, 1833), 163-64.

                              1834

Angelo, Henry. Angelo's Picnic; or Table Talk. London: John
    Ebers, 1834. [Reminiscences of the fencing master.]

Baker, W. H. The Merits of Pope, and the Poets of the Reign of
    Queen Anne, Compared with those of Byron, and the Poets of
    the Last Thirty Years ... Being the Essay to Which the
    Prize, Given by the Nottingham Literary Society Was Awarded,
    April 14, 1834. Nottingham: J. Staveley, 1834.

Blessington, Marguerite Power Farmer Gardiner, Countess of.
    Conversations of Lord Byron with the Countess of Blessington.
    London: H. Colburn, 1834. [First published serially.] A
    later edition has title, A Journal of the Conversations of Lord
    Byron with the Countess of Blessington, A New Edition, Re-
    vised and Annotated. To Which is Prefixed a Contemporary
    Sketch of Lady Blessington, by Her Sister, and a Memoir of
    Her, by the Editor of this Edition. London: Bentley & Son,
    1893.

Reviews:
    Monthly Review, 4th ser., I (Jan., 1834), 97-109.
    New Monthly Magazine, 2nd ser., XL (Jan., 1834), 97-98.
    Gentleman's Magazine, n.s., I (April, 1834), 347-58; ibid.,
        n.s., I (June, 1834), 583-93.

Browne, James Hamilton. "Voyage from Leghorn to Cephalonia
    with Lord Byron," Blackwood's, XXXV (Jan., 1834), 56-57.

_____. "A Narrative of a Visit to the Seat of War in Greece,"
    Blackwood's, XXXVI (Sept., 1834), 392-407.

Brydges, Sir Egerton. The Autobiography, Times, Opinion, and
    Contemporaries of Sir Egerton Brydges. 2 vols. London:
    Cochrane and M'Crone, 1834.

Byroniana. The Opinions of Lord Byron on Men, Manners, and
    Things; with the Parish Clerk's Album, Kept at His Burial
    Place, Hucknall Torkard. London: Hamilton, Adams, 1834.

Carlyle, Thomas. Sartor Resartus. London: James Fraser, 1834.

"Cowper and Byron," Atheneum, Aug. 9, 1834, pp. 594-95.

Galt, John. The Literary Life and Miscellanies of John Galt.
    3 vols. Edinburgh: Blackwood; London: T. Cadell, 1834.

Medwin, Thomas. The Angler in Wales; or, Days and Nights of
    Sportsmen. 2 vols. London: Richard Bentley, 1834. [Con-
    tains some anecdotes of Lord Byron.]

Taylor, Sir Henry. "Preface," Philip Van Artevelde, a Dramatic
    Romance in two parts. 2 vols. London: E. Moxon, 1834.
    Vol. I, pp. iv-xvi. [An anti-Byronic estimate.]

                                    1835

Bulwer-Lytton, Henry. "Life of Lord Byron," The Complete Works
    of Lord Byron. Reprinted from the Last London Edition, Con-
    taining besides, the Notes and Illustrations by Moore, W.
    Scott, Campbell, ... To Which is Prefixed a Life, by Henry
    Lytton-Bulwer. Paris: A. & W. Galignani, 1835; 1837;
    1842. Pp. xi-xxxiii. Rptd. in *Select Poetical Works of
    Lord Byron, London: Adam Scott, 1848; The Poetical Works
    of Lord Byron, Containing "The Giaour," "Bride of Abydos"
    ... Also Several Attributed and Suppressed Poems not In-
    cluded in other Editions, London: Henry G. Bohn, 1851, pp.
    xi-xlviii; Johnson's Lives of the English Poets, Completed by
    William Hazlitt, 4 vols., London: Nathaniel Cooke, the Na-
    tional Illustrated Library, 1854, IV, 204-40.

Butler, William Joseph. "An Essay on the Poetry of Pope and
     Byron, " Roche Abbey, and Other Poems, with a Few Essays
     in Prose, Which Have Been Read before the Literary Society
     of Nottingham. Nottingham: J. Hicklin, 1835. Pp. 27-47.

D. , A. "Conversations of an American with Lord Byron, " New
     Monthly Magazine, 2nd ser. , XLV (Oct. , 1835), 193-203,
     291-302. [Reminiscences of an American woman who met
     him in Florence.]

Mackintosh, Sir James. Memoirs of the Life of Sir James Mackin-
     tosh, ed. Robert James Mackintosh. 2 vols. London: E.
     Moxon, 1835.

[Stith, Catherine P.] "Lord Byron, " Knickerbocker, VI (Aug. ,
     1835), 171-72.

Willis, Nathaniel Parker. Pencillings by the Way: Written During
     Some Years of Residence and Travel in France, Italy, Greece,
     Asia Minor, Turkey, and England. 3 vols. London: John
     Macrone, 1835.

1836

"Byron and his Traducers, " American Monthly Magazine, n. s. , II
     (Nov. 1836), 491-98. [Tries to determine the origin of the
     dislike for Byron. A defence.]

Chateaubriand, Francois Auguste René, Vicomte. Sketches of Eng-
     lish Literature; with Considerations on the Spirit of the
     Times, Men and Revolutions. 2 vols. London: H. Colburn,
     1836. [A few critical comments.]

Mitford, John. The Private Life of Lord Byron: Comprising His
     Voluptuous Amours, Secret Intrigues, and Close Connection
     with Various Ladies of Rank and Fame, in Scotland and Lon-
     don, at Eton, Harrow, Cambridge, Paris, Rome, Venice, etc.
     London: H. Smith, 1836.

Ruskin, John. "Essay on Literature, " 1836 [Byron, Shakespeare
     excepted, the greatest poet that ever lived.] First published
     in The Works of John Ruskin, eds. E. T. Cook and Alex-
     ander Wedderburn. "Library Edition. " 39 vols. London:
     George Allen; New York: Longmans, Green & Co. , 1903-
     1912. Vol. I, pp. 357-75.

1837

"Byron's Memoirs, " New Monthly Magazine, 2nd ser. , LI (Sept. ,
     1837), 131-32.

Cottle, Joseph. Early Recollections; Chiefly Relating to the Late
    S. T. Coleridge, during His Long Residence in Bristol. 2
    vols. London: Longman, Rees, and Hamilton, Adams & Co.,
    1837.

Cunningham, George Godfrey. "Lord Byron," Lives of Eminent
    and Illustrious Englishmen. 8 vols. Glasgow: A. Fullarton
    & Co., 1837. Vol. VIII, pp. 295-305.

Lockhart, J. Gibson. Memoirs of the Life of Sir Walter Scott.
    7 vols. Edinburgh: R. Cadell; London: John Murray, 1837-
    1838.

Simmons, James W. "Byron and Lady Blessington," Southern Lite-
    rary Journal, III (Feb., 1837), 414-19. [Remarks suggested
    by Lady Blessington's Conversations.]

Spencer, Archdeacon. "On the Life and Writings of Lord Byron."
    Keepsake, 1837, pp. 211-19.

Tuckerman, Henry Theodore. "Byronia [sic]," Italian Sketch-book.
    Boston: Light & Stearns, 1837. Pp. 211-17.

                                1838

Bulwer-Lytton, Edward. "The Present State of Poetry," Monthly
    Chronicle, I (June, 1838), 309-16. Rptd. in his Critical and
    Miscellaneous Writings. 2 vols. Philadelphia: Lea &
    Blanchard, 1841. Vol. I, pp. 334-50.

Carlyle, Thomas. Critical and Miscellaneous Essays. 4 vols.
    Boston: J. Munroe & Co., 1838-1839. [Scattered references.]

Chorley, Henry F. "Lord Byron," The Authors of England. A
    Series of Medallion Portraits of Modern Literary Characters.
    Engraved from the Works of British Artists by Achille Collas.
    With Illustrative Notes. London: Charles Tilt, 1838. Pp.
    17-26.

Driver, Henry Austen. Byron and "The Abbey." A Few Remarks
    Upon the Poet, Elicited by the Rejection of His Statue by the
    Dean of Westminster: with Suggestions for the Erection of a
    National Edifice to Contain the Monument of Our Great Men.
    London: Longman, 1838.

Grimaldi, Joseph. Memoirs of Joseph Grimaldi, ed. Charles
    Dickens. 2 vols. London: R. Bentley, 1838. [Touches on
    Byron's acquaintance with Grimaldi the clown.]

Knighton, Lady Dorothea Hawker. Memoirs of Sir William Knighton,
    Keeper of the Privy Purse during the Reign of King George
    the Fourth. 2 vols. London: R. Bentley, 1838. [A note of

a conversation between Byron and Sir William, his medical
attendant for a while, in Vol. I, pp. 422-23.]

1839

Blessington, Marguerite Power Farmer Gardiner, Countess of.
"Thoughts on Byron Suggested by a Picture Representing His
Contemplation of the Coliseum," Keepsake, 1839, pp. 180-83.
Rptd. in The Lottery of Life. 3 vols. London: Henry Col-
burn, 1844. III, pp. 251-58.

_____. The Idler in Italy. 2 vols. London: Henry Colburn,
1839.

Brent, H. J. "Byron and His Contemporaries," National Magazine
and Republican Review (Washington), May, 1839, pp. 77-83.
[On Bulwer-Lytton's Life of Byron, but not exactly a review.]

"The Horse in Byron's Mazeppa," Blackwood's, XLVI (Aug., 1839),
174.

Lewis, M[atthew] G[regory]. The Life and Correspondence of M.
G. Lewis, with Many Pieces in Prose and Verse, Never be-
fore Published, ed. Mrs. Margaret Baron-Wilson. London:
Henry Colburn, 1839.

"The Life of Byron," The Complete Works of Lord Byron, including the Suppressed Poems, and Supplementary Pieces Selected
from His Papers after His Death, in One Volume. Paris:
Garnier, 1839. Pp. ix-xxiii.

[Mazzini, Joseph]. "Byron and Goethe," Monthly Chronicle, IV
(Sept., 1839), 242-54. A different translation in Life and
Writings of Joseph Mazzini. 6 vols. London: Smith & Elder 1864-1870. Vol. VI, pp. 61-97. Rptd. in Essays: Selected from the Writings, Literary, Political, and Religious
of Joseph Mazzini. London: W. Scott, 1887. Pp. 83-108.

"Modern English Poetry: Byron, Shelley and Wordsworth," American Biblical Repository, 2nd ser., I (Jan., 1839), 206-38.

Thoughts on What Has Been Called Sensibility of the Imagination,
with Practical Illustrations from the Lives of Petrarch,
Sterne, and Byron; and on Other Subjects. London: Simpkin,
Marshall, 1839.

"Visit to the Chateau of Chillon; Ball at the Tuilleries, Countess
Guiccioli, etc.," Bentley's Miscellany, V (1839), 30-33.

3. DECLINE IN INTEREST AND REPUTATION
1840-1868

1840

B. "Byron's Voyage to Lisbon," Mirror, XXXV (Feb. 22, 1840), 132.

Bunn, Alfred. The Stage: Both Before and Behind the Scenes. 2 vols. London: Lea & Blanchard, 1840. [Bunn was a producer of Byron's plays.]

"Conversations at Weimar upon Lord Byron," Fraser's Magazine, XXII (Nov., 1840), 573-77. [A discussion in the presence of Goethe.]

Dudley, John William Ward, 1st Earl of. Letters of the Earl of Dudley to the Bishop of Llandaff. London: John Murray, 1840. [See especially Letters III, X, XXIV.]

Richardson, David Lester. "On Byron's Opinion of Pope," Literary Leaves, or, Prose and Verse, Chiefly Written in India. Calcutta: Messrs. Thacker & Co., 1840. Vol. I, pp. 123-34.

"The Spirit Pervading the Poetry of Byron," Fireside Companion (1840), 66-70. [An analysis of Byron's misanthropy, which, the author states, is but disguised vanity and love of the world.]

Taylor, Catharine. Letters from Italy to a Younger Sister. 2 vols. London: John Murray, 1840-1841.

W., H. N. "Lord Byron: A Sketch of His Character," Southern Literary Messenger, VI (Jan., 1840), 34-36.

1841

"Byron and Zuleika," Mirror, XXXVII (Jan. 30, 1841), 77-79. [Translated from the French of Benedict Galles for The Mirror.]

H. "Lord Byron," Southern Literary Messenger, VII (Jan., 1841), 32.

Thackeray, William Makepeace. "Memorials of Gormandizing,"
Fraser's Magazine, XXIII (June, 1841), 710-25. [Anti-
Byronic.]

1842

B., J. "The Childe Harold and The Excursion. Does Not Wordsworth's Excursion Contain Poetry of a Higher Grade and More
Finished Execution than Byron's Childe Harold?" London University Magazine, I (April, 1842), 31-63. [Argues in the
affirmative.]

F., T. L. "The Stars that Have Set in the 19th Century: Byron,"
Democratic Review, n. s., X (March, 1842), 225-38.

H., F. A. "Byron's Heroines," Mirror, XL (July 30, 1842), 83-
84.

1843

Carlyle, Thomas. "Lord Byron," Knickerbocker Magazine, XXI
(March, 1843), 199-212. [Collected from the various writings of Carlyle by Francis Copcutt.]

_____. Past and Present. Boston: C. C. Little & J. Brown,
1843.

Holland, John. The Psalmists of Britain: Records, Biographical
and Literary of upwards of 150 Authors Who Have Rendered
the Whole or Parts of the Book of Psalms into English Verse.
With Specimens of the Different Versions and a General Introduction. 2 vols. London: R. Groombridge, 1843. [See
especially Vol. II, pp. 285-87.]

"The Poets of England Who Have Died Young. No. V: Byron in
Greece," Cambridge University Magazine, II (1843), 470-83.

Ruskin, John. Modern Painters. 5 vols. London: Smith, Elder
& Co., 1843-1860.

1844

Broughton, John Cam Hobhouse, Lord. Remarks on the Exclusion
of Lord Byron's Monument from Westminster Abbey. London:
Privately Printed, 1844.

"Burns and Byron," Tait's Edinburgh Magazine, 2nd ser., XI
(Oct., 1844), 622-23.

Chambers, Robert. "Byron," Cyclopaedia of English Literature.
2 vols. Edinburgh: William & Robert Chambers, 1844.
Vol. II, pp. 386-95.

Gordon, Thomas. History of the Greek Revolution. 2 vols. Edinburgh: W. Blackwood; London: T. Cadell, 1844.

Jesse, Captain William. The Life of George Brummell, Esq.,
Commonly Called Beau Brummell. 2 vols. London: Saunders & Otley, 1844.

                              1845

Griswold, Rufus W. "Byron," The Poets and Poetry of England in
the 19th Century. New York: P. F. Collier, [1845]. Pp.
216-17.

Headley, Joel Tyler. Letters from Italy. New York: Wiley &
Putnam, 1845. [In them Headley refers to Byron's life in
Genoa.]

Kinglake, Alexander William. Eōthen; or, Traces of Travel Brought
Home from the East. New York: Wiley & Putnam, 1845.
[Anecdote of Byron in the East.]

Méryon, Charles Lewis. Memoirs of Lady Hester Stanhope, as
Related by Herself in Conversation with Her Physician. 3
vols. London: Colburn, 1845.

Richardson, David Lester. Literary Chit-chat, with Miscellaneous
Poems and an Appendix of Prose Papers. Calcutta: Messrs.
Thacker & Co., 1845.
It contains:
"Lord Byron and His Lady," pp. 118-25.
"Sir Walter Scott and Lord Byron," pp. 168-79.

Tuckerman, Henry Theodore. "Thoughts on the Poets. No. VII:
Byron," Columbian Magazine, III (June, 1845), 275-78. Rptd.
in his Thoughts on the Poets. New York: C. S. Francis,
1846. Pp. 165-74.

Whipple, E. P. "Characteristics of Lord Byron," NAR, LX (Jan.,
1845), 64-86. Rptd. in his Characteristics of Men of Genius,
2 vols. London: Chapman Bros., 1847, I, 245-73; Essays
and Reviews, 2 vols., Boston: Houghton Mifflin, 1850, I,
267-98.

                              1846

Armstrong, James Leslie. The Life of Lord Byron. London:
William Walker, 1846.

Hunt, Leigh. Stories from the Italian Poets. 3 vols. New York:
    Wiley & Putnam, 1846. [See especially Vol. I, pp. 283-314,
    on the Morgante Maggiore.]

Ossoli, Margaret Fuller. Papers on Literature and Art. 2 vols.
    New York: Wiley & Putnam, 1846. [See especially Vol. I,
    pp. 74-81.]

Thackeray, William Makepeace. Notes of a Journey from Cornhill
    to Grand Cairo. London: Chapman & Hall, 1846. [Byron
    never wrote from the heart and was far from being a native
    poet.]

                                1847

Gilfillan, George. "Lord Byron," Tait's Edinburgh Magazine, 2nd
    ser., XIV (July, 1847), 447-54. Rptd. in Eclectic Magazine,
    XI (Aug., 1847), 556-65; Gilfillan's A Second Gallery of Lite-
    rary Portraits, 2nd series, Edinburgh: J. Hogg, 1852, pp.
    27-41.

Medwin, Thomas. The Life of Percy Bysshe Shelley. 2 vols.
    London: Thomas Cautley Newby, 1847.

"The Two Devils: or the Satan of Milton and Lucifer of Byron
    Compared," Knickerbocker Magazine, XXX (1847), 150-55.

                                1848

"Byron's Address to the Ocean," Blackwood's, LXIV (Oct., 1848),
    499-514.

Collins, William Wilkie. Memoirs of the Life of William Collins,
    with Selections from His Journal and Correspondence. 2
    vols. London: Longman, Brown, Green & Longmans, 1848.
    [Anecdotes.]

Jeffrey, Francis. Contributions to the "Edinburgh Review." 3
    vols. London: Longman, Brown, Green and Longmans, 1848.
    It contains:
        Review of Childe Harold's Pilgrimage, III, II, 453-69. Rptd.
            from ER, XXVII (Dec., 1816), 277-310.
        Review of Manfred, II, 128-42. Rptd. from ER, XXVIII
            (Aug., 1817), 418-31.
        Review of Sardanapalus, The Two Foscari, Cain, II, 87-127.
            Rptd. from ER, XXXVI (Feb., 1822), 413-52.

Poe, Edgar Allan. "The Rationale of Verse," Southern Literary
    Messenger," XIV (Nov., 1848), 673-82. Rptd. in The Works
    of Edgar Allan Poe, ed. J. H. Ingram, Edinburgh: A. & C.,
    Black, 1874. III, 246-51.

1849

Barham, Harris Dalton. The Life and Remains of Theodore Edward Hook. 2 vols. London: Richard Bentley, 1849. [An
   anecdote about Byron at Harrow.]

"Byron and Burns," Southern Literary Messenger, XV (March,
   1849), 165-70.

Campbell, Thomas. Life and Letters, ed. William Beattie. 3
   vols. London: Moxon, 1849. [Material about his defense of
   Lady Byron.]

The Inedited Works of Lord Byron, Now First Published from His
   Letters, Journals, and Other Manuscripts in the Possession
   of His Son, Major George Gordon Byron. New York: G. G.
   Byron, R. Martin, 1849.
   Review:
   Literary World (New York), V (Nov. 17, 1849), 422-23; ibid.,
      VI (Feb. 9, 1850), 125-26.

Leatham, William Henry. "Byron, and the Poets of the 19th Century," Concluding Sequel to Lectures Delivered at Literary
   and Mechanics' Institution. London: Longman, Brown, Green
   & Longmans, 1849. Pp. 32-43.

Patmore, P. G. "Personal Recollections of the Late Lady Blessington," Bentley's Miscellany, XXVI (Oct., 1849), 162-75.

Southey, Charles Cuthbert (ed.). The Life and Correspondence of
   the Late Robert Southey. 6 vols. London: Longman, 1849-
   1850.

1850

Anderson, William. "Life of Lord Byron," The Works of Lord
   Byron. 2 vols. Edinburgh: A. Fullarton & Co., [1850].
   Pp. vii-ccxxiv.

Cunningham, Allan. "Life of Lord Byron," Lord Byron's Poetical
   Works. London: Charles Daly, 1850. Pp. iii-xii. Rptd.
   in Lord Byron's "Don Juan," Philadelphia: Willis P. Hazard,
   1856; Lord Byron's Poetical Works, Philadelphia: Davis,
   Porter & Coates, 1866.

Emdee. "Passage in Lara," N&Q, 1st ser., I (Feb. 23, 1850),
   262. [Wonders what Lara saw in his hall that midnight when
   he so alarmed his household with "A sound, a voice, a
   shriek, a fearful call--a long loud shriek and silence," and
   if the Kaled of Lara is not the Gulnare of The Giaour.] Cf.
   Ç. B., ibid., 1st ser., I (March 16, 1850), 324; A. G.,

1st ser. , I (May 4, 1850), 443. [Both give their interpretations.]

Giles, Henry. Lectures and Essays. 2 vols. Boston: Ticknor,
Reed & Fields, 1850.
It contains:
"The Moral Philosophy of Byron's Life, " I, 93-135.
"The Moral Spirit of Byron's Genius, " I, 136-65.

Goethe, Johann Wolfgang von. Conversations of Goethe with Eckermann and Soret, trans. John Oxenford. 2 vols. London:
Smith & Elder, 1850.

Hunt, James Henry Leigh. The Autobiography of Leigh Hunt; with
Reminiscences of Friends and Contemporaries. 3 vols. London: Smith, Elder & Co. , 1850.

Melanion. "Plagiarisms, or Parallel Passages, " N&Q, 1st ser. ,
I (Jan. 12, 1850), 163; ibid. , 1st ser. , I (Feb. 23, 1850),
260. Cf. T. R. M. , ibid. , 1st ser. , I (March 9, 1850),
299. [From Burton and La Rochefoucauld, in Childe Harold.]

Roberts, Arthur. The Life, Letters and Opinions of William
Roberts, Esq. London: Seeleys, 1850. [British Review reviewer.]

Schoolboy. "Byron and Tacitus, " N&Q, 1st ser. , I (April 13,
1850), 390. [Finds a parallel between line 912 of The Bride
of Abydos, "Mark! Where his carriage and his conquest
cease/He makes a solitude, and calls it--peace, " and a
speech of Galgacus.] Cf. W. , ibid. , 1st ser. , I (April 27,
1850), 417. [Wonders where Lord Byron stole stanzas 1, 2,
3, and 4, of The Bride of Abydos, Canto II. Agrees with
Schoolboy, but points out that Byron probably considered the
parallel too well known to acknowledge.] H. W. , ibid. , 1st
ser. , I (May 11, 1850), 462. [Cautions Schoolboy against
reading Byron.]

W. , C. B. "Byron's Birthplace, " N&Q, 1st ser. , II (Nov. 16,
1850), 410. [He was born at 24, Holles St. , and christened
in the small parish church of St. Marylebone.]

1851

Borderer. "Upon the Description of the Medicean Venus in the
4th Canto of Childe Harold's Pilgrimage, stanzas li and lii, "
N&Q, 1st ser. , IV (Aug. 2, 1851), 83. [Thinks it comes
from Lucretius rather than from Ovid.]

Clark, Davis W. "Lord Byron," Deathbed Scenes. New York:
    Lane & Scott, 1851. Pp. 557-59.

Comstock, John L. History of the Greek Revolution. Hartford:
    Silas Andrus & Sons, 1851.

Hare, Augustus William, and Julius Charles Hare. Guesses at
    Truth. Boston: Ticknor, Fields, 1851. [Byron "the prince
    of egotists."]

Henry, James, M.D. "Criticism on the Style of Lord Byron, in
    a Letter to the Editor of Notes and Queries," The Unripe
    Windfalls in Prose and Verse. Dublin: Printed at the Uni-
    versity Press, 1851. [No pagination for this article.]

Moir, David Macbeth. "Byron," Sketches of the Poetical Litera-
    ture of the Past Half Century, in Six Lectures. Edinburgh:
    William Blackwood, 1851. Pp. 162-78.

An Old Bengal Civilian. "Son of the Morning," N&Q, 1st ser.,
    IV (Sept. 20, 1851), 209. [Who was the Son of the Morning
    mentioned in Childe Harold's Pilgrimage, II, iii?] Cf. G. L.
    S., ibid., 1st ser., IV (Oct. 25, 1851), 330; W. W., ibid.,
    1st ser., IV (Nov. 15, 1851), 391. [Give their opinions.]
    An Old Bengal Civilian, ibid., 1st ser., V (Feb. 7, 1852),
    137. [Says the phrase is an orientalism for travellers, in
    allusion to their early rising to avoid the heat of the midday
    sun.]

Smith, T. C. "Byron," N&Q, 1st ser., III (April 26, 1851), 320-
    21. [Poetical coincidences with Thomas Randolph's Jealous
    Lovers, and also with Carew, Lee, and Smollet.]

W., T. "Stanza in Childe Harold," N&Q, 1st ser., IV (Sept. 27,
    1851), 223-25. [Finds lines 4 and 5 of Childe Harold's Pil-
    grimage, IV, clxxxii, "Thy waters wasted them while they
    were free/And many a tyrant since," difficult to understand.]
    Cf. Jas. Crossley, ibid., 1st ser., IV (Oct. 11, 1851), 285;
    T. W., ibid., 1st ser., IV (Oct. 25, 1851), 323-24; Priscian,
    ibid., 1st ser., IV (Oct. 25, 1851), 324-25; Mortimer Col-
    lins, ibid., 1st ser., IV (Oct. 25, 1851), 325; W. W., ibid.,
    1st ser., IV (Oct. 25, 1851), 325; S. Hickson, ibid., 1st
    ser., IV (Nov. 15, 1851), 386; W. W., ibid., 1st ser., IV
    (Nov. 15, 1851), 386-87; Leon, ibid., 1st ser., IV (Dec. 27,
    1851), 508; S. Williamson, ibid., 1st ser., VIII (Sept. 10,
    1853), 258; J. S. Warden, ibid., 1st ser., IX (May 20, 1854),
    481-83; Cervus, ibid., 1st ser., X (Oct. 14, 1854), 314-15;
    W. S. B., ibid., 1st ser., X (Nov. 25, 1854), 434. [Schol-
    ars offer different interpretations of the lines.]

Wordsworth, William. Memoirs of William Wordsworth, ed.
    Christopher Wordsworth. 2 vols. London: Edward Moxon,
    1851.

"Wordsworth, Byron, Scott and Shelley," Harper's Magazine, III
(Sept., 1851), 502-505.

1852

Aeldric. "Something New about Byron," Graham's Magazine, XLI
(Oct., 1852), 384-89. [Much of Byron's popularity was due
to the intrinsic merits of his productions.]

Belfast, Frederick Richard Chichester, Earl of. "Byron," Poets
and Poetry of the 19th Century. London: Longman & Co.,
1852. Pp. 135-65.

"Lady Blessington," Irish Quarterly Review, II (Dec., 1852), 782-
92.

Cockburn, Henry. Life of Lord Jeffrey, with a Selection from His
Correspondence. 2 vols. Edinburgh: A. & C. Black, 1852.

Gilfillan, George. "Lord Byron," Exeter Hall Lectures, VII (Feb.
3, 1852), 409-33.

Jerdan, William. The Autobiography of William Jerdan, M.R.S.L.,
Corresponding Member of the Real Academia de la Historia
of Spain, etc., etc., With Reminiscences and Correspondence
during the Last Fifty Years. 4 vols. London: Arthur Hall,
Virtue & Co., 1852-1853. [Byron's plagiarisms and "memoirs."]

Mitford, Mary Russell. Recollections of a Literary Life; and Selections from My Favorite Poets and Prose Writers. 3 vols.
London: Richard Bentley, 1852.

Ossoli, Margaret Fuller. Memoirs of Margaret Fuller Ossoli.
2 vols. Boston: Phillips, Sampson & Co., 1852. [Con-
siders Thorwaldsen's Byron "the truly beautiful, the ideal
Byron."]

Shelley, Percy Bysshe. The Letters of Percy Bysshe Shelley, with
an Introductory Essay by Robert Browning. London: E.
Moxon, 1852. [Forged letters with references to Byron.]

Warden, J. S. "Siege of Corinth," N&Q, 1st ser., V (June 5,
1852), 534. [Corrects a point in Dr. Moir's Sketches on the
Poetical Literature of the Past Half Century. Thinks that
the visit of Francesca is a supernatural one.]

White, William. The Calumnies of the "Atheneum" Journal Exposed.
Mr. White's Letter to Mr. Murray on the Subject of the Byron, Shelley and Keats Manuscripts. London: W. White,
1852. [Prompted by "Literary Forgeries," Atheneum, March
6, 1852, pp. 278-79.]

1853

Alison, Sir Archibald. "Sir Walter Scott and Lord Byron," Pen
    and Pencil, I (Feb. 12, 1853), 198-200.

"The Destruction of Lord Byron's Memoirs," QR, XCIII (July,
    1853), 311-14. [Letter from the late John Murray to Sir
    Robert Wilmot Horton.]

"An Event in the Life of Lord Byron, by the Author of 'The Un-
    holy Wish,'" New Monthly Magazine, XCIX (Sept., 1853),
    138-50. [A shorter version from the one that appeared in
    Court Journal, Sept. 12, 1829.]

Hillard, George S. "Lord Byron," Six Months in Italy. Boston:
    Ticknor, Reed & Fields, 1853. Pp. 428-36.

Kingsley, Charles. "Thoughts on Shelley and Byron," Fraser's
    Magazine, XLVIII (Nov., 1853), 568-76. Rptd. in his Mis-
    cellanies, 2 vols. London: John W. Parker & Sons, 1859,
    I, 304-24; New Miscellanies, Boston: Ticknor & Fields,
    1860, pp. 106-25.

Moore, Thomas. Memoirs, Journal and Correspondence of Thomas
    Moore, ed. Lord John Russell. 8 vols. Boston: Little,
    Brown & Co., 1853-1856.

"Recollections of Ravenna," Fraser's Magazine, XLVIII (Aug.,
    1853), 186-97.

Russell, William. "Byron," Extraordinary Men: Their Boyhood
    and Early Life. London: Ingram, Cooke & Co., 1853. Pp.
    211-27.

Uneda. "Byron Noticed," N&Q, 1st ser., VIII (July 16, 1853), 55.
    [Asks what relation to the poet was the Lord Byron men-
    tioned in the Apology for the Life of George Ann Bellamy.]

W., I. "Immoral Works by Byron," N&Q, 1st ser., VII (Jan. 15,
    1853), 66. [Calls attention to the 1500 line poem to Thomas
    Moore, called Don Leon.]

Whipple, Edwin P. Lectures on Subjects Connected with Literature
    and Life. Boston: Ticknor, Reed & Fields, 1853.

Willis, N. Parker. Summer Cruise in the Mediterranean. Lon-
    don: T. Nelson, 1853. [Reprint of a great part of the first
    two volumes of Willis's Pencillings by the Way. See especial-
    ly Letter XXII, pp. 196-99.]

1854

Hannay, James. "Byron," Satire and Satirists. London: D. Bogue, 1854. Pp. 241-57.

Lister, T. H. "Byron," Encyclopaedia Britannica. 8th ed. Edinburgh: A. & C. Black, 1854. Vol. VI, pp. 37-42. Rptd. in The Poetical Works of Lord Byron. 10 vols. Boston: Houghton, Mifflin & Co., 1860. Pp. xi-xxxv.

Moore, Thomas. Notes from the Letters of Thomas Moore to His Music Publisher, James Power. New York: Redfield, 1854.

Opie, Amelia. Memorials of the Life of Amelia Opie, Selected and Arranged from Her Letters, Diaries and Other Manuscripts, ed. Cecilia Lucy Brightwell. 2nd ed. Norwich: Fletcher & Alexander; London: Longman, Brown & Co., 1854. [Reminiscences of Lord Byron whom she probably met in 1812.]

Patmore, Peter George. My Friends and Acquaintances; Being Memorials, Mind Portraits, and Personal Recollections of Deceased Celebrities of the 19th Century: With Selections from their Unpublished Letters. 3 vols. London: Saunders & Otley, 1854.

Ruskin, John. Lectures on Architecture and Painting. London: Smith, Elder & Co., 1854.

Sigma. "Byron and La Rochefoucauld," N&Q, 1st ser., IX (April 15, 1854), 347. Cf. Henry H. Breen, ibid., 1st ser., IX (June 10, 1854), 553; C. Forbes, ibid., 1st ser., X (July 8, 1854), 37. [Give parallel passages between them.]

Stowe, Harriet Beecher. Sunny Memories of Foreign Lands. London: Piper, Stephenson & Spence, 1854. [On her meeting Lady Byron.]

Wilson, John. Noctes Ambrosianae, with Memoirs and Notes by R. Shelton Mackenzie. 5 vols. New York: Redfield, 1854. [A series of imaginary colloquies written by Prof. Wilson, containing remarks on Byron's life and works.]
The following items are relevant to Byron:
"Christopher in the Tent," I, 1-30. Rptd. from Blackwood's, V (Aug., 1819), 597-613*.
"Noctes Ambrosianae, No. I," I, 129-54. Rptd. from Blackwood's, XI (March, 1822), 369-*371.
"Noctes Ambrosianae, No. III," I, 175-97. Rptd. from Blackwood's, XI (May, 1822), 601-18.
"Noctes Ambrosianae, No. IV," I, 198-225. Rptd. from Blackwood's, XII (July, 1822), 100-14.
"Noctes Ambrosianae, No. VI," I, 256-73. Rptd. from Blackwood's, XII (Dec., 1822), 693-709.

"Noctes Ambrosianae, No. XV," I, 432-56.   Rptd. from
   Blackwood's, XV (June, 1824), 706-24.
"Noctes Ambrosianae, No. XVI," I, 457-86.   Rptd. from
   Blackwood's, XVI (Aug., 1824), 231-50.
"Noctes Ambrosianae, No. XVII," II, 1-24.   Rptd. from
   Blackwood's, XVI (Nov., 1824), 585-601.
"Noctes Ambrosianae, No. XIX," II, 50-78.   Rptd. from
   Blackwood's, XVII (March, 1825), 366-84.
"Noctes Ambrosianae, No. XXII," II, 117-29.   Rptd. from
   Blackwood's, XVIII (Oct., 1825), 500-508.
"Noctes Ambrosianae, No. XLIX," IV, 1-41.   Rptd. from
   Blackwood's, XXVII (May, 1830), 802-20.

                              1855

A.   "Childe Harold and Gerusalemme Liberata," N&Q, 1st ser.,
     XII (July 14, 1855), 26. [Notices a parallel between Childe
     Harold, IV, lxxviii, and Gerusalemme Liberata, XV, xx.]

Crue, William M.   "Byron: Sardanapalus," N&Q, 1st ser., XI
     (March 10, 1855), 184. [Has a copy of a Latin translation
     of Diodorus Siculus, printed at Leyden, 1559, with Byron's
     autograph. The chapter dealing with Sardanapalus is heavily
     annotated and underlined. A copy that Byron used.]

Eric.   "Lord Byron's Monody on the Death of Sheridan," N&Q, 1st
     ser., XI (June 2, 1855), 423. [Wonders if the closing lines
     are from Ariosto.] Cf. Desultory Reader, ibid., 1st ser.,
     XI (June 30, 1855), 514. [Both think they come from Arios-
     to.]

Holland, Lady Elizabeth Vassall Fox.   A Memoir of the Reverend
     Sydney Smith, by His Daughter Lady Holland, with a Selection
     from His Letters, ed. Mrs. Austin. 2 vols. London: Long-
     man, Brown & Co., 1855.

Macray, John.   "Lord Byron," N&Q, 1st ser., XI (May 5, 1855),
     348. [Anecdotes of his youth.]

Madden, R. R.   The Literary Life and Correspondence of the
     Countess of Blessington. 3 vols. London: T. C. Newby,
     1855.

"Misprints," Household Words, XI (April 7, 1855), 232-38. [Some
     misprints in Byron.]

The Odoherty Papers, annotated by Dr. Shelton Mackenzie. 2 vols.
     New York: Redfield, 1855-57.

Reed, Henry.   "Byron," Lectures on English Literature from
     Chaucer to Tennyson. Philadelphia: Parry & McMillan,
     1855. Pp. 272-92.

Typo. "Lord Byron: His Character," London Investigator, II
(Nov., 1855), 113-18; ibid., II (Dec., 1855), 129-33.

Warden, J. S. "Lord Byron and the Hippopotamus," N&Q, 1st
ser., XII (July 14, 1855), 28. [He must have seen a tapir
instead of a hippopotamus at Exeter Change in 1813.] Cf.
J. T. C., ibid., 1st ser., XII (Aug. 11, 1855), 112.
[Wants to know where he can find the journal in which Byron
mentions having seen a hippopotamus.]

1856

Alison, Sir Archibald. "Scott, Campbell and Byron," Miscellaneous
Essays. Boston: Phillips, Sampson & Co., 1856. Pp. 160-
61. [A rather bombastic essay in which Byron is considered
the poet of passion.]

B., J. M. "Lord Byron's Verses on Sam Rogers in 'Question and
Answer,'" N&Q, 2nd ser., I (March 29, 1856), 253. [Did
Byron really write this poem?]

Burke, James. Life of Thomas Moore. Dublin: J. Duffy, 1856.

Ferguson, John Clarke. Lecture on the Writings and Genius of
Byron. Carlisle: A. Thurman, 1856.

Goodrich, Samuel Griswold. Recollections of a Lifetime. 2 vols.
New York: Miller, Orton & Milligan, 1856.

Rogers, Samuel. Recollections of the Table Talk of Samuel Rogers.
To Which Is Added Porsoniana, ed. Alexander Dyce. New
York: Appleton, 1856.

S., F. "On Sir Archibald Alison's Views of Lord Byron," Fraser's
Magazine, LIV (Aug., 1856), 154-69.

1857

Cleveland, Charles Dexter. "George Gordon Byron," English Literature of the Nineteenth Century. Philadelphia: E. C. & J.
Biddle, 1857. Pp. 115-29.

Irving, Washington. Life and Letters, ed. Pierre M. Irving. 3
vols. New York: G. P. Putnam's Sons, 1857.

"Life of Lord Byron," The Poetical Works of Lord Byron. Edinburgh: Houlston & Wright, 1857. Pp. iii-xiv.

"Literary Men of the Last Half Century," Bentley's Miscellany,
XLI (April, 1857), 343-54.

Napier, William Francis Patrick. The Life and Opinions of Gene-
    ral Sir Charles James Napier. 4 vols. London: John Mur-
    ray, 1857. [Reminiscences of the commander of British
    troops at Cephalonia.]

Reed, Henry. "Byron," Lectures on the British Poets. Philadel-
    phia: Parry & McMillan, 1857. Vol. II, pp. 163-93.

Ruskin, John. Notes on the Turner Collection at Marlborough
    House. London: Smith and Elder, 1857.

Threlkeld. "Was Byron or Scott the Greater Poet?" British Con-
    troversionalist, 2nd ser., IV (1857), 21-26, 68-71, 130-35.

Webster, Daniel. The Private Correspondence of Daniel Webster,
    ed. Fletch Webster. 2 vols. Boston: Little, Brown & Co.,
    1857. [A letter to George Ticknor, April 8, 1833, about
    Moore's Life of Byron, in Vol. I, p. 333.]

                                1858

D. "English Bards and Scotch Reviewers," N&Q, 2nd ser., VI
    (Oct. 16, 1858), 302-303. [On Byron and Ridge, his first
    printer, and 1st edition of Fugitive Pieces.] Cf. Douglas W.
    Seymour, " 'D. of Rotherwood,' An Old Correspondent of
    N&Q," ibid., CLXX (Jan. 25, 1936), 64. [Wants help in
    tracing Fugitive Pieces, or an earlier correspondent who
    signed himself D. Rotherwood.] Gilbert H. Doane, ibid.,
    CLXX (March 7, 1936), 179. [Says that D. of Rotherwood
    may have had at hand the edition that is now at the Pierpont
    Morgan Library. Also asserts that there are four surviving
    copies of the first edition of Fugitive Pieces.]

Gordon, George H. "Byron Note," N&Q, 2nd ser., V (March 20,
    1858), 231-32. [On Byron and Mary Duff.]

O., J. "Parodies on Scott and Byron," N&Q, 2nd ser., VI (Sept.
    11, 1858), 206. [Lists Erasmus' The Outlaw as a parody of
    The Bride of Abydos.]

R., J. "Byron and Aeschylus," N&Q, 2nd ser., V (June 5, 1858),
    454. [Passage in English Bards and Scotch Reviewers begin-
    ning, "So the struck eagle, stretched upon the plain," may
    come from Aeschylus's The Fragments, No. 123.] Cf. Beta,
    ibid., 2nd ser., V (June 19, 1858), 507. [Thinks it comes,
    not from Aeschylus, but from Waller's verses "To a Lady
    Singing a Song of His Composing."] John R. Garstin, ibid.,
    2nd ser., VI (July 10, 1858), 35. [Says Byron was not
    enough acquainted with Aeschylus. Waller more plausible.]
    T. C. Smith, "Byron and Henry Kirke White," ibid., 2nd
    ser., VI (July 24, 1858), 78. [Thinks it may come from Sir
    Roger L'Estrange's Fables of Aesop and Other Eminent
    Mythologists.]

Redding, Cyrus. Fifty Years' Recollections, Literary and Personal. 3 vols. London: Charles J. Skeet, 1858.

Robertson, Frederick William. Lectures and Addresses on Literary and Social Topics. London: Smith, Elder & Co., 1858.

Trelawny, Edward John. Recollections of the Last Days of Shelley and Byron. Boston: Ticknor & Fields, 1858. Subsequently published, with additions and changes, under the title, Records of Shelley, Byron and the Author. 2 vols. London: B. M. Pickering, 1878.
Reviews:
Atheneum, Feb. 27, 1858, pp. 267-69.
Westminster Review, 2nd ser., XIII (April, 1858), 350-69.
Rptd. in Living Age, LVII (May 22, 1858), 580-91.
Richard Garnett, Fortnightly Review, XXIX (June, 1878), 850-66.

1859

Allibone, Samuel Austin. "Byron," A Critical Dictionary of English Literature and British and American Authors. 3 vols. Philadelphia: Childs & Peterson, 1859. Vol. I, pp. 319-24.

Broughton, John Cam Hobhouse, Lord. Italy: Remarks Made in Several Visits from the Year 1816 to 1854. 2 vols. London: John Murray, 1859.

Ellis, Sarah Stickney. "The Mother of Lord Byron," The Mothers of Great Men. London: 1859. [I have consulted the Chatto & Windus edition of 1874. Pp. 378-98.]

[Fitzpatrick, William J.] "Lady Morgan," Irish Quarterly Review, IX (July, 1859), 380-512*. Rptd. with some slight alterations and additions under the title, The Friends, Foes and Adventures of Lady Morgan. Dublin: W. B. Kelly, 1859.

Leighton, Alexander. "The Life of Lord Byron," The Poetical Works of Lord Byron. New York: W. W. Swayne, 1859? Pp. 5-12. Rptd. in The Poetical Works of Lord Byron, with Illustrations by Keeley Halswelle, Edinburgh: William P. Nimmo, London: Simpkin, Marshall & Co., 1861, 1870, 1872, pp. 5-14; The Poetical Works of Lord Byron, 10 vols., Boston: James R. Osgood & Co., 1871, pp. xi-xxxv; The Poetical Works of Lord Byron, Reprinted from the Original Editions, with Life, Explanatory Notes, etc., "The Albion Edition," London: F. Warne & Co., 1881, 1890, pp. v-xii; The Poetical Works of Lord Byron, with Memoir and Explanatory Notes, New York: Thomas Y. Crowell & Co., 1884, 189-?, pp. v-xiv.

Shelley, Percy Bysshe. The Shelley Memorials from Authentic
    Sources, ed. Lady Jane Shelley. London: Smith, Elder &
    Co., 1859.

                              1860

De Vericour. "Notes on Marino Faliero," Dublin University Maga-
    zine, LV (April, 1860), 461-68.

Fitzhugh, G. "Milton, Byron and Southey," De Bow's Commercial
    Review, XXIX (Oct., 1860), 430-40. [On The Vision of Judg-
    ment.]

Leslie, Charles Robert. Autobiographical Recollections, ed. with
    a Prefatory Essay on Leslie as an Artist, and Selections
    from His Correspondence by Tom Taylor, Esq. 2 vols.
    London: John Murray, 1860.

Redding, Cyrus. Literary Reminiscences and Memoirs of Thomas
    Campbell. London: Charles J. Skeet, 1860.

St. Swithin. "Byron and Ridge, His First Publisher," N&Q, 2nd
    ser., X (Nov. 10, 1860), 362-63. [Three letters to Ridge
    never before published, dated Dorant's Hotel, Albemarle St.,
    Jan. 12, 1807; Trinity College, Cambridge, Nov. 29, 1807;
    Dorant's Hotel, Feb. 11, 1808.]

                              1861

"Byrons of Newstead," All the Year Round, V (June 15, 1861),
    282-85.

Finlay, George. History of the Greek Revolution. 2 vols. Edin-
    burgh: W. Blackwood & Sons, 1861.

Jaydee. "Marino Faliero," N&Q, 2nd ser., XII (July 6, 1861),
    19. [Asks who has the MS, to see whether Byron was really
    responsible for the bad grammar in the line "Their heads
    may sodden in the sun."]

Knight, Cornelia. Autobiography of Miss Cornelia Knight, Lady
    Companion to the Princess Charlotte of Wales, with Extracts
    from Her Journals and Anecdote Books. 2 vols. London:
    W. H. Allen & Co., 1861.

[Martineau, Harriet]. "Lady Byron and Mrs. Stowe," Atlantic
    Monthly, VII (Feb., 1861), 185-95.

Piozzi, Mrs. Hester Lynch Thrale. Autobiography. Letters and
    Literary Remains of Mrs. Piozzi, ed. A. Hayward. 2 vols.
    Boston: Ticknor, Fields & Co., 1861.

Robertson, John. "The Poet Byron in a Snow-storm," Atheneum, Nov. 9, 1861, p. 618. [Tells how Byron was nearly lost in a graveyard during a snowstorm when he was a small boy.]

1862

Ainger, Alfred. "Byron's Plagiarisms," N&Q, 3rd ser., II (Dec. 13, 1862), 465-66. [Perhaps the description of the storm at sea and the shipwreck in Don Juan is from Rabelais.]

C., W. "Byron's School Days," N&Q, 3rd ser., II (Nov. 29, 1862), 426-27.

Fr. "Byron's Early Poems," N&Q, 3rd ser., II (Nov. 1, 1862), 346. [On a genuine volume of Poems on Various Occasions, presentation copy to Mr. Pigot.]

Gronow, Captain R. H. "Lord Byron," Reminiscences of Captain Gronow, Being Anecdotes of the Camp, the Court, and the Clubs. London: Smith, Elder & Co., 1862. Pp. 208-12.

Hunt, Leigh. The Correspondence of Leigh Hunt, ed. Thornton Leigh Hunt. 2 vols. London: Smith, Elder & Co., 1862.

Morgan, Lady Sydney. Lady Morgan's Memoirs: Autobiography, Diaries and Correspondence, ed. W. H. Dixon. 2 vols. W. H. Allen & Co., 1862.

1863

Culkin, Peter. "Byron's Plagiarisms," N&Q, 3rd ser., III (Jan. 17, 1863), 55-56. [From Donne's Satires and Mme. de Staël's Corinne, Byron borrowed part of stanzas clxxxii and clxxxix of Childe Harold, IV.]

Pearson, Charles Henry. On the Early Byron and Robert de Barum. London: J. B. Nichols, 1863.

Redding, Cyrus. Yesterday and Today. 3 vols. London: T. Cautley Newby, 1863.

1864

Knight, Charles. Passages of a Working Life during Half a Century: With a Prelude of Early Reminiscences. 3 vols. London: Bradbury & Evans, 1864-1865. [On the injunction forbidding the publication of Dallas' Correspondence of Lord Byron with a Friend.]

Marsden, John Howard. A Brief Memoir of the Life and Writings of William Martin Leake. London: Privately Printed by Whittingham & Wilkins, 1864.

Smith, T. C. "Byroniana," N&Q, 3rd ser., VI (Sept. 24, 1864), 245-46. [His first letter, dated Newstead Abbey, Nov. 8, 1798, and the MS of "Epitaph on a Beautiful Boy" are in the Library of Trinity College.] Cf. Job Y. B. Workard, ibid., 3rd ser., VI (Oct. 8, 1864), 298. [Wonders if the last line of the "Epitaph on a Beautiful Boy" is the original of the inscription found on tombstones that reads: "She sparkled, was exhaled, and went to heaven."]

Turner, Charles Edward. "Byron and Shelley," Our Great Writers: A Course of Lectures upon English Literature. 2 vols. St. Petersburgh: A. Minx, 1864-1865. Vol. II, pp. 262-80.

1865

B., J. "Notes on Fly-leaves," N&Q, 3rd ser., VIII (Dec. 23, 1865), 522. [On a blank page of a copy of Byron's Corsair was written the following: "On Wordsworth's Poems (said to be written by Byron), Here lie the poems of W. W. /There let them lie and ne'er trouble you /trouble you."] Cf. X. Y. Z., ibid., 3rd ser., IX (Jan. 20, 1866), 66-67. [Says that lines appeared in substance in a pseudo Peter Bell, which he proceeds to outline. Article also deals with attacks on Wordsworth to be found in Don Juan.] Silax, ibid., 3rd ser., IX (Feb. 10, 1866), 127. [Did the parody not appear in Blackwood's?] Fitzhopkins, ibid., 3rd ser., IX (Feb. 10, 1866), 127. [Reynolds may have written this parody.]

Berry, Mary. Extracts of the Journals and Correspondence of Miss Berry, from the Years 1783 to 1852, ed. Lady Theresa Lewis. 3 vols. London: Longmans & Co., 1865. [On her acquaintance with Lord Byron whom she met at Lady Glenbervie's in 1812.]

Eassie, W. "Rogers and Byron," N&Q, 3rd ser., VIII (July 22, 1865), 73. [Did Byron write the verses beginning, "Pleasures of Memory! Oh! supremely blest, /And Justly proud, beyond a poet's praise?"] Cf. Lyttleton, ibid., 3rd ser., VIII (July 29, 1865), 98. [Yes.] C. G. Prowett and William J. Thoms, ibid., 3rd ser., VIII (Aug. 5, 1865), 114. [No.]

Timbs, John. "The Eccentricities of Byron," Romance of London. Strange Stories, Scenes and Remarkable Persons of the Great Town. 3 vols. London: Frederick Warne & Co., 1865. Vol. III, pp. 275-76. [Extracted from The Table Talk of Samuel Rogers.]

*Williams, Stephen Frederick. "On Modern Poetry. --Byron's
Manfred," Essayist, 1865, pp. 51-60.

1866

Brown, Matthew. "The Deformed and the Stricken," Good Words,
VII (Nov., 1866), 737-40. [Touches on Byron's lameness.]

Grant, Charles. The Last Hundred Years of English Literature.
London: Williams and Norgate, 1886. Pp. 62-75.

Gronow, Captain R. H. "Lord Byron and Dan Mackinnon," Captain
Gronow's Last Recollections; Being the Fourth and Final
Series of His Reminiscences and Anecdotes. London: Smith,
Elder & Co., 1866. Pp. 100-102. [On the relationship of
these two "dandies."]

Jameson, Anna Brownell Murphy. Studies, Stories and Memoirs.
Boston: Ticknor & Fields, 1866. [It has a review of Eckermann's Conversations with Goethe, with passages on Byron.]

Morley, Henry. The Journal of a London Playgoer from 1851 to
1866. London: G. Routledge & Sons, 1866. [Manfred on the
stage.]

Swinburne, Algernon Charles. "Preface," A Selection from the
Works of Lord Byron. London: Edward Moxon & Co., 1866.
Pp. v-xxix. Rptd. in Essays and Studies. London: Chatto
& Windus, 1875. Pp. 238-58.

1867

Alger, William R. "Byron," The Solitudes of Nature and of Man;
or, The Loneliness of Human Life. Boston: Roberts Bros.,
1867. Pp. 289-304.

Arnold, Matthew. On the Study of Celtic Literature. London:
Smith, Elder & Co., 1867.

Bowring, John. "The Byron Album," N&Q, 3rd ser., XII (Sept.
18, 1867), 241. [An album containing 28 inscriptions in verse
and 36 in prose has disappeared from Hucknall Torkard.]

Buckton, T. J. "False Quantity in Don Juan," N&Q, 3rd ser.,
XII (Aug. 17, 1867), 127. [In the line "And so Zoe spent
her's, as most women do."] Cf. E. B. Nicholson, R. M. C.
and H. B. C., ibid., 3rd ser., XII (Sept. 7, 1867), 197.
[Offer different corrections to the line.] E. L. S., ibid.,
3rd ser., XII (Oct. 5, 1867), 275. [Says that the problem
arises because Byron made Zoe rhyme with snowy and Chloe.]

H., S. "The Conquest of Alhama," N&Q, 3rd ser., XII (Nov. 16, 1867), 391. [Wonders what text Byron followed in his translation of this ballad.] Cf. C. J., ibid., 4th ser., I (Feb. 15, 1868), 162-63. [Gives three ballads mentioned in Pérez de Hita's Guerras Civiles de Granada as possible sources.]

Hazlitt, William Carew. Memoirs of William Hazlitt. With Portions of His Correspondence. 2 vols. London: Richard Bentley, 1867. [Refers to Byron and The Liberal.]

R., A. C. "Byron's Lameness," N&Q, 3rd ser., XII (Sept. 21, 1867), 225. [Wonders what bathing costume Byron wore so that Trelawny did not know until Byron's death the cause of his lameness.]

                                  1868

"Byron in Venice," Once a Week (London), 3rd ser., II (Oct. 10, 1868), 287-90.

McCann, Walter E. "Byronism," Galaxy, V (June 1868), 777-81. [Tries to account for the existence of Byronism and to trace its origin.]

Thomas, Ralph. "Lord Byron," N&Q, 4th ser., I (March 21, 1868), 267. [Pamphlets and squibs on Byron.] Cf. H. Tiedman and James Bladon, ibid., 4th ser., I (April 25, 1868), 397. [Add a few items.]

4. REVIVAL OF INTEREST, 1869-1897

1869

Austin, Alfred. A Vindication of Lord Byron. London: Chapman & Hall, 1869. [Occasioned by Mrs. Stowe's article.]

"Byron at Venice," Atheneum, May 22, 1869, p. 702. [A letter by Richard B. Hoppner, dated at Versailles, May, 1869, stating that Byron went to Greece to get away from Teresa.]

"Byron at Work," Chamber's (Edinburgh) Journal, 4th ser., VI, Part II (Oct. 9, 1869), 645-50. Rptd. in Living Age, CIII (Nov. 20, 1869), 464-69. [Lord Byron as a literary workman.]

"The Byron Case," Saturday Review, XXVIII (Sept. 11, 1869), 343-44; ibid., XXVIII (Sept. 25, 1869), 404-406. [On Lord Lindsay's letters to the Times on Mrs. Stowe's book.]

"The Byron Scandal," Atheneum, Sept. 11, 1869, p. 336. [Pleads for reservation of judgment so long as nothing is proved in Mrs. Stowe's assertions.]

"The Byron Scandal," Tomahawk, V (Sept. 18, 1869), 125-26. [On Mrs. Stowe's revelations.]

"The Byron Story in England," Harper's Weekly, XIII (Oct. 16, 1869), 658-59. [Summarizes the generally negative attitude of the British press about Mrs. Stowe's disclosures, but takes the attitude that the revelation was permissible and a laudable contribution to literary history.]

"Byron versus Stowe," Tomahawk, V (Oct. 2, 1869), 150-51.

"The Byronizers," Spectator, XLII, Part II (Sept. 25, 1869), 1121-22.

"The Byrons and Their Latest Biographer," St. James's Magazine, 2nd ser., IV (Nov., 1869), 133-36. [Finds repugnant the motives of Mrs. Stowe in disclosing Lady Byron's confessions.]

"Byron's Daughter," Argosy, VIII (Nov. 1, 1869), 358-61. [Cor-

respondence between Byron's daughter, Lady Lovelace, and
Mr. Andrew Crosse.]

C. , L. S. "Lady Byron," New Monthly Magazine, CXLIV (April,
    1869), 400-403.

Chance, F. "Byron's Memoirs," N&Q, 4th ser. , IV (Nov. 6,
    1869), 388-89. [Quotes from Teresa's Recollections that
    Lady Blessington had made copies of his memoirs, and also
    that Byron had written five additional cantos of Don Juan.]

Clough, Arthur Hugh. The Poems and Prose Remains of Arthur
    Hugh Clough, with a Selection from His Letters and a Mem-
    oir, ed. His Wife. 2 vols. London: Macmillan & Co. ,
    1869.

"The Countess Guiccioli," Galaxy, VIII (Oct. , 1869), 558-62.

Dodge, N. S. "A Lost Chapter of History," Lippincott's, III
    (June, 1869), 666-73. [Byron's memoirs.]

E. "Lady Byron and Mrs. Beecher Stowe, " Broadway (London),
    2nd ser. , III (Oct. , 1869), 167-85.

"Editions of Byron and Byronana [sic]," American Bibliopolist, I
    (Dec. , 1869), 378-82.

Ellcee. "Byron and Dr. Lavender," N&Q, 4th ser. , III (March 27,
    1869), 284. [Dr. Lavender, the quack doctor with whom By-
    ron lived in Nottingham in an attempt to cure his foot de-
    formity, showed little consideration for Byron, to the point
    of sending him after beer for the family dinner.] Cf. P. P. ,
    ibid. , 4th ser. , III (May, 1869), 418. [Asks for confirma-
    tion of this anecdote.] Ellcee, ibid. , 4th ser. , III (June 12,
    1869), 561. [Says he has the anecdote from a reliable source
    and witness.]

Este. "Byroniana: Sequel to Don Juan," N&Q, 4th ser. , IV (Aug.
    21, 1869), 157. [Who wrote Sequel to Don Juan and An
    Apology for Don Juan?] Cf. S. H. , ibid. , 4th ser. , V
    (March 26, 1870), 329. [An Apology was written by Rev.
    John W. Thomas.]

[Fleck, Dudley]. Light at Last. The Byron Mystery! Mrs.
    Beecher Stowe and Her True History of Lady Byron's Life.
    The Early Life of Lord Byron, Strange Mental Affliction.
    The Solution of Lord Byron's Connection with His Half-sister,
    Augusta. The Real Cause of the Separation Between Lord
    and Lady Byron. His Poems, etc. London: Elliot, 1869.
    [Refuses to believe Mrs. Stowe.]

Forster, John. Walter Savage Landor, a Biography. 8 vols.
    London: Chapman & Hall, 1869.

Fox, John C. "The Bride of Abydos," Temple Bar, XXVIII (Dec.,
1869), 61-91. Rptd. with corrections and additions in his
Vindication of Lady Byron. London: Richard Bentley, 1871.
Pp. 137-205.

_____. "The Character of Lady Byron," Temple Bar, XXVII
(Oct., 1869), 334-54. Rptd. with corrections and additions
in his Vindication of Lady Byron. London: Richard Bentley,
1871. Pp. 69-136.

_____. "Lord Byron," Temple Bar, XXV (Feb., 1869), 364-71.
Rptd. in Eclectic Magazine, LXXII (May, 1869), 547-53.
[First of a series of attacks on Byron by John Fox.]

_____. "Lord Byron's Married Life," Temple Bar, XXVI (June,
1869), 364-93. Rptd. in his Vindication of Lady Byron. London: Richard Bentley, 1871. Pp. 1-68. [The crime of incest is first publicly charged on Lord Byron.]

Friswell, James Hain. "Lord Byron," Essays on English Writers.
London: Sampson Low & Marston, 1869. Pp. 317-27.

Guiccioli, Teresa Gamba, Countess. My Recollections of Lord By-
ron; and Those of Eyewitnesses of His Life, trans. Hubert
E. H. Jerningham. London: Bentley, 1869.
Reviews:
Atheneum, May 16, 1868, pp. 687-89; ibid., April 5, 1873,
p. 439.
Saturday Review, XXV (May 30, 1868), 720-22; ibid., XXV
(June 13, 1868), 788-90.
Every Saturday (Boston), V (June 13, 1868), 745-49.
W. Stigand, Belgravia, VII (Feb., 1869), 491-512.
Chamber's (Edinburgh) Journal, 4th ser., VI, Part I (March
27, 1869), 198-202.
[John Paget], Blackwood's, CVI (July, 1869), 24-33. Rptd.
in Living Age, CII (Aug. 14, 1869), 428-35; Paradoxes and
Puzzles, Historical, Judicial, and Literary. Edinburgh
and London: Blackwood & Sons, 1874. Pp. 264-82.

H., F. C. "Unpublished Letter of Lord Byron," N&Q, 4th ser.,
IV (Sept. 25, 1869), 250-51. [To Douglas Kinnaird, dated
"13bre (sic) 27th, 1823; not in Moore.]

Holtermann, Adolf. "Cain, a Mystery," Critically Examined.
Brunswick: Frederic Vieweg, 1869.

Hone, Heinrich. Remarks on Lord Byron's Life, Character and
Opinions. Munster: Coppewrath, 1869.

"In Defence of Lord Byron," New Monthly Magazine, CXLV (Oct.,
1869), 475-78. [Against Mrs. Stowe's accusations.]

L.   "America--Mrs. Stowe," Atheneum, Sept. 18, 1869, p. 373.
     [Mrs. Stowe's book the great topic of discussion in America.]

L., P. A.   "Unpublished Letter of Byron," N&Q, 4th ser., IV
     (Oct. 9, 1869), 291. [Dated Genoa, April 19, 1823, to a
     correspondent in Leghorn.]

"Lady Byron and Mrs. Stowe," Nation, IX (Sept. 23, 1869), 251-
     52; ibid., IX (Sept. 30, 1869), 271; ibid., IX (Nov. 4, 1869),
     388; ibid., IX (Nov. 18, 1869), 436.

"Lady Noel Byron and Mrs. Beecher Stowe, a Short Chapter of
     'Ifs,' " New Monthly Magazine, CXLV (Oct., 1869), 447-49.

"The Late Lord Byron," Academy, I (Oct. 9, 1869), 1. [Byron's
     letter on the separation drawn up by Byron in Aug., 1817, at
     La Mira, near Venice.] Cf. "Lord Byron and The Academy,"
     Saturday Review, XXVIII (Oct. 16, 1869), 509-10. [On the
     document about the separation drawn by Byron in Venice:
     Why should we believe its contents when he had such disre-
     gard for truth?]

"Letters, &c., of Lord Byron," Sharpe's London Magazine, XLIX
     (Jan., 1869), 10-14; ibid., XLIX (Feb., 1869), 72-74; ibid.,
     XLIX (March, 1869), 123-24; ibid., XLIX (April, 1869), 179-
     81; ibid., XLIX (May, 1869), 235-36; ibid., XLIX (June,
     1869), 291-93; ibid., L (July, 1869), 14-16.

Life of Lady Byron, Compiled from the Best Authorities, together
     with a Summary of the "True Story" Told by Mrs. Harriet
     Beecher Stowe. With Descriptive Matter--Private Letters--
     and Full Particulars of the Great Scandal, to Which is Ap-
     pended a Vindication of Lord Byron, with Correct Portraits
     of Lord and Lady Byron, Their Daughter Ada, and Mrs.
     Stowe. London: G. Purkess, [1869].

"Lord and Lady Byron," Argosy, VIII (Oct. 1, 1869), 274-89.

"Lord Byron," Dublin University Magazine, LXXIII (March, 1869),
     270-86.

"Lord Byron Vindicated," Fraser's Magazine, LXXX (Nov., 1869),
     598-617. [Rejoinder to Mrs. Stowe's True Story.]

Lucas, Samuel (comp.). The Stowe-Byron Controversy: A Com-
     plete Resumé of All That Has Been Written and Said upon the
     Subject, Re-printed from "The Times," "Saturday Review,"
     "Daily News," "Pall Mall Gazette," "Daily Telegraph," etc.
     Together with an Impartial Review of the Merits of the Case.
     By the Editor of "Once a Week." London: Thomas Cooper
     & Co., [1869]. [Also attributed to Eneas Sweetland Dallas.]

M., J. P. "Byron at Banff," N&Q, 4th ser., IV (July 10, 1869), 29-30. [When at Banff, Byron the boy used to play tricks on its inhabitants.]

Mackay, Charles. Medora Leigh; a History and an Autobiography. With an Introduction, and a Commentary on the Charges Brought Against Lord Byron by Mrs. Beecher Stowe. London: Richard Bentley, 1869.

Martineau, Harriet. "Lady Noel Byron," Biographical Sketches. London: Macmillan, 1869. Pp. 282-91.

"Mrs. Beecher Stowe and Lady Byron," Spectator, XLII, Part II (Sept. 4, 1869), 1038-39.

*Moore, J. Sheridan. Byron; His Biographers and Critics; Being the Substance of a Discourse Delivered before the Australian Patriotic Association. Sidney: John Ferguson, 1869.

Mysterious. "Mrs. Beecher Stowe on Lord Byron," Will o' the Wisps, II (Sept. 4, 1869), 294.

An Octogenerian. "Personal Recollections," Under the Crown, Jan., 1869, pp. 69-76. [Recollections of a Harrow school fellow who was also lame.] Rptd. in Living Age, C (Feb. 13, 1869), 416-20.

An Old Irish Lady. "Byron and His 'Memoir,'" N&Q, 4th ser., IV (Nov. 6, 1869), 385-86.

[Palmer, Samuel, according to the Harvard Library Catalogue.] Byron Painted by His Compeers; or, All about Lord Byron, from His Marriage to His Death, as Given in the Various Newspapers of His Day, Shewing wherein the American Novelist Gives a Truthful Account, and Wherein She Draws on Her Own Morbid Imagination. London: Palmer, 1869.

[Quincey, E.]. "The Byron Horror," Nation, IX (Aug. 26, 1869), 167. [A dissection of Mrs. Stowe's article, pointing out some errors.]

————. "Was it Mystification?" Nation, IX (Sept. 2, 1869), 189. [Mrs. Stowe should have let the truth die with her.]

Redding, Cyrus. "Byron and His Libeller," New Monthly Magazine, CXLV (Dec., 1869), 686-92. [Deals severely with Lady Byron and Mrs. Stowe.]

————. "Lord Byron," New Monthly Magazine, CXLV (Nov., 1869), 497-504. [Against Mrs. Stowe's judgment.]

Robinson, Henry Crabb. Diary, Reminiscences and Correspondence, ed. Thomas Sadler. 3 vols. London: Macmillan & Co., 1869.

Russell, W. Clark. The Book of Authors. A Collection of Criti-
    cisms, and Mots, Personal Descriptions, etc., etc., etc.,
    Wholly Referring to English Men of Letters in Every Age of
    English Literature. London: Frederick Warne & Co.,
    [1869?]

S., O. "A Minor Byron Mystery," N&Q, 4th ser., IV (Oct. 23,
    1869), 333-34. [Was the name of Lady Byron's confidential
    friend, Clermont, Claremont, or Charlemont?]

"Sketch of the Life of Lord Byron," The Poetical Works of Lord
    Byron, with Life and Portrait and Sixteen Illustrations. By
    F. Gilbert. London: J. Dicks, 1869. Pp. ix-xv.

"Some Recollections Connected with Byron's Name," New Monthly
    Magazine, CXLIV (May, 1869), 598-610. [Anecdotes of By-
    ron's mother, wife, daughter, and grandson.]

Stowe, Harriet Elizabeth. "The True Story of Lady Byron's Life,"
    Macmillan, XX (Sept., 1869), 377-96. Rptd. in Atlantic
    Monthly, XXIV (Sept., 1869), 295-313.
    Reviews:
        Saturday Review, XXVIII (Sept. 4, 1869), 311-14.
        [A. Hayward], QR, CXXVII (Oct., 1869), 211-33.
        QR, CXXVII (Oct., 1869), 400-44. Rptd. in Living Age,
            CIII (Nov. 20, 1869), 486-508.
        Englishwoman's Domestic Magazine, VIII (Oct. 1, 1869), 194-
            97.
    See also:
        "The True Story of Mrs. Shakespeare's Life," Gentleman's
            Magazine, CCXXVII (Dec., 1869), 63-73. [A squib ridi-
            culing Harriet Beecher Stowe's "True Story of Lady By-
            ron's Life."] Rptd. separately, Boston: Loring Publish-
            ers, 1869.
        Cobb, Clarence F. The Vision of Judgment Revived. Wash-
            ington, D.C., Jan. 19, 1870. [A "rhyme" handling Mrs.
            Stowe without gloves. A satire in two Cantos.]

T., "Interesting Letter of Byron," N&Q, 4th ser., III (June 5,
    1869), 524-25. [Two letters to J. J. Coulmann, one of them
    dated at Genoa, July 12, 1823; not printed by Moore.]

[Tupper, John Lucas]. The True Story of Lord and Lady Byron,
    as Told by Lord Macaulay, Thomas Moore, Leigh Hunt, Lord
    Lindsay, the Countess of Blessington, Thomas Lindsay, the
    Countess Guiccioli, by Lady Byron, and by the Poet Himself,
    in Answer to Mrs. Beecher Stowe. London: John Camden
    Hotten, [1869?].

W., L. R. "Byron's Mystifications," Nation, IX (Sept. 9, 1869),
    210. [A plea not to trust Byron's confessions of evil-doing
    too seriously.]

Wilson, James Grant. The Life and Letters of FitzGreene Halleck.
    New York: D. Appleton & Co., 1869. [On Halleck's early
    biographical memoir of Byron.]

1870

Austin, Alfred. The Poetry of the Period. London: Richard
    Bentley, 1870.

Bernard, Edward. Pedigree of George Gordon, 6th Lord Byron of
    the Family of Burun, or Buron or Byron. London: C. Wil-
    son, 1870.

[Brougham, Marcus]. Autobiography of the Best Abused Man in
    the World. London: Griffith, Farran & Co., 187? [In
    Missolonghi was found an iron box with several letters and
    the autobiography written in Armenian.]

Broughton, John Cam Hobhouse, Lord. A Contemporary Account
    of the Separation of Lord and Lady Byron. Also of the De-
    struction of Lord Byron's Memoirs. London: Privately
    Printed, 1870. Rptd. in his Recollections of a Long Life, ed.
    Lady Dorchester. 6 vols. London: John Murray, 1909-
    1911. Vol. II, pp. 191-366.

"Byron and the Controversy," American Bibliopolist, II (Feb.,
    1870), 69-74. [A series of reprints from other periodicals
    on various aspects of Byron, but mainly on the Stowe contro-
    versy.]

Ellis, A. S. "Shelley and Byron," N&Q, 4th ser., VI (Dec. 3,
    1870), 473. [A note on their common descent from William
    Sidney.]

Elze, Karl. Lord Byron, A Biography. London: David Nutt &
    Co., 1870. Another edition: Lord Byron: A Biography.
    With a Critical Essay on His Place in Literature. Trans-
    lated with the Author's Sanction, and Edited with Notes.
    With Portrait and Facsimile. London: John Murray, 1872.
    Reviews:
    Atheneum, June 25, 1870, pp. 829-30.
    Abraham Hayward, QR, CXXXI (Oct., 1871), 354-92. Rptd.
    in Eclectic Magazine, 2nd ser., XV (Jan., 1872), 1-20;
    as "Byron and Tennyson," in his Sketches of Eminent
    Statesmen and Writers, with Other Essays, 2 vols., Lon-
    don: John Murray, 1880, II, 305-59. Cf. Andrew Lang,
    "Criticism of Eulogy of Byron's Poetry published in the
    Quarterly Review, 1872," Critic, XXIV (March 3, 1894),
    152; ibid., XXIV (March 17, 1894), 188; A Canadian, ibid.,
    XXIV (March 31, 1894), 216. [The latter an answer to
    Lang.]
    N&Q, 4th ser., IX (Feb. 10, 1872), 131.

J. R. Dennet, Nation, XIV (April 4, 1872), 218-19.

Grant, James. Memoirs of Sir George Sinclair, Bart. of Ulbster.
London: Tinsley Bros., 1870. [Pp. 12-17 contain anecdotes
about Byron.]

H., F. C. "Lord Byron's English Bards and Scotch Reviewers,"
N&Q, 4th ser., VI (Oct. 29, 1870), 368. [Was Lord
Brougham the reviewer of Hours of Idleness?] Cf. Anonymous, ibid., 4th ser., VI (Nov. 19, 1870), 449. [Jeffrey
was.] James Henry Dixon, ibid., 4th ser., VI (Dec. 3,
1870), 480. [Lord Brougham.] J. A. Picton, ibid., 4th ser.,
VI (Dec. 24, 1870), 554. [An extension and correction of
previous items.] J. S., ibid., 4th ser., VII (Jan. 7, 1871),
23. [Jeffrey.] J. H., ibid., 4th ser., VII (Jan. 7, 1871),
23-24. [Jeffrey.] James H. Dixon, ibid., VII (Feb. 4, 1871),
106. [Finds Byron's dicta on poets of small value. The controversy, though still entitled "Lord Byron's English Bards
and Scotch Reviewers," now turns to a polemic on Lord Byron's taste in poetry.] Anonymous, ibid., 4th ser., VII
(March 4, 1871), 197; James H. Dixon, ibid., 4th ser., VII
(April 22, 1871), 351; Archdeacon Watson, ibid., 4th ser.,
VII (May 20, 1871), 441; J. N., ibid., 4th ser., VIII (Aug.
5, 1871), 111. [The latter proves conclusively that the review was not written by Jeffrey.]

Kindt, Hermann. "Goethe on Lord Byron and Walter Scott," N&Q
4th ser., V (Jan. 1, 1870), 10-13. [Translates passages
from a volume of Goethe's Conversations with Kanzler F. V.
Müller.] William M. Rossetti, ibid., 4th ser., V (Jan. 22,
1870), 106. [Finds it grotesque in Goethe to run down so
great a man as Shelley for not admiring the Poem on the
Death of General Moore, which Byron had not written after
all.] W. F., ibid., 4th ser., V (April 9, 1870), 365-66.
[A Mr. Boxwell mentioned by Müller in his Conversations
may have been Joseph Green Cogswell, who was a professor
at Harvard University and first superintendent of the Astor
Library in New York.] F. C. H., ibid., 4th ser., V (May
28, 1870), 503-504. [Translates verses which Goethe sent to
Byron at Leghorn, and which had appeared in German in Moore's
Life of Byron.]

"Lady Byron and Mrs. Beecher Stowe," New Monthly Magazine,
CXLVI (Feb., 1870), 217-19.

Lamb, James J. "Lord Byron's 'Irish Lady,'" N&Q, 4th ser., V
(Jan. 22, 1870), 89. [Who is this lady?] Cf. D. V., ibid.,
4th ser., V (Feb. 5, 1870), 160. [Lady Charlemont, daughter of William Bermingham.]

Minto, William. "Memoir," The Poetical Works of Lord Byron.
Collected and Arranged with Notes by Sir Walter Scott, Lord
Jeffrey, Professor Wilson, Thomas Moore, William Gifford,

Rev. George Crabbe, Bishop Herber, J. G. Lockhart, Lord
Brougham, Thomas Campbell. New and Complete Edition.
Philadelphia: Porter & Coates, 187-. Pp. vii-xxii.

"Mrs. Beecher Stowe's Vindication," Argosy, IX (April 1, 1870),
  269-87.

Morley, John. "Byron," Fortnightly Review, XIV (Dec., 1870),
  650-73. Rptd., largely amplified, in his Critical Miscellanies. London: Chapman & Hall, 1871. Pp. 251-90.

Outis. "The True Story" of Mrs. Stowe. London: Mann Nephews,
  1870.

Paget, John. "Lord Byron and His Calumniators," Blackwood's,
  CVII (Jan., 1870), 123-38; "Postscript to 'Lord Byron and
  His Calumniators,'" ibid., CVII (Feb., 1870), 267-68.
  Rptd. in his Paradoxes and Puzzles. Historical, Judicial,
  and Literary. Edinburgh: William Blackwood, 1874. Pp.
  283-314.

Pebody, Charles. "The Edinburgh Reviewers: Francis Jeffrey,
  Sydney Smith, Lord Macaulay," Gentleman's Magazine,
  CCXXVII (Oct., 1870), 547-61.

Piesse, Septimus. "Chillon," N&Q, 4th ser., VI (July 16, 1870),
  45. [The name "Byron" engraved on a stone column at Chillon; a vandal had carved "H. B. Stowe" near his name.] Cf.
  James Henry Dixon, ibid., 4th ser., VI (Aug. 20, 1870),
  162. [Says that Byron did not carve his name, whereas Mrs.
  Stowe did.]

" 'The Prisoner of Chillon,' " All the Year Round, n.s., IV (July
  16, 1870), 150-56.

Quilibet, Philip. "Byron, Man and Poet," Galaxy, IX (Feb., 1870),
  275-77.

"A Retrospective Glance at the Byron Controversy," Light or Darkness? A Poem. With Remarks on Lord Byron's Detractors.
  London: Smart & Allen, 1870. Pp. 31-83.

Rossetti, William Michael. "Prefatory Note," The Poetical Works
  of Lord Byron. London: E. Moxon, Son & Co., 1870. Pp.
  ix-xx. Rptd. in his Lives of Famous Men. London: E.
  Moxon, Son & Co., 1878. Pp. 287-307.

Scott, Sir Walter. The Miscellaneous Works of Sir Walter Scott,
  Bart. 30 vols. London: Whittaker; Edinburgh: Adam &
  Charles Black, 1870.
  It contains:
    Review of Childe Harold's Pilgrimage, Canto III and The
      Prisoner of Chillon, Vol. IV, pp. 376-99. Rptd. from QR,

XVI (Oct. , 1816), 172-208.
Review of Childe Harold's Pilgrimage, Canto IV, Vol. XVII,
    pp. 337-66. Rptd. from QR, XIX (April, 1818), 215-32.

Stowe, Harriet Beecher. Lady Byron Vindicated. A History of
    the Byron Controversy, from Its Beginning in 1816, to the
    Present Time. London: Sampson Low, 1870.
    Reviews:
    Abraham Hayward, QR, CXXVIII (Jan. , 1870), 218-50.
    [E. L. Godkin], Nation, X (Jan. 13, 1870), 24-25.
    Saturday Review, XXIX (Jan. 29, 1870), 140-44. Rptd. in
        Living Age, CIV (March 5, 1870), 625-34.
    Cyrus Redding, New Monthly Magazine, CXLVI (March, 1870),
        352-66.
    Argosy, IX (April 1, 1870), 269-87.

"The Tendency of Byron's Poetry," Broadway (London), 2nd ser. ,
    IV (March, 1870), 54-69.

1871

Browne, C. Elliott. "Manuscript Journal Mentioned by Byron,"
    N&Q, 4th ser. , VIII (July 1, 1871), 8. [In Lady Blessing-
    ton's Conversations.] Cf. P. A. L. and H. W. L. , ibid. ,
    4th ser. , VIII (Aug. 19, 1871), 147-48. [Count D'Orsay's.]

C[ollier], J[ohn] P[ayne]. An Old Man's Diary, Forty Years Ago;
    for 1832-1833. For Strictly Private Circulation. 4 vols.
    London: Thomas Richards, 1871-1872.

De Wilde, G. J. "'Young Gallant Howard,'" N&Q, 4th ser. , VII
    (May 20, 1871), 428. [The prototype of young gallant Howard
    in Byron's Childe Harold III is in Guarini's Pastor Fido.]

Fox, John Charles, I. Vindication of Lady Byron. London:
    Richard Bentley, 1871. [Mostly rptd. from Temple Bar,
    1869.]

"Glimpses of Fashionable Life in the Time of Byron and Peter-
    sham," Tinsley's Magazine, IX (Oct. , 1871), 298-312.

Hall, Samuel Carter. A Book of Memories of Great Men and Wo-
    men of the Age, from Personal Acquaintance. London: Vir-
    tue & Co. , 1871.

L'Estrange, Alfred Guy. The Literary Life of the Rev. William
    Harness. London: Hurst & Blackett, 1871. [Reminiscences
    of a Harrow school friend.]

"Life of Lord Byron," The Poetical Works of Lord Byron. 10
    vols. Boston: James R. Osgood & Co. , 1871.

Mackenzie, Robert Shelton. Sir Walter Scott: The Story of His
    Life. Boston: James R. Osgood & Co. , 1871.

Rinck. Comparison of the Lyrical Poems of Thomas Moore and
    Lord Byron. Köhn: Franz Greven, 1871.

Taine, Hippolyte Adolphe. "Lord Byron," A History of English
    Literature, trans. H. Van Laun. 2 vols. New York: Holt
    & Williams, 1871. Vol. II, pp. 271-312.

1872

"Byron and Shelley," Temple Bar, XXXIV (March, 1872), 30-49.

Carlyle, Thomas. Critical and Miscellaneous Essays. 7 vols.
    London: Chapman and Hall, 1872.

"A Century of Great Poets, from 1750 Downwards. No. VII: Lord
    Byron," Blackwood's, CXII (July, 1872), 49-72. Rptd. in
    Living Age, CXIV (Aug. 17, 1872), 387-404; Eclectic Maga-
    zine, LXXIX (Oct. , 1872), 385-403.

Cocke, W. Archer. "Byron and Shelley," Southern Magazine, XI
    (Oct. , 1872), 496-506.

Frere, John Hookham. The Works of the Right Hon. John Hook-
    ham Frere, in Verse and Prose, now First Collected with a
    Prefatory Memoir by his Nephews, W. E. and Sir Bartle
    Frere. 2 vols. London: B. M. Pickering, 1872.

Graham, John Murray. An Historical View of Literature and Art
    in Great Britain. London: Longmans, Green & Co. , 1872.

Holland, Sir Henry. Recollections of a Past Life. London: Long-
    mans, Green & Co. , 1872.

Jacox, Francis. Aspects of Authorship; or, Book Marks and Book-
    makers. London: Hodder & Stoughton, 1872. [Many refer-
    ences to Byron and his sayings to illustrate.]

Locker, Frederick. "Meter of Beppo and Don Juan," N&Q, 4th
    ser. , X (Sept. 7, 1872), 185. [Sees similarity between them
    and C. B. Stapylton's Herodians of Alexandria, 1652.] Cf.
    W. F. Howlett, ibid. , 4th ser. , X (Sept. 14, 1872), 212.
    [Quotes verses by Sir John Harington, written a bit earlier
    than Stapylton's, also very similar in meter to Beppo and
    Don Juan.] Julian Sharman, ibid. , 4th ser. , X (Sept. 28,
    1872), 251-52. [Says that the vein of sarcastic drollery of
    Beppo and Don Juan are in Whistlecraft and Berni.]

Paget, J. "Lord Byron," Every Saturday, 2nd ser. , II (Aug. 3,
    1872), 117-26.

Pebody, Charles. "Byron," Authors at Work. London: William
    H. Allen, 1872. Pp. 247-79.

Schultess-Young, H. S. (ed.). "Introduction," The Unpublished
    Letters of Lord Byron. London: Richard Bentley & Son,
    1872. Pp. 1-74. [It also contains "Recollections of Lord
    Byron," pp. 234-45.]

                                1873

Arnould, Sir Joseph. Memoir of Thomas, First Lord Denman.
    2 vols. London: Longmans, Green & Co., 1873.

B., H. "Lines Addressed to Mr. Hobhouse: 'Mors Janua Vitae,'"
    N&Q, 4th ser., XII (Oct. 25, 1873), 329. [Wonders if these
    lines on Hobhouse's election to Westminster are Byron's.]
    Cf. H. P. D., ibid., 4th ser., XII (Nov. 1, 1873), 357.
    [They are to be found in the Paris edition of 1828, among
    "Attributed poems."] Ellcee, ibid., 5th ser., I (Jan. 17,
    1874), 56-57. [Asserts that they were published in The
    Liberal, Verse and Prose from the South.]

"Byron and His Worshippers," Saturday Review, XXXV (Jan. 18,
    1873), 71-72. Rptd. in American Bibliopolist, V (Jan.,
    1873), 23-24. [A summing up of the "lay-lie" controversy
    which had appeared in the London Times, occasioned by a
    line in Childe Harold's Pilgrimage, Canto IV, cclxxx.]

Clarke, J. S. "Lord Byron: His Genius and Character," Sketches
    of Character. Downpatrick, [Ireland]: Published at the "Re-
    corder" Office, 1873. Pp. 137-67.

Coppée, Henry. "The New Romantic Poetry: Byron and Moore,"
    English Literature Considered as an Interpreter of English
    History. Philadelphia: Claxton, Remsen & Haffelfinger,
    1873. Pp. 384-90.

Curwen, Henry. "John Murray," A History of Booksellers, the Old
    and the New. London: Chatto & Windus, 1873. Pp. 159-98.

Devey, Joseph. "Byron," A Comparative Estimate of Modern Poets.
    London: E. Moxon, Son & Co., 1873. Pp. 184-211.

Duyckinck, E. A. "Lord Byron," Portrait Gallery of Eminent
    Men and Women. 2 vols. New York: Johnson Wilson & Co.,
    1873. Vol. I, pp. 507-28.

Hadley, James. "Are the Writings of Lord Byron Immoral in
    Their Tendency?" Essays Philological and Critical. New
    York: Holt & Williams, 1873. [Yes. His moral character
    had an injurious effect on his literary character.]

Jacox, Francis. Traits of Character and Notes of Incident in Bible
Story. London: Hodder & Stoughton, 1873.

Noel, Roden. "Lord Byron and His Times, " St. Paul's Magazine,
XIII (Nov. , 1873), 555-77; ibid. , XIII (Dec. , 1873), 618-38.
Rptd. in his Essays on Poetry and Poets. London: K. Paul,
Trench & Co. , 1886. Pp. 50-113.

Picton, J. A. "Lord Byron's Address to the Ocean, " N&Q, 4th
ser. , XI (Feb. 8, 1873), 110. Cf. Makrocheir, ibid. , 5th
ser. , IV (Nov. 27, 1875), 431-32; R. E. E. W. , "Byron:
Childe Harold, " N&Q, 7th ser. , II (Nov. 6, 1886), 366; Wm.
Gurner, ibid. , 7th ser. , III (Jan. 1, 1887), 14; W. F. P.
Stockley, ibid. , 11th ser. , IX (June 27, 1914), 506; C. C. B. ,
ibid. , 11th ser. , X (Aug. 22, 1914), 158. [On the meaning
and grammar of Childe Harold, IV, cclxxx, "and dashed him
again to earth. -there let him lay. "]

Presley, James T. "Lord Byron, " N&Q, 4th ser. , XI (Feb. 1,
1873), 91-92. [Two illustrations of the impression produced
by his death.]

Sealy, Louis. " 'My Days Are in the Yellow Leaf,' " N&Q, 4th ser. ,
XI (March 22, 1873), 238. [Who wrote this poem?]. Cf.
Cumee O'Lynn, ibid. , 4th ser. , XI (April 12, 1873), 312.
[Byron.]

Smith, Mary R. Darby. "My Reminiscences of Mme. la Marquise
de Boissy, " Victorian Magazine, XXII (Nov. , 1873), 1-24.

T. , W. M. "A King Who Buys and Sells, " N&Q, 4th ser. , XII
(Dec. 6, 1873), 449. [Does this line from Canto III of Don
Juan allude to Louis Phillipe?] Cf. J. W. E. , ibid. , 4th
ser. , XII (Dec. 27, 1873), 520. [It alludes to Louis XVIII,
although it could also allude to Louise Phillipe.]

W. , J. W. "Childe Harold, IV, lxxxi, " N&Q, 4th ser. , XI (April
5, 1873), 279. [In the line, "Night's daughter, Ignorance,
hath wrapt and wrap, " do we have carelessness or should the
line read, "hath wrapt- doth wrap"?]

Williams, Sparks H. N&Q, 4th ser. , XI (Jan. 11, 1873), 48.
[The MS in his possession shows that Byron wrote 'Thy
waters washed them power while they were free, ' rather than
'Thy waters wasted them while they were free.]

1874

Bascom, John. Philosophy of English Literature. New York: G.
P. Putnam's Sons, 1874. Pp. 249-54. [Considers Byron's
works immoral.]

Blair, David. "Byron and Chalmers," N&Q, 5th ser., I (May 23,
    1874), 405. [Childe Harold's Pilgrimage, IV, v, is closely
    parallel to Chalmer's Sermon, "On the Expulsive Power of
    New Affection."]

C. "Lord Byron in Scotland," N&Q, 5th ser., I (Jan. 24, 1874),
    65. [Life of Dr. Guthrie makes a mistake. Byron was
    never in Scotland after 1798.]

Chorley, Henry Fothergill. Personal Reminiscences by Chorley,
    Planche, and Young, ed. Richard Henry Stoddard. ("Bric-a-
    Brac Series," No. 1.) New York: Scribner, Armstrong &
    Co., 1874. [Some Byron anecdotes.]

"The Cycle of English Song." Temple Bar, XL (March, 1874),
    478-94. [Place of Byron in English poetry.]

Field, Maunsell B. Memories of Many Men and of Some Women:
    Being Personal Recollections of Emperors, Kings, Queens,
    Princes. New York: Harper & Bros., 1874. [Contains
    anecdotes of Byron's journey in the East in 1810.]

Greville, C. C. F. The Greville Memoirs: A Journal of the
    Reigns of King George the Fourth and King William the
    Fourth, ed. Henry Reeve. 3 vols. London: Longmans,
    Green & Co., 1874.

Liechtenstein, Marie Henrietta Norberta. Holland House. 2 vols.
    London: Macmillan & Co., 1874.

London Hermit [pseud. for Walter Parke]. "Manfred, Poem and
    Drama," Dublin University Magazine, LXXXIII (April, 1874),
    502-508. Rptd. in his Peeps at Life; and Studies in My Cell.
    London: Simpkin, Marshall & Co., 1875. Pp. 97-108.

Mathews, William. The Great Conversers and Other Essays.
    Chicago: S. C. Griggs & Co., 1874.

Rassmann, V. A Critical Analysis of Lord Byron's "English Bards
    and Scotch Reviewers." Rüdesheim: A. Fischer, 1874.

Russell, William Clark. The Book of Table-Talk. Selections from
    the Conversations of Poets, Philosophers, Statesmen, Divines,
    etc. With Notes and Memoirs. London: G. Routledge, 1874.
    Pp. 353-67. [Anthology of table-talk with no sources given.]

Scott, William B. "Preliminary Memoir," The Complete Poetical
    Works of Lord Byron. London: G. Routledge, 1874. Pp.
    9-15. Reissued in 1883 and 1890.

Smith, Bernhard. "Byron," N&Q, 5th ser., I (June 13, 1874),
    465. [Notices two blunders in The Siege of Corinth: 1) In
    the beginning lines, "In the year since Jesus died for men/

Eighteen hundred years and ten, " Byron dates the Christian
era from the death of Christ rather than His birth; and 2) the
lines where Byron has the soldiers partake of the holy wine
at communion which they could not do because they were Roman Catholic.] Cf. W. A. C., ibid., 5th ser., II (July 18,
1874), 50-51. [Says that the first lines do not really belong
to the Siege, but are lines "intended for the opening of The
Siege of Corinth"; they were written in imitation of Christabel. Furthermore, he calls attention to Cole's War Eclogue,
Fire, Famine, and Slaughter as source for a passage in Byron.] K. P. D. E., ibid., 5th ser., II (July 18, 1874), 51.
[Doubts that there is a mistake in the second passage; in the
East, Roman Catholics receive communion both ways.] William
Whiston, ibid., 5th ser., II (Aug. 29, 1874), 177. [Says that
W. A. C. is wrong in saying that the lines are not from the
Siege of Corinth. Furthermore he asserts that Byron had not
read Christabel.] C. A. Ward, ibid., 5th ser., II (Nov. 14,
1874), 393. [Byron was influenced by Christabel in the first
12 lines of stanza xix.] W. Whiston, ibid., III (March 13,
1875), 216. [Byron did not mean to give the impression that
he had been the originator of the ideas expressed in stanza
xix.]

Timbs, John.   Anecdote Lives of the Water Wits and Humorists.
    2 vols.   London: Richard Bentley & Son, 1874.   [References
    to Byron.   Quotes poems in which Byron refers to Coleridge.]

Willowby, Raseim.   "The Byron Mystery.   Alnaby Hall: Where
    Byron Spent His Honeymoon, " Claude and Etheline and Other
    Poems.   Bombay: Cooper & Co., 1874.   Pp. 130-34.

1875

Bain, Alexander.   "Biographical Memoir of Dr. Neil Arnott, "
    Transactions of the Aberdeen Philosophical Society, I 1875),
    138.   [In a footnote on this page Bain says that Byron stood
    seventeenth in his class in Aberdeen, thus correcting Moore.]

"Byron at Willis's Rooms, " World, July 21, 1875, pp. 8-9.
    [Protestation against the Byron Monument.]

"The Byron Memorial, " Saturday Review, XL (July 24, 1875), 107-
    109.

C.   "Byron's Books, " N&Q, 5th ser., IV (Aug. 7, 1875), 109.
    [Was there a public sale of his books?] Cf. William Platt,
    ibid., 5th ser., IV (Aug. 28, 1875), 175. [There most sure-
    ly was; quotes letters to Mr. Murray.] Este, ibid., 5th ser.,
    IV (Sept. 18, 1875), 238.   [Sold by auction by Mr. Evans, at
    93, Pall Mall, on Friday, July 6, 1827.]

Castelar, Emilio. Life of Lord Byron and Other Sketches, trans.
    Mrs. Arthur Arnold. London: Tinsley Bros. , 1875.
    Review:
    W. M. Rossetti, Academy, XI (Jan. 20, 1877), 47.

Goddard, Julia. "Byron's Manfred, " St. James's Magazine, 3rd
    ser. , XIV (Dec. , 1875), 254-64.

Gostwick, Joseph. "Byron," English Poets. Twelve Essays.
    New York: Stroefer & Kirchner, 1875. Pp. 173-90.

Harness, William. "Lord Byron," Personal Reminiscences by
    Barham, Harness, and Hodder, ed. Richard Henry Stoddard.
    ("Bric-a-Brac Series, " No. 4.) New York: Scribner, Arm-
    strong, 1875. Pp. 179-96. [Contains the substance of Har-
    ness's recollections of Byron.]

Macready, William Charles. Macready's Reminiscences and Selec-
    tions from His Diaries and Letters, ed. Sir Frederick Pol-
    lock. 2 vols. London: Macmillan & Co. , 1875.

Matthiae, Otto. Characteristics of Lord Byron. Berlin: Trow-
    itzsch & Sohn, 1875.

Parke, Walter. "A Monument to Byron," Dublin University Maga-
    zine, LXXXV, Part II (Dec. , 1875), 727-31. Rptd. in his
    Peeps at Life; and Studies in My Cell. London: Simpkin,
    Marshall & Co. , 1875. Pp. 185-92.

_____. "The Morality of Don Juan," Dublin University Magazine,
    LXXXV, Part I (May, 1875), 630-37. Rptd. in his Peeps at
    Life; and Studies in My Cell. London: Simpkin, Marshall &
    Co. , 1875. Pp. 193-204.

Peacock, Thomas Love. The Works of Thomas Love Peacock, ed.
    Henry Cole. 3 vols. London: Richard Bentley & Son, 1875.

Scharf, Lewis. Poetry and Genius of Pope with the Poetry and
    Genius of Byron Compared. Wien: Druck von Carl Gerold's
    Sohn, 1875. Rptd. in his Chips from English Literature.
    Aschersleben: E. Schlegel, 1881. Pp. 1-24.

Stigand, William. The Life, Work and Opinions of Heinrich Heine.
    London: Longmans, Green & Co. , 1875.

Stoddard, Richard Henry (ed.). Personal Recollections of Lamb.
    Hazlitt, and Others. ("Bric-a-Brac Series, " No. 9.) New
    York: Scribner, Armstrong & Co. , 1875.

Taylor, John. Personal Reminiscences by O'Keeffe, Kelly, and
    Taylor, ed. Richard Henry Stoddard. ("Bric-a-Brac Series, "
    No. 8.) New York: Scribner, Armstrong & Co. , 1875.

1876

A., T. J. "Poets the Masters of Language: Lord Byron," N&Q,
5th ser., V (April 22, 1876), 326. [Byron thought that Teos
was an island.]

*B., A. G. "Lord Byron," Fascination, I (Jan., 1876), 19-24.

B., R. E. "Bonivard, 'The Prisoner of Chillon,' " Fraser's
Magazine, XCIII (May, 1876), 582-87.

Bennett, De Robigne Mortimer. "Byron," The World's Sages, Infi-
dels and Thinkers. New York: The Truth Seeker Co., 1876.
Pp. 706-10.

Blair, D. "Byron and Beaumarchais," N&Q, 5th ser., VI (Aug.
12, 1876), 126. [Notices a parallel between Don Juan and
The Barber of Seville.]

Fields, James Thomas. Old Acquaintance: Barry Cornwall and
Some of His Friends. Boston: J. R. Osgood & Co., 1876.

Gatty, Alfred. "Poets the Masters of Language: Lord Byron,"
N&Q, 5th ser., V (Jan. 8, 1876), 37. [Notices the use of
sung for sang in "The Isles of Greece."]

Haydon, Benjamin Robert. Correspondence and Table Talk; with
a Memoir by His Son Frederick Wordsworth Haydon, 2 vols.
London: Chatto & Windus, 1876.

M., W. T. "Lord Byron's English Bards and Scotch Reviewers,"
N&Q, 5th ser., VI (July 15, 1876), 49. [Wants proof of au-
thorship of review of Hours of Idleness which appeared in the
Edinburgh Review.]

Mackay, George Eric. Lord Byron at the Armenian Convent.
Venice: Office of the "Polyglotta," 1876.

Minto, William. "Lord Byron," Encyclopaedia Britannica. 9th ed.
Boston: Little & Brown, 1876. Vol. IV, pp. 604-12.

_____. "Lord Byron and 'Thyrza,' " Atheneum, Sept. 2, 1876,
pp. 306-307. [She was the girl who used to ride with him in
1808 and whom he introduced as his younger brother.]

Noremac, W. T. "Byron and Shakespeare," N&Q, 5th ser., V
(April 29, 1876), 345. [Byron did read Shakespeare; cites
four parallels as evidence.] Cf. J. L. Walker, ibid., 5th
ser., V (May 13, 1876), 393. [Further evidence.]

"The Proposed Memorial of Byron," Fraser's Magazine, XCIII
(Feb., 1876), 246-60. [Disraeli's speech at Willis's Rooms,
July 17, 1876, asking for a Byron monument. Rest of the
essay is essentially anti-Byronic.]

"Shall Byron Have a Statue?" Punch, LXXI (Nov. 18, 1876), 212.
    [Letters to the editor expressing approval and disapproval of
    the project to have a Byron monument.]

Ticknor, George. Life, Letters and Journals, ed. G. S. Hillard.
    2 vols. Boston: James R. Osgood & Co., 1876. [Recollec-
    tions of a Harvard man, son of a wealthy Bostonian.]

Trevelyan, Sir George O. The Life and Letters of Lord Macaulay.
    2 vols. New York: Harper & Bros., 1876.

W., E. D. "Unpublished Story of Lord Byron and Mary Chaworth,"
    Lippincott's, XVIII (Nov., 1876), 637-39.

                                  1877

Alston, R. "Byron's Hebrew Melodies," Charing Cross Magazine,
    2nd ser., V (Nov., 1877), 135-40.

Bowring, Sir John, "Lord Byron," Autobiographical Recollections.
    London: H. S. King & Co., 1877. Pp. 344-47.

Browning, Elizabeth Barrett. Letters of Elizabeth Barrett Brown-
    ing Addressed to Richard Hengist Horne, with a Preface and
    a Memoir by Richard Henry Stoddard. New York: James
    Miller, 1877.

"The Byron Memorial," Saturday Review, XLIII (June 16, 1877),
    734-35. [On Disraeli's speech at Willis's Rooms in favor of
    a Byron statue. Article against monument.]

Cornwall, Barry [pseud. for Bryan Waller Procter]. An autobio-
    graphical Fragment and Biographical Notes, ed. C. Patmore.
    Boston: Robert Bros., 1877. [This volume seems to contain
    two letters not included in Prothero, Murray, or Quennell,
    dated Pisa, 1822, and Genoa, March 5, 1823.]

Dowden, Edward. "The French Revolution and Literature," CR,
    XXX (June, 1877), 120-41. Rptd. in his Studies in Literature
    1789-1877. London: Kegan Paul, Trench & Co., 1882. Pp.
    1-43.

Finlay, George. A History of Greece, ed. Rev. H. F. Tozer.
    Oxford: Clarendon Press, 1877.

Fraxi, Pisanus [pseud. for Henry Spencer Ashbee]. Index Librorum
    Prohibitoru [sic.], Being Notes Bio-Biblio-Icono-graphical and
    Critical, on Curious and Uncommon Books. London: Private-
    ly Printed, 1877. [On the Don Leon Poems.]

Köhler, A. A Glance at Lord Byron as a Dramatist. Ostern,
    1877.

Lennox, Lord William Pitt. "Byron," Celebrities I Have Known;
   with Episodes Political, Social, Sporting, and Theatrical.
   2nd ser. London: Hurst & Blackett, 1877. Vol. I, pp. 80-
   84.

L'Estrange, Alfred Guy K. "On Byron," History of English Humor.
   2 vols. London: Hurst & Blackett, 1877. Vol. II, pp. 184-
   95.

Perry, Thomas Sergeant. "German Influence in English Literature," Atlantic Monthly, XL (Aug., 1877), 129-47. [On Byron, pp. 138-43.]

Pocock, Crawford J. "Letter of Lord Byron," N&Q, 5th ser.,
   VIII (July 14, 1877), 26. [Dated March 6, 1814, in his collection.]

Sharp, William. Life of Percy Bysshe Shelley. "Great Writers."
   London: W. Scott, 1877.

Sinclair, Thomas. The Mount: Speech from Its England Heights.
   London: Trübner & Co., 1877. [References to Byron.]

Smith, George Barnett. Shelley: A Critical Biography. Edinburgh: D. Douglas, 1877.

Stoddard, Richard Henry. Anecdote Biography of Percy Bysshe
   Shelley. New York: Scribner, Armstrong & Co., 1877.

Vyvyan, E. R. "Author Wanted," N&Q, 5th ser., VII (June 23,
   1877), 489. [For the continuation or sequel to Don Juan.]
   Cf. H. J. Daniel, "A Sequel to Don Juan," ibid., 5th ser.,
   VII (June 30, 1877), 519. [Claims he wrote a seventeenth
   Canto.]

Warren, J. Leicester. "Byron and Shelley in the Environs of Ge-
   neva during the Summer of 1816," N&Q, 5th ser., VIII (July
   7, 1877), 1-2; ibid., 5th ser., VIII (July 14, 1877), 23-24.
   [After their removal from the Hôtel de Sécheron, "the Shelley
   party alone occupied Mont Alègre and Byron only occupied
   Diodati."] Cf. Dudley Carey Elives, ibid., 5th ser., VIII
   (Aug. 11, 1877), 115; Thus., "Villa Diodati," ibid., 5th ser.,
   VIII (Aug. 11, 1877), 115. [Both items about Villa Diodati.]

_____. "Byron's English Bards and Scotch Reviewers," N&Q,
   5th ser., VII (Feb. 24, 1877), 145; ibid., 5th ser., VII
   (March 17, 1877), 203-204. [Gives early editions of English
   Bards and Scotch Reviewers.] Cf. W. M. Tartt, ibid., 5th
   ser., VII (April 14, 1877), 296. [Makes a correction to
   above.] J. Leicester Warren, ibid., 5th ser., VII (May 5,
   1877), 355. [Gives the date of the 2nd edition.]

274 Bibliography

_____. "MSS of Childe Harold, Canto III," Atheneum, June 2,
1877, pp. 703-704.

1878

Bede, Cuthbert. "Byron's The Prisoner of Chillon," N&Q, 5th
    ser., IX (April 6, 1878), 268. [Wonders if Byron is correct
    in saying that the dungeon was 'below the surface of the
    lake?"] Cf. Septimius Piesse and A. J. M., ibid., 5th ser.,
    IX (May 25, 1878), 419. [Say that Byron does not imply that
    the whole dungeon was under or below the level of the lake.]

Hodgson, James T. Memoir of the Rev. Francis Hodgson. 2 vols.
    London: Macmillan & Co., 1878.

Mayer, S. R. Townshend. "Lady Caroline Lamb," Temple Bar,
    LIII (June, 1878), 174-92.

Moore, Thomas. Prose and Verse, Humorous, Satirical, and
    Sentimental. With Suppressed Passages from the Memoirs of
    Lord Byron. Chiefly from the Author's Manuscript and All
    Hitherto Inedited and Uncollected. With Notes and Introduc-
    tion by Richard Herne Shepherd. London: Chatto & Windus,
    1878.

Proctor, Fred. "Byron's Beauties," Charing Cross Magazine, 2nd
    ser., V (Feb., 1878), 385-88. [Description of the particular
    charms of some of Byron's romantic heroines.]

Rogers, Charles. "Lord Byron," N&Q, 5th ser., X (Oct. 26,
    1878), 326. [A letter dated Cephalonia, Aug. 26, 1823, to
    Captain Wright Know, Governor of Ithaca.]

Sergeant, Lewis. New Greece. London: Cassell, Petter & Gal-
    pin, 1878.

Smith, Mary Rebecca Darby. Recollections of Two Distinguished
    Persons: La Marquise de Boissy and the Count de Waldeck.
    Philadelphia: J. B. Lippincott & Co., 1878.

Torrens, William McCullagh. Memoirs of the Right Honourable
    William, second Viscount Melbourne. London: Macmillan &
    Co., 1878.

1879

Bagehot, Walter. "Wordsworth, Tennyson and Browning, or The
    Pure, the Ornate and the Grotesque in Poetry," Literary
    Studies, ed. Richard Holt Hutton. 3 vols. London: Long-
    mans, Green & Co., 1879. Vol. II, pp. 326-81. [Harsh
    judgment on the Oriental Tales.]

"The Byron Monument," Fraser's Magazine, XCIX (May, 1879),
665-66. [Proposes several quotations from Byron's works
which could be used as inscriptions to his monument, all of
which make evident that Byron is not worthy of a statue.]

C., X. "Pronunciation of Lord Byron's Name," N&Q, 5th ser.,
XI (March 29, 1879), 246. [According to Sir William Knighton,
it is pronounced with a long i.] Cf. Richard Edgcumbe, ibid.,
5th ser., XI (April 12, 1879), 296. [Medwin said that Byron
pronounced it Byrne when speaking of his wife.] H. Buxton
Forman, ibid., 5th ser., XI (May 3, 1879), 356. [He pro-
nounces it with a long i, rejecting Medwin's evidence.]

Deshler, Charles Dunham. "Byron's Sonnets," Afternoon with the
Poets. New York: Harper & Bros., 1879. Pp. 220-21.

Dixon, James. "Byron's English Bards and Scotch Reviewers,"
N&Q, 5th ser., XII (Sept. 20, 1879), 226-27. [In the opening lines, "Still must I hear? Shall hoarse Fitzgerald bawl /
His creaking couplets in a tavern hall?" he would prefer the
word croaking instead of creaking.] Cf. Frederick Rule,
ibid., 5th ser., XII (Nov. 1, 1879), 355. [He prefers creaking.] John Murray, ibid., XII (Nov. 8, 1879), 377. [Says
that Byron first wrote maudlin, but ran it through and put
creaking instead when he added the first 96 lines for the first
time in the third edition.] John Murray, ibid., 5th ser., XII
(Nov. 15, 1879), 392. [Corrects previous statement by saying that the 96 lines were added to the second, not to the
third edition of the poem.]

Dorling, W. "The Late John Sheppard and Lord Byron--an Incident," Sunday Magazine, VI (Nov., 1879), 818-21. [On the
letters exchanged between the two men.]

Hamilton, Walter. The Poets Laureate of England; Being a History
of the Office of Poet Laureate, Biographical Notice of Its
Holders and a Collection of the Satires, Epigrams and Lam-
poons Directed Against Them. London: E. Stock, 1879.

Kemble, Frances Anne. Records of a Girlhood. New York:
Henry Holt & Co., 1879.

"Lord Byron's Life and Literary Labors," The Poems and Dramas
of Lord Byron. New York: The Arundel Printing and Publishing Co., 1879. Pp. v-xi.

Perry, Thomas Sergeant. "Recent Criticism of Byron," International Review, VII (Sept., 1879), 282-93.

St. Swithin. "The Byron Separation," N&Q, 5th ser., XI (April 5,
1879), 266-67. [Reprints a cut from The Yorkshire Gazette
giving an account of the separation by Mrs. Morrell.] Cf.
Richard Edgcumbe, ibid., 5th ser., XI (April 19, 1879), 311-

12. [Corrects the article above.] J. M., ibid., XI (May 3,
1879), 350. [Prints document drawn up by Byron at La Mira,
Aug. 9, 1817.] J. Russell, ibid., 5th ser., XI (May 3,
1879), 350. [Says that Mrs. Morrell's and Medwin's account
of the separation are very similar.]

Symonds, John Addington. Shelley. "English Men of Letters."
New York: Harper & Bros., 1879.

1880

"Byron's 'Ianthe,' " ILN, LXXVI (March 27, 1880), 291. [Identi-
fies her as Charlotte Bacon.]

*Elliot, Arthur H. [pseud. for William Davenport Adams]. "By-
ron and His Contemporaries," The Witty and Humorous Side
of the English Poets. With a Variety of Specimens Arranged
in Periods. London: Sampson Low, Marston, Searle and
Rivington, 1880. Pp. 181-221.

Ingram, John H. Edgar Allan Poe, His Life, Letters and Opinions. 2 vols. London: John Hogg, 1880.

James, Ralph N. "The Duel between Lord Byron and Mr. Chaworth," N&Q, 6th ser., I (Jan. 31, 1880), 94. [Quotes incident from Gentleman's Magazine, Jan., 1765.] Cf. William
Platt, ibid., 6th ser., I (Feb. 14, 1880), 142. [Adds a report about the same by Horace Walpole.]

Jaydee. "Anecdote of Byron by Colonel Napier," N&Q, 6th ser.,
I (April 3, 1880), 276. [Asks in what publication by Colonel
Napier is to be found the story about Byron's head being so
small.] Cf. Richard Edgcumbe, ibid., 6th ser., I (May 8,
1880), 383. [Moore alludes to this anecdote in his Life of
Byron. He quotes it from Byroniana.] Jaydee, ibid., 6th
ser., I (May 22, 1880), 426. [But did Napier write Byroniana?] Richard Edgcumbe, ibid., 6th ser., II (July 24, 1880),
77. [Moore quoted from the MS of Byroniana (never published), but that is where the anecdote appeared.] William
Kelly, ibid., 6th ser., II (Aug. 14, 1880), 125. [Draws attention to the book by that name that appeared in 1834.]

Jebb, Sir Richard Claverhouse. "Byron in Greece," Modern
Greece. London: Macmillan Co., 1880. Pp. 143-83.

Nichol, John. Byron. "English Men of Letters Series." London:
Macmillan, 1880.
Reviews:
Francis F. Browne, Dial, I (Oct., 1880), 112-14.
J. M. Hart, Nation, XXXI (Nov. 11, 1880), 344-45.
Harper's Magazine, LXII (Dec., 1880), 145-46.
[A. Symons], QR, CXCII (July, 1900), 25-44.

Ruskin, John. "Fiction--Fair and Foul," Nineteenth Century, VIII
    (Sept., 1880), 394-410; ibid., VIII (Nov., 1880), 748-60.
    Rptd. in his Works, eds. Sir E. T. Cooke and A. D. O.
    Wedderburn. London: G. Allen; New York: Longmans,
    Green & Co., 1903-1912. Vol. XXXIV, pp. 322-69.

*Symes, John Elliotson. "Byron," Syllabus of Lectures on English
    Poetry, 1785-1825. "University Extension Series." Cardiff:
    W. Lewis, 1880. [Lectures 7 and 8.]

Symonds, John Addington. "Lord Byron," The English Poets, ed.
    T. H. Ward. 4 vols. London: Macmillan, 1880. Vol. IV,
    pp. 244-303.

Todhunter, John. A Study of Shelley. London: Kegan Paul & Co.,
    1880.

Vecchi, A[ugusto] V[ittorio]. "The Eagle's Nest of the Italian
    Navy," Minerva, II (Oct., 1880), 447-58. [Mentions some
    local memories of Shelley and Byron.]

1881

Arnold, Matthew (ed.). "Preface," Poetry of Byron. London:
    Macmillan & Co., 1881. Pp. vii-xxxi. Rptd. in his Essays
    in Criticism, 2nd ser., London: Macmillan & Co., 1888,
    pp. 163-204; Toward Today, ed. Erich Albert Walter, Chica-
    go: Scott, Foresman & Co., 1938, pp. 247-59; Matthew Ar-
    nold: Poetry and Prose, Oxford: The Clarendon Press,
    1939, pp. 714-30.
    Reviews:
        Macmillan's Magazine, XLIII (March, 1881), 367-77. Rptd.
        in Living Age, CXLIX (April 16, 1881), 131-39; Appleton's
        Journal, XXV (May, 1881), 413-20.
    W. E. Henley, Atheneum, June 25, 1881, pp. 839-40. Rptd.
        in Views and Reviews, Vol. V of The Works of William
        Ernest Henley. 7 vols. London: David Nutt, 1908, pp.
        65-73.
    Alfred Austin, QR, CLIV (July, 1882), 53-82. Rptd. as "By-
        ron and Wordsworth," in his The Bridling of Pegasus.
        London: Macmillan, 1910. Pp. 78-138.
    Saturday Review, LII (July 23, 1881), 110-12.

Baker, Walter C. "Byron," N&Q, 6th ser., III (May 21, 1881),
    408. [Wants an explication of "Fortune, fame, power, life,
    have named themselves a star," from Childe Harold's Pilgrim-
    age, III, lxxxviii.] Cf. Este, ibid., 6th ser., III (June 25,
    1881), 516; H. Krebs, ibid., 6th ser., III (June 25, 1881),
    517. [Both give explications.]

"Byron in Greece," Temple Bar, LXII (May, 1881), 100-108.

Edgcumbe, Richard. "Lord Byron at Missolonghi," N&Q, 6th ser.,
III (June 11, 1881), 462-63.

_____. "Palm Sunday at Missolonghi," N&Q, 6th ser., IV
(July 16, 1881), 46. [Byron is not forgotten in Missolonghi.
Article written from data furnished by Mr. Colnaghi, Consul
at Missolonghi.]

Fields, James Thomas. James T. Fields. Biographical Notes
and Personal Sketches with Unpublished Fragments and Tributes from Men and Women of Letters. Boston: Houghton,
Mifflin & Co., 1881. [Editor of Atlantic Monthly; references
to Byron.]

Fitzgerald, Percy. The Life of George the Fourth, Including His
Letters and Opinions with a View of the Men, Manners and
Politics of His Reign. 2 vols. London: Tinsley Bros., 1881.

Gilfillan, George. Sketches Literary and Theological, Being Se-
lections from an Unpublished Manuscript of the Late Rev.
George Gilfillan, ed. Frank Henderson. Edinburgh: David
Douglas, 1881.

Lennox, Lord William Pitt. Plays, Players and Playhouses at
Home and Abroad, with Anecdotes of the Drama and the Stage.
London: Hurst & Blackett, 1881. [References to Byron's
dramas.]

Rutherford, Mark [pseud. for W. Hale White]. "Byron, Goethe,
and Matthew Arnold," CR, XL (Aug., 1881), 179-85. Rptd.
in Appleton's Journal, XXVI (Oct., 1881), 335-39; White's
Pages from a Journal, London: Unwin, 1900, pp. 133-48.

Shepherd, R. H. and C. N. Williamson (eds.). Memoirs of the
Life and Writings of Thomas Carlyle. 2 vols. London: W.
H. Allen, 1881.

Sinker, Robert. "The Statue of Byron in the Library of Trinity
College, Cambridge," N&Q, 6th ser., IV (Nov. 26, 1881),
421-23. Rptd. in his The Byron Statue in The Library of
Trinity College, Cambridge. Cambridge: Deighton, Bell &
Co., 1891. Pp. 125-34.

Southey, Robert. The Correspondence of Robert Southey with
Caroline Bowles. To Which Are Added: Correspondence with
Shelley and Southey's Dreams, ed. Edward Dowden. "Dublin
University Series." Dublin: Hodges, Figgis & Co., London:
Longmans, Green & Co., 1881.

Stevens, Abel. Madame de Staël. A Study of Her Life and Times.
New York: Harper & Bros., 1881.

Stirling, Edward. Old Drury Lane. London: Chatto & Windus, 1881.

W. , H. E. "Edward John Trelawny," Temple Bar, LXIII (Nov. , 1881), 325-42. Cf. Frances Power Cobbe, "Clubfoot of Byron," ibid., LXIV (Feb. , 1882), 317-18. [Says that Byron's lameness consisted merely of an ordinary slightly clubbed foot.] Richard Edgcumbe, "Letter to the Editor of Temple Bar, on a recent article on E. J. Trelawny, anent Byron's Lameness," ibid. , LXVI (Nov. , 1882), 431-32. [Defends Trelawny against accusations of untruthfulness.]

Wedgwood, H. "A Neat Set-down of Byron," N&Q, 6th ser. , III (Jan. 15, 1881), 44. [An anecdote of how Byron was once put down about his comments on Venice.] Cf. Richard Edgcumbe, ibid. , 6th ser. , III (Jan. 22, 1881), 70. [Takes anecdote with a grain of salt.]

1882

Brown, Cornelius. "Lord Byron," Lives of Nottinghamshire Worthies. London: H. Sotheran & Co. , 1882. Pp. 309-19.

Cotterill, Henry B. "Byron," An Introduction to the Study of Poetry. London: Kegan, Paul, Trench & Co. , 1882. Pp. 269-97.

Edgcumbe, Richard. Edward Trelawny, a Biographical Sketch. Plymouth: W. H. Luke, 1882.

"False Coins in Poetry," Blackwood's, CXXXI (June, 1882), 727-40. [Touches on Byron's "Address to the Ocean."]

Fitzgerald, Percy. A New History of the English Stage. 2 vols. London: Tinsley Bros. , 1882.

Fox, Caroline. Memories of Old Friends; Being Extracts from the Journals and Letters of Caroline Fox from 1835 to 1871, ed. Horace N. Pym. London: Smith, Elder & Co. , 1882. [Contains some anecdotes about Byron.]

L'Estrange, A. Guy (ed.). The Friendships of Mary Russell Mitford, as Recorded in Letters from Her Literary Correspondents. 2 vols. London: Hurst & Blackett, 1882.

Nadal, E. S. "Byron," Essays at Home and Elsewhere. London: Macmillan & Co. , 1882. Pp. 42-85.

_____. "Lord Byron," Critic (N. Y.), II (March 25, 1882), 81-83; ibid. , II (April 8, 1882), 95-97.

Oliphant, Margaret. "Byron," Literary History of England in the
   End of the 18th Century and Beginning of the 19th Century.
   3 vols. New York: Macmillan, 1882. Vol. III, pp. 44-132.

Rossetti, William Michael. "Talks with Trelawny," Atheneum,
   July 15, 1882, pp. 78-79. [Jottings from Rossetti's Diary.]

Saintsbury, George. A Short History of English Literature. Oxford: Clarendon Press, 1882.

*Worthington, W. R. Lord Byron. A Paper Read Before the New
   Ferry Literary and Debating Society, on Tuesday, Dec. 6,
   1881. Carlisle: Printed by Hudson Scott, for Private Circulation Only, 1882.

                                 1883

Ashbee, H. S. "The Rest of Don Juan," Bibliographer, IV (July,
   1883), 25-28. [On Henry Morford's The Rest of Don Juan,
   Inscribed to the Shade of Byron.]

B., G. F. R. "Lord Byron and the Harrow and Eton Match," N&Q,
   6th ser., VIII (July 21, 1883), 45. [Byron made 7 runs in the
   first innings and 2 in the second.] Cf. F. L., ibid., 6th
   ser., VIII (Sept. 8, 1883), 197. [Reports about somebody who
   had seen the game.]

Bates, William. The Maclise Portrait Gallery of Illustrious Literary Characters, with Memoirs. London: Chatto & Windus,
   1883.

Bulwer-Lytton, Edward. The Life, Letters, and Literary Remains
   of Edward Bulwer-Lytton. An Autobiography edited with additions by his son, Edward Robert Bulwer-Lytton. 2 vols.
   London: Kegan Paul, French & Co., 1883. [Caroline and
   Byron.]

"Byron's Letters," Atheneum, Aug. 18, 1883, pp. 206-11. [Main-
   ly letters of Mrs. Byron and Mrs. Leigh; but on p. 208
   there is one of Lord Byron to his wife: his last letter to her
   on leaving England in 1816. No date. Some of those letters
   are preserved at the British Museum.]

Caine, T. Hall. "A Review of the First Reviewers of the 'Lake,'
   'Satanic,' and 'Cockney,' School," Cobwebs of Criticism.
   London: Elliott Stock, 1883. Pp. 91-119. [He incorporates
   part of his review of Jeaffreson's The Real Lord Byron, from
   Academy, XXIII (May 26, 1883), 357-58.]

Cantù, Cesare. Lord Byron and His Works; a Biography and Essay, edited with notes by A. Kinloch. London: George Red-
   way, 1883.

Chalmers, J. "Lord Byron's Foot," Lancet, Part I (June 2, 1883), pp. 975-76.

Dennis, John. "Lord Byron," Heroes of Literature: English Poets, a Book for Young Readers. London: Society for Promoting Christian Knowledge, 1883. Pp. 344-64.

Edgcumbe, Richard. "Byron's Version of 'Tu Mi Chamas,'" N&Q, 6th ser., VII (Jan. 20, 1883), 46. [Prints the verses found in Lady Lansdowne's album at Bowood.]

_____. History of the Byron Memorial. London: Effingham Wilson, 1883.

_____. "Montbovon to Thun in 1816," N&Q, 6th ser., VIII (Sept. 29, 1883), 247. [Tried to trace the old route, following Byron's journal of his and Hobhouse's journey to Thun in 1816, but was not successful.] Cf. W. A. B. Coolidge, ibid., 12th ser., III (May, 1917), 301-302. [Explains the route.]

Hollingshead, John. "Manfred on the Stage," Footlights. London: Chapman & Hall, 1883. Pp. 178-90.

Jeaffreson, John Cordy. The Real Lord Byron. New Views of the Poet's Life. London: Hurst & Blackett, 1883.
Reviews:
Atheneum, May 12, 1883, pp. 595-97.
Lancet, Part I (May 19, 1883), 872-74. Cf. ibid., (June 9, 1883), p. 1022.
H. Hall Caine, Academy, XXIII (May 26, 1883), 357-58.
Literary World (Boston), XIV (June 16, 1883), 187; ibid., XIV (Oct. 6, 1883), 326. [Reviews the controversy between Jeaffreson and Froude.]
Saturday Review, LV (June 16, 1883), 773-74.
Abraham Hayward, QR, CLVI (July, 1883), 90-131. Rptd. in Living Age, CLVIII (Aug. 25, 1883), 451-73. Cf. John Cordy Jeaffreson, Atheneum, Aug. 4, 1883, pp. 143-45. [Answers Hayward.] Ibid., Aug. 18, 1883, pp. 204-205. [On the destruction of Byron's Memoirs.]
British Quarterly, LXXVIII (July 1, 1883), 175-78.
J. A. Froude, Nineteenth Century, XIV (Aug., 1883), 228-42. Cf. J. C. Jeaffreson, Atheneum, Sept. 1, 1883, pp. 273-75; ibid., Sept. 22, 1883, p. 366.
Harper's New Monthly, LXVII (Aug., 1883), 473-74.
G. S. Venables, Fortnightly Review, XL (Aug., 1883), 189-202.
J. M. Hart, Nation, XXXVII (Aug. 16, 1883), 143-45.
Spectator, LVI (Nov. 10, 1883), 1451-52.

"Lord Byron and His Critics," Gentleman's Magazine, CCLV (Oct., 1883), 414. [About The Real Lord Byron and the quarrels ensuing between Froude and Jeaffreson.]

282 Bibliography

"Lord Byron on Ireland," Today, I (June, 1883), 121-25.

Morrison, Alfred. "Byron," The Collection of Autograph Letters and Historical Documents, Formed Between 1865 and 1882 by Alfred Morrison. 6 vols. London: Printed for Private Circulation only, 1883. Vol. I, pp. 142-51.

Muir, H. Skey. "Notes on Medwin's Conversations of Lord Byron, by Sir C. J. Napier and Trelawny," N&Q, 6th ser., VII (Feb. 3, 1883), 81-82. [Marginal notes written by Napier and Trelawny.]

Nichols, John, and J. C. Jeaffreson. "Outline of the Life of Byron," The Complete Poetical and Dramatic Works of Lord Byron. "The Newstead Edition." Philadelphia: E. Claxton & Co., 1883. Pp. ix-lx.

Nicoll, Henry J. Landmarks of English Literature. New York: D. Appleton & Co., 1883. Pp. 310-16.

Smith, G. Barnett. "Lady Caroline Lamb," Gentleman's Magazine, CCLV (Oct., 1883), 337-58.

1884

*Andrews, Samuel. Our Great Writers. London: E. Stock, 1884.

Axon, William Edward A. "Byron's Influence on European Literature," Papers of the Manchester Literary Club, X (Oct., 1884), 323-29. Rptd. in his Stray Chapters on Literature, Folklore and Archaeology. Manchester: John Heywood, 1888. Pp. 47-56.

B., A. "Who Was Thyrza?" Atheneum, July 5, 1884, pp. 14-15. [There was no historical Thyrza for the Thyrza of his poems.]

Bayne, Thomas. "Scottish Proverb in Don Juan, XI, lxxvii," N&Q, 6th ser., X (Oct. 4, 1884), 266. [Asks for explanation of "Caw me, caw thee."] Cf. Walter W. Skeat, ibid., 6th ser., X (Oct. 18, 1884), 315; F. C. Birbeck Terry, ibid., 6th ser., X (Dec. 13, 1884), 472; J. Carrick Moore, ibid., 6th ser., XI (Jan. 10, 1885), 33; W. F. P., ibid., 6th ser., XI (Jan. 17, 1885), 58; F. Chance, ibid., 6th ser., XII (Oct. 31, 1885), 358; Frederick E. Sawyer, ibid., 7th ser., IV (Oct. 8, 1887), 293. [Offer several explanations.]

Byron, George Gordon, Lord. Letters Written by Lord Byron during His Residence at Missolonghi. January to April 1824, to Mr. Samuel Barff at Zante. Naples: Tipografia Desanctis, 1884. [Dated as follows: Jan. 23, 1824 (in Italian); Jan. 24, 1824; Feb. 21, 1824; March 5, 1824; March 9, 1833 (sic); March 10, 1824; March 19, 1824; March 22, 1824; March 26, 1824; April 6, 1824; April 9, 1824.]

Croker, John Wilson. The Crocker Papers. The Correspondence
and Diaries of the Late Right Honourable John Wilson Croker, ed. L. L. Jennings. 2 vols. New York: Scribner's
Sons, 1884.

"The Destruction of Byron's Memoirs," Atheneum, May 24, 1884,
pp. 662-63. [Seven letters on the subject by Augusta Leigh,
Lady Byron, and Mr. Wilmot Horton.]

Dixon, J. "Don Juan, XV, lxvi," N&Q, 6th ser., IX (June 28,
1884), 510. ["Then there were God knows what all' Alle-
mande, / A l'espagnole, timbale and salpicon." Did Byron
mean to write "Timbale, and salpicon a l'Espagnole," for
purposes of rhyme?] Cf. ibid., 6th ser., X (July 19, 1884),
56. [States that this "seemingly incorrect form" appeared in
the 1846 one volume edition by Murray.] G. F. R. B., ibid.,
6th ser., X (July 26, 1884), 76. [Byron never saw canto
printed.] Fred Rule, ibid., 6th ser., X (Aug. 16, 1884),
134. [Murray alone has answer in MS.] H. Gibson, ibid.,
6th ser., X (Dec. 20, 1884), 506. [Explains "salpicon."]

Hamilton, Herbert Bruce. Inaugural Essay on the Portrayal of the
Life and Character of Lord Byron in a Novel by B. Disraeli
entitled "Venetia." Leipzig: Printed by Gustav Schmidt,
1884.

Hamilton, Walter. "Byron," Parodies of the Works of English and
American Authors. 6 vols. London: Reeves & Turner,
1884-1889. Vol. III, pp. 190-229.

Heine, Heinrich. Memoirs, and Some Newly Discovered Fragments
of His Writings, with an Introductory Essay by Thomas W.
Evans. London: John Bell & Sons, 1884.

Hoffmann, Frederick August. "Byron," Poetry: Its Origin, Nature
and History. 2 vols. London: Thurgate & Sons, 1884.
Vol. I, pp. 441-65.

Jowett, Henry. Byron. Oxford: Privately Printed, [1884]. [Pa-
per read before the Aylesbury Debating Society on the mo-
tion: "That the character and writings of Lord Byron have
been unduly traduced." Argues in the affirmative.]

Lord, John. "Lord Byron," Nineteenth Century Writers. Vol.
VIII of Beacon Lights of History. 8 vols. New York: Fordes
Howard & Hulbert, 1884. Pp. 135-87.

Maginn, William. A Gallery of Illustrious Literary Characters,
Drawn by the Late Daniel Maclise and Accompanied by No-
tices Chiefly by the Late William Maginn, ed. W. Bates.
London: Chatto & Windus, 1884.

Malmsbury, James Harris, 1st Earl of. Memoirs of an Ex-Minister, an Autobiography. 2 vols. London: Longmans, Green & Co., 1884.

Miller, Joaquin. Memorie and Rime. New York: Funk & Wagnalls, 1884. [Contains an anecdote of a visit to Byron's tomb on Sept. 25, 1870.]

Muir, H. Skey. "Byroniana," N&Q, 6th ser., IX (Feb. 2, 1884), 81-82. [Among his father's papers he discovered some memoranda of Lord Byron's conversations in Cephalonia.]

Rusticus, Mus. "A letter of Lord Byron," N&Q, 6th ser., IX (March 8, 1884), 186-87. [Letter to Dr. Bowring found in Antiquarian Magazine, dated Oct. 7, 1823.] Cf. Este, ibid., 6th ser., IX (March 29, 1884), 254. [Has a holograph letter of Byron dated March 30, 1824, offers to send a copy of it.] Fred W. Joy, ibid., 6th ser., IX (April 12, 1884), 285. [Another letter to Dr. Bowring, dated Oct. 13, 1823, in his collection at Cathedral Library, Ely.] Richard Edgcumbe, ibid., 6th ser., IX (April 12, 1884), 290. [Says that the letter found in Antiquarian Magazine by Rusticus had already appeared in Moore's Life and Letters, dated Dec. 7, 1823.] Richard Edgcumbe, ibid., 6th ser., IX (May 3, 1884), 356. [Letter in Joy's collection also had appeared in Moore's Life, p. 604.] Fred W. Joy, ibid., 6th ser., IX (May 10, 1884), 375. [Accepts Edgcumbe's reproof about his carelessness.]

Sawyer, Frederick E. "Princess Charlotte and Whig Views," N&Q, 6th ser., X (Oct. 25, 1884), 328. [When did Byron write "Lines to a Lady Weeping?" When and where did the incident occur?] Cf. Edward Solly, ibid., 6th ser., X (Nov. 8, 1884), 369-70. [Circumstances took place at a dinner given by the Prince Regent at Carlton House on Jan. 22, 1812.]

Swinburne, A. C. "Wordsworth and Byron," Nineteenth Century, XV (April, 1884), 583-609; ibid., XV (May, 1884), 764-90. Rptd. in Complete Works of Algernon Charles Swinburne, eds. Sir Edmund Gosse and Thomas James Wise. 20 vols. London: William Heineman; New York: G. Wells, 1926. Vol. XIV, pp. 155-244.

1885

Burges, Sir James Bland. Selections from the Letters and Correspondence of Sir James Bland Burges, Bart., with Notices of His Life, ed. James Hutton. London: John Murray, 1885. [It contains two letters of Lady Milbanke addressed to Burges, relating to Lord and Lady Byron.]

"The Byron Quarto of 1806 and its Variants," Atheneum, Nov. 21, 1885, 669-70. Cf. ibid., Dec. 5, 1885, pp. 731-33; Richard

Edgcumbe, ibid., Dec. 12, 1885, p. 769; H. Buxton Forman,
ibid., Dec. 19, 1885, p. 807; William Cronin, ibid., Dec.
26, 1885, p. 842; H. Buxton Forman, ibid., Jan. 9, 1886,
pp. 67-68; Richard Edgcumbe and Francis Harvey, ibid.,
Jan. 16, 1886, pp. 101-102; H. Buxton Forman, ibid., Jan.
23, 1886, p. 137.

Courthope, William John. "The Revival of Romance: Scott, Byron,
Shelley," National Review, V (April, 1885), 220-37. Rptd.
in his The Liberal Movement in English Literature. London:
John Murray, 1885. Pp. 111-56.

Dawson, George. "Poe and Byron," Biographical Lectures, ed.
George St. Clair. London: Kegan Paul, Trench & Co.,
1885. Pp. 225-34.

Edgcumbe, Richard. "Hours of Idleness," N&Q, 6th ser., XII
(Nov. 14, 1885), 386. [Early copies.] Cf. A. A., ibid.,
6th ser., XII (Dec. 26, 1886), 520; W. F. Marsh Jackson,
ibid., 7th ser., I (Jan. 30, 1886), 95. [Describe their first
editions.]

Hogg, James T. Memorials of James Hogg, the Ettrick Shepherd,
ed. Mrs. M. G. Garden. London: Alexander Gardner, 1885.

Jeaffreson, John Cordy. "Letters," Atheneum, Sept. 19, 1885,
pp. 369-72. [Twenty-four letters written by Mrs. Leigh to
Rev. Francis Hodgson between the date of her brother's engagement to Miss Milbanke and the end of July 1824, with
evidence against the Stowe scandal. Alfred Morrison has
them.] Cf. Buxton Forman, ibid., Sept. 26, 1885, p. 401.
[Says that letters had appeared in Hodgson's Memoirs.]
John Cordy Jeaffreson and Sam. Timmius, ibid., Oct. 3,
1885, p. 436. [Say that collation of letters shows variants
from Hodgson's version.]

_____. The Real Shelley. 2 vols. London: Hurst & Blackett,
1885.

Maginn, William. Miscellanies: Prose and Verse, ed. R. W.
Montagu. 2 vols. London: Sampson Low, Marston, Searle
& Rivington, 1885.

Mason, Edward Tuckerman. "Byron," Personal Traits of British
Authors: Byron, Shelley, Moore, etc. 4 vols. New York:
C. Scribner's Sons, 1885. Vol. I, pp. 5-71.

Norton, G. "The Might-have-been Old Age of Byron," Nation, XL
(Jan. 22, 1885), 69-70. [His old age might have been tran-
quil, and probably he would have become "the enlightener of
nations," if he had lived to Goethe's age.]

Ruskin, John. Praeterita; Outlines of Scenes and Thoughts Perhaps
    Worthy of Memory in my Past Life. New York: John Wiley
    & Sons, 1885-1889.

Tozer, Henry F. (ed.). "Introduction and Notes, " Childe Harold's
    Pilgrimage. Oxford: The Clarendon Press, 1885. Pp. 7-
    48. Rptd. in 1891 and 1907.

                                1886

Arnold, Frederick. "Lady Byron, " Robertson of Brighton. With
    Some Notices of His Times and Contemporaries. London:
    Ward & Downey, 1886. Pp. 153-95.

Blackledge, Geo. "Finden's Illustrations to The Life and Works of
    Lord Byron, " N&Q, 7th ser. , I (April 3, 1886), 269.
    [Wants information as to the completeness of his volumes.]
    Cf. W. E. Buckley, G. F. R. B. , and Emily Barclay, ibid. ,
    7th ser. , I (April 17, 1886), 311; Alpha, ibid. , 7th ser. , II
    (Aug. 14, 1886), 137; W. H. Halliday and Alpha, ibid. , 7th
    ser. , II (Sept. 4, 1886), 198. [Describe their editions.]

Blind, Mathilde (ed.). "Introductory Notice, " Poetical Works of
    Lord Byron. "The Canterbury Poets. " 2 vols. London:
    Walter Scott, 1886. Pp. vii-xxviii.

Byron-Shelley-Keats. In Memoriam. Endowed Yearly Prizes.
    Prize Essays by Competitors. With Life Incidents of the
    Foundress, Rose Mary Crawshay. Breconshire: Mrs. Craw-
    shay, Cathedine, Bwlch, 1886.
    It contains:
    Kate Cashin, "Byron's 'Fare Thee Well, ' " pp. 43-51.
    Maria H. Russell, "Lines on Hearing Lady Byron was Ill, "
    pp. 52-56.

Carlyle, Thomas. Early Letters of Thomas Carlyle, ed. Charles
    Eliot Norton. 2 vols. London: Macmillan & Co. , 1886.

Gerard, William. Byron Re-Studied in His Dramas; Being a Con-
    tribution towards a Definitive Estimate of His Genius: An
    Essay. London: F. V. White, 1886.

Glover, Mrs. E. W. The Morning Star of Annesley; or, a Poet's
    Love. Mary Chaworth and Lord Byron. Port Huron, Mich. :
    Sunday Commercial Book and Job Print, 1886.

J. "Corinth's Pedagogue, " N&Q, 7th ser. , II (July 3, 1886), 8.
    [Who is the "Corinth's Pedagogue" in the Ode to Napoleon,
    st. xiv?] Cf. ibid. , 7th ser. , II (July 3, 1886), 8. [Editor
    says he was Dionysius the younger.]

Jerningham, Hubert E. H. "Reminiscences of an Attache. Part

IV, " Blackwood's, CXXXIX (Jan., 1886), 101-105. Rptd. in his Reminiscences of an Attaché. Edinburgh: William Blackwood, 1886. [Reports conversations with Countess Guiccioli, mainly about Byron and Allegra.]

Lamb, Charles. Letters of Charles Lamb, with Some Account of the Writer, His Friends and Correspondents, and Explanatory Notes by the Late Sir Thomas Noon Talfour, D. C. L., one of His Executors. An Entirely New Edition Carefully Revised and Greatly Enlarged by W. Carew Hazlitt. 2 vols. London: George Bell & Sons, 1886.

R., M. H. "Homer and Byron," N&Q, 7th ser., II (Nov. 27, 1886), 426. [An echo from The Iliad.] Cf. F. C. Birbeck Terry, ibid., 7th ser., III (Feb. 12, 1887), 137. [Line shows more of Pope than of Homer.]

Roberts, W. "Poems Attributed to Byron," N&Q, 7th ser., II (Sept. 4, 1886), 183-84. [Gives a list.] Cf. W. O. W., ibid., 7th ser., II (Sept. 25, 1886), 253; J. Carrick Moore, ibid., 7th ser., II (Oct. 9, 1886), 298; Frederick Rule, Richard Edgcumbe and William Fraser, ibid., 7th ser., II (Nov. 13, 1886), 389-90; J. Dixon, ibid., 7th ser., II (Dec. 4, 1886), 457; R. R., ibid., 7th ser., III (Jan. 8, 1887), 33; A. J. M., ibid., 7th ser., III (Jan. 22, 1887), 73; St. Swithin, ibid., III (Feb. 19, 1887), 158; W. Roberts, ibid., 7th ser., IV (July 23, 1887), 77. [Additions to first list.]

Rossetti, William Michael. Memoir of Shelley. London: Richard Clay & Sons, 1886.

Stephen, Leslie (ed.). "Lord Byron," Dictionary of National Biography. 63 vols. London: Smith, Elder & Co., 1886. Vol. VIII, pp. 132-57.

Taylor, John. "Byron Bibliography," N&Q, 7th ser., I (Jan. 16, 1886), 42-44. [Lists items.] Cf. Richard Edgcumbe, ibid., 7th ser., I (April 3, 1886), 265; ibid., 7th ser., I (May 29, 1886), 425; ibid., 7th ser., II (July 3, 1886), 3-4; ibid., 7th ser., II (July 31, 1886), 86; ibid., 7th ser., II (Aug. 21, 1886), 143; ibid., 7th ser., II (Sept. 4, 1886), 196; ibid., 7th ser., II (Sept. 11, 1886), 206; ibid., II (Oct. 9, 1886), 284-85. [Edgcumbe contributes his own list of items for a Byron bibliography as well as the classification he would use.]

Winter, William. "Relics of Lord Byron," Shakespeare's England. Edinburgh: D. Douglas, 1886. Pp. 98-103.

1887

Blind, Mathilde (ed.). "Introduction," The Letters of Lord Byron. London: Walter Scott, 1887. Pp. v-xvi.

Brandl, Alois Leonhard. Coleridge and the English Romantic
    School, ed. Lady Eastlake. London: John Murray, 1887.

Briscoe, John Potter. "Byroniana," Home Chimes, n. s. , No. 19,
    (Aug. , 1887), 59-67. [Anecdotes, conversations and poetry.]

"The Byron Quarto in Facsimile," Atheneum, April 23, 1887, p.
    545.

"Byron's Werner," Saturday Review, LXIII (May 28, 1887), 767.

Dowden, Edward. The Life of Percy Bysshe Shelley.   2 vols.
    London: Kegan Paul, Trench & Co. , 1887.

Edgcumbe, Richard. "The Sobriquet 'Albé,' " N&Q, 7th ser. , III
    (May 28, 1887), 425. [Suggests that it may come from Alber-
    marle St.] Cf. A. H. , ibid. , 7th ser. , IV (July 16, 1887),
    53. [Thinks he adopted it because he was blood brother by
    adoption of the Albanesers.]

Glover, Mrs. E. W. Lord Byron and His Daughter.   Port Huron,
    Mich. : Sunday Commercial Book and Job Print, 1887.

Goethe, Johann Wolfgang von. Goethe's Letters to Zelter, with
    Extracts from Those of Zelter to Goethe, Selected, Trans-
    lated and Annotated by A. D. Coleridge.   London: G. Bell
    & Sons, 1887.

Greenough, Francis Boot. Letters of Horatio Greenough to His
    Brother Henry Greenough. Boston: Ticknor & Co. , 1887.
    [Pp. 93-94 contain an anecdote of Byron's visit to an Ameri-
    can man of war.]

Griswold, Hattie Tyng. "Lord Byron," Home Life of Great Au-
    thors. Chicago: A. C. McClurg, 1887. Pp. 94-101.

Hale, Edward Everett (ed.). "Byron," Lights of Two Centuries.
    "Standard Biographies Series. " New York: A. S. Barnes &
    Co. , 1887. Pp. 461-72.

Hamerton, Philip Gilbert. Books Which Have Influenced Me.
    ("British Weekly Extras," No. 1.) London: Office of the
    British Weekly, 1887.

Hayman, Henry D. "The Byron Ladies, " National Review, IX
    (June, 1887), 484-98.

Mackay, Charles. "Medora Leigh," Through the Long Day; or,
    Memorial of a Literary Life during Half a Century.   2 vols.
    London: W. H. Allen & Co. , 1887. Vol. II, pp. 372-78.

Milbanke, Ralph Gordon Noel, Earl of Lovelace. Lady Noel Byron.
    and the Leighs: Some Authentic Records of Certain Circum-

stances in the Lives of Augusta Leigh and Others of Her
Family, that Concerned Anne Isabella, Lady Byron, in the
Course of Forty Years after Her Separation. London: W.
Clowes & Son, 1887.

Morrill, Justin Smith. "Byron," Self-Consciousness of Noted Persons. Boston: Ticknor & Co., 1887. Pp. 158-61.

Roberts, W. "Some Poems Attributed to Byron," N&Q, 7th ser.,
IV (July 23, 1887), 77. [Announces article to appear in Walford's Antiquarian.]

_____. "Some Poems Attributed to Byron," Walford's Antiquari-
an Magazine, XII (1887), 101-106. [Gives a list of these
poems.]

Saunders, Frederick. The Story of Some Famous Books. New
York: A. C. Armstrong & Son, 1887. [Pp. 155-59 deal with
The Prisoner of Chillon.]

Stoddard, Richard H. "Lord Byron," New Princeton Review, 5th
ser., IV (Sept. 1887), 145-62.

Wake, Henry T. "Byron's Childe Harold," N&Q, 7th ser., IV
(Nov. 12, 1887), 389. [In the 1818 Zwickau edition of the
poem that once belonged to Byron, there is a note, perhaps
in his handwriting, indicating that a stanza is omitted between stanzas cxxxiv and cxxxv. Wonders if it is known
which stanza was omitted.] Cf. Edward Marshall, ibid., 7th
ser., IV (Dec. 24, 1887), 512. [Says that in a footnote to
the 17 vol. Murray edition of 1832 is given the text of the
omitted stanza.] G. F. R. B., ibid., 7th ser., IV (Dec. 24,
1887), 512. [Quotes the stanza as it appears in Murray's
The Poetical Works of Lord Byron, 1855.] Richard Edgcumbe, ibid., 8th ser., VIII (Aug. 10, 1895), 101. [The
stanza was omitted because Byron used the word Bat by which
Caroline Lamb was widely known in London society.] Everard
H. Coleman, ibid., 8th ser., VIII (Oct. 26, 1895), 336.
[The suppression of this stanza had been noted before. The
stanza is to be found in, among others, the Murray 10 vol.
edition of 1851.]

Wotton, Mabel E. (ed.). "Byron," Word Portraits of Famous Writers. London: Richard Bentley, 1887. Pp. 47-50.

1888

Althaus, Friedrich. "On the Personal Relations between Goethe
and Byron," Publications of the English Goethe Society, IV
(1888), 1-23.

Byron-Shelley-Keats. In Memoriam. Endowed Yearly Prizes for
the Best Essay in English, Written by a Woman of Any Na-
tion. Prize Essays No. 2. Breconshire: Rose Mary Craw-
shay, Cathedine, Bwlch, 1888.
It contains:
Marie Balfour, "The Vision of Judgment," pp. 19-25.
Eliza May, "The Bride of Abydos," pp. 12-18.
C. E. Montizambert, " 'The Prayer of Nature,' " pp. 7-11.

Downing, W. H. "Byron's Poems," N&Q, 7th ser., V (June 16,
1888), 468. [An 1820 edition of his works published in Philadelphia by M. Thomas.]

Fields, Mrs. James T. A Shelf of Old Books, New York: C.
Scribner's Sons, 1888. [Has a letter from Byron to Murray,
dated Oct. 26, 1821.]

Frey, Albert Romer. Sobriquets and Nicknames. Boston: Tick-
nor & Co., 1888. [Byron was known by such sobriquets as
'The Balaam of Baron,' 'Bard of Corsair,' 'The Comus of
Poetry,' 'Damaetas,' 'Don Jose, Don Juan,' 'A Literary Vas-
sal,' 'Lord Glenarvon,' 'The Mockingbird of our Parnassian
Ornithology.']

Harney, Geo. Julian. "Byron, Shelley, Keats," N&Q, 7th ser., VI
(July 28, 1888), 64. [About the Mrs. Rose Mary Crawshay
Prize Essays on Byron, Keats and Shelley.]

Lamb, Charles. The Letters of Charles Lamb, ed. Alfred Ainger.
2 vols. London: Macmillan & Co., 1888.

Lane-Poole, Stanley. The Life of the Right Honourable Stratford
Canning, Viscount Stratford de Redcliffe. From His Memoirs
and Private and Official Papers. 2 vols. London: Longmans,
Green & Co., 1888. [Reminisces about Harrow cricket match
in which Byron took part.]

Lee, A. Collingwood. "Byron," N&Q, 7th ser., V (March 31, 1888),
246. [Misprint in "The Prisoner of Chillon," st. iii. "Pined
in heart" should read "joined in heart." Also notices "wasted"
for "washed" in Childe Harold, IV, clxxxii.] Cf. J. A. Picton, ibid., 7th ser., V (April 28, 1888), 335-36. [Satisfied
with "wasted."] Richard Edgcumbe, ibid., 7th ser., V
(April 28, 1888), 336. [Gives the correct line which reads
"washed."]

"Lord Byron at Seaham," Monthly Chronicle of North Country Lore
and Legend, II (Feb., 1888), 65-68. [A biographical account
of the courtship and marriage of Byron and Anne Milbank.]

Merrydew, J. T. (ed.). Love Letters of Famous Men and Women.
2 vols. London: Remington & Co., 1888.

Murphy, Rev. M. A. "The Poetry of Byron," Irish Ecclesiastical
    Record, 3rd ser., IX (Dec., 1888), 1084-1108.

Norcross, John E. "Byron," N&Q, 7th ser., VI (Nov. 10, 1888),
    369. [His copy of the Ode to Napoleon Buonaparte has 16
    stanzas and omits the tribute to Washington.] Cf. Frederick
    Rule, ibid., 7th ser., VI (Dec. 22, 1888), 493. [Says that
    in Murray's edition the ode consists of 19 stanzas.] J. Cuth-
    bert Welch, ibid., 7th ser., X (Aug. 23, 1890), 158. [Won-
    ders if an additional stanza published in The Morning Chron-
    icle, April 28, 1814, is by Byron or only an imitation.]

Sharpe, Charles Kirkpatrick. Letters from and to Charles Kirk-
    patrick Sharpe, ed. A. Allardyce, with a Memoir by W. K.
    R. Bedford. 2 vols. London: W. Blackwood, 1888. [About
    Byron's mother's infatuation with her husband-to-be.]

Stedman, Edmund Clarence. Victorian Poets. Boston: Houghton
    Mifflin & Co., 1888. [Byron contrasted with Tennyson and
    Swinburne.]

Taylor, Henry. Correspondence of Henry Taylor, ed. Edward
    Dowden. London: Longmans, Green & Co., 1888. [Contains
    a letter of Wordsworth's charging Byron with plagiarism.]

Winchester, C. T. "Byron," Methodist Review, 5th ser., IV
    (Sept., 1888), 666-86.

Woodberry, George E. "Byron's Centenary," Nation, XLVI (Jan.
    26, 1888), 66-68. Rptd. in his Makers of Literature, New
    York: Macmillan, 1900, pp. 371-85; Literary Essays, New
    York: Harcourt Brace & Co., 1920, pp. 49-58.

                                1889

Canning, Albert Stratford George. Literary Influence in British
    History; An Historical Sketch. London: W. H. Allen, 1889.

Clayden, Peter William. Rogers and His Contemporaries. 2 vols.
    London: Smith, Elder & Co., 1889.

D., W. "Death of Medora," N&Q, 7th ser., VIII (Oct. 19, 1889),
    305. [Thinks it was caused by lightning. Bases his inter-
    pretation on the lines: "The lightning came, that blast hath
    blighted both,/The granite's firmness and the Lily's Growth."]
    Cf. Frederick Rule and E. A. D., ibid., 7th ser., VIII (Nov.
    9, 1889), 377-78. [Both disagree with his interpretation.
    Think that the lightning is metaphorical, not literal.]

Frothingham, Washington, and Charlemagne Tower. "Byron,"
    Our Book. New York: G. W. Dillingham; London: S. Low,
    Son & Co., 1889. Pp. 264-86.

Howitt, Mary. An Autobiography, ed. Margaret Howitt. 2 vols.
    Boston: Houghton Mifflin & Co. , 1889. [Byron's death and
    funeral.]

Marshall, Mrs. Julian. The Life and Letters of Mary Wollstone-
    craft Shelley. London: R. Bentley & Son, 1889.

Melbourne, William Lamb, 2nd Viscount. Lord Melbourne's Papers,
    ed. Lloyd Charles Sanders, with a Preface by the Earl Cow-
    per. London: Longmans, Green & Co. , 1889.

Welch, J. Cuthbert. "Byron's 'Monody on the Death of Sheridan, ' "
    N&Q, 7th ser. , VII (Feb. 9, 1889), 108. [Asks if it was
    issued with or without paper covers. Also what other first
    editions of Byron were issued in paper covers and not boards.]
    Cf. F. W. D. , ibid. , 7th ser. , VII (March 30, 1889), 255.
    [Gives a list.] J. C. Welch, ibid. , 7th ser. , VII (May 11,
    1889), 377. [Lists first editions of Byron's works issued in
    wrappers.]

                                1890

Anderson, J. P. "Bibliography," in Roden Noel, Life of Lord By-
    ron. London: Scott, 1890. Pp. i-xxxviii.

Bolton, Mrs. Sarah Knowles. "Lord Byron," Famous English Au-
    thors of the 19th Century. New York: Thomas Y. Crowell
    & Co. , 1890. Pp. 102-141.

Brooks, Sarah Warner. "Byron and Moore," English Poetry and
    Poets. Boston: Estes & Lauriat, 1890. Pp. 368-87.

Dowden, Edward. "English Men and Women of Letters. No. 9:
    Byron," Atalanta, III (June, 1890), 577-81.

Dunckley, Henry. Lord Melbourne. London: S. Low, Marston,
    Searle & Rivington, 1890.

Noel, Roden. Life of Lord Byron. "Great Writers Series. " Lon-
    don: Walter Scott, 1890.
    Reviews:
    Scots Observer, IV (June 12, 1890), 128.
    Saturday Review, LXX (Aug. 2, 1890), 140-41.

Peacock, Edward. "Byron," N&Q, 7th ser. , X (July 5, 1890), 8.
    [On the third edition of English Bards and Scotch Reviewers.]
    Cf. J. C. Welch, ibid. , 7th ser. , X (Aug. 16, 1890), 135-
    36. [There were two issues of the third edition.]

Reid, Thomas Wemyss. The Life, Letters, Friendships of Richard
    Monckton Milnes, 1st Lord Houghton. 2 vols. London:
    Cassell & Co. , 1890.

Scott, Sir Walter. The Journal of Sir Walter Scott, from the Ori-
    ginal Manuscript at Abbotsford. 2 vols. Edinburgh: D.
    Douglas, 1890.

Stevenson, E. Early Reviews of Great Writers. London: Walter
    Scott, 1890.
    It contains:
        Lord Brougham, a review of Hours of Idleness, pp. 53-60.
        Rptd. from ER, XI (Jan., 1808), 285-89.
        John Wilson, a review of Childe Harold's Pilgrimage, III,
            pp. 168-95. Rptd. from ER, XXX (June, 1818), 87-120.

Story, William Wetmore. Conversations in a Studio. 2 vols.
    Boston: Houghton Mifflin & Co., 1890. [See especially Vol.
    I, p. 233.]

Tew, E. L. H. "Mutiny on the Bounty," N&Q, 7th ser., X (Aug.
    2, 1890), 86. [Announcing the death of the sister of Midship-
    man Stewart; he was the prototype of Byron's young Arcadian
    in The Island.] Cf. John Pickford, ibid., 7th ser., X (Sept.
    13, 1890), 213. [Says he fails to find allusion to George
    Stewart in his copy of The Island.] Frederick Rule, and R.
    M. Spence, ibid., 7th ser., X (Oct. 11, 1890), 291-92.
    [Pickford's copy is probably a first edition, and it may not
    contain a footnote to canto II, st. viii, identifying George
    Stewart.] John Pickford, ibid., 7th ser., X (Nov. 22, 1890),
    412. [Describes his copy and accepts views given by Rule
    and Spence.]

Wharton, Grace, and Wharton, Philip [pseud. for Katherin B.
    Thomson and J. C. Thomson]. The Queens of Society. 2
    vols. London: J. W. Jarvis & Son, 1890. [On Caroline
    Lamb and Byron.]

                                1891

Bancroft, George. "A Day with Lord Byron," History of the Battle
    of Lake Erie and Miscellaneous Papers. New York: R. Bon-
    ner's Sons, 1891. Pp. 190-210. [Reminiscences of the
    American historian.]

Blaikie, W. G. "Lord Byron's Early School Days," Harper's New
    Monthly Magazine, LXXXIII (Aug., 1891), 409-16.

Blumenthal, Friedrich. Lord Byron's Mystery "Cain" and Its Re-
    lation to Milton's "Paradise Lost" and Gessner's "Death of
    Abel." Oldenburg: Gerhard Stalling, 1891.

Buchanan, Robert. "Scott and Byron," ILN, XCIX (Dec. 5, 1891),
    734. Cf. Andrew Lang, "The Futility of Criticism," ibid.,
    XCIX (Dec. 19, 1891), 803. ['Byron was great, with astonish-
    ing blemishes, with long lapses, and wonderful examples of
    the art of sinking. So was Scott.']

Dees, R. R. "Lord Byron," N&Q, 7th ser., XI (Jan. 10, 1891),
    27. [Asks who was the editor of the edition of Byron's Life
    and Works, in 17 volumes, published by Murray in 1834 and
    1835.] Cf. F. W. D., ibid., 7th ser., XI (Jan. 24, 1891),
    77. [Says it was a reissue of Moore's edition.] R. R. Dees,
    ibid., 7th ser., XI (Feb. 7, 1891), 118. [Thinks it was John
    Wright.] Thomas Ewing, ibid., XI (Feb. 28, 1891), 177.
    [Says it was not Moore.] John Murray, ibid., 7th ser., XI
    (March 14, 1891), 213. [Categorically says it was John
    Wright.] F. W. D., ibid., 7th ser., XI (May 16, 1891),
    394; Thomas J. Ewing, ibid., 7th ser., XI (June 13, 1891),
    474-75. [Exchanges reproofs with F. W. D.]

Hayman, Henry. "Glimpses of Byron, with Some Reflections on
    them," Murray's Magazine, X (Oct., 1891), 611-25. Rptd.
    in Living Age, CXCII (Jan. 2, 1892), 41-49.

Ross, Janet. "Byron at Pisa," Nineteenth Century, XXX (Nov.,
    1891), 753-63. [On his political activities in Pisa. A letter
    dated Pisa, March 27, 1822, to Mr. E. J. Dawkins, at the
    Archives in Stato at Florence, here printed for the first time.]

S., J. B. "Byron's Love Letters," N&Q, 7th ser., XI (June 27,
    1891), 508. [Wonders if there are any extant and where they
    can be found.] Cf. J. Cuthbert Welch, ibid., 7th ser., XII
    (July 25, 1891), 72. [Directs him to Love Letters of Famous
    Men and Women in the Past and Present Century, ed. J. T.
    Merrydew, 1888.]

Scherer, Edmond. Essays on English Literature, trans. G. W.
    Saintsbury. New York: Scribner's Sons, 1891.

Smiles, Samuel. A Publisher and His Friends: Memoir and Cor-
    respondence of the Late John Murray, with an Account of the
    Origin and Progress of the House, 1768-1843. 2 vols. Lon-
    don: John Murray, 1891.

Wake, Henry T. "Byroniana," N&Q, 7th ser., XII (Sept. 5, 1891),
    182-83. [Notes written by Byron in a copy of Anna Seward's
    Memoirs of the Life of Dr. Darwin, 1804.]

Winter, William. "Byron," Gray Days and Gold. New York:
    Macmillan & Co., 1891. Pp. 279-87. [Byron, the uncompro-
    mising friend of liberty.]

1892

Bouchier, Jonathan. "Childe Harold: Ianthe," N&Q, 8th ser., I
    (Jan. 30, 1892), 87. [Did he make a mistake in saying that
    Ianthe means a lily?] Cf. Dnargel, ibid., 8th ser., I (Feb.
    20, 1892), 157. [Byron did not really say that Ianthe meant
    a lily. We are faced by a problem of punctuation.] C. C.

B. , ibid. , 8th ser. , I (Feb. 20, 1892), 157. [Says that
Landor uses Ianthe as a substitute for Jane.] G. Fielding
Blandford, ibid. , 8th ser. , I (March 19, 1892), 233. [Thinks
the punctuation is as Dnargel gives it.]

Crosse, Cornelia A. H. Red Letter Days of My Life. 2 vols.
London: Richard Bentley & Son, 1892.

Hugo, Victor Marie, Comte. "Lord Byron, apropos of his death, "
Things Seen and Essays. Vol. XXII of Victor Hugo's Works.
30 vols. Boston: Estes & Lauriat, 1892. Pp. 320-29.

McCrackan, W. D. "The True Bonnivard, the 'Prisoner of Chillon, ' " New England Magazine, n. s. , VI (July 1892), 615-22.

Mather, Marshall. "Byron, the Pessimist, " Popular Studies of
19th Century Poets. London: F. Warne & Co. , 1892. Pp.
75-98.

Sharp, William. The Life and Letters of Joseph Severn. New
York: Charles Scribner's Sons, 1892.

Stedman, Edmund Clarence. The Nature and Elements of Poetry.
Boston: Houghton, Mifflin & Co. , 1892.

Swanwick, Anna. "Lord Byron, " Poets the Interpreters of Their
Age. London: George Bell & Sons, 1892. Pp. 289-99.

                            1893

Allingham, William. "Disraeli's Monument to Byron, " Varieties
in Prose. 3 vols. London: Longmans, Green & Co. , 1893.
Vol. III, pp. 279-312.

"A Byronic Fragment, " Atheneum, April 29, 1893, p. 537. [On
the fragment beginning, "What matter the pangs of a husband
and father. " Internal evidence of the fragment seems to indicate that the two "Charity Ball" stanzas of the standard
edition of Byron's Works (Moore's and Murray's 10 vol. edition) were selected for publication from a satirical piece of
seven stanzas.]

Dole, Nathan Haskell. "Biographical Sketch, " Selected Poems of
Lord Byron, ed. Matthew Arnold. New York: T. Y. Crowell
& Co. , 1893. Pp. vii-lxxi.

Elliott, S. R. "Sonority of Byron, " Critic, XXII (May 13, 1893),
303-304.

Graham, William. "Chats with Jane Clairmont, " Nineteenth Century, XXXIV (Nov. , 1893), 753-69; ibid. , XXXV (Jan. , 1894),

76-90. [Incorporated in his Last Links with Shelley and Byron.] Cf. "The Duty of Forgetting," Spectator, LXXI (Nov.
4, 1893), 626.

Hickey, E. H. "How it Strikes a Contemporary; Impression of
Byron," Atheneum, Jan. 14, 1893, p. 54. ["He was a little
man; he was lame."]

Monkhouse, William Cosmo. Life of Leigh Hunt. "Great Writers
Series." London: Walter Scott, Ltd., 1893.

Morrison, Alfred. "Byron," The Collection of Autograph Letters
and Historical Documents formed by Alfred Morrison. 2nd
series, 1882-1893. 7 vols. London: Printed for Private
Circulation, 1893-1897. Vol. I, pp. 446-56.

Phelps, W. L. The Beginnings of the English Romantic Period.
Boston: Ginn & Co., 1893.

Price, C. A. "Famous Poets, I: Byron," Belgravia, LXXX (Jan.,
1893), 137-52.

Roe, John C. Some Obscure and Disputed Points in Byronic Biography. Leipzig: Printed by Oswald Schmidt, 1893.

Stopes, Charlotte Carmichael. "The First Byron of Newstead Abbey," Atheneum, Sept. 2, 1893, pp. 322-23.

Tomlinson, C. "Sir Walter Scott and Ariosto," N&Q, 8th ser.,
IV (Aug. 26, 1893), 172. [In the line, "And broke the die in
moulding Sheridan," Byron echoes Ariosto.] Cf. R. R.,
ibid., 8th ser., IV (Sept. 9, 1893), 218. [Others had borrowed this thought before Byron.] J. Dixon, ibid., 8th ser.,
IV (Oct. 14, 1893), 316. [Says that Byron confused casting
with stamping.]

"Unpublished Letters of Byron," Bookworm (London), VI (1893),
45-48. [Three letters: 1) to Hodgson, dated Nov. 3, 1808;
2) to Sir James Wedderburn, dated Feb. 10, 1823; 3) to
John Hunt, dated Genoa, March 17, 1823.]

                                  1894

Beddoes, Thomas Lovell. Letters, ed. Edmund Gosse. London:
Elkin Mathews & John Lane, 1894.

C., J. D. "English Bards and Scotch Reviewers," Atheneum,
May 5, 1894, pp. 578-79. [On the bibliography of this satire: different editions.] Cf. John Bagguley, ibid., May 12,
1894, p 614; Bertram Dobell, ibid., May 19, 1894, p. 646;
John Murray, ibid., May 26, 1894, p. 680; E. H. Bates,
ibid., June 2, 1894, pp. 710-11; John Murray, J. R. Bagguley,

Robert Griffin, Bertram Dobell, Roland J. A. Shelley, ibid.,
June 9, 1894, pp. 741-42; J. D. C., ibid., June 16, 1894,
p. 774; W. Spencer, ibid., June 23, 1894, pp. 804-805;
Barry E. Milner, ibid., July 7, 1894, p. 32.

Campbell, James Dykes. Samuel Taylor Coleridge, a Narrative of
the Events of His Life, with a Memoir of the Author by Leslie Stephen. London: Macmillan & Co., 1894.

Granville, Harriet Leveson-Gower, Countess. Letters of Harriet,
Countess Granville, 1810-1845, ed. the Hon. F. Leveson
Gower, 2 vols. London: Longmans, Green & Co., 1894.

Hayman, Henry. "Lord Byron and the Greek Patriots," Harper's
New Monthly Magazine, LXXXVIII (Feb., 1894), 365-70.
[Reprints a previously unpublished letter of Byron to Barff,
dated April 9, 1824.]

Jeaffreson, John Cordy. A Book of Recollections. 2 vols. London: Hurst & Blackett, 1894.

Lowell, James Russell. Letters, ed. Charles Eliot Norton. 2
vols. New York: Harper & Bros., 1894.

_____. The Writings of James Russell Lowell. 10 vols. Bos-
ton: Houghton Mifflin & Co., 1894.

Minto, William. "Byron," Literature of the Georgian Era. London: William Blackwood & Sons, 1894. Pp. 215-33.

Peters, Robert J. Lord Byron. A Study in Heredity and Environment. Tifflin, Ohio: E. R. Good & Bros., 1894.

Ruskin, John. Letters Addressed to a College Friend during the
Years 1840-1845. New York: Macmillan & Co.; London:
G. Allen, 1894.

Scott, Sir Walter. Familiar Letters of Sir Walter Scott. 2 vols.
Boston: Houghton Mifflin & Co., 1894.

Slater, J. H. "Lord Byron," Early Editions: A Bibliographical
Survey of the Works of Some Popular Modern Authors. London: Kegan Paul, Trench, Trübner & Co., 1894. Pp. 62-
69.

Thayer, William Roscoe. The Dawn of Italian Independence. Italy
from the Congress of Vienna, 1814, to the Fall of Venice,
1849. 2 vols. Boston: Houghton Mifflin & Co., 1894.

Wake, Henry T. "Byroniana," N&Q, 8th ser., VI (Aug. 25, 1894),
144-45. [Transcribes a poem, "The Mountain Violet," and
wonders if it is Byron's.] Cf. Jaydee, ibid., 8th ser., VI
(Sept. 8, 1894), 194. [Does not think it is a Byron poem.]

Richard Edgcumbe, ibid. , 8th ser. , VI (Nov. 3, 1894), 355.
[Asks several questions of Wake.] Richard Edgcumbe, ibid. ,
8th ser. , VI (Dec. 29, 1894), 515. [Gives his reasons for
thinking that it is a Byron poem.] John Pickford, ibid. , 8th
ser. , VI (Dec. 29, 1894), 516. [Quotes a stanza "I saw
thee weep," from Hebrew Melodies, also about a violet.]
E. Yardley, ibid. , 8th ser. , VII (Feb. 16, 1895), 138.
[Thinks that the lines quoted by Pickford are like Walter
Scott's "The Lord of the Isles," also published in 1815.]

1895

Coleridge, Samuel Taylor. Letters of Samuel Taylor Coleridge,
    ed. E. H. Coleridge. 2 vols. London: Heineman, 1895.

De Morgan, Sophia Elizabeth. Threescore Years and Ten. Remi-
    niscences of the Late Sophia Elizabeth De Morgan, to Which
    are Added Letters to and from Her Husband, the Late Augus-
    tus De Morgan, and Others, ed. Mary A. De Morgan. Lon-
    don: Richard Bentley & Son, 1895. [Much on Lady Byron.]

Edgeworth, Maria. Life and Letters, ed. Augustus J. C. Hare.
    Boston: Mifflin & Co. , 1895.

Fisher, Mary. "Byron," Twenty Five Letters on English Authors.
    Chicago: S. C. Griggs & Co. , 1895. Pp. 224-32.

Hamann, Albert. A Short History of the Life and Works of Lord
    Byron, from a Course of Lectures Held at the Victoria Lyce-
    um. Berlin: Gaertner, 1895.

Layard, G. S. "Lord Byron and Ianthe," N&Q, 8th ser. , VIII
    (July 6, 1895), 8. [Asks to be enlightened about Ianthe.]
    Cf. J. W. , ibid. , 8th ser. , VIII (July 20, 1895), 58. [She
    was Lady Charlotte Harley, daughter of the Earl of Oxford.
    He refers Layard to Murray's complete edition of Lord By-
    ron's Poems and Moore's Life for further information.]

Peacock, Edward. "Black Banditti," N&Q, 8th ser. , VIII (Dec. 14,
    1895), 464. [The words "Black Banditti" in the Deformed
    Transformed are a reminiscence of the same phrase to be
    found in Robert Fergusson's "Daft Days."]

Rossetti, Dante Gabriel. Dante Gabriel Rossetti: His Family
    Letters. With a Memoir by William Michael Rossetti. 2 vols.
    Boston: Roberts Brothers, 1895.

Scudder, Vida Dutton. The Life of the Spirit in the Modern English
    Poets. Boston & New York: Houghton, Mifflin Co. , 1895.

White, Greenough. "A Study of Modern Pessimism," SR, IV (Nov. ,
    1895), 102-15.

1896

Butler, Samuel.   Life and Letters of Dr. Samuel Butler, ed. Samuel Butler. 2 vols. London: John Murray, 1896. [A letter
from Lord Byron (original in the possession of Mrs. G. L.
Bridges and Miss Butler), dated 4 Bennet St., St. James,
Oct. 20, 1813, is in Vol. I, pp. 89-90.]

Dixon, William Macneille. "The Spirit of Poetry in Revolt:
Burns, Byron, Elliott," English Poetry from Blake to Brown-
ing. "University Extension Series." London: Methuen &
Co., 1896. Pp. 45-73.

Henley, William Ernest (ed.). "Introduction," The Works of Lord
Byron. Vol. I. Letters, 1804-1813. London: William
Heinemann, 1896. Pp. iii-xxi. [No more published.]
Reviews:
   Academy, L (Dec. 19, 1896), 551-52.
   Andrew Lang, Bookman (London), XI (Jan., 1897), 114-16.
      Rptd. in Bookman, V (March, 1897), 63-66.
   Atheneum, Jan. 2, 1897, pp. 7-8. Cf. ibid., Jan. 9, 1897,
      p. 50. [A reply by Henley.]
   Saturday Review, LXXXIII (Jan. 9, 1897), 42-43.
   Critic, XXX (March 6, 1897), 163-64.
   Literary World (Boston), XXVIII (April 3, 1897), 100-101.
      Cf. Henry Abbey, ibid., XXVIII (April 17, 1897), 125-26;
      Francis Howard Williams, Jessie B. Rittenhouse, and B.
      W. Pencock, ibid., XXVIII (May 15, 1897), 163. [Reac-
      tions to original review and to Abbey.]
   Melville B. Anderson, Dial, XXIII (Sept. 1, 1897), 113-16.
   Walter Sichel, Fortnightly Review, LXX (April, 1898), 231-
      48. [Also a review of The Works of Lord Byron, ed. R.
      E. Prothero. Letters and Journals, I.]
   Nation, LXVII (April 18, 1898), 131-33.

Jerningham, Frances Dillon. The Jerningham Letters, 1780-1843,
ed. Egerton Castle. London: Richard Bentley, 1896. [In
one of the letters to Lady Bedingfeld, she narrates Caroline
Lamb's attempt at stabbing herself at Lady Heathcote's party.]

Johnson, Reginald Brimley. Leigh Hunt. London: S. Sonnenschein & Co.; New York: Macmillan & Co., 1896.

Knight, William Angus. Memoir of John Nichol, Professor of
English Literature in the University of Glasgow. Glasgow:
James McLehose & Sons, 1896.

Lang, Andrew. "From a Scottish Workshop," ILN, CIX (Oct. 24,
1896), 546. Cf. "Culture and Byron," Scribner's Magazine,
XX (Sept., 1896), 385-86. [Assails Lang's strictures on Byron.]

Molloy, Joseph Fitzgerald. The Most Gorgeous Lady Blessington.
2 vols. London: Downey & Co., 1896.

Percival, William. "Conversation in Hades between Lord Byron
and H. de Balzac," SR, IV (May, 1896), 377-80. [Byron
shocked on finding out that Saintsbury does not consider him
a great poet.]

Platt, Jas. "Pronunciation of 'Giaour,'" N&Q, 8th ser., IX (May
16, 1896), 386. Cf. Walter W. Skeat, ibid., 8th ser., IX
(May 23, 1896), 418; Jas. Platt, ibid., 8th ser., IX (June
20, 1896), 491-92; Killigrew, ibid., 8th ser., X (July 4,
1896), 11-12; Killigrew, ibid., 8th ser., X (Aug. 8, 1896),
120-21; W. F. Prideaux, ibid., 8th ser., X (Sept. 19, 1896),
240-41; P. Maxwell, ibid., 8th ser., X (Oct. 10, 1896), 302-
303; Richard H. Thornton, ibid., 8th ser., XI (Jan. 2, 1897),
13; F. C. B. Terry, ibid., 8th ser., XII (July 3, 1897), 12;
W. F. Prideaux, ibid., 8th ser., XII (Aug. 21, 1897), 151.

Rae, W. Fraser. Sheridan: A Biography. 2 vols. New York:
Henry Holt & Co., 1896.

Salt, Henry Stephens. Percy Bysshe Shelley, Poet and Pioneer.
London: W. Reeves, 1896.

Smith, Lewis Worthington. "The Literature of Dreams," Poet
Lore, VIII (May, 1896), 233-43. [Touches on Byron's "The
Dream."]

Warner, Charles Dudley. "Lord Byron," Library of the World's
Best Literature, Ancient and Modern. 30 vols. New York:
R. S. Peale & J. A. Hill, 1896. Vol. V, pp. 2935-43.

Warren, Ina Russelle. "Lord Byron," Magazine of Poetry, VIII
(April, 1896), 167-68.

                                  1897

Barbey d'Aurevilly, Jules Amedée. Of Dandyism and of George
Brummell, translated from the French by Douglas Ainslie.
London: J. M. Dent; Boston: Copeland & Day, 1897.

Bayne, Thomas. "Byron's Beppo," N&Q, 8th ser., XII (July 3,
1897), 5. [Gives credit to Frere's Whistlecraft, Tennant's
Anste Fair, and Fairfax's Tasso for the meter.] Cf. E.
Yardley, ibid., 8th ser., XII (July 31, 1897), 94. [Says
that Spenser used this meter.]

Browning, Elizabeth Barrett. Letters, ed. Frederick G. Kenyon.
London: Smith & Elder, 1897.

"Byron, the Poet, Byron the Man," Literary World (Boston),
XXVIII (May 15, 1897), 163.

Dowden, E. "Renewed Revolutionary Advance," The French Revolution and English Literature. New York: Scribner, 1897.
Pp. 243-85.

Eddy, F. M. "Relics of Byron," Munsey, XVII (June, 1897), 330-
42. [About the collection of Byron souvenirs gathered by
Senhor Salvador de Mendonca, Brazilian Minister at Washington.]

Fields, Mrs. James T. Life and Letters of Harriet Beecher
Stowe. London: Sampson Low, Marston & Co., 1897.

Gamlin, Hilda. "The Homecoming of the Remains of Lord Byron,"
N&Q, 8th ser., XI (May 29, 1897), 421-22. Cf. G. Yarrow
Baldock, ibid., 8th ser., XI (June 12, 1897), 470. [Says
that Byron's heart remained in Greece.] E. Walford, ibid.,
8th ser., XI (June 12, 1897), 471. [Adds a few notes to
Gamlin above.] John T. Page, ibid., 8th ser., XII (July 10,
1897), 37-38. [Then, what about the inscription in his tomb
that says his heart is there?] J. P. Stilwell, ibid., 8th ser.,
XII (Sept. 18, 1897), 237. [Says his remains were disem-
barked at the stairs of old Westminster Bridge, not at the
Temple or Whitehall stairs.]

Gennadius, J. "Byron and the Greeks," English Illustrated Magazine, XVII (June, 1897), 289-90.

Hazlitt, William Carew. The Lambs, Their Lives, Their Friends,
and Their Correspondence. New Particulars and New Material. London: Elkin Mathews, 1897.

Herford, Charles Harold. The Age of Wordsworth. London: G.
Bell, 1897.

Keene, H. G. "Waterloo," Westminster Review, CXLVIII (July,
1897), 37-47. [Deals with Napoleon and the stanzas in
Childe Harold's Pilgrimage referring to him.]

Lang, Andrew. The Life and Letters of John Gibson Lockhart.
2 vols. London: John C. Nimmo; New York: Charles
Scribner's Son, 1897.

Lee, Robert. Extracts from the Diary of Dr. Robert Lee. London: Privately Printed by Messrs. Hatchard, 1897. [The
physician of Lord Melbourne reminisces about Byron.]

Mitchell, Donald. "Lord Byron," The Later Georges to Victoria.
Vol. IV of English Lands, Letters and Kings. 4 vols. London: Elkin Mathews, 1897. Pp. 187-252.

Oliphant, Margaret. Annals of a Publishing House. William
    Blackwood and His Sons, Their Magazine and Friends. 3
    vols. Edinburgh and London: William Blackwood & Sons,
    1897-98.

Palgrave, Francis. Landscape in Poetry from Homer to Tennyson.
    London: Macmillan Co., 1897. ['Byron's love of landscape
    was a passion, deep and sincere perhaps as that of any
    poet. "]

Phillips, Walter Alison. The War of Greek Independence. London:
    Smith, Elder & Co., 1897.

Rossetti, Dante Gabriel. Letters of Dante Gabriel Rossetti to W.
    Allingham. London: T. F. Unwin, 1897.

Sanborn, F. B. "Lord Byron in the Greek Revolution," Scribner's
    Magazine, XXII (Sept., 1897), 345-59.

_____. "Odysseus and Trelawny, A Sequel to Byron's Grecian
    Career," Scribner's Magazine, XXI (April, 1897), 504-17.

Sergeant, Lewis. Greece in the 19th Century, A Record of Hellenic
    Emancipation and Progress, 1821-1897. London: T. Fisher
    Unwin, 1897.

Talman, John. "Lord Byron Reconsidered," Midland Monthly (Des
    Moines), VIII (July, 1897), 32-35.

5. INCENTIVE TO SCHOLARSHIP, 1898-1921

1898

*B., J. M. Newark as a Publishing Town. Newark: For Private Circulation Only, 1898. [Reprinted from The Newark Advertiser.]

Biagi, Guido. The Last Days of Percy Bysshe Shelley. New Details from Unpublished Documents. London: T. F. Unwin, 1898.

Bouchier, Jonathan. "Byron and Napoleon," N&Q, 9th ser., II (Sept. 3, 1898), 186.

Bulloch, John Malcolm. "The Duffs and the Gordons. Brains, Bravery, and Byron," Scottish Notes and Queries, XI (May, 1898), 161-64.

_____. "The Gay Gordons: A Study in Inherited Prestige," Blackwood's, CLXIII (Feb., 1898), 245-61. [On the maternal ancestry of Byron.]

_____. "The Lucky Duffs," English Illustrated Magazine, XIX (June, 1898), 235-46.

Coleridge, Ernest Hartley (ed.). The Works of Lord Byron.[1] A New Revised and Enlarged Edition, with Illustrations (including Portraits). Poetry. Vol. I. London: John Murray, 1898. Rptd. New York: Charles Scribner's Sons, 1918 & 1922.
  Reviews:
    Saturday Review, LXXXV (April 30, 1898), 576.
    Lionel Pigot Johnson, Academy, LIII (May 7, 1898), 489-90. Rptd., with slight revisions, in his Post Liminium; Essays and Critical Papers, ed. Thomas Whittemore. London: E. Mathews, 1911, pp. 193-200.
    Francis Thompson, Outlook (London), I (May 7, 1898), 434-35. Rptd. as "The New Byron," in Literary Criticisms, Newly Discovered and Collected by Rev. Terence L. Connolly. New York: E. P. Dutton, 1948. Pp. 112-16.
    Atheneum, May 14, 1898, pp. 621-23. Cf. E. H. Coleridge,

---

[1]Additional volumes of this edition will be referred to hereafter as Poetry, with the appropriate volume number and date following it.

ibid., May 28, 1898, p. 694. [A protestation of the review.]

Richard Garnett, Bookman (London), XIV (June, 1898), 71-72.
Rptd. in part in Bookman, VII (July, 1898), 424-25. [Also
a review of The Works of Lord Byron: Letters and Journals, I.]

Critic, XXXII (June 11, 1898), 385.

F. J. Gregg, Book Buyer, XVI (July, 1898), 483-87. [Also
a review of The Works of Lord Byron: Letters and Journals, I.]

G. L. Kittredge, Nation, LXVII (Aug. 18, 1898), 131-32.
[Also a review of Henley's The Works of Lord Byron and
of The Works of Lord Byron: Letters and Journals, I.]

Dial, XXVI (May 16, 1899), 330-32. [Also a review of The
Works of Lord Byron: Letters and Journals, I and II.]

[A. Symons], QR, CXCII (July, 1900), 25-44. [Also a review of The Works of Lord Byron: Poetry, II, and Letters
and Journals, I-III.]

[A. C. Lyall], ER, CXCII (Oct., 1900), 358-81. Rptd. in
Living Age, CCXXVIII or n. s. X (Jan. 19, 1901), 137-53;
Studies in Literature and History, London: John Murray,
1915, pp. 177-209. [Also a review of The Works of Lord
Byron: Letters and Journals, I and II.]

Edgcumbe, Richard. "A Byronic Fragment," Atheneum, Oct. 15,
1898, p. 530. ["Ossian's Address to the Sun." The Harvard
Version printed for purposes of comparison with the Newstead
version. Suggests that perhaps the Harvard MS is the first
draft of his translation.] Cf. W. E. G. G., ibid., Oct. 29,
1898, p. 609. [Collated the two poems and does not think
one is a draft of the other. The shorter Newstead version
is generally nearer to the original.] Richard Edgcumbe, ibid.,
Nov. 19, 1898, p. 714. [Makes some points for the authenticity of the Harvard copy, once in his possession.]

Foster, Vere Henry Lewis. The Two Duchesses: Family Correspondence, 1777-1859. London: Blackie & Sons, 1898. [Im-
pressions.]

Graham, William. Last Links with Byron, Shelley and Keats.
London: L. Smithers & Co., 1898.
Review:
Saturday Review, LXXXVII (Jan. 21, 1899), 87.
See also:
E. L. H. Tew, "Mr. Graham and Jane Clairmont," N&Q,
11th ser., II (Aug. 6, 1910), 108-109; ibid., 11th ser.,
VIII (Sept. 20, 1913), 228; H. Londsdale, ibid., 11th ser.,
VIII (Sept. 27, 1913), 249.

Hebb, John. "Byron and Shelley in Pisa," N&Q, 9th ser., I
(Feb. 19, 1898), 142-43.

Johnson, Charles Frederick. Elements of Literary Criticism.
New York: Harper & Bros. , 1898.

Kiernan, Jas. G. "Degeneracy Stigmata as Basis of Morbid Suspicion: A Study of Byron and Sir Walter Scott," Alienist and
Neurologist, XIX (Jan. , 1898), 40-55; ibid. , XIX (July, 1898),
447-56; ibid. , XIX (Oct. , 1898), 589-98; ibid. , XX (April,
1899), 175-86; ibid. , XX (Oct. , 1899), 565-71; ibid. , XX
(July, 1900), 419-31; ibid. , XXI (Jan. , 1901), 50-57; ibid. ,
XXI (April, 1901), 287-304; ibid. , XXI (Oct. , 1901), 668-88.

"Lameness of Byron," Literary World (Boston), XXIX (July 23,
1898), 232.

M. , W. "Was Byron a Dandy?" Academy, LIV (July 30, 1898),
113-14. [He was a dandy only on certain days.]

Matthews, Brander. "New Trials for Old Favorites," Forum,
XXV (Aug. , 1898), 749-60. [There are signs of a revolution
in Byron's favor.]

More, Paul Elmer. "The Wholesome Revival of Byron," Atlantic
Monthly, LXXXII (Dec. , 1898), 801-809. Rptd. , in revised
form and in combination with a review of The Works of Lord
Byron: Poetry, IV, from Independent, LIII (Oct. 3, 1901),
2359-60, as "Biographical Sketch" in The Complete Poetical
Works of Lord Byron. New York: Houghton Mifflin, 1905.
Pp. xi-xxi.

Murray, John, IV. "Lord Byron," Vol. VII of A Reference Catalogue of British and Foreign Autographs and Manuscripts, ed.
T. J. Wise. London: One hundred copies only printed for
distribution to Members of the Society of Archivists, 1898.

Phillips, Stephen. "The Poetry of Byron. An Anniversary Study,"
Cornhill Magazine, LXXVII (Jan. , 1898), 16-26.

Pratt, Alice Edwards. "Byron's Use of Color," The Use of Color
in the Verse of the English Romantic Poets. Chicago: The
University of Chicago Press, 1898. Pp. 61-68.

Prothero, Rowland E. "Childhood and School Days of Byron,"
Nineteenth Century, XLIII (Jan. , 1898), 61-81.

_____ (ed.). The Works of Lord Byron. [1] A New Revised and
Enlarged Edition, with Illustrations (including Portraits).
Letters and Journals. Vol. I. London: John Murray, 1898.
Rptd. New York: Charles Scribner's Sons, 1918 and 1922.
Reviews:
Academy, LIII (May 21, 1898), 541-42.

[1]Additional volumes of this edition will be referred to hereafter as
Letters and Journals, with the appropriate volume number and date.

Richard Garnett. See Coleridge, Poetry, I, 1898.
Saturday Review, LXXXV (June 11, 1898), 782-83.
Atheneum, June 18, 1898, pp. 781-82.
F. J. Gregg. See Coleridge, Poetry, I, 1898.
Critic, XXXIII (July, 1898), 74-78.
Literary World (Boston), XXIX (July 23, 1898), 230-31.
Walter Sichel, Fortnightly Review, LXX (Aug. , 1898), 231-48.
  [Also a review of Henley's The Works of Lord Byron,
  1896.]
G. L. Kittredge. See Coleridge, Poetry, I, 1898.
Dial. See Coleridge, Poetry, I, 1898.
G. S. Street, Blackwood's, CLXVI (Nov. , 1899), 620-30.
  [Also a review of The Works of Lord Byron: Letters and
  Journals, II and III.] Rptd. together with a review of The
  Works of Lord Byron: Letters and Journals, IV-VI,
  Blackwood's, CLXX (Dec. , 1901), 761-71, as "Books and
  Men: Byron to 1816. Byron 1816-1824," in his A Book
  of Essays. Westminster: A. Constable & Co. , 1902, pp.
  67-119.
[A. Symons]. See Coleridge, Poetry, I, 1898.
[A. C. Lyall]. See Coleridge, Poetry, I, 1898.

_____ (ed.). Letters and Journals, II, 1898.
Reviews:
  Academy, LV (Dec. 10, 1898), 413-15.
  Saturday Review, LXXXVI (Dec. 10, 1898), 787.
  Bookman (London), XV (Jan. , 1899), 112-13.
  Atheneum, Jan. 14, 1899, pp. 43-44.
  Critic, XXXIV (March, 1899), 282.
  Dial. See Coleridge, Poetry, I, 1898.
  G. L. Kittredge, Nation, LXIX (July 13, 1899), 34-35. [Al-
    so a review of The Works of Lord Byron: Poetry, II.]
  G. S. Street. See Prothero, Letters and Journals, I, 1898.
  [A. Symons]. See Coleridge, Poetry, I, 1898.
  [A. C. Lyall]. See Coleridge, Poetry, I, 1898.

Trent, W. P. "The Byron Revival," Forum, XXVI (Oct. , 1898),
  242-56. Rptd. in his The Authority of Criticism. New York:
  C. Scribner's Sons, 1899. Pp. 205-36.

                              1899

Beavan, Arthur H. James and Horace Smith ... A Family Narrative Based upon Hitherto Unpublished and Private Diaries,
  Letters, and Other Documents. London: Hurst and Blackett,
  1899.

Beers, Henry A. A History of English Romanticism in the 19th
  Century. New York: Holt, 1899.

Browning, Robert and Elizabeth Barrett Browning. The Letters of
  Robert Browning and Elizabeth Barrett Browning, ed. Robert

Weidmann Barret Browning. 2 vols. New York: Harper & Bros., 1899.

Bryant, John Ebenezer. "Lord Byron," Home Study Circle, ed. Seymour Eaton. New York: The Doubleday and McClure Co., 1899. Pp. 215-92.

Bulloch, J. M. "Byron's Maternal Grandfather," N&Q, 9th ser., IV (July 8, 1899), 27. [Did he drown himself?] Cf. A. R. Bayley, ibid., 9th ser., X (July 19, 1902), p. 52. [Cites Prothero and Stephen to support suicide.] T. C. F., ibid., 9th ser., X (Aug. 2, 1902), 97. [Says that a burial entry in the 'Registers' of Bath Abbey does not refer to the cause of death.]

Coleridge, Ernest Hartley (ed.). Poetry, II, 1899.
   Reviews:
   Atheneum, June 10, 1899, pp. 713-14.
   Bookman (London), XVI (July, 1899), 104.
   Nation, LXIX (July 13, 1899), 34-35.
   Spectator, LXXXIII (Aug. 19, 1899), 254-55. [Also a review of The Works of Lord Byron: Letters and Journals, III.]
   M. B. Anderson, Dial, XXVII (Dec. 1, 1899), 420-21. [Also a review of The Works of Lord Byron: Letters and Journals, III.]

Gates, Lewis Edwards. "Francis Jeffrey," Three Studies in Literature. New York: The Macmillan Co., 1899. Pp. 1-63.

Gower, Leveson F. "Did Byron Write Werner?" Nineteenth Century, XLVI (Aug., 1899), 243-50. [Argues that the Duchess of Devonshire wrote it, who gave the MS to Lady Caroline Lamb.]

Hancock, Albert Elmer. "Byron," The French Revolution and the English Poets. New York: H. Holt & Co., 1899. Pp. 78-118.

L., H. "The Spectre of Byron at Venice," Academy, LVI (June 24, 1899), 685. [His spirit pervades Italy.]

Moore, Thomas. "Thomas Moore" Anecdotes, ed. Wilmot Harrison. London: Jarrold & Sons, 1899.

Prothero, Rowland E. (ed.). Letters and Journals, III, 1899.
   Reviews:
   Atheneum, July 22, 1899, pp. 117-18.
   Saturday Review, LXXXVIII (Aug. 5, 1899), 170-71.
   Academy, LVII (Aug. 12, 1899), 151-52.
   Spectator. See Coleridge, Poetry, II, 1899.
   M. B. Anderson. See Coleridge, Poetry, II, 1899.
   G. L. Kittredge, Nation, LXXI (Aug. 23, 1900), 154-56.
   [Also a review of The Works of Lord Byron: Poetry, III.]

G. S. Street. See Prothero, Letters and Journals, I, 1898.
[A. Symons]. See Coleridge, Poetry, I, 1898.

Redgrave, Gilbert R. "The First Four Editions of English Bards
    and Scotch Reviewers," Library (London), n. s., I (Dec. 1,
    1899), 18-25. [Published about the middle of March 1809.]

Ross, Adelaide. "Reminiscences of Lady Byron," Nineteenth Cen-
    tury, XLV (May, 1899), 821-32.

Tweedie, Ethel Brilliana Harley. George Harley, F. R. S. The
    Life of a London Physician, ed. his daughter. London: The
    Scientific Press, 1899. [Contains references to Byron.]

Winchester, Caleb Thomas. Some Principles of Literary Criticism.
    New York: The Macmillan Co., 1899.

1900

Amstel, A. van. "The True Story of the Prisoner of Chillon,"
    Nineteenth Century, XLVII (May, 1900), 821-29.

Bowen, Anna M. "Byron's Influence upon Goethe," Dial, XXVIII
    (March 1, 1900), 144-47.

Byers, Samuel H. M. Twenty Years in Europe. Chicago: Rand,
    McNally & Co., 1900.

"Byron as Self-critic," Academy, LIX (Aug. 11, 1900), 113-14.
    [Extracts from his letters show Byron as a critic of his
    Manfred, as play and poetry.]

Carpenter, Frederick Ives (ed.). "Introduction," Selections from
    the Poetry of Lord Byron. New York: H. Holt, 1900. Pp.
    v-lviii.

Clark, John Scott. "Byron," A Study of English and American
    Poets, A Laboratory Method. New York: C. Scribner's
    Sons, 1900. Pp. 370-410. [A selection of excerpts from
    Byron critics of the nineteenth century.]

Coleridge, Ernest Hartley (ed.). Poetry, III, 1900.
    Reviews:
    Atheneum, June 23, 1900, pp. 775-76.
    Saturday Review, LXXXIX (June 30, 1900), 813-14.
    Francis Thompson, Academy, LVIII (June 30, 1900), 548-49.
        Rptd. as "Byron of Tinsel and Splendours," in The Real
        Robert Louis Stevenson and Other Critical Essays, ed.
        Terence L. Connolly. New York: University Publishers,
        Inc., 1959. Pp. 96-99.
    G. L. Kittredge. See Prothero, Letters and Journals, III,
        1899.

Richard Garnett, Bookman (London), XVIII (Sept., 1900), 180-81.

Keith, Abijah. "The Sword of Lord Byron," Proceedings of the Vermont Historical Society, Oct. 16 and Nov. 7, 1900, pp. 91-92.

Omond, Thomas S. The Romantic Triumph. London: W. Blackwood & Sons, 1900.

Patmore, Coventry. Memoirs and Correspondence, ed. Basil Champneys. 2 vols. London: George Bell & Sons, 1900.

Prothero, Rowland E. (ed.). Letters and Journals, IV, 1900. Reviews:
  Atheneum, Aug. 11, 1900, pp. 175-77. Cf. ibid., Aug. 25, 1900, p. 253.
  Richard Garnett. See Coleridge, Poetry, III, 1900.
  Saturday Review, XCI (June 1, 1901), 707. [Also a review of The Works of Lord Byron: Letters and Journals, V.]
  G. S. Street, Blackwood's, CLXX (Dec., 1901), 761-71. [Also a review of The Works of Lord Byron: Letters and Journals, V and VI.] Rptd., together with a review of The Works of Lord Byron: Letters and Journals I-III, Blackwood's, CLXVI (Nov., 1899), 620-30, as "Books and Men: Byron to 1816. Byron 1816-1824," in his A Book of Essays. Westminster: A. Constable & Co., 1902. Pp. 67-119.

Robinson, William Clarke. British Poets of the Revolutionary Age: Burns, Byron, Moore, Scott, Shelley, Wordsworth, 1776-1848. Delivered as University Extension Lectures. Belfast: Sold by Olley & Co., 1900. [Each lecture is paged separately.]

Rutherford, Mark [pseud. for William Hale White]. Pages from a Journal. London: Unwin, 1900.
  It contains:
  "The Morality of Byron's Poetry, and The Corsair," pp. 125-32.
  "Byron, Goethe and Matthew Arnold," pp. 133-48. Rptd. from CR, XL (Aug., 1881), 179-85.

Scott, Mary Augusta. "Mary Chaworth's Daughter," Nation, LXX (Feb. 22, 1900), 144-45.

Sharp, Robert F. "Byron, the Man," Architects of English Literature; Biographical Sketches of Great Writers from Shakespeare to Tennyson. New York: E. P. Dutton & Co.; London: S. Sonnenschein & Co., 1900. Pp. 186-201.

Stoddard, R. H. (ed.). "Introduction," The Works of Lord Byron, with His Letters and Journals and His Life by Thomas

Moore. 16 vols. London: Francis A. Nicolls & Co. ,
[1900]. Pp. xix-xl.

Wratislaw, Theodore. Algernon Charles Swinburne. London:
Greening & Co. , 1900.

1901

Brandes, Georg Morris Cohen. Main Currents in 19th Century
Literature, trans. Diana White and Mary Morrison from the
Danish. 6 vols. London: W. Heinemann, 1901-1905.
It contains:
"Byron: His Self-Absorption," IV, 292-99.
"Byron: The Passionate Personality," IV, 251-92.
"Byron: The Revolutionary Spirit," IV, 300-318.
"Byron's Death," IV, 358-64.
"Comic and Tragic Realism," IV, 319-41.
"Culmination of Naturalism," IV, 342-57.
"Influence of Byron," VI, 30-33.

Coleridge, Ernest Hartley (ed.). Poetry, IV, 1901.
Reviews:
Atheneum, July 27, 1901, pp. 113-14.
Richard Garnett, Bookman (London), XX (Sept. , 1901), 180.
Paul Elmer More, Independent, LIII (Oct. 3, 1901), 2359-60.
Partly incorporated in the "Biographical Sketch" that ap-
pears in The Complete Poetical Works of Lord Byron.
New York: Houghton Mifflin, 1905. Pp. xi-xxi.
G. L. Kittredge, Nation, LXXIII (Dec. 12, 1901), 457-58.

Courthope, William John. "Byron and Tennyson," Life in Poetry;
Law in Taste. London: Macmillan & Co. , 1901. Pp. 388-
418.

Edgcumbe, Richard. " 'Stanzas to the Po,' " Atheneum, Aug. 24,
1901, pp. 252-53. [An interpretation.]

Garnett, Richard. "Shelley and Beaconsfield," Essays of an Ex-
Librarian. London: William Heinemann, 1901. Pp. 101-25.

L. , W. F. "Byron's Poem on Greece," N&Q, 9th ser. , VII
(April 27, 1901), 328. [Asks if somebody can supply him
with the poem written by a lady in answer to Byron's poem
on Greece.] Cf. Charles Green, ibid. , 9th ser. , VII (June
15, 1901), 475. [Quotes the poem.]

Levi, Eugenia. "Byron and Petrarch," Atheneum, July 20, 1901,
pp. 95-96. [Did Byron translate Petrarch's "The Death of
Mago," Book VI of his Africa?] Cf. Irving W. Way, ibid. ,
Aug. 17, 1901, p. 222. [Says that in his copy of Foscolo's
Essays on Petrarch, the name of Byron is crossed out and
that of Medwin substituted.] Richard Edgcumbe, ibid. , Sept.

7, 1901, p. 318. [Says that Medwin may have been the translator.]

Prothero, Rowland E. (ed.). Letters and Journals, V, 1901.
  Reviews:
    B. B. B. , Academy, LX (Feb. 16, 1901), 147-48. Cf. Edward Hutton, ibid. , LX (Feb. 23, 1901), 171.
    Atheneum, April 13, 1901, pp. 455-57. Cf. , ibid. , April 20, 1901, p. 501; ibid. , April 27, 1901, p. 531.
    Richard Garnett, Bookman (London), XX (May, 1901), 52-53. [Also a review of The Works of Lord Byron: Letters and Journals, V.]
    Saturday Review. See Prothero, Letters and Journals, IV, 1900.
    G. S. Street. See Prothero, Letters and Journals, IV, 1900.

_____. (ed.). Letters and Journals, VI, 1901.
  Reviews:
    Atheneum, Nov. 30, 1901, pp. 725-26.
    G. S. Street. See Prothero, Letters and Journals, IV, 1900.
    Richard Garnett, Bookman (London), XXI (Dec. , 1901), 87-88. Rptd. in Bookman, XIV (Feb. , 1902), 587-88.
    G. L. Kittredge. See Coleridge, Poetry, IV, 1901.

Schuyler, Eugene. "Shelley with Byron, " Italian Influences. London: Sampson Low, Marston & Co. , 1901. Pp. 135-55.

Scudder, Horace Elisha. James Russell Lowell: A Biography. 2 vols. Boston: Houghton Mifflin & Co. , 1901.

Young, John Russell. Men and Memories; Personal Reminiscences. 2 vols. New York: F. T. Neely, 1901.

1902

Blake, C. J. "Byron's Marino Faliero, " Great Thoughts from Master Minds, 5th ser. , II (Dec. , 1902), 131-32.

Bulloch, John Malcolm. House of Gordon Gight. Aberdeen: Printed for the New Spalding Club, 1902.

Chesterton, G. K. "The Optimism of Byron, " Twelve Types. London: A. L. Humphreys, 1902. Pp. 31-44. Rptd. in his Varied Types. New York: Dodd, Mead & Co. , 1903, pp. 29-39; Five Types, London: Arthur L. Humphreys, 1910, pp. 1-14.

Coleridge, Ernest Hartley (ed.). Poetry, V, 1902.
  Reviews:
    Richard Garnett, Bookman (London), XXII (May, 1902), 60-61.
    Atheneum, May 24, 1902, pp. 647-48.

Dawson, William James. "Lord Byron," The Makers of Modern
English. New York: T. Whittaker, 1902. Pp. 26-35. Rptd.
as The Makers of English Poetry. New York: F. H. Revell
Co., 1906. Pp. 35-44. [Pity will "always be the predomi-
nant feeling of the world towards him," if it considers the environment of his life.]

Edgar, Pelham. "The Nature Poetry of Byron and Shelley,"
Canadian Magazine, XIX (May, 1902), 18-24.

Herrmann, Albert. A Grammatical Inquiry into the Language of
Lord Byron. Berlin: R. Gaertners, 1902.

Hughes, Charles Hamilton. "A Neuro-Psychologist's Plea for Byron," Alienist and Neurologist, XXIII (Aug., 1902), 349-51.
["He became intellectually overwrought and instinctively sought
the reaction of reckless psychical and physical dissipation for
relief from pangs of cerebrasthenic brain fag and general nervous exhaustion."]

Laughlin, Clara Elizabeth. "Variously Estimated Byron and His
Life of Unrest," Stories of Authors' Loves. 2 vols. Philadelphia: J. B. Lippincott Co., 1902. Vol. II, pp. 201-51.

Moulton, Charles Wells (ed.). "Byron," Library of Literary
Criticism of English and American Authors. 8 vols. Buffa-
lo: The Moulton Publishing Company, 1902. Vol. IV, pp.
731-66. [A collection of passages from different books dealing with Byron.]

Paston, George [pseud. for Emily Morse Symonds]. "An American
in England," Sidelights on the Georgian Period. London:
Methuen & Co., 1902. Pp. 281-300. [On Ticknor's acquaintance with Byron.]

"The Persistence of Byron," Academy, LXII (April 26, 1902), 435-
36. [Deals with the burial of Byron.]

Poe, Edgar Allan. The Works of Edgar Allan Poe, eds. Edmund
Clarence Stedman and George Edward Woodberry. 10 vols.
New York: Charles Scribner's Sons, 1902. [Scattered com-
ments.]

Repplier, Agnes. "Allegra," Atlantic Monthly, LXXXIX (April,
1902), 466-70. Rptd. in her Compromises. Boston: Houghton Mifflin & Co., 1904, pp. 240-77; Eight Decades; Essays
and Episodes. Boston: Houghton Mifflin & Co., 1937, pp.
199-222.

Saintsbury, George. A History of Criticism and Literary Taste in
Europe. 3 vols. Edinburgh: W. Blackwood, 1902.

Schauffler, R. "Two New Byron Letters," Book Buyer, XXIV
(April, 1902), 199-200. [To Mrs. Stith, dated at Villa Du-
puis, May 22, 1822, and another to Major Stith.]

Whitman, Walt. The Complete Writings of Walt Whitman. 10
vols. New York: G. P. Putnam's Sons, 1902-1903. [Scat-
tered references.]

Williams, Edward Ellerker. The Journal of Edward Ellerker Williams, Companion of Shelley and Byron in 1821 and 1822,
with an introduction by R. Garnett. London: E. Mathews,
1902.

1903

Bowles, Ralph Hartt (ed.). "Introduction," Byron's Shorter Poems.
New York: The Macmillan Co., 1903. Pp. xiii-xxxviii.

Cockerell, Charles Robert. Travels in Southern Europe and the
Levant, 1810-1817. The Journal of Charles Robert Cockerell,
R. A., ed. Samuel Pepys Cockerell. London: Longmans,
Green & Co., 1903. [Contains references to Byron whom
Cockerell met in the East in 1810-1811.]

Coleridge, Ernest Hartley (ed.). Poetry, VI, 1903.
Reviews:
TLS, April 24, 1903, p. 125.
[Francis Thompson], Academy, LXIV (May 2, 1903), 439-40.
Rptd. as "Poet's Table Talk," in Literary Criticisms,
Newly Discovered and Collected by Rev. Terence L. Con-
nolly. New York: E. P. Dutton, 1948. Pp. 112-16.
Richard Garnett, Bookman (London), XXIV (Aug., 1903), pp.
183-84.
Atheneum, Aug. 15, 1903, pp. 209-10.
Paul Elmer More, Independent, LV (Aug. 27, 1903), 2049-52.
Rptd. as "A Note on Byron's Don Juan," in his Shelburne
Essays, 3rd ser. New York: G. P. Putnam's Sons, 1906,
166-76.
G. L. Kittredge, Nation, LXXVII (Oct. 8, 1903), 285-86.

De Mille, A. B. Literature in the Century. London: W. & R.
Chambers; Philadelphia: The Bradley-Garretson Co., 1903.

Garnett, Richard. "The 'John Bull' Letter to Lord Byron,"
Atheneum, March 7, 1903, pp. 304-305. [Thinks John Black
is the author.]

_____, and Edmund Gosse. "Byron," English Literature, an
Illustrated Record. 4 vols. New York: Macmillan, 1903-
1904. Vol. IV, pp. 107-22.

K., L. L. "Byroniana," N&Q, 9th ser., XI (June 6, 1903), 444.
[Byron at Ferrara?] Cf. Richard Edgcumbe, ibid., 9th ser.,
XI (June 20, 1903), 492-93. [Denial.] L. L. K., ibid.,
9th ser., XI (July 4, 1903), 18. [Insists that he was at
Ferrara.] Richard Edgcumbe, ibid., 9th ser., XI (July 18,
1903), 91. [Apologizes for his mistake.]

"A New Poem by Byron," Bookman, XVIII (Sept., 1903), pp. 71-
78. ["King of the Humbugs," heavily annotated, found in
a drawer.]

Pudbres, Anna. "Lord Byron: The Admirer and Imitator of Al-
fieri," Englische Studien, XXXIII (1903), 40-83.

Rebec, George. "Byron and Morals," International Journal of
Ethics, XIV (Oct., 1903), 39-54.

Rossetti, William Michael. Rossetti Papers, 1862-1870. New
York: C. Scribner's Sons, 1903.

Trowbridge, John Townsend. My Own Story. Boston: Houghton,
Mifflin & Co., 1903.

Watts-Dunton, Theodore. "Byron," Chamber's Cyclopaedia of
English Literature. New edition. 3 vols. London: W. &
R. Chambers, 1903. Vol. III, pp. 118-35.

Woodberry, George Edward. The Torch: Eight Lectures on Race
Power in Literature. New York: McClure, Phillips & Co.,
1903.

                                    1904

Bonnell, Cedric. Lord Byron. Some Passages in the Career of
"Our Mightiest Minstrel," Ranged and Arranged by Cedric
Bonnell. ("Lions of Lambkinville" Series, No. 12.) 1904 [Rptd.
from the Nottinghamshire Express, July 1 and 8, 1904.]

Bulloch, J. M. "England and Lord Byron," The Lamp, XXIX
(Aug., 1904), 24-26. [Byron neglected in England.]

Coleridge, E. H. "Lord Byron," Transactions of the Royal Society
of Literature, 2nd ser., XXV (1904), 127-50.

_____ (ed.). Poetry, VII, 1904.
Reviews:
    Bookman (London), XXVI (May, 1904), 64.
    Atheneum, May 21, 1904, pp. 645-46; ibid., June 4, 1904,
        pp. 714-15. Cf. E. H. Coleridge, ibid., June 11, 1904,
        p. 753.
    Saturday Review, XCVII (May 21, 1904), 660-61.
    M. B. Anderson, Dial, XXXVI (June 16, 1904), 389-90.

[Review of the thirteen volumes.]
John Churton Collins, QR, CCII (April, 1905), 429-57. Rptd.
as "The Works of Lord Byron," in his Studies in Poetry
and Criticism. London: George Bell & Co., 1905. Pp.
78-123. [Review of the thirteen volumes.]

Corbett, F. St. John. "Lord Byron," History of British Poetry.
London: Gay & Bird, 1904. Pp. 424-38.

Creevey, Thomas. The Creevey Papers. A Selection from the
Correspondence and Diaries of the Late Thomas Creevey,
M. P., ed. Sir Herbert Maxwell. 2 vols. London: John
Murray, 1904. [Byron and Glenarvon.]

Duff, J. Wight (ed.). "Introduction," Byron: Selected Poetry.
Edinburgh: W. Blackwood, 1904. Pp. ix-lxi.

Forman, H. B. "Early Poems of Byron Authenticated," Atheneum,
June 11, 1904, pp. 752-53. ["Adieu to Sweet Mary for ever,"
and "O Memory, Torture Me No More."]

Gwynn, Stephen Lucius. "Byron," The Masters of English Literature. London: Macmillan & Co., 1904. Pp. 308-28.

H., W. B. "Byroniana," N&Q, 10th ser., I (June 18, 1904), 488.
[Who was the author of A Sequel to Don Juan?] Cf. P. J. F.
Gantillon, ibid., 10th ser., II (July 16, 1904), 55. [G. W.
M. Reynolds.]

Haney, John Louis (ed.). Early Reviews of English Poets. Philadelphia: The Egerton Press, 1904.
   It contains:
   Lord Brougham. "A Review of Hours of Idleness," pp. 94-
   100. Rptd. from ER, XI (Jan., 1808), 285-89.
   "A review of Childe Harold's Pilgrimage, I and II," pp. 101-
   14. Rptd. from Christian Observer, XI (June, 1812), pp.
   376-87.

Kindon, J. "Byron versus Spenser," International Journal of
Ethics, XIV (April, 1904), 362-77.

"The King of the Humbugs," Good Words, XLV (July, 1904), 467-
73; ibid., XLV (Aug., 1904), 579-87. [A Byron find.]

Kuhns, L. Oscar. "Byron," Dante and the English Poets from Chaucer
to Tennyson. New York: H. Holt & Co., 1904. Pp. 150-72.

Sharp, William. Literary Geography. London: Officers of the
"Pall Mall Publications," 1904.

Sichel, Walter. Disraeli: A Study in Personality and Ideas. London: Methuen & Co., 1904.

Spermologos. "Byron's Works Abroad," Saturday Review, XCVII
    (March 12, 1904), 331-32. [Byron best known of English
    poets throughout Eastern Europe where editions of his works
    are in stock everywhere.]

Symons, A. (ed.). "Introduction," Byron: Poems. London:
    Blackie & Son, 1904. Pp. iii-ix.

                                    1905

Bayne, Thomas. "Byron and Moore: A Parallelism," N&Q, 10th
    ser., III (May 27, 1905), 406. [Between a Byron letter to
    Hoppner, dated July 2, 1819, and a passage in Lalla Rookh.]

Bettany, W. A. (arranger) The Confessions of Lord Byron. A
    Collection of His Private Opinions of Men and Matters, Taken
    from the New and Enlarged Edition of His Letters and Jour-
    nals. London: John Murray, 1905.
  Reviews:
    TLS, July 7, 1905, p. 217.
    Current Literature, XXXIX (Sept., 1905), 266-69.
    Thomas Seccombe, Bookman (London) XXIX (Oct., 1905), 29-
        30.
    Anna B. McMahan, Dial XXXIX (Oct. 16, 1905), 235-36.
    Nation, LXXXI (Nov. 30, 1905), 450-51.

Coleridge, Ernest Hartley (ed.). "Introduction," The Poetical
    Works of Lord Byron. The Only Complete and Copyright
    Text in One Volume. London: John Murray, 1905. Pp. ix-
    lxi. Rptd. in 1931.
  Reviews:
    Academy, LXX (Jan. 6, 1906), 5-6.
    Atheneum, Jan. 6, 1906, pp. 14-15.

Dorsey, A. V. "Lord Byron's 'Caro,'" Bookman, XXI (May,
    1905), 240-49. [Touches on Byron's relations with Caroline
    Lamb.]

Dudley, John William Ward, 1st Earl of. Letters to "Ivy" from
    the First Earl of Dudley, ed. S. H. Romilly. London:
    Longmans, Green & Co., 1905.

Duff, J. Wight. "Byron," Bookman (London), XXIX (Oct., 1905),
    pp. 9-14. [This issue of Bookman contains many portraits
    of Byron too.]

Ernle, Rowland E. Prothero, Lord. "The Goddess of Wisdom and
    Lady Caroline Lamb," MR, XIX (June, 1905), 12-28.

Gerothwohl, M. A. "The Ethics of Don Juan," Fortnightly Review,
    LXXXIII (June, 1905), 1061-74.

Gwynn, Stephen. Thomas Moore. London: Macmillan & Co.,
    1905.

Holland, Henry Richard Vassall, 3rd Lord. Further Memoirs of
    the Whig Party, 1807-1821, ed. Lord Stavordale. London:
    John Murray, 1905.

Lamb, Charles. The Letters of Charles Lamb, in Which Many
    Mutilated Words and Passages Have Been Restored to Their
    Original Form; with Letters Never before Published and
    Facsimiles of Original MS Letters and Poems, with an Intro-
    duction by Henry M. Harper. 5 vols. Boston: The Biblio-
    phile Society, 1905.

Leonard, William Ellery. Byron and Byronism in America. ("Co-
    lumbia University Studies in English," ser. II, Vol. I.) New
    York: Columbia University Press, 1905.

Lovelace, Ralph Gordon Noel Milbank, 2nd Earl of. Astarte: A
    Fragment of Truth concerning George Gordon Byron, 6th Lord
    Byron, Recorded by His Grandson. London: Printed at the
    Chiswick Press, 1905. New Edition, revised with many addi-
    tional letters, ed. Mary Countess of Lovelace. London:
    Christophers, 1921.

McMahan, Anna Benneson. With Shelley in Italy; Being a Selection
    of the Poems and Letters of Percy Bysshe Shelley Which Have
    to Do with His Life in Italy from 1818 to 1822. Chicago:
    McClurg & Co., 1905.

More, Paul Elmer (ed.). "Biographical Sketch," The Complete
    Poetical Works of Lord Byron. Boston: Houghton Mifflin
    Co., 1905. Pp. xi-xxi. [A revision and combination of two
    earlier articles; see Paul Elmer More, 1898, 1901.]

Morley, John. "An Address at the Opening of the Manchester Pub-
    lic Library," Herrig's Archiv, CXIV (1905), 167-68. [Quotes
    from The Manchester Guardian, Dec. 19, 1904.]

Noel, Roden. "Byron," The Poets and the Poetry of the Nineteenth
    Century, ed. Alfred Henry Miles. 12 vols. London: Rout-
    ledge & Sons, 1905. Vol. II, pp. 363-86.

Paston, George [pseud. for Emily Morse Symonds]. R. B. Haydon
    and His Friends. London: James Nisbet & Co., 1905.

Street, George Slythe. "Don Juan," Books and Things: A Collec-
    tion of Stray Remarks. London: Duckworth, 1905. Pp. 48-
    60.

1906

Bulwer-Lytton, Edward Robert.   Personal and Literary Letters of
      Robert Lytton, ed. Lady Betty Balfour.   2 vols.   London:
      Longmans, Green, 1906.   [Contains a good appreciation of
      Byron by both Lytton and his father.]

Cooper, Lane.   "A Dissertation upon Northern Lights," MLN, XXI
      (Feb., 1906), 44-46.   Rptd. in his Late Harvest.   Ithaca,
      N.Y.: Cornell University Press, 1952.   Pp. 47-51.   [A co-
      incidence in imagery between the first eight lines of Words-
      worth's Complaint of a Forsaken Indian Woman and Byron's
      Mazeppa, stanza xi, beginning: "We sped like meteors
      through the sky/When with its crackling sound the night/Is
      chequer'd with the northern light."]

Ernle, Rowland E. Prothero, Lord.   "Lord Lovelace on the Sepa-
      ration of Byron and Lady Byron," MR, XXII (March, 1906),
      11-18.   Rptd. in Lord Byron and his Detractors.   London:
      Ballantyne, 1906, 89-98.   [Reply to Lovelace's Astarte.]

Kassel, Charles.   "Byron: A Study in Heredity," Arena, XXXVI
      (Aug., 1906), 175-78.

Lamington, Alexander.   In the Days of the Dandies.   London:
      Eveleigh Nash, 1906.

Lawrence, Thomas.   Sir Thomas Lawrence's Letter-bag, ed.
      George S. Layard.   London: George Allen, 1906.   [Several
      references to Byron and one letter about him.]

McMahan, Anna Benneson (ed.).   With Byron in Italy; Being a Se-
      lection of the Poems and Letters of Lord Byron Which Have
      to Do with His Life in Italy from 1816 to 1823.   Chicago:
      A. C. McClurg, 1906.

Murray, John, IV.   "Lord Byron and Lord Lovelace," MR, XXII
      (Feb., 1906), 19-40.   [Refutation of Astarte, with special
      reference to his attack upon the Murrays.]   Rptd. in Lord
      Byron and His Detractors.   London: Ballantyne & Co.,
      1906.   Pp. 63-88.

"Musings without Method," Blackwood's, CLXXIX (March, 1906),
      419-23.   [On the Astarte and Stowe Controversy.]

Norgate, Gerald Le Grys.   The Life of Sir Walter Scott.   London:
      Methuen & Co., 1906.

[Pember, E. H.]   "Astarte," Lord Byron and His Detractors.
      London: Ballantyne, 1906.   Pp. 1-61.   [Case for the de-
      fence in the Astarte controversy.   Brings about a verdict of
      not guilty for Byron and Augusta.]

Ramsden, Lady Helen Guendolen. Correspondence of Two Brothers: Edward Adolphus, Eleventh Duke of Somerset, and His
Brother, Lord Webb Seymour, 1800-1819, and after. London: Longmans, Green & Co., 1906. [On page 117, there
is an unpublished letter written by Byron to the Duchess of
Somerset, Aug. 15, 1813.]

Reid, Stuart J. Life and Letters of the 1st Earl of Durham, 1792-
1840. 2 vols. London: Longmans, Green & Co., 1906.
[Includes an unpublished poem by Byron, dated Jan., 1812,
beginning "Again deceived! Again betrayed!"]

Rossetti, William Michael. Some Reminiscences. 2 vols. London: Brown, Langham & Co., 1906.

Strachan, L. R. M. "Byron and Greek Grammar," N&Q, 10th
ser., V (Feb. 3, 1906), 93-94. [He wrote an Armenian
grammar.]

Whishaw, John. The "Pope" of Holland House. Selections from
the Correspondence of John Whishaw and His Friends 1813-
1840, ed. Lady Seymour. London: T. Fisher Unwin, 1906.

1907

Ball, Margaret. Sir Walter Scott as a Critic of Literature. New
York: Columbia University Press, 1907.

Chandler, Frank Wadleigh. The Literature of Roguery. Boston:
Houghton, Mifflin & Co., 1907.

Coleridge, Ernest Hartley. "Byron," Poet's Country, ed. Andrew
Lang. Philadelphia: Lippincott, 1907. Pp. 46-65.

Farrer, James A. "The Forged Letters of Byron and Shelley,"
Literary Forgeries, with an Introduction by Andrew Lang.
London: Longman, Green & Co., 1907. Pp. 175-90.

Hill, Julian. "Lord Byron," Great English Poets. London: E.
Grant Richards, 1907. Pp. 232-47. [His reputation was
"made in Germany"; Byron not a melodist, but a "tune-
monger."]

Huchon, René. George Crabbe and His Times, 1754-1832, a Critical and Biographical Study, trans. Frederick Clarke. London: John Murray, 1907.

Jerrold, Walter. Thomas Hood: His Life and Times. London:
Alston Rivers, 1907. [Scattered references.]

Krueger, G. "Childe Harold," N&Q, 10th ser., VIII (Nov. 30,
1907), 430. [The sense nor the construction of Childe

Harold's Pilgrimage, IV, stanza clxxxii, are clear to him.]
Cf. Thomas Bayne, F. A. Russell, R. C. Bostock, John B.
Wainwright, C. Lawrence Ford, ibid., 10th ser., VIII (Dec.
21, 1907), 495-96. [Several explications given in separate
articles.]

Leonard, William Ellery. Byron and Byronism in America. New
York: Columbia University Press, 1907.

Moorman, F. W. "Byron," The Nineteenth Century. Vol. XII of
The Cambridge History of English Literature, eds. A. W.
Ward and A. R. Waller. 14 vols. Cambridge, [Eng.]: The
University Press, 1907. Pp. 34-62.

Nicoll, William Robertson, and Thomas Seccombe. "Lord Byron,"
A History of English Literature. New York: Dodd, Mead &
Co., 1907. Pp. 970-86.

Payne, William Morton. "Byron," The Greater English Poets of
the 19th Century. New York: H. Holt & Co., 1907. Pp.
64-95. [On Byronism, the personality and the work of Byron.]

Pyre, J. F. A. "Byron in Our Day," Atlantic Monthly, XCIX
(April, 1907), 542-52. [A revaluation of Byron.]

Rannie, David Watson. Wordsworth and His Circle. New York:
G. P. Putnam's Sons, 1907.

Stebbing, William. "Byron," The Poets--Geoffrey Chaucer to Alfred
Tennyson. 2 vols. London: Oxford University Press, 1907.
Vol. II, pp. 89-102. Rptd. Five Centuries of English Verse.
2 vols. London: H. Frowde, 1913. Pp. 92-105.

Stephen, Leslie (ed.). "Introduction," The Complete Poetical
Works of Lord Byron. New York: Macmillan, 1907. Pp.
xv-xliv.

Street, George Slythe. "Ghosts of Piccadilly," MR, XXVI (Jan.,
1907), 71-79. Rptd. in Putnam's Magazine, I (Feb., 1907),
535-49. [Anecdotes associated with 81, Piccadilly, Site of a
club to which Byron belonged.] Rptd. with some changes in
his Ghosts of Piccadilly. London: A. Constable & Co., 1907.
Pp. 91-106.

Tucker, Thomas George. The Foreign Debt of English Literature.
London: Bell & Sons, 1907.

Uhlemayr, B. "Introduction," Lord Byron. "Cain, a Mystery,"
with Introduction, Notes and Appendix. Nürnberg: C. Koch,
1907. Pp. iii-xvii.

Vaughan, C. E.   The Romantic Revolt.   New York: C. Scribner's
      Sons, 1907.

Wordsworth, William.   Letters of the Wordsworth Family from
      1787 to 1855.   Collected and edited by William Knight.   3
      vols.   Boston: Ginn & Co., 1907.

1908

Bancroft, George.   Life and Letters of George Bancroft, ed. M. A.
      De Wolfe Howe.   2 vols.   New York: Charles Scribner's
      Sons, 1908.   [The American scholar reminisces about Byron
      whom he met in 1822.]

Bielschowsky, Albert.   The Life of Goethe.   Authorized translation
      from the German by William A. Cooper.   3 vols.   New York:
      G. P. Putnam; London: The Knickerbocker Press, 1908.

Bury, Lady Charlotte Campbell.   The Diary of a Lady-in Waiting,
      ed. A. F. Steuart.   2 vols.   London: J. Lane, 1908.

Churchman, Philip.   "Espronceda, Byron and Ossian," MLN, XXIII
      (Jan., 1908), 13-16.   [Both men versified the same passage
      from Ossian.]

Conant, Martha Pike.   The Oriental Tale in England in the 18th
      Century.   New York: The Columbia University Press, 1908.

Cooper, Lane.   "Notes on Byron and Shelley," MLN, XXIII (April,
      1908), 118-19.   Rptd. in his Late Harvest.   Ithaca, N. Y.:
      Cornell University Press, 1952.   Pp. 125-27.   [The reactions
      of Byron and Shelley to the death of Keats.]

Courtney, William Prideaux.   The Secrets of Our National Litera-
      ture.   London: Archibald Constable & Co., 1908.

Henley, William Ernest.   Essays.   Vol. IV of The Works of Wil-
      liam Ernest Henley.   7 vols.   London: David Nutt, 1908.
      It contains:
            "Byron's World," pp. 1-167.
            "Pippin," pp. 168-85.   [On Lady Byron and Byron.]

Magnus, Laurie.   "Byron and Carlyle," Transactions of the Royal
      Society of Literature, 2nd ser., XXVIII (1908), 235-52.
      ["Carlyle was a Byron moralized ... or Byron was a sensu-
      ous Carlyle."]

Mead, William Edward.   "Italy in English Poetry," PMLA, XXIII
      (1908), 421-70.

Sanders, Lloyd.   The Holland House Circle.   London: Methuen &
      Co., 1908.

Shorter, Clement K.   The Brontës: Life and Letters.   2 vols.
    London: Hodder & Stoughton, 1908.

Waxman, Samuel M.   "The Don Juan Legend in Literature,"
    Journal of American Folklore, XXI (1908), 184-204.

Wiehr, Josef.   "The Relations of Grabbe to Byron," JEGP, VII
    (July, 1908), 134-49.   [Grabbe's Gotland was probably influ-
    enced by Cain.]

                                    1909

Bagot, Captain Josceline (ed.).   George Canning and His Friends.
    2 vols.   London: John Murray, 1909.   [Byron and the Greek
    War.]

Broughton, John Cam Hobhouse, Lord.   Recollections of a Long
    Life, ed. Lady Dorchester.   6 vols.   London: John Murray,
    1909-1911.

Bruce, J. Douglas.   "Lord Byron's 'Stanzas to the Po,' " MLN,
    XXIV (Dec., 1909), 258-59.

Campbell, K.   "Poe's Indebtedness to Byron," Nation, LXXXVIII
    (March 11, 1909), 248-49.

Carlyle, Thomas.   The Love Letters of Thomas Carlyle and Jane
    Welsh, ed. Alexander Carlyle.   2 vols.   London: John Lane,
    1909.

Churchman, Philip H.   "Byron and Espronceda," Revue Hispanique,
    XX (1909), 5-210.   [Similarities between the Spanish Byron &
    Byron.]
    Review:
    R. Schevill, MLN, XXVII (Jan., 1912), 28-30.

_____.   "Byron and Shakespeare," MLN, XXIV (April, 1909),
    126-27.

_____.   "Lord Byron's Experiences in the Spanish Peninsula in
    1809," Bulletin Hispanique, 4th ser., XI (janvier-mars, 1909),
    55-95; ibid., XI (avril-juin, 1909), 125-71.

Edgcumbe, Richard.   Byron: The Last Phase.   New York: Charles
    Scribner's Sons, 1909.
    Reviews:
    TLS, Oct. 21, 1909, p. 386.
    Spectator, CIII (Oct. 23, 1909), 645-46.
    Paul Elmer More, Nation, LXXXIX (Nov., 4, 1909), 431-33.
    Saturday Review, CVIII (Nov. 6, 1909), 568-69.
    QR, CCXII (Jan., 1910), 1-31.
    SR, XIX (July, 1911), 363-69.

Gabrielson, Arvid. Rime as the Criterion of the Pronunciation of Spenser, Pope, Byron and Swinburne. Uppsala: Almqvist & Wiksells, 1909.

Garnett, Richard. A History of Italian Literature. New York: D. Appleton & Co., 1909. [On Morgante Maggiore.]

Hauhart, William Frederic. "The Attitude of Eminent Literary Men of England toward Goethe's Faust. Byron," The Reception of Goethe's "Faust" in England in the First Half of the 19th Century. New York: Columbia University Press, 1909. Pp. 69-74.

Herz, N. "Byron's Bride of Abydos," N&Q, 10th ser., XI (June 5, 1909), 445. [Of bibliographical interest: a first edition.]

Lane-Poole, Stanley. "Byron and Stratford Canning," Atheneum, Aug. 7, 1909, p. 154. [Relates an incident that took place in Turkey between Byron and Canning.]

Long, William J. "George Gordon Lord Byron," English Literature: Its History and Its Significance for the Life of the English Speaking World. Boston, New York: Ginn & Co., 1909. Pp. 405-410.

MacCum, Florence. "Lord Byron," Sir Walter Scott's Friends. Edinburgh: William Blackwood & Sons, 1909. Pp. 403-17.

Mason, Caroline Atwater. The Spell of Italy. Boston: L. C. Page & Co., 1909.

Orr, Lyndon. "Famous Affinities of History," Munsey, XLI (April, 1909), 64-68. [Lord Byron and the Countess Guiccioli.]

Ross, Janet, and Nelly Erichsen. The Story of Pisa. London: J. M. Dent, 1909.

"Some Byron Crumbs: 'The Irish Avatar' Again," Atheneum, June 26, 1909, pp. 756-57.

Symons, Arthur. "Byron," The Romantic Movement in English Poetry. New York: E. P. Dutton & Co.; London: A. Constable & Co., 1909. Pp. 239-63.

Toynbee, Paget Jackson. "Byron," Dante in English Literature from Chaucer to Carey. London: Methuen, 1909. Vol. II, pp. 31-55.

Toynbee, William. Glimpses of the Twenties. London: A. Constable & Co., 1909.

1910

Austin, Alfred.   The Bridling of Pegasus.   London: Macmillan
    Ltd. , 1910.
    It contains:
        "Byron and Wordsworth, " pp. 78-138.   Rptd. from QR, CLIV
        (July, 1882), 53-82.
    "The Essentials of Good Poetry, " pp. 1-27.

    _____ . "Byron in Italy, " National Review, LV (July, 1910),
        776-85.

Bruce, J. Douglas.   "Lord Byron's 'Stanzas to the Po, ' Again, "
    MLN, XXV (Jan. , 1910), 31-32.

Byron, May Clarissa Gillington.   A Day with Lord Byron.   London:
    Hodder & Stoughton, 1910.   [A composite "typical" Byron
    day.]

Chapman, Edward Mortimer.   "The Apostles of Revolt: Byron and
    Shelley, " English Literature in Account with Religion: 1800-
    1900.   Boston: Houghton Mifflin Co. , 1910.   Pp. 91-109.

Chubb, Edwin Watts.   "Byron as Swimmer and Feaster, " Stories
    of Authors, British and American.   New York: Sturgis &
    Walton Co. , 1910.   Pp. 64-70.

Churchman, Philip H.   "The Beginnings of Byronism in Spain, "
    Revue Hispanique, XXIII (Sept. , 1910), 333-69.

Clutton-Brock, A.   Shelley: The Man and the Poet.   London:
    Methuen Co. , 1910.

Coleridge, Ernest Hartley.   "Byron, " Encyclopaedia Britannica.
    11th ed.   New York: Encyclopaedia Britannica, Inc. , 1910.
    Vol. VI, pp. 897-905.

Courthope, William John.   "The Poetry of Romantic Self-represen-
    tation: Byron, " A History of English Poetry.   London:
    Macmillan, 1910.   Vol. VI, pp. 232-77.

Giles, Edith.   "Byron's 'Prisoner of Chillon, ' " Journal of Education
    (Boston), LXXI (April 14, 1910), 405; ibid. , LXXI (April 21,
    1910), 430-31.

Glenbervie, Sylvester Douglas, Baron.   The Glenbervie Journals,
    ed. Walter Sichel.   London: Constable & Co. , 1910.   [On
    the Drury Lane Speech and the subsequent publication of the
    Rejected and the Accepted Addresses.]

Gribble, Francis.   The Love Affairs of Lord Byron.   New York:
    Scribner's, 1910.

Reviews:
Atheneum, Nov. 5, 1910, p. 554.
Graham Berry, Bookman, XXXII (Dec., 1910), 413-17.
George B. Rose, SR, XIX (July, 1911), 363-69.

Griffin, W. Hall, and Harry Christopher Minchin. The Life of
Robert Browning, with Notices of His Writings, His Family
and His Friends. London: Methuen & Co., 1910.

Hill, Constance. Maria Edgeworth and Her Circle in the Days of
Buonaparte and Bourbon. London: John Lane, 1910.

Jeffrey, Francis. "Lord Byron," Literary Criticism, ed. D. N.
Smith. London: Henry Frowde, 1910. Pp. 147-79. [A reprint of Jeffrey's reviews of Childe Harold's Pilgrimage, III,
and Sardanapalus.]

Lang, Andrew. "Byron and Mary Chaworth," Fortnightly Review,
XCIV (Aug., 1910), 268-80. [An answer to the Edgcumbe
theory.]

Miller, Barnette. Leigh Hunt's Relations with Byron, Shelley and
Keats. New York: The Columbia University Press, 1910.

Monypenny, William Flavelle. The Life of Benjamin Disraeli. 6
vols. New York: The Macmillan Co., 1910-1920.

"Musings without Method," Blackwood's, CLXXXVII (Feb., 1910),
294-308. [Byron a Tory in disguise.]

Pancoast, Henry S. and Percy Van Dyke Shelly. "Lord Byron,"
A First Book in English Literature. New York: H. Holt &
Co., 1910. Pp. 347-53.

Previté-Orton, Charles William. Political Satire in English Poetry.
Cambridge, [Eng.]: Cambridge University Press, 1910.

Reid, Whitelaw. Byron: Address at the University College of
Nottingham. London: Harrison & Sons, 1910. Rptd. Fortnightly Review, XCV (Jan. 2, 1911), 129-43; Reid's American
and English Studies, 2 vols. New York: Scribner, 1913. II,
165-89. Cf. "The Worst and the Best in Byron," Current
Literature, L (March, 1911), 330-32. [A summary of this
lecture.]

Roberts, Richard Ellis. "Byron," Samuel Rogers and His Circle.
London: Methuen & Co., 1910. Pp. 180-208.

Roe, Frederick William. Thomas Carlyle as a Critic of Literature.
New York: Columbia University Press, 1910.

Saintsbury, George. History of English Prosody. 3 vols. London: Macmillan, 1910. Vol. III, pp. 95-102.

Thomas, Edward. Feminine Influence on the Poets. London:
    Martin Secker, 1910.

Trelawny, Edward John. Letters of Edward John Trelawny. Lon-
    don: H. Frowde, 1910.

Trent, William P. (ed.). "Introduction," The Poems and Plays of
    Lord Byron. 3 vols. London: J. M. Dent & Sons; New
    York: E. P. Dutton & Co., 1910. Pp. v-xi. New revised
    edition, London: Dent, 1948, with a preface by Guy Pocock,
    pp. xii-xvii.

Woodberry, George Edward. "Byron," The Inspiration of Poetry.
    New York: Macmillan, 1910. Pp. 85-112. [Byron as a
    continental poet.]

                                1911

Angeli, Helen Rossetti. Shelley and His Friends in Italy. London:
    Methuen & Co., 1911.

Austin, Alfred. Autobiography. London: Macmillan & Co., 1911.
    [On his Vindication of Lord Byron, written to answer Mrs.
    Stowe's book, and on the correspondence he received praising
    it.]

Boynton, P. H. "London of Byron and Lamb," Chautauquan, LXII
    (March, 1911), 33-42. Rptd. in his London in English Litera-
    ture. Chicago: The University of Chicago Press, 1913.
    Pp. 192-217.

Brecknock, Albert. The Pilgrim Poet: Lord Byron of Newstead.
    London: Francis Griffiths, 1911.

Cook, Edward T. The Life of John Ruskin. 2 vols. London:
    George Allen & Co., 1911.

Cory, Herbert E. "Spenser, Thomson, and Romanticism," PMLA,
    XXVI (1911), 51-91. [Byron was influenced by Beattie's
    The Minstrel.]

Freeman, Alexander Martin. Thomas Love Peacock, a Critical
    Study. New York: Mitchell Kennerley, 1911.

Gribble, Francis. The Romantic Life of Shelley and the Sequel.
    New York: G. P. Putnam's Sons, 1911.

Hazlitt, William Carew. The Hazlitts: An Account of Their Origin
    and Descent. Edinburgh: Ballantyne, Hanson & Co., 1911.

Jack, Adolphus Alfred. "Byron," Poetry and Prose; Being Essays
    on Modern English Poetry. London: Constable & Co., 1911.

Pp. 122-45. [Byron's work representative of oratorical poetry.]

Polidori, J. W.   The Diary of Dr. John William Polidori, 1816,
Relating to Byron, Shelley, etc., ed. William Michael Rossetti. London: Elkin Mathews, 1911.

Saintsbury, George. A History of English Criticism. Edinburgh:
William Blackwood & Sons, 1911.

Shore, William Teignmouth. D'Orsay; or, the Complete Dandy.
New York: Brentano's; London: John Long, 1911.

Thomas, Edward. Feminine Influence on the Poets. New York:
John Lane, 1911. [On the Byron women.]

Van Doren, Carl. The Life of Thomas Love Peacock. London:
J. M. Dent; New York: E. P. Dutton, 1911.

Winter, William. "Byron," Gray Days and Gold. New York:
Moffat, Yard & Co., 1911. Pp. 279-87.

1912

B., G. "Byron and the Sidney Family," N&Q, 11th ser., V (April
6, 1912), 286. [Was Sir Philip Sidney an ancestor of Byron?]
Cf. A. R. Bayley, ibid., 11th ser., V (May 11, 1912), 378.
[Yes, and gives genealogy.]

Carlton, W. N. C. (ed.). Poems and Letters of Lord Byron,
edited from the Original Manuscripts in the Possession of
W. K. Bixby, of St. Louis. Chicago: Society of Defobs,
1912.
It contains the following letters:
To James Cawthorn, dated July 7, 1811.
To J. W. Croker, dated July 13, 1813.
To J. Wedderburn Webster, dated March 2, 1814.
To R. B. Hoppner, dated Nov. 20, 1817.
To Douglas Kinnaird, dated Nov. 28, 1819.
To R. B. Hoppner, dated March 31, 1820.
To Douglas Kinnaird, dated April 2, 1820.
To John Murray?, dated May 5, 1821.
To R. B. Hoppner, dated May 21, 1821.
To John Murray?, dated Oct. 3, 1821.
To Sir Godfrey Webster, dated Aug. 28, 1822.
To Captain J. Hay, dated Sept. 1, 1822.
To Sir Godfrey Webster, dated Nov. 28, 1822.
To R. B. Hoppner, dated Jan. 2, 1823.

Compton-Rickett, Arthur. "Byron," A History of English Literature. London: T. C. & E. C. Jack; New York: Dodge Publishing Co., 1912. Pp. 81-82.

Dixon, William Macneile. English Epic and Heroic Poetry. Lon-
     don: J. M. Dent & Sons; New York: E. P. Dutton, 1912.

Elton, Oliver. "Byron," A Survey of English Literature, 1780-
     1880. London: Edward Arnold, 1912. Vol. II, pp. 135-82.

Forman, H. Buxton. "Byron's Hours of Idleness. An Old Ques-
     tion Approximately Settled," Atheneum, April 27, 1912, p.
     469.

_____. "Byron's Moriah, a 'flat burglary,' " Atheneum, Aug.
     24, 1912, p. 193. [Moriah in "The First Kiss of Love,"
     in Fugitive Pieces, is the goddess of Folly, but Byron prob-
     ably cancelled it in his Poems on Various Occasions because
     somebody told him he had picked it up from Christopher
     Anstey's New Bath Guide.]

Fuess, C. M. Lord Byron as a Satirist in Verse. New York:
     Columbia University Press, 1912.
     Review:
     Lane Cooper, Dial, LIV (Jan. 16, 1913), 49-51. Rptd. in
        his Late Harvest. Ithaca, N.Y.: Cornell University Press,
        1952. Pp. 128-34.

Howe, Will D. (ed.). "Introduction," Byron: Select Poems, in-
     cluding "Mazeppa," "The Prisoner of Chillon," the Fourth
     Canto of "Childe Harold." New York: Scribner's Sons, 1912.
     Pp. vii-xvii.

Knott, John. The Last Illness of Lord Byron: A Study in the
     Borderland of Genius and Madness, of Cosmical Inspiration
     and Pathological Psychology. St. Paul, Minnesota: Volks-
     zeitung Printing Co., 1912.
     Review:
     Atheneum, March 9, 1912, p. 282.

Lang, Andrew. "Byron," A History of English Literature from
     Beowulf to Swinburne. London: Longmans, Green & Co.,
     1912. Pp. 519-25.

Mayne, Ethel Colburn. Byron. 2 vols. New York: Scribner's
     Sons, 1912. New edition: New York: Scribner, 1924.
     Reviews:
     Atheneum, Nov. 2, 1912, p. 511.
     TLS, Nov. 14, 1912, p. 505.
     Spectator, CIX (Nov. 23, 1912), 858-59.
     Current Opinion, LIV (Feb., 1913), 146-48.
     Samuel Chew, MLN, XXVIII (March, 1913), 85-86.
     Nation, XCVI (May 8, 1913), 476-77.
     Samuel Chew, SRL, II (Oct. 31, 1925), 256.

Meredith, George. Letters of George Meredith, Collected and
     Edited by His Son. 2 vols. New York: C. Scribner's Sons,
     1912. [Passing references.]

Neilson, William Allan. Essentials of Poetry. Boston: Houghton
    Mifflin Co. , 1912.

Reed, Edward Bliss. English Lyrical Poetry from Its Origins to
    the Present Time. New Haven: Yale University Press,
    1912.

1913

Bayley, A. R. "Byron and the Hobhouse Manuscript," N&Q, 11th
    ser. , VIII (July 19, 1913), 51. [It was printed by Lady Dor-
    chester in 1909, in her edition of Lord Broughton's Recollec-
    tions of a Long Life, II, 190, et seq.]

Broadley, A. M. , and Walter Jerrold. The Romance of an Elder-
    ly Poet. London: Stanley Paul & Co. , 1913. [George
    Crabbe's correspondence with Elizabeth Charter.]

Bulwer-Lytton, Edward Robert. The Life of Edward Bulwer, First
    Lord Lytton. 2 vols. London: Macmillan & Co. , 1913.

"Byron and Swinburne," Poetry Review, II (May, 1913), 201-204.

Chew, Samuel. "Byron and Croly," MLN, XXVIII (Nov. , 1913),
    201-203. [Finds Childe Harold, IV, indebted to George
    Croly's Paris in 1815.]

Craig, Hardin (ed.). "Introduction," Byron's "Childe Harold,"
    Cantos III and IV, "The Prisoner of Chillon" and Other Poems.
    New York: H. Holt & Co. , 1913. Pp. vii-xxiv.

Dick, William (ed.). Byron and His Poetry: Selections with Com-
    mentaries. "Poetry and Life Series," No. 15. London:
    George Harrap, 1913.

Halleck, Reuben. "George Noel Gordon, Lord Byron," Halleck's
    New English Literature. New York: American Book Co. ,
    1913. Pp. 406-16.

Hamel, Frank. Lady Hester Lucy Stanhope. New York: Cassell
    & Co. , 1913.

Mason, Caroline Atwater. "Authors in Italy," The Spell of Italy.
    Boston: L. C. Page & Co. , 1913. Pp. 334-72.

More, Paul Elmer. The Drift of Romanticism. Boston: Houghton
    Mifflin, 1913.

Phillips, Stephen. "The Tonic of Byron," Poetry Review, II (April,
    1913), 195-96.

Pignatorre, George. "Byron and Greece," Chambers, 7th ser.,
    III (Jan. 25, 1913), 122-25.

Russell, Rollo. Early Correspondence of Lord John Russell, 1805-
    1840. 2 vols. London: T. Fisher Unwin, 1913.

Schelling, Felix E. The English Lyric. Boston: Houghton Mifflin
    Co., 1913.

Shelley, Lady Frances. The Diary of Frances Shelley, ed.
    Richard Edgcumbe. London: John Murray, 1913.

Spencer-Stanhope, Lady Elizabeth. The Letter-bag of Lady Eliza-
    beth Spencer-Stanhope, Compiled from the Cannon Hall Papers,
    1806-1873, by A. M. W. Stirling. London: John Lane, 1913.

Vincent, Leon Henry. "Episodes in the Life of a Noble Poet
    (Lord Byron)," Dandies and Men of Letters. Boston: Hough-
    ton Mifflin Co., 1913. Pp. 77-114.

Wingfield-Stratford, Esmé. The History of English Patriotism. 2
    vols. London: John Lane, 1913.

Woods, Matthew. "Lord Byron," In Spite of Epilepsy; Being a Re-
    view of the Lives of Three Great Epileptics--Julius Caesar,
    Mahammed, Lord Byron. New York: The Cosmopolitan
    Press, 1913. Pp. 191-305.

                                1914

Chew, Samuel C. "Notes on Byron," MLN, XXIX (April, 1914),
    105-107. [Adds some annotations to Coleridge's Don Juan
    and makes a correction in Coleridge's edition of Byron.]

_____. The Relation of Lord Byron to the Drama of the Roman-
    tic Period. Göttingen: Vendenhoeck & Ruprecht; Baltimore:
    The Johns Hopkins Press, 1914.

Cruse, Amy. "Byron's Childe Harold," English Literature through
    the Ages: Beowulf to Stevenson. London: G. G. Harrap &
    Co., 1914. Pp. 412-22. Rptd. in her Famous English Books
    and Their Stories. London: G. G. Harrap, 1926. Pp. 186-
    95.

Gauss, C. "Byron's Indebtedness to La Fontaine," Nation, XCIX
    (Oct. 8, 1914), 431.

Hunt, Theodore W. English Literary Miscellany. 2nd Series.
    Oberlin, Ohio: Bibliotheca Sacra Company, 1914.

Johnson, Reginald B. (ed.). "On Byron," Famous Reviews. Lon-
    don: Sir I. Pitman & Sons, 1914. Pp. 57-59. [A reprint

of Lord Brougham's review of Byron's Hours of Idleness
from the Edinburgh Review.]

Kingsley, Maud E.   "Examination Questions for Byron's 'Prisoner
of Chillon' and 'Mazeppa, ' " Education, XXXIV (Feb. , 1914),
386-87.

Monahan, Michael.   'Byron, " At the Sign of the Van.   New York:
M. Kennerley, 1914.   Pp. 311-15.

Parrott, Edward.   "Lord Byron, " The Pageant of English Literature.   New York: Sully & Kleinteich, 1914.   Pp. 359-67.

Porterfield, A. W.   "Poets as Heroes in Dramatic Works in German Literature, " MP, XII (June, 1914), 65-99; ibid. , XII
(Nov. , 1914), 297-311.

Scrimgeour, J. C.   (ed.).   "Introduction, " Childe Harold's Pilgrimage, Cantos I and II.   London: Macmillan, 1914.   Pp. xi-
xliii.

Smith, Harry Bache.   A Sentimental Library, Comprising Books
formerly Owned by Famous Writers, Presentation Copies,
Manuscripts and Drawings.   Collected and Described by Harry
Bache Smith, with Fifty-six Illustrations.   New York: The
De Vinne Press, 1914.   Rptd. New York: Scribner's, 1924.
It contains the following letters:
To George Byron, dated Feb. 24, 1801, from Dulwich Grove.
To Rev. Francis Hodgson, dated Oct. 3, 1810, from Patras.
To Rev. Francis Hodgson, the last letter before he left Eng-
land.   [Unpublished.]
To R. B. Hoppner, dated April 3, 1821, from Ravenna.
To John Bowring, dated March 30, 1824, from Missolonghi.
[Unpublished.]

Türck, Hermann.   "Lord Byron's Delineation of the Superman in
Manfred, " The Man of Genius.   London: Adam & Charles
Black, 1914.   Pp. 179-197.

1915

Chew, Samuel.   The Dramas of Lord Byron.   Göttingen: Venden-
hoeck & Ruprecht; Baltimore: The Johns Hopkins Press,
1915.
Review:
William Ellery Leonard, MLN, XXXI (Jan. , 1916), 42-47.

Corelli, Marie.   'Byron--the Man and the Poet, " T. P. 's Weekly,
XXVI (Oct. 9, 1915), 339-40; ibid. , XXVI (Oct. 16, 1915),
363-64.

Dalton, Moray. "Childe Harold and the Carbonari," Spectator,
    CXV (Oct. 16, 1915), 501-502.

De Sélincourt, Ernest. English Poets and the National Ideal. Lon-
    don: Oxford University Press, 1915.

Dobell, Bertram. "A Farrago Libelli, a Byron? Discovery,"
    English Review, XXI (Aug., 1915), 1-24. [Attributes to By-
    ron a manuscript translation of the first satire of Juvenal.]
    Cf. Samuel Chew, "Did Byron Write A Farrago Libelli?"
    MLN, XXXI (May, 1916), 287-91. [A refutation.]

Dowling, Theodore Edward, and Edwin Fletcher. Hellenism in
    England, a Short History of the Greek People in This Country
    from the Earliest Times to the Present Day. London: Faith
    Press; Milwaukee: Young Churchman, 1915.

From the Unpublished Letters of Lord Byron. Venice: In the Is-
    land of S. Lazzaro, 1915.

Hearn, Lafcadio. Interpretations of Literature. 2 vols. New
    York: Dodd, Mead & Co., 1915.
    It contains:
    "Byron," I, 111-23.
    "Culling from Byron," I, 124-40. Rptd. in his On Poets.
    Tokyo: The Hokuseido Press, 1934. Pp. 542-72.

Lounsbury, Thomas R. Life and Times of Tennyson. New Haven:
    Yale University Press, 1915.

Meester, Marie E. de. "Oriental Influences in the English Litera-
    ture of the Nineteenth Century," Anglistische Forschungen,
    XLVI (1915), 33-38.

Mitford, Mary Russell. Mary Russell Mitford; Correspondence
    with Charles Boner and John Ruskin, ed. Elizabeth Lee.
    Chicago: Rand McNally & Co., 1915.

                                1916

Chew, Samuel. "Unpublished Letters of Lord Byron," MLN, XXXI
    (Nov., 1916), 446-47. [A letter, dated Dec. 12, 1821, which
    he found in Quatrich's Catalogue for June 1916 (No. 344).]

Chubb, Edwin Watts. "Byron," Masters of English Literature.
    Chicago: A. C. McClurg & Co., 1916. Pp. 183-205.

Coleridge, Stephen. An Evening in My Library. Among the Eng-
    lish Poets. London: John Lane, 1916.

Collison-Morley, Lacy. "Some English Poets in Modern Italian
    Literature," MLR, XI (Jan., 1916), 48-60.

Cooke, Margaret W. "Schiller's Robbers in England," MLR, XI
    (April, 1916), 156-75. [On Werner.]

Granville, G. Leveson-Gower, First Earl. Private Correspondence,
    1781-1821, ed. Castalia, Countess Granville. 2 vols. Lon-
    don: John Murray, 1916.

Haller, William. "Byron and the British Conscience," SR, XXIV
    (Jan., 1916), 1-18. [Byron was always at loggerheads with
    the inconsistent British conscience for condoning the offences
    of his youth and damning him for other offences that he him-
    self did not consider too serious.]

Levi, A. R. (ed.). "Preface," Childe Harold and Minor Poems.
    Milan: Fratelli Treves, 1916. Pp. ix-xv.

Powys, John Cowper. "Byron," Suspended Judgments, Essays on
    Books and Sensations. New York: G. Arnold Shaw, 1916.
    Pp. 179-309.

Scott, J. A. "The Refrain in Byron's 'Maid of Athens,' " Classi-
    cal Journal, XI (March, 1916), 368-69. [Thinks that refrain
    means "My Zoe, I Love You."] Cf. T. Macartney, ibid.,
    XI (June, 1916), 552-53. [Disagrees with Scott. Thinks it
    means, "My Life, I Love Thee."]

Sichel, Walter. "Byron as a War Poet," Fortnightly Review, CV
    (Jan., 1916), 127-33.

Strunk, W., Jr. "Byron and His Travels," N&Q, 12th ser., II
    (Dec. 2, 1916), 447. [Did he visit Calais or Lucca?] Cf.
    C. C. B., ibid., 12th ser., II (Dec. 30, 1916), 535. [No,
    he simply thought of visiting Lucca.]

Thayer, Mary Rebecca. "Lord Byron," The Influence of Horace
    on the Chief English Poets of the 19th Century. ("Cornell
    Studies in English," Vol. 2.) New Haven: Yale University
    Press, 1916. Pp. 69-84.

Whitcomb, Edna Pearle. Oriental Diction and Theme in English
    Verse, 1740-1840. ("Bulletin of the University of Kansas,
    Humanistic Series," Vol. 2, No. 1.) Lawrence: The Uni-
    versity Press, 1916.

                            1917

Baker, H. T. "Sensationalism of Byron," MLN, XXXII (April,
    1917), 249. [His love of energy and action seems to culmi-
    nate in the word lightning.]

Birch, Lionel. "Byron," Papers of the Manchester Literary Club,
    XLIII (1917), 282-98.

Browning, Oscar. 'Byron and Ovid," TLS, Oct. 25, 1917, p. 518.
    [A parallel from Don Juan.]

Buell, L. M. 'Byron and Shelley," MLN, XXXII (May, 1917),
    312-13. [A comparison of passages on the Promethean
    theme.]

Colvin, Sidney. John Keats: His Life and Poetry, His Friends,
    Critics and After Fame. New York: Charles Scribner's
    Sons, 1917.

Ingpen, Roger. Shelley in England. New Facts and Letters from
    the Shelley-Whitton Papers. 2 vols. Boston: Houghton
    Mifflin Co., 1917.

Northup, C. S. 'Byron and Gray," MLN, XXXII (May, 1917), 310-
    12. [Who translated Gray into Armenian in Beauties of Eng-
    lish Poets, 1852?]

Pierce, Frederick E. "The Hellenic Current in English 19th
    Century Poetry," JEGP, XVI (1917), 103-35.

Stauffer, Ruth M. 'Byron and Shelley in Italy," Poet Lore,
    XXVIII (Autumn, 1917), 554-66; ibid., XXVIII (Winter, 1917),
    703-21.

                                1918

Cairns, William B. British Criticism of American Writings, 1783-
    1815. ("University of Wisconsin Studies in Language and
    Literature," No. 1.) Madison: University of Wisconsin,
    1918. [Touches on Byron's opinions of American writers.]

Calvert, F. R. J. 'Byron in Greece," TLS, June 6, 1918, p.
    264. [A letter in the archives at Hydra, from Frank Hastings
    to Captain Hamilton, referring to the then recent death of
    Byron.]

Chew, Samuel. 'Byron in Fiction," N&Q, 12th ser., IV (Jan.,
    1918), 10. [Lists novels in which Byron is a character.]
    Cf. M. H. Dodds, ibid., 12th ser., IV (Feb., 1918), 60;
    Samuel Chew, ibid., 12th ser., V (March, 1919), 80. [Addi-
    tions to Chew's first article.]

_____. 'Byroniana," MLN, XXXIII (May, 1918), 306-309.
    [On the Prometheus theme; also about Beauties of English
    Poets, Lord Byron's Armenian Exercises and Poetry, and
    Mackay's Lord Byron at the Armenian Convent.]

_____. 'Byron-Shelley Hoax," Nation, CVII (Aug. 24, 1918),
    199-200. [On A Narrative of Lord Byron's Voyage to Corsica
    and Sardinia.]

_____ . "An Original Letter of Byron," Nation, CVI (April 18,
   1918), 473-74. [Dated Nov. 14, 1813, to W. Baldwin, not
   published in Prothero.]

Dawson, W. J.   "Byron's Letters," Encyclopedia Americana.
   New York: The Encyclopedia Americana Corporation, 1918.
   Pp. 102.

Eversley, G. J.   "Some Reminiscences," Cornhill Magazine,
   CXVIII (Nov. , 1918), 471-82.   [On Lord Byron and his physician in Greece, Dr. Millingen.]   Cf. ibid. , CXIX (May, 1919),
   560. [An addition to the above.]

Harper, Henry Howard.   Byron's Malach Hamoves.   A Commentary
   on Leigh Hunt's Work Entitled "Lord Byron and Some of His
   Contemporaries. "   Boston: Privately Printed, 1918.   Revised
   edition, Boston: Torch Press, 1933.

"Lord Byron," University Library of Autobiography.   New York:
   F. Tyler Daniels Co. , 1918.   Pp. 335-48.

Moore, Olin H.   "The Romanticism of Guy de Maupassant," PMLA,
   XXXIII (1918), 97-134.   [On Don Juan and Bel Ami, p. 112.]

Pierce, Frederick E.   Currents and Eddies in the English Romantic Generation.   New Haven: Yale University Press, 1918.

Pierpont, Robert.   "Austrians as 'Huns, ' " N&Q, 12th ser. , IV
   (Jan. , 1918), 25.   [Byron uses the name Huns for Austrians
   and not for Germans.]

Trent, William Peterfield.   "Byron," Encyclopedia Americana.
   New York: The Encyclopedia Americana Corporation, 1918.
   Vol. V, pp. 97-101.   Rptd. in 1948.

"The War Lord's Fall," Spectator, CXXI (Nov. 16, 1918), 543-44.
   [On Byron's "Ode to Napoleon. "]

                                   1919

Andrews, J. T.   "Byron's Don Juan, Cantos XVII and XVIII," N&Q,
   12th ser. , V (July, 1919), 179.   [Has a copy of Cantos XVII
   and XVIII, printed by Duncombe of Little Queen St. , Holborne,
   with the date, 1825, added in pencil.   Mentions some of his
   sets of Byron's Don Juan.]   Cf. Herbert C. Roe, ibid. , 12th
   ser. , V (Sept. , 1919), 240.   [Says that his copy must be one
   of the sequels mentioned by Coleridge in his bibliography.
   Also cites editions of Don Juan, none of them published with
   Byron's name.]   W. B. H. , ibid. , V (Sept. , 1919), 240-41.
   [Wonders if the eleven cantos promised by Reynolds in the advertisement to the Sequel were ever published.]

Babbitt, Irving. Rousseau and Romanticism. Boston: Houghton
    Mifflin, 1919.

*Bealby, George. Thoughts on Byron. London: R. Folkard &
    Son, 1919?

Brooke, Stopford. "Byron's Cain," Hibbert Journal, XVIII (Oct.,
    1919), 74-94. Rptd. in his Naturalism in English Poetry.
    London: J. M. Dent, 1920. Pp. 269-99.

Chew, Samuel. "The Byron Apocrypha," N&Q, 12th ser., V (May,
    1919), 113-15; ibid., 12th ser., V (June, 1919), 143-45.
    Rptd., with corrections and amplifications, in his Byron in
    England: His Fame and Afterfame. London: J. Murray,
    1924. Pp. 169-93.

_____. "Centenary of Don Juan," American Journal of Philol-
    ogy, XL (April, 1919), 117-52. Rptd., with revisions and
    corrections, in his Byron in England: His Fame and After-
    fame. London: J. Murray, 1924. Pp. 27-75.

_____. "The Pamphlets of the Byron Separation," MLN, XXXIV
    (March, 1919), 155-62. Rptd., enlarged and revised, in his
    Byron in England: His Fame and Afterfame. London: J.
    Murray, 1924. Pp. 19-26.

Dalgado, D. G. Lord Byron's Childe Harold's Pilgrimage to Portu-
    gal Critically Examined. Lisboa: Imprensa Nacional, 1919.

Hopman, Frits. "Some Aspects of Lord Byron's Character and
    Poetry," ES, I (Aug., 1919), 102-104; ibid., I (Sept., 1919),
    147-49.

Masaryk, Thomas G. The Spirit of Russia. 2 vols. London:
    George Allen & Unwin; New York: The Macmillan Co., 1919.

Mordell, Albert. The Erotic Motive in Literature. New York:
    Boni & Liveright, 1919. New revised edition, New York:
    Collier Books, 1962.

Phillips, Walter Clarke. "The Byronic Hero," Dickens, Reade
    and Collins: Sensation Novelists. ("Columbia University
    Studies in English and Comparative Literature," No. 67.)
    New York: Columbia University Press, 1919. Pp. 155-64.

Price, Lawrence Marsden. "Byron," English German Literary In-
    fluences. Berkeley, Calif.: The University of California
    Press, 1919. Pp. 517-39.

Roe, Herbert C. The Rare Quarto Edition of Lord Byron's "Fugi-
    tive Pieces," Described by Herbert C. Roe. With a Note on
    the Pigot Family. Nottingham: Printed for private circula-
    tion, 1919.

Sokolow, Nahun. History of Zionism. 2 vols. London: Longmans, Green & Co., 1919. [Chap. xviii, in Vol. I, discusses Byron's influence upon the movement in the cause of
liberty in Italy and Greece.]

Waugh, Alec. "Byron's Love Affairs," John O'London's Weekly,
II (Nov. 8, 1919), 120.

1920

A., B. "Byron and His Mother-in-law," Saturday Review, CXXIX
(Jan. 24, 1920), 84.

Brooke, Stopford Augustus. Naturalism in English Poetry. Lon-
don: J. M. Dent, 1920.
It contains:
"Cain," pp. 269-99.
"The Poetry of Byron," pp. 243-67.
"Wordsworth, Shelley, Byron," pp. 165-94.

Brown, P. Hume. Life of Goethe. 2 vols. New York: Henry
Holt, 1920.

"Byron," Saturday Review, CXXIX (Jan. 17, 1920), 55-56.

Ferriman, Z. Duckett. Some English Philhellenes. No. 8: Lord
Byron. London: The Anglo-Hellenic League, 1920.

Grierson, Sir H. J. C. "Lord Byron: Arnold and Swinburne,"
Proceedings of the British Academy, IX (1919-1920), 431-61.
("The Warton Lecture on English Poetry," No. 11.) Rptd. in
his The Background of English Literature. London: Chatto
& Windus, 1925. Pp. 68-114.

Hewitt, E. P. "Byron and Westminster Abbey," National Review,
LXXVI (Oct., 1920), 276-87. [Exclusion of Byron from
Westminster Abbey not justified.] Cf. H. de F. Montgomery,
ibid., LXXVI (Nov., 1920, 429. [Protests against Hewitt's
treatment of Lady Byron.] E. P. Hewitt, ibid., LXXVI
(Dec., 1920), 551-54. [Makes a few general observations
about Astarte, and answers Montgomery.]

Hibbert, H. A Playgoer's Memories. London: Grant Richards,
1920. [Refers to stage productions of Byron's Mazeppa.]

Ker, William Paton. The Art of Poetry. Oxford: The Clarendon
Press, 1920.

Le Gallienne, Richard. "Introduction," Lord Byron. 3 vols. New
York: The Cooperative Publication Society, 192? Pp. 1-14.

Lockwood, Frank C. "Byron the Revolutionist," Methodist Review,
CIII (March-April, 1920), 220-30.

Lovelace, Mary Caroline Wortley, Countess of. Ralph, Earl of
Lovelace, a Memoir. London: Christophers, 1920.

Murray, John, IV. "Byron's Letters," Saturday Review, CXXIX
(Jan. 31, 1920), 107. [Murray says that the originals were
never in his grandfather's possession; he was, therefore,
not responsible for the asterisks.]

Peers, E. A. "Sidelights on Byronism in Spain," Revue Hispanique,
L (Dec., 1920), 359-66.

Reynolds, George F., and Garland Greever. "Lord Byron," The
Facts and Background of Literature. New York: The Century
Co., 1920. Pp. 153-55.

Sichel, Walter. "The Humor of Byron," Nineteenth Century and
After, LXXXVIII (Dec., 1920), 1026-36.

Thompson, A. H. (ed.). "Introduction," Selections from the Poems
of Lord Byron. Cambridge, [Eng.]: University Press, 1920.
Pp. xii-xliv.

Trelawny, Edward John. The Relations of Lord Byron and Augusta
Leigh. With a Comparison of the Characters of Byron and
Shelley and a Rebuke to Jane Clairmont on Her Hatred of the
Former. London: Printed for private circulation only by
Richard Clay, 1920.

_____. The Relations of P. B. Shelley with His Two Wives,
Harriet and Mary, and a Comment on the Character of Lady
Byron. London: Richard Clay & Son, 1920. [Letter II on
Byron and Lady Byron.]

Wendell, Barrett. The Traditions of European Literature. New
York: C. Scribner's Sons, 1920.

Williamson, Claude C. H. "A Wayward Genius, Byron," Writers
of Three Centuries, 1789-1914. London: Grant Richards,
1920. Pp. 78-85.

1921

Airlie, Mabell Frances Elizabeth Ogilvy, Countess of. In Whig
Society, 1775-1818. London: Hodder & Stoughton, 1921.

Bennett, Arnold. "Byron on the Stage," Things That Have Interested Me. 1st Series. London: Chatto & Windus, 1921.
Pp. 210-11. [On Manfred.]

Dark, Sidney. "Byron and Caroline Lamb," John O'London's Weekly, VI (Nov. 26, 1921), 236.

Douglas, Sir George. "Don Juan in Literature and Music," Cornhill Magazine, CXXIV (July, 1921), 96-104.

Ernle, Rowland E. Prothero, Baron. "The End of the Byron Mystery," Nineteenth Century and After, XC (Aug. , 1921), 207-18. [The second Astarte, in the eyes of Lord Ernle, makes it less easy to maintain the innocence of Byron and Augusta Leigh, the unpublished letters to Lady Melbourne materially strengthening the charge of incest previous to the marriage.]

Francis, Henry Thomas. "Byron Papers," TLS, Sept. 1, 1921, p. 517. [Location of letters to Harry Drury? They were believed to be indecent and Francis advised against publication. Where are they?]

Goethe, Johann Wolfgang von. Literary Essays; a Selection in English, arranged by J. E. Spingarn. New York: Harcourt, Brace & Co. , 1921.
   It contains:
   "Byron's Don Juan," pp. 205-207.
   "Byron's Manfred," pp. 202-204.
   "Lord Byron," pp. 283-86. [From Conversations with Eckermann.]

Graham, Walter. "Politics of the Greater Romantic Poets," PMLA, XXXVI (March, 1921), 60-78.

_____. Tory Criticism in the "Quarterly Review," 1809-1853. New York: Columbia University Press, 1921.

"A Hundred Years Ago. 1821: Byron at Pisa," N&A, XXIX (April 30, 1921), 175.

Husluck, F. W. "Byron and Colonel Rooke," Saturday Review, CXXXI (June 11, 1921), 480-81. [Byron's visit to Mitylene.]

Loane, George G. "Byron and the N. E. D. ," TLS, April 21, 1921, p. 260. [Says that out of 15 passages that he marked out of 300 pages of Byron, he found 10 quoted in the N. E. D. and four usages were worthy of comment.]

Lovelace, Ralph Gordon Noel Milbanke, 2nd Earl of. Astarte: A Fragment of Truth concerning George Gordon Byron, 6th Lord Byron. New Edition, With Many Additional Letters, ed. Mary Countess of Lovelace. London: Christophers, 1921.
   Reviews:
   Thomas Moult, English Review, XXXIII (July, 1921), 74-76.
   TLS, July 14, 1921, p. 445.
   Stewart Marsh Ellis, Saturday Review, CXXXII (July 16, 1921), 88-89. Rptd. as "Byron and His Sister," in his Mainly Victorian. London: Hutchinson & Co. , 1925. Pp. 241-44.
   Blackwood's, CCX (Aug. , 1921), 285-88.

N&A, XXIX (Aug. 6, 1921), 682-83.
Samuel Chew, Nation, CXIII (Aug. 24, 1921), 207-208.
Current Opinion, LXXI (Oct. , 1921), 507-10.
J. A. Strahan, ER, CCXXXIV (Oct. , 1921), 331-45; ibid. ,
    CCXXXV (Jan. , 1922), 76-89.
E. P. Hewitt, National Review, LXXVIII (Oct. , 1921), 218-
    30. [Considers Astarte an unfair and unnatural attack on
    both Lord and Lady Byron.] Cf. Harold Child, "Lady
    Byron and Augusta Leigh, " ibid. , LXXVIII (Jan. , 1922),
    641-49. [An attack on the reviews by Hewitt and Strahan
    above.] E. P. Hewitt, ibid. , LXXIX (March, 1922), 125-
    30. [A reply.] Hugh de F. Montgomery, ibid. , LXXIX
    (June, 1922), 629-31. [A rejoinder.]
"Affable Hawk, " NS, XVIII (Feb. 25, 1922), 593.
See also:
    R. C. K. Ensor, NS, XVII (May 7, 1921), 128. [Thinks
    that Astarte in Manfred is Mary Chaworth.]
    Richard Edgcumbe, TLS, Aug. 11, 1921, pp. 516-17. [Evi-
    dence published in Astarte is incomplete.]
    _____, ibid. , Sept. 22, 1921, pp. 612-13. [Reply to the
    criticism of his Byron: The Last Phase, made by Lord
    Lovelace in his book Astarte.]

Mordell, Albert. The Literature of Ecstasy. New York: Boni &
    Liveright, 1921.

Murray, John. "Two Passages in Childe Harold, " TLS, Aug. 25,
    1921, p. 548. [Says that he discovered proofs of Canto IV,
    with Byron's correction of "washed them power" to "wafted
    them" in the third line of stanza clxxxii. Also calls atten-
    tion to the last line of stanza clxxx, "there let him lay. "
    Furthermore says that when Gifford suggested a change in the
    line at the end of st. clxxxvii, "Without a grave, unearthed,
    uncoffined and unknown, " Byron accepted it. Line now reads,
    "Without a grave, unknelled, uncoffined and unknown. "] Cf.
    George Greenwood, ibid. , Sept. 1, 1921, p. 564. [Proposes
    a change from lay to pray in the line "There let him lay. "]
    N. W. Hill, ibid. , Nov. 3, 1921, p. 716. [Proposes, "Thy
    waters washed their power, while they were free, " as an al-
    ternative to the line in st. clxxxii.]

Paulton, J. M. "A Byron Relic, " TLS, Nov. 17, 1921, p. 752.
    [In a letter to the editor he encloses some lines, "Lord By-
    ron upon His Guide. "]

Unamuno, Miguel de. The Tragic Sense of Life in Men and in
    Peoples, trans. Crawford Flitch. London: Macmillan & Co. ,
    1921. [On Cain.]

Ward, Col. B. R. "Poem that Made a Revolution, " John O'Lon-
    don's Weekly, V (April 23, 1921), 73. [Byron and the cen-
    tenary of the Greek rising.]

Whitman, Walt. Uncollected Poetry and Prose of Walt Whitman.
2 vols. New York: Doubleday, Page & Co. , 1921.

Whitten, Wilfred. "Where Does Byron Stand Now?" John O'London's Weekly, IV (April 2, 1921), 807-808.

Woodberry, George E. Literary Memoirs of the 19th Century.
New York: Harcourt, Brace & Co. , 1921.

Young, Stark. "Mental Goodness, " NAR, CCXIV (July, 1921), 76-
82. Rptd. in his The Three Fountains. New York: Charles
Scribner's Sons, 1924. Pp. 60-74. [By mental goodness he
means that instead of "forgiving Byron, it is better to understand the facts. "]

1922

Airlie, Mabell Frances Elizabeth Oglivy, Countess of. Lady Palmerston and Her Times. 2 vols. London: Hodder & Stoughton, 1922. [Mainly on Byron's marriage and separation.]

Butler, Edward K. Illustrated Catalogue of Notable First Editions
of English Authors, Collected by Edward K. Butler of Ja-
maica Plain, Mass. New York: The American Art Association, 1922.

Cairns, William B. British Criticisms of American Writings,
1815-1833. ("University of Wisconsin Studies in Language
and Literature, " No. 14.) Madison: University of Wisconsin, 1922. [On Byron's comments on American writers.]

Clavel, A. "Byron and Corsica, " N&Q, 12th ser. , X (April 8,
1922), 270. [Did Byron make a tour in Corsica in 1821?]
Cf. Willoughby Maycock, ibid. , X (April 22, 1922), 312.
[No.]

Duff, John Wight. Byron and Aberdeen, a Plea for a Memorial of
the Byron House. Aberdeen: Taylor & Henderson, 1922.

E. "Byron's Lameness, " N&Q, 12th ser. , XI (Sept. 20, 1922),
272. [What was the real nature of Byron's lameness? Is
Trelawny a reliable witness?] Cf. John Murray, ibid. , XI
(Oct. 14, 1922), 316. [Suggests that E. turn to Vol. I, p.
11 of Prothero's Letters and Journals.] C. J. P. , ibid. , XI
(Oct. 21, 1922), 339. [Left leg was shorter than the right
one.] E. , ibid. , XI (Nov. 4, 1922), 375. [Draws attention
to the Sheldrake article in New Monthly Magazine for 1830.]

Edgcumbe, Richard. "The Byron Controversy, " National Review,
LXXIX (July, 1922), 788-89. [Lady Byron did not consider
Augusta the cause of all her unhappiness.]

Gerould, Katherine F. "Men, Women and the Byron-complex,"
    Atlantic Monthly, CXXX (Sept. , 1922), 289-95. [Thoughts
    provoked by the critics' preoccupation with Byron's life,
    rather than with his poetry.] Rptd. in her Ringside Seats.
    New York: Dodd, Mead & Co. , 1937. Pp. 20-32.

Graham, Walter. "Byron and Campbell," N&Q, 12th ser. , X
    (Jan. 21, 1922), 45-46. [Campbell's debt to Byron.]

Havens, Raymond D.   The Influence of Milton on English Poetry.
    Cambridge: Harvard University Press, 1922.

Lehman, B. H.   "The Doctrine of 'Leadership' in the Greater Ro-
    mantic Poets," PMLA, XXXVII (June, 1922), 639-61.

Lynd, Robert.   "Byron Once More," Books and Authors.   London:
    R. Cobden-Sanderson, 1922. Pp. 68-75. [Perhaps the comic
    Byron, as revealed in his letters, is the immortal Byron.]

Miller, Joaquin.   Trelawny with Shelley and Byron.   Pompton
    Lakes, N.J. : The Biblio Co. , 1922.

Miller, William.   A History of the Greek People.   London: Me-
    thuen & Co. , 1922.

Monahan, Michael.   "Black Friar," An Attic Dreamer.   New York:
    M. Kennerley, 1922. Pp. 144-51. [The worst has been said
    about Byron.   Touches on Mrs. Stowe and Lord Lovelace.]

Murray, John (ed.).   Lord Byron's Correspondence, Chiefly with
    Lady Melbourne, Mr. Hobhouse, The Hon. Douglas Kinnaird,
    and P. B. Shelley.   With Portraits.   2 vols.   London: John
    Murray, 1922.
    Reviews:
    TLS, Feb. 16, 1922, pp. 97-98.   Cf. Maurice H. FitzGerald,
        ibid. , Feb. 23, 1922, p. 125. [Corrects a line of the
        preceding review.]
    N&A, XXX (Feb. 25, 1922), 796-97.
    "Affable Hawk," NS, XVIII (Feb. 25, 1922), 593.
    Spectator, CXXVIII (Feb. 25, 1922), 239-40.
    John O'London's Weekly, VI (March 11, 1922), 755.
    Bookman (London), LXII (April, 1922), 29-30.
    Lord Ernle, QR, CCXXXVII (April, 1922), 430-50.
    Maurice Hewlett, London Mercury, V (April, 1922), 664-66.
        Rptd. as "Byron at His Worst," in his Extemporary Essays,
        London: Oxford University Press, 1922. Pp. 94-100.
        Cf. E. Marsh, ibid. , VI (May, 1922), 83-84. [Refers to
        this review in his letter to the editor.]
    NYTBR, April 2, 1922, pp. 3, 24.
    Samuel Chew, Nation, CXIV (April 12, 1922), 442.
    Stewart M. Ellis, Fortnightly Review, CXVII (April 15, 1922),
        668-78.   Rptd. as "The New Byron Letters," in his Main-
        ly Victorian.   London: Hutchinson & Co. , 1925. Pp. 230-

40. Cf. E. P. Hewitt, ibid. , CXVIII (Nov. , 1922), 876-
79. [An answer to Ellis.] S. M. Ellis, ibid. , CXVIII
(Dec. , 1922), 1050-51. [A rejoiner to Hewitt.]
P. Lubbock, Independent, CVIII (April 15, 1922), 364. [Para-
phrased as "Why Byron Still Holds Our Imagination, " in
Current Opinion, LXXII (June, 1922), 811-14.]
Bookman, LV (May, 1922), 298-99.
Edward Liveing, Discovery, III (May, 1922), 134-36.
Howard M. Jones, Freeman, V (June 7, 1922), 306-308.
William Rose Benét, Literary Review, II (July 15, 1922),
801-802.
John Erskine, Outlook, CXXXI (July 26, 1922), 533-34.
Stark Young, NR, XXXII (Sept. 27, 1922), Pt. II, 12-14.
Partly rptd. in "The Magic World of Stark Young, " NR,
CXLVIII (Jan. 26, 1963), 21-23.
Stewart Mitchell, Dial, LXXIII (Oct. , 1922), 453-55.
Frederick E. Pierce, Yale Review, XIII (Oct. , 1923), 169-71.
See also:
R. C. Ensor, NS, XVIII (March 4, 1922), 617. [A letter to
the editor.]

Peers, E. Allison. "The Earliest Notice of Byron in Spain, "
Revue de Litterature Comparée, II (Jan. , 1922), 113-16.
[Most of the article is in Spanish.]

Prescott, Frederick Clarke. The Poetic Mind. New York: The
Macmillan Co. , 1922.

Quiller-Couch, Sir Arthur. "Byron, " Studies in Literature. 2nd
series. New York: Putnam, 1922. Pp. 3-31. [From an
address given at University College, Nottingham.] Rptd. in
"Q" Anthology, ed. F. Brittain. London: J. M. Dent, 1948.
Pp. 399-405. [An abridged version.]

Quintana, Ricardo B. "The Satiric Mood in Byron, " Washington
University Studies, "Humanities Series, " IX (April, 1922),
211-31.

Reilley, Joseph J. "Letters of Tom Moore's Noble Poet, " Catholic
World, CXVI (Nov. , 1922), 180-88. [Byron as revealed in
his letters a man of common clay and not always a "noble
poet. "]

Squire, John Collings. "Byron, " Books Reviewed. New York:
George H. Doran, 1922. Pp. 129-35. [A review of Astarte
from the Observer.]

Street, George Slythe. "Byron Reconsidered, " Nineteenth Century,
XCI (May, 1922), 774-81. [Byron as revealed in his letters.
A stern revaluation.]

Wainwright, John B. "Byron and the Royal Society, " N&Q, 12th
ser. , X (June 3, 1922), 430. [When was Byron elected

Fellow of the Royal Society?] Cf. G. N. W., ibid., 12th
  ser., X (June 24, 1922), 498. [On Jan. 11, 1816.]

Werner, A. "The Byron Problem," NS, XIX (June 3, 1922), 235-
  36. [Letter to the editor motivated by Astarte and Lord Byron's Correspondence. He maintains that Byron had been
  married to Thyrza in 1809.]

White, Newman I. "The English Romantic Writers as Dramatists,"
  SR, XXX (April-June, 1922), 206-15.

                                1923

Benson, Adolph B. "Catherine Potter Stith and Her Meeting with
  Lord Byron, with Unpublished Letters of Lord Byron, Tre-
  lawny, Thomas Sully and L. Gaylord Clark," SAQ, XXII
  (Jan., 1923), 10-22. [A Philadelphian who met Byron in
  Leghorn.]

Blankner, Fredericka. "The Influence of Italy upon Lord Byron
  as Shown in Extracts from His Poems and Letters," Colum-
  bus, XXI (April, 1923), 21-27.

Cameron, H. Charles. "The Lameness of Lord Byron," British
  Medical Journal, Part I, March 31, 1923, pp. 564-65. [Ab-
  stract of an address delivered at a Social evening of the
  Royal Society of Medicine on March 21st, 1923.] A similar
  abstract to be found in Lancet, Part I, March 31, 1923, pp.
  678-79. Rptd. with some additions in N&Q, CXLVI (April 19,
  1924), 281-85. Cf. E., ibid., CXLVI (May 31, 1924), 400-
  401.

D'Olivet, Fabre. Cain, A Dramatic Mystery in Three Acts by
  Lord Byron, Translated into French Verse and Refuted in a
  Series of Philosophical and Critical Remarks Preceded by a
  Letter Addressed to Lord Byron, upon the Motives and the
  Purpose of this Work. Done into English by Nayán Louise
  Redfield. New York: G. P. Putnam's Sons, 1923.

Draper, Frederick W. M. The Rise and Fall of the French Romantic Drama, with Special Reference to the Influence of
  Shakespeare, Scott and Byron. London: Constable & Co.,
  1923.

Drinkwater, John. "Byron," The Outline of Literature. 2 vols.
  London: G. Newnes, 1923-24. Vol. II, 372-80.

Goode, Clement Tyson. Byron as Critic. Weimar: R. Wagner
  Sohn, 1923.
  Reviews:
    Clarke S. Northup, Cornell Alumni News, XXVI (April 24,
    1924), 374.

Howard M. Jones, JEGP, XXIV (April, 1925), 295-99.

Grierson, H. J. C. Address at the Presentation to Aberdeen
    Grammar School of A Statue of Lord Byron. Aberdeen:
    Printed at the Rosemount Press, 1923. Rptd. in his Essays
    and Addresses. London: Chatto & Windus, 1940. Pp. 1-18.

—————— (ed.). "Preface," Poems of Lord Byron, Selected and
    Arranged in Chronological Order with a Preface. London:
    Chatto & Windus, 1923. Pp. v-xxviii.
    Review:
    Lord Ernle, QR, CCXLI (April, 1924), 229-53.

Holland, Henry Edward V. Fox, 4th Baron. The Journal of the
    Hon. Henry Edward Fox, 1818-1830, ed. Earl of Ilchester.
    London: T. Butterworth Ltd., 1923.

Kephala, Euphrosine. "A Link with Byron," Spectator, CXXX
    (May 23, 1923), 884. [His grandfather had seen Byron in
    Greece one day.]

Ker, William Paton. "Byron," The Criterion, II (Oct., 1923), 1-
    15. Rptd. in his Collected Essays. London: Macmillan &
    Co., 1925. Vol. I, pp. 207-23. [Deals with Goethe's opin-
    ion of Byron, Byron as a lyrical poet, and the possible re-
    semblances between Byron and Edward Young.]

Krumbhaar, E. B. "On the Post-mortem Examination of the Body
    of Lord Byron," Annals of Medical History, V (Sept., 1923),
    283-84.

Krummel, Charles A. "Byron and Goethe," SAQ, XXII (July, 1923),
    246-56.

Paget, Walpurga Ehrengarde Helena, Lady. Embassies of Other
    Days, and Further Recollections. 2 vols. New York: George
    H. Doran Co., 1923. Vol. I, p. 245. [A Byron anecdote.]

Ponsonby, Arthur. "Byron," English Diaries: A Review of Eng-
    lish Diaries from the 16th to the 20th Century. London:
    Methuen & Co., 1923. Pp. 264-71. [On Byron's Journal
    from Nov. 14, 1813, to April 19, 1814; his Alps Expedition
    Journal, 1816, and his January-February, 1821, Journal.]

Statham, H. Heathcote. "Byron's Place in Poetry," SR, XXXI
    (July, 1923), 296-312.

Symons, Arthur. "Paradoxes on Poets," Dramatis Personae. In-
    dianapolis: The Bobbs-Merril Co., 1923. Pp. 351-58. [In
    comic verse (Don Juan), he showed mastery over form and
    found "a genius for rhyme and a genius for plain statement."]

Whitten, Wilfred. "Byron About Town," John O'London's Weekly,
    V (April 28, 1923), 119.

Wilson, David Alec. Carlyle till Marriage, 1795-1826. London:
    K. Paul, Trench, Trübner & Co., 1923.

Woollen, W. H. "Last Links with Byron, Shelley & Keats," N&Q,
    CXLV (Oct. 27, 1923), 323. [Points out some errors in
    Graham's work.]

6. CENTENNIAL, 1924-1925

1924

''[Account of the Bringing of Byron's Remains from London to Hucknall Torkard],'' N&Q, CXLVII (July 19, 1924), 40.

Bellamy, Robert Lowe. Byron, the Man. London: K. Paul, 1924.
Review:
Edward Shanks, London Mercury, X (July, 1924), 325-27.

Belloc, Hillaire. ''On Byron,'' NS, XXIII (May 31, 1924), 222-23.
Rptd. as ''Talking of Byron,'' in his Short Talks with the Dead
and Others. Kensington: The Cayne Press, 1926. Pp. 31-
37. [In Byron's poetry there was ''marriage of intelligence
with the magic of words.'' We are to blame for the shifts in
his popularity.]

Birrell, Augustine. ''Byron, a Century After,'' Literary Review,
IV (April 12, 1924), 659-60. [Byron has stood his test.]

_____. ''Byron's Letters,'' More Obiter Dicta. New York:
Scribner, 1924. Pp. 59-69. [A review of Lord Byron's
Correspondence, rptd. from The Times (London), Feb.,
1922.]

Brandes, Georg. Wolfgang Goethe. Authorized translation by
Allen W. Porterfield. 2 vols. New York: Nicholas L.
Brown, 1924.

Briscoe, Walter A. ''Byron as Politician,'' CR, CXXV (April,
1924), 460-67.

_____. ''Byron's First Printers,'' Bookman (London), LXVI
(May, 1924), 101.

_____. (ed.). Byron, the Poet: A Collection of Addresses and
Essays. A Centenary Volume. London: G. Routledge &
Sons, 1924. [Of the items found in this book, those marked
with an asterisk are reprints of articles already listed in this
bibliography and their original date of publication appears in
parentheses following the title. The others are either addresses delivered mostly in Nottingham prior to publication
of this book, or essays written expressly to be published
here.]

It contains:
Shirley C. Atchley, "Byron in Greece," pp. 131-52.
Sir Squire Bancroft and William Archer, "Byron on the Stage,"
    pp. 161-80.
Walter A. Briscoe, "Byron as Poet Laureate," pp. 153-57.
_____, "Byron's Happy Years," pp. 201-15.
_____, "A Prince of Lovers," pp. 222-35.
Marie Corelli, "The Genius of Byron, pp. 86-88.
W. Macneillie Dixon, "Byron," pp. 94-95.
*William Fletcher, "Byron's Last Illness and Death," (1824),
    pp. 276-81.
Frank Granger, "The Moral Influence of Byron," pp. 91-93.
_____, "Shakespeare and Byron," pp. 158-60.
C. L. Graves, "A Hundred Years After," pp. 239-40.
H. J. C. Grierson, "Byron and English Society," pp. 55-85.
Viscount Haldane, "Byron and Goethe," pp. 35-54.
J. A. Hammerton, "Byron's First Romance," from The
    Sketch (1897), pp. 216-21.
_____, "At Byron's Grave," from British Weekly (1898),
    pp. 282-87.
William Howitt & others, "The Byron Mystery. The Case
    for the Defence," pp. 241-75.
Edmund Huntsman, "Byron the Poet," pp. 37-54.
*Sir Arthur Quiller Couch, "Byron, a Study," (1922), pp. 3-
    29.
*Hon. Whitelaw Reid, "The Fame of Byron," (1910), pp. 30-34.
*Cecil Roberts, "Byron in Venice," (1924), pp. 105-130.
_____, "A Ghost of Venice," pp. 236-38. [A poem.]
*Herbert C. Roe, "Byron's Fugitive Pieces," (1919), pp. 181-
    89.
*George Saintsbury, "Byron as Prosodist," (1910), pp. 89-90.
*Wilfred Whitten, "Byron About Town," (1923), pp. 99-104.
Reviews:
ER, CCXXXIX (April, 1924), 342-57.
N&A, XXXV (April 5, 1924), 18.
TLS, Feb. 21, 1924, p. 108.

_____. "Sorrows of Byron," Bookman (London), LXVI (April,
    1924), 5-7. [The theme of sorrow pervades his life and his
    poetry.]

Burdett, Osbert. "Verdict on Byron," Outlook (London), LIII
    (April 19, 1924), 264-65. [His genius was in prose, as evi-
    denced in his letters and journals.]

"Byron and His Doctor," Living Age, CCCXXI (June 21, 1924),
    1209-10.

"Byron and the United States," World's Work, XLVIII (July, 1924),
    249-50.

"The Byron Centenary," Poetry Review, XV (July-Aug., 1924),
    205-10.

"The Byron Centenary. The Greek National Celebrations," Poetry
   Review, XV (Sept. -Oct. , 1924), 346-47.

"Byron Centenary Celebrations," Near East, XXV (May 8, 1924),
   481-82.

"Byron, Devil's Disciple," Nation, CXVIII (April 30, 1924), 495-
   96. [Byron as a person is no longer more important than
   his poetry. Favorable change in attitude towards him in the
   Jazz Age.]

"Byron Legend. Celebrating Missolonghi and the Afterglow,"
   Current Opinion, LXXVI (May, 1924), 649-50.

"Byron's Lameness and Death," British Medical Journal, I (April
   19, 1924), 719-20.

Caclamos, Demetrius. The Centenary of Byron's Death in England:
   Addresses Delivered by Demetrius Caclamos. London: Pri-
   vately Printed, 1924. Rptd. in his Greece in Peace and War.
   London: P. L. Humphries & Co. , 1942. Pp. 61-81.

Campbell, Olwen Ward. Shelley and the Unromantics. London:
   Methuen & Co. , 1924.

The Celebration of the Centenary of Lord Byron's Death by the
   University of Athens, 1824-1924. [Some items are in Greek
   only; others are bi-lingual and are recorded here.] A.
   Andreades and others. "Centenary Speech," pp. 42-54.
   John Drinkwater. Ode to Byron, p. 34. [Rptd. from The
      Times, April 19, 1924, p. 11.]
   Simos Menardos. "Centenary Speech," pp. 17-33. Rptd. as
      "Byron in Greece" in Poetry Review, XV (Aug. , 1924),
      211-20.
   Costis Palamas, Ode to Byron, pp. 37-41. Rptd. in Poetry
      Review, XV (Aug. , 1924), 223-24.

"The Centenary of Byron's Death. His Last Illness," British
   Medical Journal, I (April 19, 1924), 724-26.

Chancellor, E. Beresford. "Byron in London," English Review,
   XXXVIII (April, 1924), 465-71.

Chew, Samuel C. "Byron in America," American Mercury, I
   (March, 1924), 335-44.

_____. Byron in England: His Fame and Afterfame. London:
   J. Murray, 1924.
   Reviews:
      TLS, March 6, 1924, p. 141.
      Lord Ernle, QR, CCXLI (April, 1924), 229-53.
      C. E. Lawrence, ER, CCXXXIX (April, 1924), 342-57.
      V. Rendall, Saturday Review, CXXXVII (April 19, 1924), 406-

408.
F. V. Keys, NAR, CCXIX (June, 1924), 905-908.
Edward Shanks, London Mercury, X (June, 1924), 218-20.
W. E. Leonard, Nation, CXIX (July 9, 1924), 50-51.
Howard M. Jones, NR, XL (Oct. 1, 1924), Pt. II, 6-7.
_____, MLN, XL (March, 1925), 176-78.
Harold Nicolson, N&A, XXXV (April 5, 1927), 18.

Clark, Cumberland. Byron Centenary Celebration, 1824-1924.
    Lectures on Byron's Life and Works. London: Wass,
    Pritchard & Co., 1924. Rptd. in his Dickens and Democra-
    cy, and Other Studies. London: C. Palmer, 1930. Pp.
    109-71.

Cleworth, Joseph. "The Byron Centenary," Transactions of the
    Rochdale Literary and Scientific Society, XV (1923-1925), 71-
    75.

Crundell, H. W. "A Poem by Byron," London Mercury, X (Aug.,
    1924), 409-10. ["Lines- to her who can best understand
    them," attributed to Byron.]

Edgar, Pelham. "The Centenary of Byron (1788-1824)," Dalhousie
    Review, IV (April, 1924), 98-101. [In spite of his faults 'he
    is still not only the most glittering, but the most potent per-
    sonality of his age."]

Elliott, G. R. "Byron and the Comic Spirit," PMLA, XXXIX
    (Dec., 1924), 897-909. Rptd. in his The Cycle of Modern
    Poetry. Princeton: Princeton University Press, 1929.
    Pp. 25-37.

Ernle, Rowland E. Prothero, Baron. "Byron: The Cosmopolitan
    Poet," Poetry Review, XV (Aug., 1924), 221-23.

Fox, Sir John C. The Byron Mystery. London: G. Richards,
    1924.
    Reviews:
    TLS, Nov. 13, 1924, p. 726.
    Harold Nicolson, N&A, XXXVI (Nov. 22, 1924), 300.
    Chartres Biron, London Mercury, XII (May, 1925), 104-106.

Garrod, Heathcote William. Byron: 1824-1924. Oxford: The
    Clarendon Press, 1924. Rptd. in his The Profession of
    Poetry and Other Lectures. Oxford: The Clarendon Press,
    1929. Pp. 49-65.

Gay, H. Nelson. " 'Mio Byron' and a Fair-haired Romagnola,"
    NYTBR, April 13, 1924, pp. 2-3, 24. [Byron and Teresa.]

Gingerich, S. F. "Byron," Essays in the Romantic Poets. New
    York: The Macmillan Co., 1924. Pp. 243-76.

Grey, Rowland. "Imagined Byrons," Cornhill Magazine, CXXIX (April, 1924), 392-400. [Byron in fiction.]

Grierson, H. J. C. "Lord Byron," N&A, XXXV (April 19, 1924), 81-83. [Although he is the least of the romantics in that he is the most negative and an imperfect artist, except in satire, we cannot overlook Byron because he reminds thinkers and dreamers "of what the world really is, of the greatness of the task of interpreting and reforming it."]

Griffith, R. H., and H. M. Jones. A Descriptive Catalogue of an Exhibition of Manuscripts and First Editions of Lord Byron. Austin, Texas: The University of Texas Press, 1924.

Henson, Herbert H. Byron. Cambridge, [Eng.]: The University Press, 1924. [The Rede Lecture for 1924.]
Reviews:
N&Q, CXLVI (May 17, 1924), 370.
F. H. Pughe, Englische Studien, LIX (1925), 107-11.

Herford, C. H. "Lord Byron," Holborn Review, n.s., XV (April, 1924), 145-58.

Hewitt, E. "Our Neglected Debt to Byron," National Review, LXXXIII (March, 1924), 86-88. [Pleads for a bust or monument of Byron in Westminster Abbey.]

Hopman, F. J. "Byron: Some Characteristics of His Poetry," ES, VI (April, 1924), 49-60.

_____. "Byron: Some Personal Characteristics," ES, VI (Feb., 1924), 1-12.

Jones, Howard M. "Byron Centenary," Yale Review, XIII (July, 1924), 730-45.

_____. "The Influence of Byron," Texas Review, IX (April, 1924), 170-96.

Kempling, W. Bailey. "Lord Byron in Monumental Record," Fortnightly Review, CXXI (April, 1924), 476-81. ["No English poet, Shakespeare alone exempt, has so many monuments to his fame."]

Le Gallienne, Richard. "Lord Byron, 1824-1924," NYTBR, April 13, 1924, pp. 1, 22.

"Lord Byron, 1788-1824," TLS, April 10, 1924, pp. 213-14. [Leading article.]

MacDonald, William. "Viewing Byron in His Meteoric Course," Literary Digest International Book Review, II (Oct., 1924), 790-91, 793.

McKillop, Alan D. "The Power of Byron," NR, XXXVIII (April 16, 1924), 201-203. [His reputation lies in his satires.]

Maurois, André. Ariel: A Shelley Romance, trans. Ella D'Arcy, London: John Lane Ltd., 1924.

Milne, James. "Byron and the Murrays," A London Book Window. London: John Lane, 1924. Pp. 93-102.

Minchin, H. C. "Byron: Flame and Power," Fortnightly Review, CXXI (April, 1924), 465-75. ["Byron's writing is instinct with power as well as with the flaming gift of satire."]

Mirsky, D. S. "Byron," London Mercury, IX (April, 1924), 603-16.

Monroe, H. "Byron," Poetry, XXIV (April, 1924), 32-40.

Moore, T. Sturge. "Byron's Vision of Judgment," London Mercury, X (Sept., 1924), 520-21.

Morgan, Myrtis. "Lord Byron. 'Crede Byron,'" Libertarian, II (Feb., 1924), 91-100.

Murray, John. Byron and John Murray. London: John Murray, 1924.

_____. "The Popularity of Byron," Cornhill Magazine, CXXIX (April, 1924), 384-91. Rptd. in Living Age, CCCXXI (May 10, 1924), 913-17.

Nash, J. V. "Byron: After 100 Years," Open Court, XXXVIII (July, 1924), 395-405.

Nicolson, Harold. Byron: The Last Journey, April 1823-April 1824. London: Constable, 1924. New edition with a supplementary chapter, 1940.
    Reviews:
        TLS, March 6, 1924, p. 141.
        Clive Bell, N&A, XXXIV (March 15, 1924), 836, 838. Rptd. in NR, XXXIX (May 28, 1924), 25.
        C. E. Lawrence, ER, CCXXXIX (April, 1924), 342-57.
        Edward Shanks, London Mercury, IX (April, 1924), 662-64.
        Saturday Review, CXXXVII (April 19, 1924), 406.
        Samuel Chew, Nation, CXIX (Aug. 6, 1924), 149.
        Edmund Wilson, Dial, LXXVIII (June, 1925), 511-14. Rptd. as "Byron in the Twenties," in his Shores of Light. New York: Farrar, Strauss & Young, 1952. Pp. 62-67.
        TLS, June 22, 1940, p. 304. [Review of new edition with a supplementary chapter.]
    See also:
        Leonard W. Mackail, "The Cause of Byron's Death," TLS, April 24, 1924, p. 253. [Quotes opinion of William Osler

that it was meningitis.]
P. P. Howe, "Byron, the Last Journey," TLS, June 5, 1924,
p. 356. [A letter to the editor in which he corrects a detail in Nicolson's work about the Hunt brothers.]

Partridge, Eric. The French Romantics' Knowledge of English
Literature. 1820-1848. Paris: Edouard Champion, 1924.

Pemberton, William B. "Byron in the Field," Fighting Forces, I
(June, 1924), 265-75. [Byron and his disillusionment with
the Greek War of Independence.]

Pierce, Frederick E. "Byron and this Century," Literary Review,
IV (April 26, 1924), 701-702.

Pigot, C. Becher. "Lord Byron at Southwell," N&Q, CXLVI (May
17, 1924), 358.

Ratchford, Fannie E. "Byron's First Composition of the English
Bards and Scotch Reviewers," Texas Review, IX (April, 1924),
250-54. [Makes a study of textual changes in English Bards
& Scotch Reviewers.]

_____. "Notes on Byron," UTSE, IV (March 15, 1924), 88-96.
[Concerns Byron's quarrel with Southey and Murray.]

Raymond, Dora Neill. The Political Career of Lord Byron. New
York: H. Holt & Co., 1924.
Reviews:
W. E. Leonard, Nation, CXIX (July 9, 1924), 50-51.
Outlook, CXXXVII (July 16, 1924), 444.
H. M. Jones, NR, XL (Oct. 1, 1924), Pt. II, 6-7.
Edmund Wilson, Dial, LXXVIII (June, 1925), 511-14. Rptd.
as "Byron in the Twenties," in his Shores of Light. New
York: Farrar, Strauss & Young, 1952. Pp. 62-67.
TLS, July 23, 1925, p. 497.
Saturday Review, CXL (Aug. 1, 1925), 137.
Augustine Birrell, NS, XXV (Aug. 29, 1925), 553-54.

Rice, Richard Ashley. "Lord Byron's British Reputation," Smith
College Studies in Modern Languages, V (Jan., 1924), 1-26.

Roberts, C. "Byron in Venice," Fortnightly Review, CXXI (Jan.,
1924), 60-74.

Roberts, R. Ellis. "Critical Sketch," Bookman (London), LXVI
(April, 1924), 1-5.

Rose, William. From Goethe to Byron: The Development of
'Weltschmerz' in German Literature. London: G. Routledge,
1924.

354   Bibliography

Saintsbury, George E. B. A Last Scrapbook. London: Macmillan
    & Co. , 1924. [Pp. 37-52, et passim.]

Smith, Harry B. "Byron: His Books and Autographs," Scribner's
    Magazine, LXXVI (Sept. , 1924), 237-50. [Letters in his
    possession.]

Spender, Harold. Byron and Greece. London: J. Murray; New
    York: Scribner, 1924.
    Reviews:
    Edward Shanks, London Mercury, X (June, 1924), 218-20.
    Samuel Chew, Nation, CXIX (Aug. 6, 1924), 149.
    Howard M. Jones, NR, XL (Oct. 1, 1924), Pt. II, 6-7.

Strachey, J. St. Loe. "Dancing and the Poets," London Mercury,
    X (Oct. , 1924), 597-604. [On Byron's "The Waltz."]

Strahan, J. A. "Byron's Biographer," Blackwood's, CCXV (April,
    1924), 574-82. [On Thomas Moore.]

Stuckey, Norman. "Celebrating a Byron Centenary," Literary Di-
    gest International Book Review, II (April, 1924), 365, 367.

Symon, James David. Byron in Perspective. London: M. Secker,
    1924.
    Reviews:
    TLS, April 24, 1924, p. 251.
    Edward Shanks, London Mercury, X (June, 1924), 218-20.
    SRL, II (Oct. 17, 1925), 221.
    Newman I. White, SAQ, XXV (Oct. , 1926), 440-42.

Taylor, W. D. "Byron," Queen's Quarterly, XXXII (July-Aug. -
    Sept. , 1924), 1-13. [Some remarks suggested by Symon's
    Byron in Perspective and Nicolson's Byron: The Last Jour-
    ney.]

Teignmouth, Henry Noel Shore, 5th Baron. "Byron's Suliote Body-
    guard," Nineteenth Century, XCV (April, 1924), 541-54.

Thompson, Elbert. "The Interest of English Poets in Italian Free-
    dom," PQ, III (July, 1924), 172-91.

Whibley, Charles. "The Letters of an Englishman. Byron and
    Westminster Abbey," English Review, XXXIX (Aug. , 1924),
    216-20.

White, G. H. "Byron's Armenian Translations," N&Q, CXLVI
    (April 5, 1924), 250. [Bibliographical description of Beauties
    of English Poets. Venice: In the Island of St. Lazzaro,
    1852.] Cf. S. F. , and Harmatopegos, ibid. , CXLVI (April
    19, 1924), 292. [Reminisce about their visit to St. Lazzaro.]

Williamson, G. C. 'Byron Exhibition," Spectator, CXXXIII (Nov. 8, 1924), 681-82. [A write-up of the First Edition Club Exhibition to take place in 1925.]

Wilson, Harriette. The Memoirs of Harriette Wilson, Written by Herself. 2 vols. London: Privately Printed, 1924. [Contains spurious recollections of Byron whom this courtesan never met.]

Wood, Clement. Byron and the Women He Loved. Girard, Kan.: Haldeman-Julius & Co., 1924.

Woodbridge, Benjamin M. "Bel Ami and Madame Walter," MLN, XXXIX (March, 1924), 185-87. [Sees no necessary relation between Bel Ami and Don Juan, or between Mme. Walter, a character in the novel, and Donna Julia.]

1925

Barber, T. G., and C. H. H. Mitchell. "The Byron International Memorial Fund," London Mercury, XII (Aug., 1925), 413-14. [Announcing the creation of a Memorial Committee.]

Barrington, E. [pseud. for Lily Moresly Adams Beck]. Glorious Apollo. New York: Dodd, Mead & Co., 1925. [A sensational biography, really fiction.]
Review:
SRL, II (Aug. 29, 1925), 89-90.

Bertie, Charles H. 'Byron's Hebrew Melodies," TLS, July 2, 1925, p. 448. [None of the MSS are in Australia; Nathan probably never took them with him.]

Blacket, J. "Joseph Blacket and His Links to Byron." London Quarterly Review, CXLIII (Jan., 1925), 26-40. [A young shoemaker in London, writer of verses, a protegé of Miss Milbanke, attacked by Byron in English Bards and Scotch Reviewers, about whom Byron always referred in disparaging terms.]

Boyd, Ernest. "A New Way with Old Masterpieces, IV: Lord Byron," Harper, CL (May, 1925), 730-38. Rptd. in his Literary Blasphemies. New York: Harper & Bros., 1927. Pp. 106-135. [Though hostile to Byron, Boyd finds him deserving of immortality.]

Buckland, C. S. B. "A Letter to Byron," TLS, Jan. 22, 1925, p. 56. [From Hoppner, dated from Venice, Sept. 22, 1820, now to be found in Vol. XCVIII of the Liverpool Papers at the British Museum; quotes the entire letter.]

"Byron--1824-1924, " Poetry Review, XVI (Feb. , 1925), 69-70.

"Byron's Last Writing," Living Age, CCCXXV (May 16, 1925), 383-
84.

Cassity, J. H. "Psychopathological Glimpses of Lord Byron, "
Psychoanalytic Review, XII (1925), 397-413. [Calls attention
to a few of the psychopathological features of Lord Byron's
personality, "with special reference to the etiological motivation of both his literary productions and his singular behavior. "]

Chambers, R. W. Ruskin (and Others) on Byron. ("Pamphlet of
the English Association" No. 62.) Oxford: Oxford University
Press, 1925. Rptd. in his Man's Unconquerable Mind. London: J. Cape, 1939. Pp. 311-41.

Chancellor, Edwin B. "The Rejected Addresses, " Literary Diver-
sions. London: Dulau & Co. , 1925. Pp. 169-174. [On the
origin of The Rejected Addresses and the reason for the
title.]

Drinkwater, John. The Pilgrim of Eternity: Byron--A Conflict.
New York: George H. Doran Co. , 1925.
Reviews:
Spectator, CXXXV (Nov. 21, 1925), 938.
TLS, Nov. 26, 1925, p. 791.
Allan Nevins, Bookman, LXII (Dec. , 1925), 488-89.
N&A, XXXVIII (Dec. 19, 1925), 442.
Ernest Boyd, Independent, CXVI (Jan. 9, 1926), 49.
Samuel Chew, SRL, II (Jan. 30, 1926), 525.
London Mercury, XIV (July, 1926), 315-17.
W. E. H. , SR, XXXIV (July-Sept. , 1926), 344-45.
Newman I. White, SAQ, XXV (Oct. , 1926), 440-42.
Martha Boyard, Literary Digest International Book Review,
IV (Nov. , 1926), 764, 766.
Edward Shanks, Saturday Review, CXL (Dec. 6, 1926), 662-
63.

Elton, Oliver. "The Present Value of Byron, " RES, I (Jan. ,
1925), 24-39. Rptd. in his Essays and Addresses. New
York: Longmans Green & Co. ; London: Edward Arnold &
Co. , 1939. Pp. 44-69.

"First Editions of Lord Byron, " London Mercury, XI (April, 1925),
641. [Exhibitions of MSS and first editions held in 1924.]

Forsythe, Robert S. "Byron's Lines on Hoppner, " TLS, March 5,
1925, p. 156. [Reports another copy of this jeux d'esprit
besides the ones mentioned in the First Edition Club catalogue. Wonders if his volume is genuine.]

Furniss, Harry. Paradise in Piccadilly: The Story of Albany.

London: John Lane, The Bodley Head; New York: Dodd,
Mead & Co., 1925. [Byron wrote Lara and "Ode to Napoleon" in his Albany Apartment.]

Gosse, Sir Edmund W. "Shelley's Widow," Silhouettes. London:
W. Heinemann, 1925. Pp. 231-38.

Grierson, H. J. C. The Background of English Literature, Classi-
cal and Romantic and Other Collected Essays and Addresses.
London: Chatto & Windus, 1925.
It contains:
    "Byron and English Society," pp. 167-99. Rptd. from Byron,
    the Poet, ed. Walter A. Briscoe, 1924.
    "Lord Byron: Arnold and Swinburne," pp. 68-114. Rptd.
    from Proceedings of the British Academy, 1925, pp. 431-
    61.

Hewitt, R. M. Byron's Melancholy. "Byron Foundation Lecture."
Nottingham: University of Nottingham, 1925.

[Irving, Washington]. An Unwritten Drama of Lord Byron; with
an Introduction by Thomas Ollive Mabbot, Ph.D. Metuchen,
N.J.: C. F. Heartman, 1925. [Gives the general plan of
a dramatic poem, projected but not written by Lord Byron.
Irving's article was originally contributed to The Gift: A
Christmas and New Year's Present for 1836.]

King, R. W. "Italian Influence on English Scholarship and Literature during the Romantic Revival," MLR, XX (July, 1925),
295-304; ibid., XXI (Jan., 1926), 24-33.

Lowell, Amy. John Keats. 2 vols. Boston: Houghton Mifflin &
Co., 1925.

*Lynch, Bohun. "Lord Byron's Screen," The Prize Ring. London:
Country Life Ltd., 1925. Pp. 30-46.

Mabbott, Thomas O. "Byron Reference Found," N&Q, CXLVIII
(May 9, 1925), 331. [Discovery of French original of epigram: "Ægle, poet and beauty."]

McIntyre, Clara F. "The Later Career of the Elizabethan Villain-
Hero," PMLA, XL (Sept., 1925), 874-80. [Byron's heroes
have the characteristics of Mrs. Radcliffe's.]

Money, Leo Chiozza. "Had Byron a Musical Ear?" Poetry Review, XVI (Jan.-Feb., 1925), 23-26. [Maintains that "there
is more true music in Don Juan alone than in all the jingles
Swinburne ever wrote."]

Moore, Thomas. Tom Moore's Diary; a Selection Edited with an
Introduction by J. B. Priestley. Cambridge, [Eng.]: The
University Press, 1925.

Pickering, Leslie P.   Lord Byron, Leigh Hunt and the 'Liberal.'
    London: Drane's Ltd. , 1925.

Robertson, John G.   "Goethe and Byron," Publications of the Eng-
    lish Goethe Society, n. s. , II (1925), 1-132.
    Reviews:
    London Mercury, XIV (July, 1926), 315-17.
    L. A. Willoughby, MLR, XXI (Oct. , 1926), 461-62.
    William Rose, RES, III (Jan. , 1927), 106-10.

Robinson, John George.   The Reconciliation of Classic and Roman-
    tic. Cambridge, [Eng.]: Bowes & Bowes, 1925.

Rusk, Ralph Leslie.   The Literature of the Middle Western Fron-
    tier. 2 vols. ("Columbia University Studies in English and
    Comparative Literature," No. 45.) New York: Columbia
    University Press, 1925. [Byron among the poets read.]

Sinclair, Upton.   "The First Lord of Letters," Mammonart: An
    Essay in Economic Interpretation. Pasadena, Calif. : The
    Author, 1925. Pp. 175-78. [Having a clear eye and a clear
    brain, he could see the truth and spoke it to all Europe, thus
    helping revolt and the fight for freedom.]

Symon, James D.   "Byron and Deeside: The Facts and the Le-
    gends, " Deeside Field, II (1925), 24-28.

Tinker, C. Brewster.   "Assault upon the Poets, " Yale Review,
    XIV (July, 1925), 625-44. Rptd. in American Criticism, ed.
    W. A. Drake, New York: Harcourt Brace & Co. , 1926, pp.
    265-90; Tinker's The Good Estate of Poetry, Boston: Little,
    Brown & Co. , 1929, pp. 3-33. [On Nicolson's attack on By-
    ron in his Byron: The Last Journey. Cautions against the
    use of facts of a poet's life in the interpretation of his poe-
    try.]

Walker, Hugh.   English Satire and Satirists.   New York: E. P.
    Dutton, 1925.

Wright, Peter.   "The Centenary of Byron's Death, " Portraits and
    Criticism. London: Eveleigh Nash & Grayson, Ltd. , 1925.
    Pp. 177-82.

7. LITERARY PAUSE, 1926-1934

<u>1926</u>

Abercrombie, Lascelles. <u>Romanticism.</u> London: M. Secker, 1926.

Allen, Hervey. Israfel. <u>The Life and Times of Edgar Allan Poe.</u> 2 vols. New York: George H. Doran & Co., 1926.

Atkins, Elizabeth. "Points of Contact between Byron and Socrates," <u>PMLA</u>, XLI (June, 1926), 402-23.

Benham, Allen R. "Byron and His Contemporaries," <u>Personalist,</u> VII (July, 1926), 185-96.

Bewdley, Stanley Baldwin, Earl of. "Byron," <u>On England and Other Addresses.</u> London: P. Allan & Co., 1926. Pp. 123-25. [In his death he established his immortality.]

Boas, Guy. "Lord Byron," <u>Dryden, Pope and Byron, Compared and Contrasted,</u> ed. Sir Henry Newbolt. London: Thomas Nelson & Sons, 1926. Pp. 157-67.

Bowles, William Lisle. <u>A Wiltshire Parson and His Friends: The Correspondence of William Lisle Bowles,</u> ed. Garland Greever. London: Constable & Co., 1926.

Brecknock, Albert. <u>Byron: A Study of the Poet in the Light of New Discoveries.</u> London: C. Palmer, 1926.

Brinton, Clarence Crane. "Second Generation of Revolt: Byron and Shelley," <u>Political Ideas of the English Romanticists.</u> London: Oxford University Press, 1926. Pp. 147-95.

"Byron and Shelley," <u>N&Q</u>, CLI (July 17, 1926), 37. [Relations of Walter Savage Landor and Byron.]

Calverton, V. F. <u>Sex Expression in Literature.</u> New York: Boni & Liveright, 1926.

Collins, V. H. "Quotations in Byron's Letters," <u>N&Q</u>, CLI (Sept. 18, 1926), 207. [Asks for references to quotations.]

360   Bibliography

Quotations found:
Edward Bensly and Geo. T. Walsh, ibid., CLI (Oct. 2, 1926), 246.
Walter Worrall, ibid., CLI (Oct. 16, 1926), 285.

Dargan, E. Preston. "Byron's Fame in France," VQR, II (Oct., 1926), 530-41.

De Beer, E. S., and Walter Seton. "Byroniana: The Archives of the London Greek Committee," Nineteenth Century, C (Sept., 1926), 396-412.

E., O. "Byron and Canova's Helen," TLS, Sept. 23, 1926, p. 632. [Proposes emendation of lines in The Works of Lord Byron, ed. E. H. Coleridge, Poetry, IV, 536, from "From what nature could, but would not, do/And Beauty and Canova can," to "What Nature would, but could not, do,/And Beauty and Canova can."] Cf. John Murray, ibid., Sept. 30, 1926, p. 654. [Says MS is very clear and Prothero right.]

Gordon, Armistead Churchill. Allegra; the Story of Byron and Miss Clairmont. New York: Minton, Balch & Co., 1926.
Reviews:
Outlook, CXLIV (Nov. 3, 1926), 314.
Agnes Repplier, Forum, LXXVII (March, 1927), 474-75.
TLS, Sept. 15, 1927, p. 621.

Haydon, Benjamin Robert. Autobiography and Memoirs, 1786-1846, ed. Tom Taylor. 2 vols. London: P. Davis, 1926. [On Byron's memoirs.]

Jones, Howard Mumford. "The Author of Two Byron Apocrypha," MLN, XLI (Feb., 1926), 129-31. [Farewell to England and Pilgrimage to the Holy Land attributed to an American imitator.]

Littlefield, Walter (comp.). "Introduction," With Byron in Love. New York: J. H. Sears & Co., 1926. Pp. 7-24. [Aside from the introduction, the rest is primary source material.]

Miller, William. The English in Athens before 1921. London: The Anglo Hellenic League, 1926.

Monahan, Michael. "Byron: The Last Phase," Nemesis. New York: Frank-Maurice, 1926. Pp. 16-33. [A review of Astarte.]

Mordell, Albert. "Remarks on Don Juan by Lord Byron," Notorious Literary Attacks. New York: Boni & Liveright, 1926. Pp. 83-92. [A reprint from Blackwood's, V (Aug., 1819), 512-18.]

Otto, William N. "Assignment Lesson: On the Castle of Chillon,"
    English Journal, XV (May, 1926), 367-72.

Pocock, Guy Noel. "Byron," The Little Room. New York: E. P.
    Dutton, 1926. Pp. 184-91.

Powell, A. E. [Mrs. E. R. Dodds]. The Romantic Theory of
    Poetry. New York: Longmans, Green & Co., 1926.

Shelley, Percy Bysshe. The Complete Works of Shelley, eds.
    Roger Ingpen and Walter E. Peck. 10 vols. London: Pub-
    lished for the Julian Editions by E. Benn, Ltd.; New York:
    C. Scribner's Sons, 1926-1930.

Stokoe, Frank Woodyer. "Byron," German Influence in the English
    Romantic Period, 1788-1818. Cambridge, [Eng.]: Cambridge
    University Press, 1926. Pp. 159-74.

Trilling, Lionel. "A Friend of Byron," Menorah Journal, XII
    (Aug., 1926), 371-83. [On Isaac Nathan.]

Waller, R. D. "Introduction on the Italian Poets and Their Eng-
    lish Imitators, Including Byron," The Monks and the Giants,
    by John Hookham Frere. Manchester: The University Press;
    London: Longmans, Green & Co., 1926. Pp. 1-57.
    Review:
    "J. H. Frere, Byron and Keats," TLS, Nov. 11, 1926,
        p. 790.

                                1927

Auslander, Joseph. "Childe Harold," The Winged Horse; the Story
    of the Poets and Their Poetry. Garden City, N.Y.: Double-
    day, Page & Co., 1927. Pp. 255-64.

Babcock, R. W. "Inception and Reception of Byron's Cain," SAQ,
    XXVI (April, 1927), 178-88.

Batho, Edith. The Ettrick Shepherd. Cambridge: Cambridge Uni-
    versity Press, 1927.

Bennett, James O. "Childe Harold's Pilgrimage," Much Loved
    Books; Best Sellers of the Ages. New York: Boni & Live-
    right, 1927. Pp. 109-14.

"Byron's Lameness," Mentor, XV (May, 1927), 63.

Caskey, J. Homer. "Tracing an Epigram," MLN, XLII (May,
    1927), 323. [Wonders if the epigram by Edward Moore in-
    spired a line in English Bards and Scotch Reviewers, or if
    perhaps they had a common source.]

Cazamian, Louis. "Byron," A History of English Literature, eds.
    Emile Legouis and Louis Cazamian, translated by W. D.
    MacInness and the Author. New York: The Macmillan Co. ,
    1927. Vol. II, pp. 295-99. Revised edition with revised
    bibliographies, in one volume. London: J. M. Dent & Sons,
    1954. Pp. 1044-51.

Collins, Vere Henry (ed.). "Introduction," Lord Byron in His
    Letters: Selections from His Letters and Journals. London:
    John Murray, 1927. Pp. v-xii.
  Reviews:
    SRL, CXLIII (April 9, 1927), 567.
    N&A, XLI (April 23, 1927), 86.
    TLS, Aug. 4, 1927, p. 531.
    Samuel Chew, Yale Review, XVII (Oct. , 1927), 195-97.

Crump, Geoffrey H. "Byron," Poets of the Romantic Revival.
    London: George G. Harrap & Co. , 1927. Pp. 125-38.

Dodd, Lee Wilson. "Notorieties," The Golden Complex, a Defence
    of Inferiority. New York: John Day Co. , 1927. Pp. 55-73.
    [Considers Byron as the supreme example of the beneficent
    workings of the golden complex; i. e. , inferiority complex.]

Dole, Nathan Haskell. "Biographical Sketch and Notes," The Com-
    plete Works of Lord Byron. New York: T. J. Crowell,
    1927. Pp. iii-xxiv.

Elliott, Maude. Lord Byron's Helmet. Boston: Houghton, Mifflin
    & Co. , 1927.

Greville, Charles Cavendish Fulke. The Greville Diary, including
    Passages hitherto Withheld from Publication, ed. Philip Whit-
    well Wilson. 2 vols. Garden City, N. Y. : Doubleday, Page
    & Co. , 1927.

Hammond, G. T. "Byron's Borrowings," Spectator, CXXXIX (Nov.
    26, 1927), 924-25. [Reprints extracts from The United Ser-
    vice Journal, 1829, dealing with Don Juan's shipwreck.]

Hearn, Lafcadio. "Byron," A History of English Literature. 2
    vols. Tokyo: The Hokuseido Press, 1927. Vol. II, pp. 518-
    26.

Hespelt, E. H. "Irving's Version of Byron's 'The Isles of Greece,' "
    MLN, XLII (Feb. , 1927), 111. [Variations from the Cole-
    ridge text.]

Irving, Washington. Notes while Preparing Sketch Book &c. , 1817,
    ed. Stanley T. Williams. New Haven: Yale University Press,
    1927.

Ludwig, Emil. "Lord Byron and Lassalle," Genius and Character.
New York: Harcourt Brace & Co., 1927. Pp. 213-42.

M., H. W. "The Printing of Canto IV of Byron's Childe Harold:
A Bibliographical Study," Yale University Library Gazette,
I (Jan., 1927), 39-41.

Mayfield, John S. Notes on Lord Byron's Infirmity. N.P.: Privately Printed, 1927.

Peck, Walter Edwin. Shelley: His Life and Work, 2 vols. London: Ernest Benn, 1927.

Powell, D. "Byron's Oratory," Quarterly Journal of Speech Education, XIII (Nov., 1927), 424-32.

Railo, Eino. The Haunted Castle. A Study of the Elements of
English Romanticism. London: Routledge & Sons; New York:
E. P. Dutton & Co., 1927.

Rennes, Jacob Johan van. Bowles, Byron and the Pope Controversy. New York: G. E. Steckert, 1927.

Ristine, Frank (ed.). "Introduction," Don Juan. "Modern Readers'
Series." New York: The Macmillan Co., 1927. Pp. v-
xvii.

Robinson, Henry Crabb. The Correspondence of Henry Crabb
Robinson with the Wordsworth Circle (1808-1886), ed. Edith
J. Morley. 2 vols. Oxford: The Clarendon Press, 1927.

S. "A Difficulty in Byron's The Siege of Corinth," N&Q, CLII
(April 16, 1927), 279-80. [In the opening lines, "In the year
since Jesus died for men/Eighteen Hundred years and ten/
We were a gallant company," Byron would have been nineteen
years in the tomb in 1843, when according to the poem he
roamed about the Peloponnese.] Cf. Edward Bensly, ibid.,
CLII (April 30, 1927), 319. [Says that Byron made the
Christian era date from the death of Christ by mistake.]
Edward Broadbent, ibid., CLII (June 4, 1927), 412. [Re-
ports that Coleridge in Poetry, III, says that "the metrical
rendering of the date (miscalculated from the death instead
of the birth) may be traced to the opening lines of an old
ballad," which he quotes.]

Sawyer, Charles J., and F. J. Darton. "Byron," English Books,
1475-1900, a Signpost for Collectors. 2 vols. Westminster:
C. J. Sawyer, Ltd., 1927. Vol. II, pp. 67-75. [On variations in different editions of Byron's works. Lists the very
rare editions.]

Stein, Harold. "A Note on the Versification of Childe Harold,"
MLN, XLII (Jan., 1927), 34-35.

Treitschke, Heinrich G.   "Byron," Fortnightly Review, CXXVIII
    (Nov., 1927), 621-36.   [Article translated into English by
    Mrs. C. E. Barrett.   Byron and his antagonism to English
    Society.]

                                    1928

Beck, Richard.   "Grimür Thomsen: A Pioneer Byron Student,"
    JEGP, XXVII (April, 1928), 70-82.   [An Icelandic poet-
    admirer of Byron, one of the first to introduce Byron to
    Scandinavia and one who shows influence of Byron.]

Blunden, Edmund C.   Leigh Hunt's "Examiner" Examined.   Lon-
    don: Cobden-Sanderson, 1928.

Brightfield, Myron F.   Theodore Hook and His Novels.   Cambridge,
    Mass.: Harvard University Press, 1928.   [Byron's opinion
    of the drama of his day; an anecdote of Hook and Byron at
    Harrow.]

Chesterton, G. K.   "On Byron and Tom Moore," Generally Speak-
    ing, a Book of Essays.   London: Methuen & Co., 1928.
    Pp. 268-73.

Clark, Kenneth M.   The Gothic Revival, an Essay in the History
    of Taste.   London: Constable & Co., 1928.

Collins, A. S.   The Profession of Letters.   A Study of the Rela-
    tion of Author to Patron, Publisher and Public, 1780-1832.
    London: Routledge, 1928.

Collins, V. H.   "Allusions in Byron's Letters.   Sources Wanted,"
    N&Q, CLIV (March 10, 1928), 171.
    Allusions found:
      H. G. Howarth, ibid., CLXXI (Dec. 5, 1936), 401-403.
      Edward Bensly, ibid., CLXXI (Dec. 12, 1936), 424.
      Hibernicus, ibid., CLXXI (Dec. 19, 1936), 446.
      R. G. Howarth, ibid., CLXXI (Dec. 26, 1936), 462-63.
      T. O. M., ibid., CLXXII (Jan. 2, 1937), 14.
      R. G. Howarth, ibid., CLXXII (May 1, 1937), 321.
      _____, ibid., CLXXIII (Sept. 11, 1937), 187-88.
      _____, ibid., CLXXIV (April 9, 1938), 260-61.

_____.   "Allusions in Byron's Letters.   Sources Wanted," N&Q,
    CLIV (April 7, 1928), 245.
    Allusions found:
      R. G. Howarth, ibid., CLXXI (Dec. 26, 1936), 462-63.

_____.   "References in Byron's Letters," N&Q, CLIV (May 5,
    1928), 316.   [Asks for the sources of some references.]
    References found:
      John R. Magrath, Edward Bensly and V. R., ibid., CLIV

(May 19, 1928), 355.

Charles E. Stratton, ibid., CLV (July 7, 1928), 14.

R. G. Howarth, ibid., CLXXI (Dec. 5, 1936), 401-403.

Edward Bensly, ibid., CLXXI (Dec. 12, 1936), 424.

Hibernicus, ibid., CLXXI (Dec. 19, 1936), 446.

R. G. Howarth, ibid., CLXXI (Dec. 26, 1936), 462-63.

T. O. M., ibid., CLXXII (Jan. 2, 1937), 14.

R. G. Howarth, ibid., CLXXII (May 1, 1937), 321.

_____, ibid., CLXXII (May 15, 1937), 349-51.

_____, ibid., CLXXIII (Sept. 11, 1937), 187-88.

_____, ibid., CLXXIV (April 9, 1938), 260-61.

Ernle, Rowland E. Prothero, Baron. "Introduction," The Ravenna Journal; Mainly Compiled at Ravenna in 1821 and Now for the First Time Issued in Book Form. London: The First Edition Club, 1928. Pp. 3-21.

Erskine, John. "Don Juan," The Delight of Great Books. Indianapolis: The Bobbs-Merrill Co., 1928. Pp. 203-20.

_____. "A Romantic Autobiography: Don Juan," Delineator, CXII (Jan., 1928), 49, 87-89.

Fairchild, Hoxie Neale. The Noble Savage; a Study in Romantic Naturalism. New York: Columbia University Press, 1928.

Foerster, Norman. American Criticism. Boston: Houghton Mifflin Co., 1928.

Glenbervie, Sylvester Douglas, Baron. The Diaries of Sylvester Douglas, ed. Francis Bickley. 2 vols. London: Constable & Co.; Boston: Houghton Mifflin Co., 1928.

Gore, John. " 'When We Two Parted': A Byron Mystery Resolved," Cornhill, CXXXVII (Jan., 1928), 39-53. [Prints unpublished letters to Lady Hardy from Albaro, 1822-1823, in which Byron revealed that he had written the poem for Lady Frances Webster.]

Green, Andrew J. "Did Byron Write the Poem 'To Lady Caroline Lamb'?" PQ, VII (Oct., 1928), 338-44. [The evidence presented seems to point to the authenticity of this poem.]

Grierson, H. J. C. "Scott, Byron, Shelley, Keats," Lyrical Poetry from Blake to Hardy. London: The Hogarth Press, 1928. Pp. 39-64.

Harrison, John S. The Vital Interpretation of English Literature. Indianapolis: John S. Harrison, 1928.

Johnson, R. B. (ed.). Shelley-Leigh Hunt: How Friendship Made History. London: Ingpen & Grant, 1928.

Ker, William Paton. Form and Style in Poetry. London: Macmillan & Co., 1928.

Ludwig, Emil. Goethe: The History of a Man, 1749-1832.
Translated from the German by Ethel Colburn Mayne. New
York: G. P. Putnam's; London: The Knickerbocker Press,
1928.

Newton, Annabel. Wordsworth in Early American Criticism. Chicago: The University of Chicago Press, 1928. [Touches on
Byron's death and its effect on America.]

Paull, H. M. Literary Ethics: A Study in the Growth of the
Literary Conscience. London: T. Butterworth, Ltd., 1928.
[On the piracy of Byron's Don Juan and Cain and the injunc-
tions to stop it. Also touches on Byron's plagiarisms.]

Ryan, M. J. "The Adventures of Lord Byron's Prefaces," Bookman's Journal, 3rd ser., XVI (1928), 419-30. [Additional
notes to Byron's bibliography.]

Steuart, Francis. "The Mount Coffee-House," N&Q, CLV (Sept. 8,
1928), 171. [Wants to know what Lord Glenbervie meant
when he wrote in his diary that Byron was living in Villa
Diodatti with the wife of the man who kept the Mount Coffee-
House.] Cf. G. C. Moore Smith, ibid., CLV (Sept. 22,
1928), 208-209. [Says that Shelley's first wife, Harriet West-
brook, was the daughter of the landlord of the Mount Coffee-
House in Grovenor Square. Glenbervie made the mistake of
thinking that Claire Clairmont was the mother of Harriet.]
W. Courthope Forman, ibid., CLV (Sept. 22, 1928), 209.
[Gives history of the Mount.] W. Courthope Forman, ibid.,
CLV (Oct. 6, 1928), 247. [Thinks Claire Clairmont was
Mrs. Shelley.]

Summers, Alphonsus Joseph. "Byron's 'Lovely Rosa' (Charlotte
Dacri)," Essays in Petto. London: The Fortune Press,
1928. Pp. 57-73. [Sister of the "Maid of Athens."]

Willoughby, D. "Revaluations," Outlook (London), LXI (April 28,
1928), 528-29. ['His vision was limited to our globe, and
clear only for its human inhabitants."]

Wilson, Romer [pseud. for Florence Roma Muir O'Brien]. All
Alone: The Life and Private History of Emily Jane Brontë.
London: Chatto & Windus, 1928. Pp. 113-16. [On Byron's
influence on this Victorian novelist and poet.]

Wise, Thomas J. A Byron Library: a Catalogue of Printed Books,
Manuscripts and Autograph Letters by George Gordon Noel,
Baron Byron. With an Introduction by Ethel C. Mayne. Lon-
don: Printed for Private Circulation Only, 1928.

1929

Beck, Richard. "Gisli Brynjülfsson: An Icelandic Imitator of
    Childe Harold's Pilgrimage," JEGP, XXVIII (April, 1929),
    220-37.

*Carter, Frederick (ed.). "Introduction," Manfred. London:
    Franfolico Press, 1929.

Clutton-Brock, A. Shelley: The Man and the Poet. London:
    Methuen & Co., 1929.

Flower, Robin E. W. Byron and Ossian. "Byron Foundation Lec-
    ture." Nottingham: University of Nottingham, 1929.

F[otheringham], D. R. "Byron on the Stage and Byron in Fiction,"
    Poetry Review, XX (March-April, 1929), 140-44. [Calls at-
    tention to Alicia Ramsey's play Byron, and Howard Gordon
    Page's The Shattered Harp.]

Garvin, James Louis. "Byron," The Hundred Best English Essays,
    ed. Frederick Edwin S. Birkenhead. London: Cassell & Co.,
    1929. Pp. 781-801. [A reprint of two articles from the
    Observer, April 6 and 13, 1924.]

Hubbell, Jay B. The Enjoyment of Literature. New York: The
    Macmillan Co., 1929.

Maurois, Andre. "Don Juan; or, The Youth of Byron," Forum,
    LXXXII (Aug., 1929), 65-71; ibid., LXXXII (Sept., 1929),
    183-92; ibid., LXXXII (Oct., 1929), 250-56; ibid., LXXXII
    (Nov., 1929), 309-16; ibid., LXXXII (Dec., 1929), 378-84;
    ibid., LXXXIII (Jan., 1930), 53-59; ibid., LXXXIII (Feb.,
    1930), 114-21. Rptd. as Maurois' Byron. New York: D.
    Appleton, 1930.

Mayne, Ethel Colburn. The Life and Letters of Anne Isabella,
    Lady Noel Byron. London: Constable & Co., 1929.
    Reviews:
        Spectator, CXLII (June 29, 1929), 1017-18.
        Leonard Woolf, N&A, XLV (July 6, 1929), 478.
        T. E. W., Saturday Review, CXLVIII (July 20, 1929), 74.
        R. Edgcumbe, National Review, CIX (Sept., 1929), 73-83.
        Robert Sencourt, Criterion, IX (Oct., 1929), 122-27.
        Stark Young, NR, LX (Oct. 2, 1929), 174-76.
        R. E. Larsson, Commonweal, XI (Nov. 20, 1929), 86-87.
        F. E. Pierce, Yale Review, XIX (Winter, 1930), 404-406.
        N. I. White, SAQ, XXIX (Jan., 1930), 103-106.
        Samuel Chew, SRL, VI (March 22, 1930), 839.

Petrovic, Ilija. "Byron and the Yugoslavs," Slavonic Review, VIII
    (June, 1929), 144-55. [The popularization of Byron among

the Yugoslavs was due to Lermontov, Mickiewicz, and Pushkin.]

Ponsonby, Sir John.   The Ponsonby Family.   London: The Medici
    Society, 1929.   [On Caroline Lamb and Byron.]

Reynolds, George F.   "George Gordon Byron," English Literature
    in Fact and Story.   New York: The Century Co., 1929.
    Pp. 305-10.

Sommervell, D. C.   English Thought in the 19th Century.   London:
    Methuen & Co., 1929.

Stuart-Young, John M.   "Lord Byron," The Immortal Nine: An
    Introduction to the Poetry of the Last Century.   London: F.
    Wright, 1929.   Pp. 79-94.

Terry, Howard L.   "Byron's Monument to His Dog," Mentor, XVII
    (Aug., 1929), 66.

Tillett, Nettie S.   "The Unholy Alliance of Pisa," SAQ, XXVIII
    (Jan., 1929), 27-44.

Van Dyke, Henry.   "Rebellious Poet," The Man behind the Book:
    Essays in Understanding.   New York: C. Scribner's Sons,
    1929.   Pp. 147-73.

Van Nosdall, George A.   "The Most Romantic Figure in English
    Literature," American Collector, VI (April, 1929), 12-15.

Wiegler, Paul.   "Apotheosis (Byron)," Genius in Love and Death,
    trans. Carl Raushenbush.   New York: A & C. Boni, 1929.
    Pp. 13-24.

Witty, P. A., and H. C. Lehman.   "Nervous Instability and Gen-
    ius; Poetry and Fiction," Journal of Abnormal Psychology,
    XXIV (April-June, 1929), 82-84.

Wolfe, Humbert.   Notes on English Verse Satires.   London: The
    Hogarth Press, 1929.   [On Byron's The Vision of Judgment.]

Wood, C. A.   "Julius Millingen, Lord Byron's Physician," Annals
    of Medical History, n.s., I (May, 1929), 260-69.

1930

Adkins, Nelson Frederick.   Fitz-Greene Halleck: An Early Knick-
    erbocker, Wit, and Poet.   New Haven: Yale University
    Press; London: Oxford University Press, 1930.

Bernbaum, Ernest.   "Byron," Anthology of Romanticism and Guide
    through the Romantic Movement.   5 vols.   New York: Nelson,

1930. Vol. I, pp. 275-315. Rptd. in his Guide through the Romantic Movement. Second Edition Revised and Enlarged. New York: Ronald Press, 1949. Pp. 187-213.

Blunden, Edmund. Leigh Hunt: A Biography. London: Cobden-Sanderson, 1930. Rptd. in America under the title, Leigh Hunt and His Circle. New York: Harper & Bros., 1930.

Butler, Lady Eleanor. The Hamwood Papers of the Ladies of Llangollen and Caroline Hamilton, ed. G. H. Bell. London: Macmillan & Co., 1930.

Byron and Shelley in Italy. Rome: Ente Nazionale Industrie Turistische, 193-?

Clark, Roy Benjamin. William Gifford, Tory Satirist, Critic and Editor. New York: Columbia University Press, 1930.

Closs, August. "Fancy and Imagination: Romanticism in Byron's Childe Harold's Pilgrimage," Poetry Review, XXI (July-Aug., 1930), 269-76.

Cruse, Amy. The Englishman and His Books in the Early 19th Century. London: George G. Harrap & Co., 1930.

Ernle, Rowland E. Prothero, Baron. "Lady Byron and Her Separation," QR, CCLIV (Jan., 1930), 15-36.

Fagnani, Emma Everett. The Art Life of a 19th Century Portrait Painter, Joseph Fagnani, 1819-1873. Paris: H. Clarke, 1930.

Farrand, M. L. "Udolpho and Childe Harold," MLN, XLV (April, 1930), 220-31.

Flower, R. E. W. "Letters," British Museum Quarterly, V (1930), 63. [The British Museum contained only the letters to Hanson. Forty-nine letters, to J. C. Hobhouse and Douglas Kinnaird (1817-1819), were bequeathed by John Murray.]

Fotheringham, D. R. "Byron through French Eyes," Poetry Review, XXI (July-Aug., 1930), 277-83.

Fox, John C., II. "The Character of Lady Noel Byron," National Review, XCIV (Jan., 1930), 700-709. [Reviews some publications about Lady Byron: i.e., Astarte, Mayne's Life, and others.]

Gray, J. R. L. "Poet of the High Places," Cairngorm Club Journal, XII (Jan., 1930), 142-45. [Byron the first poet to give us the true poetry of the mountains in full measure.]

Griggs, Earl Leslie. "Coleridge and Byron; with Five hitherto
    Unpublished Letters written by Coleridge to Byron," PMLA,
    XLV (Dec., 1930), 1085-97.

Gwyn, Stephen. The Life of Sir Walter Scott. London: T. But-
    terworth, 1930.

Hazlitt, William. The Complete Works of William Hazlitt, ed.
    P. P. Howe, after the edition of A. R. Waller and Arnold
    Glover. 21 vols. London & Toronto: J. M. Dent & Sons,
    1930-34.
    It contains the following reviews of works of Byron:
    Review of Childe Harold's Pilgrimage, Canto IV, Vol. XIX,
        pp. 35-43. Rptd. from Yellow Dwarf, May 2, 1818, pp.
        142-44.
    Review of Heaven and Earth, Vol. XVI, pp. 411-15. Rptd.
        from ER, XXXVIII (Feb., 1823), 27-48.
    Review of Letter to **** ***** on the Reverend Bowles'
        Strictures on the Life and Writings of Pope, Vol. XIX,
        pp. 62-84. Rptd. from London Magazine, III (June, 1821),
        593-607.
    Review of Marino Faliero, Vol. XIX, pp. 44-51. Rptd. from
        London Magazine, III (May, 1821), 550-54.

Lovat-Fraser, J. A. "With Disraeli in Italy," CR, CXXXVIII
    (Aug., 1930), 192-99. [On his visit to Italy in 1826, Dis-
    raeli was so under the influence of Byron that he not only
    imitated Byron in all he could, but he also visited all the
    places there associated with Byron.]

Lovelace, Edith. "A Missing Byron MS," TLS, Jan. 23, 1930,
    p. 60. [A Beppo MS which belonged to the Lovelaces. Re-
    quests information as to its whereabouts.]

Massingham, Harold John. The Friend of Shelley. A Memoir of
    Edward John Trelawny. New York: D. Appleton & Co.,
    1930.

Mathews, Elkin. Byron and Byroniana: A Catalogue of Books.
    London: Elkin Mathews, Ltd., 1930.

Maurois, Andre. Byron, trans. Hamish Miles. New York: D.
    Appleton & Co., 1930.
    Reviews:
    T. E. Welby, Week End Review, March 1, 1930, pp. 18, 20.
    Saturday Review, CXLIX (March 8, 1930), 295-96.
    TLS, March 13, 1930, p. 209.
    D. McCarthy, SRL, VI (March 22, 1930), 844-45.
    F. Birrell, N&A, XLVII (April, 1930), 52.
    Bookman, LXXI (April, 1930), 225-26.
    Wilfred Gibson, Bookman (London), LXXVIII (April, 1930),
        5-7.
    Clennel Wilkinson, London Mercury, XXI (April, 1930), 568-

70.
J. Wood Krutch, Nation, CXXX (April 16, 1930), 460.
F. E. Pierce, Yale Review, XIX (June, 1930), 827-28.
Stark Young, NR, LXIII (June 4, 1930), 70-71.
E. Wagenknecht, VQR, VI (July, 1930), 431-42.
N. I. White, SAQ, XXIX (July, 1930), 343-44.
ES, XII (Aug. , 1930), 129-38.

Metcalf, John Calvin. "Moore's Life of Byron," The Stream of
English Biography. Readings in Representative Biographies.
New York: The Century Co. , 1930. Pp. 196-97. [It also
contains a chapter from Moore's Life of Byron, pp. 198-209.]

Miles, Hamish (ed.). "Introduction," Selections from Byron. London: J. Cape, 1930. Pp. 7-13.

Moody, William Vaughn, and Robert Morss Lovett. "Triumph of
Romanticism," A History of English Literature. New York:
Scribner's Sons, 1930. Pp. 271-74.

Newman, Bertram. Lord Melbourne. London: Macmillan & Co. ,
1930.

Peck, Edwin Walter (ed.). "Introduction," Seventeen Letters of
George Noel Byron, to an Unknown Lady, 1811-1817. New
York: Covici, Friede, 1930. Pp. 9-24.

Petrie, Sir Charles. The Life of George Canning. London: Eyre
& Spottiswoode, 1930. [Touches on their acquaintance.]

Praz, Mario. "Recent Byron Literature," ES, XII (Aug. , 1930),
129-38. [A review of books by Du Bois, Maurois, Mayne,
and Estève.]

Salt, Henry Stephen. Company I Have Kept. London: George
Allen & Unwin, 1930.

Scott, Sir Walter. The Private Letter-books of Sir Walter Scott,
ed. Wilfred G. Partington. London: Hodder & Stoughton,
1930.

Vines, Sherard. The Course of English Classicism from the Tudor
to the Victorian Age. London: Leonard & Virginia Woolf,
1930.

Whiting, Mary B. "The Heart of Calantia," Bookman (London),
LXXVII (Jan. , 1930), 228-30. [Lady Caroline's Glenarvon.]

1931

Babbitt, Irving. "Romanticism and the Orient," Bookman, LXXIV
(Dec. , 1931), 349-57.

Barnard, Cyril. "Byron: A Criticism of Matthew Arnold's Essay," Englische Studien, LXV (1931), 211-16.

Butler, E. M. Sheridan, A Ghost Story. London: Constable & Co., 1931.

Butterwick, J. C. "A Note on the First Editions of Manfred," Book Collector's Quarterly, No. 3 (June, 1931), 39-42.

Cruse, Amy. "The Romance of Love and Gloom," The Golden Road in English Literature; from Beowulf to Bernard Shaw. New York: Thomas Y. Crowell, 1931. Pp. 468-74.

Fairchild, Hoxie Neale. The Romantic Quest. New York: Columbia University Press, 1931.
    It contains:
        "Byron and Transcendentalism," pp. 362-72.
        "Younger Generation," pp. 218-36.

Friedell, E. "Byron and the Romantics," Living Age, CCCXXXIX (Feb., 1931), 618-20. [Translated from the Vossische Zeitung, a Berlin Liberal Daily.]

"Greece and Byron; the Gift of Newstead Abbey," Near East, XL (July 23, 1931), 90. [The day's program and part of Venizelos' speech.]

Irving, Washington. Journal of Washington Irving (1823-1824), ed. Stanley T. Williams. Cambridge: Harvard University Press, 1931. [In his entry for Feb. 1, 1824, we find comments on Byron's manner of composition and a talk of Irving with Captain Medwin about Byron.]

Jones, Fred L. "Adonais: The Source of xxvii-xxviii," MLN, XLVI (April, 1931), 236-39. [The ideas originated in a letter by Byron to Shelley on April 26, 1821.]

Kemble, James. "Byron: His Lameness and His Last Illness," QR, CCLVII (Oct., 1931), 231-43. Rptd. in Idols and Invalids. London: Methuen & Co., 1933. Pp. 3-26.

Kessel, Marcel. "A Byron Inscription," TLS, July 23, 1931, p. 583. ["H. P. E. D. S. G. G. B.," in Byron's autograph inscription on the copy of Fugitive Pieces in the Pierpont Morgan Library, stand for "Haec poemata ex dono sunt--Georgii Gordon Byron."]

King, Lucille. "The Influence of Shakespeare on Byron's Marino Faliero," UTSE, XI (1931), 48-55.

Kitchin, George. A Survey of Burlesque and Parody in English.

Edinburgh: Oliver & Boyd, 1931.

Levin, Harry. The Broken Column; a Study in Romantic Hellenism. Cambridge, Mass.: Harvard University Press, 1931.

Lockhart, John Gibson. Lockhart's Literary Criticism, ed. M. Clive Hildyard. Oxford: Basil Blackwell, 1931.

Low, D. M. "The Text of Byron's Letters," TLS, Dec. 10, 1931, p. 1006. [Some corrections to the letters of Lord Byron's Correspondence.]

McPeek, James A. S. "A Note on 'So We'll Go No More A-Roving,'" MLN, XLVI (Feb., 1931), 118-19.

Nevinson, Henry W. "Two Contrasts in Lives," NSN, II (July 25, 1931), 108-109. Rptd. in Essays of the Year, 1931-1932, by Various Authors. London: The Argonaut Press, 1932. Pp. 67-75. [Holds that his death in Missolonghi raised him high above his contemporaries who surpassed him in poetic art.]

Nicolson, Harold. "If Byron Had Become King of Greece," If, or, History Rewritten, ed. John Collings Squire. New York: The Viking Press, 1931. Pp. 221-55. [A review of the Gamba Papers.]

Rudwin, Maximilian J. The Devil in Legend and Literature. London: The Open Court, 1931. [Reference to Byron as one of the vindicators of the devil in English literature.]

Salomon, Louis B. The Devil Take Her; a Study of the Rebellious Lover in English Poetry. Philadelphia: University of Pennsylvania Press, 1931. [Byron among the poets who wrote about woman's fickleness.]

Schwartz, Jacob. "Byron," Eleven Hundred Obscure Points. London: The Ulysses Bookshop, 1931. Pp. 8-11. [Collates 44 first editions of Byron's works.]

Smith, Earl C. "Byron and the Countess Guiccioli," PMLA, XLVI (Dec., 1931), 1221-27.

Spencer, W. M. "A Byron Query," TLS, Nov. 12, 1931, p. 894. [Who was the virtuous person for whom Byron wrote, "Bright be the place of thy soul?"]

Spink, G. W. "J. C. von Zedlitz and Byron," MLR, XXVI (Aug., 1931), 348-50. [About his Todtenkranze (1859), and its similarities to Childe Harold.]

Thomas, Percy. "Byron," Aspects of Literary Theory and Practice: 1550-1870. London: Heath Cranton, Ltd., 1931. Pp. 135-45.

Veniselos, H. E. M. "Byron and Greece," Poetry Review, XXII
    (Sept. -Oct. , 1931), 374-80.

Walmsley, D. M. (ed.). "Introduction," Selections from Byron:
    Poetry and Prose. London: Methuen, 1931. Pp. 1-14.

Watson, Edmund Henry L. (ed.). "George Gordon, Lord Byron,"
    Contemporary Comments; Writers of the Early 19th Century
    as they Appeared to Each Other. London: Eyre & Spottis-
    woode, 1931. Pp. 45-74.

Wise, Thomas James. "A Byron Query," TLS, April 30, 1931,
    p. 347. [Who was Dr. Rennell?] Cf. Wasey Sterry, ibid. ,
    Dec. 10, 1931, p. 1006. [He was the Dean of Winchester.]

                                1932

Baker, A. T. "Byron and Hugo," French Quarterly, XIV (Sept. ,
    1932), 80-84. [Byron's 'Fragment' from Occasional Pieces
    of some influence on Hugo.]

Boyd, James. Goethe's Knowledge of English Literature. Oxford:
    Clarendon Press, 1932.

Bradford, Gamaliel. "The Glory of Sin: Byron," Saints and Sin-
    ners. Boston: Houghton Mifflin Co. , 1932. Pp. 223-54.

Brewer, Luther A. My Leigh Hunt Library: The Holograph
    Letters. Cedar Rapids, Ia. : Privately Printed by the Torch
    Press, 1932.

Bruce, K. C. "Byron and Lamartine," N&Q, CLXII (Feb. 27,
    1932), 152. [Meeting with Lamartine did not take place.]

Buchan, John. Sir Walter Scott. New York: Coward McCann,
    1932.

"Byron's Death," Poetry Review, XXIII (Jan. -Feb. , 1932), 77.

Du Bos, Charles. Byron and the Need of Fatality, trans. Ethel
    Colburn Mayne. London: Putnam, 1932.
    Reviews:
        Geoffrey West, Bookman (London), LXXXII (May, 1932), 109.
        Richard Church, Spectator, CXLVIII (May 28, 1932), 768-69.
        Eric Blair, New Adelphi, IV (Sept. , 1932), 873-75.
        TLS, Sept. 8, 1932, p. 626.

Hearnshaw, Fossey J. C. (ed.). The Social and Political Ideas of
    Some Representative Thinkers of the Age of Reaction and Re-
    construction, 1815-1865. London: G. G. Harrap & Co. ,
    1932.

Jenkins, Elizabeth. Lady Caroline Lamb. Boston: Little, Brown
    & Co. , 1932.

Mabbott, T. O. "Byron and Chatterton: A Parallel, " N&Q, CLXII
    (March 19, 1932), 207. [Between the opening of "Monody on
    Sheridan" and the couplet in "Narva and Mored, " 11. 43-44.]
    Cf. T. O. Mabbott, ibid. , CXCI (Dec. 28, 1946), 281. [Re-
    peats his views of 1932.]

Monroe, Harriet. "Byron, " Poets and Their Art. New York:
    The Macmillan Co. , 1932. Pp. 183-90.

Neumann, Robert. "Lord Byron Plays Lord Byron, " Passion, Six
    Literary Marriages, translated from the German by Brian W.
    Downs. New York: Harcourt Brace & Co. , 1932. Pp. 151-
    75.

"Note on 'Dal Diario Inedito di Alessandro Guiccioli, ' " N&Q,
    CLXIII (Sept. 3, 1932), 164. [Contains a letter from Byron
    dated August, 1820.]

Oliver, John W. The Life of William Beckford. London: Oxford
    University Press, 1932.

Olybrius. "An Obscure Letter of Lord Byron, " N&Q, CLXIII (Nov.
    19, 1932), p. 67. [A letter dated Dec. 14, 1807, written
    from Trinity College, to Mr. Ridge about addition of some
    lines to "Thoughts Suggested by a College Examination, " ap-
    peared in reduced facsimile in a catalogue of books of James
    F. Drake, New York.]

Partington, Wilfred. "Don Juan and His Swarm of Queer Offspring, "
    Bookman, LXXV (Oct. , 1932), supp. iii-iv, vii.

Paston, George [pseud. for Emily Morse Symonds]. At John Mur-
    ray's: Records of a Literary Circle, 1843-1892. London:
    John Murray, 1932.

Price, L. M. The Reception of English Literature in Germany.
    Berkeley, Calif. : University of California Press, 1932.

Rascoe, Burton. "Byron, the Yearning, " Titans of Literature from
    Homer to the Present. New York: G. P. Putnam's Sons,
    1932. Pp. 329-36.

Scott, Sir Walter. The Letters of Sir Walter Scott, ed. H. J. C.
    Grierson. 12 vols. London: Constable & Co. , 1932-37.

_____ . Sir Walter Scott's Post Bag; More Stories and Sidelights
    from His Unpublished Letter-books. London: John Murray,
    1932.

Sickels, Eleanor M.   The Gloomy Egoist, Moods and Themes of
    Melancholy from Gray to Keats.   New York: Columbia Uni-
    versity Press, 1932.

Simmons, E. J.   "Byron and a Greek Maid," MLR, XXVII (July,
    1932), 318-23.

Sutro, Alfred.   Which: Lord Byron or Lord Byron; a Bet.   San
    Francisco: Privately Printed, 1932.

Tibble, J. W., and Anne Tibble.   John Clare: A Life.   New
    York: Oxford University Press, 1932.

Weaver, Bennett.   Towards the Understanding of Shelley.   Ann
    Arbor: University of Michigan Press, 1932.

Wise, Thomas J.   A Bibliography of the Writings in Verse and
    Prose of George Gordon Noel, Baron Byron, with Letters Il-
    lustrating His Life and Work and His Attitude Towards Keats.
    2 vols.   London: Printed for Private Circulation Only, 1932-
    1933.
    Reviews:
       TLS, Sept. 15, 1932, p. 642.
       TLS, Sept. 21, 1933, p. 636.
       TLS, March 19, 1964, p. 244.
    See also:
       John Carter, ibid., Sept. 29, 1932, p. 696; Gilbert H. Doane,
       ibid., Nov. 17, 1932, p. 864; Thomas J. Wise, ibid.,
       Dec. 1, 1932, p. 928; John Carter, ibid., April 27, 1933,
       p. 300; John Carter, ibid., May 4, 1933, p. 316.

                                    1933

"A. L. S., dated at Rome, June 28, 1821," The Autograph Album, I
    (Dec., 1933), 39.   [Addressee unknown.]

Elton, Oliver.   The English Muse, a Sketch.   London: G. Bell &
    Sons, 1933.

Evans, Selina C.   "A Contemporary Opinion of Byron's Adventures,"
    N&Q, CLXIV (Feb. 4, 1933), 74-75.   [A letter written by a
    George Hall to his brother, minimizing Byron's achievements.]

Griggs, Earl Leslie.   Unpublished Letters of Samuel Taylor Cole-
    ridge.   2 vols.   New Haven: Yale University Press, 1933.

Hearn, Lafcadio.   "Byron," Poets and Poems.   Tokyo: Hokuseido,
    1933.   Pp. 86-103.

Hogg, Thomas Jefferson.   The Life of Percy Bysshe Shelley as
    Comprised in "The Life of Shelley" by Thomas Jefferson
    Hogg.   "The Recollections of Shelley and Byron" by Edward

Trelawny. "Memoirs of Shelley" by Thomas Love Peacock,
with an Introduction by Humbert Wolfe. 2 vols. London:
J. M. Dent, 1933.

"Magnificent Byron Letter of American Interest," The Autograph
Album, I (June, 1933), 24-25. [A. L. S. dated at Genoa,
June 21, 1823, and addressed to E. Church, Esq., Consul at
Geneva.]

Maurois, André. "Introduction," Letters of George Gordon, 6th
Lord Byron, ed. Robert Guy Howarth. London: J. M. Dent,
1933. Pp. v-x.
Reviews:
SRL, X (Feb. 24, 1933), 509.
TLS, Nov. 2, 1933, p. 755.
E. B. Sturgis, Week End Review, VIII (Nov. 18, 1933), 526.
A. Waugh, Bookman, LXXXV (Dec., 1933), 225-26.
E. L. Getchell, Education, LIV (May, 1934), 573-74.
H. Gregory, NR, LXXIX (July 11, 1934), 242-43. Rptd. as
"Lord Byron: The Poet as Letter-Writer," in his Spirit
of Time and Place. New York: Morton, 1973. Pp. 33-
41.

Praz, Mario. "The Metamorphoses of Satan," The Romantic Agony. London: Oxford University Press, 1933. Pp. 51-91.

Rice, Richard Ashley (ed.). "Introduction," The Best of Byron.
New York: Thomas Nelson and Sons, 1933. Pp. 1-27.

Rice, Warner G. "Early English Travellers to Greece and the
Levant," Essays and Studies in English and Comparative
Literature, X (1933), 205-60.

Sadleir, Michael T. H. Blessington-D'Orsay: A Masquerade.
London: Constable & Co., 1933. Rptd. in America under
the title, The Strange Life of Lady Blessington. Boston:
Little, Brown & Co., 1933. A new edition, revised and enlarged, 1947.

Schramm, Wilbur L. "What shall we say of Byron?" English
Journal, XXII (Oct., 1933), 666-71. [A defence of Byron.]
Cf. Carl J. Weber, ibid., XXIII (April, 1934), 328-29.
[Points out inaccuracies in the article above.]

Seymour, W. Douglas. "Byron's Juvenilia," TLS, Dec. 28, 1933,
p. 924. [Wants to know the adventures of the copy of Fugitive Pieces before it got to the Pierpont Morgan Library.]

Strachey, Giles Lytton. "Byron, Shelley, Keats and Lamb,"
Characters and Commentaries. New York: Harcourt Brace
& Co., 1933. Pp. 50-64. Rptd. in his Literary Essays.
New York: Harcourt Brace & Co., 1949. Pp. 276-89.

Weller, Earle. Autobiography of John Keats. Stanford, Calif.:
    Stanford University Press, 1933.

1934

Clarke, Isabel Constance. Shelley and Byron: A Tragic Friend-
    ship. London: Hutchinson & Co., Ltd., 1934.
    Review:
    TLS, June 7, 1934, p. 404.

Evans, Sir Benjamin Ifor. English Poetry in the 19th Century.
    London: Oxford University Press, 1934.

Haslip, Joan. Lady Hester Stanhope; a Biography. London: Cob-
    den-Sanderson, 1934. [On the course of the relationship be-
    tween her and Byron which began in Athens.]

Hawkes, Charles Pascoe. "George Gordon Byron," Authors-at-
    Arms: The Soldiering of Six Great Writers. London:
    Macmillan & Co., 1934. Pp. 179-218.

Hogg, Thomas Jefferson. After Shelley; the Letters of Thomas
    Jefferson Hogg to Jane Williams, ed. with a Biographical
    Introduction by Sylva Norman. London: Oxford University
    Press, 1934.

Howarth, R. G. "Byron's Reading," TLS, March 15, 1934, p. 194.
    Cf. E. Bensly, ibid., March 29, 1934, p. 229.

Jones, Claude E. "An American Lara," N&Q, CLXVII (Oct. 20,
    1934), 276. [Of bibliographical interest.]

Jones, Frederick L. "Byron's Last Poem," SP, XXXI (July,
    1934), 487-89. [Finds similarities between the feelings ex-
    pressed in his "On This Day I Complete My Thirty-Sixth
    Birthday," and thoughts spoken by Macbeth.]

Kessel, Marcel. "Byron's Juvenilia," TLS, Feb. 15, 1934, p. 112.

Kirtlan, E. J. B. "The Relative Position of Keats, Shelley and
    Byron as Poets," London Quarterly Review, CLIX (April,
    1934), 233-37. [Byron not the greatest of the three. Ad-
    verse criticism of Byron.]

Marshall, Roderick. Italy in English Literature, 1755-1815. New
    York: Columbia University Press, 1934.

Nesbitt, George L. Benthamite Reviewing: The First Twelve
    Years of the "Westminster Review," 1824-1836. New York:
    Columbia University Press, 1934.

Nevinson, Henry Woodd. " 'The Pilgrim of Eternity': How Being
    at Newstead Abbey, I felt the Presence of Byron, Whose

Heroic End I Witnessed on my Way Through Aetolia, " In the
Dark Backward. London: G. Routledge & Sons, 1934. Pp.
184-202. [Finds Byron a man who "had shaken the self-
complacent presumption of Church and Society" in England.]

Parsons, Coleman Oscar. "Three Byron Letters, " N&Q, CLXVI
(May 26, 1934), 366-67. [Dated Spring, 1812, to Moore;
Nov. 22, 1813, to James Wedderburn Webster; July, 1820?
to Hoppner. They found their way into the Watson Autograph
Collection in the National Library of Scotland.]

Paston, George [pseud. for Emily Morse Symonds]. "New Light
on Byron's Loves, with Excerpts from Letters, " Cornhill,
CXLIX (April, 1934), 385-400; ibid. , CXLIX (May, 1934),
513-27; ibid. , CXLIX (June, 1934), 641-55; ibid. , CL (July,
1934), 1-16; ibid. , CL (Aug. , 1934), 129-44; ibid. , CL
(Sept. , 1934), 257-76. Rptd. as "To Lord Byron, " Feminine Profiles. Based upon Unpublished Letters, 1807-1824,
eds. George Paston and Peter Quennell. London: John Murray, 1939.

Pratt, Willis W. "A Lost Review of Manfred, " TLS, May 10,
1934, p. 342. [From The Day and New Times, June 23,
1817, in a scrapbook in his possession.] Cf. George Harwell,
ibid. , Aug. 2, 1934, p. 541. [Says that the review mentioned by Pratt was published in Gentleman's Magazine,
LXXXVII (July, 1817), 4, with two alterations.]

Quennell, Peter. Byron. "Great Lives Series. " London: Duck-
worth, 1934.
Reviews:
K. John, NSN, VII (Feb. 10, 1934), 198.
TLS, March 1, 1934, p. 141.
John Sparrow, Spectator, CLII (June 15, 1934), 932.
N. I. White, SAQ, XXXIV (April, 1935), 228-30.

Sherwood, Margaret. Undercurrents of Influence in English Romantic Poetry. Cambridge, Mass. : Harvard University Press,
1934.

Stowe, Lyman Beecher. Saints, Sinners and Beechers. Indianapolis: The Bobbs-Merrill Co. , 1934. [On the Stowe-Byron
controversy.]

Swann, Elsie. Christopher North--John Wilson. Edinburgh & London: Oliver & Boyd, 1934.

Thrall, Miriam M. H. Rebellious Fraser's. New York: Columbia University Press, 1934. [On Fraser's attacks on Byron.]

Vare, Daniele. "Byron and the Guiccioli, in the 'Memorie della
famiglia Guiccioli by the Marchesse Guiccioli, ' " QR, CCLXII
(April, 1934), 206-26.

8. MODERN CRITICAL BEGINNINGS, 1935-1945

1935

Armour, Richard Willard. Barry Cornwall, a Biography of Bryan Waller Procter. Boston: Meador Publishing Co., 1935.

Bredvold, Louis Ignatius (ed.). "Introductory Essay," Lord Byron: "Don Juan" and Other Satirical Poems. "The Odyssey Series in Literature." New York: Odyssey Press, 1935. Pp. v-xxxv.

Calvert, William J. Byron: Romantic Paradox. Chapel Hill: The University of North Carolina Press, 1935.
Reviews:
    E. L. Walton, NYTBR, March 10, 1935, p. 2.
    N. I. White, SAQ, XXXIV (April, 1935), 228-30.
    Samuel Chew, SRL, XI (April 20, 1935), 636.
    M. D. Zabel, MP, XXXII (May, 1935), 435-36.
    Lionel Trilling, Nation, CXLI (July 10, 1935), 52-53.
    N&Q, CLXIX (July 27, 1935), 70.
    TLS, Oct. 17, 1935, p. 647.
    G. Kitchin, MLR, XXXI (April, 1936), 262.
    Jacob Zeitlin, JEGP, XXXV (July, 1936), 446-48.

De la Mare, Walter. Early One Morning in the Spring. Chapters on Children and Childhood as It Is Revealed in Particular in Early Memories and in Early Writings. New York: Macmillan Co., 1935. [Byron's childhood; Mary Duff.]

Doane, G. H. "Byron's Letter to the Editor of My Grandmother's Review, 1819," Bibliographical Notes and Queries, I (Jan., 1935), 8. [A letter from Thomas Moore to John Murray on this point.]

Garratt, G. T. Lord Brougham. London: Macmillan & Co., 1935.

Guérard, Albert. Literature and Society. Boston: Lothrop, Lee & Shepard Co., 1935.

Kemble, J. "The Lameness of Lord Byron," West London Medical Journal, XL (1935), 33-41.

Macbeth, Gilbert. John Gibson Lockhart: A Critical Study. ("University of Illinois Bulletin, Vol. XXXII (Feb. 26, 1931)," No.
26.) Urbana, Illinois: University of Illinois, 1935.

MacCall, Seamus. Thomas Moore. London: G. Duckworth & Co.,
Dublin: The Talbot Press, 1935.

Motter, T. H. Vail. "Byron's Werner Re-estimated: A Neglected
Chapter in Nineteenth Century Stage History," Essays in
Dramatic Literature by Various Authors. The Parrott Pre-
sentation Volume, by Pupils of Prof. Thomas Marc Parrott
of Princeton University, ed. Hardin Craig. Princeton:
Princeton University Press, 1935. Pp. 243-75.

Origo, Iris. Allegra. London: Leonard and Virginia Woolf at
the Hogarth Press, 1935. Rptd. with revisions in A Measure
of Love. New York: Pantheon Books, 1957. Pp. 15-87.
Review:
TLS, Nov. 23, 1935, p. 759.

_____. "Conte Alessandro Guiccioli, a Husband," London Mer-
cury, XXXII (Aug., 1935), 343-52.

_____. Leopardi, A Study in Solitude. London: Oxford Uni-
versity Press, 1935.

Osgood, Charles G. "Byron," The Voice of England. A History
of English Literature. New York: Harpers & Bros., 1935.
Pp. 431-37.

Quennell, Peter. "Byron and Harriette Wilson," Cornhill, CLI
(April, 1935), 415-26. [Her letters to him.]

_____. Byron: The Years of Fame. New York: The Viking
Press, 1935.
Reviews:
TLS, Oct. 17, 1935, p. 647.
John Sparrow, Spectator, CLV (Oct. 18, 1935), 615.
Clive Bell, NSN, X (Oct. 26, 1935), 606.
E. C. Mayne, London Mercury, XXXIII (Nov., 1935), 70-71.
Samuel Chew, SRL, XIII (Nov. 23, 1935), 5-6.
H. S. Canby, Book of the Month Club News, Dec., 1935,
p. 7.
C. Wright, NYTBR, Dec. 1, 1935, pp. 5, 22.
R. M. Lovett, NR, LXXXV (Dec. 18, 1935), 176-77.
Bernice Kenyon, Scribner's, XCIX (Jan., 1936), 2.
Frederick Dupee, Nation, CXLII (Jan. 29, 1936), 136.
TLS, Aug. 5, 1954, p. 505.

Rendall, Vernon. "Byron: An Emendation," TLS, Dec. 21, 1935,
p. 879. [Suggests a change from plant to plat in the lines
from "Churchill's Grave," "... and I asked/The Gardener

of that ground, why it might be That for this plant strangers
his memory tasked..."]

Scheidacker, Frances. Lord Byron and Mary Chaworth. Brooklyn,
     N. Y. : The Author, 1935.

Smith, Chard Powers. Annals of the Poets. New York: Charles
     Scribner, 1935. [Personal traits of Byron.]

Thompson, L. C. More Magic Dethroned (On the Influence of
     Shelley on Byron and Keats). London: Warner Press, 1935.

Williams, Stanley Thomas. The Life of Washington Irving. New
     York: Oxford University Press, 1935.

Winwar, Frances. The Romantic Rebels. Boston: Little, Brown
     & Co. , 1935.

                                    1936

Aubin, R. A. "Imitations of Childe Harold," Englische Studien,
     LXX, No. 3, (1936), 432-33. [Pieces not recorded by Chew.]

_____ . Topographical Poetry in 18th Century England. New
     York: The Modern Language Association of America, 1936.
     [Byron among the poets who wrote descriptive poetry and top-
     ographical poetry; i. e. , poetry with specifically named lo-
     calities.]

Barnard, Ellsworth. Shelley's Religion. Minneapolis, Minnesota:
     The University of Minnesota Press, 1936.

Beach, Joseph Warren. The Concept of Nature in 19th Century
     English Poetry. New York: The Macmillan Co. , 1936.

Boyle, Sir Edward C. G. "Byron, the Last Journey of All,"
     Biographical Essays, 1790-1890. London: Oxford University
     Press, 1936. Pp. 135-48.

Brown, Wallace Cable. "Popularity of English Travel Books about
     the Near East, 1775-1825," PQ, XV (Jan. , 1936), 70-80.

Chew, Samuel C. (ed.). "Introduction," "Childe Harold's Pilgrimage"
     and Other Romantic Poems. New York: Odyssey Press,
     1936. Pp. ix-xxxiv.

Coleridge, Samuel Taylor. Coleridge's Miscellaneous Criticism,
     ed. Thomas Middleton Raysor. London: Constable & Co. ,
     1936.

Emden, Paul Herman. Regency Pageant. London: Hodder &
     Stoughton, 1936.

Finney, Claude Lee. The Evolution of Keats's Poetry. 2 vols.
    Cambridge, Mass.: Harvard University Press, 1936.

Grabo, Carl. The Magic Plant. The Growth of Shelley's Thought.
    Chapel Hill: The University of North Carolina Press, 1936.

Howarth, R. G. "Allusions in Byron's Letters. Sources Wanted,"
    N&Q, CLXXI (Nov. 28, 1936), 388.
    Allusions found:
        E. Bensly, ibid., CLXXI (Dec. 12, 1936), 424.
        Hibernicus, ibid., CLXXI (Dec. 19, 1936), 446.
        R. G. Howarth, ibid., CLXXI (Dec. 26, 1936), 462-63.
        T. O. M., ibid., CLXXII (Jan. 2, 1937), 14.
        R. G. Howarth, ibid., CLXXII (May 1, 1937), 321.
        _____, ibid., CLXXII (May 15, 1937), 349-51.
        Montague Summers, ibid., CLXXIII (Nov. 13, 1937), 357.
        R. G. Howarth, ibid., CLXXIV (April 9, 1938), 260-61.

Karnosh, L. J. "The Insanities of Famous Men," The Journal of
    the Indiana State Medical Association, XXIX (Jan., 1936), 1-
    8.

Kelly, Blanch Mary. "Byron," The Well of English. New York:
    Harper & Bros., 1936. Pp. 179-82.

Leavis, Frank Raymond. "Byron's Satire," Revaluation: Tradition
    and Development in English Poetry. London: Chatto & Win-
    dus, 1936. Pp. 148-53.

Lucas, Frank Lawrence. The Decline and Fall of the Romantic
    Ideal. New York: Macmillan & Co., 1936.

McCarthy, W. H., Jr. "First Edition of Byron's Corsair,"
    Colophon, n. s., II (Autumn, 1936), 51-59.

Mead, George. Movements of Thought in the 19th Century. Chi-
    cago: University of Chicago Press, 1936.

Penn, Virginia. "Philhellenism in England, 1821-1827," Slavonic
    Review, XIV (Jan., 1936), 363-71; ibid., XIV (April, 1936),
    647-60.

Redfern, Joan. "A Precursor of Byron," TLS, July 25, 1936,
    p. 620. [Berni as Byron's precursor.]

Repplier, Agnes. "House of Laughter, the Holland House Circle,"
    Atlantic Monthly, CLVIII (July, 1936), 18-27.

Romilly, Lady Anne. Romilly-Edgeworth Letters, 1813-1818, with
    an Introduction and Notes by Samuel Henry Romilly. London:
    John Murray, 1936.

Sen, Amiyakumar. "The Byronic Hero," Calcutta Review, 3rd
    ser., LXI (Oct., 1936), 76-90; ibid., LXI (Nov., 1936), 231-
    39; ibid., LXI (Dec., 1936), 353-60.

Smith, F. P. "An Unpublished Poem by Byron?" N&Q, CLXXI
    (Dec. 5, 1936), 405. [Stanzas "To Her Who Best Can Under-
    stand Them,"--said to be by Byron--copied in Washington
    Irving's commonplace-book. Has anyone seen the 19 stanzas
    in print?]

Thane, Elswyth. Young Mr. Disraeli. New York: Harcourt,
    Brace & Co., 1936.

Thirkell, Angela Mackail. The Fortunes of Harriette. London:
    Hamish Hamilton, 1936. [A Regency courtesan who wrote to
    Byron, but whom he never met.]

                                1937

App, A. J. "How Six Famous Poets Were Treated," Catholic
    World, CXLIV (Feb., 1937), 582-89. [Deals with Byron's
    clash with the reviewers.]

Barnard, Ellsworth. Shelley's Religion. Minneapolis, Minnesota:
    University of Minnesota Press, 1937.

Basler, R. P. "Byronism in Poe's 'To One in Paradise,' " AL,
    IX (May, 1937), 232-36.

_____. "The Publication Date and Source of Byron's 'Transla-
    tion of a Romaic Love Song,' " MLN, LII (Nov., 1937), 503.

Bennett, Joan (ed.). "Introduction," Byron: Satirical and Critical
    Poems. Cambridge, [Eng.]: At the University Press, 1937.
    Pp. ix-xiv. Notes, pp. 185-214.

Bond, Richard (ed.). The Marlay Letters, 1778-1820. London:
    Constable & Co., 1937. [Gossip about Byron at Bologna.]

Brown, Wallace Cable. "Byron and English Interest in the Near
    East," SP, XXXIV (Jan., 1937), 55-64.

_____. "English Travel Books and Minor Poetry about the Near
    East, 1775-1825," PQ, XVI (July, 1937), 249-71.

Bush, Douglas. "Byron," Mythology and the Romantic Tradition in
    English Poetry. Cambridge, Mass.: Harvard University
    Press, 1937. Pp. 71-80.

Carnegie, Dale. "The 'Perfect Lover' Who Chewed Tobacco, Bit
    his Fingernails, and Drank Wine out of Human Skulls," Five

Minute Biographies. New York: Greenberg, 1937. Pp. 253-56.

Colum, Mary M. From These Roots: The Ideas that Have Made Modern Literature. New York: C. Scribner's Sons; London: C. Scribner's Sons, Ltd., 1937.

Cook, Davidson. "Byron's 'Fare Thee Well'--Unrecorded Editions," TLS, Sept. 18, 1937, p. 680. Cf. Graham Pollard, "Pirated Collections of Byron," ibid., Oct. 16, 1937, p. 764. [Gives additions and commentaries.]

Eliot, T. S. "Byron," From Anne to Victoria, ed. Bonamy Dobrée. London: Cassell & Co., 1937. Pp. 601-19. Rptd. in his On Poets and Poetry. New York: Farrar, Straus & Cudahy, 1957. Pp. 223-39.

Gilbertson, Catherine. Harriet Beecher Stowe. New York: D. Appleton-Century Co., 1937.

Harwell, George. "Three Poems Attributed to Byron," MP, XXXV (Nov., 1937), 173-77. [Contained in the seven scrapbooks at Duke.]

Hewlett, Dorothy. A Life of John Keats. London: Hurst & Blackett, 1937.

Howarth, R. G. "Allusions in Byron's Letters: Sources Wanted," N&Q, CLXXIII (Sept. 25, 1937), 227; ibid., CLXXIII (Oct. 2, 1937), 241.
Allusions found:
T. C. C., ibid., CLXXIII (Oct. 9, 1937), 268.
E. Bensly and H. Kendra Baker, ibid., CLXXIII (Oct. 16, 1937), 285.
Montague Summers, ibid., CLXXIII (Nov. 13, 1937), 357.
R. G. Howarth, ibid., CLXXIV (April 9, 1938), 260-61.

Ilchester, Giles Stephan Holland Fox-Strangways, Earl of. The Home of the Hollands, 1605-1820. New York: E. P. Dutton & Co., 1937.

Johnson, Edgar. One Mighty Torrent; the Drama of Biography. New York City: Stackpole Sons, 1937.

Jones, Howard Mumford. The Harp That Once. A Chronicle of the Life of Thomas Moore. New York: Henry Holt & Co., 1937.

McElderry, B. R., Jr. "Byron's Interest in the Americas," Research Studies of the State College of Washington, V (Sept., 1937), 145-78.

Mowatt, Robert B.   The Romantic Age; Europe in the Early 19th
    Century.   London: George G. Harrap & Co. , 1937.

Nicolson, Harold.   "Mr. William Fletcher," Small Talk.   New
    York: Harcourt Brace & Co. , 1937.   Pp. 63-75.

Scott, Sir Walter.   The Correspondence of Sir Walter Scott and
    Charles Robert Maturin, eds. F. E. Ratchford and W. H.
    McCarthy, Jr.   Austin, Texas: The University of Texas
    Press, 1937.

Strong, Leonard Alfred G.   The Minstrel Boy. A Portrait of Tom
    Moore.   London: Hodder & Stoughton, 1937.

Thorpe, Dorothea Mary Roby, Lady Charnwood.   Call Back Yes-
    terday.   A Book of Old Letters Chosen from her Collection
    with Some Memories of her Own and a Preface by Sir John
    Squire.   London: Eyre and Spottiswoode, 1937.

Wellek, René.   "Mácha and Byron," Slavonic Review, XV (Jan. ,
    1937), 400-12.

                                1938

Armstrong, Margaret.   Fanny Kemble: A Passionate Victorian.
    New York: The Macmillan Co. , 1938.   [On her fascination
    with the writings of Byron.]

Blyton, William J.   "-And Realist Poets," We Are Observed.   A
    Mirror to English Character.   London: John Murray, 1938.

Bowen, Marjorie [pseud. for Gabrielle Margaret Campbell Long].
    "Byron," World's Wonder and Other Essays.   London: Hutch-
    inson & Co. , 1938.   Pp. 139-53.

Boyajan, Zabelle C.   "Missolonghi," CR, CLIII (June, 1938), 711-
    17.

Brown, Wallace Cable.   "Prose Fiction and English Interest in the
    Near East, 1775-1825," PMLA, LIII (Sept. , 1938), 827-36.

Caclamos, Demetrius.   "Some Byron Relics," N&Q, CLXXIV
    (June 11, 1938), 417-21. [Mentions several relics and as-
    serts that Byron's heart is in Greece.] Cf. Sydney Race,
    ibid. , CLXXV (July 9, 1938), 32; Demetrius Caclamos, ibid. ,
    CLXXV (July 23, 1938), 64; Sydney Race, ibid. , CLXXV
    (Sept. 3, 1938), 175-76. Sydney Race, ibid. , CLXXVII (Aug.
    26, 1939), 159. [An exchange of opinions.]

Chew, Samuel.   "Notes on Some False Byrons," N&Q, CLXXV
    (Aug. 20, 1938), 132-33. [Identifies the writers of some By-
    ron apocrypha.]

Daiches, David. Literature and Society. London: Victor Gol-
    lancz, 1938.

Farrison, W. Edward. "The Popularity of Byron's Metrical
    Tales," Quarterly Journal of Florida A & M University, VII
    (April, 1938), 5-7.

Ford, Ford Madox. The March of Literature, from Confucius'
    Day to Our Own. New York: The Dial Press, 1938.

Grierson, Sir H. J. C. Sir Walter Scott, Bart. New York:
    Columbia University Press; London: Constable & Co. , 1938.

Grylls, Rosalie Glynn. Mary Shelley, A Biography. London:
    Oxford University Press, 1938.

Hartley, Lodwick C. "Byron in Provincial America: A Possible
    Allusion," N&Q, CLXXIV (May 28, 1938), 385. [An echo of
    the Byron separation in the Georgetown, S. C. , Gazette, for
    Wednesday, May 15, 1816.]

Hewlett, Dorothy. A Life of John Keats. New York: The Bobbs-
    Merrill Co. , 1938.

Jamil, M. Tahir. "Philosophy in Lord Byron," Calcutta Review,
    LXVIII (Aug. , 1938), 132-42; ibid. , LXVIII (Sept. , 1938),
    274-82; ibid. , LXIX (Oct. , 1938), 31-40.

Lissner, Alice Sanders. "Byron and the Theatre," Emerson Quar-
    terly, XVIII (June, 1938), 9-10, 13-14.

Marjarum, Edward Wayne. Byron as Skeptic and Believer.
    Princeton: Princeton University Press, 1938.

Olybrius. "A Letter of Byron," N&Q, CLXXIV (April 9, 1938),
    261. [From Byron to Lord Erskine, Sept. 10, 1823, copied
    from a recent catalog of Goodspeed's Book Shop, Boston.]

"On Byron's Birthday. The Unburnt Autobiography," TLS, Jan. 22,
    1938, pp. 49-50. Cf. A. K. Woodward, ibid. , Jan. 29,
    1938, p. 76; John Murray, ibid. , Feb. 5, 1938, p. 92; Ralph
    M. Wardle, ibid. , March 19, 1938, p. 188; A. K. Woodward,
    ibid. , April 9, 1938, p. 252.

Pope-Hennessy, Una. "Byron and an American," TLS, April 23,
    1938, p. 280. [About the American who visited Byron in
    Missolonghi as he lay sick.]

Quennell, Peter. "Byron and Henrietta," Cornhill, CLVII (April,
    1938), 475-92. [Henrietta d'Ussieres' correspondence with
    Byron.]

Robinson, Henry Crabb. Henry Crabb Robinson on Books and
    Their Writers, ed. Edith J. Morley. 3 vols. London:
    J. M. Dent & Sons, 1938.

Russell, Bertrand. "Aristocratic Rebels. Byron and the Modern
    World," SRL, XVII (Feb. 12, 1938), 2-4, 16, 18. Rptd. in
    Saturday Review Treasury. New York: Simon & Schuster,
    1957. Pp. 172-81. Rptd., with some omissions, in Journal
    of the History of Ideas, I (Jan., 1940), 24-37; with some
    variations from this version, in A History of Western Philos-
    ophy, New York: Simon & Schuster, 1945, pp. 746-52.

Waller, J. "A Defence of Don Juan," Poetry Review, XXIX (July-
    Aug., 1938), 273-77.

Williams, Charles. "Extracts from a Sorbonne Lecture on Byron
    and Byronism," The British Institute of the University of
    Paris Bulletin, April, 1938, pp. 13-19.

Wilson, P. N. "Byron Still Flings a Challenge to Tyranny," NYTM,
    Jan. 23, 1938, pp. 7, 23. [After 150 years, his words ring
    sharply.]

Woodward, E. L. The Age of Reform, 1815-1870. Oxford: At
    the Clarendon Press, 1938.

                            1939

Austen, John. The Story of Don Juan: A Study of the Legend and
    of the Hero. London: Martin Secker, 1939.

Bottrall, Ronald. "Byron and the Colloquial Tradition in English
    Poetry," Criterion, XVIII (Jan., 1939), 204-24.

Bronowski, Jacob. The Poet's Defence. Cambridge, [Eng.]: The
    University Press, 1939.

Brown, Helen. "Influence of Byron on Emily Brontë," MLR,
    XXXIV (July, 1939), 374-81.

Cecil, Lord David. The Young Melbourne and the Story of His
    Marriage with Caroline Lamb. London: Constable & Co.,
    1939.

Clement, N. H. Romanticism in France. ("The Revolving Fund
    Series," Vol. IX.) New York: The Modern Language Asso-
    ciation of America, 1939.

Erdman, David V. "Byron's Stage-Fright: The History of His Am-
    bition and Fear of Writing for the Stage," ELH, VI (Sept.,
    1939), 219-43.

Foss, Kenelm. Here Lies Richard Brinsley Sheridan. London: Martin Secker, 1939.

Freemantle, Alan Frederick. England in the 19th Century, 1806-1810. London: George Allen & Unwin Ltd., 1939.

Grylls, R. Glynn. Claire Clairmont, Mother of Byron's Allegra. London: John Murray, 1939.
Reviews:
TLS, May 20, 1939, p. 300.
Sylva Norman, Spectator, CLXII (June 9, 1939), 1009.

Knight, G. Wilson. "Two Eternities: An Essay on Byron," Burning Oracle; Studies in Poetry of Action. London: Oxford University Press, 1939. Pp. 197-288.

Ladu, Arthur I. "Note on Childe Harold and 'Thanatopsis,' " AL, XI (March, 1939), 80-81.

MacColl, Archie. "Byron and His Publisher," Listener, XXI (Jan. 5, 1939), 40-41.

McKenzie, Harriet Margaret. Byron's Laughter in Life and Poetry. London: Lymanhouse, 1939.

Mayne, Ethel Colburn. A Regency Chapter: Lady Bessborough and Her Friendships. London: Macmillan & Co., 1939.

Morphopoulos, P. "Byron's Translations and Use of Modern Greek Writings," MLN, LIV (May, 1939), 317-26.

Nicolson, H. "An Addition to Byron's Biography," Nineteenth Century and After, CXXV (June, 1939), 687-99. [On Hobhouse's relations to Byron and Moore.]

Phillips, George. "Elliott's The Giaour," RES, XV (Oct., 1939), 422-31. [On Ebenezer Elliott's satire of Byron's Giaour.]

Powell, Desmond. "Byron's Foreign Critics," Colorado-Wyoming Journal of Letters, Feb., 1939, pp. 13-46. [A survey of German, French and American criticism, which was, in general, more favorable than the English criticism.]

Rubin, Joseph Jay. "Whitman on Byron, Scott and Sentiment," N&Q, CLXXVI (March 11, 1939), 171.

Russell, James Anderson. Dutch Poetry and English. Amsterdam: H. J. Paris, 1939. [Byron's influence on Dutch poetry.]

Scheidacker, Frances Moor. "Lord Byron's Memoranda," National Review, CXIII (Aug., 1939), 245-48. Rptd. as The Case of Lord Byron's "Memoranda." New York: The Author, 1940. [Refuses to believe that all copies of Byron's memoirs were destroyed.]

Sen, D. K. "Byron: A Retrospect and an Estimate," Modern Review, LXV (Jan., 1939), 52-55.

Smith, Byron Porter. Islam in English Literature. Beirut, Lebanon: Printed at the American Press, 1939.

Strout, Alan L. "Robert Mudie on Byron," N&Q, CLXXVI (May 27, 1939), 365. [His healthy defence of Byron in Attic Fragments of 1825, entitled "Death and Character of Byron," may have been written a year earlier.]

Trilling, Lionel. Matthew Arnold. New York: W. W. Norton & Co., 1939.

Villiers, Marjorie. The Grand Whiggery. London: John Murray, 1939.

1940

Armour, Richard W., and Raymond Howes (eds.). Coleridge, the Talker. Ithaca, N.Y.: Cornell University Press, 1940.

Armstrong, Margaret N. Trelawny: A Man's Life. New York: The Macmillan Co., 1940. London: Robert Hale, 1941.

Bacon, Leonard. "Pale Caste of Thought; Fashions in Intellectualism," SRL, XXII (July 20, 1940), 11-13. [Byron was the first to use the noun intellectual in its modern sense, even in its mocking connotation.]

Bessborough, Henrietta Frances Ponsonby, Countess of. Lady Bessborough and Her Family Circle, ed. Earl of Bessborough in collaboration with A. Aspinall. London: John Murray, 1940. [Letters of Caroline Lamb, her daughter, about Lord Byron.]

Brightfield, Myron F. John Wilson Croker. Berkeley, Calif.: University of California Press, 1940.

Clark, Harry Hayden. "Literary Criticism in the North American Review, 1815-1835," Transactions of the Wisconsin Academy of Science, Arts and Letters, XXXII (1940), 299-350.

Dyson, H. V. D., and John Butt. Augustans and Romantics, 1689-1830. London: Cresset Press, 1940.

E., J. "Childe Harold's Pilgrimage," More Books, XV (Nov., 1940), 385-86.

Evans, Sir Benjamin I. "Wordsworth, Coleridge, Byron and Scott," Tradition and Romanticism, Studies in English Poetry

from Chaucer to W. B. Yeats. London: Methuen & Co.,
1940. Pp. 109-28.

Guérard, Albert. Preface to World Literature. New York: Henry
Holt & Co., 1940.

Hentschel, Cedric. The Byronic Teuton. Aspects of German Pessimism, 1800-1933. London: Methuen & Co., 1940.

Irvine, Magnus. "Byron: the First True European," The Unceas-
ing Quest. London: Thynne, 1940. Pp. 41-69. [Byron reflects an epoch in English history and culture. Byron's appeal to Europe marks him off uniquely from other English
poets.]

McGing, M. E. "Possible Source of the Female Disguise in Byron's Don Juan," MLN, LV (Jan., 1940), 39-42. [Cantos V
and VI probably based on Miss Tully's Narrative of Ten
Years' Residence at Tripoli in Africa.]

Neff, Emery Edward. A Revolution in European Poetry, 1660-
1900. New York: Columbia University Press, 1940.

Nitchie, Elizabeth. The Reverend Colonel Finch. New York:
Columbia University Press, 1940.

Phillips, Olga S. Isaac Nathan, Friend of Byron. London: Minerva Publishing Co., 1940. Pp. 37-83.

"Poetry Corner: Scott and Byron," Scholastic, XXXVII (Dec. 9,
1940), 25, 28.

Power, Julia. Shelley in America in the Nineteenth Century: His
Relation to American Critical Thought and His Influence.
Lincoln: University of Nebraska Press, 1940.

Quennell, Peter. "Byron in Venice," Horizon, II (Dec., 1940),
300-17; ibid., III (Jan., 1941), 47-62.

Quiller-Couch, Sir Arthur. "Introduction," Byron, Poetry and
Prose; with Essays by Scott, Hazlitt, Macaulay, etc. With an
Introduction by Sir Arthur Quiller-Couch and notes by D.
Nichol Smith. Oxford: The Clarendon Press, 1940. Pp. iii-
xi.

S., W. W. "Lèmpriere and Keats," N&Q, CLXXVIII (June 15,
1940), 427-28. [Byron was right in the letter, wrong in the
spirit, when he spoke of Keats as versifying Lemprière's
Dictionary.]

Seary, E. R. "A Sequel to Don Juan," MLR, XXXV (Oct., 1940),
526-29. [George Longmore's Don Juan, A Sequel, Cantos
XIX and XX, in the Fairbridge Collection of the South African

Library, Cape Town, should not be entirely forgotten as a continuation.]

Spence, Lewis. "Byron and Greece," Scots Magazine, XXXIV (Dec., 1940), 187-96.

Strout, Alan Lang. "Lockhart on Don Juan," TLS, Nov. 30, 1940, p. 608. [Publishes letters of Lockhart and Croker now in the William L. Clements Library of the University of Michigan. Identifies Lockhart as the author of the Letters to the Right Hon. Lord Byron.]

White, Newman I. Shelley. 2 vols. New York: Alfred A. Knopf, 1940.

Wiener, Harold S. L. "Byron and the East: Literary Sources of the 'Turkish Tales,'" Nineteenth Century Studies in Honor of C. S. Northup, ed. Herbert John Davis. Ithaca, N.Y.: Cornell University Press, 1940. Pp. 89-129.

Worcester, David. The Art of Satire. Cambridge, Mass.: Harvard University Press, 1940.

                                 1941

Armour, Richard W. "Byron's Message for Today," SRL, XXIII (April 5, 1941), 11.

Askwith, Betty. Keats. London: Collins, 1941.

Attwater, Donald. "Byron and the Monks; Armenian Mekhitarist Order of San Lazzaro, off Venice," Commonweal, XXXIV (Aug. 29, 1941), 441-43.

Caclamos, Demetrius. "Was Byron a Philhellene?," Cambridge Review, LXII (Jan. 31, 1941), 210-12. [Argues in the affirmative against Harold Nicolson's view.] Rptd. in his Greece in Peace and War. London: P. Lund, Humphries & Co., 1942. Pp. 54-60.

Cline, C. L. "Unpublished Notes on the Romantic Poets by Isaac D'Israeli," UTSE, 1941, pp. 138-46.

Erdman, David V. "Lord Byron and the Genteel Reformers," PMLA, LVI (Dec., 1941), 1065-94. [An account of Byron's political connections and activities.]

French, Ruth E. "Lord Byron in Romantic Music," Etude, LIX (Feb., 1941), 78, 128.

Gerritsen, John. "Lord Byron's Name," ES, XXII (Feb., 1941), 24-25. [George Gordon Noel Byron, 6th Baron Byron of Rochdale.]

Harkness, David James. Lincoln and Byron, Lovers of Liberty.
Harrogate, [Tenn.]: Lincoln Memorial University, 1941.

Havens, Raymond D. The Mind of a Poet. Baltimore: The
Johns Hopkins Press, 1941.

Jones, Joseph Jay. "Lord Byron on America," UTSE, 1941, pp.
121-37.

Knight, G. Wilson. The Starlit Dome: Studies in the Poetry of
Vision, with an Introduction by W. F. Jackson Knight and an
Appendix on Spiritualism and Poetry. London: Oxford Uni-
versity Press, 1941.

Larrabee, Stephen A. "Byron's Return from Greece," MLN, LVI
(Dec., 1941), 618-19. [Byron returned from his first trip
aboard the Hydra which bore the Elgin Marbles. Bases his
assertion on C. R. Cockerell's Travels in Southern Europe
and the Levant and on the Elgin papers.]

Marchand, Leslie A. The Athenaeum, a Mirror of Victorian Culture. Chapel Hill: The University of North Carolina Press,
1941.

Palfrey, Thomas R. "Lady Byron and Louise Swanton Belloc's
Lord Byron," ES, XXIII (Feb., 1941), 19-22.

Phillips, William John. France on Byron. Philadelphia: University of Pennsylvania Press, 1941.
Review:
    G. Kitchin, MLR, XXXVIII (April, 1943), 168-69.

Pope-Hennessy, Dame Una B. "The Byrons at Seaham," Durham
Company. London: Chatto & Windus, 1941. Pp. 23-80.

Quennell, Peter. "Byron in Greece," Geographical Magazine, XII
(March, 1941), 301-13.

_____. Byron in Italy. London: Collins; New York: Viking
Press, 1941.
Reviews:
    Margaret Armstrong, NYHTBR, Nov. 9, 1941, p. 3.
    Time, XXXVIII (Nov. 10, 1941), 98, 100-102.
    M. D. Zabel, NR, CV (Nov. 17, 1941), 673-74.
    R. Ellis Roberts, SRL, XXIV (Nov. 29, 1941), 13.
    TLS, Dec. 6, 1941, pp. 607-608.
    Lionel Trilling, Nation, CLIV (May 2, 1942), 520-21.
    Frances Winwar, NYTBR, July 25, 1942, p. 12.

Quinlan, Maurice J. Victorian Prelude. New York: Columbia
University Press, 1941.

Sampson, George. "Byron," The Concise Cambridge History of
English Literature. Cambridge: Cambridge University Press,
1941. Pp. 626-31.

Siegel, Paul. " 'A Paradise Within Thee,' in Milton, Byron, and
Shelley," MLN, LVI (Dec., 1941), 615-17. [The injunction
given by Lucifer to Cain in Cain, II, ii, 463-64, "Think and
endure," is the promise of an internal world different from
that of Adam or Laon, in that thinking makes man master the
universe and "rise above the dust of which he is composed."]

"Tenbury Discoveries, No. III," TLS, Sept. 20, 1941, p. 476.
[A letter from Byron to Hoppner, dated Dec. 7, 1819.]

Thomas, Henry [pseud. for Henry Thomas Schnittkind], and Dana
Lee Thomas. "Byron," Living Biographies of Great Poets.
Garden City, N.Y.: Garden City Publishing Co., 1941.
Pp. 123-35.

Wellesley, Dorothy. Byron. London: W. Collins, 1941.

Wilson, Forrest. Crusader in Crinoline. Philadelphia: J. B.
Lippincott Co., 1941. [Harriet Beecher Stowe.]

1942

Blunden, Edmund. "Romantic Poetry and the Fine Arts," Proceedings of the British Academy, XXVIII (1942), 101-18. ["Wharton Lecture on English Poetry."]

"Byron's Day," TLS, June 6, 1942, p. 283. [Byron has been neglected by his countrymen while considered, on the Continent,
as one of the greatest of English writers. The time has
come to open 'thy Byron.']

Clifford, James L. "Robert Merry: A pre-Byronic Hero," Bulletin of the John Rylands Library, XXVII (1942-43), 74-96.

Cline, C. L. "A Byron Poem?" TLS, Feb. 7, 1942, p. 67.
[The poem, 'Literal Version of a Later Literal Effusion,'
found among Disraeli's papers at Hughenden Manor.]
See also:
    W. N. Brown, ibid., Feb. 14, 1942, p. 84. [Does not think
    Cline's find is genuine because "the construction is loose
    and lacks Byron's smoothness." Says he burned similar
    spurious Byron MSS.]
    Lord Wentworth, ibid., March 7, 1942, p. 116. [Not genuine
    because it 'lacks his command of scansion and facility of
    piercing wit."]
    Duncan Gray, ibid., March 14, 1942, p. 128. [Also denies
    attribution to Byron but asks from Brown why he destroyed
    MSS attributed to Byron.]
    W. N. Brown, ibid., March 28, 1942, p. 157. [Says that he
    destroyed them because they were pornographic and obscene.]

Dykes, Eva Beatrice. The Negro in English Romantic Thought.
Washington, D. C. : The Associated Publishers, Inc. , 1942.

Erdman, David V. "Lord Byron as Rinaldo, " PMLA, LVII (March,
1942), 189-231. [A survey of Byron's brief political career,
and the role played by Lady Oxford.]

Evans, Sir Benjamin Ifor. English Literature: Values and Traditions. London: Allen & Unwin, 1942.

Johnson, Edward D. H. "A Political Interpretation of Byron's
Marino Faliero, " MLQ, III (Sept. 1942), 417-25. [Thinks
Byron's play is a mirror of the political affairs of England
and Italy in 1820.]

Mazzini, Giuseppe. "Byron, Poet of the United Nations, " SRL,
XXV (July 25, 1942), 10. [Drawn from his essay "Byron and
Goethe. "]

Stoll, E. E. "Heroes and Villains: Shakespeare, Middleton, Byron and Dickens, " RES, XVIII (July, 1942), 257-69.

Strout, Alan L. "John Bull's Letter to Lord Byron, " N&Q,
CLXXXIII (Nov. 21, 1942), 317. [Asks for source of three
quotations in this letter.] Cf. G. G. L. , ibid. , CLXXXIV
(Jan. 2, 1943), 23. [Gives sources.]

Tillotson, Geoffrey. "Flecker and Byron, " N&Q, CLXXXIII (Nov.
21, 1942), 312-13. [Parallels between Tenebris Interlucentem
and "The Prisoner of Chillon. "]

"Westernization of Russia, " TLS, Jan. 24, 1942, p. 42. [During
the decades 1820-1840, Byron heads the list of foreign literary
favorites with 143 Russian renderings of his works.]

Wiener, Harold S. L. "A Correction in Byron Scholarship, " MLN,
LVII (June, 1942), 465-66. [The review of Sir William Gell's
Geography and Antiquities of Maca and Itinerary of Greece
which appeared in the Monthly Review, August, 1811, was
written by Francis Hodgson and not by Byron as stated by
E. H. Coleridge.]

1943

The Athenians: Being Correspondence between Thomas Jefferson
Hogg and His Friends Thomas Love Peacock, Leigh Hunt,
Percy Bysshe Shelley and Others, ed. Walter Sidney Scott.
London: Golden Cockerell Press, 1943.

B. , K. J. "Keats and Byron, " N&Q, CLXXXV (Aug. 14, 1943),
110. [Wonders if the lines, "I am free from Men of Pleasure's Cares, /By dint of feelings far more deep than theirs, "
attributed by Keats to Byron, are really Byron's.]

Barzun, Jacques Martin. Romanticism and the Modern Ego. Bos-
    ton: Little, Brown & Co., 1943.

Casson, Stanley. Greece and Britain. London: Collins, 1943.

Hamilton, George H. "Eugene Delacroix and Lord Byron," Gazette
    des Beaux Arts, 6th ser., XXIII (Feb., 1943), 99-110.

"John Murray, 1778-1843, 'The Anax of Publishers,' " TLS, June
    26, 1943, 308.

Larrabee, S. A. "Byron and Art," English Bards and Grecian
    Marbles. New York: Columbia University Press, 1943.
    Pp. 149-74.

McElderry, B. R., Jr. "Byron's Epitaph to Boatswain," MLN,
    LVIII (Nov. 1943), 553-54.

Maurois, André. "The Ethics of Biography," English Institute An-
    nual for 1942. New York: Columbia University Press, 1943.
    Pp. 6-28.

_____. "Lord Byron," The Torch of Freedom, eds. E. Ludwig
    and H. B. Kranz. New York: Farrar & Rinehart, 1943.
    Pp. 129-45.

Nicolson, Harold. "Marginal Comment: [Quality of Byron's Re-
    nown"], Spectator, CLXX (May 14, 1943), 450.

_____. The Poetry of Byron. London: Oxford University
    Press, 1943. [English Association Presidential Address.]
    Reviews:
    N&Q, CLXXXV (Sept. 25, 1943), 209-10.
    TLS, Oct. 23, 1943, p. 511.

Olybrius. "Byron: An Uncollected Couplet?" N&Q, CLXXXIV
    (May 22, 1943), 316. [About "Bold Robert Speer was Bony's
    bad precursor/Bob was a bloody dog, but Bonapart's a wors-
    er," which Moore picked up at W. Harness's house but which
    he left out when he wrote Byron's life.]

Poston, M. L. "Byron's 'Lines to E. N. Long,' " TLS, Aug. 7,
    1943, p. 384. [Says he has another MS which differs from
    the Newstead MS and from the accepted text.] Cf. Anthony
    Hammond, ibid., Oct. 9, 1943, p. 492. [Raises some im-
    portant questions.]

Sitwell, Edith. A Poet's Notebook. London: Macmillan & Co.,
    1943. [Considers "So We'll Go No More A-Roving" great
    poetry.]

Stuart, Dorothy Margaret. Regency Roundabout. London: Mac-
    millan & Co., 1943.

Warner, Oliver. "Glimpses of Byron as Seen by Frederick Chamier," QR, CCLXXX (April, 1943), 203-11. [In his autobiography, The Life of a Sailor.]

White, Newman I. "The Development, Use and Abuse of Interpretation in Biography," English Institute Annual for 1942. New
York: Columbia University Press, 1943. Pp. 29-58.

<u>1944</u>

B., B. "A Browning-Byron Parallel," N&Q, CLXXXVI (March 25,
1944), 160. [Between Bishop Blougram's Apology and Childe
Harold's Pilgrimage, IV, stanza xxiii, already hit upon by
E. H. Coleridge.]

_____. "Byron and Barrabas," N&Q, CLXXXVI (Feb. 26, 1944),
114. [Thomas Campbell said "Now Barrabas was a publisher,"
not Byron.]

_____. "Byron, Patmore and Alice Meynell," N&Q, CLXXXVI
(June 3, 1944), 267-68. [Points of contact between them.]

Beach, Joseph Warren. A Romantic View of Poetry. Minneapolis:
The University of Minnesota Press, 1944.

Cecil, Lord David. "The English Poets," Romance of English
Literature, ed. W. J. Turner. New York: Hastings House,
1944. Pp. 52-53.

Frye, Northrop. "The Nature of Satire," UTQ, XIV (Oct., 1944),
75-89.

Gray, Duncan. "Medora Leigh's Daughter," TLS, April 1, 1944,
p. 163.

Gregory, Horace. "On Prose Written by Poets, and, in Particular,
on Byron's Letters," Shield of Achilles. New York: Harcourt, Brace & Co., 1944. Pp. 33-44.

Grierson, Sir H. J. C., and James C. Smith. "Byron," A Critical
History of English Poetry. London: Chatto & Windus, 1944.
Pp. 372-82.

Guerard, Albert, Jr. "Prometheus and the Aeolian Lyre," Yale
Review, XXXIII (March, 1944), 482-97. [On the Promethean
individualism of the romantics.]

Hamilton, George Heard. "Hamlet or Childe Harold?" Gazette des
Beaux Arts, 6th ser., XXVI (Dec., 1944), 365-86.

Hellman, George S. "A New Byron Discovery: The Unknown
Farewell to His Wife," SRL, XXVII (Jan. 1, 1944), 11-12.

["To Her Who Can Best Understand Them" attributed by
Washington Irving to Byron.] In this connection,
See also:
Milton Ellis, May F. Hoisington, Alice I. McLaughlin, John
H. White, and Homer E. Woodbridge, "The Byron Discovery," ibid., XXVII (Jan. 29, 1944), 13-14. [In separate letters to the editor, they protest against Hellman's
assertiveness.]
Louise S. Boas, "Objection Offered," ibid., XXVII (March 4,
1944), 15. [Corrects Hellman on two points.]
John N. White, "Further Byronia," ibid., XXVII (March 18,
1944), 16. [Raises some interesting questions related to
the Hellman essay.]

Hussey, Richard. "A Quotation by Byron," N&Q, CLXXXVII
(July 15, 1944), 35. [Wants the origin of "Nam vita gaudet
mortua floribus."] Cf. Richard Hussey, ibid., CLXXXVIII
(Feb. 24, 1945), 85. [Found the origin of quote in Cowley.]
W. A. Thorpe, ibid., CLXXXVIII (April 7, 1945), 151.
[Makes an addition to Hussey.]

_____. "Some More Notes on 'King,'" N&Q, CLXXXVII (Oct.
7, 1944), 156-57. [Gives sources of quotations and allusions
in Byron.]

Johnson, E. D. H. "Don Juan in England," ELH, XI (June, 1944),
135-53.

Mineka, Francis E. The Dissidence of Dissent; The Monthly Repository, 1806-1836. Chapel Hill: University of North Carolina Press, 1944.

[Morgan, Charles]. "The English View of Byron," TLS, Jan. 22,
1944, p. 39.

Peyre, Henri. Writers and Their Critics: A Study of Misunder-
standing. Ithaca, N.Y.: Cornell University Press, 1944.

Shelley, Mary. The Letters of Mary Shelley, ed. Frederick L.
Jones. Norman, Oklahoma: Oklahoma University Press,
1944.

W., R. G. "'Blood, Sweat and Tears.' Its Source in Byron?"
N&Q, CLXXXVI (March 25, 1944), 160. [Perhaps from The
Age of Bronze, XIV.]

Ward, W. S. "Byron's Hours of Idleness and Other than Scotch
Reviewers," MLN, LIX (Dec., 1944), 547-50. [Analyzes 16
contemporary reviews, out of which 11 are quite favorable
to Byron.]

Wise, Thomas J. Letters of Thomas J. Wise to John Henry Wrenn,
ed. Fannie Ratchford. New York: Alfred A. Knopf, 1944.

1945

B., D. G. "Byron, Gray and Dante," N&Q, CLXXXVIII (June 16,
    1945), 257. [Wonders if Byron read Gray in some disgrace-
    ful edition printed without Gray's notes.]

Blom, Eric. Music in England. Harmondsworth, Middlesex (Eng.);
    New York: Penguin Books, 1945.

Boyd, Elizabeth. Byron's "Don Juan." New Brunswick, N.J.:
    Rutgers University Press, 1945.
    Reviews:
      TLS, Sept. 1, 1945, p. 414.
      TLS, Nov. 14, 1958, p. 662.

Brouzas, C. G. "Teresa Macri, the 'Maid of Athens,' " Transac-
    tions of the American Philological Association, LXXVI (1945),
    xxxi-xxxii.

Dawson, Christopher M. "Byron and a Greek Folk Song," Yale
    University Library Gazette, XX (July, 1945), 14-18. ["I en-
    ter Your Garden, Most Beautiful Haidée." See next entry.]

_____, and A. E. Raubitschek. "A Greek Folksong Copied for
    Lord Byron," Hesperia, XIV (Jan. -March, 1945), 33-57.
    [Miss Dudu Roque copied it for him. Byron's translation in
    its original draft was purchased by Prof. C. Tinker in 1944.
    An abstract of this article may also be found in the American
    Journal of Archaeology, XLIX (Oct., 1945), 590-91.]

De Ullmann, S. "Romanticism and Synaesthesia: A Comparative
    Study of Sense Transfer in Keats and Byron; a Linguistic-
    Semantic Interpretation," PMLA, LX (Sept., 1945), 811-27.

Gray, Austin K. Teresa, or Her Demon Lover. New York: C.
    Scribner's Sons, 1945. Rptd. in England under the title,
    Teresa: The Story of Byron's Last Mistress. London: G.
    G. Harrap, 1948.
    Reviews:
      Leonard Bacon, SRL, XXVIII (Oct. 13, 1945), 64, 66.
      Carlos Baker, NYTBR, Nov. 4, 1945, p. 1.
      TLS, Feb. 14, 1948, p. 96.

Hudson, A. P. "Byron and the Ballad," SP, XLII (July, 1945),
    594-608. Rptd. in Studies in Language and Literature, ed.
    George R. Coffman. Chapel Hill: The University of North
    Carolina Press, 1945. Pp. 216-30.

Lea, Frank A. Shelley and the Romantic Revolution. London:
    Routledge, 1945.

Liljegren, S. B. Essence and Attitude in English Romanticism.
    Uppsala: Almqvist and Wiksells boktryckeri ab Leipzig, 1945.

It contains:
"Disraeli, Don Juan and Byron," pp. 155-70.
"The Psychology of the Byronic Hero and His Heart," pp. 94-
   120.

Little, Arthur. "Byron Reconsidered," Studies, XXXIV (June,
   1945), 222-30. [Recalls the circumstances of Byron's exile
   and deals with his religion, ethics, conscience, and need for
   expiation which finally took him to Greece.]

Matenko, Percy. "The Goethe, Schiller and Byron Translations of
   the Saaling Album," MLQ, VI (March, 1945), 53-69. [Prints
   the text of the exorcism scene from Manfred translated into
   German by Julie and Marianne Saaling.]

Namier, L. B. "The Poet Journalist," TLS, Sept. 15, 1945, p.
   439. [Goethe thought that if Byron had been able to work off
   his negative feelings in speeches in the House of Lords, he
   would have emerged a purer poet.]

Nelson, Lawrence E. "Satanic School," Our Roving Bible; Tracking
   Its Influence through English and American Life. New York:
   Abingdon-Cokesbury Press, 1945. Pp. 150-56. [On The
   Vision of Judgment.]

Simmons, Jack. Southey. London: Collins, 1945.

Smith, Robert Metcalf. The Shelley Legend. New York: Charles
   Scribner's Sons, 1945.

Super, R. H. "Landor and the Satanic School," SP, XLII (Oct.,
   1945), 793-810. [Landor's opinion of Byron and Byron's of
   Landor.]

Trueblood, Paul Graham. The Flowering of Byron's Genius:
   Studies in Byron's "Don Juan." Palo Alto, Calif.: Stanford
   University Press, 1945.
   Reviews:
      Carlos Baker, NYTBR, July 15, 1945, p. 8.
      Samuel Chew, MLN, LXI (March, 1946), 210-11.
      R. A. Rice, JEGP, XLVI (July, 1947), 329-30.

Ward, William S. "English Conservatism toward Poetry, 1780-
   1820," PMLA, LX (June, 1945), 386-98. [Scott and Byron
   were censured for their lack of neoclassical precedent in
   what they produced, and also for their heroes and their sentiments.]

9. BYRONIC REORIENTATION: RENAISSANCE IN PRIMARY SOURCE MATERIALS, 1946-1956

1946

Bebbington, W. G. "Byron Now," Poetry Review, XXXVII (April-May, 1946), 113-19. [Thinks that Byron's poetry and its message will come into its own again, "more contemporary than any poetry of our time."] Cf. Mary V. Kernick, ibid., XXXVII (June-July, 1946), 238-41. [Takes issue with Mr. Bebbington's "Byronade." Finds Byron the Man contemptible.] H. L. Senior, ibid., XXXVII (Oct. -Dec., 1946), 394-96. [Defends Mr. Bebbington and Byron.]

Blunden, Edmund. "Shelley and Byron at Geneva," Profiles from Notable Modern Biographies and Autobiographies, ed. Leonard R. Gribble. London: S. Low, Marston & Co., 1946. Pp. 145-57. [A chapter from Blunden's Shelley.]

————. Shelley, a Life Story. London: Collins, 1946.

Caclamos, Demetrius. "Byron and the Countess Guiccioli," N&Q, CXCI (Aug. 10, 1946), 64. [The Marquis de Boissy, Teresa's second husband, was proud of the fact that she had been Byron's lover.]

Cameron, John. "Byron's Association with Scotland," Dalhousie Review, XXVI (April, 1946), 57-63.

Eaves, T. C. Duncan. "A Note on Lord Byron's Selected Works, 1823," Library, 5th ser., I (June, 1946), 70-72. [A two volume edition by Murray not recorded by E. H. Coleridge.]

Fairchild, Hoxie Neale. "Byron and Monk Lewis," TLS, May 11, 1946, p. 223. [Perhaps Monk Lewis's "Farewell to Spain" may have suggested the melancholy part of Canto II, xviii-xx, of Don Juan as well as the seasickness of Juan.]

Gray, Duncan. The Life and Work of Lord Byron. ("Newstead Abbey Publications," No. 4.) Nottingham: Corporation of Nottingham, 1946.

Greenberg, Herbert. "Two Versions of Byron's Poem, 'Ossian's Address to the Sun,'" N&Q, CXC (June 15, 1946), 256-57.

401

Gregor, D. B. "Plagiarism or Parallelism?" N&Q, CXCI (July
    27, 1946), 24-25. [A possible source for Manfred: Vincenzo
    Monti's A Don Sigismondo Chigi.] Cf. D. B. Gregor, ibid.,
    CXCIV (March 5, 1949), 95-96.

_____. "An Unpublished Letter of the Countess Guiccioli Re-
    ferring to Byron," N&Q, CXC (June 29, 1946), 266. [Ad-
    dressed to Dr. Vacca of Pisa, requesting him to send a pre-
    scription to relieve pain on Byron's skin.]

Grierson, H. J. C. and J. C. Smith. "Byron," A Critical History
    of English Poetry. New York: Oxford University Press,
    1946. Pp. 380-81.

Holland, Elizabeth Vassal Fox, Lady. Elizabeth, Lady Holland, to
    Her Son, 1821-1845, ed. Earl of Ilchester. London: John
    Murray, 1946.

Howarth, Robert G. "Byromania," Literary Particles: Essays on
    Books and Authors. London: Angus & Robertson, 1946.
    Pp. 1-5. [On George Paston's Feminine Profiles.]

Keith, C. "Byron's Letters," Queen's Quarterly, LIII (Winter,
    1946-47), 468-77.

Mabbott, T. O. "Byron's 'On This Day I Complete My 36th Year,'"
    Explicator, IV (March, 1946), item 36. Cf. Arthur Dickson,
    ibid., V (Nov., 1946), item 15. [Adds a point to Mabbott's
    comment.]

_____. "Chatterton and Byron: A Reminiscence?" N&Q, CXCI
    (Dec. 28, 1946), 281. [In the opening couplet of Byron's
    Monody on the Death of Sheridan there is, perhaps, an echo
    of Chatterton's Naiva and Mored, ll. 43-44.]

Macaulay, Rose. "The Regrettable Discovery," They Went to
    Portugal. London: Jonathan Cape, 1946. Pp. 165-174.
    [Contains a chapter on Byron's visit to Portugal, and the ac-
    count of it in Childe Harold.]

Madariaga, Salvador de. Don Juan as a European Figure. "Byron
    Foundation Lecture." Nottingham: University College, 1946.
    Reviews:
    TLS, Oct. 12, 1946, p. 498.
    N&Q, CXCI (Dec. 19, 1946), 264.

Oake, Mary Elizabeth. "Byron and Shelley," Poetry Review,
    XXXVII (Aug.-Sept., 1946), 315-16.

Roberts, Cecil E. M. "Byron and the U.S. S(hip) 'Constitution,'"
    And So to America. London: Hodder & Stoughton, 1946.
    Pp. 303-17.

Robertson, J. Minto. "Burns and Byron--a Comparison," The
    Robert Burns Annual and Chronicle. Kilmarnock: The Burns
    Federation, 1946. Pp. 29-40.

Rollins, Hyder Edward. Keats' Reputation in America to 1848.
    Cambridge, Mass.: Harvard University Press, 1946.

Sencourt, Robert. "Byron and Shelley at the Lake of Geneva,"
    QR, CCLXXXIV (April, 1946), 209-21.

Shipley, Joseph T. (ed.). "George Gordon, Lord Byron," Ency-
    clopedia of Literature. New York: Philosophical Library,
    1946. Pp. 243-44.

Thackeray, William M. The Letters and Private Papers of Wil-
    liam M. Thackeray, ed. Gordon N. Ray. 4 vols. Cambridge,
    Mass.: Harvard University Press, 1946. [Scattered men-
    tions.]

Van Doren, Mark. "Don Juan," The Noble Voice, a Study of Ten
    Great Poems. New York: H. Holt & Co., 1946. Pp. 283-
    302.

1947

Barrell, Joseph. Shelley and the Thought of His Time: A Study
    in the History of Ideas. ("Yale Studies in English," No.
    106.) New Haven: Yale University Press, 1947.

Brouzas, C. G. "Teresa Macri, the 'Maid of Athens,'" West Vir-
    ginia University Bulletin Philological Papers, V (May, 1947),
    1-31.

Daghlian, Philip B. "Byron's 'Observations on an Article in
    Blackwood's Magazine,'" RES, XXIII (April, 1947), 123-30.

De Sélincourt, E. "Byron," Wordsworthian and Other Studies.
    Oxford: Clarendon Press, 1947. Pp. 105-28. [Considers
    what Byron was to himself and to his own time. By concen-
    trating in himself, he reflects in all his writings the "disap-
    pointed aspirations, the failure, the sorrow of his time."]

Erdman, David V. "Byron and Revolt in England," Science and
    Society, XI (Summer, 1947), 234-48. [For Byron, revolution
    was inevitable.]

Evans, Bertrand. Gothic Drama from Walpole to Shelley. ("Uni-
    versity of California Publications in English," Vol. 18.)
    Berkeley, Calif.: University of California Press, 1947.

_____. "Manfred's Remorse and Dramatic Tradition," PMLA,
    LXII (Sept., 1947), 752-73.

Frye, Northrop. Fearful Symmetry, a Study of William Blake.
    Princeton, N.J.: Princeton University Press, 1947.

Grace, William J. "The Social Idea in the English Romantic
    Poet," Thought, XXII (Sept. , 1947), 461-82.

Henkin, Leo J. "Pugilism and the Poets," MLQ, VIII (March,
    1947), 69-79.

James, Henry. The Notebooks of Henry James, eds. F. O. Mat-
    thiessen and Kenneth B. Murdock. New York: Oxford Uni-
    versity Press, 1947.

Mackerness, E. D. "Byron, the Satirist," CR, CLXXII (Aug. ,
    1947), 112-18.

Marchand, Leslie A. "On Writing a New Life of Byron," Listener,
    XXXVIII (Oct. 23, 1947), 721-22.

Parker, W. M. "Charles Ollier to William Blackwood," TLS,
    June 7, 1947, p. 288. ["The pretended 'Life' was nothing
    more than blank paper. "]

Pratt, Willis W. Lord Byron and His Circle. A Calendar of MSS
    in the University of Texas Library. Austin, Texas: The
    University of Texas Press, 1947.
    Reviews:
    TLS, June 26, 1948, p. 361.
    Frank H. Ristine, MLQ, X (Sept. , 1949), 411-12.

_____ . "Mr. Dalby and the Romantics," UTSE, 1947, pp. 90-
    107. [On the relationship between this bookseller and the
    poets.]

Sencourt, Robert. "Byron and Shelley in Venice," QR, CCLXXXV
    (Jan. , 1947), 84-97. [Article draws on White's Shelley.]

Shelley, Mary. Mary Shelley's Journal, ed. Frederick L. Jones,
    Norman, Oklahoma: University of Oklahoma Press, 1947.

Steffan, Truman G. "Byron at Work on Canto I of Don Juan," MP,
    XLIV (Feb. , 1947), 141-64.

_____ . "The Byron Poetry Manuscripts in the Library of the
    University of Texas," MLQ, VIII (June, 1947), 194-210.
    [Surveys 59 Mss.]

_____ . "The Token-Web, the Sea-Sodom and Canto I of Don
    Juan," UTSE, 1947, pp. 108-68. [On some circumstances
    that contributed to the composition of the first canto of Don
    Juan.]

Strout, Alan L. (ed.). John Bull's Letter to Lord Byron. Nor-
man, Oklahoma: University of Oklahoma Press, 1947.
[Finds Lockhart the author of this letter.]
Reviews:
Henry Cavendish, NYTBR, Nov. 30, 1947, p. 18.
N&Q, CXCIII (March 20, 1948), 131.
TLS, Oct. 2, 1948, p. 559.
Samuel Chew, MLN, LXIII (Dec., 1948), 568-69.
Ima Honaker-Herron, Southwest Review, XXXIII (Winter,
1948), 89-90.
TLS, March 3, 1950, p. 138.

Ticknor, George. "Wanderjahre: 1815-1819," Discovery of Europe,
ed. Philip Rhav. Boston: Houghton Mifflin Co., 1947. Pp.
63-93. [Extracts from Ticknor's Journal, relating to Byron.]

Warner, Oliver. "Captain Chamier and Byron," Captains and Kings,
a Group of Miniatures. London: George Allen & Unwin,
1947. Pp. 134-44.

1948

Baker, Carlos. Shelley's Major Poetry: The Fabric of a Vision.
Princeton: Princeton University Press, 1948.

Bandy, W. T. "Lord Byron and Lady Blessington: A Bibliographical Note," PQ, XXVII (April, 1948), 186-87. [Byron's lines
to Lady Blessington had appeared prior to their publication in
Moore's Letters and Journals in Les Annales Romantiques for
1827-1828, and in a review of the French Annals in Monthly
Magazine, n.s. VII (Feb., 1829), 137-43. Prints the corrected version of the Monthly Magazine.]

Borst, William A. Lord Byron's First Pilgrimage. ("Yale Studies
in English," Vol. 109.) New Haven: Yale University Press,
1948.
Reviews:
Carlos Baker, NYTBR, Dec. 12, 1948, p. 19.
TLS, March 3, 1950, p. 138.
T. Guy Steffan, MLN, LXVI (Feb., 1951), 121-23.
Leslie Marchand, MLQ, XII (March, 1951), 113-14.

Chew, Samuel. "Byron," The Nineteenth Century and After, 1798-
1939. Part IV of A Literary History of England, ed. A. C.
Baugh. New York: Appleton-Century-Crofts, 1948. Pp.
1218-29. Also issued separately as The Nineteenth Century
and After, 1798-1939. New York: Appleton-Century-Crofts,
1948. Pp. 1218-29.

Evans, Margiad. "Byron and Emily Brontë," Life and Letters,
LVII (June, 1948), 193-216.

Fuller, Roy (ed.). "Introduction," Byron for Today. London:
    Porcupine Press, 1948. Pp. 7-15.
    Review:
    TLS, July 15, 1949, p. 453.

Gordon, R. K. "William Hazlitt on Some of His Contemporaries,"
    Proceedings and Transactions of the Royal Society of Canada,
    3rd. ser., XLII, sec. ii, 1948, pp. 1-12.

Greig, James A. Francis Jeffrey of the "Edinburgh Review."
    Edinburgh: Oliver & Boyd, 1948.

James, David Gwilym. The Romantic Comedy. London: Oxford
    University Press, 1948.

Jordan, Hoover H. "Byron and Moore," MLQ, IX (Dec., 1948),
    429-39.

Joyce, Michael. My Friend H. London: Murray, 1948. [On
    Hobhouse.]

Marchand, Leslie A. "Byron's Beppo," Spectator, CLXXX (April
    16, 1948), 468.

Martin, Leonard Cyril. Byron's Lyrics. "Byron Foundation Lec-
    ture." Nottingham: University of Nottingham, 1948.
    Reviews:
    C. S. Sisson, MLR, XLIV (Jan., 1949), 144.
    W. D. Thomas, RES, n. s., II (July, 1951), 298-99.

Nicolson, Harold. "Marginal Comment: [An Imaginary Conversa-
    tion with Byron in 1948]," Spectator, CLXXX (May 14, 1948),
    584.

Origo, Iris. "Byron's Last Attachment," Listener, XXXIX (June
    24, 1948), 1014-15.

Osborne, W. A. "Be a Byron When You Travel," Rotarian, LXXII
    (April, 1948), 17. [By seeking out the best in the land you
    are visiting.]

Pratt, Willis W. Byron at Southwell: The Making of a Poet, with
    New Poems, and Letters from the Rare Books Collection of
    the University of Texas. Austin, Texas: The University of
    Texas Press, 1948.
    Reviews:
    TLS, June 26, 1948, p. 361.
    Ima Honaker-Herron, Southwest Review, XXXIII (Autumn,
        1948), 418-20.
    Vivian de Sola Pinto, MLR, XLIV (Jan., 1949), 114-15.
    Frank H. Ristine, MLQ, X (Sept., 1949), 411-12.

Rollins, Hyder Edward (ed.). The Keats Circle. Letters and Papers, 1816-1879. Cambridge, Mass.: Harvard University
Press, 1948.

Rosa, Sister M. "Romanticism in Annette van Droste-Hülshoff,"
MLJ, XXXII (April, 1948), 279-87. [Her debt to Byron and
others.]

Steffan, Truman G. "An Early Byron Ms. in the Pierpont Morgan
Library, 'The Edinburgh Ladies Petition,' " UTSE, 1948, pp.
146-76.

_____. "Ms. Rhyme Revision of Canto I of Don Juan," N&Q,
CXCIII (June 12, 1948), 244-46.

Vulliamy, Colwyn Edward. Byron, with a View of the Kingdom of
Cant and a Dissection of the Byronic Ego. London: Michael
Joseph, 1948.
Review:
Margiad Evans, Life and Letters, LVIII (July, 1948), 62-64.

1949

Baily, Francis Evans. The Love Story of Lady Palmerston. London: Hutchinson & Co., 1949.

Bandy, W. T. "First Printing of Byron's Stanzas on the Death of
the Duke of Dorset," MLR, XLIV (Jan., 1949), 93-94. [It
appeared with some variants from the known text in the Edinburgh Annual Register for 1824. Bandy gives the text.]

Bertocci, Angelo Philip. "An Animal of the Higher Species: By-
ron," Charles Du Bos and English Literature: A Critic and
His Orientation. New York: King's Crown Press, 1949.
Pp. 168-92.

Bewley, Marius. "The Colloquial Mode of Byron," Scrutiny, XVI
(March, 1949), 8-23. [Finds that the English quality of style
in such poems as Beppo, The Vision of Judgment and Don
Juan is of more importance than the Italian influence on them.]

Bottome, Phyllis. "Neurosis as a Handicap to Genius," Life and
Letters, LXI (May, 1949), 100-109. Rptd. in Literature and
Psychology, V (May, 1955), 20-25; Not in Our Stars, London:
Faber & Faber, 1955. Pp. 135-46.

Bowra, C. Maurice. "Don Juan," The Romantic Imagination.
Cambridge, Mass.: Harvard University Press, 1949. Pp.
149-73.

Brouzas, C. G. "Byron's 'Maid of Athens': Her Family and Surroundings," West Virginia University Bulletin Philological
Papers, VII (June, 1949), 1-65.

Cameron, H. C. "The Mystery of Byron's Lameness," Listener, XLI (April 28, 1949), 703-704. [Mr. Cameron thinks Byron suffered from a mild form of Little's Disease in which there is no deformity and no weakness or loss of power, but movements are stiff, awkward and uncontrolled, with a complete lack of precision.]

*Dickinson, Patrick (ed.). "Introduction," Byron: Poems. London: The Grey Walls Press, 1949.

Entwistle, W. J. "The Byronism of Lermontov's A Hero of Our Times," Comparative Literature, I (Spring, 1949), 140-46.

Fairchild, Hoxie Neale. "Byron," Religious Trends in English Poetry. Vol. III: 1780-1830, Romantic Faith. New York: Columbia University Press, 1949. Pp. 388-451.

Hamilton, George Heard. "Delacroix, Byron and the English Illustrators," Gazette des Beaux Arts, 6th ser., XXXVI (Oct., 1949), 261-78.

Hennig, John. "Early English Translations of Goethe's Essays on Byron," MLR, XLIV (July, 1949), 360-71. Cf. D. F. S. Scott's reply to Hennig, ibid., XLV (Oct., 1950), 519.

Highet, Gilbert. The Classical Tradition; Greek and Roman Influences on Western Literature. New York: Oxford University Press, 1949.

Kronenberger, Louis. "Introduction," Don Juan, New York: Modern Library, 1949. Pp. v-xiii. Rptd., partially, as "Byron 'Turned Pose into Poetry,'" NYTBR, Oct. 30, 1949, pp. 5, 48; Kronenberger's The Republic of Letters; Essays on Various Writers, New York: Knopf, 1955, pp. 144-53; Modern Literary Criticism: An Anthology, ed. Irving Howe, Boston: Beacon, 1958, pp. 396-403; as Byron's Don Juan, in The Polished Surface: Essays in the Literature of Wordliness. New York: Knopf, 1969, pp. 151-60.

Lovell, Ernest J., Jr. Byron: The Record of a Quest. Studies in a Poet's Concept and Treatment of Nature. Austin, Texas: University of Texas Press, 1949.
   Reviews:
      N&Q, CXCV (June 24, 1950), 286.
      C. A. Bodelsen, ES, XXXI (Aug., 1950), 147-48.
      N. P. Stallknecht, SAQ, XLIX (Oct., 1950), 546-47.
      J. M. S. Tompkins, MLR, XLVI (April, 1951), 265-66.
      Leslie A. Marchand, MLQ, XIII (June, 1952), 216-17.
      Choice, III (Oct., 1966), 644.

_____. "Byron's The Island and Maturin's Melmoth the Wanderer," N&Q, CXCIV (Nov. 12, 1949), 497-99.

Marchand, Leslie A. "Lord Byron and Count Alborghetti," PMLA, LXIV (Dec., 1949), 976-1007. [Eight unpublished letters of Byron to Alborghetti and 19 of the Count to Byron.]

Nicolson, Harold. "The Byron Curse Echoes Again," NYTM, March 27, 1949, pp. 12-13, 33, 35. [On the Elgin Marbles.]

_____. "Marginal Comment: [Byron and the Elgin Marbles Row]," Spectator, CLXXXII (Jan. 21, 1949), 77.

Notopolous, James A. The Platonism of Shelley. A Study of Platonism and the Poetic Mind. Durham, N.C.: Duke University Press, 1949.

Origo, Iris. "My Only and Last Love: Byron's Unpublished Letters to Countess Teresa Guiccioli," Atlantic Monthly, CLXXXIII (March, 1949), 19-28; ibid., CLXXXIII (April, 1949), 34-40; ibid., CLXXXIII (May, 1949), 39-44; ibid., CLXXXIII (June, 1949), 39-44. Published in book form under the title, The Last Attachment. London: J. Cape & John Murray, 1949.
Reviews:
TLS, Sept. 16, 1949, p. 600.
J. Squire, ILN, CCXV (Sept. 17, 1949), 412.
V. S. Pritchett, NSN, XXXVIII (Oct. 1, 1949), 360.
Carlos Baker, NYTBR, Oct. 23, 1949, p. 48.
Samuel Chew, NYHTBR, Nov. 6, 1949, p. 8.
Robert Halsband, SRL, XXXIII (Jan. 7, 1950), 9.
Richard D. Altick, VQR, XXVI (Spring, 1950), 311-16.
Joseph Sagmaster, KR, XII (Spring, 1950), 360-68.
Paul G. Trueblood, K-SJ, I (Jan., 1952), 115-16.

Pratt, Willis W. "Byron and Elizabeth Pigot," Library Chronicle of the University of Texas, III (Summer, 1949), 146-61. [On the influence of the young woman from Southwell who, according to Mr. Pratt, played an important role in Byron's development as a poet.]

_____. "An Italian Pocket Notebook of Lord Byron," UTSE, XXVIII (1949), 195-212. [In this account book, Byron recorded his household expenses from Dec., 1819, till July, 1820. After that date, Teresa got hold of it and made her own entries.]

Pyles, Thomas. "Margarita, Marianna and the Countess of Blessington," N&Q, CXCIV (May 14, 1949), 209-10. [Disagrees with Michael Sadleir's identification, in his Blessington-D'Orsay: A Masquerade, of Byron's mistresses as they appear in Mrs. Gore's Cecil. The three references to Lady Blessington must be cut to two.]

Quennell, Peter. "Introduction," Don Juan. London: John Lehman, 1949. Pp. v-xii.

Samuels, D. G. "Some Byronic Influences in Spanish Poetry, 1870-1880," Hispanic Review, XVII (Oct., 1949), 290-307.

_____. "Some Dubious Spanish Translations of Byron for 1829," Hispanic Review, XVII (Jan., 1949), 73-75.

Steffan, Truman G. "Byron Furbishing Canto I of Don Juan," MP, XLVI (May, 1949), 217-41. [Revisions in the MS.] Rptd. with corrections and additions in The Making of a Masterpiece. Vol. I of Byron's "Don Juan": A Variorum Edition, eds. Truman G. Steffan and Willis W. Pratt. 4 vols. Austin, Texas: University of Texas Press, 1957. Pp. 130-80.

_____. "Extent of Ms. Revision of Canto I of Don Juan," SP, XLVI (July, 1949), 440-52. [Byron revised the beginning of Canto I much more than he was willing to admit.] Rptd. with corrections and additions in The Making of a Masterpiece. Vol. I of Byron's "Don Juan": A Variorum Edition, eds. Truman G. Steffan and Willis W. Pratt. 4 vols. Austin, Texas: University of Texas Press, 1957. Pp. 100-14.

Stiling, Frank, and Bruno Meinecke. "Byron's Don Juan, X, xli," Explicator, VII (March, 1949), item 36. [Explicates the pharmacology of this stanza.]

Stout, George Dumas. The Political History of Leigh Hunt's "Examiner." Together with an Account of "The Book." Saint Louis: Washington University Studies--New Series, No. 19, 1949.

Straumann, Heinrich. Byron and Switzerland. "Byron Foundation Lecture." Nottingham: Nottingham University, 1949.
Reviews:
Harold Nicolson, Spectator, CLXXXII (May 13, 1949), 641.
G. R. de Beer, MLR, XLV (Jan., 1950), 80-82.
C. A. Bodelsen, ES, XXXI (Dec., 1950), 239.
W. D. Thomas, RES, n.s., II (July, 1951), 298-99.

Tsanoff, Radoslav. The Ways of Genius. New York: Harper & Bros., 1949. [Byron's use of imagination in Sardanapalus.]

Viëtor, Karl. Goethe, the Poet. Cambridge, [Mass.]: Harvard University Press, 1949.

Vincent, E. R. Byron, Hobhouse and Foscolo. New York: Macmillan, 1949.
Reviews:
TLS, Dec. 2, 1949, p. 788.
John Purves, Italian Studies, V (1950), 68-72.
N&Q, CXCV (March 4, 1950), 109-10.
Dublin Magazine, XXV (April-June, 1950), 78-79.
Terence Spencer, MLR, XLV (Oct., 1950), 591.

C. A. Bodelsen, ES, XXXI (Dec., 1950), 226-27.
Ernest H. Wilkins, Romanic Review, XLI (Dec., 1950), 305-306.
John Purves, RES, n.s., II (Oct., 1951), 391-94.
Paul G. Trueblood, MLQ, XII (Dec., 1951), 502-503.

Ward, W. S. "Lord Byron and 'My Grandmother's Review,'"
    MLN, LXIV (Jan., 1949), 25-29. [On the reaction of William
    Roberts, editor of The British Review, to Byron's lines in
    Canto I, stanzas cci-ccx, claiming that he had bribed him to
    secure a favorable review of Don Juan.]

Wiley, Autrey Nell. "Byron's 'Incomparable Oil Macassar,'" N&Q,
    CXCIV (Nov. 12, 1949), 499-500. [In Don Juan, Canto I, st.
    xvii, ll. 135-36. Wonders if it was an advertisement.]

Wimsatt, William K. "The Structure of Romantic Nature Imagery,"
    The Age of Johnson: Essays Presented to Chauncery Brew-
    ster Tinker. New Haven: Yale University Press; London:
    Oxford University Press, 1949. Pp. 291-303. Rptd. in his
    The Verbal Icon: Studies in the Meaning of Poetry and Two
    Preliminary Essays Written in collaboration with Monroe C.
    Beardsley. Lexington: University of Kentucky, 1954. Pp.
    103-16.

Wormhoudt, A. "Byron," The Demon Lover: A Psychological Ap-
    proach to Literature. New York: Exposition Press, 1949.
    Pp. 113-45.

1950

Altick, Richard Daniel. "On the Trail of Byron," The Scholar Ad-
    venturers. New York: Macmillan, 1950. Pp. 270-88. [On
    Marchand's experiences while collecting Byron material for
    his biography.]

Arbuthnot, Harriet. The Journal of Mrs. Arbuthnot, 1820-1832,
    eds. Francis Banford and the Duke of Wellington. London:
    Macmillan & Co., 1950. [Gossip about Byron's vices and
    Caroline Lamb's reaction to Medwin's Conversations.]

Beach, Joseph Warren. "George Gordon, Lord Byron," English
    Literature of the 19th and the Early 20th Centuries, 1798 to
    the First World War. Vol. IV of A History of English Liter-
    ature, ed. Hardin Craig. 4 vols. New York: Oxford Uni-
    versity Press, 1950. Pp. 476-79.

Brouzas, C. G. "Whittington's Letters to Mariana Macri, Sister
    of the 'Maid of Athens,'" Proceedings of the West Virginia
    Academy of Science, XXII (1950), 107-15.

412   Bibliography

Bryant, Arthur. The Age of Elegance, 1812-1822. London: Collins, 1950.

Bush, Douglas. Science and English Poetry: A Historical Sketch, 1590-1950. New York: Oxford University Press; London: Geoffrey Cumberlege, 1950.

Butler, Eliza M. Byron and Goethe. 'Byron Foundation Lecture." Nottingham: University of Nottingham, 1950.

Cameron, Kenneth Neill. The Young Shelley. New York: The Macmillan Co., 1950.

Dowden, Wilfred S. "The Consistency of Byron's Social Doctrine," Rice Institute Pamphlet, XXXVII (Oct., 1950), 18-44. [He was consistent in his hatred of oppression.]

Evans, Sir Benjamin Ifor. A Short History of English Drama. London: Staples Press, 1950.

Friederich, Werner Paul. "Dante and English Romanticism," Dante's Fame Abroad. Rome: Storia e Letterature; Chapel Hill: University of North Carolina, 1950. Pp. 229-95.

Grylls, R. Glynn. Trelawny. London: Constable, 1950.

Havens, Raymond D. 'Discontinuity in Literary Development. The Case of English Romanticism," SP, XLVII (Jan., 1950), 101-11.

Heath-Stubbs, John. The Darkling Plain: A Study of the Later Fortunes of Romanticism in English Poetry from George Darley to W. B. Yeats. London: Eyre & Spottiswoode, 1950. [Touches on George Darley's detestation of Byron's dramas.]

Jones, Frederick L. "A Byron Letter," N&Q, CXCV (June 10, 1950), 252. [Dated June 27th, 1816, the MS owned by Dr. Frank Read of Philadelphia.]

Jones, W. Powell. "Sir Egerton Brydges on Lord Byron," Huntington Library Quarterly, XIII (May, 1950), 325-37. [Gives the text of the letter in the Huntington Library.]

Knight, G. Wilson. "The Plays of Lord Byron," TLS, Feb. 3, 1950, p. 80.

Looker, Samuel Joseph. Shelley, Trelawny and Henley, a Study of Three Titans. Worthing: Published under the Worthing Art Development Scheme by Aldridge Bros., 1950.

Magarshack, David. Stanislavsky, a Life. London: McGibbon & Kee, 1950. [On his production of Cain.]

Origo, Iris. "Byron, Teresa Guiccioli and Fanny Silvestrini,"
KSMB, III (1950), 9-18. [Mme. Silvestrini played the go-
between in the Byron-Guiccioli affair.]

Pound, Ezra. The Letters of Ezra Pound, 1907-1941, ed. D. D.
Paige. New York: Harcourt Brace & Co., 1950.

Praz, Mario. "The Ashes of a Rose," Mandrake, II (1950-1951),
31-35. [About Byron's letters to Teresa Guiccioli.]

Quennell, Peter (ed.). Byron: A Self-portrait. Letters and Dia-
ries, 1798-1824, with hitherto Unpublished Letters. 2 vols.
London: John Murray; New York: Scribner, 1950.
Reviews:
H. W. Garrod, Spectator, LXXXII (Jan. 27, 1950), 114-16.
Sir John Squire, ILN, CCXVI (Feb. 18, 1950), 250.
Eric Gillet, National and English Review, CXXXIV (March,
1950), 226-31.
Listener, XLIII (March 2, 1950), 399.
TLS, March 3, 1950, p. 138.
Samuel Chew, NYHTBR, April 16, 1950, p. 6.
William A. Borst, SRL, XXXIII (May 20, 1950), 28-29.
Leslie A. Marchand, NYTBR, June 4, 1950, p. 17.
Ernest Jones, Nation, CLXXI (July 22, 1950), 88-89.
The Month, n. s., IV (Sept., 1950), 193-94.
Lunn, A., Tablet, CXCVII (Feb. 15, 1951), 129.

_____ (ed.). Byron: Selections from Poetry, Letters and Jour-
nals. London: Nonesuch Press, 1950.
Review:
TLS, March 3, 1950, p. 138.

Rulfs, Donald J. "The Romantic Writers and Edmund Kean," MLQ,
XI (Dec., 1950), 425-37. [On Byron's admiration for Kean
and their relation to Drury Lane.]

Samuels, D. G. "Critical Appreciations of Byron in Spain, 1900-
1929," Hispanic Review, XVIII (Oct., 1950), 302-18.

Scott, Noel. "Byron in the Provinces," QR, CCLXXXVIII (April,
1950), 217-28. [Deals with his popularity in the Home Countries as evidenced by favorable reviews in The Windsor and
Eton Express and General Advertiser.]

Wardle, R. M. "The Motive for Byron's 'George Russell of A,'"
MLN, LXV (March, 1950), 179-83. [Thinks that this prose
fragment was an attack upon Blackwood's, occasioned by certain of the contents of that periodical for Nov., 1821.]

White, Newman I. "Our Ancient Contemporaries, the Romantic
Poets," Library Notes, No. 24 (July, 1950), 19-34.

Whittier, John Greenleaf. Whittier on Writers and Writing: The
    Uncollected Critical Writings of John Greenleaf Whittier, eds.
    Edwin H. Cady and Harry H. Clark. Syracuse: Syracuse
    University Press, 1950.
    It contains:
        "Lord Byron," pp. 38-40. Rptd. from Essex Gazette, May
            1830.
        "Moore's Byron, Vol. II," pp. 70-71. Rptd. from New Eng-
            land Weekly Review, Feb. 14, 1831.
        "Poetry- Reminiscence- Lord Byron," pp. 99-105. Rptd.
            from New England Magazine, Aug., 1832.

Whitton, Charlotte. "Lord Byron on Vampires," Queen's Quarter-
    ly, LVII (Winter, 1950), 474-78. [Reprints Byron's letter to
    Galignani dated April 27, 1819.]

                              1951

Bartlett, Phyllis Brooks. Poems in Process. New York: Oxford
    University Press, 1951. [On Byron's habits of composition:
    he had the reputation of being one of the easiest of writers.]

Bett, W. R. "Lord Byron: Lameness and Genius," The Infirmi-
    ties of Genius. London: Christopher Johnson, 1951. Pp.
    149-60.

"Books and the Festival," TLS, May 11, 1951, p. 300. [Three MS
    Cantos of Don Juan on exhibition at the Victoria and Albert
    Museum.]

Bostetter, Edward E. (ed.). "Introduction," Byron: Selected Poe-
    try and Letters. New York: Holt, Rinehart & Winston, 1951.
    Pp. v-xxxi.

Bowra, C. M. Inspiration and Poetry, Cambridge, [Eng.]: Cam-
    bridge University Press, 1951.

Bridge, Alex. "Sir James Bacon and Byron," TLS, March 16,
    1951, p. 165. [The editor of Memoirs of the Life and Writ-
    ings of Lord Byron, "George Clinton, Esq.," was really
    James Bacon.]

Buckley, Jerome Hamilton. The Victorian Temper: A Study in
    Literary Culture. Cambridge, Mass.: Harvard University
    Press; London: Allen & Unwin, 1951.

Clare, John. The Prose of John Clare. Eds. J. W. Tibble and
    Anne Tibble. London: Routledge, 1951.

Doughty, Oswald. "Dante and the English Romantic Poets,"
    English Miscellany, II (1951), 125-69.

Dowden, Wilfred S. "Harold the Exile--Another Item in the List of Byroniana," N&Q, CXCVI (Oct. 13, 1951), 447-48. [An anonymous novel based on Byron's early life.]

_____. "A Jacobin Journal's View of Lord Byron," SP, XLVIII (Jan., 1951), 56-66. [The reviews from the Monthly Magazine.]

Ehrsam, Theodore G. Major Byron, the Incredible Career of a Literary Forger. New York: C. S. Boesen, 1951.

Gisborne, Maria. Maria Gisborne and Edward E. Williams, Shelley's Friends: Their Journals and Letters, ed. Frederick L. Jones. Norman, Oklahoma: University of Oklahoma Press, 1951.

Gregor, D. B. "Byron's Knowledge of Armenian," N&Q, CXCVI (July 21, 1951), 316-20.

Hauser, Arnold. The Social History of Art, trans. in collaboration with the author by Stanley Godman. 2 vols. London: Routledge, 1951. [On the Byronic hero.]

James, D. G. Byron and Shelley. "Byron Foundation Lecture." Nottingham: University of Nottingham, 1951.

Lovell, E. J. "Byron and the Byronic Hero in the Novels of Mary Shelley," UTSE, XXX (1951), 158-83.

_____. "Byron and La Nouvelle Heloïse: Two Parallel Paradoxes," MLN, LXVI (Nov., 1951), 459-61.

Lucas, F. L. Literature and Psychology. London: Cassell & Co., 1951.

Marchand, Leslie A. (ed.). "Introduction," Byron: Selected Poetry. New York: Modern Library, 1951. Pp. v-xvi.

Nicolson, Harold. "Marginal Comment: [Byron, the Swimmer]," Spectator, CLXXXVII (Sept. 21, 1951), 359.

Pafford, Ward. "The Date of Hours of Idleness," N&Q, CXCVI (Aug. 4, 1951), 339-40. [Sets its publication on the final week of June, 1807.] Cf. Ward Pafford, ibid., CXCVI (Oct. 27, 1951), 476-77. [A copy of Hours of Idleness inscribed to Byron's mother, June 25, 1807, makes the date ascribed in previous article conclusive.]

Pearson, Hesketh. Dizzy; the Life and Personality of Benjamin Disraeli, Earl of Beaconsfield. New York: Harper & Bros., 1951.

Pratt, Willis W. "Byron's Fantastic Will of 1811," Library Chronicle of the University of Texas, IV (Summer, 1951), 75-81.

Read, Herbert. Byron. ("Writers and Their Work," No. 10.)
London: Published for the British Council and the National
Book League by Longmans, Green, 1951. Rptd. in his True
Voice of Feeling: Studies in English Romantic Poetry. Lon-
don: Faber; New York: Pantheon Books, 1953. Pp. 288-
310.

Sangiorgi, Roberto Benaglia. "Giambattista Casti's Novelle Gallanti
and Lord Byron's Beppo," Italica, XXVIII (Dec., 1951), 261-
69.

Scott, Winifred. Jefferson Hogg. London: Jonathan Cape, 1951.

Sencourt, Robert. "Certain Affinities of Turner," QR, CCLXXXIX
(Oct., 1951), 487-99. [Affinities with Byron, Shelley and
Wordsworth.]

Spencer, Terence. "A Byron Plagiarism from Dryden," N&Q,
CXCVI (April 14, 1951), 164. [Some lines in Marino Faliero
resemble a passage in Dryden's Epistle Dedicatory to "The
Rival Ladies," to the Right Honorable Roger, Earl of Orrery.]

Tillotson, Geoffrey. Criticism and the 19th Century. London:
The Athlone Press, 1951.

Ure, Peter. "Beckford's Dwarf and Don Juan, V, lxxxvii-xciv,"
N&Q, CXCVI (March 31, 1951), 143-44. [The dwarf-mutes
of this canto may owe their existence "to a report of one of
Caliph Beckford's extravagances rather than to an experience,
real or imagined, during his own Eastern travels."]

Whalley, George. "Coleridge and John Murray," QR, CCLXXXIX
(April, 1951), 253-66. [On the relationship of Byron and
Coleridge, and on Byron's request that Thomas Moore review
Coleridge's "two volumes of Poesy and Biography."]

White, N. I., F. L. Jones, and K. N. Cameron. An Examination
of "The Shelley Legend." Philadelphia: University of Pennsylvania Press, 1951.

Wilson, June. Green Shadows: The Life of John Clare. London:
Hodder & Stoughton, 1951.

1952

Bishop, Morchard [pseud. for Oliver Stonor]. "Introduction," Recollections of the Table Talk of Samuel Rogers. First Collected by the Rev. Alexander Dyce. London: Richards,
1952.

Bernbaum, Ernest. "A Critical Sketch of Important Books and Articles Concerning Keats, Shelley, Byron and Hunt, published in 1940-1950," K-SJ, I (Jan., 1952), 73-85.

Blunden, Edmund. "A Lover of Books, J. W. Dalby (1799-1880)," Etudes Anglaises, V (Août, 1952), 193-201. [The bookseller.]

Brown, W. N. "Lord Byron and the Borderland of Genius and Insanity," Medical World (London), LXXVII (Sept. 26, 1952), 96-98.

Bush, Douglas. English Poetry: The Main Currents from Chaucer to the Present. Oxford and New York: Oxford University Press, 1952.

Cline, Clarence Lee. Byron, Shelley and Their Pisan Circle. London: John Murray, 1952.
    Reviews:
        Edmund Blunden, Spectator, CLXXXVIII (May 9, 1952), 620, 622.
        TLS, June 13, 1952, p. 388.
        N&Q, CXCVII (July 19, 1952), 309.
        Robert Halsband, SRL, XXXV (Aug. 2, 1952), 33-34.
        D. Ferguson, NYHTBR, Aug. 3, 1952, p. 4.
        D. J. Gordon, NSN, XLIV (Sept. 27, 1952), 358.
        Leslie A. Marchand, NYTBR, Nov. 9, 1952, p. 59.
        _____. K-SJ, II (Jan., 1953), 113-14.
        Emma G. Salter, CR, CLXXXIII (April, 1953), 255.
        VQR, XXIX (Winter, 1953), xviii.
        G. G., Personalist, XXXV (Spring, 1954), 196-97.
        K. N. Cameron, MLN, LXIX (March, 1954), 200-201.

Connely, Willard. Count D'Orsay: The Dandy of Dandies. London: Cassell, 1952.

Cooper, Dorothy J. "The Romantics and Emily Brontë," Transactions of the Brontë Society, XII (1952), 106-12.

Dale, P. M. "Byron," Medical Biographies: The Ailments of Thirty-three Famous Persons. Norman, Oklahoma: University of Oklahoma Press, 1952. Pp. 176-83.

Davie, Donald. Purity of Diction in English Verse. London: Chatto & Windus, 1952.

Downs, Brian W. "Anglo-Norwegian Literary Relations, 1867-1900," MLR, XLVII (Oct., 1952), 449-94. [On criticism and translation of Byron.]

Estrich, Robert M., and Hans Sperber. Three Keys to Language. New York: Rinehart, 1952. [A discussion of Manfred on pp. 219-22.]

Fiess, Edward. "Melville as a Reader and Student of Byron," AL, XXIV (May, 1952), 186-94.

Forman, Maurice Buxton. The Letters of John Keats. London: Geoffrey Cumberlege, 1952.

*Forster, H. B. "Byron's Romaic," Symposium Published by the British Academy at Patras, IV (Spring, 1952), 37-41.

George, Mary Dorothy. Catalogue of Political and Personal Satires Preserved in the Department of Prints and Drawings in the British Museum. Vol. X: 1820-1827. London: British Museum, 1952.

Hamilton, George Heard. "Delacroix's Memorial to Byron," Burlington Magazine, XCIV (Sept., 1952), 257-61. [His painting, "La Grèce expirant sur les ruines de Missolonghi," and others, were influenced by his reading of Byron.]

Haüsermann, Hans Walter. The Genevese Background: Studies of Shelley, Francis Danby, Maria Edgeworth, Ruskin, Meredith and Joseph Conrad in Geneva, with hitherto Unpublished Letters. London: Routledge & Kegan Paul, 1952.

Knight, G. Wilson. Lord Byron: Christian Virtues. London: Routledge, Paul, 1952.
Reviews:
    Helen Gardner, NSN, XLIV (Nov. 29, 1952), 658. Cf. G. Wilson Knight, ibid., XLIV (Dec. 20, 1952), 757. [Answers H. Gardner's review of his book.]
    John Davenport, Twentieth Century, CLII (Dec., 1952), 532-34.
    TLS, Dec. 19, 1952, p. 838. Cf. G. Wilson Knight, ibid., Jan. 2, 1953, p. 9. [Answers some points in the TLS review of his book.] Ibid., Jan. 9, 1953, p. 25. [Reviewer answers Knight.]
    Listener, XLIX (Feb. 26, 1953), 359, 361.
    John Jones, Blackfriars, XXXIV (April, 1953), 203-204.
    V. de Sola Pinto, English, IX (Summer, 1953), 189-90.
    Edgar Johnson, NYTBR, Aug. 9, 1953, pp. 4, 15.
    Samuel Chew, NYHTBR, Aug. 30, 1953, p. 6.
    W. E. Garrison, Christian Century, LXX (Sept. 16, 1953), 1054.
    R. W. King, RES, n.s., V (Jan., 1954), 96-98. Cf. G. Wilson Knight, RES, n.s., V (July, 1954), 271-73. [Reply to King's review.]
    Howard Nemerov, Hudson Review, VII (Summer, 1954), 285-91. Rptd. as "Poetry and Life: Lord Byron," in his Poetry and Fiction: Essays. New Brunswick: Rutgers University Press, 1963. Pp. 34-41.
    E. D. Johnson, Yale Review, XLIII (Winter, 1954), 301.
    C. G. Thayer, Books Abroad, XXVIII (Winter, 1954), 82-83.

Robert J. O'Connell, Thought, XXIX (Winter, 1954-1955),
    612-13.
  B. R. McElderry, Personalist, XXXVI (Winter, 1955), 84-85.

Lefevre, Carl. "Lord Byron's Fiery Convert of Revenge," SP,
    XLIX (July, 1952), 468-87. [A study of four Byronic heroes
    who revenge themselves on their peers by allying themselves
    with the mob with whom they have nothing in common.]

Marchand, Leslie A. "Recent Byron Scholarship," English Mis-
    cellany, III (1952), 125-39. Rptd. with revisions and addi-
    tions in Essays in Literary History, Presented to J. Milton
    French, eds. Rudolf Kirk and C. F. Main. New Brunswick,
    N.J.: Rutgers University Press, 1961. Pp. 127-48.

_____. "Trelawny on the Death of Shelley," KSMB, IV (1952),
    9-34.

Origo, Iris. "The Innocent Miss Francis and the Truly Noble
    Lord Byron," K-SJ, I (Jan., 1952), 1-9. [Eliza Francis
    and her meeting with Byron.]

Pafford, Ward. "Byron's 'To Those Ladies': An Unpublished
    Poem," K-SJ, I (Jan., 1952), 65-69. [Prints the text of
    this poem of 12 quatrains from the MS in the Yale Library.]

Peacock, Ronald. "Novalis and Schopenhauer: A Critical Transi-
    tion in Romanticism," German Studies Presented to Leonard
    Ashley Willoughby. Oxford: Blackwell, 1952. Pp. 133-43.

Raymond, Ernest. Two Gentlemen of Rome: The Story of Keats
    and Shelley. London: Cassell, 1952.

Robertson, Lorraine. "The Journal and Notebooks of Claire Clair-
    mont, Unpublished Passages," KSMB, IV (1952), 35-47.

Scharper, P. J. "Hemingway, Byron, the Adolescent Hero,"
    America, LXXXVIII (Dec. 13, 1952), 303-304. ["The Byronic
    hero was fashioned on an essentially adolescent pattern--more
    subtle, slightly more intellectual than Hemingway's pattern,
    but essentially adolescent."]

Slater, J. "Byron's Hebrew Melodies," SP, XLIX (Jan., 1952),
    75-94.

Smelser, Marshall. "Byron's Knowledge of Daniel Boone's Wilder-
    ness Patriarchy," N&Q, CXCVII (March 15, 1952), 112-14.
    [The reference to Boone in Canto VIII of Don Juan comes from
    H. M. Brackenbridge's Views of Louisiana.]

Steffan, Truman Guy. "Byron and Murder in Ravenna," N&Q,
    CXCVII (April 26, 1952), 184-86. [An investigation of the
    assassination of the Military Commandant of Ravenna, del

Pinto, near Byron's house.   Byron was so impressed by the
murder that he included an account of it in Canto V, stanzas
xxxiii to xxxix.]   Rptd. in The Making of a Masterpiece.
Vol. I of Byron's "Don Juan": A Variorum Edition, eds.   Truman G. Steffan and Willis W. Pratt. 4 vols. Austin, Texas:
University of Texas Press, 1957. Pp. 80-85.

_____. "Byron's Focus of Revision in His Compositions of Don
Juan, " UTSE, XXXI (1952), 57-67. Rptd. with additions and
omissions in The Making of a Masterpiece.   Vol. I of Byron's "Don Juan": A Variorum Edition, eds. Truman G. Steffan and Willis W. Pratt. 4 vols. Austin, Texas: University
of Texas Press, 1957. Pp. 115-29.

Trelawny, Edward John.   The Last Days of Shelley and Byron,
Being the Complete Text of Trelawny's "Recollections, " ed. ,
with Additions from Contemporary Sources, by J. E. Mor-
purgo.   New York: Philosophical Library; London: Folio
Society, 1952.
Reviews:
TLS, Dec. 5, 1952, p. 798.
Betty Miller, Twentieth Century, CLIII (Feb. , 1953), 155-56.
Robert Halsband, SRL, XXXVI (May 9, 1953), 48.
Robert L. Cline, JEGP, LIII (Jan. , 1954), 130-31.
Truman Guy Steffan, K-SJ, III (Winter, 1954), 67-73.

Trewin, J. C. "Without Meeting Byron, " ILN, CCI (Nov. 8,
1952), 780. [On William Douglas Home's play Caro William
in which Byron does not appear.]

W. , R. "His Cause Was Freedom, " South African Banker's Journal, XLIX (Sept. , 1952), 274-75.

Wilson, Edmund. "Byron in the Twenties, " The Shores of Light.
New York: Farrar, Straus & Young, 1952.
It contains:
"Byron and His Biographers, " pp. 62-67. Rptd. from Dial,
LXXVIII (June, 1925), 511-14.
"The New Byron Letters, " pp. 57-62. Rptd. from New York
Herald Tribune, July 2, 1922, Part V, p. 4.

Woodring, Carl Ray. Victorian Samplers: William and Mary Howitt. Lawrence, Kansas: University of Kansas Press, 1952.
[Byron's neighbors in Nottingham and their conflicting attitudes toward Byron's poetry and reputation.]

Yohannan, John D. "The Persian Poetry Fad in England, 1770-
1825, " Comparative Literature, IV (Spring, 1952), 137-60.

1953

Abrams, Meyer Howard. The Mirror and the Lamp: Romantic
    Theory and the Critical Tradition. London: Oxford Univer-
    sity Press, 1953.

Ashe, Dora Jean. "Byron's Alleged Part in the Production of
    Coleridge's Remorse," N&Q, CXCVIII (Jan. , 1953), 33-36.
    [Byron did not take part in this production since he was not
    a member of the Drury Lane Committee in 1812.]

Austin, James C. Fields of the "Atlantic Monthly. " San Marino,
    Calif. : The Huntington Library, 1953. [References to Lady
    Byron.]

Barzun, Jacques (ed.). "Introduction: Byron and the Byronic in
    History," Selected Letters of Lord Byron. "Great Letters
    Series. " New York: Farrar, Straus and Young, 1953. Pp.
    vii-xli. Rptd. with some omissions in Atlantic Monthly,
    CXCII (Aug. , 1953), 47-52; The Energies of Art. New York:
    Harper, 1956. Pp. 49-80.
    Reviews:
        George Genzmer, NYHTBR, July 26, 1953, p. 5.
        Time, LXII (Aug. 3, 1953), 71-72.
        Edgar Johnson, NYTBR, Aug. 9, 1953, pp. 4, 15.
        Robert Halsband, SRL, XXXVI (Oct. 3, 1953), 36, 52.
        New Yorker, XXIX (Dec. 5, 1953), 218-19.
        Dudley Fitts, NR, CXXX (Jan. 11, 1954), 21.
        Howard Nemerov, Hudson Review, VII (Summer, 1954), 285-
            91. Rptd. as "Poetry and Life: Lord Byron," in his
            Poetry and Fiction: Essays. New Brunswick: Rutgers
            University Press, 1963. Pp. 34-41.
        Hugh Kenner, Poetry, LXXXIV (Aug. , 1954), 296-304.

Bauer, Josephine. "The London Magazine, 1820-1829, " Anglistica.
    I (1953), 1-363.

Bebbington, W. G. "The Two Foscari, " English, IX (Autumn, 1953
    1953), 201-206.

Binder, Pearl. Muffs and Morals. London: Harrap; Toronto:
    Clarke, Irwin, 1953.

Brown, T. J. "The Detection of Faked Literary MSS, " Book Col-
    lector, II (Spring, 1953), 6-23. [Considers the points to be
    taken into account when examining a suspect document.
    Prints facsimile illustration of Byron's handwriting.]

Bruce, Ian. Lavallette Bruce, His Adventures and Intrigues Be-
    fore and After Waterloo. London: Hamish Hamilton, 1953.
    [Michael Bruce's association with Caroline Lamb who told
    him of her affair with Byron.]

Bryant, J. Ernest. Genius and Epilepsy: Brief Sketches of Great
    Men Who Had Both. Concord, Mass.: Ye Old Depot Press,
    1953.

Chesterton, G. K. "Romantic Love," A Handful of Authors:
    Essays on Books and Writers, ed. Dorothy Collins. New
    York: Sheed & Ward, 1953. Pp. 193-96.

Dixon, Raymond J. Granger's Index to Poetry. 4th edition. New
    York: Columbia University Press, 1953.

Filipovic, Rudolf. "Anglo-Croatian Literary Relations in the 19th
    Century," Slavonic and East European Review, XXXII (Dec.,
    1953), 92-107. [After Shakespeare, Byron is the most popu-
    lar English poet in Croatia.]

Forster, H. B. "Byron and Nicholas Karvellas," K-SJ, II (Jan.,
    1953), 73-77. [A letter sent to a Greek patriot, May 14,
    1823.]

Gates, Payson G. "A Leigh Hunt-Byron Letter," K-SJ, II (Jan.,
    1953), 11-17. [About the first number of The Liberal.]

Hough, G. G. "Byron," The Romantic Poets. London: Hutchin-
    son; New York: Longmans, 1953. Pp. 97-121.

Knight, G. Wilson. Byron's Dramatic Prose. "Byron Foundation
    Lecture." Nottingham: University of Nottingham, 1953.

Liljegren, S. B. "Byron and Greece," Studies Presented to David
    Moore Robinson on His Seventieth Birthday, eds. George E.
    Mylonas and Doris Raymond. 2 vols. St. Louis, Mo.:
    Washington University, 1951-1953. Vol. II, pp. 726-31.

Lovell, Ernest J., Jr. "Byron and Mary Shelley," K-SJ, II (Jan.,
    1953), 35-49. [On their relationship.]

Macaulay, Rose. Pleasures of Ruins. London: Weidenfeld &
    Nicolson, 1953. [Byron as dreamer.]

Masefield, Muriel. Peacocks and Primroses. A Survey of Dis-
    raeli's Novels. London: Geoffrey Bles, 1953.

Montagu-Nathan, M. "Pushkin's Debt to English Literature," CR,
    CLXXXIII (May, 1953), 303-307.

Nitchie, Elizabeth. Mary Shelley, Author of "Frankenstein." New
    Brunswick: Rutgers University Press, 1953.

Norman, Sylva. "Leigh Hunt, Moore and Byron," TLS, Jan. 2,
    1953, p. 16. [About a Leigh Hunt notebook in which he jotted
    down notes while reading Moore's Life of Byron and which are
    related to the Tatler reviews of this life.]

Price, Lawrence Marsden. English Literature in Germany. ("Publications in Modern Philology," Vol. 37.) Berkeley and Los Angeles: University of California, 1953.

Quennell, Peter. "The Romantic Catastrophe," The Golden Horizon, ed. together with an introduction by Cyril Connolly. New York: University Books, 1953. Pp. 528-43.

Read, Sir Herbert E. "Byron," The True Voice of Feeling: Studies in English Romantic Poetry. London: Faber; New York: Pantheon Books, 1953. Pp. 288-319.

Roe, Ivan. Shelley: The Last Phase. London: Hutchinson, 1953.

Rubinstein, Annette T. "Byron," The Great Tradition in English Literature from Shakespeare to Shaw. New York: The Citadel Press, 1953. Pp. 493-516.

Sarmiento, E. "A Parallel between Lord Byron and Fray Luis de Leon," RES, n.s., IV (July, 1953), 267-73. [Finds a parallel between "When Coldness Wraps This Suffering Clay" and "El aire se serena."]

Small, Harold A. The Field of His Fame: A Ramble in the Curious History of Charles Wolfe's Poem "The Burial of Sir John Moore." ("University of California Publications: English Studies," No. 5.) Berkeley and Los Angeles: University of California Press, 1953.

Smith, Sydney. The Letters of Sydney Smith, ed. Nowell C. Smith. 2 vols. Oxford: Clarendon Press, 1953.

Steffan, T. G. "The Devil a Bit of Our Beppo," PQ, XXXII (April, 1953), 154-71. [Analysis of the MS and a comparison between the MS and the first edition.] Rptd. in Byron: A Collection of Critical Essays, ed. Paul West. Englewood Cliffs, N.J.: Prentice-Hall, 1963. Pp. 65-82.

Strout, Alan L. "Knights of the Burning Epistle (The Blackwood Papers in the National Library of Scotland)," Studia Neophilogica, XXVI (1953-1954), 77-98.

Stuart, Dorothy Margaret. "The Prince Regent and the Poets," Portrait of the Prince Regent. London: Methuen: 1953. Pp. 123-46. Rptd. in Essays by Divers Hands, n.s., XXVII (1955), 109-28. ["Of all the poets, major and minor, who delighted in using their poetical fists upon the Prince Regent, Byron had the hardest punch at command."]

"The Thunder's Roll," TLS, Nov. 13, 1953, p. 725. [Leading article: Byron's fame is on the ascent again.]

Vincent, E. R. Ugo Foscolo: An Italian in Regency England.
  Cambridge, [Eng.]: Cambridge University Press, 1953.

Wain, John (ed.). Contemporary Reviews of Romantic Poetry.
  London: George G. Harrap & Co., 1953.
  It contains:
    Sir Walter Scott, "Review of Childe Harold's Pilgrimage, III,"
      pp. 116-32. Rptd. from QR, XVI (Oct., 1916), 172-208.
    Francis Jeffrey, "Review of Childe Harold's Pilgrimage, III,"
      pp. 142-48. Rptd. from ER, XXVII (Dec., 1816), 277-
      310.
    John Wilson, "Review of Manfred," pp. 136-39. Rptd. from
      Blackwood's, I (June, 1817), 289-95.
    Sir Walter Scott, "Review of Childe Harold's Pilgrimage, IV,"
      pp. 132-36. Rptd. from QR, XIX (April, 1818), 215-32.
    J. G. Lockhart, "Review of Don Juan," pp. 148-53. Rptd.
      from Blackwood's, V (Aug., 1819), 512-18*. [See original
      review.]
    Francis Jeffrey, "Review of Byron's Plays," pp. 139-42.
      Rptd. from ER, XXXVI (Feb., 1822), 413-52.

Woolf, Virginia. A Writer's Diary, ed. Leonard Woolf. London:
  Hogarth Press, 1953. [Critical opinions on Byron.]

Zall, Paul M. "Lord Eldon's Censorship," PMLA, LXVIII (June,
  1953), 436-43. [On the Chancellor's principles in refusing
  copyright to Murray, Shelley, etc., when he considered the
  writings were injurious.]

                                  1954

Bates, Madison C. "Two New Letters of Keats and Byron," K-SJ,
  III (Winter, 1954), 75-88. [To Dr. James Alexander, on loan
  in the Houghton Library at Harvard University.]

Boas, Guy. "Great Englishmen at School," Essays and Studies,
  n.s., VII (1954), 1-41. [Byron at Harrow.]

Bourke, John. The Sea as Symbol in British Poetry. Eton: Alden
  & Blackwell, 1954. [Byron uses the ocean to symbolize eternity.]

Browning, Elizabeth Barrett. Elizabeth Barrett Browning to Miss
  Mitford: The Unpublished Letters of Elizabeth Barrett Brown-
  ing to Mary Russell Mitford, ed. Betty Miller. London:
  Murray, 1954.

Butler, P. R. "Byron's Rivers," QR, CCXCII (April, 1954), 215-
  26. ["River-mentions" in Byron.]

Butter, Peter. Shelley's Idols of the Cave. Edinburgh: At the
  University Press, 1954.

Cecil, Lord David.   Lord M. or the Later Life of Lord Melbourne.
    London: Constable, 1954.

Cline, Clarence L.   'Byron and Southey: A Repressed Rejoinder,''
    K-SJ, III (Winter, 1954), 27-38.   [A letter, dated Pisa, Feb.
    5, 1822, to the editor of the Courier, which Byron never
    sent, printed in full for the first time.]

Dobrée, Bonamy.   The Broken Cistern.   London: Cohen & West,
    1954.   [Mention of Byron.]

Ehrsam, Theodore.   "Major Byron,'' Book Collector, III (Spring,
    1954), 69-71.

Eliot, George [pseud. for Mary Ann Evans].   The George Eliot
    Letters, ed. Gordon S. Haight.   7 vols.   New Haven: Yale
    University Press; London: Cumberlege, 1954-55.

Erdman, David V.   Blake, Prophet against Empire: A Poet's In-
    terpretation of the History of His Own Times.   Princeton:
    Princeton University Press, 1954.   [On their political views.]

Foerster, Donald M.   "The Critical Attack upon the Epic in the
    English Romantic Movement,'' PMLA, LXIX (June, 1954),
    432-47.

Foster, Charles H.   "Vindication of a Friend,'' The Rungless Lad-
    der: Harriet Beecher Stowe and New England Puritanism.
    Durham, N.C.:   Duke University Press, 1954.   Pp. 219-26.

Fussell, Edwin Sill.   Edwin Arlington Robinson: The Literary
    Background of a Traditional Poet.   Berkeley: University of
    California Press, 1954.

George, M. Dorothy.   Catalogue of Political and Personal Satires
    Preserved in the Department of Prints and Drawings in the
    British Museum.   Vol. XI: 1828-1832.   London: British
    Museum, 1954.

Glover, A. S. B. (ed.).   "Introduction,'' Byron: A Selection from
    His Poems.   London: Penguin Books, 1954.
    Review:
    Kingsley Amis, Spectator, CXCIII (Dec. 31, 1954), 831-32.

Grove's Dictionary of Music and Musicians, ed. Eric Blom.   5th
    ed.   9 vols.   London: Macmillan; New York: St. Martin's,
    1954.   [Musical settings of, and music inspired by Byron's
    poetry.]

Hamilton, Charles.   "Eleven Ways to Spot a Forgery,'' Amateur
    Book Collector, V (Dec., 1954), 9-12.   [Comments on Byron
    forgeries.]

Hamilton, George Heard. "The Iconographical Origins of Dela-
croix's 'Liberty Leading the People,' " Studies in Art and
Literature for Belle da Costa Greene, ed. Dorothy Miner.
Princeton: Princeton University Press, 1954. Pp. 55-66.

Highet, Gilbert. "The Poet and His Vulture, " A Clerk of Oxen-
ford: Essays on Literature and Life. New York: Oxford
University Press, 1954. Pp. 117-24. Rptd. as "Byron:
The Poet and His Vulture, " in his The Powers of Poetry,
New York: Oxford University Press, 1960, pp. 82-90. [On
Byron's starvation diet and on the influence that his desire to
be thin may have had on his poetry.]

Hopkins, Kenneth.   The Poets Laureate.   London: Bodley Head,
1954.   [Byron's reaction to the laureateship.]

Knight, G. Wilson.   "The Book of Life: On Byron's Adulation of
Pope, " Laureate of Peace: On the Genius of Alexander Pope.
London: Routledge, 1954.   Pp. 113-64.

_____. "Don Leon Poems," TLS, June 4, 1954, p. 368. [Sug-
gests George Colman as the author of these poems which
were first published in 1866.] Cf. Samuel C. Chew, ibid. ,
July 9, 1954, p. 447. [Reminds Knight of his own treatment
of the Don Leon Poems in his Byron in England.]

_____. "Who Wrote Don Leon?" Twentieth Century, CLVI
(July, 1954), 67-79.

Lockhead, Marion.   John Gibson Lockhart.   London: John Murray,
1954.

Lovell, Ernest J. , Jr. (ed.).   His Very Self and Voice: Collected
Conversations of Lord Byron.   New York: Macmillan, 1954.
Reviews:
    Library Journal, LXXIX (Nov. 1, 1954), 2098.
    Carlos Baker, NYTBR, Nov. 28, 1954, p. 4.
    Samuel C. Chew, NYHTBR, Nov. 28, 1954, p. 5.
    Paul G. Trueblood, SRL, XXXVII (Dec. 11, 1954), 21.
    Thomas D. Jarrett, Phylon, XVI (First quarter, 1955), 119.
    Time, LXV (Jan. 3, 1955), 72-74.
    V. S. Pritchett, NSN, LI (Jan. 8, 1955), 46-47.
    TLS, Feb. 25, 1955, p. 118.
    United States Quarterly Book Review, XI (March, 1955), 12.
    Jacob Korg, Nation, CLXXXV (March 19, 1955), 244-45.
    Robert Martin Adams, Hudson Review, VIII (Summer, 1955),
        288-94.
    Ima H. Herron, Southwest Review, XL (Summer, 1955), 276-
        78.
    Garland Greever, Personalist, XXXVI (Autumn, 1955), 423-
        24.
    Leslie Marchand, K-SJ, IV (Winter, 1955), 97-99.
    Desmond Powell, Arizona Quarterly, XI (Winter, 1955), 365-

66.
Alec Lucas, Queen's Quarterly, LXII (Winter, 1956), 630.
S. C. Wilcox, Books Abroad, XXX (Winter, 1956), 92.
Reed Whittenmore, Poetry, LXXXVII (March, 1956), 372-76.
Rptd. as "Childe Byron," in his Fascination of the Abomi-
nation. Poems, Stories and Essays. New York: Mac-
millan, 1963. Pp. 306-12.
Marie A. U. White, SAQ, LV (April, 1956), 249-50.
C. A. Bodelsen, ES, XLII (April, 1961), 119-20.

McEachran, F. (ed.). Spells. Oxford: Blackwell, 1954.

Norman, Arthur M. Z. "Dialogue in Byron's Dramas," N&Q,
CXCIX (July, 1954), 304-306. [It has buoyancy and dramatic
quality.

Norman, Sylva. Flight of the Skylark; the Development of Shelley's
Reputation. Norman, Oklahoma: University of Oklahoma
Press, 1954.

Packe, Michael St. John. The Life of John Stuart Mill. London:
Secker & Warburg; New York: Macmillan, 1954.

Poulet, Georges. "Timelessness and Romanticism," Journal of the
History of Ideas, XV (Jan., 1954), 3-22. Rptd. in Ideas in
Cultural Perspective, eds. Philip Paul Wiener and Aaron No-
land. New Brunswick: Rutgers University Press, 1962. Pp.
658-77.

Raynor, Henry. "The Fortunate Travellers," Fortnightly, CLXXXI
(March, 1954), 188-201. ["After a life in which travel was a
drug, a sedative for an uneasy conscience and a preventative
against self-knowledge, the last purposeful, idealistic journey
(to Greece), ended in failure."]

Spencer, Terence. "Byron's Poetical Inheritance of Philhellenism,"
Fair Greece, Sad Relic: Literary Philhellenism from Shakespeare to Byron. London: Weidenfeld & Nicolson, 1954. Pp.
247-94.

Stanford, W. B. The Ulysses Theme: A Study in the Adaptability
of a Traditional Hero. Oxford: Blackwell, 1954.

Steffan, Truman G. "Trelawny Trepanned," K-SJ, III (Winter,
1954), 67-73.

Strout, Alan L. "Some Miscellaneous Letters Concerning Blackwood's Magazine," N&Q, CXCIX (July, 1954), 309-12.

Super, Robert Henry. Walter Savage Landor. New York: New
York University Press, 1954.

Taft, Kendall B. "Byronic Background of Emerson's 'Good Bye,' "
    New England Quarterly, XXVII (Dec. , 1954), 525-27.

Templeton, Edith. The Surprise of Cremona. London: Eyre &
    Spottiswoode, 1954. [Comments on Byron provoked by a
    visit to Ravenna.]

Tompkins, Peter. "Byron's Shoes," New Yorker, XXX (Oct. 16,
    1954), 70-84.

Trevelyan, G. M. A Layman's Love of Letters. London: Long-
    mans Green, 1954. [Adopts opposite position from Arnold
    in his estimate of Byron.]

Unwin, Rayner. The Rural Muse: Studies in the Peasant Poetry
    of England. London: Allen & Unwin, 1954.

Wheelwright, Philip Ellis. The Burning Fountain: A Study in the
    Language of Symbolism. Bloomington: Indiana University
    Press, 1954. [Discusses "The Isles of Greece. "]

Wicker, C. V. "Byron as Parodist, " MLN, LXIX (May, 1954),
    320-21.

Yeats, William Butler. Letters, ed. Allan Wade. London: Ru-
    pert Hart-Davis, 1954. [Scattered comments.]

                                    1955

Adam Mickiewicz, 1798-1955: In Commemoration of the Centenary
    of His Death. Zurich: Unesco, 1955.
    It contains:
    Jean Fabre, "Adam Mickiewicz and European Romanticism, "
        pp. 37-59.
    Giovanni Maver, "Adam Mickiewicz and Italy, " pp. 115-141.

Ball, Patricia M. "Byronic Drama, " Orpheus, II (Jan. -May,
    1955), 25-31. [A revaluation of Byron's plays.]

Bhattacherje, Mohini Mohan. "Byron--the Poet of Movement and
    Passion, " Calcutta Review, CXXXV (May, 1955), 155-67.

Blunden, Edmund. "Fragment of Byronism," Etudes Anglaises,
    VIII (janvier-mars, 1955), 32-42. [The poetic notebook of an
    English traveller in Italy at the time of Byron containing
    stanzas in the manner of Beppo and Don Juan.]

Browning, Elizabeth Barrett. Elizabeth Barrett to Mr. Boyd: Un-
    published Letters of Elizabeth Barrett Browning to Hugh
    Stuart Boyd, ed. Barbara P. McCarthy. New Haven: Yale
    University Press, 1955.

Butler, Eliza M. "Byron, Goethe and Professor Benecke," Publications of the English Goethe Society, n. s., XXIV (1955), 77-100. [Byron's dedication of Sardanapalus to Goethe.]

*Crawford, Thomas. "The Edinburgh Review and Romantic Poetry (1802-1829)," Auckland University College Bulletin No. 47: English Series No. 8, 1955.

Dakin, Douglas. British and American Philhellenes during the War of Greek Independence, 1821-1833. Salonika, Greece: Society for Macedonia Studies, 1955.

Davie, Donald. Articulate Energy: An Inquiry into the Syntax of English Poetry. London: Routledge & K. Paul, 1955.

De Baun, Vincent C. "Temple Bar: Index of Victorian Middleclass Thought," Journal of the Rutgers University Library, XIX (Dec., 1955), 6-16. [Byron was the second most popular figure with the magazine.]

Dowden, Wilfred S. "Austrian Surveillance of Byron in Greece," Anglo-Americana, ed. Karl Brunner. Wiener Beitrage zur Englischen Philologie, LXII (1955), 37-41.

_____. "Byron and the Austrian Censorship," K-SJ, IV (Winter, 1955), 67-75.

Duncan-Jones, Caroline M. Miss Mitford and Mr. Harness: Records of a Friendship. London: S. P. C. K., 1955.

Findlater, Richard [pseud. for Kenneth Bruce F. Bain]. Grimaldi: King of Clowns. London: MacGibbon & Kee, 1955. [On the acquaintance of Grimaldi the clown and Byron.]

Gannon, Patricio. "Zante," Blackwood's, CCLXXVII (March, 1955), 238-45. [Prints the text of a letter to N. Karvellas, which, however, had already been published by H. B. Forster in K-SJ, II (1953), 76-77.]

Graves, Robert. The Crowning Privilege. London: Cassell, 1955.

Greene, Marc T. "Byron's Island Refuge," American Mercury, LXXXI (July, 1955), 20. [The convent of the Mechitarist Fathers, San Lazzaro.]

Grigson, Geoffrey, and Charles Harvard Gibbs-Smith. "Dear Adorable Lord Byron," People: A Volume of the Good, Bad, Great and Eccentric People Who Illustrate the Admirable Diversity of Man. New York: Hawthorn, 1955, pp. 54-55.

Groom, Bernard. The Diction of Poetry from Spenser to Bridges. Toronto: The University of Toronto Press, 1955.

Hamilton, Charles. "Authors of the Romantic Age," Hobbies, LX
    (March, 1955), 108-109. [On autograph collecting.]

_____. "Beware the Facsimile!" Amateur Book Collector, V
    (April, 1955), 3-4. [On Byron's letter to Galignani on The
    Vampyre.]

House, Humphry.   All in Due Time.   London: Rupert Hart-Davis,
    1955.

Huscher, Herbert.   "Claire Clairmont's Lost Russian Journal and
    Some Further Glimpses of Her Later Life," KSMB, VI (1955),
    35-47.

In Memory of Lord Byron's Sojourn at St. Lazarus.   Venice: St.
    Lazzaro, 1955. [A series of Byron's letters all mentioning
    the Armenian Convent.]

LeComte, Edward S.   Dictionary of Last Words.   New York:
    Philosophical Library, 1955.

Lee, Amice.   Laurels and Rosemary: The Life of William and
    Mary Howitt.   London: Cumberlege, 1955. [On William's
    visit to Newstead Abbey.   Also references to Byron's burial.]

Lombard, C. M.   "Byron and Lamartine," N&Q, CC (Feb. , 1955),
    81-82.

Majut, Rudolf.   "Some Literary Affiliation of George Büchner with
    England," MLR, L (Jan. , 1955), 30-43.

Marchand, Leslie A.   "A Note on the Burning of Shelley's Body,"
    KSMB, VI (1955), 1-3.

Maxoudian, Noubar.   "Lord Byron and the Armenians," Armenian
    Review, VIII (Winter, 1955-1956), 47-48.

Neilson, Francis.   "The Corn Law Rhymes," American Journal of
    Economics and Sociology, X (July, 1955), 407-15.   Rptd. in
    The Cultural Tradition and Other Essays.   New York: Robert
    Schalbenbach Foundation, 1957.   Pp. 125-35. [Poems on
    economic and social matters.]

Nicoll, Allardyce.   Early Nineteenth Century Drama: 1800-1850.
    Vol. IV of A History of English Drama: 1660-1900.   5 vols.
    Cambridge, [Eng.]: Cambridge University Press, 1955.

Notopoulos, James A.   "New Sources on Byron at Missolonghi,"
    K-SJ, IV (Winter, 1955), 31-45. [Greek material dealing with
    Byron's last phase.]

Press, John.   The Fire and the Fountain: An Essay on Poetry.
    London: Cumberlege, 1955. [Critical comments.]

Ruskin, John. Ruskin's Letters from Venice, 1851-1852, ed. John
    Lewis Bradley. ("Yale Studies in English," Vol. 129.) New
    Haven: Yale University Press; London: Cumberlege, 1955.

Santayana, George. The Letters of George Santayana, ed. Daniel
    Cory. New York: Scribner, 1955. [Scattered references.]

Scott, Noel. "Byron and the Stage," QR, CCXCIII (Oct., 1955),
    496-503. [Discusses reviews of Byron's dramas in the
    Windsor and Eton Express and General Advertiser.]

Sells, A. Lytton. Animal Poetry in French and English Literature
    and the Greek Tradition. ("Indiana University Publications:
    Humanities Series," No. 32.) Bloomington, Indiana: Indiana
    University Press, 1955.

Spearman, Diana. "New Byron Letters," National and English Re-
    view, CXLIV (May, 1955), 279-83. [Five letters addressed
    to Robert Wilmot, March 11-14, 1816.]

Stavrou, Constantine N. "Milton, Byron and the Devil," Univer-
    sity of Kansas City Review, XXI (March, 1955), 153-59.
    [Differences between Byron's devil and Milton's.]

Stein, Gisela. The Inspiration Motif in the Works of Franz Grill-
    parzer, with Special Consideration of "Libussa." The Hague:
    M. Nijhoff, 1955. [Grillparzer's concept of inspiration is
    compared with that of Byron.]

Stuart, Dorothy Margaret. Dearest Bess: The Life and Times of
    Lady Elizabeth Foster, Afterwards Duchess of Devonshire.
    London: Methuen, 1955. [Caroline's mother and Byron.]

Switzer, Richard. "Lord Ruthwen and the Vampires," French Re-
    view, XXIX (Dec., 1955), 107-12. [On Polidori's The Vam-
    pire and its relation to Byron's projected ghost story.]

Ward, A. C. "The Triple Peak: Byron," Blake to Bernard Shaw.
    Vol. III of Illustrated History of English Literature. 3 vols.
    London: Longmans, Green, 1955. Pp. 95-102.

Wasserman, Earl R. "Byron and Sterne," MLN, LXX (Jan.,
    1955), 25. [On the influence of Tristram Shandy, Vol. IV,
    on Don Juan, II, xviii-xx.]

Welland, Denis S. R. "Mark Twain the Great Victorian," Chicago
    Review, IX (Fall, 1955), 101-109. [On Mark Twain's esti-
    mate of Byron.]

Wellek, René. A History of Modern Criticism, 1750-1950. Vol.
    II: The Romantic Age. Vol. III: The Age of Transition.
    Vol. IV: The Later Nineteenth Century. 5 vols. New
    Haven: Yale University Press, 1955-1965.

Willoughby, L. A. "Goethe Looks at the English," MLR, L (Oct.,
1955), 464-84.

Wilson, Harriette. The Game of Hearts. Harriette Wilson's Memoirs, ed. Lesley Blanch. New York: Simon & Schuster,
1955.

                                    1956

Apel, Gudrun. "A Byronic Hero in Slovak Literature," Slavonic
and East European Review, XXXIV (June, 1956), 338-54.

Ashe, Dora Jean. "Coleridge, Byron, and Schiller's Der
Geisterseher," N&Q, CCI (Oct., 1956), 436-38. ["Oscar of
Alva," in Hours of Idleness, 1807, and Coleridge's Osorio,
later known as Remorse, based on Schiller.]

Barzun, Jacques. "Byron and the Byronic in History," The Ener-
gies of Art: Studies in Authors, Classic and Modern. New
York: Harper, 1956. Pp. 49-80.

Bebbington, W. G. "The Most Remarkable Man of His Age, Byron
in The Windsor and Eton Express and General Advertiser,"
KSMB, VII (1956), 27-31.

Berry, C. L. "Byron in Venice, 1819," N&Q, CCI (Sept., 1956),
396-97. [A contemporary account by an unknown hand.]

Bigland, Eileen. Lord Byron. London: Cassell, 1956. Rptd. in
America under the title, Passion for Excitement; The Life
and Personality of the Incredible Lord Byron. New York:
Coward-McCann, 1956.
Reviews:
TLS, Sept. 28, 1956, p. 574.
Charles J. Rolo, Atlantic Monthly, CXCVIII (Nov., 1956),
105-106.
Carlos Baker, NYTBR, Dec. 23, 1956, p. 6.
Robert Halsband, SRL, XL (July 27, 1957), 19.
Willis Pratt, K-SJ, VI (Winter, 1957), 117-18.

Blanch, Lesley. "Loti-land," Cornhill Magazine, CLXVIII (Spring,
1956), 388-404. ["Exoticism" for Byron was "a medium, a
way to exalt and dramatize the tragedies of his character."]

Blunden, Edmund. "Lord Byron: Some Early Biographies," KSMB,
VII (1956), 1-3.

Brooks, Elmer L. "Byron and the London Magazine," K-SJ, V
(Winter, 1956), 49-67.

_____. "Don Juan: Early Moral Judgments," N&Q, CCI
(March, 1956), 117-18. [John Scott, not Harry Franklin in

Blackwood's, X (Aug., 1821), 107-15, was the first to defend Don Juan against the charge of immorality.]

Butler, E. M. Byron and Goethe: Analysis of a Passion. London: Bowes & Bowes, 1956.
Reviews:
Anthony Cronin, T&T, XXXVII (Nov. 3, 1956), 1335.
Listener, LVI (Nov. 8, 1956), 763.
TLS, Nov. 30, 1956, p. 714.
E. Muir, NSN, LII (Dec. 1, 1956), 718.
QR, CCXCV (Jan., 1957), 116-17.
W. H. Bruford, Cambridge Review, LXXVIII (Jan. 26, 1957), 307.
C. Brooke-Rose, London Magazine, IV (April, 1957), 19.
Howard Sergeant, CR, CXCI (June, 1957), 380-81.
Robin Atthill, English, XI (Autumn, 1957), 234-35.
L. A. Willoughby, German Life and Letters, XI (Oct., 1957), 72-73.

Byrns, Richard H. "Some Unpublished Works of De Quincey," PMLA, LXXI (Dec., 1956), 990-1003. [Passage on Byron.]

Cady, Edwin H. The Road to Realism: The Early Years 1837-1885 of William Dean Howells. Syracuse: Syracuse University Press, 1956. [On the publication of Harriet Beecher Stowe's article in the Atlantic Magazine.]

Court, Glyn. "Berlioz and Byron in Harold in Italy," Music Review, XVII (Aug., 1956), 229-36. [Negligible influence of Byron on Berlioz's life or work.]

Duncan, Robert W. "Byron and the London Literary Gazette," Boston University Studies in English, II (Winter, 1956), 240-50. [Its evaluation of Byron was rather confused.]

Gaster, Beryl. "Red Letter Days," CR, CXC (Dec., 1956), 357-60. [On Lady Blessington's meeting with Byron.]

Gittings, Robert. "Byron and Keats's Eremite," KSMB, VII (1956), 7-10. ["Bright Star" is related to Childe Harold passage.]

_____. The Mask of Keats, a Study of Problems. Cambridge, Mass.: Harvard University Press, 1956.

Gray, Duncan, and Violet Walker. "Benjamin Robert Haydon on Byron and Others," KSMB, VII (1956), 14-26. [Haydon's comments written in his copy of Medwin's Journal of the Conversations of Lord Byron.]

Green-Armytage, R. N. "T. N. Talfourd," TLS, May 18, 1956, p. 297. [Though Talfourd made a long speech supporting Wordsworth, his literary club voted Byron a greater poet.]

Grenier, Cynthia.   "The Art of Fiction: An Interview with William
    Faulkner," Accent, XVI (Summer, 1956), 167-77. [He had a
    taste for Byron.]

Griffith, Ben W., Jr.   "The Revolt of Islam and Byron's The Cor-
    sair," N&Q, CCI (June, 1956), 265. [Acknowledgment by
    Shelley of a borrowing from Byron's poem.]

Guthke, Karl S.   "C. M. Wieland and M. G. Lewis," Neophilologus,
    XL (1956), 231-33. [Lewis a link between German literature
    and Byron.]

Hough, Graham.   Two Exiles: Lord Byron and D. H. Lawrence.
    "Byron Foundation Lecture." Nottingham: University of
    Nottingham, 1956. Rptd. in Image and Experience: Studies
    in a Literary Revolution. London: Duckworth, 1960. Pp.
    133-59.

Hunt, Leigh.   Leigh Hunt's Criticism, eds. Lawrence Houston
    Houtchens and Carolyn Washburn Houtchens. New York:
    Columbia University Press, 1956.
    It contains:
    "Distressing Circumstances in High Life," pp. 95-102.   Rptd.
       from the Examiner, April 21, 1816, pp. 247-50.
    "Sketches of the Living Poets, Lord Byron," pp. 153-58.
       Rptd. from the Examiner, July 29, 1821, pp. 472-74.
    "Lord Byron, Mr. Moore and Mr. Leigh Hunt with Original
       Letters not in Mr. Moore's Work," pp. 302-43.   Rptd.
       from the Tatler, II (Jan. 11, 1831), 441-42.

Jones, Claude E.   "Byron and Others--A Russian Source," N&Q,
    CCI (July, 1956), 306. [A Russian article on Byron's activi-
    ties in the Greek revolt that can be found in Vol. 87 of the
    Krasnyi Arkhiv.]

Kahn, Sholom J.   "Whitman's 'Black Lucifer': Some Possible
    Sources," PMLA, LXXI (Dec., 1956), 932-44.

Kindilien, Carlin T.   American Poetry in the 1890's.   Providence:
    Brown University Press, 1956.   [Influence of Byron.]

Knight, G. Wilson.   "Colman and Don Leon," Twentieth Century,
    CLIX (June, 1956), 562-73. [Colman the author of this poem.]

Kristof, Ladis K.   "Lord Byron and the Monks of St. Lazarus,"
    Armenian Review, IX (Spring, 1956), 65-76.

Lee, Laurie.   "A Walk in Warsaw," Encounter, VI (Feb., 1956),
    5-13. [A Polish poet is editing a two-volume translation of
    the works of Lord Byron.]

Marchand, Leslie A.   "Byron's Lameness," KSMB, VII (1956), 32-
    42. [Byron had a club-foot.]

Nicolson, Harold. The English Sense of Humor and Other Essays. London: Constable, 1956.

Olney, Clarke. "Glenarvon Revisited," University of Kansas City Review, XXII (June, 1956), 271-76.

Overmeyer, Grace. America's First Hamlet. New York: New York University Press, 1956. [John Howard Payne's relation to Byron.]

Pageard, R., and G. W. Ribbans. "Heine and Byron in the Semanario Popular," Bulletin of Hispanic Studies, XXXIII (April, 1956), 78-86. [Byron noticed profusely in this periodical.]

Praz, Mario. The Hero in Eclipse in Victorian Fiction, translated from the Italian by Angus Davidson. London: Cumberlege, 1956.

Riewald, J. G. "Laureates in Elysium: Sir William Davenant and Robert Southey," ES, XXXVII (June, 1956), 133-40. [Parallels between Vision of Judgment and Flecknoe's poem on Davenant, Voyage.]

Rogers, Neville. Shelley at Work. Oxford: At the Clarendon Press, 1956.

Rogers, Samuel. The Italian Journal of Samuel Rogers, ed. J. R. Hale. London: Faber & Faber, 1956.

Rowell, George. The Victorian Theatre, a Survey. London: Oxford University Press, 1956. [The dramas of Byron.]

Ruskin, John. The Diaries of John Ruskin, eds. Joan Evans and John Howard Whitehouse. 3 vols. Oxford: Clarendon Press, 1956-1959. [Allusions to Byron.]

Rutherford, Andrew. "An Early Ms of English Bards and Scotch Reviewers," KSMB, VII (1956), 11-13.

St. John-Stevas, Norman. Obscenity and the Law. London: Secker & Warburg, 1956. [On the reaction to Don Juan, I and II.]

Shaw, Joseph T. "Byron, the Byronic Tradition of the Romantic Verse Tale in Russian, and Lermontov's Mtsyri," Indiana Slavic Studies, I (1956), 165-90.

Shipley, Joseph T. "Cain," Guide to Great Plays. Washington: Public Affairs Press, 1956. Pp. 130-31.

Trewin, John C. Verse Drama since 1800. ("Readers' Guides," 2nd ser., No. 8.) Cambridge, [Eng.]: Cambridge University Press, Published for the National Book League, 1956.

Watts, Charles Henry, II. Thomas Holley Chivers: His Literary
    Career and His Poetry. Athens: University of Georgia
    Press, 1956. [Byron's influence on Chivers is noted.]

Whatmough, Joshua. "A Byron Legend: Style and Authenticity,"
    Poetic, Scientific and Other Forms of Discourse. Berkeley,
    Calif.: University of California Press, 1956. Pp. 153-82.
    [A statistical study of the style of two letters Byron sent to
    James Dearden to determine their authenticity, might cast
    light on the legend prevalent in Rochdale that Byron went to
    England in 1823 to transact the sale of his Rochdale property.
    Legend also has it that Byron was in Rochdale with Mary Cha-
    worth in 1803.]

Whitley, Alvin. "Byron as 'Pacificator': A New Letter," KSMB,
    VII (1956), 4-6. [A letter to Lady Frances Wedderburn Web-
    ster, dated Genoa, Feb. 21, 1823.]

Willey, Basil. More 19th Century Studies. London: Chatto &
    Windus, 1956.

Wormhoudt, Arthur. "The Five Layer Structure of Sublimation
    and Literary Analysis," American Imago, XIII (Summer,
    1956), 205-19. [On Manfred.]

10. BALANCE RESTORED: RENAISSANCE
IN BIOGRAPHY AND CRITICISM,
1957-1972

1957

Abrams, M. H. "The Correspondent Breeze: A Romantic Metaphor," KR, XIX (Winter, 1957), 113-30.

Adelman, Seymour. "The Pugilist and the Poet," General Magazine and Historical Chronicle, LIX (Spring, 1957), 7-16.
[On Byron's interest in boxing.]

Altick, Richard D. The English Common Reader: A Social History
of the Mass Reading Public 1800-1900. Chicago: University
of Chicago Press, 1957.

Blumenthal, Walter Hart. "Barbs and Bludgeons," American Book
Collector, VII (June, 1957), 23-31. [Mentions Henry Brougham's attack on Hours of Idleness.]

Brand, Charles Peter. Italy and the English Romantics; the
Italianate Fashion in Early 19th Century England. Cambridge,
[Eng.]: Cambridge University Press, 1957.

Briggs, Thomas Henry. Poetry and Its Enjoyment. New York:
Columbia University Press, 1957.

Clive, John. Scotch Reviewers: The "Edinburgh Review," 1802-
1815. Cambridge, Mass. : Harvard University Press; London: Faber, 1957.

Frye, Northrop. The Anatomy of Criticism. Princeton: Princeton University Press, 1957.

Gauss, Christian F. "Byron," The Papers of Christian Gauss,
eds. Katherine Gauss Jackson and Hiram Haydn. New York:
Random House, 1957. Pp. 177-88. [A lecture given Nov. 5,
1914.]

Gell, Sir William. Reminiscences of Sir Walter Scott's Residence
in Italy, 1832, ed. James C. Corson. London: Nelson,
1957.

437

George, Daniel [pseud. for Daniel George Bunting] (ed.). A Book of Anecdotes Illustrating Varieties of Experience in the Lives of the Illustrious and the Obscure. London: Hulton Press, 1957.

Gettman, Royal A. "Colburn-Bentley and the March of Intellect," Studies in Bibliography, IX (1957), 197-213. [Touches on what went on behind the scenes before the publication of Galt's Life of Byron for the National Library.]

Gillies, Alexander. Goethe's "Faust:" An Interpretation. Oxford: Blackwell, 1957.

Grigson, Geoffrey, and Charles Harvard Gibbs-Smith (eds.). Ideas: A Volume of Ideas, Notions and Emotions, Clear or Confused, Which Have Moved the Minds of Men. New York: Hawthorn Books, 1957.

Houtchens, Carolyn Washburn, and Lawrence Huston Houtchens, eds. The English Romantic Poets and Essayists; a Review of Research and Criticism. New York: Modern Language Association of America, 1957. Rpt. New York University Press, 1966.

Joyce, James. Letters of James Joyce, ed. Stuart Gilbert. Vol. I. New York: Viking, 1957.

Jump, J. D. "Lord Byron," From Blake to Byron, ed. Boris Ford. ("The Pelican Guide to English Literature," Vol. V.) Harmondsworth: Penguin, 1957. Pp. 240-57.

Kaser, David. Messrs. Carey and Lee of Philadelphia: A Study in the History of the Booktrade. Philadelphia: Pennsylvania University Press, 1957. [On American reprints of Byron's works.]

Kermode, Frank. Romantic Image. London: Routledge and K. Paul, 1957.

Knight, G. Wilson. Lord Byron's Marriage, The Evidence of Asterisks. London: Routledge and Kegan Paul; New York: Macmillan, 1957.
    Reviews:
    John Jones, NSN, LIII (Feb. 2, 1957), 147-48.
    Listener, LVII (Feb. 7, 1957), 237.
    John Davenport, Spectator, CXCVIII (Feb. 8, 1957), 180, 182.
    TLS, Feb. 8, 1957, p. 82. Cf. Malcolm Elwin, ibid., March 1, 1957, p. 129. [Takes issue with this review.]
    The Reviewer, ibid., March 1, 1957, p. 129. [Answers Elwin.]
    A.[nthony] P.[owell]. Punch, CCXXXII (Feb. 27, 1957), 313.
    Eric Gillet, National and English Review, CXLVIII (March, 1957), 145.

Richard Rees, Twentieth Century, CLXI (March, 1957), 308,
   310.
C. Brooke-Rose, London Magazine, IV (April, 1957), 61-64.
V. de Sola Pinto, N&Q, CCII (April, 1957), 182.
Harry Moore, NR, CXXXVI (April 29, 1957), 18-19.
Gerald Meath, Blackfriars, XXXVIII (June, 1957), 275-76.
Robert Halsband, SRL, XL (July 27, 1957), 19.
Dallas Kenmore, Poetry Review, XLVIII (July-Sept., 1957),
   168.
Hardin McD. Goodman, English Journal, XLVI (Sept., 1957),
   371.
Andrew Rutherford, Essays in Criticism, VIII (Jan., 1958),
   88-97. Cf. G. Wilson Knight, ibid., VIII (Oct., 1958),
   453-56. [Answers some of Rutherford's "misrepresenta-
   tions."]
David Erdman, PQ, XXXVII (April, 1958), 147-48.
V. de Sola Pinto, RES, n.s., IX (May, 1958), 224-25.
Bruce R. McElderry, Personalist, XXXIX (Summer, 1958),
   318-19.
See also:
   L. M. Tristam, TLS, March 8, 1957, p. 145. [Requests
   material facetiously to prove that Byron never existed.]
   G. Wilson Knight, ibid., March 22, 1957, p. 177.
   [Prints a letter (Nov. 29, 1920) of the 10th Lord Byron
   who criticized Astarte and its conclusions.]

Langbaum, Robert. The Poetry of Experience: The Dramatic
   Monologue in Modern Literary Tradition. London: Chatto &
   Windus, 1957. [Critical comments on Byron.]

Larrabee, Stephen A. Hellas Observed: The American Experience
   of Greece, 1775-1865. New York: New York University
   Press, 1957.

Lavrin, Janko. "Some Notes on Lermontov's Romanticism." Slavonic and East European Review, XXXVI (Dec., 1957), 68-
   80. [On Lermontov's debt to Byron.]

Lewitter, L. R. "Mazeppa," History Today, VII (Sept., 1957),
   590-96.

McCollom, William G. Tragedy. New York: Macmillan, 1957.
   [On Marino Faliero.]

Marchand, Leslie A. Byron: A Biography. New York: Knopf,
   1957.
   Reviews:
      Carlos Baker, NYTBR, Oct. 20, 1957, pp. 1, 44.
      Samuel Chew, NYHTBR, Oct. 20, 1957, p. 3.
      DeLancey Ferguson, SRL, XL (Oct. 26, 1957), 20-21.
      Peter Quennell, Nation, CLXXXV (Nov. 9, 1957), 326-27.
      Nora Magid, Commonweal, LXVII (Nov. 29, 1957), 234-36.
      Leon Edel, NR, CXXXVII (Dec. 2, 1957), 17-18.

Iris Origo, K-SJ, VII (Winter, 1958), 97-100.
Francis G. Townsend, English Journal, XLVII (Feb., 1958),
    104.
TLS, March 7, 1958, pp. 121-22. Cf. Myra Curtis, ibid.,
    March 14, 1958, p. 139. [Refers to this review.] The
    reviewer, ibid., March 14, 1958, p. 139. [Answer to
    Miss Curtis.] G. Wilson Knight, ibid., March 21, 1957,
    p. 153. [Suggests that Marchand has been misguided about
    the incest.]
John Jones, NSN, LV (March 15, 1958), 341-42.
Listener, LIX (March 20, 1958), 509-10.
W. W. Robson, Spectator, CC (March 21, 1958), 365.
David V. Erdman, PQ, XXXVII (April, 1958), 148-49.
W. H. Auden, New Yorker, XXXIV (April 26, 1958), 133-36,
    139-46, 149-50.
A. Noyes, CR, CXCIII (May, 1958), 232-38.
E. Lovell, Jr., SAQ, LVII (Summer, 1958), 325-32.
John Wain, London Magazine, V (July, 1958), 44-57. Rptd.
    as "Byron: The Search for Identity," in his Essays on
    Literature and Ideas. London: Macmillan, 1963, pp. 85-
    102.
Louis Simpson, Hudson Review, XI (Autumn, 1958), 451-54.
Carl R. Woodring, VQR, XXXIV (Winter, 1958), 138-40.

Marshall, William H. "The Misdating of a Letter: An Exonera-
    tion of Byron," N&Q, CCII (March, 1957), 122-23. [From
    duplicity towards the Hunts.]

Miller, Perry, Charles Poore, and Lyman Bryson. "Lord Byron,
    Don Juan," Invitation to Learning Reader, VI (1957), 371-78.

Morton, Henry C. V. A Traveller in Rome. New York: Dodd,
    Mead; London: Methuen, 1957.

*Mukoyama, Yasuko. "The Historical Background of Byron's Sar-
    danapalus," Journal of Aoyama Gakuin Women's Junior Col-
    lege, No. 8 (Nov., 1957), 1-12.

Origo, Iris. A Measure of Love. New York: Pantheon Books,
    1957.
    It contains:
        "Allegra," pp. 15-87, a reprint, with revisions, of her book,
        Allegra, London: Hogarth Press, 1935.
        "The Lady in the Gondola," pp. 91-114, a sketch of Byron's
        friend, Countess Maria Benzon.

R., S. "Byron Queries," N&Q, CCII (Aug., 1957), 360. [Where
    is printed the letter that Byron wrote purporting to be Fletcher
    that Crabb Robinson mentions in his diary? Also inquires
    about "Lines Written by a Miss Baker."] Cf. C. A. T.,
    ibid., CCIII (Feb., 1958), 89. [Letter written by Byron pur-
    porting to be his valet was to John Cam Hobhouse, from
    Venice, June, 1818, printed in Prothero's Letters and Journals,

IV, 234-36. The pamphlet by Miss Baker is "Lines Addressed to a Noble Lord, by one of the Small Fry. "]

Robson, W. W. "Byron as Poet," Proceedings of the British
Academy, XLIII (1957), 25-62. Rptd. London: Oxford Uni-
versity Press, 1957; Critical Essays, London: Routledge &
K. Paul, 1966, pp. 148-88.

Sanders, Charles Richard. Lytton Strachey, His Mind and Art.
New Haven: Yale University Press, 1957.

Scott, A. F. The Poet's Craft: A Course in the Critical Appreciation of Poetry. Cambridge, [Eng.]: Cambridge University
Press, 1957.

Short, Clarice. "Joyce's 'A Little Cloud,'" MLN, LXXII (April,
1957), 275-78. [On the similarities between Byron's Prisoner
of Chillon and Joyce's Chandler.]

Siegfried, Joan. "Romantic Artist as a Portrait Painter," Marsyas:
Studies in the History of Art, VIII (1957-1959), 34-42. [Dis-
cusses Gericault's "Imagined Portrait of Lord Byron" now at
Montpellier Museum.]

Steffan, Truman G. , and Willis W. Pratt (eds.). Byron's "Don
Juan": A Variorum Edition. 4 vols. Austin, Texas: Uni-
versity of Texas Press, 1957.
Reviews:
Calvin C. Smith, Southwest Review, XLII (Autumn, 1957),
354-56.
John Ciardi, SRL, XL (Dec. 28, 1957), 14-15.
Samuel Chew, K-SJ, VII (Winter, 1958), 100-102.
VQR, XXXIV (Winter, 1958), xvi.
TLS, March 7, 1958, pp. 121-22.
Edward E. Bostetter, PQ, XXXVII (April, 1958), 149-50.
Carl R. Woodring, JEGP, LVII (April, 1958), 348-55.
Helen Gardner, London Magazine, V (July, 1958), 58-65.
Leslie Marchand, MLN, LXXIV (May, 1959), 453-55.

Strout, Alan L. "Blunders about Blackwood," N&Q, CCII (June,
1957), 263-65. [Maginn did not write the poetical "Critique
of Lord Byron" of April 1822. Strout attributes it to Colonel
John Matthews.]

Taplin, Gardner B. The Life of Elizabeth Barrett Browning. New
Haven: Yale University Press; London: John Murray, 1957.

Taylor, Robert H. Authors at Work. New York: Grolier Club,
1957. [Reproduces excerpts from several Byron MSS.]

Thorpe, Clarence C. , Carlos Baker, and Bennett Weaver (eds.).
The Major English Romantic Poets: A Symposium in Reappraisal. Carbondale: Southern Illinois University Press,

1957.
It contains:
  Ernest J. Lovell, Jr., "Irony and Image in Byron's Don
  Juan," pp. 129-48.
  Leslie A. Marchand, "Byron and the Modern Spirit," pp. 162-
  66.
  Willis W. Pratt, "Byron and Some Current Patterns of
  Thought," pp. 149-61.

Trewin, John C. The Night Has Been Unruly. London: Hale,
  1957. [Touches on some of the theatrical connections of Byron.]

Varma, Devendra P. The Gothic Flame, Being a History of the
  Gothic Novel. London: Barker, 1957.

Wilson, Milton. Shelley's Later Poetry: A Study of His Prophetic
  Imagination. New York: Columbia University Press, 1957.

Woodring, Carl. "Byron in Musical Comedy," K-SJ, VI (Winter,
  1957), 2. [A Paris performance of Les Amours de Don Juan.]

Woodward, Helen Beal. "The Smitten Female," Mademoiselle,
  XLV (July, 1957), 64-68, 103-104. [Byron, the most romantic of men idolized by women.]

Worthington, Mabel P. "Byron's Don Juan: Certain Psychological
  Aspects," Literature and Psychology, VII (Aug., 1957), 50-
  55. [In Don Juan Byron gave expression to the myth of growing up.]

Wright, Herbert G. Boccaccio in England from Chaucer to Tennyson. London: Athlone, 1957. [Passing references.]

                                1958

Agnew, L. R. C. "In Search of Jeffrey," American Book Collect-
  or, VIII, No. 5, (1958), 3-11.

Battenhouse, Henry M. "Lord Byron," English Romantic Writers.
  Great Neck, New York: Barrows Educational Series, 1958.
  Pp. 125-63.

Beardsley, Monroe C. Aesthetics: Problems in the Philosophy of
  Criticism. New York: Harcourt, Brace, 1958.

Birkenhead, Sheila. "In the Days of Lewis and Byron," Peace in
  Piccadilly. The Story of Albany. New York: Reynal; London: Hamilton, 1958. Pp. 69-115.

Boyd, Elizabeth. Byron's "Don Juan." London: Routledge &
  Kegan Paul; New York: Humanities Press, 1958. [A reissue
  of a book published in 1945 by Rutgers University.]

Bridge, A. "Byron's The Corsair," Book Collector, VII (Summer, 1958), 191. [Variants of the first edition.]

Britton, Karl. "John Stuart Mill: A Debating Speech on Wordsworth, 1829," Cambridge Review, LXXIX (March 8, 1958), 418-20, 423. [The MS notes of Mill's speech have been found and are here discussed as are his remarks on Byron.]

Carb, Nathan R. E., Jr. "Byron as Critic: Not a Neoclassicist," West Virginia University Bulletin Philological Papers, XI (May, 1958), 16-21. [Byron lacks consistency to be classed as a neoclassic critic.]

Carnall, Geoffrey. "Matthew Arnold's 'Great Critical Effort,'" Essays in Criticism, VIII (July, 1958), 256-68. [Questions Arnold's dictum on Byron.]

Corrigan, Beatrice. "The Byron-Hobhouse Translation of Pellico's Francesca," Italica, XXXV (Dec., 1958), 235-41.

Craig, Alec. "The Law and Lord Byron," Essays in Criticism, VIII (July, 1958), 345-46. [Prompted by Knight's Lord Byron's Marriage.

De Beer, Gavin. "A Byron Letter at Leningrad," TLS, May 16, 1958, p. 269. [Reproduces a letter to Mr. Trevannion, dated Oct. 15, 1816.]

Elwin, Malcolm. Landor: A Replevin. London: MacDonald, 1958.

Everett, Edwin M. "Lord Byron's Lakist Interlude," SP, LV (Jan., 1958), 62-75. [On the parallels between "The Prisoner of Chillon" and The Ancient Mariner.]

Farwell, Beatrice. "Sources for Delacroix's 'Death of Sardanapalus,'" Art Bulletin, XL (March, 1958), 66-71.

Foakes, R. A. The Romantic Assertion. A Study of the Language of 19th Century Poetry. New Haven: Yale University Press; London: Methuen, 1958.

Franzero, Carlo Maria. Beau Brummell: His Life and Times. New York: The John Day Co., 1958. [Byron's and Brummell's idea of each other.]

Grandsen, K. W. "The Spoken Word: Auden on Byron," Listener, LIX (May 22, 1958), 876. [A summary of a lecture on Don Juan given in Oxford on May 12, 1958.]

Gröndahl, I. C. "Henrik Wergeland and England," German Life and Letters, XI (July, 1958), 268-92. [Byron influenced this Norwegian poet.]

Hale, Leslie. John Philpot Currant: His Life and Times. London: Cape, 1958.

Hemlow, Joyce. The History of Fanny Burney. Oxford: Clarendon Press, 1958. [A remark of Byron on Fanny Burney.]

Herold, J. Christopher. Mistress to an Age: A Life of Madame de Staël. Indianapolis: The Bobbs-Merrill Co., 1958.

Hopkins, Kenneth. Portraits in Satire. London: Barrie Books, 1958. ["Last large-scale satirist in English."]

Howes, Alan B. Yorick and the Critics: Sterne's Reputation in England, 1760-1868. ("Yale Studies in English," Vol. 139.) New Haven: Yale University Press, 1958.

Jamison, William A. "Arnold and the Romantics," Anglistica, X (1958), 58-83. [Arnold's judgment of Byron.]

Kinghorn, Alexander M. "The Poet as Philosopher," Dalhousie Review, XXXVII (Winter, 1958), 348-56. [Byron professed a distaste for philosophy.]

Kovalev, Y. V. "The Literature of Chartism," Victorian Studies, II (Dec., 1958), 117-38. [Byron had some influence on Chartist literature.]

Kroeber, A. L. "Parts of Speech in Periods of Poetry," PMLA, LXXIII (Sept., 1958), 309-14.

Liljegren, S. B. "Lord Byron and Greece," Revue de Litterature Comparée, XXXII (janvier-mars, 1958), 66-73.

McAleer, Edward C. The Sensitive Plant, a Life of Lady Mount Cashell. Chapel Hill: The University of North Carolina Press, 1958. [Claire Clairmont and Byron in Italy.]

Marchand, Leslie A. (ed.) "Introduction," Don Juan. Boston: Houghton Mifflin, 1958. Pp. v-xiv.

Melchiori, Giorgio. Byron and Italy. "Byron Foundation Lecture." Nottingham: University of Nottingham Press, 1958.

Moore, Doris L. "The Burning of Byron's Memoirs: An Account Based on Published and Unpublished Evidence," Cornhill Magazine, CLXX (Winter, 1958-1959), 215-55. Rptd. in Atlantic Monthly, CCIV (Aug., 1959), 27-37.

Mudrick, Marvin. "Mickiewicz and the Last Epic," Spectrum, II (Spring-Summer, 1958), 83-95. [On Byron's influence on Mickiewicz.]

Nitchie, Elizabeth. "Byron, Madame de Staël and Albertino,"
K-SJ, VII (Winter, 1958), 7-8.

Powys, John Cowper. Letters of John Cowper Powys to Louis
Wilkinson, 1935-1956. London: MacDonald, 1958.

Pratt, Willis W. "A Decade of Byron Scholarship, 1946-1956. A
Selective Survey," K-SJ, VII (Winter, 1958), 69-85.

Praz, Mario. The Flaming Heart. Garden City, N.Y. : Doubleday Anchor, 1958.

Quinlan, Maurice J. "Byron's Manfred and Zoroastrianism,"
JEGP, LVII (Oct. , 1958), 726-38.

R. , S. "Medora Leigh," N&Q, CCIII (March, 1958), 105.

Rollins, Hyder Edward. The Letters of John Keats, 1814-1821.
2 vols. Cambridge, Mass. : Harvard University Press, 1958.

Ross, T. J. "Passion--Moral and Otherwise," NR, CXXXIX (Aug.
18, 1958), 23-26. [Byron used as a disreputable symbol of
sex.]

Ryals, Clyde de L. "Toward a Definition of Decadent as Applied
to British Literature of the 19th Century," Journal of Aesthetics and Art Criticism, XVII (Sept. , 1958), 85-92. [Touches
on the Byronic hero.]

Sutherland, James. English Satire. Cambridge, [Eng.]: Cambridge University Press, 1958. ["His ultimate limitation as
a satirist is that the only thing that interested him profound-
ly was himself. " Finds The Vision of Judgment his finest
work.]

Taplin, Garner B. "Critical Essays on English Writers in the
Southern Literary Messenger," Virginia in History and Tra-
dition, ed. R. C. Simonini, Jr. Farmville, Va. : Longwood
College, 1958. Pp. 43-64.

Wallace, J. W. "The Reference Paper and In-class Writing,"
College English, XIX (Jan. , 1958), 166-67. [Canto I of Don
Juan used as the basis for a class theme.]

Wiedlin, Sister M. Ethel. "Horatian Echoes in Byron's Don Juan,"
Classical Bulletin, XXXIV (Feb. , 1958), 44-45. [In Don Juan
Byron borrowed, revised, and quoted Horatian texts.]

Wittig, Kurt. The Scottish Tradition in Literature. Edinburgh:
Oliver & Boyd, 1958.

1959

Adams, J. Donald. "Speaking of Books," NYTBR, Jan. 25, 1959,
     p. 2. [Likenesses between Byron and Burns.]

Baender, Paul. "Mark Twain and the Byron Scandal," AL, XXX
     (Jan., 1959), 467-85. [About six unsigned editorials written
     for the Buffalo Express on the Stowe-Byron controversy.]

Bigland, Eileen. Mary Shelley. London: Cassell, 1959.

Blunden, Edmund C. "Byron," Three Young Poets: Critical
     Sketches of Byron, Shelley and Keats. Tokyo: Kenkyusha,
     1959. Pp. 1-30.

Buckley, Vincent. Poetry and Morality: Studies in the Criticism
     of Matthew Arnold, T. S. Eliot and F. R. Leavis. London:
     Chatto & Windus, 1959.

Coles, William A. "Magazine and Other Contributions by Mary
     Russell Mitford and Thomas Noon Talfourd," Studies in Bib-
     liography, XII (1959), 218-26. [Talfourd wrote a review of
     Werner and another of the Liberal in the Lady's Magazine,
     and one of Sardanapalus, The Two Foscari and Cain in the
     London Magazine.]

Cruttwell, Patrick. "Makers and Persons," Hudson Review, XII
     (Winter, 1959-1960), 487-507. [Byron wrote at his best when
     he abandoned his aspiration to withdraw himself from himself,
     when 'he gave up the Childe Harold poses and the attempts at
     drama and simply wrote down his moods as they came to him
     in the shameless self-parading of Don Juan."]

Currie, Haver C. "Bertrand Russell on Values, with Allusions to
     Lord Byron," Personalist, XL (Winter, 1959), 13-21.

Dakin, Douglas. British Intelligence of Events in Greece, 1824-
     1827: A Documentary Collection. Athens: Menas Myrtides,
     1959.

Drew, Elizabeth. Poetry: A Modern Guide to Its Understanding
     and Enjoyment. New York: Norton, 1959. Also in paper-
     back: Dell & Co., 1959.

Drew, Fraser. "Lord Byron in Montpelier," Vermont History,
     XXVII (Jan., 1959), 18-21. [History of Byron's sword.]

Eby, Lois. Marked for Adventure. Philadelphia: Chilton Co.,
     1959. [Byron, in spite of his handicap, found success.]

Edwards, John Hamilton, and William W. Vasse. Annotated Index
     to the Cantos of Ezra Pound, Cantos I-LXXXIV. Berkeley,
     Calif.: California University Press, 1959.

Emden, Cecil Stuart. "Reckless Brilliance," Poets in Their
    Letters. London: Oxford University Press, 1959. Pp. 121-
    44.

Faverty, Frederic Everett. "Byron's Poetical Works," Your Lite-
    rary Heritage. Philadelphia: Lippincott, 1959. Pp. 98-100.

Fraser, G. S. Vision and Rhetoric: Studies in Modern Poetry.
    London: Faber, 1959.

Frye, Northrop. "Lord Byron," Major British Writers, ed. G. B.
    Harrison. 2 vols. New York: Harcourt Brace, 1959. Vol.
    II, pp. 149-61. Rptd. in his Fables of Identity: Studies in
    Poetic Mythology. New York: Harcourt Brace, 1963. Pp.
    168-89.

Griggs, Earl Leslie. Letters of Samuel Taylor Coleridge. 4 vols.
    Oxford: At the Clarendon Press, 1959.

Heppenstall, Rayner. "Two Voices: England and the Rest," TLS,
    Aug. 7, 1959, pp. xxvi-xxxvii. [The English and the Scots
    both claim Byron.]

Hodgart, Matthew J. C., and Mabel P. Worthington. Song in the
    Works of James Joyce. New York: Columbia University
    Press, 1959. ["When We Two Parted," quoted in Finnegans
    Wake.]

Holubnychy, Lydia. "Mazeppa in Byron's Poem and in History,"
    Ukrainian Quarterly, XV (Dec., 1959), 336-45.

Knight, G. Wilson. "Byron's Dramatic Verse," TLS, Feb. 20,
    1959, p. 97.

_____. "Shakespeare and Byron's Plays," Shakespeare-Jahrbuch,
    XCV (1959), 82-97.

Lavrin, Janko. Lermontov. London: Bowes & Bowes, 1959.

Leathers, Victor. British Entertainers in France. Toronto: Uni-
    versity of Toronto Press, 1959. [Mention of performance of
    works or adaptations of works by Byron.]

Levitt, John, and Joan Levitt. The Spell of Words. London:
    Darwen Finlayson, 1959. [Gives origin of the name "Byron."]

McDonald, W. V., Jr. "Byron at Chillon," N&Q, CCIV (March,
    1959), 87. [Mentions the report of Byron's visit to Chillon
    made by Henry D. Inglis in his Switzerland, the South of
    France and the Pyrenees in 1830.]

Manning, Clarence. "Mazeppa in English Literature," Ukrainian
    Quarterly, XV (March, 1959), 133-44.

Marchand, Leslie A. "John Hunt as Byron's Publisher," K-SJ,
    VIII (Autumn, 1959), 119-32. [Uses much new manuscript
    material.]

Marshall, William H. "Eliot's The Waste Land, 182," Explicator,
    XVII (March, 1959), item 42. ["By the waters of Leman I
    sat down and wept," indebted to Byron's "By the Rivers of
    Babylon We Sat Down and Wept," and to Childe Harold, III,
    lviii and lxxxv, and to "The Prisoner of Chillon."]

_____. "Some Byron Comments on Pope and Boileau," PQ,
    XXXVIII (April, 1959), 252-53.

Moore, Doris L. "Byron, Leigh Hunt and the Shelleys. New
    Light On Certain Old Scandals," KSMB, X (1959), 20-29.
    [Tries to vindicate Byron.]

_____. The Great Byron Adventure. Philadelphia: J. B. Lip-
    pincott, 1959. [A reprint of articles that appeared in the
    London Sunday Times.]

Nabokov, Vladimir. "The Servile Path," On Translation, ed.
    Reuben A. Brower. Cambridge, Mass.: Harvard University
    Press, 1959. Pp. 97-110. [Pushkin's indebtedness to By-
    ron.]

Nicolson, Marjorie Hope. Mountain Gloom and Mountain Glory:
    The Development of the Aesthetics of the Infinite. Ithaca:
    Cornell University Press, 1959.

Nietzche, Friedrich. Nietzche: Unpublished Letters, ed. Kurt F.
    Leidecker. New York: Philosophical Library, 1959.

Nuñez, Estuardo. "The Byrons and America," Americas, XI
    (June, 1959), 28-29. [Through his grandfather's experiences,
    America seemed to Byron the essence of all that was fresh
    and alive in nature. It also appealed to his romanticism.]

O'Casey, Sean. "The Harp in the Air Still Sings," NYTM, Jan.
    11, 1959, pp. 11, 68-69. [Joy in the work of Byron.]

Pinto, Vivian de Sola. "Byron," Chambers's Encyclopaedia. Lon-
    don: George Newnes, Ltd., 1959. New edition. Vol. II,
    pp. 730-31.

Preyer, Robert. "Robert Browning: A Reading of the Early Nar-
    ratives," ELH, XXVI (Dec., 1959), 531-48.

Quennell, Peter (ed.). "Introduction," Byron: Selected Verse and
    Prose Works, Including Letters and Extracts from Lord By-
    ron's Journals and Diaries. London: Collins, 1959. Pp. 9-
    80.
    Review:
    TLS, Sept. 25, 1959, p. 546.

Rantavvara, Irma. "On Romantic Imagery in Virginia Woolf's The
    Waves with Special Reference to Antithesis," Neuphilologische
    Mitteilungen, LX (1959), 72-89.

Rapin, René. "Lausanne and Some English Writers," Etudes de
    Lettres, 2nd ser., II (July-Sept., 1959), 91-121.

Ridge, George Ross. The Hero in French Romantic Literature.
    Athens, Ga.: University of Georgia Press, 1959.

Ross, Alan. "In the Wake of the Don Juan," Saturday Book, No.
    19, (1959), 161-71. [Memories of Shelley and Byron while
    cruising along the Spezia Riviera.]

Semaan, Angele Botros. "Themes of Emily Brontë's Poetry,"
    Cairo Studies in English, 1959, pp. 118-34.

Siegrist, Ottmar K. "Timbale: An Antedating," N&Q, CCIV (Oct.,
    1959), 375. [The word Timbale was used in Don Juan fifty-
    six years before it was recorded in the OED.]

Spencer, T. J. B. Byron and the Greek Tradition. "Byron Foun-
    dation Lecture." Nottingham: University of Nottingham Press,
    1959.

Stendhal, Count of [pseud. for Marie Henri Beyle]. Selected
    Journalism from the English Reviews by Stendhal, with Trans-
    lations of Other Critical Writings, ed. and with an introduc-
    tion by Geoffrey Strickland. New York: Grove Press, Inc.,
    1959.
    It contains:
    "Memories of Lord Byron," pp. 294-99.
    "Lord Byron in Italy," pp. 300-321. [From Revue de Paris,
    1830.]

Stevenson, L. " 'My Last Duchess' and Parisina," MLN, LXXIV
    (June, 1959), 489-92.

Swinburne, Algernon Charles. The Swinburne Letters, ed. Cecil
    Y. Lang. 6 vols. New Haven: Yale University Press,
    1959-1962.

Thomas, Lowell. "Byron," The Vital Spark: 101 Outstanding
    Lives. Garden City, N.Y.: Doubleday & Co., 1959. Pp.
    408-11.

*Tomlinson, T. B. "Don Juan's Morals," Melbourne Critical Re-
    view, No. 2, (1959), 47-56.

Untermeyer, Louis. "Byron," Lives of the Poets: The Story of
    One Thousand Years of English and American Poetry. New
    York: Simon and Schuster, 1959. Pp. 383-417.

Weinstein, Leo. The Metamorphoses of Don Juan. ("Stanford
   Studies in Language and Literature," No. 18.) Stanford:
   Stanford University Press, 1959.

Wellek, René. "Hippolyte Taine's Literary Theory and Criticism,"
   Criticism, I (Winter, 1959), 1-18; ibid. , I (Spring, 1959),
   123-38.

West, Paul. "Byronic Romance and Nature's Frailty," Dalhousie
   Review, XXXIX (Summer, 1959), 219-29. [Evaluates Byron's
   romances.]

_____. "Byron's Farce with Language," Twentieth Century,
   CLXV (Feb. , 1959), 138-51. [Byron and Baudelaire.]

Wilson, Colin Henry. The Age of Defeat. London: Gollancz,
   1959. [On Byron's heroes.]

Zimmerman, Robert Lee. "Byron in The Gentleman's Magazine,"
   N&Q, CCIV (Feb. , 1959), 77. [J. C. Blaby's "Lines Written
   on Perusing Lord Byron's Poem Entitled Childe Harold" that
   Chew had found in the scrap-book of the British Museum is
   in The Gentleman's Magazine, Feb. , 1813.]

                              1960

Abrams, M. H. (ed.). English Romantic Poets. New York: Oxford University Press, 1960.
   It contains:
      R. Bottrall, "Byron: The Colloquial Tradition in English
      Poetry," pp. 210-27. Rptd. from Criterion, XVIII (Jan. ,
      1939), 204-224.
      T. S. Eliot, "Byron," pp. 196-209. Rptd. from From Anne
      to Victoria, ed. Bonamy Dobrée, London: Cassell, 1937,
      pp. 601-619.
      Ernest J. Lovell, Jr. , "Irony and Image in Don Juan," pp.
      228-46. Rptd. from The Major English Romantic Poets,
      A Symposium in Reappraisal, eds. Clarence C. Thorpe, et
      alles, Carbondale: Southern Illinois University Press, 1957,
      pp. 129-48.

Atherton, James S. The Books at the Wake: A Study of Literary
   Allusions in James Joyce's "Finnegans Wake. " New York:
   Viking, 1960.

Ball, Albert. "Byron and Charles Churchill: Further Parallels,"
   N&Q, CCV (March, 1960), 105-107. Cf. Andrew Rutherford,
   ibid. , CCV (Aug. , 1960), 315-16. [Corrects Ball's article
   on one point.]

Beaty, Frederick L. "Byron and the Story of Francesca da Rimi-
   ni," PMLA, LXXV (Sept. , 1960), 395-401. [Identifies Augusta
   Leigh with Julia and Byron with Juan.]

Behrman, S. N.   Portrait of Max: An Intimate Memoir of Sir Max
    Beerbohm.   New York: Random House, 1960. [Comments on
    Byron.]

Bostetter, Edward E.   "Byron and the Politics of Paradise,"
    PMLA, LXXV (Dec., 1960), 571-76. [A study of Cain.]

Bradford, Ernle.   The Wind of the Island.   New York: Harcourt,
    Brace, 1960.   [About a letter of Byron he saw in Palermo.]

Browne, Denis.   "The Problem of Byron's Lameness," Proceedings
    of the Royal Society of Medicine, LIII (June, 1960), 440-42.

Cammell, Charles Richard.   "Byron," The Name on the Wall.
    London: Arthur Barker, 1960.   Pp. 119-32.   [The plaque at
    No. 4 Bennet St., St. James, gave occasion to this essay.]

Cannon, Garland.   "The Literary Place of Sir William Jones,"
    Journal of the Asiatic Society, II (1960), 47-61.   [On Jones's
    influence on Byron.]

Chancellor, Paul.   "British Bards and Continental Composers,"
    Musical Quarterly, XLVI (Jan., 1960), 1-11.   [On the influ-
    ence of Byron on Schumann and Berlioz.]

Coles, William A.   "Thomas Noon Talfourd on Byron and the
    Imagination," K-SJ, IX (Autumn, 1960), 99-113.   [Talfourd
    a thorough and coherent critic of Byron and others.]

Daiches, David.   "Byron," Critical History of English Literature.
    2 vols.   New York: Ronald Press, Co., 1960.   Vol. II,
    pp. 922-32.

Dakin, Arthur Hazard.   Paul Elmer More.   Princeton, N.J. :
    Princeton University Press, 1960.

Down, Robert B. (ed.).   The First Freedom: Liberty and Justice
    in the World of Books and Reading.   Chicago: American Li-
    brary Association, 1960.   [On some of the severe early criti-
    cism of Byron.]

Dwyer, J. Thomas.   "Checklist of Primary Sources of the Byron-
    Jeffrey Relationship," N&Q, CCV (July, 1960, 256-59.

Elliott, Inez (comp.).   Index to the Henry Crabb Robinson Letters
    in Dr. Williams's Library.   Being a supplement to the Index
    in Edith Morley's "Henry Crabb Robinson on Books and Their
    Writers."   London: Dr. Williams's Trust, 1960.

Emerson, Ralph Waldo.   The Journals and Miscellaneous Notebooks
    of Ralph Waldo Emerson, ed. William H. Gilman, et al.   5
    vols.   Cambridge, Mass.: Harvard University Press, 1960-
    1965.

"Fair Greece, Sad Relic," TLS, Aug. 5, 1960, p. 497. [On
    people who wrote about Greece, Byron among others.]

Fry, Humphrey. " 'Brunswick's Fated Chieftain,' " Atlantic Month-
    ly, CCV (Feb. , 1960), 77-79. [A humorous approach to the
    Waterloo stanzas in Childe Harold's Pilgrimage.]

Haydon, Benjamin Robert. Diary, ed. Willard B. Hope. 5 vols.
    Cambridge, Mass.: Harvard University Press, 1960.

Hillyer, Robert. In Pursuit of Poetry. New York: McGraw-Hill,
    1960.

Hudson, Derek. "John Murray II: A Great Publisher," The For-
    gotten King and Other Essays. London: Constable, 1960.
    Pp. 98-103.

Hussain, Imdad. "Beckford, Wainewright, De Quincey, and Ori-
    ental Exoticism," Venture, I (Sept. , 1960), 234-48.

_____. "Oriental Elements in English Poetry, 1784-1859,"
    Venture, I (June, 1960), 156-65.

Jerman, B. R. The Young Disraeli. Princeton: Princeton Uni-
    versity Press, 1960.

"John Wain and Byron," Soviet Survey, July-Sept. , 1960, p. 76.
    [Wain's review of Marchand's Byron an example of bourgeois
    criticism.]

Jovanovich, William. Now, Barrabas. New York: Harcourt
    Brace, 1960. [On John Murray's publication of Byron's
    works.]

King-Hele, Desmond. Shelley: His Thought and Work. London:
    Macmillan & Co. , 1960. Rptd. in America under the title,
    Shelley, the Man and the Poet. New York: Yoseloff, 1960.

Kleinfield, H. L. "Infidel on Parnassus: Lord Byron and the
    North American Review," New England Quarterly, XXXIII
    (June, 1960), 164-85.

Klinck, Carl F. "The Charivari and Levi Adams," Dalhousie Re-
    view, XL (Spring, 1960), 34-42. [Influence of Byron on a
    Canadian poet.]

Knieger, Bernard. "Samuel Rogers; Forgotten Maecenas," CLA
    Journal, III (March, 1960), 187-92. [Includes a reference to
    the duel between Moore and Jeffrey which Byron ridiculed.]

Kroeber, Karl. "Byron: The Adventurous Narrative," Romantic
    Narrative Art. Madison: University of Wisconsin, 1960.

Pp. 135-67. [Finds in Byron's narrative verse a novelistic quality similar to later 19th century prose fiction.]

Lister, John. "Byron's Lameness," New England Journal of Medicine, CCLXIII (Aug. 25, 1960), 400.

Lucas, Frank Laurence. "The Literature of Greek Travel," The Greatest Problem and Other Essays. London: Cassell, 1960. Pp. 79-97.

Macdonald, Dwight (ed.). Parodies: An Anthology from Chaucer to Beerbohm--and After. New York: Random House, 1960.

Macrae, Donald G. "Opiate of the People," TLS, Oct. 21, 1960, p. 677. [Thinks phrase comes from Don Juan, II, xxxiv.]

Marshall, William Harvey. Byron, Shelley, Hunt and "The Liberal." Philadelphia: Pennsylvania University Press; London: Oxford University Press, 1960.
Reviews:
TLS, July 8, 1960, p. 434.
David Bonnell Green, MP, LVIII (Feb., 1961), 219-20.
Edward E. Bostetter, SR, LXIX (Summer, 1961), 490-500.
R. W. King, MLR, LVI (July, 1961), 472-73.
G. Robert Stange, SEL, I (Autumn, 1961), 149-66.
J. D. Jump, RES, n.s., XII (Nov., 1961), 429-30.
Kenneth N. Cameron, MLN, LXXVI (Dec., 1961), 885-86.
C. A. Bodelsen, ES, XLVIII (April, 1967), 175-76.

Melchiori, Giorgio. "Excursus IV," The Whole Mystery of Art: Pattern into Poetry in the Work of W. B. Yeats. London: Routledge & K. Paul, 1960. Pp. 277-79. [On The Deformed Transformed.]

Morris, I. V. "Grillparzer's Impressions of the English," German Life and Letters, XIV (Oct., 1960-Jan., 1961), 1-15. [He was almost bewitched by Byron.]

Morris, James. Venice. London: Faber, 1960. Published in New York: Pantheon, 1960, under title, The World of Venice.

Moussa-Mahmoud, Fatma. "Beckford, Vathek and the Oriental Tale," William Beckford of Fonthill, 1760-1844: Bicentenary Essays, ed. Patma Moussa Mahmoud. ("Supplement to Cairo Studies in English." Cairo, 1960. Pp. 63-121.

Pedrini, Lura Nancy, and Duilio T. Pedrini. "Serpent Imagery and Symbolism in the Major English Romantic Poets: Blake, Wordsworth, Coleridge, Byron, Shelley, Keats," Psychiatric Quarterly Supplement, XXXIV (1960), 189-244; ibid., XXXV (1961), 36-99.

Phelps, Gilbert. "The Early Phases of British Interest in Russian
    Literature," Slavonic and East European Review, XXXVIII
    (June, 1960), 415-30.

Priestley, J. B. Literature and Western Man. New York: Harp-
    er, 1960.

Quennell, Peter. "The Mighty Dead," The Sign of the Fish. New
    York: Viking Press; London: Collins, 1960. Pp. 150-73.
    [About writing a Byron biography.]

_____ (ed.). "Preface," Byronic Thoughts, Maxims, Reflec-
    tions, Portraits from the Prose and Verse of Lord Byron,
    ed. Peter Quennell. New York: Harcourt Brace, 1960.
    Pp. 1-9.
    Reviews:
    TLS, Nov. 4, 1960, p. 712.
    G. S. Fraser, NSN, LX (Nov. 12, 1960), 749-50.
    J. Donald Adams, NYTBR, Jan. 15, 1961, p. 2.
    English Journal, L (April, 1961), 293.
    Timothy Rogers, English, XIII (Summer, 1961), 197-98.

Randel, William. "William Haygarth: Forgotten Philhellene,"
    K-SJ, IX (Autumn, 1960), 86-90.

Ridenour, George M. The Style of "Don Juan." ("Yale Studies in
    English," Vol. 144.) New Haven: Yale University Press,
    1960.
    Reviews:
    Patrick R. Penland, Library Journal, LXXXV (April 15,
        1960), 1593.
    V. de Sola Pinto, MLR, LVI (July, 1960), 413-14.
    D. M. S., English, XIII (Autumn, 1960), 116-17.
    Willis W. Pratt, K-SJ, X (Winter, 1961), 108-10.
    Geoffrey Johnson, Poetry Review, LII (Jan. -March, 1961),
        39-40.
    Edward E. Bostetter, MLN, LXXVI (April, 1961), 365-68.
    _____, PQ, XL (April, 1961), 176-77.
    Robert F. Gleckner, Criticism, III (Summer, 1961), 265-66.
    J. D. Jump, RES, n. s., XII (Aug., 1961), 308-309.
    G. Robert Stange, SEL, I (Autumn, 1961), 155.

Riley, Susan B. "Albert Pyke as an American Don Juan," Arkan-
    sas Historical Quarterly, XIX (Autumn, 1960), 207-24. [In-
    fluence of Byron on his Prose Sketches and Poems Written in
    the Western Country.]

Sarkar, Indira. "Affinities of Nabin Sen with Byron, Rousseau and
    Hugo," Calcutta Review, CLVII (Nov., 1960), 119-30.

_____. "The Themes of Nabin Sen's Poetry," Calcutta Review,
    CLVII (Oct., 1960), 1-9. [He is the Byron of Bengal.]

Sarmiento, Edward. "On the Interpretation of Don Quixote," Bulletin of Hispanic Studies, XXXVII (July, 1960), 146-53. [Byron had a limited understanding of Cervantes' purpose.]

Shaver, C. L. "Wordsworth on Byron: An Unpublished Letter to Southey," MLN, LXXV (June, 1960), 488-90. [Gives the text of the letter on the Byron-Southey quarrel.]

Shepherd, Geoffrey. "Byron's Mastery of Convention," Venture, I (Dec., 1960), 298-312. [A good general discussion of Don Juan.]

Sherwin, Oscar. Uncorking Old Sherry; The Life and Times of Richard Brinsley Sheridan. New York: Twayne Publishers, Inc., 1960.

Sinclair, Upton B. My Lifetime in Letters. Columbia, Mo.: University of Missouri Press, 1960.

Singer, Armand E. "Don Juan in America," Kentucky Foreign Language Quarterly, VII (1960), 226-32.

Spencer, Terence J. B. Byron and the Greek Tradition. "Byron Foundation Lecture." Nottingham: University of Nottingham Press, 1960.

Stead, William F. "Byron and Keats," TLS, June 17, 1960, p. 385. [Thinks that Werner is indebted to The Eve of St. Agnes.] Cf. F. C. Tighe, ibid., June 24, 1960, p. 401. [Points to Newstead Abbey as inspiration for this drama.]

Stuart, Dorothy Margaret. "Much Exposed to Authors," Essays by Divers Hands, n.s., XXX (1960), 19-35. [Byron and his attitude to the Duke of Wellington.]

Sypher, Wylie. Rococo to Cubism in Art and Literature. New York: Random House, 1960.

Thaler, Alvin. " 'With All Deliberate Speed': Byron, Shakespeare, et al.," Tennessee Studies in Literature, V (1960), 111-18. Rptd. in Tennessee Law Review, XXVII (Summer, 1960), 510-17. [Byron's use of this phrase.]

Waterman, Margaret. "Some Advice to Copy Writers," Atlantic Monthly, CCVI (Sept., 1960), 96. ["She Walks in Beauty" could be used as a commercial for nylons.]

Weevers, Theodoor. Poetry of the Netherlands in Its European Context, 1170-1930. London: Athlone Press, 1960.

Wells, Nannie Katharin. George Gordon, Lord Byron: A Scottish Genius. Abingdon-on-Thames: Abbey Press, 1960.

West, Paul. Byron and the Spoiler's Art. London: Chatto &
     Windus, 1960.
Reviews:
     Patricia Ball, Twentieth Century, CLXVIII (Oct. , 1960), 328-
     36.
John Hollander, Spectator, CCV (Oct. 14, 1960), 569.
Economist, CXCVII (Oct. 29, 1960), 458.
TLS, Nov. 4, 1960, p. 712.
G. S. Fraser, NSN, LX (Nov. 12, 1960), 749-50.
Michael Swan, Listener, LXIV (Dec. 24, 1960), 951.
William K. Seymour, Books and Bookmen, VI (Jan. , 1961),
     32-33.
Burton A. Robie, Library Journal, LXXXVI (Jan. 15, 1961),
     242.
J. D. Jump, Critical Quarterly, III (Spring, 1961), 92.
John Bayley, London Magazine, n. s. , I (April, 1961), 85-87.
Edward E. Bostetter, PQ, XL (April, 1961), 177-78.
_____ , SR, LXIX (Summer, 1961), 490-500.
Donald Reiman, SAQ, LX (Summer, 1961), 371-72.
Timothy Rogers, English, XII (Summer, 1961), 197-98.
R. S. Woof, UTQ, XXX (July, 1961), 417-18.
VQR, XXXVII (Autumn, 1961), cxxvi.
G. Robert Stange, SEL, I (Autumn, 1961), 154-55.
V. de Sola Pinto, MLR, LVI (Oct. , 1961), 595-97.
Frederick T. Wood, ES, XLII (Dec. , 1961), 402.
William H. Marshall, KSJ, XI (1962), 101-103.
Patrick Crutwell, Hudson Review, XIV (Winter, 1961-1962),
     598-606.
A. H. Elliott, RES, n. s. , XIII (Feb. , 1962), 82-83.
H. S. Whittier, Dalhousie Review, XLII (Summer, 1962), 254-
     56.

_____ . "Byron and the World of Things: An Ingenious Disre-
     gard, " KSMB, XI (1960), 21-32. [Imagery and language main-
     ly in Don Juan.]

Wolf, Edwin, II, and John F. Fleming. Rosenbach: A Biography.
     Cleveland: World Publishing Co. , 1960. [Experiences of a
     book collector.]

Wright, George Thaddeus. The Poet in the Poem: The Personae
     of Eliot, Yeats, and Pound. Berkeley: University of Cali-
     fornia Press, 1960. [Pp. 94-97 on Byron's self-mockery.]

                              1961

Adams, J. Donald. "Speaking of Books, " NYTBR, July 16, 1961,
     p. 2. [Hemingway, the Byron of our time.]

Barber, Giles. "Galignani's and the Publication of English Books
     in France from 1800 to 1852, " Library, 5th ser. , XVI (Dec. ,
     1961), 267-86. [Books much cheaper when produced in

France; e.g., Mazeppa sold at 2s 1d, as compared with the
English price of 5s 6d.]

Barlow, Samuel. "The Artist in Politics," The Astonished Muse.
New York: John Day, 1961. Pp. 201-74.

Barr, D. J. "Byron: An Allusion to Les Liaisons Dangereuses,"
N&Q, CCVI (Jan., 1961), 20. ["One gets tired of everything,
my angel," says Valmont in Byron's Journal. It comes from
"On s'ennuie de tout, mon Ange."]

Blackstone, Bernard. "Guilt and Retribution in Byron's Sea Poems,"
Review of English Literature, II (Jan., 1961), 58-69.

Bloom, Harold. "George Gordon, Lord Byron," The Visionary Company: A Reading of English Romantic Poetry. New York:
Doubleday, 1961. Pp. 232-74.

_____. "Napoleon and Prometheus: The Romantic Myth of Or-
ganic Energy," Yale French Studies, No. 26, (1961), 79-82.

Cacciatore, Vera. Shelley and Byron in Pisa. Turin: Edizioni
Rai Radiotelevisione Italiana, 1961.

Cameron, Kenneth Neill (ed.). Shelley and His Circle, 1773-1882.
8 vols. Cambridge, Mass.: Harvard University Press, 1961.

Chorley, Katharine. Arthur Hugh Clough: The Uncommitted Mind:
A Study of His Life and Poetry. Oxford: Clarendon Press,
1961. [Passing references.]

Conrad, Barnaby. Famous Last Words. Garden City, N.Y.:
Doubleday, 1961.

Courthion, Pierre. Romanticism, trans. Stuart Gilbert. Lausanne: Skira, 1961. [Discusses Delacroix's admiration for
Byron.]

Graham, Cuthbert. "The Boyhood of Byron," Listener, LXVI
(Oct. 26, 1961), 654-57. [Byron in Scotland.]

Jones, W. T. The Romantic Syndrome: Toward a New Method in
Cultural Anthropology and History of Ideas. The Hague:
Nijhoff, 1961.

King, Seth S. "Again the Issue of the Elgin Marbles," NYTM,
June 25, 1961, pp. 22-27. [Some of Byron's observations.]

Klein, J. W. "Byron's Neglected Plays," Drama, ser. 3, No. 63
(Winter, 1961), pp. 34-36. [Discusses Byron's plays and
makes a plea for their production on the stage.]

Laski, Marghanita. Ecstasy: A Study of Some Secular and Religious Experiences. Bloomington: Indiana University, 1961.

Lytton, Noel Anthony Scawen, Earl of. Wilfred Scawen Blunt: A
Memoir by His Grandson. London: MacDonald, 1961.

Marshall, William H. "Accretive Structure of Byron's The Giaour,"
MLN, LXXVI (June, 1961), 502-509.

_____. "The Byron Controversy Again," Literature and Psychol-
ogy, XI (Summer, 1961), 68-69. [The alleged incest with his
half sister should not be of critical relevance for Byron's
poetry.]

_____. "Byron's Parisina and the Function of Psychoanalytic
Criticism," Personalist XLII (Spring, 1961), 213-23. [A
psychoanalytic analysis "should yield a sense of the structure
and tension in the work arising from the interaction of the
characters at a level beneath that of the conscious and explicit."]

_____. "A Reading of Byron's Mazeppa," MLN, LXXVI (Feb.,
1961), 120-24.

_____. "Reference to a Popular Tradition in Don Juan and
Mazeppa," N&Q, CCVI (June, 1961), 224-25. [The belief that
cuckolds "are given ready entrance into Heaven."]

Moore, Doris L. The Late Lord Byron: Posthumous Dramas.
Philadelphia: Lippincott, 1961.
Reviews:
Sir Harold Nicolson, Listener, LXVI (July 13, 1961), 67.
John Bayley, Spectator, CCVII (July 14, 1961), 63-64.
Kay Dick, Punch, CCXLI (July 19, 1961), 116-17.
Andrew Rutherford, NSN, LXII (July 21, 1961), 90.
TLS, July 21, 1961, p. 450.
C. Petrie, ILN, CCXXXIX (July 11, 1961), 127.
Christopher Salvesen, T&T, XLII (Aug. 17, 1961), 1363.
DeLancey Ferguson, NYHT, Aug. 20, 1961, p. 4.
Leslie A. Marchand, SRL, XLIV (Sept. 2, 1961), 21.
Carlos Baker, NYTBR, Oct. 8, 1961, pp. 6, 45.
W. S. Merwin, Nation, CXCIII (Nov. 4, 1961), 355-56.
A. L. Bader, Antioch Review, XXI (Winter, 1961-1962), 520-
22.
Ernest J. Lovell, Jr., KR, XXIV (Winter, 1961), 162-67.
Phoebe Adams, Atlantic Monthly, CCIX (Jan., 1962), 99.
David V. Erdman, College English, XXIII (Feb., 1962), 414.
Frederick T. Wood, ES, XLIII (Aug., 1962), 272.
Jack Stillinger, SEL, II (Autumn, 1962), 513-14.
E. E. Bostetter, PQ, XLI (Oct., 1962), 661-62.
Leslie Marchand, VQR, XXXVIII (Winter, 1962), 147-50.
George Ridenour, Yale Review, LI (Winter, 1962), 321-24.
Harris W. Rudman, Books Abroad, XXVI (Winter, 1962), 85.

David Bonnel Green, K-SJ, XII (Winter, 1963), 115-16.
See also the following items all centering around this book and
the Lovelace Papers.
G. Wilson Knight, TLS, July 28, 1961, p. 465.
Doris Langley Moore, ibid., Aug. 4, 1961, p. 481.
Malcolm Elwin, ibid., Aug. 4, 1961, p. 487.
G. Wilson Knight, ibid., Aug. 11, 1961, p. 515.
Earl of Lytton, ibid., Aug. 25, 1961, p. 565.
Keith Walker, ibid., Sept. 1, 1961, p. 581.
Raymond Mortimer, ibid., Sept. 8, 1961, p. 597.
Doris Langley Moore, ibid., Sept. 8, 1961, p. 597.
G. Wilson Knight, ibid., Sept. 15, 1961, p. 613.
R. Glynn Grylls, ibid., Sept. 15, 1961, p. 613.
Earl of Lytton, ibid., Sept. 22, 1961, p. 629.
Charles H. Gibbs-Smith, ibid., Sept. 29, 1961, p. 645.
Earl of Lytton, ibid., Oct. 6, 1961, p. 663.
Doris Langley Moore, ibid., Oct. 13, 1961, p. 683.
Malcolm Elwin, ibid., Oct. 20, 1961, p. 753.
Doris Langley Moore, ibid., Oct. 27, 1961, p. 771.
The reviewer, ibid., Nov. 3, 1961, p. 789.

Moore, John Cecil. You English Words. London: Collins, 1961.

Moussa-Mahmoud, Fatma. "Orientals in Picaresque: A Chapter in
the History of the Oriental Tale in England," Cairo Studies in
English, 1961-1962, pp. 145-88. [Byron and his supposed
authorship of Anastasius are discussed.]

New, Chester W. The Life of Henry Brougham to 1830. Oxford:
Clarendon Press, 1961.

Nicolson, Harold. "The Romantic Revolt," Horizon (N.Y.), III
(July, 1961), 58-88.

Parks, Edd Winfield. William Gilmore Simms as Literary Critic.
("University of Georgia Monographs," No. 7.) Athens: University of Georgia, 1961. [Simms' criticism of Byron.]

Peck, Louis Francis. A Life of Matthew G. Lewis. Cambridge,
Mass.: Harvard University Press, 1961.

Philbrick, Thomas. James Fenimore Cooper and the Development
of American Sea Fiction. Cambridge, Mass.: Harvard University Press, 1961. [Byron's influence on his sea novels.]

Prescott, William Hickling. The Literary Memoranda of William
Hickling Prescott, ed. C. Harvey Gardiner. 2 vols. Nor-
man, Oklahoma: University of Oklahoma Press, 1961. [Vol.
I, pp. 48-49 deal with Don Juan.]

Putter, Irving. The Pessimism of Leconte de Lisle. The Work
and the Time. ("University of California Publications in
Modern Philology," Vol. XLII, No. 2.) Berkeley: University

of California Press, 1961. [Cain's influence on his Quain.]

Richards, Bernard G. "Lord Byron and Myself: From a Projected Book of Memoirs," Jewish Affairs (Johannesburg), XVI
(Oct., 1961), 22-26.

Russell, James Anderson. Dutch Romantic Poetry: The English
Influence. Bradford: Broadacre Books, 1961.

Rutherford, Andrew. Byron: A Critical Study. Edinburgh: Oli-
ver & Boyd, 1961.
Reviews:
V. de Sola Pinto, MLR, LVII (April, 1961), 252-54.
F. W. Bateson, NS, LXI (June 2, 1961), 885-86. Cf. Edwin
Morgan, ibid., LXI (June 9, 1961), 914. [A reply to
Bateson.]
Peter Quennell, Spectator, CCVI (June 9, 1961), 845.
A. Y. Garr, T&T, XLII (June 15, 1961), 994.
Graham Hough, Listener, LXV (June 15, 1961), 1057.
TLS, June 23, 1961, p. 388.
Kay Dick, Punch, CCXLI (July 19, 1961), 116-17.
QR, CCXCIX (Oct., 1961), 471.
John R. Willingham, Library Journal, LXXXVI (Oct. 1,
1961), 3284.
John A. M. Rillie, Library Review, Winter 1962, p. 251.
Bernice Slote, College English, XXIII (April, 1962), 605.
Timothy Rogers, English, XIV (Spring, 1962), 26-27.
Jack Stillinger, Books Abroad, XXXVI (Spring, 1962), 201.
F[rancis] C[hristiansen], Personalist, XLIII (Summer, 1962),
417-18.
Ernest J. Lovell, Jr., SAQ, LXI (Summer, 1962), 432.
H. S. Whittier, Dalhousie Review, XLII (Summer, 1962), 254-
56.
Frederick T. Wood, ES, XLIII (Aug., 1962), 272-73.
E. E. Bostetter, PQ, XLI (Oct., 1962), 662-63.
Jack Stillinger, SEL, II (Autumn, 1962), 513.
Kathleen V. Richardson, Poetry Review, LII (Oct.-Dec.,
1961), 234-35.
J. D. Jump, RES, n.s., XIII (Nov., 1962), 421-22.
Leslie Marchand, VQR, XXXVIII (Winter, 1962), 147-50.
George Ridenour, Yale Review, LI (Winter, 1962), 321-24.

_____. "The Influence of Hobhouse on Childe Harold's
Pilgrimage, Canto IV," RES, n.s., XII (Nov., 1961),
391-97. [His part in the composition of Canto IV was not
great.]

Saveson, J. E. "Shelley's Julian and Maddalo," K-SJ, X (1961),
53-58.

Shaw, J. T. "Byron, Chênedollé and Lermontov's 'Dying Gladia-
tor,'" Studies in Honor of John C. Hodges and John Levi
Thaler, eds. Richard B. Davis and John L. Lievsay.

Knoxville: The University of Tennessee Press, 1961. Pp.
1-10.

Stallknecht, Newton P. , and Frenz Horst (eds.). Comparative
Literature: Methods and Perspective. Carbondale: Southern
Illinois University Press, 1961.

Steiner, George. The Death of Tragedy. New York: Knopf,
1961. [Byron's dramas as precursors of modern drama.]

Thompson, Karl F. "Beckford, Byron and Henley, " Etudes
Anglaises, XIV (July-Sept. , 1961), 225-28.

Thomson, Paul van Kuykendall. Francis Thompson: A Critical
Biography. New York: Nelson, 1961. [On his criticism of
Byron's work.]

Viets, Henry R. "John William Polidori, M. D. and Lord Byron--
a Brief Interlude in 1816, " New England Journal of Medicine,
CCLXIV (March 16, 1961), 553-57.

Wayman, Dorothy G. "Byron and the Franciscans, " KSMB, XII
(1961), 7-8. [Corrects lines in Don Juan, VI, xvi.]

Woodring, Carl R. Politics in the Poetry of Coleridge. Madison:
The University of Wisconsin Press, 1961.

Woods, Ralph Lewis. Famous Poems and the Little-known Stories
behind Them. New York: Hawthorn, 1961. [Gives the background of "When We Two Parted, " "I Speak Not, I trace Not,
I breathe Not Thy Name, " "Fare Thee Well, " "So We'll Go
No More A-Roving, " "Maid of Athens. "]

1962

Ajami, Wadad Iskander. "Rousseau and Byron, " American Book
Collector, XII (Summer, 1962), 26-32.

Alexander, Boyd. England's Wealthiest Son: A Study of William
Beckford. London: Centaur, 1962.

Allott, Kenneth. "Arnold's Empedocles on Etna and Byron's Manfred, " N&Q, CCVII (Aug. , 1962), 300-302.

Amarasinghe, Upali. Dryden and Pope in the Early Nineteenth
Century: A Study of Changing Literary Taste, 1800-1930.
Cambridge [Eng.]: At the University Press, 1962.

Angles, Robert. "Commonplace Byron, " Music and Musicians, X
(July, 1962), 45.

"Association Notes," English, XIV (Spring, 1962), 40-41. [A summary of a lecture by G. Wilson Knight on "Byron as a Man
of Letters," delivered Sept. 23, 1962.]

Auden, W. H. "Don Juan," The Dyer's Hand and Other Essays.
New York: Random House, 1962. Pp. 386-406.

Baker, Herschel. William Hazlitt. Cambridge, Mass.: Harvard
University Press, 1962.

Beaty, Frederick L. "The Placement of Two Rejected Stanzas in
Don Juan," N&Q, CCVII (Nov., 1962), 422-23. [Places them
after stanza ccx rather than after stanza ccxi.]

Blackstone, Bernard. The Lost Travellers: A Romantic Theme
with Variations. London: Longmans, 1962. [A study of the
theme of travel in Byron, especially Childe Harold.]

Blunden, Edmund. Addresses on General Subjects Connected with
English Literature, Given at Tokyo University and Elsewhere
in 1948. Tokyo: Kenkyusha, 1962.

Boas, Louise Schutz. Harriet Shelley: Five Long Years. London:
Oxford University Press, 1962.

Bose, Amalendu. Chroniclers of Life: Studies in Early Victorian
Poetry. Bombay: Orient Longmans, 1962. [Byron's influence.]

Bullough, Geoffrey. Mirror of Minds: Changing Psychological Be-
liefs in English Poetry. London: Athlone, 1962. [Touches
on Byron's belief that nature is poetic mainly because of the
human associations connected with it.]

Calvert, William J. Byron: Romantic Paradox. New York: Russell & Russell, 1962. [A reprint of a book published in 1935
by University of North Carolina Press.]

Creeger, George R. (ed.). "Introduction," Byron. "The Laurel
Poetry Series." New York: Dell Publishing Co., 1962. Pp.
7-26.

Davies, Hugh Sykes. "Byron," From Blake to Browning. Vol. II
of The Poets and Their Critics. 2 vols. London: Hutchinson, 1962. Pp. 101-44.

De Beer, Gavin. "Byron on the Burning of Shelley," KSMB, XIII
(1962), 8-11.

_____. "Meshes of the Byronic Net in Switzerland," ES, XLIII
(Oct., 1962), 384-95.

Dobrée, Bonamy. Byron's Dramas. "Byron Foundation Lecture."
   Nottingham: University of Nottingham Press, 1962. [Rptd.
   in his Milton to Ouida. London: Cass, 1970. Pp. 116-39.]

Dowden, Wilfred S. "Byron through Austrian Eyes," Anglo-German
   and American-German Crosscurrents, eds. Philip Allison
   Shelley and Arthur O. Lewis, Jr. Chapel Hill: University of
   North Carolina, 1962. Vol. II, pp. 175-224.

Edel, Leon. Henry James, 1882-1895: The Middle Years. Philadelphia: Lippincott, 1962.

Elwin, Malcolm. Lord Byron's Wife. London: Macdonald, 1962.
   Reviews:
      Richard Whittington-Egan, Books and Bookmen, VIII (Nov.,
      1962), 25. Cf. Malcolm Elwin, "Pre-Strachey View of
      Biography," ibid., VIII (Jan., 1963), 11. [An answer to
      Whittington-Egan's review.]
   TLS, Nov. 23, 1962, p. 890.
   Earl of Lytton, T&T, XLIII (Dec. 6-13, 1962), 19.
   Sylvia Plath, NS, LXIV (Dec. 7, 1962), 828-29.
   Edward Lucie-Smith, Listener, LXVIII (Dec. 13, 1962), 1019.
   Twentieth Century, CLXXI (Winter, 1962-1963), 174.
   C. Petrie, ILN, CCXLI (Dec. 22, 1962), 1011.
   Peter Quennell, NYTBR, April 28, 1963, pp. 6, 14.
   DeLancey Ferguson, NYHTBR, May 5, 1963, pp. 6, 11.
   Harry T. Moore, SRL, XLVI (May 11, 1963), 29-30.
   New Yorker, XXXIX (May 11, 1963), 180-81.
   John A. M. Rillie, Library Review, Summer, 1963, p. 85.
   Carl Woodring, VQR, XXXIX (Summer, 1963), 506-509.
   E. E. Bostetter, PQ, XLII (Oct., 1963), 451-52.
   F. T. Wood, ES, XLIV (Oct., 1963), 385-86.
   Ernest Lovell, Jr., K-SJ, XIII (Winter, 1964), 105-107.
   R. H. Super, SEL, IV (Autumn, 1964), 670-71.
   See also the controversy motivated by this book and published in
      the form of letters to the editor of the Times Literary Sup-
      plement.
   G. Wilson Knight, TLS, Dec. 7, 1962, p. 955.
   Malcolm Elwin, ibid., Dec. 14, 1962, p. 973.
   Michael Joyce, ibid., Dec. 14, 1962, p. 973.
   Doris Langley Moore, ibid., Dec. 14, 1962, p. 973.
   Myra Curtis, ibid., Dec. 21, 1962, p. 989.
   G. Wilson Knight, ibid., Dec. 21, 1962, p. 989.
   Peter Eaton, ibid., Jan. 4, 1963, p. 9.
   Malcolm Elwin, ibid., Jan. 4, 1963, p. 9.
   F. Dickins, ibid., Jan. 11, 1963, p. 32.
   Michael Joyce, ibid., Jan. 11, 1963, p. 32.
   G. Wilson Knight, ibid., Jan. 11, 1963, p. 32.
   Malcolm Elwin, ibid., Jan. 18, 1963, p. 41.
   F. A. Whiting, ibid., Jan. 18, 1963, p. 41.

Erdman, David V. "Byron and 'the New Force of the People,'"
   K-SJ, XI (Winter, 1962), 47-64. [Byron's attitude toward
   radicals.]

Evans, Sir [Benjamin] Ifor. English Literature: Values and Tra-
    ditions. London: Allen & Unwin; New York: Barnes &
    Noble, 1962. [A revised edition of the work published in
    1942.]

"A Filtered Picture: China's Foreign Reading before--and after
    the Revolution," TLS, Sept. 21, 1962, pp. 740-41. [The
    Chinese were interested in Byron.]

Foerster, Donald M. The Fortunes of Epic Poetry: A Study in
    English and American Criticism, 1750-1950. Washington:
    Catholic University, 1962.

Graham, Victor E. "The Pelican as Image and Symbol," Revue
    de Littérature Comparée, XXXVI (April-June, 1962), 235-43.

Harmon, Maurice. "Little Chandler and Byron's 'First Poem,'"
    Threshold, No. 17 (1962), 59-61. [In Joyce's "A Little
    Cloud."]

Hartman, Geoffrey H. "Romanticism and 'Anti-Self-conscious-
    ness,'" Centennial Review of Arts and Science, VI (1962),
    553-65.

Highet, Gilbert. The Anatomy of Satire. Princeton: Princeton
    University Press, 1962. [On The Vision of Judgment.]

Hopkins, Kenneth. English Poetry: A Short History. Philadel-
    phia: Lippincott, 1962.

Horn, Andràs. Byron's "Don Juan" and the 18th Century Novel.
    ("Schweizer Anglistische Arbeiten [Swiss Studies in English],"
    No. 51.) Bern: Francke Verlag, 1962.

Kleinfield, H. L. "Washington Irving at Newstead Abbey," Bulletin
    of the New York Public Library, LXVI (April, 1962), 244-49.

Knight, G. Wilson. "Byron," The Golden Labyrinth: A Study of
    British Drama. London: Phoenix House, 1962. Pp. 229-39.

_____. "Byron and Hamlet," Bulletin of the John Rylands Li-
    brary, XLV (Sept., 1962), 115-47. Rptd. as "A Regency
    Hamlet," in his Byron and Shakespeare. London: Routledge
    & Kegan Paul, 1966. Pp. 73-116.

_____. The Christian Renaissance, with Interpretations of
    Dante, Shakespeare and Goethe and new discussions of Oscar
    Wilde, and the Gospel of Thomas. London: Methuen; New
    York: Norton, 1962.

Lawrence, D. H. The Collected Letters of D. H. Lawrence, ed.
    Harry T. Moore. 2 vols. New York: Viking, 1962.

Livermore, Ann Lapraik.   "Byron and Emily Brontë," QR, CCC
     (July, 1962), 337-44.

Lloyd, Quentin.   "Famous Publishing Houses--III, Where Byron
     Met Sir Walter Scott," T&T, XLIII (Nov. 15-22, 1962), 24-
     25.

Losh, James.   The Diaries and Correspondence of James Losh,
     ed. Edward Hughes. Vol. I: Diary, 1811-1823. Vol. II:
     Diary, 1824-1833; Letters to Charles, 2nd Earl Grey and
     Henry Brougham.   ("Publications of the Surtees Society,"
     Vols. CLXXI and CLXXIV.) Durham: Andrews & Co.; Lon-
     don: Quaritch, 1962-1963.

"The Lovelace Papers," Listener, LXVIII (Sept. 27, 1962), 465-
     66. [Gives a brief account of their origin.]

Lovell, Ernest J., Jr.   Captain Medwin: Friend of Byron and
     Shelley. Austin, Texas: The University of Texas Press;
     London: Macdonald, 1962.

McCullough, Norman Verrle.   The Negro in English Literature: A
     Critical Introduction. Ilfracombe: Arthur H. Stockwell,
     1962.

Mahoney, John L.   "Byron's Admiration of Pope: A Romantic
     Paradox," Discourse, V (Summer, 1962), 309-15. [Byron's
     was "the admiration of a man who felt that it was too late
     to change his own poetry, but not too late to defend Pope's
     poetical merits against the often unjustified onslaughts of the
     day."]

Marjarum, Edward Wayne.   Byron as Skeptic and Believer. New
     York: Russell and Russell, 1962. [A reprint of a book pub-
     lished in 1938 by Princeton University Press.]

Marshall, William H.   "An Early Misattribution to Byron: Hunt's
     The Feast of the Poets," N&Q, CCVII (May, 1962), 180-
     82.

_____. Structure of Byron's Major Poems. Philadelphia: Uni-
     versity of Pennsylvania Press, 1962.
     Reviews:
         Carl Woodring, VQR, XXXIX (Summer, 1963), 506-509.
         Ralph Lawrence, English, XIV (Autumn, 1963), 247.
         Morse Peckham, SEL, III (Autumn, 1963), 603-604.
         E. E. Bostetter, PQ, XLII (Oct., 1963), 453.
         Leslie A. Marchand, K-SJ, XIII (Winter, 1964), 104-
             105.
         T. G. Steffan, JEGP, LXIII (April, 1964), 376-78.
         Paul West, MLR, LIX (April, 1964), 280-81.

James V. Baker, Criticism, VI (Spring, 1964), 187-89.
Andrew Rutherford, RES, n. s., XVI (Feb., 1965), 89-90

May, Frederick. "Ugo Foscolo's 'Parallel between Dante and
    Petrarch' in Two Literary Periodicals of 1821," Italian
    Studies Presented to E. R. Vincent, eds. C. P. Brand, et.
    al. Cambridge: W. Heffer, 1962. Pp. 219-25. [A review
    of Byron's The Prophecy of Dante in the June, 1821, issue of
    The New Monthly Magazine quotes and paraphrases passages
    from Foscolo's 'Parallel.']

Mras, George. "Literary Sources of Delacroix's Conception of the
    Sketch and the Imagination," Art Bulletin, XLIV (June, 1962),
    103-11.

*Mukoyama, Yasuko. "A Study of Lord Byron," Journal of Aoyama
    Gakuin Women's Junior College, No. 16 (Nov., 1962), 13-30.

Munby, Alan N. L. The Cult of the Autograph Letter in England.
    London: Athlone, 1962.

Murray, David Leslie. "Lord Byron," Scenes and Silhouettes.
    London: J. Cape, 1962. Pp. 210-24.

Nowottny, Winifred. The Language Poets Use. New York: Oxford
    University Press; London: Athlone, 1962.

Pafford, Ward. "Byron and the Mind of Man: Childe Harold, III
    and IV, and Manfred," Studies in Romanticism, I (Winter,
    1962), 105-27. [His exploration of the poetic imagination.]

Parks, Edd Winfield. Ante-Bellum Southern Literary Critics.
    Athens, Ga.: Georgia University Press, 1962.

Peckham, Morse. Beyond the Tragic Vision: The Quest for Iden-
    tity in the 19th Century. New York: Braziller, 1962. [Dis-
    cusses Don Juan.]

Piper, Herbert Walter. The Active Universe: Pantheism and the
    Concept of Imagination in the English Romantic Poets. Lon-
    don: Athlone, 1962.

Stevenson, Robert Scott. "The Lameness of Lord Byron," Famous
    Illnesses in History. London: Eyre & Spottiswoode, 1962.
    Pp. 117-27.

Thorslev, Peter Larsen. The Byronic Hero: Types and Proto-
    types. Minneapolis: University of Minnesota Press, 1962.
    Reviews:
        John R. Willingham, Library Journal, LXXXVII (June 15,
            1962), 2381-82.
        Charles T. Doughtery, College English, XXIV (April, 1963),
            588.

Melvin J. Friedman, MLJ, XLVII (May, 1963), 216-17.
James D. Merritt, Books Abroad, XXXVII (Summer, 1963), 336.
Derek Stanford, English, XIV (Summer, 1963), 202.
Morse Peckham, SEL, III (Autumn, 1963), 603-604.
Edward E. Bostetter, PQ, XLII (Oct., 1963), 453-54.
Paul West, MLR, LVIII (Oct., 1963), 567-68.
C. T. P., American Book Collector, XIV (Nov., 1963), 3-4.
Wolfgang B. Fleischman, Comparative Literature Studies, I (1964), 73-75.
Barbara Hardy, British Journal of Aesthetics, IV (Jan., 1964), 83-84.
J. D. Jump, RES, n.s., XV (Feb., 1964), 100-101.
Andrew Rutherford, JEGP, LXIII (Oct., 1964), 814-16.

Trueblood, Paul Graham. The Flowering of Byron's Genius: Studies in Byron's "Don Juan." New York: Russell & Russell, 1962. [A reprint of a book first published in 1945 by Stanford University Press.]

Wagenknecht, Edward Charles. Washington Irving: Moderation Displayed. New York: Ocford University Press, 1962.

Wellek, René. "Italian Criticism in the Thirties and Forties: From Scalvini to Tenca," Italian Quarterly, VI (Summer, 1962), 3-25. [Reference to their evaluation of Byron.]

*Wells, Nannie Katharin. Byron Comments on the 20th Century. [Collieston, Aberdeenshire]: Michael Slains, 1962.

Wilde, Oscar. Letters, ed. Rupert Hart-Davis. London: Rupert-Hart-Davis, 1962. [Scattered references to Byron.]

Woodring, Carl R. "New Light on Byron, Trelawny and Lady Hester Stanhope," Columbia Library Columns, XI (May, 1962), 9-18. [MS diary in John Howard Paine's hand entitled "Reminiscencies (sic) of Cursory Visits to Various Places in and round the Shores of the Mediterranean."]

1963

Adams, Hazard. The Context of Poetry. Boston: Little, Brown, 1963.

Anderson, George K. "The Legend of the Wandering Jew," Books at Brown, XIX (May, 1963), 143-59.

Auden, W. H. (ed.). "Introduction," Byron: Selected Poetry and Prose. "Signet Classic Poetry Series." New York: New American Library, 1963. Pp. vii-xxiv.

Barrows, Herbert. "Convention and Novelty in the Romantic Generation's Experience of Italy," Bulletin of the New York Public
Library, LXVII (June, 1963), 360-75.

Beaty, Frederick L. "Byron's Concept of Ideal Love," K-SJ, XII
(Winter, 1963), 37-54.

Benton, Richard P. "Is Poe's 'The Assignation' a Hoax?" Nineteenth Century Fiction, XVIII (Sept., 1963), 193-97. [Thinks
that it was inspired by the Byron-Guiccioli affair.]

Berenson, Bernhard. Sunset and Twilight. From the Diaries of
1947-1958, ed. Nicky Mariano. New York: Harcourt Brace,
1963.

Beyer, Werner W. "Byron, and Sotheby, and Wieland's Eroticism,"
The Enchanted Forest. New York: Barnes & Noble, 1963.
Pp. 246-58.

Borrow, K. T., and Dorothy Hewlett. "Byron: A Link with Australia," KSMB, XIV (1963), 17-20. [A carriage of his that
was sent to Australia.]

Bostetter, Edward E. "Byron," The Romantic Ventriloquists:
Wordsworth, Coleridge, Keats, Shelley and Byron. Seattle:
University of Washington Press, 1963. Pp. 241-301.

Brown, Calvin. "Monosyllables in English Verse," SEL, III
(Autumn, 1963), 473-91.

Butler, Maria Hogan. "An Examination of Byron's revision of
Manfred, Act III," SP, LX (Oct., 1963), 627-36.

Childers, William C. "A Note on the Dedication of Don Juan,"
K-SJ, XII (Winter, 1963), 9. [The spelling pye in the last
line of stanza i may allude to a pun by George Steevens on
the name of the poet laureate Henry James Pye.]

Cogswell, Fred. "Scott - Byron," Studies in Scottish Literature,
I (Oct., 1963), 131-32. [Reproduces from the MS by Galt
an incomplete sketch of Scott and Byron. MS is item
000930-934 in the Dominion National Archives, Ottawa.]

Day, Martin. "The Poetry of Byron," History of English Literature 1660-1837. New York: Doubleday & Co., 1963. Pp.
390-411.

Eliot, George [pseud. for Mary Ann Evans]. Essays by George
Eliot, ed. Thomas Pinney. New York: Columbia University
Press, 1963.

Feinberg, Leonard. The Satirist: His Temperament, Motivation,
and Influence. Ames: Iowa State University, 1963.

Fisher, John. Eighteen Fifteen: An End and a Beginning. London: Cassell, 1963. [On the events that took place on Byron's wedding day.]

Gottfried, Leon Albert. "The Anguish of Greatness: Byron," Matthew Arnold and the Romantics. London: Routledge & K. Paul, 1963. Pp. 75-115. [Arnold's dicta on Byron.]

Graves, Robert. "Pretense on Parnassus," Horizon (N.Y.), V (May, 1963), 81-85. ["Nine tenths of what passes as English poetry is a choice between vulgarity and banality." Takes special aim at Byron.]

Green, David Bonnell. "Byron's Cousin Trevanion," ES, XLIV (April, 1963), 119-21. [Concerns John Trevanion Purnell Bettesworth Trevanion.]

*Hachiya, Akio. "Byron's Cain and the Bible," Foreign Literary Studies of Osaka Women's College, No. 15 (Feb., 1963), 1-10.

"The Heart of a Poet," Listener, LXIX (May 21, 1963), 741. [A description of the exhumation of Byron in 1938.]

Houghton, Walter E. The Poetry of Clough: An Essay in Revaluation. New Haven: Yale University Press, 1963.

Jack, Ian. "Byron," English Literature, 1815-1832. Vol. X of The Oxford History of English Literature. Oxford: Clarendon Press, 1963. Pp. 49-76.

James, Louis. Fiction for the Working Man, 1830-1850: A Study of the Literature Produced for the Working Classes in Early Victorian Urban England. London: Oxford University Press, 1963.

Johnston, Johanna. Runaway to Heaven: The Story of Harriet Beecher Stowe. Garden City: Doubleday, 1963.

King-Hele, Desmond. Erasmus Darwin. London: Macmillan; New York: St. Martin's, 1963. [Darwin's influence on Byron.]

Loomis, Emerson Robert. "The Turning Point in Pope's Reputation: A Dispute which Preceded the Bowles-Byron Controversy," PQ, XLII (April, 1963), 242-48.

Marshall, William H. (ed.). "Introduction," The Major English Romantic Poets. New York: Washington Square Press, 1963. Pp. 235-46.

Mill, John Stuart. The Earlier Letters of John Stuart Mill, 1812-1848, ed. Francis E. Mineka. 2 vols. (Vols. XII and XIII of Collected Works of John Stuart Mill.) Toronto: Toronto University Press; London: Routledge, 1963.

Mortenson, Robert. "Another Continuation of Don Juan," Studies
    in Romanticism, II (Summer, 1963), 244-47. [An article, "A
    Touch at an Unpublished Canto of Don Juan," in the Jan.,
    1822, issue of the Newcastle Magazine, purports to give an
    account of a canto of Don Juan which was placed in the edi-
    tor's hands in Sept., 1820. A hoax.]

*Mukoyama, Yasuko. "A Study of Lord Byron," Bulletin of Aoyama
    Women's Junior College, No. 16 (1963), 13-30.

Newell, Kenneth B. "Paul Elmer More on Byron," K-SJ, XII
    (Winter, 1963), 67-74.

Orel, Harold. "Lord Byron's Debt to the Enlightenment," Studies
    in Voltaire and the 18th Century, ed. Theodore Bestermann.
    ("Transactions of the First International Congress on the En-
    lightenment III.") Geneve: Institut et musée Voltaire, 1963.
    Vol. XXVI, pp. 1275-90.

Osborn, James M. "Travel Literature and the Rise of Neo-
    Hellenism in England," Bulletin of the New York Public Li-
    brary, LXVII (May, 1963), 279-300. [Byron's role in the de-
    velopment of Romantic Hellenism and Philhellenism in Eng-
    land.]

Owen, W. J. B. "A Byronic Shipwreck in the Pacific," N&Q,
    CCVIII (July, 1963), 265-67. [Echoes of Don Juan, II, in
    Charles Reade's novel, Foul Play, chaps. x-xxv.]

Partridge, Monica. "Slavonic Themes in English Poetry of the
    19th Century," Slavonic and East European Review, XLI
    (June, 1963), 420-41.

Peyre, Henri. Literature and Sincerity. New Haven: Yale Uni-
    versity Press, 1963.

Pinto, Vivian de Sola (ed.). "Introduction," Byron's Poems. 3
    vols. London: Dent; New York: Dutton, 1963. Pp. v-xx.

Pushkin, Alexander. The Letters of Alexander Pushkin, trans.
    J. Thomas Shaw. 3 vols. Bloomington: Indiana University;
    Philadelphia: University of Pennsylvania Press, 1963.

Rodway, Allan Edwin. "Byron," The Romantic Conflict. London:
    Chatto, 1963. Pp. 195-227.

Rowland, Benjamin, Jr. The Classical Tradition in Western Art.
    Cambridge, Mass.: Harvard University Press, 1963.

Schulz, Max F. The Poetic Voices of Coleridge: A Study of His
    Desire for Spontaneity and Passion for Order. Detroit:
    Wayne State University Press, 1963.

Shahane, V. A. "Rabindranath Tagore: A Study in Romanticism,"
    Studies in Romanticism, III (Autumn, 1963), 53-64. [A study
    of influence.]

Spears, Monroe K. The Poetry of W. H. Auden: The Disenchanted
    Island. New York: Oxford University Press, 1963.

Spender, Stephen, and Donald Hall (eds.). The Concise Encyclo-
    pedia of English and American Poets and Poetry. New York:
    Hawthorn, 1963.

Stavrou, Constantine N. "Religion in Byron's Don Juan," SEL, III
    (Autumn, 1963), 567-94.

Swiggart, Peter. "Faulkner's The Sound and the Fury," Explicator,
    XXII (Dec., 1963), item 31. [Byron's 'wish' in The Sound and
    the Fury refers to Don Juan, VI, xxvii.]

Thorslev, Peter L., Jr. "The Romantic Mind Is Its Own Place,"
    Comparative Literature, XV (Summer, 1963), 250-268.

Ward, Aileen. John Keats: The Making of a Poet. New York:
    The Viking Press, 1963.

Wellek, René. Concepts of Criticism, ed. Stephen G. Nichols, Jr.
    New Haven: Yale University Press, 1963.

West, Paul (ed.). "Introduction," Byron: A Collection of Critical
    Essays. Englewood Cliffs, N.J.: Prentice-Hall, 1963. [All
    items in this book are reprints of articles, reviews or chap-
    ters of books already listed in this bibliography. Their ori-
    ginal date of publication appears in parenthesis following the
    title.]
    It contains:
        Bernard Blackstone, "Guilt and Retribution in Byron's Sea
            Poems," (1961), pp. 31-41.
        Helen Gardner, "Don Juan," from London Magazine, (1958),
            pp. 113-21. [A review of Steffan's and Pratt's Byron's
            "Don Juan": A Variorum Edition.]
        G. Highet, "The Poet and His Vulture," (1954), pp. 145-50.
        G. Wilson Knight, "The Two Eternities," (1939), pp. 15-30.
        Frank Raymond Leavis, "Byron's Satire," (1936), pp. 83-87.
        Mario Praz, "Metamorphoses of Satan," (1933), 42-49.
        George Ridenour, "Carelessly I Sing," from The Style of "Don
            Juan," (1960), pp. 122-37.
        W. W. Robson, "Byron as Improviser," (1957), pp. 88-95.
        Bertrand Russell, "Byron," (1945), pp. 151-56.
        Truman Guy Steffan, "The Devil a Bit of Our Beppo," (1953),
            pp. 65-82.
            _____, "Don Juan: A Thousand Colors," from Byron's
            "Don Juan," (1957), pp. 96-112.
        John Wain, "The Search for Identity," from London Magazine,
            (1958), pp. 157-70. [A review of Steffan's and Pratt's

Byron's "Don Juan": A Variorum Edition.]
Paul West, "The Plays," from Byron and the Spoiler's Art,
(1960), pp. 50-64.
Edmund Wilson, "Byron in the Twenties," (1952), pp. 138-44.

"Who Was Emma?" Family History (Canterbury), I (April, 1963),
114-17.

Wilson, Angus. "Evil in the English Novel," Books and Bookmen,
VIII (June, 1963), 3-6, 39-43. [Touches on the influence of
the Byronic hero.]

Wind, Edgar. Art and Anarchy. London: Faber, 1963.

1964

Baker, Paul R. "Lord Byron and the Americans in Italy," K-SJ,
XIII (Winter, 1964), 61-75. [A review of the meetings of
Byron with Americans.]

Barnett, George L. Charles Lamb: The Evolution of Elia. ("Indiana University Humanities Series," No. 53.) Bloomington:
Indiana University, 1964.

Bayley, John. "Vulgarity," British Journal of Aesthetics, IV
(Oct., 1964), 298-304.

Beebe, Maurice. Ivory Towers and Sacred Founts: The Artist as
Hero in Fiction from Goethe to Joyce. New York: New York
University Press, 1964. [Byron the diabolical rebel poet.]

Bentman, Raymond. "The Romantic Poets and Critics on Robert
Burns," Texas Studies in Literature and Language, VI
(Spring, 1964), 104-18.

Braekman, W. "Letters by Robert Southey to Sir John Taylor
Coleridge," Studia Germanica Gandensia, VI (1964), 103-230.
[There are echoes of the Southey-Byron enmity.]

Carb, Nathan R. E. "The 'Leon'-'Noel' Anagram," N&Q, CCIX
(Jan., 1964), 25.

Chew, Samuel C. The Dramas of Lord Byron. New York: Russell & Russell, 1964. [A reprint of a book published in 1915
by Johns Hopkins.]

Cohen, Ralph. The Art of Discrimination: Thomson's "The Sea-
sons," and the Language of Criticism. Berkeley: University
of California Press, 1964.

Cooke, M. G. "The Restoration Ethos of Byron's Classical Plays,"
PMLA, LXXIX (Dec., 1964), 569-78.

Deslandres, Yvonne. "Delacroix and Great Britain," Scottish Art
    Review, IX, No. 4 (1964), 18-21, 32.

De Sua, William J. Dante into English: A Study of the Transla-
    tion of "The Divine Comedy" in Britain and America. ("Uni-
    versity of North Carolina Studies in Comparative Literature,"
    No. 32.) Chapel Hill: University of North Carolina, 1964.
    [On Byron's translations from it.]

Drew, Elizabeth. "Byron," The Literature of Gossip: Nine Eng-
    lish Letter-writers. New York: Norton, 1964. Pp. 158-86.

Edwards, Herbert J., Jule A. Herne and James A. Hern. The
    Rise of Realism in the American Drama. ("University of
    Maine Studies, Second Series," No. 80.) Orono, Maine:
    University of Maine, 1964.

Eversole, Richard L. "What Did Jeffrey Mean by 'Elaborate'? A
    Note or Two on Byron Letters," N&Q, CCIX (Jan., 1964), 26.

Friesner, Donald Neil. "Ellis Bell and Israfel," Brontë Society
    Transactions, XIV (1964), 11-18.

Fuess, C. M. Lord Byron as a Satirist in Verse. New York:
    Russell and Russell, 1964. [A reprint of a book published in
    1912 by Columbia University Press.]

Green, David Bonnell. "Hanson's Partner, John Birch," K-SJ,
    XIII (Winter, 1964), 5-6.

Grønbech, Vilhelm. Religious Currents in the 19th Century, trans.
    P. M. Mitchell and W. D. Paden. Lawrence: Kansas Uni-
    versity, 1964.

Haslam, G. E. (ed.). Wise after the Event: A Catalogue of
    Books, Pamphlets, Manuscripts and Letters Relating to
    Thomas James Wise Displayed in an Exhibition in Manchester
    Central Library, September 1964. Manchester: Manchester
    Libraries Committee. 1964.

Hassall, Christopher (arranger). Ambrosia and Small Beer: The
    Record of a Correspondence between Edward March and
    Christopher Hassall. London: Longmans, 1964.

Hays, H. R. The Dangerous Sex: The Myth of Feminine Evil.
    New York: Putnam's, 1964.

Hayter, Alethea. "Landscape in English Romantic Poetry and
    Painting," Annales de la Faculté des Lettres et Sciences Hu-
    maines d'Aix, XXXVIII (1964), 269-84.

Howarth, Herbert. Notes on Some Figures behind T. S. Eliot.
    Boston: Houghton Mifflin, 1964. [Byron one of them.]

Howarth, R. G. "Byron as Dramatist," A Pot of Gillyflowers:
    Studies and Notes. Cape Town: The Author, 1964. Pp. 46-
    54.

Hudson, Frederick. "A Catalogue of the Works of Charles Villiers
    Stanford, 1852-1924," Music Review, XXV (Feb., 1964), 44-
    57. [Songs written to poems by Byron.]

*Hutchings, Richard John. Landfalls of the Romantic Poets: A
    Book for G. C. E. Students. Bath: Brodie, 1964.

Hyde, Harford Montgomery. A History of Pornography. London:
    Heinemann, 1964. [Don Leon poems.]

Johnston, Arthur. The Enchanted Ground. London: Athlone
    Press, 1964.

Jones, Frederick L. The Letters of Percy Bysshe Shelley. 2
    vols. Oxford: At the Clarendon Press, 1964.

Joseph, Michael Kennedy. Byron, the Poet. London: V. Gollancz,
    1964.
    Reviews:
    Graham Hough, Listener, LXXI (April 16, 1964), 642.
    Geoffrey Grigson, Country Life, CXXXV (April 30, 1964),
        1081.
    Stephen Haskell, Spectator, CCXII (May 8, 1964), 639.
    Francis Hope, NS, LXVII (May 8, 1964), 731-32.
    E. D. O'Brien, ILN, CCXLIV (May 16, 1964), 796.
    William K. Seymour, CR, CCV (July, 1964), 389-90.
    TLS, May 28, 1964, p. 448. Cf. Michael K. Joseph, ibid.,
        July 2, 1964, p. 571.
    Gilbert Thomas, English, XV (Autumn, 1964), 109.
    Ian Jack, Landfall, XIX (March, 1965), 89-91.
    Andrew Rutherford, MLR, LX (April, 1965), 260-61.
    E. E. B[ostetter], ELN, III (Suppl. to No. 1, Sept., 1965),
        26.
    J. D. Jump, RES, n.s., XVI (Nov., 1965), 438-39.
    Frederick T. Wood, ES, XLVI (Dec., 1965), 514.
    Frederick Beaty, K-SJ, XV (Winter, 1966), 124-26.

Lentricchia, Frank, Jr. "Byron in Boston," Emerson Society
    Quarterly, No. 37, Pt. ii (1964), 73-74. [About the contro-
    versy arising from a review of Henley's edition of Byron's
    letters which appeared in the Boston Literary World, April 3,
    1897.]

Leonard, William E. Byron and Byronism in America. New York:
    Haskell House, 1964. [A reprint of a book published in 1907
    by Columbia University Press.]

Leslie, Doris. This for Caroline. London: Heinemann, 1964.

Moore, Thomas. The Journals of Thomas Moore, 1818-1841, ed.
    Peter Quennell. New York: The Macmillan Co., 1964.

————. The Letters of Thomas Moore, ed. Wilfred S. Dowden.
    2 vols. Oxford: Clarendon Press, 1964.

Morton, Henry C. V. A Traveller in Italy. New York: Dodd,
    Mead & Co., 1964.

Nabokov, Vladimir. Notes on Prosody: From the Commentary to
    His Translation of Pushkin's "Eugene Onegin." New York:
    Pantheon, 1964.

Oldham, Ellen M. "Lord Byron and Mr. Coolidge of Boston,"
    Book Collector, XIII (Summer, 1964), 211-13. [On Joseph
    Coolidge's visit with Byron.]

Ostrowski, Witold. "Walter Scott in Poland, Part I," Studies in
    Scottish Literature, II (Oct., 1964), 87-95. [Briefly on By-
    ron's reputation in Poland.]

Pack, S. W. C. The 'Wager' Mutiny. London: Redman, 1964.
    [Byron's grandfather took part in it.]

Paolucci, Anne. "Dante's Satan and Milton's 'Byronic Hero,'"
    Italica, XLI (June, 1964), 139-49.

Parks, Edd Winfield. Edgar Allan Poe as Literary Critic. Athens,
    Ga.: Georgia University Press, 1964.

Parsons, C. R. "Eugène Delacroix and Literary Inspiration,"
    UTQ, XXXIII (Jan., 1964), 164-77.

Partridge, A. C. "Byron and Italy," English Studies in Africa,
    VII (March, 1964), 1-12. Cf. Marie Dyer, "Readers'
    Forum," ibid., VIII (March, 1965), 90-97. [Is Beppo really
    an acceptance by Byron of Italian life and manner?]

Perkins, David. Wordsworth and the Poetry of Sincerity. Cam-
    bridge, Mass.: Harvard University Press, 1964.

Rawson, C. J. "Beppo and Absalom and Achitophel: A parallel,"
    N&Q, CCIX (Jan., 1964), 25.

Ridenour, George M. "The Mode of Byron's Don Juan," PMLA,
    LXXXIX (Sept., 1964), 442-46. [Partly a criticism of Mar-
    shall's The Structure of Byron's Major Poems. Sees the
    poem as essentially comic, rather than ironic or satiric.]

Roppen, Georg, and Richard Sommer. "Byron's Pilgrimage,"
    Strangers and Pilgrims: An Essay on the Metaphor of Jour-
    ney. ("Norwegian Studies in English," No. 11.) New York:
    Humanities Press, 1964. Pp. 209-83.

Ryals, Clyde de L. Theme and Symbol in Tennyson's Poems to 1850. Philadelphia: Pennsylvania University Press, 1964.

Sanders, Charles Richard. "The Byron Closed in Sartor Resartus." Studies in Romanticism, III (Winter, 1964), 77-108. [On the Carlyles' attitude towards Byron.]

Saunders, John Whiteside. The Profession of English Letters. London: Routledge; Toronto: Toronto University Press, 1964.

Singh, G. Leopardi and the Theory of Poetry. Lexington: University of Kentucky Press, 1964.

Skelton, Robin (ed.). "Introduction," Selected Poems of Byron. London: Heinemann, 1964. Pp. 1-14. Rptd. New York: Barnes & Noble, 1966.

Van der Beets, Richard. "A Note on Dramatic Necessity and the Incest Motif in Manfred," N&Q, CCIX (Jan., 1964), 26-28. [This motif "satisfies the particular dramatic needs arising from both the Gothic tradition and the Faust legend as Byron uses them."]

Whipple, Addison B. C. The Fatal Gift of Beauty. New York: Harper & Row, 1964. [A popularized biography.]

1965

Ades, John I. "Charles Lamb's Judgment of Byron and Shelley," Papers on English Language and Literature, I (Winter, 1965), 31-38. ["Basically Lamb rejected Byron on the grounds of lack of sympathy and penchant for satire."]

Alexander, Edward. Matthew Arnold and John Stuart Mill. New York: Columbia University Press; London: Routledge & Kegan Paul, 1965.

Altick, Richard D. Lives and Letters. A History of Literary Biography in England and America. New York: Alfred Knopf, 1965.

Anderson, George K. The Legend of the Wandering Jew. Providence: Brown University Press, 1965.

Anderson, Warren D. Matthew Arnold and the Classical Tradition. Ann Arbor: The University of Michigan Press, 1965.

Barbary, James. The Young Lord Byron. New York: Roy Publishers, 1965.

Barr, D. J. "Byron and Johnson," N&Q, CCX (Dec., 1965), 464. [Asks whether a line in Childe Harold's Pilgrimage echoes the Idler, No. 42.]

Bartel, Roland. "Byron's Respect for Language." Papers on English Language and Literature, I (Autumn, 1965), 373-78.

Bateson, Frederick Wilse. "Triumph of Romanticism," A Guide to
English Literature. Garden City, N.Y.: Anchor Books,
1965. Pp. 271-74.

Bhalla, Alok. "Two Voices in Byron's Manfred," An English Miscellany, (St. Stephen's College, Delhi), III (1965), 19-32.

Booth, Michael R. English Melodrama. London: H. Jenkins,
1965.

Bunday, Murray W. "John Drinkwater and 'The Cats,'" Research
Studies of Washington State University, XXXIII (June, 1965),
37-55. [On Drinkwater's annotations in his copy of the second edition of Astarte and their relation to his Byron: The
Pilgrim of Eternity.]

Chamberlain, Robert L. George Crabbe. New York: Twayne
Publishers, 1965.

Chambers, R. W. Ruskin (and Others) on Byron. New York:
Haskell House, 1965. [A reprint of a book published in 1925
by the Oxford University Press.]

Chatman, Seymour. A Theory of Meter. The Hague: Mouton,
1965.

Chew, Samuel C. Byron in England: His Fame and Afterfame.
New York: Russell and Russell, 1965. [A reprint of a book
published in 1924 by John Murray.]

Crawley, C. W. (ed.). War and Peace in an Age of Upheaval,
1793-1830. Vol. IX of The New Cambridge Modern History.
Cambridge, [Eng.]: Cambridge University Press, 1965.

Cunningham, Gilbert F. The Divine Comedy in English: A Critical Bibliography. 2 vols. New York: Barnes and Noble,
1965, 1967.

Fussell, Paul, Jr. Poetic Meter and Poetic Form. New York:
Random House, 1965.

Gardner, Helen. T. S. Eliot and the English Poetic Tradition.
"Byron Foundation Lecture." Nottingham: University of
Nottingham, 1965.

Gleckner, Robert F. "Byron in Finnegans Wake," Twelve and a
Tilly: Essays on the Occasion of the 25th Anniversary of
Finnegans Wake, ed. Jack P. Dalton and Clive Hart. Lon-
don: Faber; Evanston: Northwestern University Press, 1965.
Pp. 40-51.

_____ . "Ruskin and Byron," ELN, III (Sept. , 1965), 47-51.
[Considers Byron's manuscript revisions of The Island, III,
ll. 63-72, in relation to Ruskin's analysis of the same
lines in the manuscript notes for Fiction, Fair and Foul.]

Goode, Clement Tyson. Byron as Critic. New York: Haskell
House, 1965. [A reprint of a book published in 1923 by R.
Wagner Sohn, in Weimar.]

Green, William Chace. The Choices of Criticism. Cambridge,
Mass. : M. I. T. , 1965.

Hassler, Donald M. "Marino Faliero, the Byronic Hero and Don
Juan," K-SJ, XIV (Winter, 1965), 55-64.

Hilles, Frederick W. , and Harold Bloom (eds.). From Sensibility
to Romanticism: Essays Presented to Frederick A. Pottle.
New York: Oxford University Press, 1965.
It contains:
    E. D. Hirsch, Jr. , "Byron and the Terrestrial Paradise,"
    pp. 467-86.
    George M. Ridenour, "Byron in 1816: Four Poems from
    Diodati," pp. 453-65.

Kernan, Alvin B. "Don Juan," The Plot of Satire. New Haven:
Yale University Press, 1965. Pp. 171-222.

Leonard, William Ellery. Byron and Byronism in America. New
York: Gordian Press, 1965. [A reprint of a book published
in 1907 by Columbia University Press.]

Lovell, Ernest J. , Jr. "Byron, Mary Shelley, and Madame de
Staël," K-SJ, XIV (Winter, 1965), 13.

Luke, Hugh J. , Jr. "Publishing of Byron's Don Juan," PMLA,
LXXX (June, 1965), 199-209. [Through the piratical editions
of this work, which fell in the hands of radical booksellers in
London, Byron acquired a radical reputation. Don Juan had
a hostile reception, but he also acquired a new reading public.]

McKemy, Kay. "Lord Byron's Toothpowder," Journal of the American Dental Association, LXXI (Dec. , 1965), 1506-1507. [On
his efforts to obtain toothpowder.]

MacNeice, Louis. Varieties in Parable. Cambridge, [Eng.]:
Cambridge University Press, 1965. [Byron's "Darkness" a
parable.]

Marchand, Leslie A. "Byron," Encyclopedia Americana. New York:
The Encyclopedia Americana Corporation, 1965. Vol. V, pp.
97b-101.

_____. "Byron," Encyclopaedia Britannica. 14th edition. Chi-
cago: William Benton, 1965. Vol. IV, pp. 509-12.

_____. Byron's Poetry: A Critical Introduction. Boston:
Houghton Mifflin, 1965. Rptd. in paperback in 1966 by River-
side Studies in Literature.
Reviews:
    Annette Park, Charles Lamb Society Bulletin, No. 189 (May,
    1966), 525-26.
    J. B. Caird, Library Review, XX (Summer, 1966), 429-30.
    Choice, III (July-Aug., 1966), 411.
    Ralph Lawrence, English, XVI (Autumn, 1966), 115.
    E. E. B[ostetter], ELN, IV (Suppl. to No. 1, Sept., 1966),
    25-26.
    TLS, LXV (Sept. 15, 1966), 855.
    W. J. B. Owen, RES, n. s., XVIII (Feb., 1967), 107-108.
    Andrew Rutherford, Cambridge Review, LXXXIX (Feb. 4,
    1967), 201.
    M. K. Joseph, Aumla, No. 27 (May, 1967), 121-22.
    Frederick T. Wood, ES, XLVIII (Aut., 1967), 366.
    John Clubbe, SAQ, LXVIII (Spring, 1969), 272.

_____. "The Land of Byron's 'Pilgrimage,' " Life International,
XXXVIII (Feb. 8, 1965), 66-71. [A summary of Byron's two
voyages to Greece.]

Matthiesen, Paul F. "Gosses's Candid 'Snapshots,' " Victorian
    Studies, VIII (June, 1965), 329-54.

Mayfield, John S. "To Whom Was It Written? Note on a Byron
    Letter," Manuscripts, XVII (Winter, 1965), 3-4. [A letter
    dated May 20, 1812, at No. 8, St. James St.?]

A Medical History of Lord Byron. Norwich, N.Y.: Eaton Labora-
    tories, 1965.

Merchant, William M. "Lord Byron: Cain: A Mystery," Creed
    and Drama: An Essay in Religious Drama. London:
    S.P.C.K., 1965. Pp. 73-80.

Merritt, James D. "Disraeli as a Byronic Poet," Victorian Poe-
    try, III (Spring, 1965), 138-39. [A poem in Alroy, derived
    from "She Walks in Beauty."]

Mogan, Joseph J., Jr. "Pierre and Manfred: Melville's Study of
    the Byronic Hero," Papers on English Language and Litera-
    ture, I (Summer, 1965), 230-40.

Moore, L. Hugh, Jr. "The Sunny South and its Literature,"
    Georgia Review, XIX (Summer, 1965), 176-85. [This maga-
    zine overlooked the usual moral objections to Byron because
    of the tremendous appeal of his melancholy personality and
    romantic death.]

Moorman, Mary. William Wordsworth: A Biography. The Later
    Years, 1803-1850. Oxford: Oxford University Press, 1965.

Pearsall, Ronald. "A Letter from Byron," Books and Bookmen,
    X (March, 1965), 46 [It was just a replica.]

Peters, Robert L. The Crowns of Apollo: Swinburne's Principles
    of Literature and Art. A Study of Victorian Criticism and
    Aesthetics. Detroit: Wayne State University, 1965.

Pratt, Willis W. Lord Byron and His Circle. A Calendar of MSS
    in the University of Texas Library. New York: Haskell
    House, 1965. [A reprint of a book published in 1945 by the
    University of Texas Press.]

Praz, Mario. "Dante in England," Forum for Modern Language
    Studies, I (April, 1965), 99-116. [On Byron's interest in
    Dante.]

Quennell, Peter. "Speaking of Books: Literary Sightseeing,"
    NYTBR, Dec. 12, 1965, pp. 2, 45.

Rieger, James. "Byron as 'Albé,' " K-SJ, XIV (Winter, 1965), 6-
    7. [This soubriquet comes from the title of Sophie Cottin's
    novel Claire d'Albé.]

Rossetti, Dante Gabriel. The Letters of Dante Gabriel Rossetti,
    eds. Oswald Doughty and John Robert Wahl. 2 vols. Ox-
    ford: At the Clarendon Press, 1965.

Roston, Murray. Prophet and Poet: The Bible and the Growth of
    Romanticism. Evanston: Northwestern University Press;
    London: Faber, 1965.

Rutherford, Andrew. Byron: A Critical Study. London: Oliver,
    1965. Toronto: Clarke, Irwin, 1965. [A paperback reprint
    of a book published in 1961 by Oliver.]

_____. Byron the Best Seller. "Byron Foundation Lecture."
    Nottingham: University of Nottingham, 1965.

Sarkar, Manojkumar. "Voice of the Haunted Ruins," Calcutta Re-
    view, CLXXV (June, 1965), 241-50.

Singer, Armand E. The Don Juan Theme: Versions and Criticism:
    A Bibliography. Morgantown, W. Va.: University of West
    Virginia Press, 1965.

Southey, Robert. New Letters of Robert Southey, ed. Kenneth
    Curry. 2 vols. New York: Columbia University Press,
    1965.

Stock, Ely. "The Biblical Context of Ethan Brand," AL, XXXVII
    (May, 1965), 115-34. [Byron's Cain is an important source
    for the appearance of Satan to Ethan Brand, and for other
    elements of the story.]

Thorslev, Peter L., Jr. "Incest as Romantic Symbol," Compara-
    tive Literature Studies, II (1965), 41-58. [The Romantic age
    developed incest into a literary symbol of the Romantic
    "psyche's love affair with self and of its tragic isolation in
    an increasingly alien world."]

Tillotson, Kathleen. "Charlotte Yonge as a Critic of Literature,"
    A Chaplet for Charlotte Yonge, eds. Georgina Battiscombe
    and Marghanita Laski. London: Cresset, 1965. Pp. 56-70.

Uden, Grant (comp.). They Looked like This: An Assembly of Au-
    thentic Word-Portraits of Men and Women in English History
    and Literature over 1900 Years. Oxford: Basil Blackwell,
    1965.

Wagenknecht, Edward Charles. Harriet Beecher Stowe: The
    Known and the Unknown. New York: Oxford University Press,
    1965.

Wellek, René. Confrontations: Studies in the Intellectual and Lite-
    rary Relations between Germany, England and the United
    States during the Nineteenth Century. Princeton: Princeton
    University Press, 1965.

Wilkie, Brian. "Byron and the Epic of Negation," Romantic Poets
    and Epic Tradition. Madison: The University of Wisconsin
    Press, 1965. Pp. 188-226.

Williams, Gwyn. "The Drowned Man in English Poetry," Litera,
    VIII (1965), 62-90. [Byron and the sea.]

Wise, Winifred E. Harriet Beecher Stowe, Woman with a Cause.
    New York: G. P. Putnam's Sons, 1965.

Woodring, Carl. "Lord Byron's Widow, 1825," Columbia Library
    Columns, XIV (May, 1965), 11-20. [About a letter that Lady
    Byron sent to Augusta Leigh on June 4, 1825, dealing with
    the burning of Byron's Memoirs.]

Wright, Austin. "The Byron of Don Juan," Six Satirists, eds. A.
    Fred Sochatoff, Norman Knox, et al. Pittsburgh, Pa.:
    Carnegie Institute of Technology, 1965. Pp. 69-84.

Young, Ione. A Concordance to the Poetry of Byron. Austin,
    Texas: Pemberton Press, 1965.
    Review:
        Leslie Marchand, K-SJ, XVI (Winter, 1967), 96-97.

1966

Adams, Robert Martin. Nil: Episodes in the Literary Conquest
of Void during the Nineteenth Century. New York: Oxford
University Press, 1966. [On 'Darkness.'']

Auden, W. H. ''Byron: The Making of a Comic Poet,'' NYRB,
VII (Aug. 18, 1966), 12-18. Rptd. The American Literary
Anthology, eds. John Hawkes, John Ashberry and William
Alfred. New York: Farrar, Straus & Giroux, 1968. Pp.
26-42.

_____, (ed.). ''Introduction,'' Selected Poetry and Prose of By-
ron. New York: New American Library, 1966. Pp. vii-
xxiv.

Bartlett, C. J. Castlereagh. New York: Scribner's, 1966.

Blake, Robert. Disraeli. London: Eyre & Spottiswoode, 1966.

Brack, O. M., Jr. ''Lord Byron, Leigh Hunt and The Liberal,
Some New Evidence,'' Books at Iowa, No. 4 (April, 1966),
36-38. [Reproduces a letter from Byron to Mary Shelley,
dated Oct. 14, 1822, which would indicate that Byron probably
disparaged Leigh Hunt in his correspondence with John Murray before Oct. 8, 1822.]

Brand, C. P. Torquato Tasso: A Study of the Poet and His Contribution to English Literature. Cambridge: Cambridge University Press, 1965.

Brown, Charles Armitage. The Letters of C. A. Brown, ed. Jack
Stillinger. Cambridge, Mass.: Harvard University Press,
1966.

Browning, Robert. Learned Lady: Letters from Robert Browning
to Mrs. Thomas FitzGerald 1876-1889, ed. Edward C.
McAleer. Cambridge, [Mass.]: Harvard University Press,
1966.

Bruffee, Kenneth A. ''The Synthetic Hero and the Narrative Structure of Childe Harold III,'' SEL, VI (Autumn, 1966), 669-788.

Buckley, Jerome Hamilton. The Triumph of Time: A Study of the
Victorian Concepts of Time, History, Progress, and Decadence. Cambridge, [Mass.]: Harvard University Press,
1966.

Burney, E. L. ''Peasant Poets, or Peasants, Poetry, Patronage
and the Pauper's Pit,'' Manchester Review, XI (1966), 59-72.

Byron, George Gordon, Lord. The Works of Lord Byron, eds.
Ernest Hartley Coleridge and Rowland E. Prothero. 13 vols.

New York: Octagon Books, 1966. [A reprint of the volumes published in 1898-1904 by John Murray in London and in 1918 and 1922 by Charles Scribner's Sons.]

Casey, John. The Language of Criticism. London: Methuen, 1966.

Clare, John. Selected Poems and Prose of John Clare, eds. Eric Robinson and Geoffrey Summerfield. London: Oxford University Press, 1966.

Colby, Reginald. Mayfair: A Town within London. London: Country Life, 1966. [On the houses that Byron was familiar with in Mayfair.]

Culler, A. Dwight. Imaginative Reason: The Poetry of Matthew Arnold. New Haven: Yale University Press, 1966.

Deen, Leonard W. "Liberty and License in Byron's Don Juan," Texas Studies in Literature and Language, VIII (Fall, 1966), 345-57.

Derry, Warren. Dr. Parr: A Portrait of the Whig Dr. Johnson. Oxford: At the Clarendon Press, 1966.

Dobrzycka, Irena. "Byron and Ireland," Studies in Language and Literature in Honor of Margaret Schlauch, eds. Mieczyslaw Brahmer, Stanislaw Helsztynski, and Julian Krzyzanowski. Warsaw: Panstwowe Wydawnictwo Naukowe, 1966. [His poetry and prose reveal a 'life long sympathy for Ireland.]

Dutt, Toru. "Toru Dutt's Letters," Indian Literature, IX (April-June, 1966), 15-23.

Elledge, W. Paul. "Imagery and Theme in Byron's Cain," K-SJ, XV (Winter, 1966), 49-57.

England, A. B. "An Echo of Prior in Don Juan," N&Q, CCXI (May, 1966), 179. [An echo from Hans Carvel.]

Erdman, David V. and Ephim G. Fogel, (eds.). Evidence for Authorship. Ithaca, New York: Cornell University Press, 1966.

Fermor, Patrick Leigh. Roumeli: Travels in Northern Greece. London: John Murray, 1966.

Fiess, Edward. "Byron's Dark Blue Ocean and Melville's Rolling Sea," ELN, III (June, 1966), 274-78.

Fletcher, Richard M. English Romantic Drama 1795-1843: A Critical History. New York: Exposition Press, Inc., 1966.

Fowler, Roger (ed.). Essays on Style and Language: Linguistic
    and Critical Approaches to Literary Style. New York: Hu-
    manities, 1966.

Gérin, Winifred. "Byron's Influence on the Brontës," KSMB,
    XVII (1966), 1-19.

Goethe, Johann Wolfgang von. Goethe: Conversations and Encoun-
    ters, eds. David Luke and Robert Pick. Chicago: Regnery,
    1966.

Gordon, David J. D. H. Lawrence as a Literary Critic. New
    Haven: Yale University Press, 1966.

Gore, John. "Clio in No Hurry," QR, CCCIV (Oct., 1966), 414-
    18. [Only in 1935 was it discovered that "When We Two
    Parted" had been written to Lady Frances Wedderburn Web-
    ster.]

Grant, Judith. A Pillage of Art. London: Robert Hale, 1966.

Hardy, Thomas. Thomas Hardy's Personal Writings: Prefaces,
    Literary Opinions, Reminiscences, ed. Harold Orel. Law-
    rence: University of Kansas, 1966.

Hudson, Arthur Palmer. "The 'Superstitious' Lord Byron," SP,
    LXII (Oct., 1966), 708-21.

Jeffrey, Lloyd N. "Lord Byron and the Classics," Classical Out-
    look, XLIII (March, 1966), 76-78.

Joyce, James. Letters of James Joyce, ed. Richard Ellman. 2
    vols. New York: Viking Press, 1966.

Knight, G. Wilson. Byron and Shakespeare. London: Routledge
    and Kegan Paul; New York: Barnes & Noble, 1966.
    Reviews:
        John Bayley, Spectator, CCXVII (Nov. 25, 1966), 690-91.
        TLS, LXVI (Feb. 23, 1967), 148.
        John D. Jump, Critical Quarterly, IX (Spring, 1967), 93-94.
        Tom Cain, Cambridge Review, LXXXIX (May 20, 1967), 354-
            356.
        Choice, IV (July-Aug., 1967), 532.
        Frederick T. Wood, ES, XLVIII (Aug., 1967), 366.
        D. V. E[rdman], ELN, V (Suppl. to No. 1, Sept., 1967), 25.
        Kurt Otten, Erasmus, XX (Oct., 1968), 603-604.
        Thomas B. Stroup, Shakespeare Quarterly, XXI (Spring, 1970),
            188-89.

_____. "Byron and Spiritualism," Light, LXXXVI (Summer, 1966),
    52-57.

Kumar, Shiv Kumar (ed.). British Romantic Poets: Recent Re-
    valuations. New York: New York University Press, 1966.
    [All items in this book are reprints.]
    It contains:
        Sir C. M. Bowra, "Don Juan," pp. 179-201. [Excerpts
        from The Romantic Imagination, 1949.]
        W. S. Dowden, "The Consistency of Byron's Social Doctrine,"
        pp. 142-57. Rptd. from Rice Institute Pamphlet, XXXVII
        (Oct. , 1950), 18-44.
        A. Rutherford, "Childe Harold's Pilgrimage: Cantos III &
        IV," [Excerpts from Byron: A Critical Study, 1961].

Lambert, Cecily. "Byron and the Maid of Athens," Country Life,
    CXL (Oct. 6, 1966), 853-55.

Lentricchia, Frank, Jr. "Harriet Beecher Stowe and the Byron
    Whirlwind," Bulletin of the New York Public Library, LXX
    (April, 1966), 218-28. [Reaction of American literary figures
    to the Stowe charges against Byron.]

Lindsay, Jack. J. M. Turner: His Life and Work. Greenwich,
    Conn. : New York Graphic Society, 1966.

Loder, Elizabeth. "Maurice Guest: Some Nineteenth-Century
    Progenitors," Southerly, XXVI, No. 2 (1966), 94-105.
    [Brief mention of the Byronic hero.]

Logan, James V. , John E. Jordan, and Northrop Frye (eds.).
    Some British Romantics: A Collection of Essays. Columbus:
    Ohio State University Press, 1966.

Lovell, Ernest J. , Jr. Byron: The Record of a Quest. Studies
    in a Poet's Concept and Treatment of Nature. Hamden,
    [Conn.]: Shoe String, 1966. [A reprint of a book published
    in 1949 by the University of Texas Press.]

McClary, Ben Harris. "The Moore-Irving Letter File," N&Q,
    CCXI (May, 1966), 181-82.

McGann, Jerome. "Childe Harold's Pilgrimage I-II: A Collation
    and Analysis," KSMB, XVII (1966), 37-54.

McLean, Malcolm D. "Mazeppa. The First Texas Horse Opera,"
    Fine Texas Horses, Their Pedigree and Performance, 1830-
    1845. Fort Worth: Texas Christian University Press, 1966.
    Pp. 45-49.

Marchand, Leslie. "Byron and Rossini," Opera News, XXX
    (March 19, 1966), 6-7. [Rossini composed "The Lament of
    the Muses for the Death of Lord Byron" and sang the part of
    Apollo himself.]

Medwin, Thomas.   Medwin's "Conversations of Lord Byron," ed.
    Ernest J. Lovell, Jr.   Princeton: Princeton University
    Press, 1966.
    Reviews:
        Peter Quennell, Spectator, CCXVII (Aug. 5, 1966), 178-79.
        Choice, III (Nov., 1966), 771.
        Peter L. Thorslev, Jr., K-SJ, XVI (1967), 97-99.
        Muriel J. Mellown, SAQ, LXVI (Spring, 1967), 284.
        E. E. B[ostetter], ELN, V (Suppl. to No. 1, Sept., 1967),
        25-26.
        John D. Jump, YES, I (1971), 290-91.

Melchiori, Barbara.   "Browning's Don Juan," Etudes Celtiques,
    XVI (Oct., 1966), 416-40.

Miliband, Marion (ed.).   "Byron--The Romantic Hero," The Ob-
    server of the Nineteenth Century: 1791-1901.   Intr. Asa
    Briggs.   London: Longmans, 1966.   Pp. 95-98.

Mras, George P.   Eugène Delacroix's Theory of Art.   Princeton:
    Princeton University Press, 1966.

Murray, John (ed.).   Lord Byron's Correspondence, Chiefly with
    Lady Melbourne, Mr. Hobhouse, The Hon. Douglas Kinnaird,
    and P. B. Shelley.   With Portraits.   2 vols.   Chester
    Springs, Pa.:   Dufour Editions, 1966.   [A reprint of a book
    published in 1922 by John Murray.]

Nicolson, Harold.   Diaries and Letters 1930-1939, ed. Nigel Nicol-
    son.   New York: Atheneum, 1966.

Pedrini, Lura Nancy, and Duilio T. Pedrini.   Serpent Imagery and
    Symbolism.   A Study of the Major English Romantic Poets.
    New Haven, Conn.:   College and University Press, 1966.

Praz, Mario.   "Byron and Foscolo," Renaissance and Modern Es-
    says, Presented to Vivian de Sola Pinto in Celebration of His
    Seventieth Birthday, ed. with the Assistance of George A.
    Panichas and Allan Rodway.   London: Routledge & Kegan
    Paul, 1966.   Pp. 101-18.

Quennell, Peter.   "Byron: The Vision of Judgment," Master
    Poems of the English Language, ed. Oscar Williams.   New
    York: Trident Press, 1966.   Pp. 521-26.

Radcliffe-Umstead, Douglas.   "Cainism and Gerard de Nerval,"
    PQ, XLV (April, 1966), 395-408.

Rawson, C. J.   "Pope Echoes in Byron's 'To Romance,' and Don
    Juan, IV, iii," N&Q, CCXI (May, 1966), 179.   [From the
    Epistle to Dr. Arbuthnot, ll. 340-41.]

Reed, Joseph W., Jr. "Moore's Byron: Myth in a Mold," English Biography in the Early Nineteenth Century. New Haven: Yale University Press, 1966. Pp. 102-26.

Rennes, Jacob Johan van. Bowles, Byron and the Pope Controversy. New York: Haskell House, 1966. [A reprint of a book published in 1927 by G. E. Steckert.]

Rhodes, Jack Lee. A Study in the Vocabulary of English Romanticism: "Joy" in the Poetry of Blake, Wordsworth, Coleridge, Shelley, Keats and Byron. Austin: University of Texas, 1966.

Richardson, Joanna. George the Magnificent: A Portrait of King George IV. New York: Harcourt, Brace & World, 1966.

Roberts, K. S. "The Marquesa De Alorna and the English Poets," Kentucky Foreign Language Quarterly, XIII, No. 3 (1966), 147-55.

Robinson, Henry Crabb. The London Theatre 1811-1866: Selections from the Diary of Henry Crabb Robinson, ed. Eluned Brown. London: Society for Theatre Research, 1966.

Rogers, Katharine M. The Troublesome Helpmate: A History of Misogyny in Literature. Seattle: University of Washington Press, 1966.

Sambrook, A. J. "A Romantic Theme: The Last Man," Forum for Modern Language Studies, II (Jan., 1966), 25-33. [Byron's "Darkness" deals with this theme.]

Schenk, H. G. The Mind of the European Romantics: An Essay in Cultural History. New York: Frederick Ungar Publishing Co., 1966.

Sheridan, Richard Brinsley. The Letters of Richard Brinsley Sheridan, ed. Cecil Price. 3 vols. Oxford: Clarendon Press, 1966.

Steffan, T. G. "A Byron Facsimile," Library Chronicle of the University of Texas, VIII (Spring, 1966), 3-7. [Letter dated April 27, 1819, from Byron to the editor of Galignani's Messenger in the Miriam Lutcher Stark Library of the University of Texas; found to be a lithographic facsimile.]

Thomson, P. W. "Byron and Edmund Kean--A Comment," Theatre Research/Recherches Théâtrales, VIII, No. 1 (1966), 17-19.

Thorlby, Anthony. The Romantic Movement. "Problems and Perspectives in History Series." London: Longmans, 1966.

Timko, Michael. Innocent Victorian: The Satiric Poetry of Arthur
    Hugh Clough. Athens, Ohio: Ohio University Press, 1966.

Todd, William B. "London Printers' Imprints, 1800-1840, " Li-
    brary, 5th ser., XXII (March, 1966), 45-59. [Imprints of
    English Bards and Scotch Reviewers.]

Untermeyer, Louis. "Legendary Lover Byron, " The Paths of Poe-
    try. Twenty-Five Poets and Their Poems. New York:
    Delacorte Press, 1966. Pp. 126-34.

Watson, George. Coleridge, the Poet. London: Routledge & K.
    Paul, 1966.

                                1967

Aarsleff, Hans. The Study of Language in England, 1780-1860.
    Princeton: Princeton University Press, 1967.

Barnes, T. R. English Verse: Voice and Movement from Wyatt
    to Yeats. Cambridge: Cambridge University Press, 1967.

Blackmur, R. P. A Primer of Ignorance, ed. Joseph Frank.
    New York: Harcourt, Brace & World, 1967. [Contrasts be-
    tween Byron and William Carlos Williams.]

Brecknock, Albert. Byron: A Study of the Poet in the Light of
    New Discoveries. New York: Haskell House, 1967. [A re-
    print of a book published in 1926 by C. Palmer.]

Briscoe, Walter A. Byron, the Poet: A Collection of Addresses
    and Essays. New York: Haskell House, 1967. [A reprint
    of a book published in 1924 by Routledge.]

Brooks, Elmer L. "Two Notes on Byron, " N&Q, CCXII (Aug. ,
    1967), 295-97. [1. Byron's Coming-of-Age Party (cele-
    brated at Newstead even though Byron was at Dorant's Hotel
    in London); 2. Byron and Schools for the Poor (Byron do-
    nated 105 pounds to the Royal Lancasterian Institution in
    1814.]

Brownstein, Rachel Mayer. 'Byron's Don Juan: Some Reasons for
    the Rhymes, " MLQ, XXVIII (June, 1967), 177-91.

Buxton, John. Byron and Shelley: A Friendship Renewed. Middle-
    town, Conn. : Center for Advanced Studies, Wesleyan Univer-
    sity, 1967.

Byrne, Clifford M. "Byron's Cyclical Interpretation of History, "
    McNeese Review (Louisiana), XVIII (1967), 11-26.

Cate, Hollins L. "Emily Dickinson and 'The Prisoner of Chillon, ' "
American N&Q, VI (Sept. , 1967), 6-7. [Only poem by Byron
she mentions in her letters. She mentions it on four occasions.]

Clark, Peter. "Henry Hallam Reconsidered, " QR, CCCV (Oct. ,
1967), 410-19.

Colby, Robert A. Fiction with a Purpose: Major and Minor Nineteenth Century Novels. Bloomington: Indiana University
Press, 1967.

Crompton, Margaret. Shelley's Dream Women. South Brunswick,
N.J. : A. S. Barnes & Co. , 1967.

Dahlberg, Edward. Epitaphs of Our Times: The Letters of Edward Dahlberg. New York: Braziller, 1967.

De Ford, Miriam Allen. Thomas Moore. New York: Twayne,
1967.

Demetz, Peter. Marx, Engels, and the Poets: Origins of Marxist
Literary Criticism, trans. Jeffrey L. Sammons. Chicago:
Univ. of Chicago Press, 1967.

Eliot, C. W. J. "Lord Byron, Early Travelers, and the Monastery at Delphi, " American Journal of Archaeology, LXXI
(July, 1967), 283-91, Plates 85-86.

Ellis, Amanda M. Rebels and Conservatives: Dorothy and William
Wordsworth and their Circle. Bloomington: Indiana Univ.
Press, 1967.

Elwin, Malcolm. The Noels and the Milbankes: Their Letters for
Twenty-Five Years, 1767-1792. London: Macdonald, 1967.

Fulford, Roger. Samuel Whitbread 1764-1815: A Study in Opposition. London: Macmillan, 1967.

Gál, István. "Shelley Plain, " New Hungarian Quarterly, VIII, No.
28 (Winter, 1967), 184-89.

Garber, Frederick. "Self, Society, Value, and the Romantic
Hero, " Comparative Literature, XIX (Fall, 1967), 321-33.

"The Gennadius Library, " TLS, May 4, 1967, p. 388. [Laurel
wreath from Byron's coffin is in the Gennadeion in Athens.]

George, M. Dorothy. Hogarth to Cruikshank: Social Change in
Graphic Satire. New York: Walker, 1967.

Gleckner, Robert F. Byron and the Ruins of Paradise. Baltimore:
The Johns Hopkins University Press, 1967.

Reviews:
  Richard Freedman, KR, XXX (1968), 299-302.
  Yale Review, LVII (Spring, 1968), xxxi-xxxii.
  G. M. Matthews, NYRB, May 23, 1968, pp. 23-28.
  Brian Wilkie, JEGP, LXVII (July, 1968), 526-29.
  E. B. B[ostetter], ELN, VI (Suppl. to No. 1, Sept., 1968), 23-24.
  William H. Marshall, SAQ, LXVII (Autumn, 1968), 709-10.
  Hermann Peschmann, English, XVII (Autumn, 1968), 104-105.
  Peter L. Thorslev, Jr., Criticism, X (Fall, 1968), 370-72.
  Carl Woodring, SEL, VIII (Autumn, 1968), 728-29.
  Choice, V (Sept., 1968), 776.
  TLS, Sept. 5, 1968, p. 949.
  Bernard Beatty, MLR, LXIV (July, 1969), 655-56.
  Jerome J. McGann, MP, LXVII (Nov., 1969), 203-07.
  Sister Thomas Becket, Thought, LXIV (Spring, 1969), 133-34.
  John D. Jump, RES, n.s., XX (May, 1969), 238-39.

Green, David Bonnell. "New Letters of John Clare to Taylor and
  Hessey," SP, LXIV (Oct., 1967), 720-34.

Hagelman, Charles W., Jr., and Robert J. Barnes (eds.). A Con-
  cordance to Byron's "Don Juan." Ithaca: Cornell University
  Press, 1967.
Reviews:
  Leslie A. Marchand, K-SJ, XVII (1968), 132-33.
  TLS, April 25, 1968, p. 442.
  English, XVII (Summer, 1968), 74.
  D. V. Erdman, ELN, VI (Suppl. to No. 1, Sept., 1968), 24-25.
  Jerome McGann, MP, LXVII (1969), 203-07.
  Jurgen Schafer, Anglia, LXXXVIII (1970), 548-52.

Hamer, Douglas. "Conversation-Notes with Sir Thomas Dyke Ac-
  land," N&Q, CCXII (Feb., 1967), 65-66. [Debate on Shelley
  v. Byron took place in Oxford Union in 1829.]

Harding, Walter. Emerson's Library. Charlottesville: University
  of Virginia Press, 1967.

Hirsch, E. D., Jr. Validity in Interpretation. New Haven: Yale
  University Press, 1967.

Holloway, John. Widening Horizons in English Verse. Evanston:
  Northwestern University, 1967. [On Byron's interest in Islam
  and in India.]

Hudson, Derek. Holland House in Kensington. London: Peter
  Davies, 1967.

Joberg, Leon. "Lord Byron's Greece: Glory Reborn," Mankind, I
  (May-June, 1967), 40-47, 74-77.

Joshi, P. C. "Subjectivism in the Nineteenth Century Poetic
    Drama," Literary Criterion, VIII (Winter, 1967), 9-18.

Jump, John D. "Literary Echoes in Byron's Don Juan," N&Q,
    CCXII (Aug. , 1967), 302. [From Milton, Shakespeare and
    Smollett.]

Keenan, Hugh T. "Another Hudibras Allusion in Byron's Don Juan,"
    N&Q, CCXII (Aug. , 1967), 301-302.

Kemper, Claudette. "Irony Anew, with Occasional Reference to
    Byron and Browning," SEL, VII (Autumn, 1967), 705-19.

Knight, G. Wilson. Lord Byron: Christian Virtues. New York:
    Barnes & Noble, 1967; London: Routledge & Kegan Paul,
    1967. [A reprint of a book published in 1952 by Routledge
    and Paul.]

_____ . Poets of Action, Incorporating Essays from "The Burn-
    ing Oracle." London: Methuen, 1967.
    It contains:
    "Byron: The Poetry," pp. 179-265. Rptd. from The Burning
        Oracle, 1939, pp. 197-288.
    "Byron's Dramatic Prose," pp. 266-93. Rptd. from his By-
        ron Foundation Lecture, 1953.

_____ . Shakespeare and Religion: Essays of Forty Years.
    London: Routledge, 1967.

Lauber, John. "Byron's Concept of Poetry," Dalhousie Review,
    XLVII (Winter 1967-1968), 526-34.

Lill, John. "Because It Is There," Texas Quarterly, X (Summer,
    1967), 215-28. [Includes descriptions of mountains by Byron.]

Lombardi, Thomas W. "Hogg to Byron to Davenport: An Unpub-
    lished Byron Letter," Bulletin of the New York Public Library,
    LXXI (Jan. , 1967), 39-46. [Dated Feb. 7, 1815.]

McClary, Ben Harris. "Another Moore Letter," N&Q, CCXII
    (Jan. 19, 1967), 24-25. [Mentioning the destruction of By-
    ron's memoirs.]

_____ . "Irving's Literary Midwifery: Five Unpublished Letters
    from British Repositories," PQ, XLVI (April, 1967), 277-83.

McDowell, Robert E. "Tirso, Byron and the Don Juan Tradition,"
    Arlington Quarterly, I (Autumn, 1967), 52-68.

McGann, Jerome J. "Byron, Teresa and Sardanapalus," KSMB,
    XVIII (1967), 7-22.

_____ . "The Composition, Revision, and Meaning of Childe Harold's Pilgrimage III," Bulletin of the New York Public Library, LXXI (Sept. , 1967), 415-30.

Madden, William A. Matthew Arnold: A Study of the Aesthetic Temperament in Victorian England. ("Indiana University Humanities Series" No. 63.) Bloomington: University of Indiana Press, 1967.

Marchand, Leslie A. (ed.). "Introduction, " The Selected Poetry of Byron. New York: Modern Library, 1967. Pp. xi-xxvii.

Marples, Morris. "Byron at Harrow, " Romantics at School: The Schooldays of Wordsworth, Coleridge, Southey, Byron, Shelley and Keats. London: Faber; New York: Barnes and Noble, 1967. Pp. 112-43.

Marshall, William H. "The Byron Will of 1809, " Library Chronicle of the University of Pennsylvania, XXXIII (Spring, 1967), 97-114. [First printing of a will dated 1809.]

_____ . The World of the Victorian Novel. South Brunswick, N.J. : A. S. Barnes, 1967.

Martin, M. H. Combe. "Byron Trouvaille?" N&Q, CCXII (Jan. , 1967), 26. [Prints verses attributed to Byron supposedly addressed to Lady Frances Wedderburn-Webster.]

Matthews, Honor. The Primal Curse: The Myth of Cain and Abel in the Theatre. New York: Schocken, 1967.

Maxwell, J. C. "Academician, " N&Q, CCXII (Aug. , 1967), 303. [In Don Juan, IX, 17, it means an Academic Philosopher; a sceptic.]

_____ . "More Literary Echoes in Don Juan, " N&Q, CCXII (Aug. , 1967), 302-303.

Miles, Josephine. Style and Proportion: The Language of Prose and Poetry. Boston: Little, Brown, 1967.

Perkins, David (ed.). "Byron, " English Romantic Writers. New York: Harcourt, Brace & World, 1967. Pp. 779-87.

Playfair, Giles. The Prodigy: A Study of the Strange Life of Master Betty. London: Secker & Warburg, 1967.

Potts, Abbie Findlay. The Elegiac Mode: Poetic Form in Wordsworth and Other Elegists. Ithaca: Cornell University Press, 1967.

Quennell, Peter. Byron: The Years of Fame. New ed. London: Collins, 1967; Rev. ed. Hamden, Conn. : Archon Books, 1967.

Reeves, James and Martin Seymour-Smith. A New Canon of English Poetry. London: Heinemann, 1967.

Rieger, James. The Mutiny Within: The Heresies of Percy Bysshe Shelley. New York: George Braziller, 1967.

Robinson, Henry Crabb. The Diary of Henry Crabb Robinson: An Abridgement, ed. Derek Hudson. London: Oxford University Press, 1967.

Shipps, Anthony W. "Alaric A. Watts," N&Q, CCXII (March, 1967), 105. [Line requested in a previous query comes from English Bards and Scotch Reviewers, 1. 67.]

_____. "Replies," N&Q, CCXII (April, 1967), 145. [The source of the quotation is in Byron's Cain, I, i, 536-37.]

_____. "Replies," N&Q, CCXII (May, 1967), 195. [Source is Byron's The Corsair, I, 159-60.]

Smidt, Kristina. Books and Men: A Short History of English and American Literature. Oslo: J. W. Cappelen, 1967.

Stallworthy, Jon. "Poet and Publisher," Review of English Literature, VIII (Jan., 1967), 39-49.

Stange, G. Robert. Matthew Arnold: The Poet as Humanist. Princeton: Princeton University Press, 1967.

Steffan, T. G. "Another Doubtful Byron Letter," N&Q, CCXII (Aug., 1967), 299-301. [The Galignani letter.]

Sundell, M. G. "'Tintern Abbey' and 'Resignation,'" Victorian Poetry, V (Winter, 1967), 255-64.

Symonds, John Addington. The Letters of John Addington Symonds, eds. Herbert M. Schueller and Robert L. Peters. Vol. I: 1844-1868. Detroit: Wayne State University, 1967.

Talmon, J. L. Romanticism and Revolt in Europe, 1815-1848. London: Thames and Hudson; New York: Harcourt, Brace, and World, 1967.

Tenenbaum, Samuel. The Incredible Beau Brummell. South Brunswick, N.J.: A. S. Barnes; London: Yoseloff, 1967.

Thomas, Clara. Love and Work Enough: The Life of Anna Jameson. Toronto: University of Toronto Press, 1967.

Thompson, James R. "Byron's Plays and Don Juan: Genre and Myth," Bucknell Review, XV (Dec., 1967), 22-38.

Thorpe, Michael. Siegfried Sassoon: A Critical Study. London:
Oxford University Press, 1967. [Byron's influence on Sassoon.]

Trease, Geoffrey. The Grand Tour. New York: Holt, Rinehart
and Winston, 1967.

Vickery, Walter N. "Byron's Don Juan and Pushkin's Eugenij One-
gin: The Question of Parallelism," Indiana Slavic Studies,
IV (1967), 181-91.

Walsh, John. Strange Harp, Strange Symphony: The Life of
Francis Thompson. New York: Hawthorn Books, 1967.

Walsh, William. Coleridge: The Work and the Relevance. New
York: Barnes and Noble; London: Chatto, 1967.

Webby, Elizabeth. "English Literature in Early Australia: 1820-
1829," Southerly, XXVII, No. 4 (1967), 226-85.

Wilson, Angus. "Evil in the English Novel," KR, XXIX (March,
1967), 167-94. [The Byronic hero in some 19th century
novels.]

                              1968

Ball, Patricia. Childe Harold's Pilgrimage, Cantos III & IV, and
The Vision of Judgment. Oxford: Blackwell, 1968.

Barton, Anne. Byron and the Mythology of Fact. Nottingham:
University of Nottingham, 1968.

Beaty, Frederick L. "Harlequin Don Juan," JEGP, LXVII (July,
1968), 395-405.

Blainey, Ann. The Farthing Poet: A Biography of Richard Hen-
gist Horne, 1802-84, A Lesser Literary Lion. London:
Longmans, 1968.

Buxton, John. Byron and Shelley: The History of a Friendship.
London: Macmillan; New York: Harcourt, 1968.
Reviews:
TLS, May 30, 1968, p. 549.
Blackwood's Magazine, CCCIII (June, 1968), 565-566.
Noami Lewis, NS, LXXV (June 28, 1968), 874-75.
Hermann Peschmann, English, XVII (Autumn, 1968), 104-105.
John Lehmann, London Magazine, VIII (May, 1969), 90-97.
John D. Jump, RES, n. s., XX (May, 1969), 237-38.
E. E. B[ostetter], ELN, VII (Suppl. to No. 1, Sept., 1969),
28.
James A. Phillips, Library Journal, XCIII (Sept. 15, 1969),
3140.
Stuart Curran, K-SJ, XX (1971), 132-34.

Clairmont, Claire. The Journals of Claire Clairmont, 1814-1827,
    ed. Marion Kingston Stocking. Cambridge [Mass.]: Harvard
    University Press, 1968.

Cline, C. L. "Sacrilege at Lucca and the Pisan Circle," Texas
    Studies in Literature and Language, IX (1968), 503-509.

Cooke, Michael G. "The Limits of Skepticism: The Byronic Af-
    firmation," K-SJ, XVII (1968), 97-111.

Cooney, Seamus. "Satire Without Dogma: Byron's Don Juan,"
    Ball State University Forum, IX (Spring, 1968), 26-30.

Doherty, Francis M. Byron. London: Evans, 1968.

Elledge, W. Paul. Byron and the Dynamics of Metaphor. Nash-
    ville: Vanderbilt University Press, 1968.
    Reviews:
        Brian Wilkie, JEGP, LXVIII (July, 1969), 535-38.
        E. E. B[ostetter], ELN, VII (Suppl. to No. 1, Sept., 1969),
            28-29.
        E. J. Lovell, Jr., MLQ, XXX (Sept., 1969), 460-62.
        Hillis J. Miller, SEL, IX (Autumn, 1969), 743.
        M. K. Joseph, Aumla, No. 32, (Nov., 1969), 251-53.
        Jerome J. McGann, MP, LXVIII (Nov., 1969), 203-07.
        Thomas L. Ashton, K-SJ, XIX (1970), pp. 136-38.
        John D. Jump, RES, XXI (Feb., 1970), 112-113.
        Bernard Beatty, N&Q, CCXVI (May, 1971), 197-98.
        Robert Gleckner, Criticism, XII (Winter, 1970), 70-72.
        Vivian de Sola Pinto, YES, I (1971), 291-92.
        Charles I. Patterson, Jr., South Atlantic Bulletin, XXXIX
            (May 1974), 132-35.

Eskin, Stanley G. "Revolution and Poetry: Some Political Pat-
    terns in the Romantic Tradition and After," CLA Journal, XI
    (March, 1968), 189-205.

French, Richard. "Sir Walter Scott and His Literary Contempo-
    raries," CLA Journal, XI (March, 1968), 248-54.

Frye, Northrop. A Study of English Romanticism. ("Studies in
    Language and Literature.") New York: Random House, 1968.

Fuller, Jean Overton. Shelley: A Biography. London: Jonathan
    Cape, 1968.

Gerus-Tarnawecky, Iraida. "Literary Onomastics," Names, XVI
    (Dec., 1968), 312-24.

Gittings, Robert. John Keats. Boston: Little, Brown & Co.,
    1968.

Goodheart, Eugene. The Cult of the Ego: The Self in Modern
    Literature. Chicago & London: University of Chicago Press,
    1968.

Gunn, Peter. My Dearest Augusta: A Biography of Augusta Leigh,
    Lord Byron's Half-Sister. London: Bodley Head; New York:
    Atheneum, 1968.

Hartman, Geoffrey H. "Romantic Poetry and the Genius Loci,"
    The Disciplines of Criticism: Essays in Literary Theory, In-
    terpretation and History, eds. Peter Demetz, Thomas Greene,
    and Lowry Nelson, Jr. New Haven: Yale University Press,
    1968. Pp. 289-314.

Hassett, Michael E. "Pope, Byron and Satiric Technique," Satire
    Newsletter, VI (Fall, 1968), 10-28.

Hayter, Alethea. Opium and the Romantic Imagination. London:
    Faber; Berkeley: University of California Press, 1968.

Hume, Robert D. "The Non-Augustan Nature of Byron's Early
    'Satires,'" Revue des Langues Vivantes, XXXIV (No. 5,
    1968), 495-503.

Huscher, Herbert. "Thomas Hope, Author of Anastasius," KSMB,
    XIX (1968), 2-13.

Jump, John D. Byron's "Don Juan": Poem or Hold-All? The
    W. D. Thomas Memorial Lecture Delivered at the University
    College of Swansea on February 6, 1968. Swansea: Univer-
    sity College of Swansea, 1968.

_____. Byron's Vision of Judgment," Bulletin of the John Ry-
    lands Library, LI (Autumn, 1968), 122-36.

_____. "Byron's Letters," Essays and Studies by Members of
    the English Association, XXI (1968), 62-79.

Lauber, John. "Don Juan as Anti-Epic," SEL, VIII (Autumn,
    1968), 607-19.

Lutyens, Mary. "The Murrays of Albermarle Street," TLS, Oct.
    24, 1968, p. 1198.

McGann, Jerome J. "Byronic Drama in Two Venetian Plays," MP,
    LXVI (Aug., 1968), 30-44.

_____. "Byron's First Tale: An Unpublished Fragment,"
    KSMB, XIX (1968), 18-23. [Presents stanzas from Byron's
    unfinished poem 'The Devil--A Tale.']

_____. Fiery Dust: Byron's Poetic Development. Chicago and
    London: University of Chicago Press, 1968.
    Reviews:
    Paul F. Moran, Library Journal, XCIII (Dec. 15, 1968),
    4656.
    E. J. Lovell, Jr., SAQ, LXVIII (Summer, 1969), 428-30.

TLS, May 1, 1969, p. 471.
E. E. B[ostetter], ELN, VII (Suppl. to No. 1, Sept., 1969),
    29-30.
Donald H. Reiman, K-SJ, XIX (1970), 144-45.
Hillis J. Miller, SEL, IX (Autumn, 1969), 742-43.
W. E. Elledge, JEGP, LXVIII (Oct., 1969), 715-16.
Robert F. Gleckner, Criticism, XII (Winter, 1970), 70-72.
Gilbert Thomas, English, XIX (Autumn, 1970), 105-106.

_____. "Staging Byron's Cain," KSMB, XIX (1968), 24-27.

Marchand, Leslie A. Byron's Poetry. Cambridge, Mass.: Har-
    vard University Press, 1968. [A reissue of a book published
    in 1965 by Houghton Mifflin.]
Review:
    Roland Bartel, Comparative Literature, XXII (Winter, 1970),
    92-93.

Marshall, William H. (ed.). "Introduction," Lord Byron: Selected
    Poems and Letters. Boston: Houghton Mifflin, 1968. Pp.
    xi-xxiv.

Moorman, Mary. William Wordsworth: A Biography. 2 vols.
    London and New York: Oxford University Press, 1968.

Mortenson, Robert. "Abel: A Mystery by Philip Dixon Hardy; An
    Answer to Lord Byron's Cain: A Mystery," KSMB, XIX
    (1968), 28-32.

_____. "Byroniana: 'Remarks on Cain' Identified," Harvard
    Library Bulletin, XVI, No. 3 (1968), 237-41.

_____. "Byron's Letter to Murray on Cain," Library Chronicle
    of the University of Pennsylvania, XXXIV (1968), 94-99.

Nurmi, Martin K. "The Prompt Copy of Charles Kean's 1838 Pro-
    duction of Byron's Sardanapalus," Serif (Kent, Ohio), V, No.
    2 (1968), 3-13.

Orel, Harold. The Development of William Butler Yeats: 1855-
    1900. ("University of Kansas Publications, Humanistic
    Studies" No. 39.) Lawrence, Kansas: University of Kansas
    Press, 1968.

P[arker], D[erek]. "The All-Night Don Juan," Poetry Review, LIX
    (Winter, 1968), 312.

Parks, Stephen. "Wraxall and Byron," TLS, Dec. 19, 1968, p.
    1433.

Pickering, Leslie P. Lord Byron, Leigh Hunt and the "Liberal."
    New York: Haskell House, 1968. [A reprint of a book pub-
    lished in 1925 by Drane's.]

Pollin, Burton R.   "Byron, Poe and Miss Matilda," Names, XVI
    (Dec. , 1968), 390-414.

_____. "Poe's 'Sonnet--To Zante': Sources and Association,"
    Comparative Literature Studies, V (Sept. , 1968), 303-15.

Quennell, Peter.   Alexander Pope: The Education of Genius, 1688-
    1728. London: Weidenfield and Nicolson, 1968.

Reddy, D. V. Sabba.   Byron's "Don Juan." Tirupati, India:
    Malico Publishers, 1968.

Roston, Murray.   "The Bible Romanticized: Byron's Cain and
    Heaven and Earth," Biblical Drama in England: From the
    Middle Ages to the Present Day.   Evanston: Northwestern
    University Press, 1968.   Pp. 198-215.

Saagpakk, Paul F.   "A Survey of Psychopathology in British Litera-
    ture from Shakespeare to Hardy," Literature and Psychology,
    XVIII (1968), 135-65.

Sifton, Paul G.   "On the European Scene," Manuscripts, XX
    (Spring, 1968), 42-44.

Sperry, Stuart M. , Jr.   "The Harolds of Berlioz and Byron,"
    Your Musical Cue (Indiana University), IV, No. 6 (1968), 3-8.

Stanford, Raney.   "The Romantic Hero and that Fatal Self-hood,"
    Centennial Review, XII (Oct. , 1968), 430-52.

Steffan, Truman G. (ed.).   Lord Byron's "Cain": Twelve Essays
    and a Text with Variants and Annotations.   Austin: Univer-
    sity of Texas Press, 1968.
    Reviews:
    Paul F. Moran, Library Journal, XCIV (June 1, 1969), 2234.
    TLS, Nov. 13, 1969, p. 1298.
    Choice, VII (March, 1970), 82.
    E. E. B[ostetter], ELN, VIII (Suppl. to No. 1, Sept. , 1970), 28.
    V. S. Pritchett, NYRB, Oct. 22, 1970, pp. 6, 8, 10.
    Kenneth A. Bruffe, MP, LXVIII (Aug. , 1970), 115-17.
    Robert Mortenson, K-SJ, XX (1971), 134-37.
    J. Drummond Bone, N&Q, CCXVI (May, 1971), 195-96.

Terry, R. C.   "Big Alfred and the Critics," TLS, Feb. 15, 1968,
    p. 157.   [In The Eustace Diamonds, Trollope satirized the
    poetry of Byron and Shelley more than Tennyson's Idylls of
    the King.]

Trelawny, E. J.   Records of Shelley, Byron, and the Author.
    New York: Benjamin Blom, 1968.   [A reprint of a book pub-
    lished in 1878 by Pickering.]

Viets, H. R.   "Printings in America of Polidori's The Vampyre
in 1819," PBSA, LXII (July, 1968), 434-35.

Wallach, Alan P.   "Cole, Byron, and the Course of Empire," Art
Bulletin, L (Dec., 1968), 375-79.

Watkins, David.   Thomas Hope, 1796-1831, and the Neoclassical
Idea. London: John Murray, 1968.

Weinstein, Mark A.   William Edmonstoune Aytoun and the Spas-
modic Controversy. New Haven: Yale University Press,
1968.

Weinstock, Herbert.   Rossini: A Biography. New York: Knopf,
1968.

1969

Anderson, Patrick.   "Childe Harold in Greece," Over the Alps:
Reflections on Travel Writing with Special Reference to the
Grand Tours of Boswell, Beckford and Byron. London:
Hart-Davis, 1969. Pp. 145-85.

Ashton, Thomas L.   "Naming Byron's Aurora Raby," ELN, VII
(Dec., 1969), 114-20. [In Don Juan, XV, 43, 45.]

_____. "Peter Parker in Perry's Paper: Two Unpublished By-
ron Letters," K-SJ, XVIII (1969), 49-59. [Dated Oct. 7th,
1814 to James Perry, and Albany, Oct. 5th, 1814.]

Ball, Patricia M.   The Central Self: A Study in Romantic and
Victorian Imagination. London: University of London; New
York: Oxford University Press, 1969.

Barker, Kathleen M. D.   "The First English Performance of Byron's Werner," MP, LXVI (May, 1969), 342-44.

Beaty, Frederick L.   "Byron on Malthus and the Population Problems," K-SJ, XVIII (1969), 17-26.

Berlioz, Hector.   The Memoirs of Hector Berlioz, ed. and trans.
David Cairns. New York: Knopf, 1969.

Borst, William A.   Lord Byron's First Pilgrimage. Hamden,
[Conn.]: Shoe String, 1969. [A reprint of a book published
in 1948 by Yale University Press.]

Bostetter, Edward E. (ed.).   "Introduction," Twentieth Century Interpretations of "Don Juan": A Collection of Critical Essays.
Englewood Cliffs, N.J.: Prentice Hall, 1969. Pp. 1-15.
[All items in this book are reprints of chapters from books
listed in this bibliography. Their original date of publication

appears in parentheses following the title.]
It contains:
 W. H. Auden, "A That-There Poet," from The New Yorker,
 (1958), pp. 16-20. [A review of Leslie Marchand's Byron:
 A Biography.]
Elizabeth F. Boyd, from Byron's "Don Juan: A Critical
 Study (1945), pp. 98-99.
T. S. Eliot, from On Poets and Poetry (1957), pp. 96-97.
Robert F. Gleckner, from Byron and the Ruins of Paradise
 (1967), pp. 109-112.
E. D. Hirsch, Jr., "Byron and the Terrestrial Paradise,"
 (1965), pp. 106-108.
M. K. Joseph, "The Artist and the Mirror: The Narrator in
 Don Juan," from Byron, the Poet (1964), pp. 29-37.
Alvin B. Kernan, "The Perspective of Satire: Don Juan,"
 from The Plot of Satire (1965), pp. 85-93.
Karl Kroeber, "Byron: The Adventurous Narrative," from
 Romantic Narrative Art, (1960), pp. 103-105.
Ernest J. Lovell, Jr., "Irony and Image in Don Juan,"
 (1957), pp. 21-28.
George M. Ridenour, "A Waste and Icy Clime," from The
 Style of "Don Juan," (1960), pp. 38-50.
Andrew Rutherford, "Don Juan: War and Realism," from
 Byron, a Critical Study (1961), pp. 51-62.
Truman Guy Steffan, "The Twice Two Thousand," from By-
 ron's "Don Juan" (1957), pp. 63-72.
Paul West, from Byron and the Spoiler's Art, (1960), pp.
 100-102.
Virginia Woolf, from A Writer's Diary (1953), p. 94.
William Butler Yeats, from a letter to H. J. C. Grierson
 (1954), p. 95.

Briscoe, Walter A. Byron, the Poet. New York: Haskell House,
 1969. [A reprint of a book published in 1924 by Routledge.]

Brouzas, C. G. Byron's Maid of Athens: Her Family and Surroundings. Folcroft, Pa.: Folcroft Press, 1969. [A reprint of an article published in 1949 by West Virginia University.]

Childers, William. "Byron's Waltz: The Germans and Their
 Georges," K-SJ, XVIII (1969), 81-95.

Clark, Sir Kenneth. "The Worship of Nature," Listener, May 8,
 1969, pp. 643-48.

Cline, Clarence L. Byron, Shelley and Their Pisan Circle. London & New York: Russell & Russell, 1969. [A reprint of a
 book published in 1952 by John Murray.]

Clubbe, John. "Byron in Switzerland," TLS, Feb. 6, 1969, p.
 135. [The Hamilton Collection at Duke University contains an
 unpublished account of Byron in 1816.]

Cockshut, A[nthony]. O. J. The Achievement of Walter Scott.
London: Collins; New York: New York University Press,
1969.

Collins, Phillip. Thomas Coomper, the Chartist: Byron and the
"Poets of the Poor." "Byron Foundation Lecture." Nottingham: University of Nottingham, 1969.

Cooke, Michael G. The Blind Man Traces the Circle: On the
Patterns and Philosophy of Byron's Poetry. Princeton, N. J. :
Princeton University Press, 1969.
Reviews:
TLS, July 10, 1969, p. 749.
Paul F. Moran, Library Journal, XCIV (June 1, 1969), 2234.
Hillis J. Miller, SEL, IX (Autumn, 1969), 743.
W. Paul Elledge, K-SJ, XIX (1970), 125-27.
Kenneth A. Bruffe, MP, LXVIII (Aug., 1970), 115-17.
E. E. B[ostetter], ELN, VIII (Suppl. to No. 1, Sept., 1970),
26.
Harold Bloom, SEL, X (Autumn, 1970), 817-29.
J. R. Mac Gillivray, UTQ, XL (Fall, 1970), 73-86.

Crozier, Alice C. "Byron," The Novels of Harriet Beecher Stowe.
New York: Oxford University Press, 1969. Pp. 194-217.

De Beer, Sir Gavin. "Byron's French Passport," KSMB, XX
(1969), 31-36. [Byron never visited France.]

Dick, William. Byron and His Poetry. Folcroft, Pa. : Folcroft
Library Editions, 1969. [A reprint of a book published in
1913 by Harrap.]

Doherty, Francis M. Byron. New York: Arco, 1969.
Reviews:
Elaine Bender, Library Journal, XCV (Jan. 15, 1970), 159.
D. V. E[rdman], ELN, VIII (Suppl. to No. 1, Sept., 1970),
27.
Patrick Roberts, RES, XXII (Feb., 1971), 107-108.

Drinkwater, John. The Pilgrim of Eternity. Port Washington,
N. Y. : Kennikat, 1969. [A reprint of a book published in
1925 by Doran.]

Du Bos, Charles. Byron and the Need of Fatality, trans. Ethel
Colburn Mayne. Folcroft, Pa. : Folcroft Library Editions,
1969. [A reprint of a book published in 1932 by Putnam.]

Frank, Frederick S. "The Demon and the Thunderstorm: Byron
and Madame de Staël," Revue de Litterature Comparée,
XLIII (1969), 320-43.

Furst, Lilian R. Romanticism in Perspective: A Comparative
Study of Aspects of the Romantic Movements in England,

France and Germany. London: Macmillan; New York: St. Martin's Press, 1969.

Gianakaris, C. J. "Tracing the Rebel in Literature," Topic 18: A Journal of the Liberal Arts, IX (Fall, 1969), 11-29.

Goode, Clement Tyson. Byron as Critic. New York: Haskell House, 1969. [A reprint of a book published in 1923 by Wagner.]

Graham, William. Last Links with Byron, Shelley and Keats. Folcroft, Pa.: Folcroft Library Editions, 1969. [A reprint of a book published in 1898 by Smithers.]

Grant, Douglas. "Byron: The Pilgrim and Don Juan," The Morality of Art: Essays Presented to G. Wilson Knight by his Colleagues and Friends, ed. D. W. Jefferson. London: Routledge; New York: Barnes & Noble, 1969. Pp. 175-84.

Gregory, Horace. "Introduction," Poems of George Gordon, Lord Byron. New York: Thomas Y. Crowell Co., 1969. Pp. 1-9.

Harris, R. W. "Childe Harold and Don Juan," Romanticism and the Social Order, 1780-1830. London: Blandford Press, 1969. Pp. 328-66.

Harvey, William R. "Charles Dickens and the Byronic Hero," Nineteenth Century Fiction, XXIV (Dec., 1969), 305-16.

Hayden, John O. "Lord Byron," The Romantic Reviewers, 1802-1824. Chicago: University of Chicago Press; London: Routledge, 1969. Pp. 134-61.

Heath-Stubbs, John. "Regency Satire," The Verse Satire. London: Oxford University Press, 1969. Pp. 82-96.

Hefferman, James A. W. Wordsworth's Theory of Poetry: The Transforming Imagination. Ithaca & London: Cornell University Press, 1969.

Hewish, John. Emily Brontë: A Critical and Biographical Study. New York: St. Martin's; London: Macmillan, 1969.

*Hibbard, Esther L. "Byron's View of Nature," Essays and Studies in English Language and Literature (Yohoku Gakuin University, Sendai, Japan), LV (1969), 1-20.

Horn, András. Byron's "Don Juan" and the Eighteenth Century Novel. Folcroft, Pa.: Folcroft Library Editions, 1969. [A reprint of a book published in 1962 by Francke Verlag.]

Hubbell, Jay B. "The Literary Apprenticeship of Edgar Allan
Poe," Southern Literary Journal, II (Fall, 1969), 99-105.

Kahn, Arthur D. "Seneca and Sardanapalus: Byron, the Don
Quixote of Neo-Classicism," SP, LXVI (July, 1969), 654-71.

Keating, L[ouis] Clark. André Maurois. New York: Twayne,
1969.

Kelliher, W. Hilton. "Byron and Brooke (Fulke Greville, Lord
Brooke)," TLS, May 29, 1969, p. 584.

Kroeber, Karl, with Alfred and Theodora Kroeber. "Life Against
Death in English Poetry: A Method of Stylistic Definitions,"
Transactions of the Wisconsin Academy of Science, Arts and
Letters, LVII (1969), 29-40. [On the frequency of the words
life and death.]

Lady Blessington's "Conversations of Lord Byron," ed. Ernest J.
Lovell, Jr. Princeton: Princeton University Press, 1969.
Reviews:
Jerome J. MacGann, MP, LXVII (Nov., 1969), 205-206.
W. Paul Elledge, ELN, VII (Suppl. to No. 1, Sept., 1969),
148-50.
Hillis J. Miller, SEL, IX (Autumn, 1969), 741.
TLS, Jan. 8, 1970, p. 28.
E. E. B[ostetter], K-SJ, XIX (1970), 127-29.
Thomas L. Ashton, SAQ, LXIX (Spring, 1970), 294-95.
Choice, VII (May, 1970), 384.
D. V. E[rdman], ELN, VIII (Suppl. to No. 1, Sept., 1970),
28.
John Buxton, RES, XXII (Feb., 1971), 102-103.

Lamberston, C. L. (ed.). "Speaking of Byron," Malahat Review,
XII (Oct., 1969), 18-42; ibid., XIII (Jan., 1970), 24-46.
[Letters from Joanna Baillie to Sir Walter Scott.]

Longford, Elizabeth. Wellington: The Years of the Sword. Vol.
I. New York: Harper & Row, 1969..

McNiece, Gerald. Shelley and the Revolutionary Idea. Cambridge,
Mass.: Harvard University Press, 1969.

Manners, G. S. "Byron on Job," TLS, Oct. 2, 1969, p. 1132.
[A letter indicating that Byron wrote a poem, "On Job,"
which inadvertently was included in a volume of poetry of
Henry Saville Shepherd.]

Margetron, Stella. Leisure and Pleasure in the Nineteenth Century.
London: Cassell, 1969.

Martin, L. C. Byron's Lyrics. Folcroft, Pa.: Folcroft Library
Editions, 1969. [A reprint of a book published in 1958 by
the University of Nottingham.]

Mayfield, John S. 'Byron's Vampyre Letter, " Hobbies, LXXIII
(Jan. , 1969), 108-109.

Mayne, Ethel Colburn. Byron. New York: Barnes & Noble, 1969.
[A reprint of the 1924 edition of a book first published in
1912 by Scribner.]

_____ . The Life and Letters of Anne Isabella, Lady Noel Byron. London: Dawsons; New York: Humanities Press, 1969.
[A reprint of a book published in 1929 by Constable.]

Merivale, Patricia. Pan the Goat God. His Myth in Modern
Times. ("Harvard University Studies in Comparative Literature," No. 30.) London: Oxford University Press, 1969.

Michaels, Leonard. 'Byron's Cain, " PMLA, LXXXIV (Jan. , 1969),
71-78.

Miller, Barnette. Leigh Hunt's Relations with Byron, Shelley and
Keats. Folcroft, Pa. : Folcroft Library Editions, 1969.
[A reprint of a book published in 1910 by Columbia.]

Miyoshi, Masao. The Divided Self: A Perspective on the Literature of the Victorians. New York: New York University
Press; London: University of London Press, Ltd. , 1969.

Mortenson, Robert. "The Copyright of Byron's Cain, " PBSA,
LXIII (1st Quarter, 1969), 5-13.

_____ . "Lord Byron and Baron Lützerode: An Important Presentation Volume, " K-SJ, XVIII (1969), 27-37. [It contains
Byron's "corrections of errors and unpublished revision of the
texts of the three plays" and also "passages omitted by Murray from the published edition of the plays without Byron's
permission. "]

Muecke, Douglas C. The Compass of Irony. London: Methuen;
New York: Barnes & Noble, 1969.

Nichol, J. Byron. New York: AMS Press, 1969. [A reprint of
a book published in 1880 by Macmillan.]

Nicolson, Harold. Byron: The Last Journey, April 1823-April
1824. Hamden, Conn. : Archon Books, 1969. [A reprint of
the second edition (1948) of a book first published in 1924
by Constable.]

_____ . The Poetry of Byron. Folcroft, Pa. : Folcroft Library
Editions, 1969. [A reprint of a book published privately in
1943.]

Nielsen, Jørgen Erik. "Byroniana, " N&Q, CCIV (Feb. , 1969), 56.
[Lord Byron. A New Tale of a Tub, appeared in a newspaper

on the island of St. Croix, Dec. 19, 1825. This was an earlier version of the anecdote which appeared in England in the Court Journal, Sept. 12, 1829 and in the New Monthly Magazine, 1853.]

_____. "Parga: A Verse Tale Attributed to Byron," ES, L (Aug., 1969), 397-405.

Ogden, James. Isaac D'Israeli. Oxford: Clarendon, 1969.

Oliver, Richard A. "Romanticism and Opera," Symposium, XXIII (Fall-Winter, 1969), 325-31.

Orel, Harold. "The Relationships between Three Poet-Dramatists and Their Public: Lord Byron, Thomas Talfour, Robert Browning," The Nineteenth Century Writer and His Audience, eds. Harold Orel and George J. Worth. Lawrence, Kansas: University of Kansas Publications, 1969. Pp. 31-49.

Paananen, Victor Niles. "Byron and the Caves of Ellora," N&Q, CCXIV (Nov., 1969), 414-16.

Panichas, George A. "G. Wilson Knight: Interpreter of Genius," English Miscellany, XX (1969), 291-312.

Pearsall, Robert Brainard. "Chronological Annotations to 250 Letters of Thomas Moore," PBSA, LXIII (April-June, 1969), 105-117.

Pinto, Vivian de Sola. Byron and Liberty. Folcroft, Pa.: Folcroft Library Editions, 1969. [A reprint of a book published in 1944 by Nottingham University.]

Piper, William B. The Heroic Couplet. Cleveland & London: Case Western Reserve University, 1969.

Plomer, William. "Byron in Westminster Abbey," Cornhill Magazine, No. 1060 (Summer, 1969), 309-312.

Pollin, Burton R. "Lord Byron as Parodist of The Battle of Blenheim," Bulletin of the New York Public Library, LXXIII (April, 1969), 215-17. [On internal and circumstantial evidence, he finds Byron the author of the parody of Southey's Battle of Blenheim called A Danish Tale, which appeared anonymously in the Morning Chronicle.]

Priestley, J. B. The Prince of Pleasure and His Regency, 1811-1820. London: Heinemann; New York: Harper & Row, 1969.

Reiman, Donald H. Percy Bysshe Shelley. New York: Twayne Publishers, 1969.

Rennes, Jacob Johan van. Bowles, Byron and the Pope Controver-
    sy. Folcroft, Pa.: Folcroft Library Editions, 1969. [A
    reprint of a book published in 1927 by G. E. Steckert.]

Richardson, Joanna. "George IV: Patron of Literature," Essays
    by Divers Hands, XXXV (1969), 128-46. [Byron respected
    his taste.]

Ridenour, George M. The Style of "Don Juan." Hamden, [Conn.]:
    Shoe String, 1969. [A reprint of a book published in 1960
    by Yale University Press.]

Robson, W. W. Byron as Poet. Folcroft, Pa.: Folcroft Library
    Editions, 1969. [A reprint of a book published in 1957 by
    Oxford University Press.]

Schmidtchen, Paul W. "Byron, the Don Juan, plus Shakespeare
    and Jonson," Hobbies, LXXIV (May, 1969), 104-105, 127.

Steffan, Truman G. "Byron and Old Clothes: An Unpublished
    Letter," N&Q, CCXIV (Nov., 1969), 416-20. [From Byron
    to Capt. Daniel Roberts, dated 28 Nov., 1822.]

_____. "Byron's Don Juan," Explicator, XXVII (April, 1969),
    item 65.

Story, Patrick L. "Byron's Death and Hazlitt's Spirit of the Age,"
    ELN, VII (Sept., 1969), 42-46.

Sundell, Michael G. "The Development of The Giaour," SEL, IX
    (Autumn, 1969), 587-99.

Swanson, Donald R. "Carlyle on the English Romantic Poets,"
    Lock Haven Review, 11 (1969), 25-32.

Symons, A. J. Bibliographical Catalogue of First Editions, Proof
    Copies and Manuscripts of Books by Lord Byron. Folcroft,
    Pa.: Folcroft, 1969. [A reprint of a book published in 1925
    by the First Edition Club.]

Thomas, Donald. A Long Time Burning: The History of Literary
    Censorship in England. London: Routledge & Kegan Paul;
    New York: Praeger, 1969.

Trease, Geoffrey. Byron: A Poet Dangerous to Know. New York:
    Holt, Rinehart & Winston, 1969.
    Review:
    TLS, Dec. 4, 1969, p. 1391.

Trewin, J. C. "The Romantic Poets in the Theater," KSMB, XX
    (1969), 21-30.

Trueblood, Paul G.   Lord Byron.   "Twayne's English Author
     Series." New York: Twayne, 1969.
     Reviews:
       J. Hillis Miller, SEL, IX (Autumn, 1969), 737-53.
       Joseph de Roco, K-SJ, XIX (1970), 141-43.
       Frank Mc Cambre, N&Q, CCXV (May, 1970), 199-200.

Tucker, Martin.   The Critical Temper.   A Survey of Modern
     Criticism on English and American Literature from the Be-
     ginning to the Twentieth Century.   3 vols.   New York:
     Frederick Ungar, 1969.   Vol. II, pp. 295-321.

Viets, Henry R., M.D.   "The London Editions of Polidori's The
     Vampyre," PBSA, LXIII (1969), 83-103.

Watson, Harold Francis.   Coasts of Treasure Island: A Study of
     the Background, and Sources for Robert Louis Stevenson's
     Romance of the Sea.   San Antonio, Texas: Naylor, 1969.

Woodhouse, Christopher Montague.   The Philhellenes.   London:
     Hodder & Stoughton, 1969.

Yarrow, P. J.   "Three Plays of 1829, or Doubts about 1830,"
     Symposium, XXIII (Fall-Winter, 1969), 373-83.   [Delavigne's
     Marino Faliero influenced by Byron's work.]

                              1970

Ashton, Thomas L.   "Byron's Metrical Tales," Book Collector,
     XIX (Autumn, 1970), 384.   [Wants to know the location of the
     holograph MS of Byron's Parisina.]

Avni, Abraham.   " 'Blue-Eyed Minerva': Byron and Pope," N&Q,
     CCXV (Oct., 1970), 389.

Baker, Harry J.   Biographical Sagas of Will Power.   New York:
     Vantage, 1970.

Bentley, G. E., Jr.   "Byron, Shelley, Wordsworth, Blake, and
     The Seaman's Recorder," Studies in Romanticism, IX (Winter,
     1970), 21-36.   [Vol. II, pp. 1-4 of The Seaman's Recorder
     of 1824-27 contains an anecdote of Byron.]

Bewley, Marius.   Masks and Mirrors: Essays in Criticism.   New
     York: Atheneum, 1970.
     It contains:
       "The Colloquial Byron," pp. 50-76.   Rptd. from Scrutiny,
       XVI (March, 1949), 8-23.
       "The Romantic Imagination and the Unromantic Byron," pp.
       77-103.

_____ (ed.). "George Gordon, Lord Byron, 1788-1824," The
English Romantic Poets: An Anthology with Commentaries.
New York: Modern Library, 1970. Pp. 406-23.

Blackstone, Bernard. Byron. Vol. I: Lyric and Romance. Har-
low, England: Published for the British Council by Longmans, 1970.

Bloom, Harold. Yeats. New York: Oxford University Press,
1970.

Blunden, Edmund C. "Byron," Three Young Poets: Critical
Sketches of Byron, Shelley and Keats. Folcroft, Pa. : Folcroft Library Editions, 1970. Pp. 1-30. [A reprint of a
book published in 1959 by Kenkyusha Press, Japan.]

Buxton, John. "The Poetry of Lord Byron," Proceedings of the
British Academy, LVI (1970), 77-92.

Chambers, R. W. Ruskin (and Others) on Byron. New York:
Haskell House, 1970. [A reprint of a book published in 1925
by Oxford University Press.]

Chew, Samuel C. Byron in England; His Fame and After Fame.
St. Clair Shores, Mich. : Scholarly Press, 1970. [A reprint of a book published in 1924 by John Murray.]

_____. The Dramas of Lord Byron. St. Clair Shores, Mich. :
Scholarly Press, 1970. [A reprint of a book published in
1915 by Johns Hopkins.]

Clearman, Mary. "A Blueprint for English Bards and Scotch Reviewers: The First Satire of Juvenal," K-SJ, XIX (1970), 87-
99.

Colville, Derek. Victorian Poetry and the Romantic Religion. Albany: State University of New York Press, 1970.

Cramb, Isobel. "Francis Peacock, 1723-1807: Dancing Master in
Aberdeen," Aberdeen University Review, XLIII (Spring, 1970),
251-61.

Davenport, John A. "The Long Pilgrimage," Intercollegiate Review,
VII (Winter, 1970-71), 79-88.

Diakanova, Nina. "Byron and the English Romantics," Zeitschrift
für Anglistik und Amerikanistik, XVIII (Jan. , 1970), 144-67.

Dobrée, Bonamy. Byron's Dramas. Folcroft, Pa. : Folcroft Library Editions, 1970. [A reprint of the Byron Foundation
Lecture of 1962.]

Donohue, Joseph W. , Jr.   Dramatic Character in the English Romantic Age.   Princeton: Princeton University Press, 1970.

Du Bos, Charles.   Byron and the Need of Fatality, trans.   Ethel
Colburn Mayne.   New York: Haskell House, 1970.   [A reprint of a book published in 1932 by Putnam.]

Earle, Kathleen.   "Portrait of Margaret, Lady Blessington, "
Queen's Quarterly, LXXVII (Summer, 1970), 236-51.

Elledge, W. Paul.   "Byron's Hungry Sinner: The Quest Motif in
Don Juan, " JEGP, LXIX (Jan. , 1970), 1-13.

Erdman, David V.   "Byron's Mock Review of Rosa Matilda's Epic
on the Prince Regent--A New Attribution, " K-SJ, XIX (1970),
101-117.   [A mock review which appeared in The Morning
Chronicle of September 2 & 12, 1812, is here attributed to
Byron.]

Faulkner, Claude Winston.   Byron's Political Verse Satire.   Folcroft, Pa. :   Folcroft Library Editions, 1970.   [A reprint of
a 1947 thesis from University of Illinois.]

Fogle, Richard Harter.   "Literary History Romanticized, " New
Literary History, I (Winter, 1970), 237-47.

Gerard, William.   Byron Re-Studied in His Dramas; Being a Con-
tribution towards a Definitive Estimate of his Genius: An
Essay.   Folcroft, Pa. :   Folcroft Library Editions, 1970.
[A reprint of a book published in 1886 by White.]

Glasgow, Eric.   "Anglo-Greek Relations, 1800-1832, " CR, CCXVI
(April, 1970), 184-88.

Grebanier, Bernard D.   The Uninhibited Byron: An Account of His
Sexual Confusion.   New York: Crown Publishers, 1970.
Reviews:
Paul Moran, Library Journal, XCV (Oct. , 1970), 3771.
H. C. Webster, Saturday Review, LIII (Oct. 17, 1970), 32.
V. S. Pritchett, NYRB, Oct. 22, 1970, pp. 6, 8, 10.
S. Rodman, National Review, XXIII (March 9, 1971), 21.
E. B. Murray, Contempora, I (May-Aug. , 1971), 47.
SAQ, LXX (Summer, 1971), 437.
Choice, VIII (June, 1971), 551.
Richard Newman, Books and Bookmen, XVI (July, 1971), 48.
Douglas Dunn, NS, July 2, 1971, pp. 22-23.
E. E. B[ostetter], ELN, IX (Suppl. to No. 1, Sept. , 1971),
36.
TLS, Oct. 22, 1971, p. 1312.

Hargreaves, Henry.   "Dr. Robert Wilson: Alumnus and Benefactor
of Marischal College--the Man and His Papers, " Aberdeen
University Review, XLIII (Autumn, 1970), 374-84.

Hearn, Lafcadio. The English Romantic Poets. Folcroft, Pa.:
    Folcroft Library Editions, 1970.

Henley, V. W. "The Trouble with Byron," Fort Hare Papers, IV,
    No. 4 (April, 1970), 25-46.

Hewitt, Barnard. History of the Theater from 1800 to the Present.
    New York: Random House, 1970.

Hough, Graham. Two Exiles: Lord Byron and D. H. Lawrence.
    Folcroft, Pa.: Folcroft Library Editions, 1970. [A reprint
    of a book published in 1956 by Nottingham.]

Kahn, Arthur D. "Byron's Single Difference with Homer and Vir-
    gil: The Redefinition of the Epic in Don Juan," Arcadia, V
    (1970), 143-62.

Kernan, Alvin B. "Don Juan: The Perspective of Satire," Ro-
    manticism and Consciousness: Essays in Criticism, ed.
    Harold Bloom. New York: Norton, 1970. Pp. 343-74. Rptd.
    from his The Plot of Satire, New Haven: Yale University
    Press, 1965, pp. 171-222.

Klein, H. M. " 'Sangrado'--Byron Before Scott," N&Q, CCXV
    (May, 1970), 174. [Byron used this word before Scott.]

Leggett, B. J. "Dante, Byron and Tennyson's 'Ulysses,' " Ten-
    nessee Studies in Literature, V (1970), 143-59.

Luke, K. McCormick. "Lord Byron's Manfred: A Study of Aliena-
    tion from Within," UTQ, XL (Fall, 1970), 15-26.

McConnell, Frank D. "Byron's Reductions: 'Much Too Poetical,' "
    ELH, XXXVII (Sept., 1970), 415-32.

Manning, Peter. "Byron's English Bards and Scotch Reviewers,"
    KSMB, XXI (1970), 7-11.

_____. "Byron's English Bards and Shelley's Adonais," N&Q,
    CCXV (Oct., 1970), 380-81.

Marchand, Leslie A. Byron: A Portrait. New York: Knopf,
    1970. [A one-volume abridgment of his three volume 1957
    work.]
    Reviews:
    V. S. Pritchett, NYRB, Oct. 22, 1970, pp. 6, 8, 10.
    Economist, CCXXXIX (April 10, 1971), 60.
    Gabriel Pearson, Spectator, May 29, 1971, pp. 733-36.
    Douglas Dunn, NS, July 2, 1971, pp. 22-23.
    E. E. B[ostetter], ELN, IX (Suppl. to No. 1, Sept., 1971),
        36.
    TLS, Oct. 22, 1971, p. 1312.

_____. "The Letters of Lord Byron," American Philosophical Society Yearbook, (1970), 657-58.

Massey, Irving J. The Uncreating World: Romanticism and the Object. Bloomington & London: Indiana University Press, 1970.

Mathaney, Margaret Heinen. "Baudelaire's Knowledge of English Literature," Revue de Littérature Comparée, XLIV (Jan. - March, 1970).

Maurois, André. Memoirs, 1885-1967, trans. from the French by Denver Lindley. New York: Harper, 1970.

Mayne, Ethel Colburn. Byron. Freeport, N.J.: Books for Libraries, 1970; New York: Barnes & Noble, 1970. [A reprint of the 1924 edition of a book published in 1912 by Scribner's.]

Meredith, George. The Letters of George Meredith, ed. C. L. Cline. 3 vols. Oxford: Clarendon, 1970.

Perella, Nicolas J. "Night and the Sublime in Giacomo Leopardi," University of California Publications in Modern Philology, XCIX (1970), 1-151.

Pratt, Willis W. Lord Byron and His Circle. A Calendar of Manuscripts in the University of Texas. New York: Haskell House, 1970. [A reprint of a book published in 1947 by the University of Texas Press.]

Pushkin, Alexander. The Critical Prose of Alexander Pushkin, with Critical Essays by Four Russian Romantic Poets, ed. and trans. Carl R. Proffer. Bloomington & London: Indiana University Press, 1970.

Quennell, Peter. Romantic England: Writing and Painting. London: Weidenfeld & Nicolson, 1970.

Raymond, Dora Neill. The Political Career of Lord Byron. Folcroft, Pa.: Folcroft Library Editions, 1970. [A reprint of a book published in 1924 by Holt.]

Reisner, Thomas A. "Cain: Two Romantic Interpretations," Culture, XXXI (June, 1970), 124-43. [Byron's Cain and Blake's Ghost of Abel.]

Robinson, Charles E. "The Devil as Doppelgänger in The Deformed Transformed: The Sources and Meaning of Byron's Unfinished Drama," Bulletin of the New York Public Library, LXXVI (March, 1970), 177-202.

Rutherford, Andrew. Byron: A Critical Study. New York:
    Barnes & Noble, 1970. [A reprint of a book published in
    1961 by Oliver & Boyd.]

_____. Byron: The Critical Heritage. London: Routledge &
    K. Paul; New York: Barnes & Noble, 1970.
    Reviews:
    TLS, May 28, 1970, p. 575. Cf. Alan Lang Strout, TLS,
        June 18, 1970, p. 662.
    A. E. Dyson, Critical Quarterly, XII (Autumn, 1970), 284,
        286.
    Rowland Smith, Dalhousie Review, L (Winter, 1970-1971),
        561-63.
    John H. Alexander, Aberdeen University Review, XLIV
        (Spring, 1971), 73-74.
    John Cronin, Studies, LX (Spring, 1971), 104-108.
    E. E. B[ostetter], ELN, IX (Suppl. to No. 1, Sept., 1971),
        37.
    A. P. Robson, Victorian Studies, XV (June, 1972), 475-80.
    Drummond Bone, N&Q, CCXVII (Aug., 1972), 314-15.

St. Clair, William. "Postscript to The Last Days of Lord Byron,"
    K-SJ, XIX (1970), 4-7. [Parry's book on Byron was co-
    authored with Thomas Hodgskin.]

Stowe, Harriet Beecher. Lady Byron Vindicated. New York:
    Haskell House, 1970. [A reprint of a book published in 1870
    by S. Low.]

Stringham, Scott. "I Due Foscari: From Byron's Play to Verdi's
    Opera," West Virginia University Philological Papers, XVII
    (June, 1970), 31-40.

Walker, Keith. "Byron," New Society, XVI (Aug. 13, 1970), 280-
    82.

Watson, J[ohn R.]. "Alpine and Proud: Byron on the Mountain
    Tops," Picturesque Landscape and English Romantic Poetry.
    London: Hutchinson Educational, Ltd., 1970. Pp. 171-83.

Wellek, René. Discriminations: Further Concepts of Criticism.
    New Haven: Yale University Press, 1970.

Wilkins, Mary C. "Lord Byron Returns to Westminster," Central
    Literary Magazine, XL (Spring, 1970), 154-57.

Wittreich, Joseph Anthony, Jr. (ed.). "George Gordon Byron
    (1788-1824)," The Romantics on Milton: Formal Essays and
    Critical Asides. Cleveland: Case Western Reserve Univer-
    sity, 1970. Pp. 515-27.

Woodhouse, C. M. "Byron and the First Helenic Tourists," Es-
    says by Divers Hands, Vol. XXXVI. London: Oxford Univer-
    sity Press, 1970. Pp. 147-66.

Woodring, Carl Ray. "Byron," Politics in English Romantic Poe-
    try. Cambridge, Mass.: Harvard University; London: Ox-
    ford University, 1970.

Zegger, R. E. "Greek Independence and the London Committee,"
    History Today, XX (April, 1970), 236-45.

1971

Abrams, M. H. Natural Supernaturalism: Tradition and Revolu-
    tion in Romantic Literature. New York: Norton; London:
    Oxford University Press, 1971.

Bayley, John. Pushkin: A Comparative Study. Cambridge:
    Cambridge University, 1971.

Beaty, Frederick L. Light from Heaven: Love in British Roman-
    tic Literature. De Kalb: Northern Illinois University Press,
    1971.
    It contains:
        "The Exaltation of Passion," pp. 132-57.
        "From Wit to Irony in Byronic Comedy," pp. 21-55.

Behler, Ernst. "Technique of Irony in Light of the Romantic
    Theory," Rice University Studies, LVII (Fall, 1971), 1-17.

Bernard, Camille. "Some Aspects of Delacroix's Orientalism,"
    Bulletin of the Cleveland Museum of Arts, LVIII (April, 1971),
    123-27.

Blackstone, Bernard. Byron. Vol. II. Literary Satire, Humor
    and Reflection. [Harlow, England]: Published for the
    British Council by Longman, 1971.

_____. Byron. Vol. III: Social Satire, Drama and Epic.
    [Harlow, England]: Published for the British Council by
    Longman, 1971.

_____. "'The Loops of Time': Spatio-Temporal Patterns in
    Childe Harold," Ariel, II, No. 4 (Oct., 1971), 5-17.

Bloom, Harold. "George Gordon, Lord Byron," The Visionary
    Company: A Reading of English Romantic Poetry. Ithaca &
    London: Cornell University Press, 1971. [A revised, en-
    larged edition of a book published in 1961 by Doubleday.]

Brogan, Howard O. "Byron's Don Juan, Canto II," Explicator,
    XXX (Nov., 1971), item 28.

Bruffee, Kenneth A. "Elegiac Romance," College English, XXXII
    (Jan., 1971), 465-76. [On Byron's fragment of a novel.]

"Byron's Don Leon," TLS, Dec. 17, 1971, p. 1581. [Don Leon
    has been included in the British Museum Catalogue.]

Clarke, Isabel C. Shelley and Byron: A Tragic Friendship. New
    York: Haskell House, 1971. [A reprint of a book published
    in 1934 by Hutchinson.]

Colwell, C. Carter. "Byron," The Tradition of British Literature.
    New York: G. P. Putnam's Sons, 1971. Pp. 266-71.

Edgeworth, Maria. Letters from England, 1813-1844, ed. Chris-
    tine Colvin. Oxford: Clarendon, 1971.

Elledge, W. Paul, and Richard L. Hoffman (eds.). Romantic and
    Victorian: Studies in Memory of William H. Marshall.
    Cranbury, N.J.: Fairleigh Dickinson University, 1971.
    It contains:
        Richard H. Fogle, "Byron and Nathaniel Hawthorne," pp. 181-
            97.
        Robert D. Hume, "The Island and the Evolution of Byron's
            Tales," pp. 158-80.
        Brian Wilkie, "Byron's Artistry and Style," pp. 129-46.
        Carl Woodring, "Nature, Art, Reason, and Imagination in
            Childe Harold," pp. 147-57.

Gérin, Winifred. Emily Brontë: A Biography. Oxford: Claren-
    don, 1971.

Hagan, John. "Enemies of Freedom in Jane Eyre," Criticism,
    XIII (Fall, 1971), 357-76.

Harson, Robert R. "Byron's 'Tintern Abbey,'" K-SJ, XX (1971),
    113-21. [His 'Epistle to Augusta.']

Hassan, M. A. "Who Was Harry Franklin?" N&Q, CCXVI (May,
    1971), 165-68. [The signer of a letter to Blackwood's Maga-
    zine of Aug., 1821, favorably reviewing Don Juan, may have
    been John Gibson Lockhart.]

Hayden, John O. Romantic Bards and British Reviewers: A Se-
    lected Edition of the Contemporary Reviews of Wordsworth,
    Coleridge, Byron, Keats and Shelley. Lincoln: University
    of Nebraska Press; London: Routledge & K. Paul, 1971.

Helmick, E. T. "Hellenism in Byron and Keats," KSMB, XXII
    (1971), 18-27.

Hooker, Charlotte S. "Byron's Misadventures in Portugal,"
    McNeese Review, XX (1971-1972), 47-51.

James, D. G. Byron and Shelley. Folcroft, Pa.: Folcroft Li-
    brary Editions, 1971. [A reprint of a book published in 1951
    by University of Nottingham.]

Jeffrey, Lloyd N. "Homeric Echoes in Byron's Don Juan," South
    Central Bulletin, XXXI (Winter, 1971), 188-92.

Knight, Frida. University Rebel: The Life of William Frend
    (1757-1841). London: Gollancz, 1971. [Frend was the pri-
    vate tutor of Annabella Milbanke.]

Knight, G. Wilson. The Burning Oracle: Studies in the Poetry of
    Action. Folcroft, Pa.: Folcroft Library Editions, 1971.
    [A reprint of a book published in 1939 by Oxford University.]

———. Neglected Powers: Essays on Nineteenth and Twentieth
    Century Literature. New York: Barnes & Noble; London:
    Routledge & Kegan Paul, 1971.
    It contains:
        "Colman and Don Leon," pp. 127-41. Rptd. from Twentieth
            Century, CLIX (June, 1956), 562-73.
        "Herbert Read and Byron," pp. 481-85. Rptd. from Malahat
            Review, IX (Jan., 1969), 130-34.
        "Who Wrote Don Leon," pp. 113-26. Rptd. from Twentieth
            Century, CLVI (July, 1954), 67-79.

Lambert, Cecily. "Fighting for Greece," Adam, International Re-
    view, CCCXLIX-CCCLI (1971), 74-77.

Moore, Doris Langley. "Byronic Dress," Costume, No. 5 (1971),
    1-13.

Morgan, Peter F. "Southey on Poetry," Tennessee Studies in
    Literature, XVI (1971), 77-89.

Mortenson, Robert. "Byron and William Harness: Early Recollec-
    tions of Lord Byron," PBSA, LXV (Jan.-March, 1971), 53-65.
    [He was an early defender of Byron. Article includes partial
    texts of five Byron letters.]

Murray, John, IV. Lord Byron and His Detractors. New York:
    Haskell House, 1971. [A reprint of a book published in 1906
    by Murray.]

Murray, Roger. "A Case for the Study of Period Styles," College
    English, XXXIII (Nov., 1971), 139-48.

Noel, Roden. Life of Lord Byron. Port Washington, N.Y.: Ken-
    nikat, 1971. [A reprint of a book published in 1890 by W.
    Scott.]

Origo, Iris. The Last Attachment: The Story of Byron and Te-
    resa Guiccioli as Told in Their Unpublished Letters and
    Other Family Papers. London: Murray, 1971. [A reprint
    of a book published in 1949 by Cape & Murray.]

Pack, Robert F. "Byron's Ode to Napoleon," Journal of the Rutgers University Library, XXXIV (June, 1971), 43-45.

Park, Roy. Hazlitt and the Spirit of the Age: Abstraction and Critical Theory. Oxford: Clarendon Press, 1971.

Reiman, Donald H. "Byron's William Parry: Post-Postscript," K-SJ, XX (1971), 21.

Ruddick, William. "Lord Byron's Historical Tragedies," Essays on Nineteenth Century British Theater: The Proceedings of a Symposium Sponsored by the Manchester University Department of Drama. London: Methuen; New York: Barnes & Noble, 1971. Pp. 83-94.

Slethaug, Gordon E. "Patterns of Imagery in 'The Prisoner of Chillon,' " Queen's Quarterly, LXXVIII (Autumn, 1971), 449-55.

Steffan, T. G. "From Cambridge to Missolonghi: Byron Letters at the University of Texas," Texas Quarterly, XIV (Autumn, 1971), 6-66.

_____ (ed.). From Cambridge to Missolonghi: Byron Letters at the University of Texas. Austin: University of Texas Press, 1971. [An offprint of above.]

Strauss, Walter A. Descent and Return: The Orphic Theme in Modern Literature. Cambridge, Mass. : Harvard University; London: Oxford University, 1971.

Sutherland, Donald. On Romanticism. New York: New York University Press, 1971.

Thompson, B. Russell. "Byron's Cain and Unamuno's Abel Sanchez: Two Faces of Heroic Anguish," Proceedings: Pacific Northwest Conference on Foreign Languages. Twenty Second Annual Meeting, April 6-17, 1971. Vol. XXII, ed. Walter C. Kraft. Corvalis: Oregon State University, 1971.

Trelawny, Edward John. Recollections of the Last Days of Shelley and Byron. Freeport, N.J. : Books for Libraries, 1971. [A reprint of a book published in 1858 by Ticknor Field.]

Vincent, E. R. Byron, Hobhouse and Foscolo. Folcroft, Pa. : Folcroft Library Editions, 1971. [A reprint of a book published in 1949 by Macmillan.]

Wallace, Irving. "The Byron Lover--English Style," The Nympho and Other Maniacs. New York: Simon & Schuster, 1971, pp. 106-27.

_____. "The Lovers," Ladies' Home Journal, LXXXVIII (Feb.,
1971), 127-33. [Excerpts from the previous entry.]

Wardle, Ralph M. Hazlitt. Lincoln: University of Nebraska
Press, 1971.

Wilkinson, Lise. "William Brockedon, F. R. S. (1787-1854),"
Notes and Records of the Royal Society of London, XXVI
(1971), 65-72.

Wolff, Tatiana (ed.). Pushkin on Literature. London: Methuen,
1971.

Woodhouse, C[hristopher] M. The Philhellenes. Rutherford, N. J.:
Fairleigh Dickinson University, 1971.

1972

Ades, John. "Criticus Redivivus: The History of Charles Lamb's
Reputation as a Critic," Charles Lamb Society Bulletin, CCXV
(July, 1972), 1-6. [Byron's views of Lamb's criticism.]

Anniah, Gowds H. H. Dramatic Poetry from Medieval to Modern
Times. Madras: Macmillan, 1972.

Ashton, Thomas L. "Byronic Lyrics for David's Harp: The Hebrew Melodies," SEL, XII (Autumn, 1972), 665-81.

_____ (ed.). Byron's "Hebrew Melodies." Austin: University
of Texas Press; London: Routledge & Kegan Paul, 1972.
Reviews:
  TLS, May 19, 1972, p. 573.
  Gilbert Thomas, English, XXI (Autumn, 1972), 114.
  Michael G. Cooke, K-SJ, XXI-XXII (1972-1973), 256-58.
  John D. Jump, YES, III (1973), 307-308.
  E. E. B[ostetter], ELN, XI (Suppl. to No. 1, Sept., 1973),
  37.
  F. W. Bateson, NYRB, Feb. 22, 1973, pp. 32-33.
  John Clubbe, SAQ, LXXII (Spring, 1973), 331-32.
  A. H. Elliott, RES, n. s., XXIV (Aug., 1973), 353-54.
  Abraham Avni, English Studies, LV (April, 1974), 166-69.

_____. "The Censorship of Byron's Marino Faliero," Huntington
Library Quarterly, XXXVI (Nov., 1972), 27-44.

Asimov, Isaac (ed.). Asimov's Annotated "Don Juan." New York:
Doubleday, 1972.

Barratt, G. R. V. Ivan Kozlov: A Study and a Setting. Toronto:
Kakkert, 1972.

Beaty, Frederick L. "Byron's Long Bow and Strong Bow," SEL,
    XII (Autumn, 1972), 653-63.

_____. " 'With Verse Like Crashaw,' " N&Q, CCXVII (Aug.,
    1972), 290-92.

Blyth, Henry. Caro: The Fatal Passion. The Life of Caroline
    Lamb. London: Rupert Hart-Davis, 1972.

Bostetter, Edward E. (ed.). "Introduction," George Gordon, Lord
    Byron: Selected Works, revised and enlarged. New York:
    Holt, Rinehart & Winston, 1972. Pp. vii-xxxvi.

Braddock, Joseph. The Green Phoenix. London: Constable, 1972.

Brogan, Howard O. "Satirist Burns and Lord Byron," Costerus,
    IV (1972), 29-48.

Chew, Samuel C. Byron in England: His Fame and After Fame.
    St. Clair Shores, Mich. : Scholarly Press, 1972. [A reprint
    of a book published in 1924 by Murray.]

Cohane, Christopher B. "An Unincorporated Emendation to Byron's
    The Vision of Judgement," N&Q, CCXVII (March, 1972), 96.

Dalgado, D. G. Lord Byron's Childe Harold's Pilgrimage to Portu-
    gal Critically Examined. Folcroft, Pa. : Folcroft Library
    Editions, 1972. [A reprint of a book published in 1919 by
    Impresa Nacional, Lisbon.]

De Porte, Michael V. "Byron's Strange Perversity of Thought,"
    MLQ, XXXIII (Dec. , 1972), 405-19.

Diakanova, Nina. "The Russian Episode in Byron's Don Juan,"
    Ariel, III (July, 1972), 50-57.

Dick, William (ed.). Byron and His Poetry: Selections with Com-
    mentaries. "Poetry and Life Series," No. 15. New York:
    AMS Press, 1972. [A reprint of a book published in 1913 by
    Harrap.]

Dudley, Edward, and Maximillian E. Novak. The Wild Man Within:
    An Image in Western Thought from the Renaissance to Ro-
    manticism. Pittsburgh: University of Pittsburgh Press, 1972.

Edgcumbe, Richard. Byron: The Last Phase. New York: Has-
    kell House, 1972. [A reprint of a book published in 1909 by
    Scribner.]

Engelberg, Edward. "The Price of Consciousness: Goethe's Faust
    and Byron's Manfred," The Unknown Distance: From Con-
    sciousness to Conscience, Goethe to Camus. Cambridge:
    Harvard University Press, 1972. Pp. 40-57.

Fox, Sir John C. The Byron Mystery. St. Clair Shores, Mich.:
    Scholarly Press, 1972. [A reprint of a book published in
    1924 by Richards.]

Gérin, Winifred. "Byron's Influence on the Brontës," Essays by
    Divers Hands. 3rd ser., Vol. XXXVII. London: Oxford
    University Press, 1972. Pp. 47-62.

Gilman, Sander L. "The Uncontrollable Steed: A Study of the
    Metamorphosis of a Literary Image." Euphorion, LXVI
    (March, 1972), 32-54.

Goode, Clement Tyson. Byron as Critic. New York: B. Frank-
    lin, 1972. [A reprint of a book published in 1923 by Wagner.]

Gose, Elliott B., Jr. "Imagination Indulged: The Irrational in the
    Nineteenth Century Novel. Montreal & London: McGill-
    Queen's University, 1972.

Gunn, Peter. "Introduction," Byron: Selected Prose. Baltimore:
    Penguin Books, 1972. Pp. 9-21.

Gurr, Andrew. "Don Byron and the Moral North," Ariel, III
    (July, 1972), 32-41.

Harson, Robert R. "A Clarification Concerning Polidori, Lord
    Byron's Physician," K-SJ, XXI-XXII (1972-73), 38-40.

Holden, David. Greece Without Columns. London: Faber &
    Faber, 1972; New York: Lippincott, 1972.

Hunt, Leigh. Lord Byron and Some of His Contemporaries, with
    Recollections of the Author's Life and His Visit to Italy.
    New York: AMS, 1972. [A reprint of a book published in
    1828 by Colburn.]

Huxley, H. H. "Bos, Bentley and Byron," Greece and Rome, 2nd
    ser., XIX (Oct., 1972), 186-89. [Bos piger in Don Juan XII,
    lxx is an allusion to Horace's Epistles I, xiv, 43.]

Inglis-Jones, Elisabeth. "A Pembrokeshire Country Family in the
    Eighteenth Century, Part 2," National Library of Wales
    Journal, XVII (Summer, 1972), 217-37; Part 3, ibid., XVII
    (Winter, 1973), 321-42.

Jeffrey, Lloyd N. Thomas Hood. "Twayne English Author Series,"
    137. New York: Twayne, 1972.

Jenkins, Elizabeth. Lady Caroline Lamb. London: Sphere, 1972.
    [A revised edition of a book published in 1932 by Little
    Brown.]

Johnson, Lee. "Delacroix and The Bride of Abydos, " Burlington
      Magazine, CXIV (Sept. , 1972), 579-85.

Jump, John D. Byron. "Routledge Author Guides. " London &
      Boston: Routledge and Kegan Paul, 1972.
      Reviews:
        Robert Chapman, Books and Bookmen, XVIII, No. 3, (1972),
          39.
        TLS, Nov. 17, 1972, p. 1398.
        William Plomer, Byron Journal, I (1973), 30-31.
        Mary McBride, Library Journal, XCVIII (Feb. 15, 1973),
          546.
        F. W. Bateson, NYRB, Feb. 22, 1973, pp. 32-33.
        Choice, X (May, 1973), 458.
        E. E. Bostetter, ELN, XI (Suppl. to No. 1, Sept. , 1973), 39.
        P. D. Fleck, Humanities Association Review, XXV (Spring,
          1974), 171-172.

Kline, Richard B. "Byron's Boat, the Morat Bones, and Mr. St.
      Aubyn, " K-SJ, XXI-XXII (1972-1973), 33-38.

Kushwaba, M. S. "Byron the Dramatist: A Reappraisal," Punjab
      University Research Bulletin, III (1972), 113-20.

McGann, Jerome J. Swinburne: An Experiment in Criticism.
      Chicago & London: Chicago University Press, 1972.

Madden, Lionel (ed.). Robert Southey: The Critical Heritage.
      London & Boston: Routledge, 1972.

Manning, Peter J. "Edmund Kean and Byron's Plays, " K-SJ, XXI-
      XXII (1972-1973), 188-206.

Maxwell, J. C. "Byron and the Bishop of Clogher, " N&Q, CCXVII
      (March, 1972), 96.

Mayne, Ethel Colburn. Byron. St. Clair Shores, Mich. : Scholar-
      ly Press, 1972. [A reprint of the 1924 edition of a book pub-
      lished in 1912 by Scribner.]

Moore, Thomas. The Life, Letters and Journals of Lord Byron by
      Thomas Moore, Collected and Arranged with Notes by Sir
      Walter Scott (and others). New and Complete Edition. St.
      Clair Shores, Mich. : Scholarly Press, 1972. [A reprint of
      the 1920 edition of a book first published in 1830 by Murray.]

Morse, J. I. "Byron's 'Ignis-Fatuus to the mind,' " N&Q, CCXVII
      (Aug. , 1972), 293-94.

Nicolson, Harold. Byron: The Last Journey, April 1823-April
      1824. St. Clair Shores, Mich. : Scholarly Press, 1972.
      [A reprint of a book published in 1924 by Constable.]

Noel, Roden. Life of Lord Byron. Folcroft, Pa.: Folcroft Li-
    brary Editions, 1972; Port Washington, N.J. & London: Kennikat,
    1972. [A reprint of a book published in 1890 by W. Scott.]

Origo, Iris. The Last Attachment: The Story of Byron and Te-
    resa Guiccioli as Told in Their Unpublished Letters and
    Other Family Papers. New York: Scribner, 1972. [A re-
    print of a book published in 1949 by Cape & Murray.]

Otten, Terry. "Byron's Cain and Werner," The Deserted Stage:
    The Search for Dramatic Form in Nineteenth Century England.
    Athens, Ohio: Ohio University Press, 1972. Pp. 41-75.

Patty, James S. "Byron and Nerval: Two Sons of Fire," Studies
    in Honor of Alfred G. Engstron. ("University of North Caro-
    lina Studies in the Romance Languages and Literatures," No.
    124.) Chapel Hill: The University of North Carolina Press,
    1972. Pp. 99-115.

Raymond, Dora Neill. The Political Career of Lord Byron. New
    York: Russell & Russell, 1972. [A reprint of a book pub-
    lished in 1924 by Holt.]

Reiman, Donald H. The Romantics Reviewed: Contemporary Re-
    views of British Romantic Writers. 9 vols. New York &
    London: Garland Publishing Co., 1972.

St. Clair, William. That Greece Might Still Be Free. The Phil-
    hellenes in the War of Independence. New York: Oxford
    University Press, 1972.

Sheraw, C. Darrell. "Coleridge, Shelley, Byron and the Devil,"
    KSMB, XXIII (1972), 6-9. [On Byron's Devil's Drive.]

Small, Christopher. Ariel like a Harpy. Shelley, Mary and
    "Frankenstein." London: Victor Gollanz, 1972.

Taborski, Boleslaw. Byron and the Theater. ("Salsburg Studies
    in English Literature, Poetic Drama," No. 1.) Austria:
    University of Salsburg, 1972.

Tibble, J. W., and Anne Tibble. John Clare: A Life. London:
    Michael Joseph, 1972.

Turney, Catherine. Byron's Daughter: A Biography of Elizabeth
    Medora Leigh. New York: Charles Scribner's, 1972.

Vincent, E. R. P. Byron, Hobhouse and Foscolo: New Documents
    in the History of a Collaboration. New York: Octagon, 1972.
    [A reprint of a book published in 1949 by Macmillan.]

Walling, William. "Tradition and Revolution: Byron's Vision of
    Judgment," The Wordsworth Circle, III (Autumn, 1972), 223-
    31.

Walton, Francis R. "Byron's Lines on John William Rizzo Hopp-
    ner," K-SJ, XXI-XXII (1972-1973), 40-42.

Widdowson, Peter. "Emily Brontë: The Romantic Novelist,"
    Modern Språk, LXVI (Feb.-March, 1972), 1-19.

Wilson, James D. "Tirso, Molière, and Byron: The Emergence
    of Don Juan as Romantic Hero," South Central Bulletin,
    XXXIII (1972), 246-48.

Wolff, Cynthia Griffin. "A Mirror for Men: Stereotypes of Wo-
    men in Literature," Massachusetts Review, XIII (Winter-
    Spring, 1972), 205-218.

EPILOGUE: 1973-1974

1973

Allentuck, Marcia. "Byron and Goethe: New Unpublished References by Henry Gally Knight," PQ, LII (Oct., 1973), 777-
79.

Antonini, Giacomo. "Impact on Italian Opera," Byron Journal, I
(1973), 21-24.

Bateson, F. W. "Byron's Baby," NYRB, XX (Feb. 22, 1973), 32-
33.

Bettany, W. A. (arranger). The Confessions of Lord Byron. A
Collection of His Private Opinions of Men and Matters, Taken
from the New and Enlarged Edition of His Letters and Journals. New York: Haskell House, 1973. [A reprint of a
book published in 1905 by John Murray.]

Blyth, Henry. Caro, the Fatal Passion: The Life of Lady Caroline Lamb. New York: Coward, McCann and Geohegan,
1973.

"The Book by Byron's Bed at Missolonghi," Byron Journal, I
(1973), 12-13. [Tasso's Jerusalem Delivered.]

Brand, C. P. "Byron and the Italians," Byron Journal, I (1973),
14-21.

Briscoe, Walter A. Byron, the Poet. Philadelphia: R. West,
1973. [A reprint of a book published in 1924 by Routledge.]

Brown, Margaret. "Byron and Shelley: The Sea, a Shared Enthusiasm," Byron Journal, I (1973), 48-49.

Byron, May Clarissa Gillington. A Day with Lord Byron. Philadelphia: R. West, 1973. [A reprint of a book published in
1910 by Hodder and Stoughton.]

Cameron, Kenneth Neill (comp.). Romantic Rebels: Essays on
    Shelley and His Circle. Cambridge: Harvard University
    Press, 1973.
    It contains:
        D. V. Erdman, "Lord Byron," pp. 161-202.
        _____, " 'Fare Thee Well'-Byron's Last Days in England,"
        pp. 203-227.

Carr, Sherwyn T. "Bunn, Byron and Manfred," Nineteenth Century
    Theater Research, I (Spring, 1973), 15-27.

Chambers, R. W. Ruskin (and Others) on Byron. Philadelphia:
    R. West, 1973. [A reprint of a book published in 1925 by
    Oxford University Press.]

Clarke, Isabel Constance. Shelley and Byron: A Tragic Friend-
    ship. Philadelphia: R. West, 1973. [A reprint of a book
    published in 1934 by Hutchinson.]

Clinton, George. Memoirs of the Life and Writings of Lord Byron.
    Philadelphia: R. West, 1973. [A reprint of a book pub-
    lished in 1825 by Robins.]

Clubbe, John. "After Missolonghi: Scott on Byron, 1824-1832,"
    Library Chronicle of the University of Pennsylvania, XXXIX
    (Winter, 1973), 18-33.

_____. "Byron and Scott," Texas Studies in Language and
    Literature, XV (Spring, 1973), 67-91.

Collins, Joseph J. "Tennyson and the Spasmodics," Victorian
    Newsletter, No. 43 (Spring, 1973), 24-28.

Corner, Martin. "Texts and Context in Arnold's Essays in Criti-
    cism," Neophilologus, LVII (April, 1973), 188-197.

Curnow, Wystan. "Romanticism and Modern American Criticism,"
    Studies in Romanticism, XII (Fall, 1973), 777-99.

Dakin, Douglas. The Greek Struggle for Independence, 1821-1833.
    Berkeley: University of California Press, 1973.

Drinkwater, John. The Pilgrim of Eternity. Folcroft, Pa. :
    Folcroft Library Editions, 1973. [A reprint of a book pub-
    lished in 1925 by George H. Doran.]

Ennis, Julian. "The Death of Byron according to The Bucks Ga-
    zette, 1824," CR, CCXXII (April, 1973), 195-99.

*Evans, Constantine. "The Adventure of the Byronic Hero," Baker
    Street Journal, XXIII (Sept. , 1973), 140-146.

Fisher, Alan S. "The Stretching of Augustan Satire: Charles
    Churchill's 'Dedication' to Warburton," JEGP, LXXII (July,
    1973), 360-77.

Fletcher, Robin. "Byron in Nineteenth Century Greek Literature,"
    The Struggle for Greek Independence. Essays to Mark the
    150th Anniversary of the Greek War of Independence. Lon-
    don: Macmillan, 1973. Pp. 224-47.

Fox, Sir John C. The Byron Mystery. Philadelphia: R. West,
    1973. [A reprint of a book published in 1924 by Richards.]

Fuess, C. M. Lord Byron as Satirist in Verse. New York:
    Haskell House, 1973. [A reprint of a book published in 1912
    by Columbia University Press.]

Galt, John. The Life of Lord Byron. Philadelphia: R. West,
    1973. [A reprint of a book published in 1830 by Colburn and
    Bentley.]

Garber, Frederick. "Byron's Giaour and the Mark of Cain,"
    Etudes Anglaises, XXVI (April-June, 1973), 150-59.

Gömöri, George. "The Myth of Byron in Norwid's Life and Work,"
    Slavonic and East European Review, LI (April, 1973), 231-
    242.

Gordon, Armistead Churchill. Allegra: The Story of Byron and
    Miss Clairmont. New York: Haskell House, 1973. [A re-
    print of a book published in 1926 by Minton and Balch.]

Gordon, Sir Cosmo. The Life and Genius of Byron. Philadelphia:
    R. West, 1973. [A reprint of a book published in 1824 by
    Knight and Lacey.]

Guiccioli, Teresa Gamba, Countess. My Recollections of Lord
    Byron, and Those of Eyewitnesses of His Life. Philadelphia:
    R. West, 1973. [A reprint of a book published in 1869 by
    R. Bentley.]

Haight, Gordon. "To Whom It May Concern--and Others," TLS,
    Jan. 26, 1973, pp. 87-89. [Mention of Byron's memoirs and
    their destruction.] Cf. R. Glynn Grylls, "Byron's Memoirs,"
    ibid., Feb. 9, 1973, p. 153.

Hannay, Prudence. "The Redoubtable Lady Holland," History To-
    day, XXIII (Feb., 1973), 94-104.

Harper, Henry Howard. Byron's Malach Hamoves. A Commen-
    tary on Leigh Hunt's Work Entitled "Lord Byron and Some of
    His Contemporaries." Folcroft, Pa.: Folcroft Library Edi-
    tions, 1973. [A reprint of the revised edition of 1933 pub-
    lished by Torch Press.]

Harwell, Thomas Meade. Studies in Relevance: Romantic and
    Victorian Writers in 1972. ("Salsburg Studies in English
    Literature, Romantic Reassessment," No. 32.) Austria:
    University of Salsburg, 1973.
    It contains:
        Laura B. Kennely, "Satire and High Society," 53-75.
        Harry W. McCraw, "Growing Up Absurd: Byron's Don Juan,"
        pp. 76-86.

Haworth, Helen E. " 'A Milk-White Lamb That Bleats'? Some
    Stereotypes of Women in Romantic Literature," Humanities
    Association Review, XXIV (Fall, 1973), 277-93.

Hibber, Christopher. George IV: Regent and King. Vol. II:
    1811-1830. London: Lane, 1973.

Hobhouse, John Cam. Historical Illustrations to the Fourth Canto
    of Childe Harold: Containing Dissertations on the Ruins of
    Rome and an Essay on Italian Literature. Folcroft, Pa.:
    Folcroft Library Editions, 1973. [A reprint of a book pub-
    lished in 1818 by Murray.]

Hoge, James O., Jr. "Lady Caroline Lamb on Byron and Her
    Own Wasted Life: Two New Letters," N&Q, CCXVIII (Sept.,
    1973), 331-32.

Hood, Thomas. The Letters of Thomas Hood, ed. Peter F. Mor-
    gan. Toronto: University of Toronto Press, 1973.

Jeafresson, John Cordy. The Real Lord Byron. New Views of
    the Poet's Life. Philadelphia: R. West, 1973. [A reprint
    of a book published in 1883 by Hurst and Blackett.]

Jump, John D. (ed.). Byron: "Childe Harold's Pilgrimage" and
    'Don Juan": A Casebook. London: Macmillan, 1973.
    Reviews:
        P. D. Fleck, Humanities Association Review, XXV (Spring,
        1974), 171-172.
        Gilbert Phelps, Byron Journal, II (1974), 60-61.

Kahn, Arthur D. "The Pastoral Byron: Arcadia in 'The Island,' "
    Arcadia, VIII (1973), 274-83.

Kirchner, Jane. The Function of the Persona in the Poetry of
    Byron. ("Salsburg Studies in English Literature, Romantic
    Reassessment," No. 15.) Austria: University of Salsburg,
    1973.

Knight, G. Wilson. "Reason for Ostracism," Byron Journal, I
    (1973), 62-63. [A letter.]

Lim, Pauline M., Jr. The Style of Lord Byron's Plays. ("Sals-
    burg Studies in English Literature, Poetic Drama," No. 3.)
    Austria: University of Salsburg, 1973.

Lister, Raymond. British Romantic Art. London: Bell, 1973.

Low, Donald A. "Byron and the 'Grecian Urn,' " TLS, Oct. 26, 1973, p. 1314.

McGann, Jerome J. "Editing Byron's Poetry," Byron Journal, I (1973), pp. 5-10.

Mackay, Charles. Medora Leigh: A History and an Autobiography. New York: AMS Press, 1973. [A reprint of a book published in 1869 by Bentley.]

Mackenzie, Harriet Margaret. Byron's Laughter in Life and Poetry. Folcroft, Pa.: Folcroft Library Editions, 1973. [A reprint of a book published in 1939 by Lymanhouse.]

McMahan, Anna Benneson (ed.). With Byron in Italy. Philadelphia: R. West, 1973. [A reprint of a book published in 1906 by McClugg.]

Marchand, Leslie A. "Byron in his Letters and Journals," Cornhill, 1076 (Summer, 1973), 40-65. [Part of the Introduction to his edition of Byron's Letters and Journals.]

_____ (ed.). "Introduction," Byron's Letters and Journals. Vol. I: 1798-1810, "In My Hot Youth"; Vol. II: 1810-1812, "Famous in My Time." London: J. Murray; Harvard University Press, 1973. Pp. 1-23.
Reviews:
  Peter Conrad, NS, LXXXVI, Sept. 28, 1973, 430-432.
  Philip Ziegler, Spectator, CCXXXI, Sept. 29, 1973, 410-411.
  TLS, Oct. 19, 1973, 1265-66.
  Joanna Richardson, History Today, XXIII, Dec., 1973, 885-886.
  Peter Grosvenor, Publisher's Weekly, Jan. 14, 1974, 83.
  Anthony Powell, Apollo, XCIX, Jan., 1974, 71.
  W. Clemons, Newsweek, Feb. 11, 1974, 91-92.
  Richard Harter Fogle, SR, LXXXII, Spring, 1974, 383-392.
  C. Clarke, Journal of European Studies, IV, Mar., 1974, 81-82.
  New Yorker, April 1, 1974, 123-24.
  William K. Seymour, CR, CCXXIV, Apr., 1974, 219-220.
  Robert F. Gleckner, Wordsworth Circle, V, Summer, 1974, 133-38.
  Stuart Curran, SEL, XIV, Autumn, 1974, 637-638.
  David V. Erdman, ELN, XII (Suppl. to No. 1, Sept., 1974), 40-41.
  B. F. Fisher, IV, American Book Collector, XXV (Sept.-Oct., 1974), 4-5.
  Ian Ferguson, Unisa English Studies, XII, Sept., 1974, 7-72.
  Andrew Rutherford, Aberdeen University Review, XLV, Autumn, 1974, 406-408.
  Dewey R. Faulkner, Yale Review, LXIV, Oct., 1974, 88-93.

Elma Dangerfield, Byron Journal, II (1974), 61-62.

Ernest J. Lovell, Jr., K-SJ, XXIV, (1975), 139-43.

_____. "Introductory Essay from his Byron's Letters and Jour-
nals," Byron Journal, I (1973), 34-46. [Slightly abridged.]

Mayne, Ethel Colburn. Byron. Philadelphia: R. West, 1973.
[A reprint of the 1924 edition published by Scribner's.]

Mesrobian, Arpena. "Lord Byron at the Armenian Monastery of
San Lazzaro," Courier (Syracuse University Library), XI,
i (1973), 27-37.

Montluzin, Emily Lorraine de. "Southey's 'Satanic School' Remarks: An Old Charge for a New Offender," K-SJ, XXI-
XXII (1972-1973), 29-33.

Moore, Thomas. Life, Letters and Journals of Lord Byron. A
complete edition collected and arranged with notes by Sir
Walter Scott, Lord Jeffrey, Professor Wilson (and others).
Philadelphia: R. West, 1973. [A reprint of the 1920 edition
of a book first published in 1880 by Murray.]

Newton, K. M. "Byronic Egoism and George Eliot's The Spanish
Gypsy," Neophilologus, LVII (Oct., 1973), 388-400.

Nichol, John. Byron. Philadelphia: R. West, 1973. [A reprint
of a book published in 1880 by Macmillan.]

Nicolson, Harold. Byron: The Last Journey, April 1823-April
1824. Philadelphia: R. West, 1973. [A reprint of the 1948
edition published by Constable.]

Nielsen, Jørgen Erik. "Byron Apocrypha," N&Q, CCXVIII (Aug.,
1973), 291-292. [A supplement to Chew's list of apocrypha.]

Noel, Roden. Life of Lord Byron. New York: AMS Press, 1973.
Folcroft, Pa.: Folcroft Library Editions, 1973. [A reprint
of a book published in 1890 by Walter Scott.]

Ober, Kenneth H., and Warren U. Ober. "Zukovskij's Translation of 'The Prisoner of Chillon,' " Slavic and East European Journal, XVII (Winter, 1973), 390-98.

Ogle, Robert B. "A Byron Contradiction: Some Light on His
Italian Study," Studies in Romanticism, XII (Winter, 1973),
436-42.

Paston, George [pseud. for Emily Morse Symonds]. "To Lord Byron": Feminine Profiles. Based Upon Unpublished Letters,
1807-1824, eds. George Paston and Peter Quennell. Folcroft,
Pa.: Folcroft Library Editions, 1973. [A reprint of a book
published in 1939 by Murray.]

Pratt, Willis W. Byron at Southwell: The Making of a Poet.
    New York: Haskell House, 1973. [A reprint of a book pub-
    lished in 1948 by University of Texas Press.]

Rainwater, Frank. Lord Byron: A Study of the Development of
    His Philosophy, with Special Emphasis Upon the Dramas.
    Folcroft, Pa.: Folcroft Library Editions, 1973. [A reprint
    of a 1949 thesis publ. by the Joint University Libraries.]

Redpath, Theodore. "Byron in Cambridge," Byron Journal, I
    (1973), 59-61.

_____. The Young Romantics and Critical Opinion, 1807-1824.
    London: Harrap, 1973.

Reiman, Donald (ed.). Shelley and His Cricle, 1773-1822. Vols.
    V & VI. Cambridge, Mass.: Harvard University Press,
    1973.

Ridenour, George M. "My Poem's Epic," Parnassus Revisited.
    Modern Critical Essays on the Epic Tradition, ed. Anthony
    C. Yu. Chicago: American Library, 1973. Pp. 303-25.
    [An excerpt from Ridenour's The Style of "Don Juan," 1963.]

Roberts, Cecil. "And Did Trelawny Lie?" Books and Bookmen,
    XIX (Oct., 1973), 62-66.

Robson, H. L. "Byron, the Milbankes and Seaham Village,"
    Antiquities of Sunderland, XXV (1970/1973), 1-25.

Robson, W. W. Byron as Poet. Folcroft, Pa.: Folcroft Library
    Editions, 1973. [A reprint of a book published in 1957 by
    Oxford University Press.]

Roe, Herbert C. The Rare Quarto Edition of Lord Byron's "Fugi-
    tive Pieces." Folcroft, Pa.: Folcroft Library Editions,
    1973. [A reprint of a book published in 1924 by Routledge.]

Sheraw, C. Darrell. "Don Juan: Byron as Un-Augustan Satirist,"
    Satire Newsletter, X (1973), 25-33.

Spencer, Terence J. B. Fair Greece! Sad Relic: Literary Phil-
    hellenism from Shakespeare to Byron. New York: Octagon,
    1974. [A reprint of a book published in 1954 by Weidenfeld
    & Nicolson.]

Spender, Harold. Byron and Greece. Philadelphia: R. West,
    1973. [A reprint of a book published in 1924 by Murray.]

Steffan, T. G. "Lord Henry's and Lady Adeline's Rank in Lord
    Byron's Don Juan," N&Q, CCXVIII (Aug., 1973), 290-91.

_____, and Eleanor, and W. W. Pratt (eds.). Lord Byron:
"Don Juan," With Introduction and Notes. Baltimore and
Harmondsworth: Penguin, 1973.
Reviews:
   TLS, May 18, 1973, p. 558.
   Thomas L. Ashton, ELN, XII, (Suppl. to No. 1, Sept., 1974),
   41-42.
   Charles W. Hagelman, Jr., South Central Bulletin, XXXIV
   (Oct., 1974), 136.
   John Clubbe, K-SJ, XXIV, 1975, 153-55.

Stevens, H. R. "Theme and Structure in Byron's Manfred: The
Biblical Basis," Unisa English Studies, XI, No. 2 (1973), 15-
22.

Trelawny, Edward John. Letters, ed. H. Buxton Forman. New
York: AMS, 1973. [A reprint of a book published in 1910
by H. Frowde.]

_____. Recollections of the Last Days of Shelley and Byron.
Philadelphia: R. West, 1973. [A reprint of a book published
in 1858 by Ticknor.]

_____. Records of Shelley, Byron and the Author, ed. with an
introduction by David Wright. Harmondsworth: Penguin,
1973. [An enlarged version of his Recollections of the Last
Days of Shelley and Byron. A reprint of a book published in
1876 by Pickering.]

Trueblood, Paul G. "Byron's Political Realism," Byron Journal, I
(1973), 50-58.

Vincent, E. R. Byron, Hobhouse and Foscolo. Folcroft, Pa.:
Folcroft Library Editions, 1973. [A reprint of a book published in 1949 by Macmillan.]

Vulliamy, Colwyn Edward. Byron, With a View of the Kingdom of
Cant and a Dissection of the Byronic Ego. New York: Haskell House, 1973; Philadelphia: R. West, 1973. [A reprint
of a book published in 1948 by Joseph.]

Wallis, Bruce. Byron: The Critical Voice. Vol. I: Introduction
and General Criticism. Vol. II: Self-Criticism and Criticism of Individuals and Works. ("Salsburg Studies in English
Literature, Romantic Reassessment," No. 20 & 21.) Austria:
University of Salsburg, 1973.

Ward, Herman M. Byron and the Magazine, 1806-1824. ("Salsburg Studies in English Literature, Romantic Reassessment,"
No. 32.) Austria: University of Salsburg, 1973.

Wardroper, John. Kings, Lords and Wicked Libellers. Satire and
Protest, 1760-1837. London: John Murray, 1973.

Wellesley, Dorothy. Byron. Folcroft, Pa.: Folcroft Library
    Editions, 1973. [A reprint of a book published in 1941 by
    Collins.]

Zegger, Robert E. John Cam Hobhouse: A Political Life, 1819-
    1852. Columbia: University of Missouri Press, 1973.

1974

Ashton, Thomas L. "Marino Faliero: Byron's 'Poetry of Politics,'"
    Studies in Romanticism, XIII (Winter, 1974), 1-13.

Babinski, Hubert F. The Mazeppa Legend in European Romanti-
    cism. New York: Columbia University Press, 1974.

Barber, Thomas G. Byron and Where He Is Buried. Folcroft,
    Pa.: Folcroft Library Editions, 1974. [A reprint of a book
    published in 1939 by Morley.]

Barratt, G. R. V. "Somov, Kozlov and Byron's Russian Triumph,"
    Canadian Review of Comparative Literature, I (1974), 104-22.

Bauer, N. Stephen. "Byron's Doubting Cain," South Atlantic Bulle-
    tin, XXXIX (May, 1974), 80-88.

Blackstone, Bernard. "Byron and Islam: The Triple Eros,"
    Journal of European Studies, IV (Dec., 1974), 325-63.

_____. "Byron and the Levels of Landscape," Ariel, V, iv
    (Oct., 1974), 3-20.

_____. "Byron's Greek Canto: The Anatomy of Freedom,"
    YES, (1974), 172-79. [On Canto II of Childe Harold's Pil-
    grimage.]

Bostetter, Edward E. "Masses and Solids: Byron's View of the
    External World," MLQ, XXXV (Sept., 1974), 257-71.

Brent, P. L. Lord Byron. Introduction by Elizabeth Longford.
    London: Weidenfeld and Nicolson, 1974.

Brogan, Howard O. "Byron So Full of Fun, Frolic, Wit and
    Whim," Huntington Library Quarterly, XXXVII (Feb., 1974),
    171-89.

_____. "Lady Byron: The Moral Clytemnestra of Her Lord,"
    Durham University Journal, LXVI (March, 1974), 146-55.

Brouzas, C. G. Byron's Maid of Athens: Her Family and Sur-
    roundings. Folcroft, Pa.: Folcroft Library Editions, 1974.
    [A reprint of a book published in 1949 by West Virginia Uni-
    versity.]

Burch, Francis F. "An Unpublished Letter of Thomas More,"
    N&Q, CCXIX (Sept., 1974), 335-36.

Burton, Anthony, and John Murdoch.   Byron: An Exhibition to
    Commemorate the 150th Anniversary of His Death in the
    Greek War of Liberation, 19 April 1824.   London: Victoria
    and Albert Museum, 1974.   Cf. Peter Conrad, TLS, May 31,
    1974, p. 584.

Butler, Eliza M.   Byron and Goethe.   Folcroft, Pa.: Folcroft
    Library Editions, 1974.   [A reprint of the Byron Foundation
    Lecture of 1949.]

"Byron and the Armenian in Graphics," Armenian Review, XXVII
    (Summer, 1974), 141-45.

Cameron, Kenneth Neill.   Shelley, the Golden Years.   Cambridge,
    [Mass.]: Harvard University Press, 1974.

Chambers, R. W.   Ruskin (and Others) on Byron.   Folcroft, Pa.:
    Folcroft Library Editions, 1974.   [A reprint of a book pub-
    lished in 1925 by Oxford University Press.]

Churchill, K. G.   "Byron and Italy," Literary Half-Yearly, XV
    (July, 1974), 67-86.

Clancy, Charles J.   Lava, Hock and Soda-Water: Byron's "Don
    Juan."   ("Salsburg Studies in English Literature: Romantic
    Reassessment Series," No. 41.) Austria: University of
    Salsburg, 1974.

_____. Review of "Don Juan" Criticism: 1900-1973.   ("Salsburg
    Studies in English Literature: Romantic Reassessment," No.
    40.) Austria: University of Salsburg, 1974.

Clayton, William.   The Byron Collection.   Derby, [Eng.]: Benrose
    Editions, 1974.

Cleverdon, Douglas.   "Lady Melbourne," TLS, Oct. 11, 1974, p.
    1127.   Cf. TLS, Oct. 25, 1974, p. 1197.

Clubbe, John.   " 'The New Prometheus of New Men': Byron's 1816
    Poems and Manfred," Nineteenth Century Literary Perspec-
    tives.   Essays in Honor of Lionel Stevenson, ed. Clyde de L.
    Ryals et al.   Durham, N.C.: Duke University Press, 1974.

Cooke, Sheila M. (comp.)   Byron Commemoration, 1974: Book-
    list.   Nottingham: Nottinghamshire County Library, 1974.

Dick, William.   Byron and His Poetry.   Folcroft, Pa.: Folcroft
    Library Editions, 1974.   [A reprint of a book published in
    1913 by George Harrap.]

Driva, Ianna. "Byron in Greece," CR, CCXXIV (April, 1974),
    189-93.

Dunn, Douglas. A Choice of Byron's Verse; Selected with an in-
    troduction. London: Faber, 1974.

Durning, Russell E. "Comparative Literature: An Essay in Defi-
    nition," Literary Half-Yearly, XV (Jan., 1974), 93-113.

Eggenschwiler, David. "The Tragic and Comic Rhythms of Man-
    fred," Studies in Romanticism, XIII (Winter, 1974), 63-77.

Ehrstine, John W. "Byron and the Metaphysics of Self-Destruc-
    tion," The Gothic Imagination: Essays in Dark Romanticism,
    ed. G. R. Thompson. Pullman: Washington State Univer-
    sity Press, 1974. Pp. 94-108.

Farrell, John P. "Arnold, Byron, and Taine." English Studies,
    LV (Oct., 1974), 435-39.

Fischer, Doucet D., and Donald H. Reiman (comps.). Byron on
    the Continent: A Memorial Exhibition, 1824-1974, Feb. -
    April 1974. New York: Carl H. Pforzheimer Library and
    the New York Public Library, 1974.

Fogle, Richard Harter. The Permanent Pleasure. Essays on
    Classics of Romanticism. Athens: University of Georgia
    Press, 1974.

Fox, John Charles. The Byron Mystery. Folcroft, Pa.: Folcroft
    Library Editions, 1974. [A reprint of a book published in
    1924 by G. Richards.]

"From Missolonghi to Apsley House: A Reappraisal of Byron,"
    Listener, XCI (May 16, 1974), 623-26.

Fuess, C. M. Lord Byron as a Satirist in Verse. "Studies in
    Byron, No. 5." New York: Haskell House, 1974. [A re-
    print of a book published in 1912 by Columbia University
    Press.]

Gömöri, George. Cyprian Norvid. New York: Twayne Publishers,
    1974.

Gordon, Archie. "Byron's Gordon Ancestors," Listener, XCII
    (Dec. 19-25, 1974), 822-24.

Gordon, Cosmo. Life and Genius of Lord Byron. Folcroft, Pa.:
    Folcroft Library Editions, 1974. [A reprint of a book pub-
    lished in 1824 by Knight & Lacey.]

Grierson, Herbert. Lord Byron: Arnold and Swinburne. Fol-
    croft, Pa.: Folcroft Library Editions, 1974. [A reprint of

a book published in 1920 by The Proceedings of the British
Academy.]

Grimble, Ian.   "Byron," New Humanist, XC (Aug., 1974), 122-23.

Grunfeld, Frederic.   "The Discovery of the Mediterranean," Horizon (N. Y.), XVI (Winter, 1974), 97-103.

Hall, Ruth.   "I Want a Hero," NS, April 26, 1974, p. 593.

Hamilton, Olive.   Paradise of Exiles: Tuscany and the British.
London: Andre Deutsch, 1974.

Haworth, Helen E.   " 'The Virtuous Romantics': Indecency, Indelicacy, Pornography and Romantic Poetry," Papers on Language
and Literature, X (Summer, 1974), 287-306.

Henson, Herbert H.   Byron. New York: Haskell House, 1974.
[A reprint of a book published in 1924 by Cambridge University Press.]

Hillier, Bevis.   "Byronic Attitudes," ILN, CCLXII (June, 1974),
47-50.

Hinkel, Howard H.   "The Byronic Pilgrimage to the Absurd,"
Midwest Quarterly, XV (Summer, 1974), 352-65.

Hoge, James O., Jr.   "Lady Caroline Lamb on Byron and Her
Own Wasted Life: Two New Letters," N&Q, CCXIX (Sept.,
1974), 331-33.

Howell, Margaret J.   "Sardanapalus," Byron Journal, II (1974),
42-53.

Jackson, Michael.   "Lord Byron: 'A Gallant Spirit and Kind One,' "
Theology, LXXVII (Nov., 1974), 578-82.

Joannides, Paul.   "A Byron Subject by Horace Vernet," Burlington
Magazine, CXVI (Nov., 1974), 668-69.

Jones, Howard Mumford.   Revolution and Romanticism. Cambridge, Mass.: Belknap Press of Harvard University Press,
1974.

Kenworthy-Browne, John.   "Byron Portrayed," Antique Collector,
XLV (July, 1974), 58-64.

Klapper, M. Roxana.   The German Literary Influence on Byron.
("Salsburg Studies in English Literature: Romantic Reassessment," No. 42.) Austria: University of Salsburg, 1974.

Lambert, Cecily.   "Most Gorgeous Lady Blessington," KSMB, XXV
(1974), 26-32.

Levik, Wilhelm. "Byron in Russia," Soviet Literature, No. 10
(1974), 159-63.

Lisbeth, Terrence L. "The Motif of Imagination in Byron's Blue-
stocking Allusions," Massachusetts Studies in English, IV
(1974-1975), 34-42.

Low, Donald A. "Byron and Europe," Journal of European Studies,
IV (Dec., 1974), 364-67.

McGann, Jerome J. "Milton and Byron," KSMB, XXV (1974), 9-
25.

Mann, Peter (trans.). "The Living Byron: On the 150th Anniversary of the Poet's Death," Soviet Literature, No. 4 (1974),
143-46.

Marchand, Leslie. Byron's Letters and Journals. Vol. III: 1813-
1814: Alas! the Love of Women! Cambridge, Mass.: Har-
vard University Press; London: Murray, 1974.
Reviews:
Philip Ziegler, Spectator, CCXXXIII (Aug. 3, 1974), 149.
P. Beer, Listener, XCII (Aug. 14, 1974), 221.
Elizabeth Longford, Books and Bookmen, XIX (Aug., 1974),
24-25.
TLS, Sept. 20, 1974, p. 992.
Joanna Richardson, History Today, XXIV (Oct., 1974), 728.
Phoebe Adams, Atlantic Monthly, CCXXXIV (Nov., 1974),
123.

Marshall, William H. Structure of Byron's Major Poems. Philadelphia: University of Pennsylvania Press, 1974. [A reprint of a book published in 1962 by University of Pennsylvania Press.]

Mesrobian, Arpena. "Lord Byron at the Armenian Monastery of
San Lazzaro," Armenian Review, XXVII (Summer, 1974), 131-
40.

Miller, Edmund. "Byron's The Vision of Judgment, Stanzas
xlviii-li," Explicator, XXXIII (Sept., 1974), item 4.

Moore, Doris Langley. "Contrasting Memories of Byron," Country
Life, CLV (May 30, 1974), 1368-69.

_____. Lord Byron: Accounts Rendered. London: John Mur-
ray, 1974.
Reviews:
Phoebe Adams, Atlantic Monthly, CCXXXIII (June, 1974),
115.
Jonathan Raban, NS, LXXXVIII (July 5, 1974), 17-18.
Joanna Richardson, History Today, XXIV (July, 1974), 511-
512.

Elizabeth Longford, Books and Bookmen, XIX (Aug., 1974),
    24-25.
Choice, XI (Nov., 1974), 1310.

Osborne, Keith, and Sheila M. Cooke (comps.). Lord Byron, 1788-
    1824. Nottingham: Nottinghamshire County Library, 1974.

Parker, David. "The Narrator of Don Juan," Ariel, V (April,
    1974), 49-58.

"Philhellenic Celebration," Blackwood's, CCCXV (April, 1974), 343-
    44.

Porter, Peter. "Byron and the Moral North: The Englishness of
    Don Juan," Encounter, XLIII (Aug., 1974), 65-72.

Powell, Anthony. "Mrs. Massingberd," TLS, July 26, 1974, p.
    801.

Quennell, Peter. Byron. New York: Haskell House, 1974. Fol-
    croft, Pa.: Folcroft Library Editions, 1974. [Reprints of a
    book published in 1934 by Duckworth Library Editions.]

_____. Byron: The Years of Fame and Byron in Italy. Lon-
    don: Collins, 1974. [The revised edition of Byron: the
    Years of Fame and a reprint of Byron in Italy published in
    1941 and 1967 respectively.]

Rainwater, Frank. Lord Byron: A Study of the Development of
    His Philosophy with Special Emphasis Upon the Dramas. Fol-
    croft, Pa.: Folcroft Library Editions, 1974. [A reprint of
    a 1949 thesis published by the Joint University Libraries.]

Reddy, D. Sabba. Byron's "Don Juan." Folcroft, Pa.: Folcroft
    Library Editions, 1974. [A reprint of a book published in
    1968 by Malico Publishers in India.]

Reisner, Thomas A. "An Echo of Byron in Shelley," N&Q,
    CCXVIII (Sept., 1974), 333.

Rutherford, Andrew. "Byron: A Pilgrim's Progress," Byron Jour-
    nal, II (1974), 6-26.

Singer, Eric. "Some Thoughts on Canto II of Byron's Don Juan,"
    Byron Journal, II (1974), 64-78.

Spence, G. W. "The Moral Ambiguity of Marino Faliero," Aumla,
    No. 4 (May, 1974), 6-17.

Sperry, Stuart M. "Byron and the Meaning of Manfred," Criticism,
    XVI (Summer, 1974), 189-202.

Story, Mark.   The Poetry of John Clare.   London: Macmillan,
      1974.

Strickland, Margot.   The Byron Women.   London: Peter Owen,
      1974.
      Reviews:
      TLS, June 14, 1974, p. 646.
      A. L. Rowse, Spectator, CCXXX (June 15, 1974), 739.
      Elizabeth Longford, Books and Bookmen, XIX (Aug., 1974),
        24-25.

Symons, A. J.   A Bibliographical Catalogue of First Editions,
      Proof Copies and Manuscripts of Books by Lord Byron Ex-
      hibited at the Fourth Exhibition Held by the First Edition
      Club, January 1925.   Folcroft, Pa.: Folcroft Library Edi-
      tions, 1974. [A reprint of a book published in 1925 by The First
      Edition Club.]

Tachell, Molly.   "Byron's 'Windsor Poetics,' " KSMB, XXV (1974),
      1-5.

Terzian, Aram.   "George Gordon, Lord Byron: The Poet and the
      Legend," Armenian Review, XXVII (Summer, 1974), 115-31.

Train, Keith.   "The Byron Family," Byron Journal, II (1974), 35-
      40.

Turney, Catherine.   Byron's Daughter: A Biography of Elizabeth
      Medora Leigh.   London: Davies, 1974.

Vulliamy, Colwyn.   Byron with a View of the Kingdom of Cant and
      a Dissection of the Byronic Ego.   New York: Haskell House,
      1974.   Folcroft, Pa.: Folcroft Library Editions, 1974.   [A
      reprint of a book published in 1948 by Joseph.]

Whitla, William.   "Sources for Browning in Byron, Blake and
      Poe," Studies in Browning and His Circle, II (1974), 7-16.

Whitlock, William.   "Byron and the Luddites," KSMB, XXV (1974),
      6-8.

Wilson, Milton.   "Travellers' Venice: Some Images for Byron and
      Shelley," UTQ, XLIII (Winter, 1974), 93-120.

Winegarten, Renée.   Writers and Revolution: The Fatal Lure of
      Action.   New York: New Viewpoints a Division of Franklin
      Watts, Inc., 1974.
      It contains:
      "Literary Revolutionism, Despotism, and Outlawry," pp. 98-
        109.
      "Revolution as Personal Salvation," pp. 82-97.

Wood, Pamela J. (ed.). Byron: Derby, Eng.: English Life,
    1974.

Zulawski, Juliusz. "Byron's Influence in Poland," Byron Journal,
    II (1974), 28-34.

PART III

APPENDICES

Appendix A

DOCTORAL DISSERTATIONS ON BYRON[1]

19th CENTURY

*Roe, John C. Some Obscure and Disputed Points on Byronic Bi-
ography. Leipzig University, 1893.

1900-1909

*Leonard, W. Ellery. Byron and Byronism in America. Colum-
bia University, 1904.

*Miller, Barnette. Leigh Hunt's Relations with Byron, Shelley and
Keats. Columbia University, 1909.

1910-1919

Chew, Samuel C. The Relation of Lord Byron to the Drama of
the Romantic Period. Johns Hopkins, 1913.

*Fuess, Claude M. Lord Byron as a Satirist in Verse. Columbia
University, 1912.

1920-1929

Calvert, William J., Jr. Byron and Shakespeare, a Study of Influence. Harvard University, 1929.

*Goode, Clement T. Byron as Critic. Cornell University, 1922.

Longueil, Alfred E. Gothic Romance, Its Influence on the Romantic Poets, Wordsworth, Keats, Coleridge, Byron and Shelley.
Harvard, 1920.

*Powell, Desmond S. Criticism of Byron in France, Germany and
America. Cornell University, 1927.

---

[1]Items marked with an asterisk have been published as separate
books.

541

Raysor, Thomas M. The Critical Theories of Byron, Shelley and
    Keats. Harvard, 1922.

1930-1939

Erdman, David V. Byron's Poetic Technique. Princeton Univer-
    sity, 1937.

Johnson, Edward D. A Study in Digression, Lord Byron in "Don
    Juan." Yale University, 1939.

*Marjarum, Edward W. Byron as Skeptic and Believer. Catholic
    University, 1931.

*Phillips, William J. France on Byron. Pennsylvania University,
    1930.

Rockel, Henry J. The Byronic Hero. Harvard University, 1932.

*Trueblood, Paul G. Studies in Byron's "Don Juan." Duke Uni-
    versity, 1935.

Wiener, Harold S. The Eastern Background of Byron's Turkish
    Tales. Yale University, 1938.

1940-1949

*Borst, William A. The First Foreign Tour of Lord Byron, 1809-
    1811. Yale University, 1945.

Day, Martin S. English Verse Satire from Churchill to Byron.
    Johns Hopkins University, 1947.

*Ehrsam, Theodore G. Major George Gordon Byron and His Shell-
    ey, Byron and Keats Forgeries. New York University, 1948.

*Faulkner, Claude W. Byron's Political Verse Satire. University
    of Illinois, 1947.

*Lovell, Ernest, Jr. Byron's Concepts and Treatment of Nature,
    a Study In Contradiction and the Record of a Failure.
    Princeton University, 1946.

*Rainwater, Frank P. Lord Byron, a Study of the Development of
    His Philosophy, with Special Emphasis upon the Dramas.
    Vanderbilt University, 1949.

Ruby, Wade. A Study of the Influence of Mortality on Byron's
    Thought and Poetry. Southern California University, 1944.

Stiling, Frank. A Commentary on Byron's "Don Juan," Cantos
VII-X. University of Michigan, 1949.

*Ward, Herman M. Byron and the Magazines, 1806-1824. Prince-
ton University, 1940.

1950-1959

Adams, Norman O., Jr. Byron and the Early Victorians--A Study
of His Poetic Influence, 1824-1855. University of Wisconsin,
1956.

Ball, Patricia M. The Poetry of Byron. University of Nottingham,
1957.

Blair, George Eldridge. The Plays of the Romantic Poets. Their
Place in Dramatic History. University of Pennsylvania, 1951.

Butler, Maria H. Lord Byron's Treatment of Fatalism and Original Sin. University of North Carolina, 1952.

Curtsinger, Eugene C., Jr. The Byronic Hero and Hawthorne's
Seekers, A Comparative Study. Notre Dame, 1955.

Fiess, Edward. Byron and Byronism in the Mind and Art of Herman Melville. University of Colorado, 1951.

Goode, Clement T. Byron's Early Romances. A Study. Vanderbilt University, 1959.

Hall, John E. Byron's Philhellenism, the Nature and Extent of
Greek Influence on His Poetry. Vanderbilt University, 1958.

Harrison, John W. The Imagery of Byron's Romantic Narratives
and Dramas. University of Colorado, 1958.

Ketchin, Samuel C. Byron's Use of Gothicism. Emory University,
1957.

Kingston, Marion J. Claire Clairmont, A Biographical and Critical
Study. Duke University, 1952.

Kline, Alfred A. The English Romantics and the American Repub-
lic: An Analysis of the Concept of America in the Works of
Blake, Burns, Wordsworth, Coleridge, Byron and Shelley.
Columbia University, 1953.

Melikian, Anahid. Byron and the Near East. University of Wisconsin, 1954.

Myers, Neil N. Romantic Rebellion in the Later Poetry of Byron,
A Study of "Don Juan." Harvard University, 1959.

Ogle, Robert B. Byron and the Bernesque Satire. University of
    Illinois, 1952.

Pafford, Ward. "English Bards and Scotch Reviewers," a Study of
    Byron's Development as a Satirist. Duke University, 1950.

*Pedrini, Lura N. Serpent Imagery and Symbolism in the Major
    English Romantic Poets: Blake, Wordsworth, Coleridge, By-
    ron, Keats, and Shelley. University of Texas, 1959.

Quick, Nicholas W. Byronism in the Victorian Novel. University
    of Texas, 1954.

Ridenour, George M. A Critical Examination of the Third and
    Fourth Cantos of Lord Byron's "Childe Harold's Pilgrimage."
    Yale University, 1955.

Ruane, Darby R. A Study of Lord Byron's Satire: "The Vision of
    Judgment." St. John's University, 1959.

Shaw, Joseph T. Byron and Lermontov. The Romantic Verse
    Tale. Notre Dame, 1955.

Spencer, T. J. The Prelude of Philhellenism, a Study of Contem-
    porary Greece in English Literature before the Time of Byron.
    Kings College, London, 1953.

Tezla, Albert. Byron's Oriental Tales, a Critical Study. Univer-
    sity of Chicago, 1952.

*Thorslev, Peter Larson, Jr. The Byronic Hero: Types and
    Prototypes. University of Minnesota, 1959.

Whittier, Henry S. Byron's "Don Juan," Natural Force Versus
    Civilized Morality. Yale University, 1958.

                            1960-1970

Bartholomew, James Reece. Byron's "Sardanapalus:" A Manuscript
    Edition. University of Texas, 1965.

Baum, Joan Mandell. The Theatrical Compositions of the Major
    English Romantic Poets. Columbia University, 1969.

Bishai, N. Z. The Light Thrown on the Poetry of Blake, Byron
    and Tennyson by the Composers Who Have Set Its Words to
    Music. University of London, 1968.

Bruffe, Kenneth A. Satan and the Sublime: The Meaning of the
    Romantic Hero. Northwestern University, 1965.

Byrne, Clifford M.   Lord Byron: His Classical Republicanism, Cyclical View of History, and Their Influence on His Work. Vanderbilt University, 1963.

Carter, Ernest John.   Byron's Historical Imagination: The Poetry of Byron Seen in Relation to Pessimistic Attitudes in Eighteenth-Century History.   Claremont University, 1966.

Caruthers, Clifford M.   A Critical Study of the Plays of Lord Byron.   University of Missouri, 1968.

Chatterton, Roylance W.   Lord Byron's Dramas: An Attempt to Reform the English Stage.   Utah University, 1963.

Christensen, Allan C.   Heroism in the Age of Reform: Byron, Goethe, and the Novels of Carlyle.   Princeton University, 1968.

Coleman, Ronald Gregg.   Cosmic Symbolism in Byron's Dramas. Vanderbilt University, 1965.

Cooke, Michael George.   Byron and the Restoration.   University of California, 1962.

Cunningham, John M., Jr.   Byron's Poetics in "Don Juan."   Duke University, 1969.

Duke, David Carroll.   American Byronism: A Study in Twentieth Century Romanticism, Idealism and Disillusionment.   University of Tennessee, 1970.

Dunn, John Joseph.   The Role of MacPherson's "Ossian" in the Development of British Romanticism.   Duke University, 1966.

Ehrstine, John W.   An Analysis of Byron's Plays.   Wayne State University, 1964.

Elledge, W. Paul.   The Enkindled Clay: Imagery and Theme in Byron's Poetry.   Tulane University, 1965.

Griffiths, Victor Segismundo.   Byron's Influence in Spanish America, 1830-1852.   University of Nebraska, 1970.

Harson, Robert R.   A Profile of John Polidori, with a New Edition of "The Vampyre."   University of Ohio, 1966.

Hoffpauir, R.   The Theory and Practice of Epic (Especially Narrative and Character) with Special References to Southey, Landor, Wordsworth, Shelley, Keats and Byron.   London University, 1969.

Holcomb, Adele M.   J. M. W. Turner's Illustrations to the Poets. University of California, L.A., 1967.

Howard, John D. , Jr. The Child-Hero in the Poetry of Blake, Shelley, Byron, Coleridge, and Wordsworth. University of Maryland, 1967.

Kahn, Arthur D. The Horatian and Juvenilian Traditions of Verse Satire in Byron's "Don Juan." New York University, 1963.

Kelly, Larry Dennis. Byron Biography: 1822-1830. University of Pennsylvania, 1969.

Kirchner, Sister Mary Evangelista, R. S. M. The Function of the Persona in the Poetry of Byron. Notre Dame University, 1965.

Lehn, Gertrude L. The Development of Byron as a Dramatist. Harvard University, 1966.

Lim, Pauline Marquez, Jr. The Style of Byron's Plays. University of California, L.A., 1967.

McGann, Jerome J. "Childe Harold's Pilgrimage" and the Poetics of Self-Expression. Yale University, 1966.

Manning, Peter J. Byron and the Stage. Yale University, 1969.

Manno, Fort Philip. The Anti-hero and the Anti-hero Mode: A Study in the Genesis and Development of the Victorian Poetical Protagonist. University of Minnesota, 1968.

Mariels, Raymond P. The Grotesque in Byron's Poetry. University of Oregon, 1967.

Mellow, John Paul. Byron's "Manfred": A Study of Sources and Ideas. Pittsburgh, 1964.

Mellown, M. J. The Development of Lord Byron's Literary Criticism and of the Literary Attitudes Revealed in His Poetry and Prose. University of London, 1965.

Merewether, John Armstrong. "The Burning Chain:" The Paradoxical Nature of Love and Women in Byron's Poetry. Wayne State University, 1969.

Michaels, Leonard. "Hail, Muse! EtCetera--An Essay on Narrative Pattern, Costume, and the Idea of the Self in Byron's "Cain" and his Tales. University of Michigan, 1968.

Miller, Arthur McA. The Last Man: A Study of the Eschatological Theme in English Poetry and Fiction from 1806 through 1839. Duke University, 1966.

Morgan, Lucretia B. Byron's Influence on Villiers de L'Isle-Adam. University of Georgia, 1965.

Morokoff, G. E. A Critical Study of Byron's "Manfred." University of Illinois, 1963.

Mortenson, Robert Laurence. Lord Byron's "Cain," A Variorum Edition. University of Pennsylvania, 1964.

Mosier, John F. Byron's "Don Juan": History as Epic. Tulane University, 1969.

Neville, W. A. The Quintessence of Byronism: A Study of "Manfred." Lehigh University, 1961.

Osterberg, Oliver Sinclaire. Protero: Form and Idea in the Metaphysical Dramas of George Gordon, Honourable Lord Byron. University of Minnesota, 1970.

Otten, Terry Ralph. The Empty Stage: A Comment on the Search for Dramatic Form in the Early Nineteenth Century. University of Ohio, 1966.

Paananen, Victor N. Byron and Browning: The Aesthetics of Skepticism. University of Wisconsin, 1967.

Pratt, John M. Byron and the Stream of Wit! Studies in the Development, Survival and Culmination of the Colloquial Mode in English Poetry. University of Pennsylvania, 1969.

Quertermous, Harry M. The Byronic Hero in the Writings of the Brontës. University of Texas, 1960.

Raizis, Marios Byron. The Prometheus Theme in British and American Poetry. New York University, 1966.

Robinson, Charles E. The Frustrated Dialectic of Byron and Shelley: Their Reciprocal Influences. Temple University, 1968.

Robinson, Forest Elmo. The Peninsular War in the Political Evolution of Five English Romantic Poets. University of Colorado, 1966.

Ross, William. Digressive Narrator and Narrative Technique in Byron's "Don Juan." University of Virginia, 1970.

Rothenberg, Jacob. 'Descensus ad Terram': The Acquisition and Reception of the Elgin Marbles. Columbia University, 1967.

*Santucho, Oscar José. A Comprehensive Bibliography of Secondary Materials in English: George Gordon, Lord Byron. Baylor University, 1968.

Sheraw, C. Darrell. Byron and the Course of Romantic Satire. Ohio University, 1970.

548   Appendices

Shirakawa, S. H. M. Lord Byron's Metrical Romances: A Study
    in Poetic Development. University of London, 1968.

Stevens, Harold Ray. Byron and the Bible: A Study of Poetic and
    Philosophic Development. University of Pennsylvania, 1964.

Thompson, James Roy. Studies in the Drama of Lord Byron.
    University of Cincinnati, 1964.

Walker, Keith McKay. Byron's Readers: A Study of Attitudes
    Towards Byron 1812-1832. Cambridge University, 1967.

Wallis, Bruce E. Lord Byron's Critical Opinions. Princeton
    University, 1969.

Whitmore, Allen P. The Major Characters of Lord Byron's
    Dramas. University of Colorado, 1967.

Wilson, Joy Lee Clark. An Edition of Thomas Moore's "Common-
    place Book." Rice University, 1967.

                            1970-1974

Asfour, Mohammad Hassan. The Crescent and the Cross: Islam
    and the Muslims in English Literature from Johnson to Byron.
    Indiana University, 1973.

Bokern, Julia B. Byron's Ladies: A Study of "Don Juan." Co-
    lumbia University, 1973.

Cameron, Alan Harwood. Byronism in Lermontov's "A Hero of
    Our Time." British Columbia, 1974.

Carroll, David Barry. Romantic Literary Theory and the Sublime.
    Rice University, 1971.

Chaing, Oscar Ching-Kuan. Idealism in Plays Written by Early
    Nineteenth Century Poets. St. John's University, 1972.

Clancy, Charles John. Byron's "Don Juan": A Comic Epic. New
    York University, 1973.

Corr, Thomas Joseph. Views of the Mind (of Reason and Imagi-
    nation) as Structural and Thematic Principles in the Works of
    Byron. Duquesne University, 1974.

D'Ambruoso, Raphael R. Byron's Development in the Use of Sa-
    tiric Verse Portraits. New York University, 1973.

Goldstein, Stephen L. Byron in Radical Tradition: A Study on the
    Intellectual Background and Controversiality of "Cain." Co-
    lumbia University, 1973.

Greene, D. Randolf.   The Romantic Prometheus: Varieties of the
    Heroic Quest.   University of Wisconsin, 1974.

Hijiva, Yukihito.   Byron and the New Promethean Man.   New Mexi-
    co, 1972.

Howard, Ida Beth Heathly.   The Byronic Hero and the Renaissance
    Hero-Villain: Analogues and Prototypes.   North Texas State
    University, 1973.

Hull, Gloria Thompson.   Women in Byron's Poetry: A Biographi-
    cal and Critical Study.   Purdue University, 1972.

Katkin, Wendy F.   The Narrator of "Don Juan": Byron's Last
    Hero.   State University of New York at Buffalo, 1973.

King, Martha Jeanne.   The Influence of Byron on Italian Culture.
    University of Wisconsin, 1973.

Klapper, Molly.   The German Literary Influence on Shelley and
    Byron with Special Reference to Goethe.   New York Univer-
    sity, 1974.

Lanier, Rene Parks, Jr.   Aspects of Sublimity in the Poetry of
    Lord Byron.   University of Tennessee, 1972.

Lombardi, Thomas W.   Byron's "Hebrew Melodies."   Columbia
    University, 1973.

McCreadie, Marsha Anne.   T. S. Eliot and the Romantic Poets:
    A Study of the Similar Poetic Themes and Methods Used by
    Eliot and Wordsworth, Coleridge, Keats, Byron and Shelley.
    University of Illinois at Urbana-Champaign, 1973.

McKoski, Martin Michael.   Byron's "Childe Harold's Pilgrimage":
    The Image of the Quest.   Florida State University, 1972.

Pemberton, Richard R.   The Romantic Irony of Lord Byron.
    University of California, 1974.

Price, Elizabeth.   Don Juan: A Chronicle of His Literary Adven-
    tures in Germanic Territory.   Washington University, 1974.

Reichley, Charles Ann.   Lampoon: Archilochus to Byron.   Vander-
    bilt University, 1971.

Rich, Douglas Denham.   Heroic Vision: A Study of Byron's Verse
    Tales.   Washington State, 1974.

Robertson, James M.   Byron's "Don Juan" and the Aristocratic
    Tradition.   Duke University, 1973.

Schroeder, Ronald Allan. Byron and the New Romance: "Childe
      Harold's Pilgrimage, I and II. Northwestern University,
      1973.

Simpson, Richard Hunt. Sympathy as Value in Byron's Poetry.
      Kent State University, 1973.

Smiehorowski, Astrid Scheper. Byron's "Don Juan": A Poet's
      Pessimistic Vision of Nature. Brown University, 1971.

Stephenson, William Alva, Jr. Henry Fielding's Influence on Lord
      Byron. Texas University, 1973.

Sullivan, Mary A. Worlds of Their Own: Space-Consciousness in
      the Works of Wordsworth, Byron, Shelley and Keats. Ohio
      State University, 1973.

Twitchell, James Buell. The Romantic Psychodrama: An Inter-
      pretation of the Rime of the Ancient Mariner, Manfred, and
      Prometheus Unbound, Act IV. University of North Carolina,
      1971.

Tyler, Anthony O. Byron's Use of Ancient History and Historians
      in "Childe Harold's Pilgrimage," "Don Juan" and "The Age of
      Bronze." Indiana University, 1973.

Wesche, Ulrich Claude. Byron and Grabbe: A Comparative Study
      of Their Works and Their Relations to European Romanticism.
      University of North Carolina, 1973.

Yax, Lawrence Donald. Ocean and Water Imagery in Byron's Poe-
      try. Case Western Reserve, 1971.

Appendix B

NOTES ON SALES, LIBRARY ACQUISITIONS AND HOLDINGS[1]

Bates, William. "Religious Opinions of Lord Byron," N&Q, 1st
ser., XII (Sept. 1, 1855), 164. [Quotes a passage of a
letter sold at £4 12s 6d by Messrs. Puttick and Simpson.]

James, Ralph N. "Byron's Letters," N&Q, 6th ser., XI (Feb. 21,
1885), 145. [Announces sale of some Byron letters to Hodgson by Messrs. Sothebys on March 2.]

"Byron and Shelley at Ravenna," Atheneum, May 26, 1894, p. 679.
[Two letters of Byron not printed by Moore, both to Count
Alborghetti, dated June 28 and August 15, 1821. For sale
at Sotheby's.]

La Rose, Pierre. "An Unpublished Poem by Byron," Atlantic
Monthly, LXXXII (Dec., 1898), 810-14. [The Poems of
Ossian, London, 1806, in 2 vols., acquired by the Harvard
Library. Extensively annotated by Byron, it also contains
his "Address to the Sun."]

Joline, Adrian H. Meditations of an Autograph Collector. New
York: Harper & Bros., 1902. [A letter from Lady Byron is
in the author's possession.]

"Shelley and Byron Autographs," Atheneum, May 25, 1912, p. 590.
[A letter from Byron to Moore, dated Dec., 1821, for sale
at Sotheby's.]

"Unpublished Letter to Hodgson," The Annual of the British School
at Athens, XXII (1916-1918), 107-109. [A letter dated Athens,
Jan. 20, 1811, at the Finlay Library at the School Hostel in
Athens.]

Healey, George Harris (comp.). The Cornell Wordsworth Collec-
tion. A Catalogue of Books and Manuscripts Presented to the
University by Mr. Victor Emmanuel, Cornell, 1919. Ithaca,
New York: Cornell University Press, 1957. [It contains a
letter to R. C. Dallas, dated Sept. 10, 1811, and another to
J. C. Hobhouse, possibly dated 1818, a MS of an unfinished

---

[1]The arrangement of this appendix is chronological.

story and two editions of English Bards and Scotch Reviewers.]

'Byron in Texas," TLS, Aug. 28, 1924, p. 528. [On the 1924
exhibition at the University of Texas.]

'Byron at the First Edition Club," TLS, Jan. 29, 1925, p. 76.

'Notes on Sales," TLS, Aug. 4, 1927, p. 536. [At Sotheby's, a
letter from Byron to Charles Gordon describing the Eton and
Harrow match, dated Aug. 4, 1805, was sold at £350 to
Messrs. Maggs, who bought it for a few old Harrovians that
will present it to the Harrow Library. Also an album containing more than 49 letters, including some from Byron,
went for £205.]

Scott, Temple, "Two Leaves from a Poet's Heart," American Collector, IV (May, 1927), 50-52. [Holograph MS of Childe
Harold's Pilgrimage, Canto III, stanzas i, ii, iii, cxv, cxvi,
and cxvii, in the library of Jerome Kern of Cedar Knolls,
Westchester.]

N&Q, CLIII (Aug. 6, 1927), 92. [Announcing that the letter bought
at Sotheby's for £350, from Byron to C. Gordon, will be presented to Harrow.]

N&Q, CLIV (Feb. 18, 1928), 110. [A rough draft of Byron's will
of 1811, bought by Maggs from Sotheby's for £160.]

'Byron and Coleridge," TLS, June 27, 1929, p. 520. [At Messrs.
Hodgsons' sale, 17 unpublished letters from Lord Byron to
Edward Dawkins, chargé d'affairs at Florence, were sold for
£122.]

'Literary Documents and Books," TLS, Jan. 9, 1930, p. 32. [At
Sotheby's were sold the autograph MS of Childe Harold, II,
st. xciii-xciv, for £240, and five early letters from Byron to
E. Noel Long.]

Lovelace, Edith. "A Missing Byron MS," TLS, Jan. 23, 1930,
p. 60. [Wants to know the whereabouts of a Beppo MS which
belonged to the Lovelaces.]

'Byron and Byroniana," TLS, Jan. 30, 1930, p. 84. [Announcing
the Mathews' Catalogue of Byroniana.] Ibid., Feb. 20, 1930,
p. 148. [Announcing a similar catalogue by Messrs. B. H.
Blackwell of Oxford.]

'Notes on Sales," TLS, Nov. 20, 1930, p. 996. [The MS of Don
Juan, Cantos X, XI, XII was sold for $6000, and Cantos II
and IV for $2750. Also gives the whereabouts of other MSS.]

"Byron and Murray," TLS, July 23, 1931, p. 588. [Describes an exhibition held in the old Court House of Marylebone by Messrs. J. and E. Bumpus with several Byron MSS.]

"Notes on Sales. Byron's 'Ode to Napoleon,'" TLS, Nov. 19, 1931, p. 920. [The last three stanzas of it fetched £150 at Sotheby's. The MS of the first 16 stanzas had been sold there for £329 in 1910.]

McCarthy, William H., Jr. "Byron and the Cause of Greek Independence: Reflections upon an Unpublished Letter of Byron, Recently Acquired through the Library Associates," Yale University Library Gazette, VIII (Jan., 1934), 100-104. [A hitherto unpublished letter to the Chairman of the Greek Committee, dated Genoa, May 21, 1823.]

Parsons, Coleman Oscar. "Three Byron Letters," N&Q, CLXVI (May 26, 1934), 366-67. [Dated Spring, 1812, to Moore; Nov. 22, 1813, to James Wedderburn Webster; July, 1820? to Hoppner. They found their way into the Watson Autograph Collection in the National Library of Scotland.]

S., E. "A Byron Letter," More Books, XIII (Nov., 1938), 430. [Autograph letter by Byron written from Athens on July 19, 1810, addressed to the bookseller William Miller, now in the Boston Public Library.]

Booth, Bradford A. "Moore to Hobhouse, an Unpublished Letter," MLN, LV (Jan., 1940), 42-45. [Letter from Newstead Abbey dated Jan. 29, 1828, in the William Andrews Clark Memorial Library (an adjunct of the University of California at L.A.]

Steffan, Truman Guy. "Autograph Letters and Documents of the Byron Circle at the Library of the University of Texas," UTSE, 1945-1946, pp. 177-99. [Catalogues 121 letters.]

_____. "Byron Autograph Letters in the Library of the University of Texas," SP, XLIII (Oct., 1946), 682-99. [Catalogues 71 letters and 3 documents.]

Kimmelman, Elaine. "First Editions of Byron," Boston Public Library Quarterly, I (Oct., 1949), 169-72. [Some valuable items acquired by the Library: Poems on Various Occasions; letter from Byron to Faulkner, dated Jan. 5, 1807; Lara; and Don Juan, I and II.]

Pratt, Willis W. "Twenty Letters of the Countess Guiccioli, Chiefly Relative to Lord Byron," UTSE, XXX (1951), 132-57.

Simkins, Thomas M., Jr. "The Byron Collection in the Rare Book Room of Duke University Library," Library Notes, Jan., 1951, pp. 14-22.

"The Berg Memorial Exhibition," TLS, Feb. 16, 1951, p. 108.
[It included MSS of Byron's Curse of Minerva and of Don
Juan, Cantos XIV and XV.]

Boyce, George K. "Modern Literary Manuscripts in the Morgan
Library," PMLA, LXVII (Feb., 1952), 3-36. [Beppo, The
Corsair, Don Juan, Cantos I-V, Manfred, Marino Faliero,
Mazeppa, "Morgante Maggiore," The Prophecy of Dante,
Werner, several shorter poems, 65 Byron letters, 75 written
by members of the Byron family, 28 concerning the Medora
Leigh controversy, and 80 letters written by or to members
of the Byron family or concerning Newstead Abbey.]

"Manuscripts Acquired during the Years 1941-1950," British Museum Quarterly, XV (1941-1950, published 1952), 18-32.
[Acquisitions include papers of Zambelli, Byron's stewart,
and Hobhouse's diaries and correspondence with Foscolo and
Peacock.]

Eaton, Vincent L. "The American Academy of Arts and Letters
Collection," Library of Congress Quarterly Journal of Current Acquisitions, X (Aug., 1953), 190-93. [A few Byron
items.]

"Notes on Sales," Book Collector, III (Autumn, 1954), 220-25. [At
Sotheby's, a holograph MS of two stanzas of Don Juan was
sold for 90, and at Christie's the holograph MS of The Girl
of Cadiz for £120.]

"New Acquisitions," Library Chronicle of the University of Texas,
V (Winter, 1954), 34. [A Byron letter, dated from Southwell, Oct. 20, 1806.]

"Recent Acquisitions," Yale University Library Gazette, XXIX (Jan.,
1955), 132. [Lists some rare volumes given by Chauncey B.
Tinker, among them, Lord Byron's Farewell to England,
Poems (New York, 1817), Miscellaneous Poems on His Domestic and Other Circumstances. London, 1825.]

Turner, Justin G. "Random Notes Written from the West Coast,"
Manuscripts, VII (Spring, 1955), 198-99. [A holograph MS
of two stanzas of Byron's Don Juan fetched $252 at the Lady
Wavertree sale.]

Gordan, John D. (comp.). "What's in a Name? Authors and
Their Pseudonyms: Notes on an Exhibition from the Berg
Collection," Bulletin of the New York Public Library, LX
(March, 1956), 107-28. [Says that Byron may have selected
the pseudonym Hornem as a warning to the husbands of waltz-
ing wives.]

Pratt, Willis W. "Lord Byron and His Circle: Recent Manuscript
Acquisitions," Library Chronicle of the University of Texas,
V (Spring, 1956), 16-25.

Voronova, T. P. "Western MSS in the Saltykov-Shchedrin Library, Leningrad," Book Collector, V (Spring, 1956), 12-18.

Bliss, Carey S. "Acquisitions, May 16-August 15, 1956," Huntington Library Quarterly, XX (Nov., 1956), 98-101. [Three letters from Byron.]

"Notes on Sales," TLS, Nov. 30, 1956, p. 720. [At Sotheby's, a first edition of The Waltz was sold for £520.]

Green, David Bonnell. "Three New Byron Letters," K-SJ, V (Winter, 1956), 97-101. [1) To R. C. Dallas, dated at Cambridge, Nov. 26, 1811; 2) To Major William Clarke, dated at Sommerville, Venice, May 12, 1819; 3) To R. B. Hoppner, dated at Ravenna, Feb. 10, 1821, the three now at Haverford College Library.]

Hoffman, Alois. "Manuscrits de Jean-Jacques Rousseau et de G. G. Byron à Prague," Philologica, IX (1957), 20-29. [Article in French. The MSS of the prologue of The Prophecy of Dante and a sonnet to Countess Guiccioli, are in the National Museum of Prague.]

Jackson, William A. Houghton Library Report of Accessions, 1952-1953. Pp. 35, 37.

"Notes on Sales," TLS, May 24, 1957, p. 328. [At Sotheby's, a copy of the third edition of Medwin's Conversations with Lord Byron profusely annotated by himself, fetched £280.]

"Notes on Sales," TLS, Sept. 6, 1957, p. 540. [At Sotheby's, the 'automanuscript' of Byron's "Darkness" brought £320.]

"Notes on Sales," Book Collector, VI (Autumn, 1957), 287-89. [A copy of Medwin's Conversations with Lord Byron, profusely annotated by the author was sold for £280.]

Marshall, William H. "A News Letter from Byron to John Hunt," N&Q, CCIII (March, 1958), 122-24. [Letter dated May 21, 1823, at Pierpont Morgan Library.]

"Notes on Sales," TLS, July 18, 1958, p. 416. [At Sotheby's, the first issue of the first edition of Marino Faliero, inscribed by Byron to Medwin, fetched £140.]

"Recent Acquisitions," Yale University Library Gazette, XXXII (April, 1958), 160-61. [A copy of E. C. Mayne's Byron with manuscript corrections for a new edition made by the author.]

Hobson, A. R. A. "Unfamiliar Libraries. V: Waddeston Manor," Book Collector, VIII (Summer, 1959), 131-39. [This collection has Augusta Leigh's copy of the first edition of the first two cantos of Childe Harold's Pilgrimage.]

Jackson, William A. "The Howe Foundation, a Generation Later,"
    Harvard Library Bulletin, XIII (Aug. , 1959), 475-77. [By-
    ron's copy of Madame de Staël's De l'Allemagne was bought
    with money supplied by this fund.]

"Notes on Sales," TLS, Aug. 21, 1959, p. 488. [At Sotheby's
    was sold for £90, a commonplace book kept by Augusta
    Leigh.]

"Notes on Sales," TLS, Nov. 20, 1959, p. 684. [At Sotheby's a
    letter from Byron to R. C. Dallas, dated Sept. 26, 1811,
    fetched £250.]

Schmitt, Albert R. "The Programmschriften Collection," Library
    Chronicle of the University of Pennsylvania, XXV (Winter,
    1959), 29-42. [Contains several items on Byron.]

Taylor, Robert H. Letters of English Authors from the Collection
    of Robert H. Taylor; A Catalogue of an Exhibition in the
    Princeton University Library, May 13 to Sept. 30, 1960.
    Princeton: Princeton University Press, 1960.

"Notes on Sales," TLS, April 15, 1960, p. 248. [At Sotheby's
    the first edition of Byron's Waltz fetched £420.]

"Letters of English Authors from the Collection of Robert H. Tay-
    lor," Princeton University Library Chronicle, XXI (Summer,
    1960), 200-36.

Jackson, William A. "Contemporary Collectors XXIV: Philip
    Hofer," Book Collector, IX (Summer, 1960), 151-64; ibid. ,
    IX (Autumn, 1960), 292-300. [Two pages of an edition of
    The Corsair illuminated by G. B. Gigola are reproduced on
    p. 297.]

Taylor, Robert H. "Fine Bold Signature," Manuscripts, XII (Sum-
    mer, 1960), 4-13. [Mentions his copies of works of Byron.]

"Notes on Sales," TLS, Aug. 5, 1960, p. 504. [At Sotheby's, a
    copy of the first edition of Poems on Various Occasions, in-
    cluding a letter of Byron's mother, dated Feb. 10, 1807, was
    sold for £280.]

"Auction Sales," American Book Collector, XI (Oct. , 1960), 17-19.
    [At Swann Galleries, four Byron items were sold as part of
    "A Gentleman's Library of Rare Books."]

Hamilton, Charles. Collecting Autographs and Manuscripts. Nor-
    man: University of Oklahoma, 1961. [Reproduces autographs
    of Byron.]

Schmitt, Albert R. (comp.) Catalogue of the Programmschriften
    Collection at the University of Pennsylvania Library. Boston:
    G. K. Hall, 1961.

"Auction Sales," American Book Collector, XI (Feb., 1961), 27-29.
[At Park-Bernet Galleries was sold a letter from Byron to
Hobhouse dated May 5, 1818, announcing the arrival of Alle-
gra, for $310.]

"Commentary," Book Collector, X (Spring, 1961), 5-17. [British
Museum has acquired 30 Byron letters and the autograph MS
of "The Devil's Drive," which had belonged to the 3rd Lord
Holland.]

"The Arents Tobacco Collection," Bulletin of the New York Public
Library, LXV (Dec., 1961), 661-70. [Proof of the popularity
of the cigar in England early in the 19th century is provided
by an excerpt from The Island.]

Kendall, L. H. "Byron: An Unpublished Letter to Shelley," MLN,
LXXVI (Dec., 1961), 708-709. [Second page of a two page
A. L. S. from Byron to Shelley, conjecturally dated July 30th,
1821, in the William Luther Lewis Collection of Rare Books
and Manuscripts at T. C. U.]

"Commentary," Book Collector, XI (Spring, 1962), 7-20. [The
"Collection Jean Davray" sold at Palais Galliera in Paris, included autograph letters and documents of Byron.]

Brown, T. J. "English Literary Autographs. XLII: Lord Byron,
1788-1824," Book Collector, XI (Summer, 1962), 205. [Most
autographs of Don Juan are in American collections. However, John Murray has fair copies of Cantos I, II, V; also
of VI, VII, VIII, written by Mary Shelley. The British Museum has a draft of VI-VII [Ashley MS 5163]; the University
of London has drafts of X-XII and XVII and fair copy of III-
IV; British Museum also has a good range of letters in the
following MSS. Egerton 2611 [1806-16]; Ashley [1813-24];
Add. 31037, ff. 15, 35, 40 [1814-24]; Add. 42093 [1816-18].

"Recent Acquisitions," Yale University Library Gazette, XXXVII
(July, 1962), 39-40; ibid., XXXVIII (Jan., 1963), 110-21.
[The autograph MS of Byron's poem beginning, "Some bards
the Theban feuds recall," a letter from Augusta to Mrs.
Knight dated July 22, n. y., and other Byron items.]

Partridge, A. C. "Hours in a Florentine Library," English Studies
in Africa, V (Sept., 1962), 156-65. [In the Biblioteca Nazionale Centrale there is a Byron letter dated March 26, 1815,
with no addressee, which apparently has not yet been published.]

"Recent Acquisitions," Library Notes: A Bulletin Issued for the
Friends of the Duke University Library, No. 36 (Dec., 1962),
20-26. [The first edition of Marino Faliero acquired by Library.]

"Auction Sales," American Book Collector, XIII (Jan., 1963), 22.
[At Parke-Bernet Galleries were sold first editions of Don
Juan for $200 and a 40 page Byron MS, "The Episode of
Nisus and Euryalus," for $3,750.]

Davis, H. M. P. "The King's School, Canterbury," Etudes
Anglaises, XVI (Jan.-March, 1963), 59-62. [Its Hugh Walpole Collection has a small pocket book of Byron and twelve
lines of a translation of Dante.]

Banks, Gordon T. "The Auction Market," Manuscripts, XV (Spring,
1963), 46-59. [A letter from Carlyle analyzing Don Juan
fetched $130, at Parke-Bernet Galleries.]

Poston, M. L. "Contemporary Collectors. XXXIV: Bibliotheca
Medici," Book Collector, XII (Spring, 1963), 44-54. [Men-
tions his collection of Byron items.]

"Notes on Sales in England and America," TLS, May 31, 1963, p.
396. [At Parke-Bernet Galleries was sold a letter from
Horace Smith to J. Reading of Colburn & Co., which refers
to Byron. It fetched $375.]

Goff, Frederick R. "Rare Books," Library of Congress Quarterly
Journal of Current Acquisitions, XX (June, 1963), 193-99.
[Eight first editions recently acquired.]

Enkvist, Nils Erik. "British and American Literary Letters in
Scandinavian Public Collections. A Survey," Acta Academiae
Aboensis, Humaniora, XXVII, No. 3, 1964. [Prints letters
of Byron.]

Ray, Gordon N. "Contemporary Collectors. XXXVII: A 19th Century Collection," Book Collector, XIII (Spring, 1964), 33-44;
ibid., XIII (Summer, 1964), 171-84. [Contains Byron items.]

"Commentary," Book Collector, XIII (Summer, 1964), 143-60.
[Reviews reprint of T. J. Wise's Bibliography of Byron.]

Walton, Francis R. "Portrait of a Bibliophile XII: Joannes Gennadius, 1884-1932," Book Collector, XIII (Autumn, 1964),
305-26. [Has a good collection of Byroniana.]

Nowell-Smith, Simon. "Contemporary Collectors. XLI: The
Ewelme Collection," Book Collector, XIV (Summer, 1965),
185-93. [In the collection are continuations of Don Juan and
nine early poems of Byron.]

"News and Notes," Papers of the Bibliographical Society of America, LIX (4th Quarter, 1965), 442-44. [About the exhibitions
from Syracuse University and at the New York Public Library, both including Byron items.]

Gordan, John D. "An Anniversary Exhibition: The Henry W. and
    Albert A. Berg Collection, 1940-1965," Bulletin of the New
    York Public Library, LXIX (Oct., 1965), 537-54. [It in-
    cludes a holograph of Cantos XIV-XV of Don Juan.]

"Auction Sales," American Book Collector, XVI (March, 1966), 29-
    31. [At Parke-Bernet, a first edition of English Bards and
    Scotch Reviewers went for $85.]

"Auction Sales," American Book Collector, XVI (May, 1966), 31.
    [At Sotheby's, a first edition of Byron's Waltz went for
    $3,920.]

"News and Comment," Book Collector, XV (Winter, 1966), 461-83.
    [A copy of Byron's Sardanapalus with Beckford's notes was
    sold at Sotheby's for £380.]

Brumbaugh, Thomas B. "A Landor Collector," Library Chronicle
    of the University of Texas, VIII (Spring, 1966), 23-27. [Con-
    tains letters to Lady Blessington and an epigram on Byron's
    marriage.]

"William Beckford in the Salesroom," TLS, Oct. 20, 1966, p. 968.
    [Beckford's annotated copy of Sardanapalus was sold for £380.]

Doherty, Francis. "An Unpublished Letter of Lady Caroline Lamb
    to Clare," N&Q, CCXII (Aug., 1967), 297-99. [In the Ar-
    chives of the University of Keele.]

Steffan, T. G. "A Byron Facsimile: A Postscript," Library Chron-
    icle of the University of Texas, VIII (Spring, 1967), 19-21.

Marshall, William H. "The Byron Collection in Memory of Meyer
    Davis, Jr.," Library Chronicle of the University of Pennsyl-
    vania, XXXIII (Winter, 1967), 8-29. [Describes collection.]

Steffan, T. G. "Some 1813 Byron Letters," K-SJ, XVI (Winter,
    1967), 9-21. [Prints letters in the Miriam Lutcher Stark
    Library of the University of Texas.]

"Auction Sales," American Book Collector, XVIII (Nov., 1967), 30.
    [Volume I of La Divina Commedia containing a 17-line in-
    scription by Byron, was sold for $625 at Parke-Bernet.]

Marshall, William H. "The Catalogue for the Sale of Byron's
    Books," Library Chronicle of the University of Pennsylvania,
    XXXIV (Winter, 1968), 24-50.

Liebert, Herman W. "The Beinecke Library, Recent Acquisition,"
    Yale University Library Gazette, XLII (April, 1968), 171-210.
    [A copy of Lady Noel Byron and the Leighs, privately printed
    by Lord Lovelace in 1887, a very rare item, was acquired
    by the Yale Beinecke Library.]

Schulz, H. C. "English Literary Manuscripts in the Huntington
   Library," Huntington Library Quarterly, XXXI (May, 1968),
   251-302. [Lists MSS. by Byron and the Countess of Blessington, et alles.]

Marshall, William H. "The Davis Collection of Byroniana," K-SJ,
   XVIII (1969), 9-11.

"Recent Acquisitions--Manuscripts," The Princeton University Library Chronicle, XXX (Autumn, 1968), 60, 63. [A letter of
   Teresa Guiccioli to Henry Wikoff.]

Lohf, Kenneth A. "Our Growing Collections," Columbia Library
   Columns, XVIII (Feb., 1969), 29-44. [Addition to its Thomas
   J. Wise Collection of letters and manuscripts relating to
   Wise's Byron Bibliography.]

Szladits, Lola L. "New in the Berg Collection: 1962-1964,"
   Bulletin of the New York Public Library, LXXIII (April, 1969),
   227-52. [Byron's MS of "Episode of Nisus and Euryalus."]

Lutz, Paul V. "Meet the Collector: Irving Wallace," Manuscripts,
   XXII (Spring, 1970), 118-24. [Wallace owns letters and manuscripts of Byron.]

Marchand, Leslie A. "An Unpublished Byron Poem," Griffon
   (Gennadius Library, Athens), No. 6 (Summer, 1970), 17-19.

Bank, George T. "The Auction Market," Manuscripts, XXII (Winter, 1970), 62-63. [An already published Byron letter of
   1823 fetched $912 at Sotheby's.]

"News and Comment," Book Collector, XIX (Winter, 1970), 506.
   [Sale of 2 brief Byron letters for £380.]

Steffan, T. G. "From Cambridge to Missolonghi: Byron Letters
   at the University of Texas," Texas Quarterly, XIV (Autumn,
   1971), 6-66.

"News and Comment," Book Collector, XXI (Spring, 1972), 117-18.
   [Sotheby's sold to Quaritch Byron's five page letter to his tutor.]

"Houghton Library Acquisitions," Harvard Library Bulletin, XX
   (Oct., 1972), 448-49. [One of only two known copies extant
   of The Irish Avatar acquired by the library.]

"List of Acquisitions, Dept. of Manuscripts, July 1970 to Dec.
   1972," British Museum Quarterly, XXXVII (Summer, 1973),
   73-77.

Appendix C

PLACES ASSOCIATED WITH BYRON[1]

Adcock, Arthur St. John. Famous Houses and Literary Shrines of London. London: J. M. Dent & Sons; New York: E. P. Dutton, 1912.

Allen, Richard. The Home and Grave of Byron; a Souvenir of Newstead Abbey, Nottinghamshire. Nottingham: Richard Allen & Son; New York: Scribner, Welford & Co., 1874.

Anderson, Robert. Aberdeen in Bygone Days. Aberdeen, 1910.

Andrew, W. "A Pilgrimage to Byron," Mirror, XXIX (Feb. 25, 1837), 113-16.

Ashpitel, Arthur. The Home and Grave of Byron; an Historical and Descriptive Account of Newstead Abbey, Annesley Hall, and Hucknall-Torkard. Also Remarks on the Architecture of Newstead Abbey. London: Longman & Co., 1837. Rptd. several times.

Bailey, Thomas. Handbook to Newstead Abbey. London: Simpkin, Marshall & Co., 1855.

Barber, Thomas Gerrard. Byron and Where He Is Buried. Hucknall: Morley, 1939.

_____. Hucknall Torkard Church. Its History and Byron Associations. Hucknall, Nottinghamshire: Henry Morley, 1925.

"Byron and Newstead Abbey," Atheneum, August 30, 1884, pp. 275-76; ibid., September 6, 1884, pp. 305-306. [On the financial difficulties concerning Newstead Abbey.]

"Byron's Grave," Saturday Review, LXIV (July 30, 1887), 150.

Chancellor, Edwin Beresford. The Literary Ghosts of London. Homes and Footprints of Famous Men and Women. London: Richards, 1933.

----
[1] Since there seemed to be no special advantage in arranging this appendix chronologically, the alphabetical order has been adopted.

"Clayton Hall: A Relic of the Chetham Family," Papers of the
    Manchester Literary Club, IV (1878), 213-15. [On the Byron
    family and Clayton Hall.]

Cunningham, Peter. Handbook of London. Past and Present. A
    New Edition Corrected and Enlarged. London: John Murray,
    1850.

Dauglish, M. G. The Harrow School Register, 1801-1900. Lon-
    don: Longmans, Green & Co., 1901.

Didier, E. L. "In the Footsteps of Byron," Munsey's Magazine,
    XIV (January, 1896), 422-31. [Scenes of Byron's wanderings
    through Europe and their influence upon his life and work.]

Drew, Fraser Bragg. "Search for Byron." Vermont Historical
    Society News and Notes, XVII (Feb., 1966), 42-44. [Describes
    visits to places associated with Byron's name.]

Fraser, Augusta Z. Livingstone and Newstead. London: John
    Murray, 1913.

Freeman, John. Literature and Locality: The Literary Topography
    of Britain and Ireland. London: Cassell, 1963. [Places
    associated with Byron.]

Galt, John. "Newstead Abbey," Monthly Magazine, 2nd ser., XVII
    (Jan., 1834), 3-4.

Gibson, William Sidney. "Byron at Newstead Abbey," Chamber's
    Edinburgh Journal, 3rd ser., XVIII (September 27, 1862),
    220-23. Rptd. in his Miscellanies, Historical and Biographi-
    cal; Being a Second Series of Essays, Lectures, and Reviews.
    London: Longman, Green, 1863. Pp. 39-49.

Gribble, Francis H. Lake Geneva and Its Literary Landmarks.
    Westminster: A. Constable & Co., 1901.

H. "A Byronian Ramble," Atheneum, August 23, 1834, pp. 627-
    28. [Annesley Hall and Hucknall Torkard.] Ibid., August 30,
    1834, pp. 640-43. [Annesley Hall.] Ibid., September 6,
    1834, pp. 657-59. [Newstead Abbey.]

Hammerton, John Alexander. Memories of Books and Places.
    London: S. Low, Marston & Co., 1928.
    It contains:
    "A Memory of Newstead Abbey," pp. 170-88.
    "Of the Romantic and Some Byronic Places," pp. 90-116.

Harland, Marion [pseud. for Virginia Hawes Terhune]. "In Ra-
    venna," Where Ghosts Walk. The Haunts of Familiar Char-
    acters in History and Literature. New York: G. P. Put-
    nam's Sons, 1899. Pp. 207-29.

Harrison, J. A. "Italian Haunts of Lord Byron," Southern Maga-
    zine, XV (July, 1874), 1-19. Rptd. in his A Group of Poets
    and Their Haunts. New York: Hurd & Houghton, 1875. Pp.
    31-68.

Hasleden, W. S. "Newstead Abbey," N&Q, 1st ser., VIII (July 2,
    1853), 2-3.

Hawthorne, Sophia Amelia Peabody. Notes in England and Italy.
    New York: G. P. Putnam & Sons, 1869. [An account of a
    visit to Newstead Abbey with anecdotes of Byron.]

"The House in Which Byron Died," Mirror, V (May 14, 1825),
    305-307.

Howitt, William. "Lord Byron," Homes and Haunts of the Most
    Eminent British Poets. 2 vols. New York: Harper & Bros.,
    1847. Vol. I, pp. 525-66.

Hubbard, Elbert. "Lord Byron," Little Journeys to the Homes of
    English Authors. New York: G. P. Putnam's Sons, 1903.
    Pp. 235-76.

"Hucknall Torkard, Byron's Last Rest," New Monthly Magazine,
    2nd ser., XXVIII (Feb., 1830), 115-20. Rptd. in Polar Star,
    III (1830), 359-61.

Hutton, Laurence. Literary Landmarks of London. Boston: Tick-
    nor & Co., 1888.

Irving, Washington. "Newstead Abbey," The Crayon Miscellany.
    3 vols. Philadelphia: Carey, Lea & Blanchard, 1835. Vol.
    II, pp. 95-230.

Laborde, Edward D. Harrow School, Yesterday and Today. Lon-
    don: Winchester Publications, 1948.

Lang, Elsie M. Literary London. London: S. Werner Laurie,
    1907.

Leatham, James. In Byron's Country. Turriff, [Aberdeenshire]:
    The Deveron Press, 191-?

Lloyd, A. J. A Guide to Newstead Abbey and Gardens. Mans-
    field: W. and J. Linney, n. d.

"Lord Byron's Palace at Venice," Mirror, XVII (Feb. 12, 1831),
    113-15.

Masson, David. Memories of Two Cities: Edinburgh and Aberdeen.
    Edinburgh: Oliphant, Anderson & Ferrier, 1911.

Matthews, H. J. "Lord Byron," Old Marylebone and Some of the
    Famous People. London: Simpkin, Marshall, 1946. P. 11.

Michie, John Grant (ed.). The Records of Invercauld, 1547-1828.
    Aberdeen: Printed for the New Spalding Club, 1901.

Miller, Joaquin. "In Lord Byron's Rooms," Literary World (Bos-
    ton), XVI (Oct., 1885), 357-58. [Newstead Abbey.]

_____. "Nights at Newstead Abbey," Harper's New Monthly
    Magazine, LXXXI (Oct., 1890), 786-92. Rptd. in Joaquin
    Miller's Poems. 6 vols. "Bear Edition." San Francisco:
    The Whitaker & Ray Co., 1909. Vol. I, pp. 215-26.

Minchin, James G. Cotton. Old Harrow Days. London: Methuen
    & Co., 1898.

Moran, Benjamin. "The Homes and Graves of Byron and Mary
    Chaworth-Nottingham-Henry Kirke White," Graham's Magazine,
    XLII (April, 1853), 471-75.

Neale, Erskine. "The Grave of Byron," The Life-Book of a La-
    bourer. London: Smith, Elder, 1839. Pp. 36-43.

"Newstead Abbey," Broadway (London), 2nd ser., IV (March, 1870),
    145-52.

"Newstead Abbey," Eliza Cook's Journal, IV (March 1, 1851), 274-
    78.

Newstead Abbey. Lord Byron. Colonel Wildman. A Reminiscence.
    Leeds: Fenteman & Sons, 1856.

"Newstead Abbey, Nottinghamshire, the Family Seat of the Byrons,"
    Nic-Nac, II (June 5, 1824), 209-14.

Parkhurst, Clint. "Home and Grave of Byron," Lakeside Monthly,
    VIII (July, 1872), 68-79.

Pettigrew, Thomas J. "On Newstead Abbey," Journal of the
    British Archaeological Association, IX (1853), 14-30.

"A Pilgrimage to Hucknall Torkard," Saturday Review, CXXXVII
    (April 19, 1924), 408-409.

Ryan, P. Austin. Newstead Abbey and the Relics of Byron: Being
    a Complete Description of Newstead Abbey, Annesley Hall,
    and Hucknall Torkard Church, with Interesting Anecdotes, and
    Incidents of the Early Life of Byron. Reprinted from the
    "Mansfield and North Nottinghamshire Advertiser," Revised
    and Enlarged. Mansfield: J. Linney, 1874.

"The Seat and the Grave of the Byrons," Kaleidoscope, n.s., X
(Sept., 1829), 70.

Skelton, Percival. "The Home and Grave of Byron," Once a Week,
II (June 2, 1860), 539-42. Rptd. in Harper's New Monthly
Magazine, XXI (Oct., 1860), 606-10.

Smith, M. Crosby. "Newstead Abbey, the Home of Byron," Munsey's Magazine, XXXIX (May, 1908), 221-30.

Thornton, Percy Melville. Harrow School and Its Surroundings.
London: W. H. Allen & Co., 1885.

Wagstaff, H. F. Handbook and Guide to Newstead Abbey, Being a
Brief History and Account of This Interesting Place, Arranged
for the Convenience of Tourists and Visitors. Hucknall:
Henry Morley, 1931.

Walford, E. "A Pilgrimage to Newstead Abbey," Gentleman's
Magazine, CCLXVI (March, 1889), 243-252.

Walker, Samuel Dutton. Rambles in the Country, with a Few Re-
marks upon the Villages on the Route. No. 1. Hucknall
Torkard and the Grave of Byron. Nottingham: Simkins and
Browne, 1863.

Whipple, A. B. C. "The Italy of Byron and Shelley," Life International, XXXIV (Feb. 11, 1963), 3, 67-79; ibid., XXXIV
(Feb. 25, 1963), 68-79.

Winter, William. Gray Days and Gold. New York: Macmillan &
Co., 1891.
It contains:
"Hucknall-Torkard Church," pp. 288-309.
"Nottingham and Newstead," pp. 260-78.

Wolfe, Theodore F. A Literary Pilgrimage among the Haunts of
Famous British Authors. Philadelphia: J. B. Lippincott Co.,
1895.
It contains:
"The Home of Childe Harold," pp. 80-90.
"Some Haunts of Byron," pp. 62-79.

_____. Literary Rambles at Home and Abroad. Philadelphia:
J. B. Lippincott, 1901.
It contains:
"Byron's Harrow: Kensal Green," pp. 140-56.
"The Grave of Childe Harold," pp. 157-69.

Wood, Metcalfe. "Pilgrimage to the Land of Byron," English Illustrated Magazine, XVI (Feb., 1897), 554-60. [Visit to Nottinghamshire.]

Appendix D

POETICAL TRIBUTES, ATTACKS, SATIRES,
EPISTLES AND ADMONITIONS

1808-1824

"Address to Byron," Scots Magazine, LXXVIII (June, 1816), 454.

Algarotti. "To Lord and Lady B-. Reunion," Champion, Oct. 6,
1816, p. 318.

Alma Mater. A Poetical Epistle from Alma Mater to Lord Byron,
Occasioned by the following lines in a Tale Called "Beppo,"
"But for those children of the 'mighty mother's,' "/The
would-be wits, and can't be gentlemen." Cambridge: E.
Goode, 1819.

Alpheus. "Lines Said to Have Been Written by a Lady to Her
Lord Soon after His Quitting England," Mirror, III (June 12,
1824), 391.

[Ash, Charles Bowker.] A Layman's Epistle to a Certain Noble-
man. London: Rodwell & Martin, 1824. [Unsigned.] Rptd.
in The Poetical Works of C. B. Ash. 2 vols. London:
Longman & Co., 1831. Vol. II, pp. 109-44. [An attack in
verse.]

Auctor. "A Lament on the Death of the Noble Poet Lord Byron,"
Examiner, May 23, 1824, pp. 329-30.

B., F. H. An Address to the Right Honourable Lord Byron, with
an Opinion on Some of His Writings. London: Printed and
Published by Wetton & Jarvis, [1817].

B., J. D. "On reading the Death of Lord Byron," Mirror, III
(May 29, 1824), 357-58.

B., R. "Lines on Lord Byron," Mirror, III (June 26, 1824), 424.

[Barker, Miss.] Lines Addressed to a Noble Lord; (His Lordship
Will Know Why.) By One of the Small Fry of the Lakes.
London: W. Pople, 1815.

Barrett, Eaton Stannard. The Talents Run Mad; or, Eighteen Hun-
    dred and Sixteen. A Satirical Poem. In Three Dialogues.
    With Notes. By the Author of All the Talents. London:
    Printed for Henry Colburn, 1816. [Pp. 23-26 attack Byron.]

Brooke, Arthur [pseud. for John Chalk Claris]. "Address to Lord
    Byron," Gentleman's Magazine, LXXXVIII, Part II (Aug.,
    1818), 148. Rptd. in his Poems. London: Longman, 1818.
    P. 140.

Brown, John. The Stage. A Poem. London: J. Souter & Hatch-
    ard, 1820.

"Byron," Edinburgh Magazine, XCIV, (Nov., 1824), 616.

"Byron and Greece," Mirror, IV (Supp. XCIX, 1824), 143.

"Byronian," London Liberal, 1821, pp. 138-39.

"Byron-Shelley," Examiner, Oct. 3, 1824, p. 635.

C. "On the Death of Lord Byron," Mirror, III (June 26, 1824),
    424.

Clark, Hewson. "Lord Byron to His Bear," Satirist, II (June,
    1808), 368.

Clarke, McDonald. The Gossip; or, A Laugh with the Ladies, a
    Grin at the Gentlemen, and Burlesques on Byron, a Senti-
    mental Satire, with Other Poems: In a Series of Numbers.
    New York: Printed by Gray & Bunce, 1823.
    It contains:
    "Byron to the Devil," pp. 103-104.
    "Lord Byron," p. 27.

Claudius. "To Lord Byron: Written in the Interval between the
    Appearance of Childe Harold and Don Juan," New England
    Galaxy, IV (Oct. 13, 1820), 4.

Cottle, Joseph. An Expostulatory Epistle to Lord Byron. London:
    Cadell & Davies, 1820. Rptd. in his Malvern Hills, with
    Minor Poems and Essays. 2 vols. London: Printed for T.
    Cadell, 1829. Vol. I, pp. 221-39.
    Review:
    Monthly Review, XCIV (Feb., 1821), 211.

Daniel, George. The Modern Dunciad, a Satire; with Notes Bio-
    graphical and Critical. London: Printed for John Rodwell
    and Effingham Wilson, 1814. Pp. 57-59.

_____. The Times; or The Prophecy. London: E. Wilson,
    1813. [Attacks Lord Byron's prologue on the opening of the
    Drury Lane.]

Delia. A Poetical Epistle from Delia: Addressed to Lord Byron.
    London: Henry Colburn, 1817.

Dutton, T. "Poetical Epistle to Lord Byron," Scourge, X (Dec. 1,
    1815), 409-11.

"Elegiac Stanzas on Lord Byron," Literary Magnet, I (1824), 319-
    20.

"Elegy on the Death of Lord Byron," European Magazine, LXXXVI
    (July, 1824), 15-16.

An Elegy on the Death of Lord Byron: Intended as an Humble but
    Sincere Tribute to the Exalted Virtues and Brilliant Talents
    of that Much Lamented Nobleman; to Which Is Prefixed a
    Dedicatory Address ... on Behalf of Suffering Greece. Lon-
    don: Royal Academy, 1824.

"Elegy on the Death of Lord Byron," Tales of Chivalry and Ro-
    mance. Edinburgh: James Robertson; London: B. Cradock
    & Joy, 1826. Pp. 291-99.

"Epigram on Lord Byron," Portfolio (Dennie), 5th ser., XIV (July,
    1822), 78.

"From a Poem Entitled 'Retrospection,'" Mirror, III (June 26,
    1824), 423-24.

"Funeral of Lord Byron," Mirror, IV (July 24, 1824), 73-74.

"Genius," Beauties of the British Poets, ed. F. Campbell. 2 vols.
    London: Edwards, 1824. Vol. I, p. 297.

Gordon, Sir Cosmo. "A Sigh for the Bard," Pamphleteer, XXIV
    (1824), 219-20.

H., S. "On the Death of Lord Byron," Literary Chronicle, VI
    (May 22, 1824), 333.

[Harley, James.] The Press, or Literary Chit-Chat. A Satire.
    London: Printed for Lupton Relfe, 1822.

Harrow School Fellow of Lord Byron. "Verses on the Death of
    Lord Byron," Mirror, IV (Supp. LXXXV, 1824), 352.

Hatt. "Elegy on the Death of Lord Byron," Literary Chronicle,
    VI (May 22, 1824), 333.

Hawkins, Joseph. "Byron, Moore and Scott," Ladies' Monthly Mu-
    seum, 3rd ser., XVI (Aug., 1822), 113-16.

Hedgehog, Humphrey [pseud. for John Agg]. "Lord V___tia to
    Lord B___n," The General-Post Bag; or News! Foreign and

Domestic. To Which is Added La Bagatelle. London:
Printed for J. Johnston, 1815. Pp. 88-92.

Hogg, James. The Pilgrims of the Sun. Philadelphia: Moses
Thomas, 1815. [Dedicated to Lord Byron.]

Holland, T. C. "To Lord Byron, (written in 1814)," Monthly Repository, XII (June, 1817), 427-28.

Howitt, William. A Poet's Thoughts at the Interment of Lord Byron. London: Printed for Baldwin, Cradock & Joy, 1824.

Hulbert, C. A. "Lines on the Death of Lord Byron in Greece,"
Literary Chronicle, VI (May 22, 1824), 333. Rptd. in
Mirror, III (May 29, 1824), 357.

Humphreys, John Doddridge. "Lines, Occasioned by Reading that
the Heart of Byron Was to Remain in Greece," American
Monthly Magazine, II (Nov., 1824), 433-34.

Hunt, Leigh. The Feast of the Poets, with Notes, and Other
Pieces in Verse. London: Printed for James Cawthorn,
1814.

_____. "To the Right Honourable Lord Byron on His Departure
for Italy and Greece," Examiner, April 21, 1816, pp. 266-67.

"Invitation from a Late Bard to a Cockney Poet," London Liberal,
I (1823), 61.

[Ireland, W. H.] "Byron," Scribbleomania; or, The Printer's
Devil's Polychronicon. A Sublime Poem. London: Printed
for Sherwood, Neely & Jones, 1815. Pp. 68-70.

Keats, John. "Sonnet to Byron," ed. Richard Monckton Miles, Lord
Houghton, Life, Letters, and Literary Remains of John Keats, ed.
2 vols. London: Edward Moxon, 1848. Vol. I, p. 13.
[Written in Dec., 1814.]

Kenealy, Edward Vaughan. A New Pantomime. London: Reeves
& Turner, 1863. [A poem containing references to Byron.]

L. "Monody on the Death of Lord Byron," New England Galaxy,
VII (July 16, 1824), front page.

L., E. "On the Death of Lord Byron," Mirror, III (June 16,
1824), 424.

L., L. E. "Stanzas Written Beneath the Portrait of Byron,
Painted by Mr. West," Bristol Public Library Scrapbook,
pp. 33-36.

L., S. "Byron, a Sonnet," Literary Chronicle, VI (July 3, 1824), 430.

L., T. "A Tribute to Lord Byron," Mirror, IV (Suppl. XCIX, 1824), 142-43.

Lady of Glasgow. "To 'Childe Harold,' " Portico, III (May, 1817), 417-19.

Lake, J. W. A Poetical Tribute to the Memory of Lord Byron. Paris: Amyot, 1824.

Lamb, Caroline. Glenarvon. In Three Volumes. London: Printed for Henry Colburn, 1816.
It contains:
  "By That Smile Which Made Me Blest," II, 194-95.
  "Curs'd Be the Fiend's Detested Art," III, 283.
  "Farewell," II, 191-92.
  "If to Lose All That Love Thee," II, 131.
  "My Heart's Fit to Break," III, 13.
  "Poor Wretch," III, 69-70.
  "Song," III, 14-15, 26.
  "This Heart Has Never Stoop'd Its Pride," II, 30-31.
  "Waters of Elle!" II, 169-70.
  "When Turf and Faggots Crackling Blaze," III, 283-85, 293.

Leathwick, J. J. "Stanzas on the Death of Lord Byron," Literary Chronicle, VI (May 29, 1824), 348-49.

Leigh, Chandos. "On the Departure of Lord Byron for the Continent," Verses. London: Privately Printed, 1816. Pp. 43-45.

"Lines on Lord Byron," Mirror, IV (Supp. XCIX, 1824), 142.

"Lines on the Death of Lord Byron," Mirror, IV (Suppl. XCIX, 1824), 142.

"Lines on the Death of Lord Byron," Mirror, III (May 29, 1824), 357. [From Morning Herald.]

"Lines to Lord Byron," Edinburgh Magazine, XCII (July, 1823), 70.

"Lines to My Friend Byron," John Bull, III (Sept. 28, 1823), 309. [Against Byron.]

"Lines upon Lord Byron's Death," Ladies' Monthly Museum, 3rd ser., XX (Aug., 1824), 117-18.

"Lines Written on and Near the Tomb of Lord Byron," Mirror, IV (Suppl. XCIX, 1824), 143.

"Lines, Written on Hearing that the Remains of Lord Byron Were to Be Brought to England, but His Heart to Remain on the Shores of Greece," Portfolio (London), III (1824), 112.

"Lord Byron," Literary Magnet, I (1824), 305-306.

"Lord Byron and Greece," Literary Gazette, July 17, 1824, pp. 458-59. [Tributes to his memory in Greece; one elegy translated into English.]

M., F. "To Lord Byron, on His Dog-Ditty," Gentleman's Magazine, LXXXV, Part I (April, 1815), 350.

Malcolm, John. "Lines on the Death of Lord Byron," Mirror, IV (Suppl. XCIX, 1824), 143.

Maude, Thomas. "Lines Addressed to Lord Byron," A Legend of Ravenswood, and Other Poems. London: Hatchard & Son, 1823. Pp. 58-60.

_____. Monody on the Death of Lord Byron. London: Printed for Hatchard, 1824.

Modern Parnassus; or, The New Art of Poetry. A Poem, Designed to Supersede the Rules of Aristotle, Horace, Longinus, Vida, Boileau, and Pope. London: Printed for J. Johnson, 1814. [Byron is attacked in the poem.]

Modern Poets. A Dialogue in Verse Containing some Strictures on the Poetry of Lord Byron, Shelley and Others. London: White, Cochrane & Co., 1813. Pp. 12-14. [On Childe Harold.]

"Monody on the Death of Lord Byron," in S. W. Simmons, An Inquiry into the Moral Character of Lord Byron. New York: Bliss & White, 1824. Pp. x-xiii.

"Monody on the Death of Lord Byron," Mirror, IV (Supp. XCIX, 1824), 144.

Moore, Thomas. "L-D B-n's Memoirs, Written by Himself. Reflections when about to Read Them," Mirror, III (Suppl. LXXXV, 1824), 349-50. Rptd. in Poetical Works, Collected by Himself. 10 vols. London: Longman, Orme, 1841. Vol. VII, pp. 301-304.

Mott, Mrs. I. H. R. Sacred Melodies, Preceded by an Admonitory Appeal to the Right Honourable Lord Byron, with Other Small Poems. London: Francis Westley, 1824.

O'Donovan, P. M. [pseud. for Thomas Love Peacock]. "Dedication to Lord Byron," Sir Proteus: A Satirical Ballad. London: Printed for T. Hookman, Jr. & E. T. Hookman, 1814.

"On the Death of Lord Byron," Kaleidoscope, n. s., IV (May 25, 1824), 396.

"On the Separation of Lord and Lady Byron," Belle Assemblée, 2nd ser., XXIX (March, 1824), 117.

"On XXXX XXXXX," Gentleman's Magazine, LXXXV, Part II (Sept., 1815), 256. [X's stand for Lord Byron.]

A Poetical Epistle to Lord Byron. London: Printed for John Miller, 1816. Rptd. in part in Portfolio, 5th ser., IV (Dec., 1817), 527-28.

Pulti, Angelica. "On the Death of Lord Byron," Literary Gazette, July 17, 1824, pp. 458-59. [Translated from the Greek; the original text is also to be found here.] Cf. Y. S. M., N&Q, 7th ser., XII (Oct. 10, 1891), 286. [Quotes this elegy from memory.]

R., I. "Stanzas on Lord Byron," Literary Magnet, I (1824), 342.

Rolls, Mrs. Henry. A Poetical Address to Lord Byron. London: Printed for W. Hone, 1816.

Smith, James, and Smith, Horace. Horace in London: Consisting of Imitations of the First Two Books of the Odes of Horace. London: Printed for John Miller, 1813.

Sortes Horatiane: A Poetical Review of Poetical Talent. London: Printed for T. Hamilton, 1814.

"Stanzas Written at the Moment Lord Byron's Remains Were Borne to the Tomb," Mirror, IV (July 24, 1824), 74.

Swifte, Edmund Lewis Lenthal. Anacreon in Dublin. With Notes, Critical, Historical, and Explanatory, Dedicated to the Right Hon. Lord Byron, and Illustrated by Engravings on Wood. London: Printed for J. J. Stockdale, 1814. [The dedication takes up 18 pages.]

Taylor, John. "On the Portrait of the Late Lord Byron Painted by Richard Westall," Gentlemen's Magazine, XCIV, Part II (Aug., 1824), 167.

Terrot, Charles Hughes. "Byron," Common Sense, a Poem. London: David Brown, 1819. Pp. 5-7.

Thompson, W. G. Lines on the Death of Lord Byron. Newcastle upon Tyne: Printed at the Mercury Press by W. A. Mitchell, 1824.

[Thomson, Charles.] Lines on the Departure of a Great Poet from This Country. London: Printed for John Booth, 1816. [Abusive of Byron.]

Timo. "Greece--Lord Byron," Mirror, III (June 26, 1824), 423.

"To Greece on the Death of Lord Byron," Mirror, IV (Suppl. XCIX,
    1824), 143-44.

"To Lord Byron," Literary Journal, I (May 17, 1818), 125. [A
    parody.]

"To Lord Byron," Satirist and Tripod, XIV (March, 1814), 192.

"To Lord Byron," Thurston's Illustrations of Lord Byron's Poem,
    "The Corsair," London: Thomas Tegg, 1814.

A Tribute to the Memory of Lord Byron.   London: Printed for
    Effingham Wilson, 1824.

Turner, Sharon. Prolusions on the Present Greatness of Britain;
    On Modern Poetry; and on the Present Aspect of the World.
    London: Longman, 1819.

Turnour, Edward John. The Warning Voice. A Sacred Poem in
    Two Cantos Addressed to Infidel Writers of Poetry.   London:
    Longman, Hurst & Co., 1818.

W., C. P. "Lines on the Death of Lord Byron," Mirror, IV
    (Suppl. XCIX, 1824), 142.

Webster, James Wedderburn. "Lines on Lord B-n's Portrait,"
    Waterloo and Other Poems. Paris: Printed by Didot Sen,
    1816. Pp. 47-48.

Wiffen, Jeremiah Holmes. Aonian Hours; and Other Poems.
    London: Longman, 1819. [See especially Canto II, stanzas
    xvii-xxii.]

Wilkinson, Isaac. "To the Rt. Hon. George Gordon Byron, Lord
    Byron," The Poetical Works of Isaac Wilkinson. Cocker-
    mouth, 1824. Pp. 15-24.

Wilmot, Robert. "Lines Addressed to Lord Byron, April, 1816,"
    Earl of Lovelace's Astarte. London: Chiswick Press, 1905.
    P. 121.

"Written in a blank leaf of Lord Byron's Bride of Abydos," New
    Monthly Magazine, X (Dec., 1818), 427-28.

1825-1839

Bagnall, Edward. Lord Byron, With Remarks on His Genius and
    Character. Osvord: D. A. Talboys, 1831. [An enlarged
    version of the next item.]

_____ . Tribute to the Memory of Lord Byron; Supposed to Be
Written in the Sculpture Room of the "Society of Arts. "
Birmingham. London: Hurst, Chance, 1830.

Beste, John Richard Digby. "Modern Poetry, " Satires and The
Beggar's Coin. London: Hurst, Chance & Co. , 1831. Pp.
89-98.

Bowles, William Lisle. "Childe Harold's Last Pilgrimage, " Days
Departed, or, Banwell Hill, and Other Poems. London:
Murray, 1829. Pp. 201-205. Rptd. in The Poetical Album,
ed. Alaric A. Watts, 2nd ser. , London: Hurst, Chance &
Co. , 1829, pp. 363-64; Poetical Works of W. L. Bowles, 2
vols. , Edinburgh: James Nichol, 1855, II, 284-86.

Brown, Solyman. "Lady Byron to Her Husband, " Specimens of
American Poetry, ed. S. Kettel. 3 vols. Boston: S. G.
Goodrich, 1829. Vol. II, pp. 351-53.

Browning, Elizabeth Barrett. "Stanzas on the Death of Lord Byron, " An Essay on Mind, with Other Poems. London: James
Duncan, 1826. Pp. 117-19.

Brydges, Sir Egerton. The Lake of Geneva, a Poem, Moral and
Descriptive, in Seven Books. With Notes Historical and Biographical. 2 vols. Geneva: A. Cherbuliez; London: Bos-
sange & Co. , 1832.

_____ . Modern Aristocracy; or, The Bard's Reception; the
Fragment of a Poem Written in March, 1830. Geneva:
Printed by A. L. Vignier, 1831.

Bulwer-Lytton, Edward. The Pilgrims of the Rhine. London:
Saunders & Otley, 1834.

Colton, C. C. "Irregular Ode on the Death of Byron, " Literary
Chronicle, VII (Dec. 10, 1825), 798. Rptd. in Mirror, VI
(Dec. 31, 1825), 439-40; The Poetical Album, ed. Alaric A.
Watts, 2nd ser. , 1829, pp. 50-53.

Dagley, R. Death's Doings; Consisting of Numerous Original Com-
positions in Prose and Verse, the Friendly Contributions of
Various Writers; Principally Intended as Illustrations of
Twenty-four Plates, Designed and Etched by R. Dagley. Bos-
ton: Charles Ewer, 1828.
    It contains:
Alfred, "The Poet, " pp. 43-44.
H. Stebbing, "Death and the Poet, " pp. 45-48.

Daniels. "The Death of Byron, " Mirror, VII (April 29, 1826), 261.

Davenport, W. "Lord Byron's Immortality; or, The Vision of
Childe Harold, " The Book of Spirits and Tales of the Dead.
London: W. C. Wright, [1825?].

Eighteen Hundred and Twenty Six. Carmen Seculare. By Some-
    body. London: Effingham Wilson, 1826. [Twenty-four lines
    on Byron.]

"Elegy and Requiem," The Astrologer of the 19th Century, or,
    Compendium of Astrology, Geomancy and Occult Philosophy.
    London: W. C. Wright, 1825. Pp. 44-46.

Elliott, Ebenezer. "Byron and Napoleon; or, They Met in Heaven,"
    New Monthly Magazine, 2nd ser., XXXII (Dec., 1831), 552-
    54.

Frazer, W. The Decay of Literature: A Poem. Glasgow: G.
    Richardson, 1835.

Graham, John. "An Epistle to Lord Byron on the Publication of
    His Cain," Poems, Chiefly Historical. Belfast: Printed for
    Stuart & Gregg, 1829. Pp. 146-50.

Hodges, Charles. "To His Most Gracious Majesty, Lewis I, King
    of Bavaria," Original Poems. Münich: Jacob Bayer, 1836.
    [This dedicatory poem contains a tribute to the memory of
    Lord Byron.]

Hogg, James. "Ode for Music on the Death of Byron," Black-
    wood's, XXI (May, 1827), 520-21.

Hood, Robin. "The RA's Monitory and Minitory Addressed to Lord
    Byron," Archery and Archness. London: T. Hurst, 1834.
    Pp. 172-95.

Jones, John. "On the Death of Lord Byron," Attempts in Verse.
    London: Murray, 1831. Pp. 306-307.

Julian [pseud.]. "Verses Written on Visiting Loch-na-Gar, in
    July, 1832," Aberdeen Magazine, II (1832), 418-21.

L., S. "Lord Byron, at His Mother's Bier," Literary Journal
    (Providence), I (Nov. 30, 1833), 215.

"The Lady of Annesley," Tait's Edinburgh Magazine, n.s., III
    (May, 1836), 309.

Lamartine, Alphonse. The French Poem of the Celebrated Al-
    phonse de Lamartine, entitled "Man," Addressed to Lord By-
    ron, Translated into English Verse, with the Original Text,
    by C. Hicks. Whitby: R. Kirby, 1837.

Landor, Walter Savage. Gebir, Count Julian and Other Poems.
    London: E. Moxon, 1831.

"Lines to the Memory of Lord Byron," Edinburgh Magazine, XCVI
    (Nov., 1825), 565-66.

Lunt, George. The Grave of Byron, with Other Poems. Boston: Hilliard, Gray, Little & Wilkins, 1826. Pp. 5-54.

M., J. C. "Ode to Byron," Dublin University Magazine, XXXV (Dec., 1835), 696-701.

Mellen, Greenville. Martyr's Triumph and Other Poems. Boston: Lilly, Wait, Colman & Holden, 1833.
It contains:
"The Light of Letters," pp. 49-64.
"Ode on Byron," pp. 199-203.

Miller, Thomas. Elegy on the Death of Lord Byron's Mary. London: Simpkin & Marshall; Nottingham; G. Simmons, [1833?].

Morpeth, George William Frederick Howard, 7th Earl of Carlisle. "Prologue," The Last Greeks; or, The Fall of Constantinople. A Tragedy. London: James Ridgway, 1828. Pp. v-vi.

Müller, Wilhelm. "On the Death of Lord Byron," translated from the German by L. F. L. Gower, [1825]. Rptd. in Janus. or, The Edinburgh Literary Almanack, Glasgow: Oliver & Boyd, 1826, pp. 388-93; Examiner, Feb. 6, 1826, pp. 84-85; The Literary Rambler: Being a Collection of the Most Popular and Entertaining Stories in the English Language, [Glasgow?]: Oliver & Boyd, 1833, pp. 388-93.

Neal, John. "The Sleeper, a Poem Written on the Day after the Funeral of Lord Byron," Specimens of American Poetry, ed. S. Kettel. 3 vols. Boston: S. G. Goodrich, 1829. Vol. III, pp. 100-102.

Neale, William Johnson. The Lauread, A Literary, Political, and Naval Satire. London: Cochrane, 1833.

O'L. "Byron," Dublin and London Magazine, II (April, 1826), 192.

"On the Death of Lord Byron," The Olla Podrida. London: Lupton Relfe, 1825. Pp. 342-44.

P., S. S. "Epigram," Poems, Addressed to Various Literary Characters. Weymouth: Printed for the Author by G. Kay, Library, Augusta Place, 1827. P. 45.

Perry, Charles James. "On the Death of Lord Byron," The House of Mornington, a Pastoral Drama; with Miscellaneous Poems. London: 1826. P. 80.

Pigott, John Dryden. Johannice: A Poem in Two Cantos. Monody on Lord Byron, and Other Poems. London: J. Hatchard & Son, 1832. Pp. 1-118.

Pollok, Robert. The Course of Time, a Poem in Ten Books.
New York: Clark & Maynard, 1827.

Prentis, Stephen. An Apology for Lord Byron. With Miscellaneous Poems. London: J. Macrone, 1836.

Reade, John Edmund. Italy: A Poem, in Six Parts: With Historical and Classical Notes. London: Saunders & Otley,
1838. [See especially Canto II, stanzas xxxvi-xlii.]

Riddell, Henry Scott. Stanzas on the Death of Lord Byron. Edinburgh: J. Anderson, 1825.

Rogers, Samuel. "Bologna," Italy, a Poem. London: T. Cadell
& E. Moxon, 1830. Pp. 97-101.

Rolls, Mrs. Henry. "Death of Lord Byron," Book of Spirits and
Tales of the Dead. London: W. C. Wright, 1825? Pp. 13-
16.

Taylor, John. Poems on Various Subjects. 2 vols. London:
Payne & Foss, 1827.
It contains:
"Inscription for the Print Representing the House in Which
Byron Died in Missolonghi," II, 83.
"The Last Words of Byron Versified," II, 120.
"Sonnet Addressed to the Late Lord Byron," I, 153.

[Tennyson, Frederick, and Tennyson, Charles.] "On the Death of
Lord Byron," Poems by Two Brothers. London: W. Simpkin
& R. Marshall, 1827. Pp. 128-30.

Thornton. "Ode on the Death of the Poet Byron," Remember Me!
A New Year's Gift or Christmas Present. London: I. Poole,
1825. Pp. 160-67.

To the Departed. Stanzas to the Memory of Lord Byron. London:
J. Hatchard, 1825.

"Verses to Lord Byron," Literary Gems. In Two Parts. Edinburgh: Printed for Hurst, Robinson & Co.; London: McLach-
lan & Stewart, 1826. P. 267.

1840-1869

B., A. M. Byron: A Poem. London: J. Gordon, 1840.

[Bennett, William Cox.] Verdicts. London: Effingham Wilson,
1852. [See especially pp. 62-64.]

Browning, Elizabeth Barrett. "A Vision of Poets, 1844," The
Poetical Works of Elizabeth Barrett Browning. New York:
T. Y. Crowell & Co., 1883.

Chivers, Thomas H. "Byron," Ladies' National Magazine, XII
(Nov., 1847), 159.

[Clarke, H. S. according to the British Museum Catalogue]. In the
Matter of the Stowe Scandal. Lord Byron's Defence. London: Published at No. 183, Strand, 1869. [Verses in imitation of Byron's style, purporting to be written from Hades.]

Elliott, Ebenezer. "Devil Byron, a Ballad," People's Journal, III
(Jan. 23, 1847), 45-46.

Julia, Aemilia [pseud. for Emily Black]. Byron; Salathiel, or the
Martyrs; and Other Poems. London: Routledge, 1855. Pp.
1-51.

Kenealy, Edward Vaughan. "Byron," Poems and Translations.
London: Reeves & Turner, 1864. Pp. 224-25.

Kent, Charles. "Byron at Newstead," Dreamland, with Other
Poems. London: Longman, Green, Longman & Roberts,
1862. Pp. 81-84.

Kenworthy, Charles. "Lines on Viewing the Marble Tablet to the
Memory of Lord Byron," Original Poems, on Miscellaneous
Subjects. Manchester: Cave & Sever, 1847. Pp. 19-21.

Lamartine, Alphonse de. "Man," A Poem Addressed to Byron,
translated by H. W. Freeland. Poems of H. W. Freeland.
London: Saunders & Otley, 1848. Pp. 144-73.

Landor, Walter Savage. Dry Sticks, Fagoted by Walter Savage
Landor. Edinburgh: J. Nichol, 1858.

_____. Heroic Idylls. London: Newby, 1863.

_____. Last Fruit off an Old Tree. London: E. Moxon, 1853.

Meadows, Lindon [pseud. for Charles Butler Greatrex]. The Byron
Oak. Written after a Recent Visit to Newstead Abbey. Privately Printed, [ca. 1860].

Miles, G. M. "Poem on Byron," Southern Review, VI (Oct.,
1869), 477-78.

Pidcock, T. [pseud. for Thomas Moore]. "The 'Living Dog' and
the 'Dead Lion,'" Poetical Works, Collected by Himself.
10 vols. London: Longman, Orme, 1841. Vol. VIII, pp.
267-68.

Tuckerman, Henry Theodore. "Lord Byron at Venice," Poems.
Boston: Ticknor, Reed & Fields, 1851. Pp. 106-107.

Urquhart, Henry John. "Lines Written on Lord Byron, in Early
　　Youth," Poems, Sacred and Classical. London: Hamilton &
　　Adams, 1845. Pp. 123-26.

[Verity, Valentine.] The Shade of Byron: A Mock Heroic Poem,
　　Containing Strange Revelations not hitherto Disclosed, with
　　Copious Notes and References. A Preface, with the Author's
　　Comments on the so-called "True" Story by Mrs. Stowe.
　　And a Repudiation of the Charges Hurled Against the Memory
　　of Lord Byron and His Beloved Sister Ada Augusta. London:
　　James Burs, 186-? Rptd. in The Poetical Works of Valen-
　　tine Verity: Containing the Shade of Byron, and Other Poems,
　　ed. S. W. Leonard. London: Elliott, 1866.

1870-1899

Blackie, John Stuart. "Lord Byron and the Armenian Convent,"
　　Messis Vitae, Gleanings of Song from a Happy Life. London:
　　Macmillan & Co., 1886. P. 164.

*Brennan, Edward. The Footprints of Albe. A Poem. Part I.
　　Rome and Florence: A Zanaboni, 1874.

Brodie, Erasmus Henry. "Byron," Sonnets. London: George
　　Bell & Sons, 1885. P. 102.

Collins, Mortimer. "Crede Byron," Punch, LXIX (July 24, 1875),
　　34.

Derry, E. "Six Days at Geneva and Chamounix," Rhymes of Road,
　　Rail, and River. Bristol: J. W. Arrowsmith, 1899. Pp.
　　5-52.

Earle, J. C. "The Death of Byron," Hawthorn, II (July, 1872),
　　37.

Lang, Andrew. "Byron," Letters to Dead Authors. London:
　　Longmans, Green & Co., 1886. Pp. 205-15.

Light or Darkness? A Poem. With Remarks on Lord Byron's
　　Detractors. London: Smart & Allen, 1870.

*Lorrimer, Laurie. To Byron. Manchester: McWhinnie & Peter-
　　son, 1870.

Manfred [pseud. for E. W. Preston, according to the Harvard Li-
　　brary Catalogue]. Lord Byron Vindicated; or, Rome and Her
　　Pilgrim. London: Simpkin, Marshall & Co., 1876. [Satiric
　　poem against Mrs. Stowe.]

Massiah, S. R. St. Clair. Byron, a Poem. N. P. 1869.

Miller, Joaquin. "At Lord Byron's Tomb," Lakeside Monthly, IX
    (March, 1873), 246-47. Rptd. in Joaquin Miller's Poems.
    "Bear Edition. " 6 vols. San Francisco: The Whitaker &
    Ray Co. , 1909. Vol. IV, pp. 191-92.

_____ . "Burns and Byron," Poems. Boston: Roberts
    Bros. , 1889. Pp. 257-66. Rptd. in Joaquin Miller's Poems.
    "Bear Edition. " 6 vols. San Francisco: The Whitaker &
    Ray Co. , 1909. Pp. 173-76.

Noel, Roden. "Byron's Grave," Songs of the Heights and Deeps.
    London: E. Stock, 1885. Pp. 177-78. Rptd. in his Life
    of Lord Byron. London: Scott, 1890. Pp. 204-207.

Ogle, John Joseph. "To Lord Byron," Nottingham Magazine, No.
    1 (Nov. 14, 1885), 3.

Rosslyn, Francis Robert St. Clair Erskine, 4th Earl of. "Byron,"
    Sonnets. London: William Blackwood, 1883. P. 57.

S. , F. R. "The Fame of Byron," Dublin University Magazine,
    n. s. , V (Feb. , 1880), 224-29.

Stedman, Edmund Clarence. "Byron," Poems, Now First Collected.
    Boston: Houghton Mifflin, 1897. Pp. 125-29.

Watson, William. "Byron, the Voluptuary," Critic, XXI (Dec. 31,
    1892), 379. Rptd. in The Collected Poems of William Wat-
    son. New York: John Lane Co. , 1899. P. 110.

_____ . Wordsworth's Grave and Other Poems. London: T.
    Fisher Unwin, 1890.

Wilde, Oscar. Ravenna, a Poem. "The Newdigate Prize Poem,
    1878, " Complete Writings of Oscar Wilde. New York: The
    Nottingham Society, 1909. Vol. V, pp. 1-17.

Williams, T. C. "To a Head of Lord Byron," Harper's Weekly,
    XXXVI (June 11, 1892), 565.

THE 20th CENTURY

Armour, Richard. "Portrait of Lord Byron," Georgia Review, IX
    (Fall, 1955), 324.

Auden, W. H. , and MacNeice, Louis. "Letter to Lord Byron,"
    Letters from Iceland. London: Faber & Faber, 1937. Pp.
    17-24, 49-59, 99-107, 200-12.

Blishen, Edward. "Byron," NSN, XLV (June 27, 1953), 788.

Blunden, Edmund. "Byroniana," Poems of Many Years. London: Collins, 1957. Pp. 269-70.

Broughton, John Cam Hobhouse, Lord. "In Memoriam: Poem," London Mercury, X (May, 1924), 5.

*Byrnes, John V. "On Reading the Controversy between Lord Byron and Mr. Bowles," Southerly, No. 3 (1961), 6-18.

Church, Richard. North of Rome. London: Hutchinson, 1960.

Ciardi, John. "George Gordon of Gight," SRL, XLI (Jan. 4, 1958), 15.

Covington, Philip. "A Letter to Lord Byron," Emory University Quarterly, XIV (June, 1958), 65-74.

Crabbe, George. "Lord Byron's Inscription upon a Newfoundland Dog," New Poems by George Crabbe, ed. Arthur Pollard. Liverpool: Liverpool University, 1960. Pp. 51-52.

Crowninshield, Frederic. "To Byron, a Sonnet," A Painter's Moods. New York: Dodd, Mead & Co., 1902. P. 28.

Drinkwater, John. "Missolonghi, April 19, 1824-1924," Times, April 19, 1924, p. 11. Rptd. in the Centenary of Byron's Death. Athens: University of Athens, 1924. Pp. 37-40. [Text in English and Greek.]

Elliott, George P. "Romantic Poets," College English, XVII (Nov., 1955), 118.

Ennis, Julian. "Advanced Level Poet," REL, VII (April, 1966), 74.

Flower, Howard. Byron is Dead. Composed for the Centenary of the Death of Byron, April 19, 1924. Hartland, Vermont: Solidarian Press, 1924.

Graves, C. L. "A Hundred Years After: Lines on Reading the New Byron Letters," Punch, CLXII (March 8, 1922), 185.

Ingalls, Jeremy. "That Greece Might Still Be Free," SRL, XXIX (Feb. 16, 1946), 25.

Johnson, Robert Underwood. "To the Spirit of Byron; Poem," Independent, LXXX (Dec. 7, 1914), 368. Rptd. in Literary Digest, LII (June 10, 1916), 1716; Johnson's Poems of War and Peace, Including the Panama Ode, The Corridors of Congress. Indianapolis: The Bobbs-Merrill Co., 1916, pp. 27-28.

Logan, John. 'Byron at Shelley's Burning," Indian P. E. N.,
    XXV (Jan., 1959), 5-6. Rptd. in his Ghosts of the Heart:
    New Poems. Chicago: University of Chicago Press, 1960.
    P. 41.

Lumsden, James. "Byron--A Rustic Boy's Estimate of Him Six and
    Fifty Years Ago." Doun i' th' Loudons, a Drama of Country
    Life and Other Pieces. Edinburgh: W. Macdonald & Co.,
    1908. Pp. 159-60.

MacDonald, Alexander James. "Byron," Star-Gazing; Metrical
    Compositions. Boston: n.p., 1907. Pp. 32-33.

McInnis, Edgar Wadwell. Byron. "The Newdigate Prize Poem,
    1925." Oxford: Basil Blackwell, 1925.

Morley, C. 'Byron and Water," SRL, XXIX (Feb. 23, 1946), 20.

Mott, E. M. 'Byron," Bookman (London), XLIV (Aug., 1913),
    Supp. 6.

Nash, Ogden. "Very Like a Whale," The Face Is Familiar; the
    Selected Verse of Ogden Nash. Boston: Little, Brown & Co.,
    1940. Pp. 104-105.

Palamas, Costis. "A Byron Centenary Ode." Poetry Review, XV
    (Aug., 1924), 223-24. Rptd. in The Celebration of the Cen-
    tenary of Lord Byron's Death - by University of Athens -
    1824-1924. Athens: University of Athens, 1924. Pp. 37-41.

Pinto, Vivian de Sola. "To Lord Byron: On Editing His Poems,
    1963," English, XV (Summer, 1964), 57.

St. Clair, George. 'Lord Byron to Tom Moore--an Epistle,"
    New Mexico Quarterly, II (Feb., 1932), 49-52.

Squire, John Collings. "If Byron Had Written 'The Passing of
    Arthur,' " Tricks of the Trade. London: Martin Secker,
    1917. Pp. 72-79.

Appendix E

IMITATIONS, CONTINUATIONS, DRAMATIZATIONS,
ADAPTATIONS, PARODIES, SATIRES, AND POEMS
OCCASIONED BY THE WORKS OF BYRON[1]

ADDRESS AT THE OPENING OF DRURY LANE THEATRE

The Genuine Rejected Addresses, Presented to the Committee of
   Management for Drury Lane Theatre; Preceded by that writ-
   ten by Lord Byron, and Adopted by the Committee. London:
   Printed and Sold by B. McMillan, 1812.
   Reviews:
      QR, VIII (Sept., 1812), 172-81.
      Antijacobin Review, XLIII (Dec., 1812), 359-73.
      Francis Hodgson, Monthly Review, 2nd ser., LXX (Feb.,
         1813), 184-89.

Smith, James, and Smith, Horace. "Cui Bono? By Lord Byron,"
   Rejected Addresses; or, The New Theatrum Poetarum. London: Printed for John Miller, 1812. Pp. 17-28.

"Address of Condolence to the Unsuccessful Candidates for the
   Drury Prize," Gentleman's Magazine, LXXXII, Part II (Nov.,
   1812), 471.

"Address XVII; 'Lord B___n to J. M___y, Bookseller,'" Accepted
   Addresses; or, Proemium Poetarum. To Which Are Added,
   Macbeth Travestie, In Three Acts, and Miscellanies. By
   Different Hands. London: Printed for Thomas Tegg, 1813.
   Pp. 50-52.

A Sequel to the "Rejected Addresses"; or, the Theatrum Poetarum
   Minorum. By Another Author. London: Printed for Sherwood, Neely, & Jones, 1813.

Hogg, James. "The Guerrilla, by Lord Byron," The Poetic Mirror, or the Living Bards of Britain. London: Printed Longman, Hurst, Rees, Orme, & Brown, 1816. Pp. 3-20.
   [Parodies written in imitation of The Rejected Addresses.]
   Review:
      John Wilson Croker, QR, XV (July, 1816), 468-75.

---

[1]The arrangement of this appendix is chronological.

BEPPO

Julius.   More News from Venice.   By Beppo, a Noble Venetian.
Translated from the Original, by Julius.   Oxford: Printed
by W. Baxter for J. Vincent, 1818.   [A continuation.]

Beppo in London: A Metropolitan Story.   London: Duncombe,
1819.   [A continuation.]

THE BRIDE OF ABYDOS

B. , H. S.   "Lines Occasioned by Reading The Bride of Abydos, "
Gentleman's Magazine, LXXXIV, Part I (June, 1814), 592.

Selim and Zuleika.   A Tragedy in Three Acts.   Vol. IV of The
New British Theatre, ed. John Galt.   London: 1814-1815.

Dimond, William.   The Bride of Abydos, a Tragick Play, in Three
Acts: As Performed at the Theatre Royal, Drury Lane.
London: Richard White, 1818.   Rptd. as The Bride of Aby-
dos: A Romantic Drama in Three Acts.   From Lord Byron's
Celebrated Poem.   Lacy's Acting Edition of English Plays,
Vol. LXX, 184-?

*Erasmus.   The Outlaw: A Tale.   Edinburgh, 1818.   [A parody.]

O. , W.   The Bride of Abydos: A Tragedy, in Five Acts.   Founded
upon "The Bride of Abydos" and "The Corsair" of Lord Byron.   London: James Harper, 1818.

Payne, J. W. H.   The Unfortunate Lovers; or, The Affecting History of Selim and Almena.   A Turkish Tale; from "The Bride
of Abydos, " of Lord Byron.   New York: Published by S.
King, 1828.   [An adaptation.]

Byron, Henry James.   The Bride of Abydos; or, The Prince, the
Pirate, and The Pearl.   An Original Oriental Burlesque Ex-
travaganza.   ("Lacy's Acting Edition of English Plays, " Vol.
XXXVI.)   London: T. H. Lacy, 1858.

CAIN

Another Cain.   A Poem.   London: Sold by Messrs. Hatchard &
Son, 1822.

Blake, William.   "To Lord Byron in the Wilderness, " The Ghost
of Abel.   A Revelation in the Vision of Jehovah, Seen by
William Blake.   London, 1822.   Rptd. in The Poetical Works
of William Blake, ed. Edwin J. Ellis.   2 vols.   London:
Chatto & Windus, 1906.   Vol. I, pp. 221-25.

Z.   "On Reading Cain, a Mystery," Gentleman's Magazine, XCII,
     Part I (Feb., 1822), 164. Rptd. in Manchester Iris, I
     (March 9, 1822), 44.

Adams, Thomas. A Scourge for Lord Byron; or, "Cain, a Mys-
     tery" Unmasked. London: T. Adams, 1823.
     Review:
     Literary Chronicle, V (June 14, 1823), 374-75.

Hardy, Philip Dixon. Abel, a Mystery. Intended as an Antidote
     to Lord Byron's Cain, a Mystery. London: B. J. Holds-
     worth; Birmingham: B. Huchon; Dublin: Martin Keene, 1823.

Wilkinson, Henry. Cain, a Poem. Intended to Be Published in
     Parts, Containing an Antidote to the Impiety and Blasphemy
     of Lord Byron's "Cain"; with Notes, etc. Part I. London:
     Published by Baldwin, Cradock & Joy, 1824.

Reade, John Edmund. Cain the Wanderer: A Vision of Heaven:
     Darkness; and Other Poems. London: Whittaker, Treacher,
     1829.

Howell, Owen. Abel, Written but with Great Humility in Reply to
     Lord Byron's "Cain." London: John Mardon, 1843.

CHILDE HAROLD'S PILGRIMAGE

Penn, Granville. Lines to Harold. Buckinghamshire: Privately
     Printed at Stoke Park, 1812. Rptd. as "Address to Lord
     Byron on the Publication of Childe Harold," in The Poetical
     Album, ed. Alaric A. Watt. 2nd ser. London: Hurst,
     Chance & Co., 1829. Pp. 207-11.

H., A. "Upon Reading Lord Byron's Reflections on the Battle of
     Talavera in Childe Harold," Gentleman's Magazine, LXXXII,
     Part I (June, 1812), 566.

Modern Poets. A Dialogue in Verse Containing Some Strictures on
     the Poetry of Lord Byron, Shelley, and Others. London:
     White, Cochrane & Co., 1813. [Pp. 12-14 deal with Childe
     Harold's Pilgrimage.]

Blaby, J. C. "Lines Written on Perusing Lord Byron's Poem en-
     titled Childe Harold," Gentleman's Magazine, LXXXIII, Part
     I (Feb., 1813), 159.

Gillies, R. P. Childe Alarique, a Poet's Reverie. With Other
     Poems. Edinburgh: Printed by James Ballantyne & Co., for
     Longman, Hurst, Rees, Orme & Browne, 1814.

Bluemantle, Mrs. Bridget. The Baron of Falconberg; or, Childe
     Harolde in Prose. London: Printed at the Minerva Press
     for A. K. Newman, 1815.

[Leigh, Chandos]. "Verses Addressed to Lord Byron after His
    Publication of Childe Harold, " Juvenile Poems. London:
    Printed by G. Sidney for F. Benedict, 1815. P. 42.

Brooke, Arthur [pseud. for John Chalk Claris]. "On Reading the
    Third Canto of Childe Harold, " Gentleman's Magazine,
    LXXXVII, Part I (Jan. , 1817), 63. Rptd. in his Poems.
    London: Longmans, 1818. P. 89.

C. , H. Prodigious!!!! Or, Childe Paddie in London. 3 vols.
    London: Printed for the Author and Sold by Wm. Lindsell,
    1818.

Childe Harold's Pilgrimage to the Dead Sea; Death on the Pale
    Horse; and Other Poems. London: Baldwin, Cradock & Joy,
    1818. [Attributed to Byron and also to Laura Sophia Temple.]

Hodgson, Francis. Childe Harold's Monitor; or, Lines Occasioned
    by the Last Canto of "Childe Harold"; Including Hints to Other
    Contemporaries. London: J. Porter, 1818.

The Last Canto of Childe Harold's Pilgrimage, with Notes. Not by
    Lord Byron. London: Printed for Effingham Wilson, 1818.
    [A new canto.]

The Soul's Pilgrimage; a Poem, Written in Reference to the Senti-
    ments of the Author of "Childe Harold's Pilgrimage." Cam-
    bridge: Printed by W. Metcalfe, 1818. [An attack on By-
    ron.]

"Fragment of a 5th Canto of Childe Harold's Pilgrimage. Dedi-
    cated to Mr. H, " Blackwood's, III (May, 1818), 201-204.
    [A parody in Spenserians.]

Childe Albert; or, the Misanthrope, and Other Poems, Imitative
    and Original. Edinburgh: John Thomson; London: Baldwin,
    Cradock & Joy, 1819.

Childe Harold in the Shades: An Infernal Romaunt. 2 cantos.
    London: T. Hookman, Sherwood & Co. , 1819.

"Lines on Reading the Last Canto of Childe Harold, " New Monthly
    Magazine, XI (July, 1819), 527-28.

Maginn, William. "Letter from Lord Byron, Enclosing the Com-
    mencement of Childe Daniel, " Blackwood's, VII (May, 1820),
    186-87. Rptd. in The Odoherty Papers, Annotated by Shelton
    Mackenzie. 2 vols. New York: Redfield, 1855-1857. Vol.
    II, pp. 50-52.

"Childe Byron's Pilgrimage: Canto I, " Bon Ton Magazine, I (June
    1, 1821), 108-21. [An imitation.]

Odoherty, Morgan [pseud. for D. M. Moir]. "Childe Paddie's
    Banishment to New Holland," Blackwood's, IX (May, 1821),
    137. Rptd. in The Odoherty Papers, Annotated by Dr. Shel-
    ton Mackenzie. 2 vols. New York: Redfield, 1855-1857.
    Vol. I, p. 237.

Deacon, W. F. [pseud. for William Gifford]. "The Childe's Pil-
    grimage," Warreniana, with Notes, Critical and Explanatory,
    by the Editor of a Quarterly Review. London: Longman,
    Hurst & Co., 1824. Pp. 81-92.

"Harold's Last Pilgrimage," Edinburgh Magazine, XCV (June, 1825),
    713-17.

Lamartine, Alphonse de. The Last Canto of Childe Harold's Pil-
    grimage. London: Printed for E. Lloyd & Son, 1827.

P., S. S. "On Reading the First Canto of Childe Harold," Poems
    Addressed to Various Literary Charactors. Weymouth:
    Printed for the Author by G. Kay, Library, Augusta Place,
    1827. Pp. 44-45.

The Pilgrimage of Ormond; or, Childe Harold in the New World.
    Charleston, S.C.: W. Riley, 1831. [An imitation.]

Lamartine, Alphonse de. The Last Canto of Harold's Pilgrimage.
    From the French of Lamartine. Rendered into English by the
    Author of "The Poetry of Earth," and Other Pieces. Dublin:
    P. Dixon Hardy, 1848. [A different version from that above.]

Childe Malverne, a Fragment. And Other Poems. London: Long-
    mans, Green, 1872.

[Gordon, Rose]. Childe Archie's Pilgrimage. London: G. Pulman,
    1873. [A parody of Byron's Childe Harold.]

Milliken, Edwin James. "Childe Chappie's Pilgrimage," Punch
    LXXXV (Aug. 11, 1883), 72; ibid., LXXXV (Aug. 18, 1883),
    84; ibid., LXXXV (Aug. 25, 1883), 96; ibid., LXXXV (Sept. 1,
    1883), 108; ibid., LXXXV (Sept. 8, 1883), 120; ibid., LXXXV
    (Sept. 15, 1883), 132; ibid., LXXXV (Sept. 22, 1883), 144.
    Rptd. Childe Chappie's Pilgrimage. Illustrated by E. J.
    Wheeler. London: Bradbury, Agnew & Co., 1883.

Aubin, R. A. "Imitations of Childe Harold," Englische Studien,
    LXX, No. 3 (1936), 432-33. [Pieces not recorded by Chew.]

Y., B. A. "Childe Harold's Pilgrimage," Punch, CCXXXIV (Jan.
    8, 1958), 91. [A parody of st. clxxxvii of Byron's Childe
    Harold.]

THE CORSAIR

[Hone, William]. Conrad, the Corsair; or, The Pirate's Isle.
    A Tale. By Lord Byron. Adapted as a Romance. London:
    William Hone, 1817.

Holland, Edwin Clifford. The Corsair: A Melodrama in Four
    Acts, Collected and Arranged for the Stage from Lord By-
    ron's Poem. Charleston: S. C. : Printed for the Author by
    A. E. Miller, 1818.

Brough, William. Conrad and Medora; or, Harlequin Corsair, and
    the Little Fairy at the Bottom of the Sea. A New Burlesque
    and Pantomine. London: Thomas H. Lacy, 1856.

DARKNESS

Despair: A Vision. Derry Down and John Bull; a Simile. Being
    Two Political Parodies on "Darkness, " and a Scene from
    "The Giaour, " by Lord Byron. Together with a Love Letter
    from John Bull to Liberty and a Farewell Address, etc.
    London: Printed for the Author by R. Hamblin, 1820.

[Wilson, John?] "Dourthiness, " Blackwood's, X (Dec. , 1821), 561-
    62. [A travesty of Byron's Darkness.]

THE DEVIL'S DRIVE, AN UNFINISHED RHAPSODY

Fry, William. The Continuation of Lord Byron's "Devil's Drive, "
    (On the Continent). London: Published by the Newsagents'
    Publishing Co. , 1820. [An unfinished continuation of Byron's
    "The Devil's Drive, an Unfinished Rhapsody, " 1813.]

DON JUAN

Don Juan, with a Biographical Account of Lord Byron and His Fam-
    ily; Anecdotes of His Lordship's Travel and Residence in
    Greece, at Geneva, etc. Including also, a Sketch of the Vam-
    pyre Family. Embellished with a Portrait of His Lordship,
    from an Original Drawing. Canto III. London: William
    Wright, 1819.
    Reviews:
    Literary Chronicle, I (Oct. 23, 1819), 353-55.
    Literary Gazette, Nov. 6, 1819, pp. 707-708.

Hone, William. Don Juan. Canto the Third. London: William
    Hone, 1819. [A continuation.]

A New Canto. London: William Wright, 1819. [A continuation.]

N., M. [pseud. for William Maginn]. "Byron's Don Juan Unread,"
    Blackwood's, VI (Nov., 1819), 194-95. [A parody of Don
    Juan, resembling "Harrow Revisited."] Rptd. in The Odoherty
    Papers. New York: Redfield, 1855-1857. Vol. I. Pp. 172-82.

Don Juan. Canto XI. London: Sherwood, Neely & Jones, 1820.
    [A continuation.]
    Review:
    Literary Gazette, Aug. 19, 1820, pp. 530-31.

Jack the Giant Queller; or, Prince Juan. London: Joseph Grove
    Library, 1820. [A mock-Don Juan.]

Milner, M. Henry. The Italian Don Juan; or, Memoirs of the
    Devil Sacripanti, the Brigand of the Apennines, translated
    freely from the Italian. London: C. Chapple, 1820.

Don Juan. Canto III. London: Printed by R. Greenlaw, Holborn,
    1821. [A continuation.]

Thornton, Alfred. Don Juan. Volume the First. With Fifteen
    Coloured Engravings. London: Thomas Kelley, 1821. [Bi-
    ography of a libertine.]

The Sultana; or, A Trip to Turkey. A Melodrama in Three Acts,
    founded on Lord Byron's "Don Juan." New York: C. N.
    Baldwin, 1822.

[Thompson, W. G.?] A Touch at an Unpublished Canto of "Don
    Juan," Newcastle Magazine, n. s. I (Jan., 1822), 19-22.

Thornton, Alfred. Don Juan. Volume the Second. Containing His
    Life in London; or a True Picture of the British Metropolis.
    London: Thomas Kelley, 1822.

Coates, Henry. The British Don Juan; Being a Narrative of the
    Singular Amours, Entertaining Adventures, Remarkable
    Travels & c., of the Hon. Edward W. Montague. London:
    G. Griffin, 1823.

[Thomas, John Wesley.] An Apology for "Don Juan," Cantos I and
    II. London: Printed by T. Green, 1824. [A satire.]

[Clason, Isaac S.] Don Juan. Cantos XVII-XVIII. New York:
    Charles Wiley, 1825. [Purports to be by Byron.]

Continuation of Don Juan. Cantos XVII-XVIII. London: G. B.
    Whittaker; Oxford: Munday & Slater, 1825.

Don Giovanni; a Poem in Two Cantos. Azim and Lilla and Other
    Pieces. London: Published by Sherwood, Jones & Co.,
    1825.

Don Juan. Cantos XVII and XVIII. London: Duncombe, 1825.
   [Included in Byron's Don Juan, with a Preface by a Clergy-
   man. London: Hodgson & Co. , 1823-1825. Vol. II.]

Juan Secundus. Canto the First. London: Miller, 1825.

[Thomas, John Wesley.] An Apology for "Don Juan," a Satirical
   Poem. 2nd ed. To Which Are Added, Stanzas on the Death
   of Lord Byron, and Other Poems. London: W. Booth, 1825.

Don Juan, Canto XVII. London: Published by the editor, 1827.

Buckstone, John Baldwin. Don Juan. A Romantic Drama in Three
   Acts. Founded on Lord Byron's Poem. London: John Dicks,
   1828.

_____. A New Don Juan! An Operatical, Poetical, Egotistical,
   Melodramatical Extravaganzical, but Strictly Moral Burletta,
   in Two Acts; Founded on Lord Byron's Celebrated Poem.
   The Dramatic and Original Music by G. H. Rodwell, Esq.
   First Performed at the Adelphi Theatre, with Distinguished
   Approbation. London: T. Richardson, 1828.

The Seventeenth Canto of Don Juan, in Continuation of the Unfinished Poem by Lord Byron. Intended as the First Canto of
   the Remaining Eight Which are Wanting to Complete that Author's Original Design of Extending the Work to Twenty Four.
   London: W. Wilson, 1829.

Ravvonspear. Don Juan. Canto XVII. London: Printed for the
   Author and Sold by Richard Carlile, 1830. [A spurious continuation.]

Canto XVII of Don Juan. By One Who Desires to Be a Very Great
   Unknown; with an Illustration by Seymour. London: James
   Gilbert, 1832.

A Minor. Rodolph: A Dramatic Fragment. Stanzas in Continuation of "Don Juan"; and Other Poems. London: T. Griffiths,
   1832.

Clarke, John. Don Juan, Cantos XVII to XXIV, in 2 vols. [This
   continuation of Don Juan was privately printed by the Author
   and never published. Chew gives the date between 1834 and
   1847.]

G----, T. The Count and His Cotempors. Part I. Cantos I, II,
   III & IV. London: Sherwood & Co. , 1837. [A continuation.]

[Clark, Charles, according to CBEL.] Georgian Revel-ations! or,
   The Most Accomplished Gentleman's Midnight Visit below
   Stairs! A Poem. Reprinted from a Clever Suppressed Work,
   Entitled "Pindaric Odes and Tales," by Peter Pindar, Esq. ,

the Younger. London, 1821. With Twenty Suppressed Stanzas of "Don Juan," In Reference to Ireland, with Byron's Own Curious Historical Notes, the Whole Written in Double Rhymes, on the Model of Casti's Stanzas, an Italian Author from Whom Byron Is Said to Have Plagiarized Many of His Beauties. From a Manuscript in the Possession of Captain Medwin, Warranted Genuine. Great Totham, Essex: Printed at Charles Clark, 1838. [The Byron section of this book was reprinted as: Some Rejected Stanzas of "Don Juan," with Byron's Own Curious Notes. The Whole Written in Double Rhymes after Casti's Manner, an Italian Author from Whom Byron Is Said to Have Plagiarized Many of His Beauties. From an Unpublished Manuscript in the Possession of Captain Medwin. A Very Limited Number Printed. Great Totham, Essex: Printed at Charles Clark's Private Press, 1845.]

Baxter, George R. Wythen. Don Juan Junior, A Poem by Byron's Ghost. London: Joseph Thomas, 1839.

Don Juan in Search of Wife. With Other Poems. London: Printed for the Author, 1839.

C[owley], W[illiam?]. Don Juan Reclaimed; or, His Peregrination Continued, from Lord Byron. Sheffield: Printed for the author, 1840.

[Reynolds, George William MacArthur.] A Sequel to Don Juan. London: Paget & Co., 1843. [Five cantos with the promise of eleven more.]

Morford, Henry. The Rest of Don Juan, Inscribed to the Shade of Byron. New York: Burges, Stringer & Co., 1846. [645 stanzas divided into 7 cantos.]

[Daniel, H. J. ? according to CBEL.] Don Juan Continued. By ******. Canto the Seventeenth. London: Published for the Author by E. Churton, 1849. [108 stanzas.]

Thomas, John Wesley. An Apology for "Don Juan," A Satirical Poem, in Two Cantos. 3rd ed. To Which is Added a Third Canto, Including Remarks on the Times. London: Partridge & Oakey, 1850. [Name of author was revealed with this edition.]

————. Byron and the Times; or, An Apology for "Don Juan." London: Partridge & Oakey, 1855.

Wilberforce, Edward, and Blanchard, Edmund Forster. "Don Juan. Canto XVII," Poems. London: Longman, Brown, Green, Longmans & Roberts, 1857. Pp. 3-22.

Byron, Henry James. Beautiful Haidée. London: Thomas H. Lacy, 1863. [Adaptation.]

Wetton, Harry W. The Termination of the 16th Canto of Lord Byron's "Don Juan." London: Trübner & Co. , 1864. [Imita-
tion.]

Thomas, John Wesley. "Introduction," Byron and the Times; or,
An Apology for "Don Juan," a Satirical Poem, in Three Can-
tos. New edition. With an Introduction on the Poetry of
Byron. London: Elliot Stock, 1867. Pp. iii-xvi.

Don Juan. Canto XVIIth. London: T. Cooper & Co.; New York:
Scribner Welford & Co. , 1870. [107 stanzas.]

Timothy Cotton. A Poem. Cantos I to III. London: Hotten,
1871. [Dedicated to the Shade of Don Juan. An imitation of
Don Juan.]

[Beeton, Samuel Orchart, according to the Yale University Library
Catalogue.] Jon Duan. A Twofold Journey with Manifold
Purposes. London: Weldon, 1874.

Byron, Gerald Noel. The New Don Juan. The Introduction by
Gerald Noel Byron. And the Last Canto of the Original Don
Juan from the Papers of the Countess Guiccioli. By George
Lord Byron. London: E. Head, 1880. [A forgery.]

Hovey, Richard. "Don Juan, Canto XVII," To the End of the
Trail. New York: Duffield & Co. , 1908. Pp. 111-30.

Squire, John Collings. "Review of the Seventeenth Canto," Collected Parodies. London: Hodder & Stoughton, 1921. Pp.
126-30. [Quotes over twenty lines of a "recently found"
canto. A hoax.]

Hewitt, Eileen. Donna Juana. A Novel in Verse. London:
George Routledge & Sons, 1925.

Wolfe, Humbert. Don J. Ewan. London: A Barker, 1937. [6
cantos and an epilogue.]

Seary, E. R. "A Sequel to Don Juan," MLR, XXXV (Oct. , 1940),
526-29. [George Longmore's Don Juan, a Sequel, Cantos
XIX and XX, in the Fairbridge Collection of the South African Library, Cape Town, should not be entirely forgotten as
a continuation.]

EPITAPH ON A NEWFOUNDLAND DOG

W. , A. "To Lord Byron, Written after Perusing His Epitaph on
a Newfoundland Dog," New Monthly Magazine, X (Dec. , 1818),
426.

THE GIAOUR

"To the Reader of a Poem Lately Published, Called The Giaour, a Turkish Tale," Spirit of the Public Journals for 1812 and 1813. London: J. Ridgway, 1814. P. 227.

Osman, A Turkish Tale. London: Printed for H. N. Batten, 1815. [An imitation of no romance in particular, though it resembles The Giaour in some points.]

Despair: A Vision. Derry Down and John Bull; A Simile. Being Two Political Parodies on "Darkness," and a Scene from "The Giaour," by Lord Byron. Together with a Love Letter from John Bull to Liberty and a Farewell Address, etc. London: Printed for the Author by R. Hamblin, 1820.

Odoherty, Morgan [pseud. for D. M. Moir]. "The Galiongee," Blackwood's, IX (May, 1821), 136. Rptd. in The Odoherty Papers, Annotated by Dr. Shelton Mackenzie. 2 vols. New York: Redfield, 1855-1857. Vol. I, p. 235.

Elliott, Ebenezer. Love: A Poem in Three Parts. To Which Is Added "The Giaour": A Satirical Poem. London: Charles Stocking, 1823.

GREECE

"The Goose," Gossip of Kentish Town, June 9, 1821, pp. 118-19. [Lord Byron's "Greece" parodied.]

MAZEPPA

Mazeppa Travestied: A Poem, with an Introductory Address to the Goddess of "Milling," and Her Worshippers, "The Fancy." London: Published by C. Chapple, 1820.

Milner, H. M. Mazeppa; or, The Wild Horse of Tartary. A Romantic Drama, in Three Acts. Dramatized from Lord Byron's Poem. ("Lacy's Acting Edition of English Plays," Vol. XCVI.)

White, C. Mazeppa, an Equestrian Burlesque, in Two Acts, Transposed and Arranged by C. White. New York: Frederick A. Brady, 1856. [In an American setting, a Negro is Satinette who had experiences like Mazeppa.]

Eschwege, H. The Knight's Tour. In a Continuous and Uninterrupted Ride over 48 Boards or 3072 Squares. Adapted from Byron's "Mazeppa." Shanklin, I.W.: Silsbury Bros., 1896. [A game of chess.]

PARISINA

Eldredge, Ruth, and Darling, Adam. Parisina: A Tragic Ro-
      mance of Ferrara, Italy. Prologue and Four Acts. Founded
      on Lord Byron's "Parisina." Denver, Colorado: Press of
      C. F. Hoeckel, 1897.

POEMS ON HIS DOMESTIC CIRCUMSTANCES

Lady Byron's Responsive "Fare Thee Well." London: Printed for
      R. Edwards, 1816.

A Reply to Fare Thee Well!!! Lines addressed to Lord Byron.
      Also "To a Sleeping Infant," by the Same. London: Printed
      by Plummer and Brewis, 1816. Another edition: London:
      R. S. Kirby, 1816.

[Tyro]. A Sketch from Public Life: A Poem Founded upon Re-
      cent Domestic Circumstances; with "Weep Not for Me!" and
      Other Poems. London: William Hone, 1816.

Cockle, Mrs. E. Lines Addressed to Lady Byron. Newcastle:
      S. Hodgson, 1817.

Reply to Lord Byron's Fare Thee Well. Newcastle: Printed by
      S. Hodgson, 1817.

[Hall, Thomas?] "Reply to Byron's Fare Thee Well," Voyage to
      India, and Other Poems, on Various Subjects. London: S.
      Odell, 1853. P. 46.

PRISONER OF CHILLON

S. "Lines on Reading The Prisoner of Chillon by Lord Byron,"
      Ladies' Monthly Museum, 3rd ser., VII (Feb., 1818), 114-16.

SARDANAPALUS

Kean, Charles. Sardanapalus. A Tragedy by Lord Byron.
      Adapted for Representation by C. K. ("Lacy's Acting Edi-
      tion of Plays, Dramas, Extravaganzas, Farces, etc.," Vol.
      XI.) London: T. H. Lacy, 1850?

Calvert, Charles. Lord Byron's Historical Tragedy of Sardana-
      palus, Arranged for Representation by Charles Calvert; and
      first Produced at the Alexandra Theatre, Liverpool, 20th
      Sept., 1875. Manchester: J. Heywood, 1875.

STANZA ON THE SILVER FOOT OF A SKULL MOUNTED AS A CUP FOR WINE

Sterndale, W. H. "To Lord Byron. On Reading his 'Stanza on
the Silver Foot of a Skull Mounted as a Cup for Wine,' "
Gentleman's Magazine, XCIV, Part I (May, 1824), 449.
Rptd. from The Leeds Intelligencer.

VISION OF JUDGMENT

Mucklegrin, Andrew. "The Vision of Parnassus," London Liberal,
I (1823), 24-42. [A satire.]

WERNER

Werner: A Tragedy of the Attic. Aristophanic, Classic, Comic,
Didactic, Domestic, Localic, Moralistic, Operatic, Terpsi-
choric (and Every Other Essential-ic) Extravaganza Class.
Interspersed with Parodies: Dedicated (not) by Permission
to an Illustrious and Well-Known Character on the Pave of
the Metropolis. By a Regular Swell Cove. London: Printed
for E. Duncombe, [ca. 1830].

Appendix F

BYRON IN DRAMA, FICTION AND POETRY

BYRON IN DRAMA

Ardaschir, K. K. The Pilgrim of Eternity, a Play. Produced at
the Duke of York's Theatre. London: November 12, 1921.

Box, Sydney, and Cox, Vivian. The Bad Lord Byron. London:
Convoy Publications Ltd., 1949.

Buttle, Myra [pseud. for Victor W. W. Purcell]. The Bitches'
Brew; or, The Plot against Bertrand Russell. London: C. A.
Watts, 1960. [In scene V of the play, the "ghost" of Byron
is made to speak.]

Cumming, Mrs. Isabel W. The Honor of the House of Murray, a
Play in One Act Based on the Life of Byron. Alabama:
University Press, 1941.

Ferber, Maurice. Lord Byron; a Play in Eight Scenes. New York:
D. Appleton & Co., 1924.

Foy, Helen. "Poor Caro!" The Best One-Act Plays of 1940, selected by J. W. Marriott. London: George G. Harrap & Co.,
1941.

[Gifford, William.] The Illiberal! Verse and Prose from the
North!! Dedicated to My Lord Byron in the South!! N. B.
To Be Continued Occasionally!! viz. as a Supplement to Each
Number of "The Liberal." London: T. Holt, 1822. [A sa-
tire on The Liberal; this pamphlet was suppressed before
publication.]

Goethe, Johann Wolfgang von. Faust: a Tragedy. Part I. Edited and annotated by F. H. Hedge, D. D. Metrical Version
by Miss Swanwick. Also a prose Translation of the same by
A. Hayward. Part II. Translated by Miss Swanwick. New
York: J. D. Williams, 1882. [In Part II, Act III, Euphorion, the child of Faust and Helena, represents Byron.]

Gorman, Arthur J. "The Youth of Don Juan," Scholastic, XXIV
(March 3, 1934), 7-8, 11.

Gould, Gerald, and Burnham, Barbara. Falling Angel, a Play in
Three Acts. London: V. Gollancz, Ltd. , 1936.

Ireland, Anthony. Byron in Piccadilly, a Play in Three Acts.
London: J. Cape, 1945.

Kitchin, Laurence. "The Trial of Lord Byron," Three on Trial.
London: Pall Mall Press, 1959. Pp. 3-57. [A play broad-
cast by BBC.]

Langley, Noel. An Elegance of Rebels, a Play in Three Acts.
London: Arthur Barker, 1959.

Lea, Fanny Heaslip. Crede Byron; a Play. New York: Dodd,
Mead & Co. , 1936.

Luby, James. Byron, a Romantic Play in Four Acts. New York:
Printed for Private Use, 1897.

Ramsey, Alicia. Byron, a Play, in Four Acts and an Epilogue.
London, 1908. [This play was produced in London, perhaps
in 1930. It also served as the source of the scenario for
the screen-play "The Prince of Lovers," 1922.]

Read, Sir Herbert. Lord Byron at the Opera: A Play for Broad-
casting. ("Herbert Read Series," No. 2.) North Harrow:
Philip Ward, 1963.

Rice, Carl Young. Love and Lord Byron: a Drama. New York:
D. Appleton-Century Co. , 1936.

Sanger, Joan. The Dark Meteor. A Play. 192-?

Stein, Gertrude. "Byron, a Play," Last Operas and Plays. New
York: Rinehart, 1949. Pp. 333-86.

Turney, Catherine. Bitter Harvest. London: H. Hamilton, 1936.

Williams, Tennessee. Camino Real. Norfolk, Conn. : New Directions, 1953.

_____ . "Lord Byron's Love Letter," Twenty Seven Wagons
Full of Cotton and Other One-act Plays. Norfolk, Conn. :
New Directions, 1945. Pp. 123-32.

Young, Stanley. Bright Rebel, a Play. 1937.

BYRON IN FICTION

Aldanov, Mark [pseud. for Mark Aleksandrovich Landau]. For
Thee the Best, trans. Nicholas Wreden. New York: C.
Scribner's Sons, 1945.

Barrett, Eaton Stannard. Six Weeks at Long's. By a Late Resi-
    dent. 3 vols. London: Printed for the Author by B. Clarke,
    1817.

Bedford, John Harman. Wanderings of Childe Harold. A Romance
    of Real Life, Interspersed with Memoirs of the English Wife,
    the Foreign Mistress, and Various Other Celebrated Charac-
    ters. 3 vols. London: Sherwood, Jones & Co., 1825.

Blessington, Marguerite Power Farmer Gardiner, Countess of.
    The Lottery of Life. 3 vols. London: Henry Colburn, 1844.

Borrow, George. Lavengro, the Scholar--the Gypsy--the Priest.
    3 vols. New York: G. P. Putnam, 1851.

_____. The Romany Rye: A Sequel to Lavengro. 2 vols.
    London: John Murray, 1857.

Disraeli, Benjamin. Contarini Fleming: A Psychological Autobi-
    ography. 4 vols. London: John Murray, 1832.

_____. Venetia, a Novel. 3 vols. London: Henry Colburn,
    1837.

_____. Vivian Grey. 5 vols. London: Henry Colburn, 1833.

Driver, Henry Austen. Harold de Burun. A Semi-Dramatic Poem;
    in Six Scenes. London: Longman, Rees, Orme, & Co.,
    1835. [Introduces the poet in his proper character to reveal
    his real character and sentiments.]

Edschmid, Kasimir. Lord Byron: The Story of a Passion, trans.
    Eveline Bennett. London: Humphrey Toulmin, 1930. Pub-
    lished in America under the title, The Passionate Rebel,
    trans. Whittaker Chambers. New York: A. & C. Boni,
    1930.
    Reviews:
    TLS, June 19, 1930, p. 510.
    Osbert Burdett, Saturday Review, CL (Aug. 16, 1930), 205.
    G. Vernon, Bookman, LXXII (Nov., 1930), 323.

Edwards, Anne. Haunted Summer. New York: Coward, McCann
    & Geoghegan, 1972.

"An Event in the Life of Lord Byron," New Monthly Magazine,
    XCIX (Oct., 1853), 138-50. Rptd. in Eclectic Magazine,
    XXX (Nov., 1853), 415-24; Argosy, VII (April 1, 1869), 273-
    89.

Gordon Page, Howard. The Shattered Harp; a Romance on the Life
    of Lord Byron. London: A. Rivers, Ltd., 1928.

Hewlett, Maurice. Bendish: A Study in Prodigality. London: Macmillan & Co., 1913.

Kenyon, F. W. The Absorbing Fire, the Byron Legend. New York: Dodd, Mead & Co., 1966.

Lamb, Caroline. Ada Reiss. 3 vols. London: John Murray, 1823.

_____. Glenarvon. 3 vols. London: Printed for Henry Colburn, 1816. Rptd. under the title, The Fatal Passion. London: C. H. Clarke, 1865.

Landor, Walter Savage. "Archdeacon Hare and Walter Landor," The Last Fruits off an Old Tree. London: Edward Moxon, 1853. Pp. 97-131.

_____. Imaginary Conversations of Literary Men and Statesmen. 2 vols. London: Taylor & Hessey, 1824.
The following are of relevance to Byron:
"Bishop Burnett and Humphrey Hardcastle," I, 153-65.
"Southey and Porson," I, 37-54.
"The Abbé Delille and Walter Landor," I, 249-310.

McLaws, Lafayette [pseud. for Emily Lafayette]. Maid of Athens. Boston: Little, Brown & Co., 1906.

Mannering, Julia [pseud. for Madeleine Bingham]. The Passionate Poet; a Romantic Story Based Upon Lord Byron's Loves and Adventures. London: Museum Press, 1951.

Marlowe, Derek. A Single Summer with L. B. London: Cape, 1969. Published in America as A Single Summer with Lord B. New York: Viking Press, 1970.

Mitford, John. "Lord Byron's Residence in the Island of Mitylene," New Monthly Magazine, X (Nov., 1818), 309-10. Rptd. in Literary Journal, I (Nov. 28, 1818), 561-62; The Vampyre; a Tale, London: Printed for Sherwood, Neely & Jones, 1819, pp. 73-84; Portfolio (Dennie), 4th ser., VII (April, 1819), 281-84; The Every Day Book, or, Everlasting Calendar of Popular Amusements, London: W. Hone, 1826, cols. 486-90, April 19, 1819; Literary Journal (Providence), I (Aug. 3, 1833), 65.

Moore, Frank Frankfort. He Loved but One; the Story of Lord Byron and Mary Chaworth. London: Eveleigh Nash, 1905. Rptd. in America under the title, Love Alone Is Lord. New York: G. P. Putnam's Sons, 1905.

"My Wedding Night; the Obnoxious Chapter in Lord Byron's Memoirs," John Bull Magazine, I (July, 1824), 19-21.

Narrative of Lord Byron's Voyage to Corsica and Sardinia, during
     the Summer and Autumn of the Year 1821. Compiled from
     Minutes Made during the Voyage by the Passengers; and Ex-
     tracts from the Journal of His Lordship's Yacht, the Mazeppa,
     Kept by Captain Benson, R.N., Commander. London: J.
     Limbird, 1824.

Paul, Howard. Lord Byron in Love, and Other Stories. London:
     J. C. Hotten, 1871? Pp. 1-54.

Peacock, Thomas Love. Headlong Hall, and Nightmare Abbey.
     London: Ward & Lock, 1856.

Prokosch, Frederick. The Missolonghi Manuscript. New York:
     Farrar, Straus & Giroux; London: W. H. Allen, 1968.
     Reviews:
     Harry T. Moore, SRL, LI (Jan. 13, 1968), 82, 87.
     Iris Origo, NYTBR, Jan. 14, 1968, pp. 5, 38.
     Phoebe Adams, Atlantic, CCXXI (Feb., 1968), 142-43.
     G. M. Matthews, NYRB, X (May 23, 1968), 23-28.
     J. A. Cuddon, Books and Bookmen, XIII (June, 1968), 33-34.
     Naomi Lewis, New Statesman, LXXV (June 28, 1968), 874-75.

Redivivus, Quevedo. A Spiritual Interview with Lord Byron. In
     Which His Lordship Gave His Opinion and Feelings about His
     New Monument and Gossip about the Literature of His Own
     and the Present Day, with Some Interesting Information about
     the Spirit World. With Notes Explanatory and Elucidatory.
     London: S. Palmer, [ca. 1840].

Rives, Hallie Ermine. The Castaway; Three Great Men Ruined in
     One Year: A King, a Cad and a Castaway. Indianapolis:
     The Bobbs-Merrill Co., 1904.

Shelley, Mary. Falkner; a Novel. 3 vols. London: Saunders &
     Otley, 1837.

_____. The Last Man. 3 vols. London: Henry Colburn, 1826.

_____. Lodore. New York: Wallis & Newell, 1835.

_____. Valperga; or, The Life and Adventures of Castruccio,
     Prince of Lucca. 3 vols. London: G. & W. B. Whittaker,
     1823.

Three Weeks at Fladongs, by a Late Visitant. 3 vols. London:
     Printed for the Author, 1817.

W., Alicia. Harold, the Exile. 3 vols. London: J. Gillet, 1819.
     [Novel in the form of letters, based on Byron's life.]

Ward, Mrs. Humphry. The Marriage of William Ashe. 2 vols.
     New York: Harper & Bros., 1905.

BYRON IN POETRY

Q., Q., and W., W. [pseud. for Francis Hodgson.] Leaves of
    Laurel, or New Probationary Odes, for the Vacant Laureate-
    ship. London: T. Beckett & J. Porter, 1813. [In it Byron
    is made to speak, pp. 8-10.]

Shelley, Percy Bysshe. The Complete Works of Shelley. Newly
    Edited by Roger Ingpen and Walter E. Peck. 10 vols. New
    York: Gordian Press; London: Ernest Benn Ltd., 1965.
    It contains:
        "Adonais," II, 389-405.
    "Julian and Maddalo," III, 179-96.

Taylor, John. Byronna, the Disappointed. A Tale of Lord Byron;
    or, The Power of the Passions. Part I. A Poem. London:
    Printed and Published for the Author by W. Rock, ca. 1830.

Wordsworth, William. "Not in the Lucid Intervals of Life," Poeti-
    cal Works, ed. W. Knight. 11 vols. Edinburgh: W. W.
    Paterson, 1882-1889. Vol. VIII, pp. 390-91. [Lines written
    with Lord Byron's character, as a poet, in mind.]

AUTHOR INDEX